Grace Moments

a daily journey with God

Sylane Mack

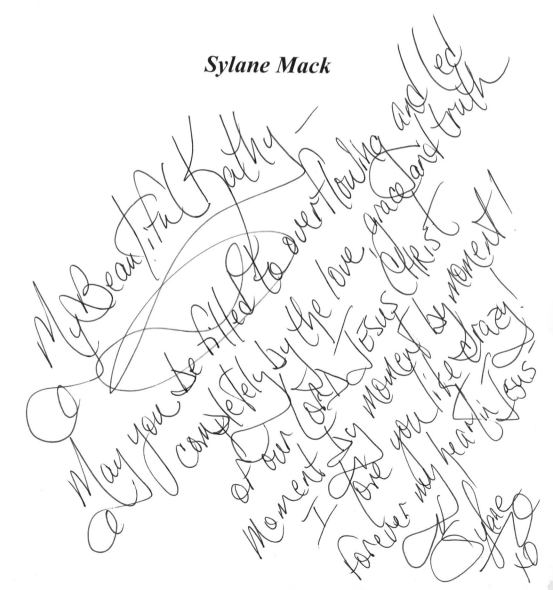

My Beautiful Kathy —

May you be filled to overflowing and led completely by the love, grace, and truth of our Lord Jesus Christ / moment by moment by moment by moment!

I love you like crazy! Forever my heart in Jesus,

Sylane

Grace Moments

a daily journey with God

Sylane Mack

Library of Congress Control Number: 2014919023
CreateSpace Independent Publishing Platform, North Charleston, SC

International Standard Book Number - 10: 1502425882
International Standard Book Number - 13: 978-1502425881
Printed in the United States of America.

To contact the ministry Transformed by Grace, Inc.:
Website: **www.transformedbygrace.org**
Email: **Info@transformedbygrace.org**
Phone: 215.497.0882
Address: PO Box 976 - Newtown, PA 18940

Cover designed by Curtis Peters.

Grace Moments – a daily journey with God

is dedicated, first and always,
to my Lord Jesus.
You hold my every moment, my every day in Your hands.
And there, I am held in Your love, grace and truth.
There, I breathe deeply and am fully alive.

– and to –

my Timmy,
my best friend, husband, lover and adventure-bringer,
you have filled each of my days with
love and encouragement, faithfulness and fun,
wisdom and strength, commitment and courage,
prayer and passion
in such beautiful and deep ways,
and oh-so-far beyond what I could ever have imagined!
And you've been doing all this for me, and with me,
since we were just kids!

– and to –

DeAnne Harland,
my precious friend, sister in Christ and in heart,
your love and prayers, hard work and humor,
insane number of texts, emails, calls and
screening of every minute detail have made you
Midwife to the birthing of Grace Moments!
And you did it all with such generosity and grace!

Dearest One,
Enter in with your soul quieted and your heart opened,
knowing that…

We all need grace. We all need moments filled with God's grace.

We need moments to slow our pace and breathe more deeply.
We need moments to hear God's words of grace and truth.
We need moments to hear God's words of encouragement,
of challenge, and of unfailing, outrageous love.

We need moments to reflect on what we truly believe as we hear
and read God's Word.

We need moments to decide what, if anything, we will do about what we
believe.

This is the purpose and passion of Grace Moments.

To give each of us these moments to quiet our souls and open our hearts so
we may more fully listen to our God.
To give each of us these moments of reflection and choice – moments of
grace and truth – as we journey daily with our God,
and each other.

My love and prayers for the journey are with each of you,
through the grace of Jesus, my Lord and King –

Sylane

A special note: Celebrating the victorious resurrection of our Lord Jesus after His sacrificial death for the forgiveness of our sins is the very foundation of our faith and the hope we have as we trust in Jesus as our Savior and Lord!

Although the dates for celebrating Easter change each year, the message of Christ's death and resurrection must be told! In 2014, the year *Grace Moments* was written, Holy Saturday and Easter Sunday were on April 19 and 20. It is on these dates that you will find reflections about these sacred days.

IN THE BEGINNING GOD

Happy New Year! The old year is past. The New Year has arrived. We have been given a new day. A new beginning with each new moment.

Many of us across the world take time to honor the transition from one year to the next. In the beginning of this New Year, many of us will make resolutions and establish plans to meet some serious and significant goals, some very personal and even adventurous goals. In the beginning we're motivated to put forth a sincere, and maybe even a little bit of a superhuman, effort to get ourselves in shape in all kinds of ways. We're determined to transform our lives physically or financially, academically or professionally, emotionally or relationally or spiritually. Maybe even in each of these ways. After all, this is the time for transformation! The clock has struck midnight! And we're in the beginning of a New Year. This thought – this biblical message of grace and truth – keeps running through my head over and over again, persistently and passionately, as I think about all the new beginning possibilities that come to us at the beginning of this New Year:

> ***In the beginning God...***
> Genesis 1:1

Say it slowly. Word by word. Think about it deeply. Think about what it would mean if each one of us wholeheartedly embraced a life transformation focusing on: *In the beginning God.* I deeply believe that each of us has been created to make choices that would honor these holy words.

Making these ***In the beginning God*** choices would mean that we would...
Seek God first.
Listen to God first.
Trust God first.
Obey God first.
Love God first.

These ***In the beginning God*** choices would be made by each of us...
In the beginning of every day and every moment of life we have been given.
In the beginning of everything we do.
In the beginning of everything we say – spoken, written and cyber-spaced.
In the beginning of every interaction with every person.
In the beginning of every choice we make.

Choosing to live in the grace and truth of ***In the beginning God*** will give each of us a deeper awareness of the gift of life we have been given, keeping us in a right relational position with our sovereign God as the loving authority and sacred author of our lives.

Choosing to live in the grace and truth of ***In the beginning God*** will fill us with the peace and power we so desperately need to live each new day – no matter what our day may bring – today and every day of this New Year!

May this New Year be one of great transformation for each of us as we choose to live out the grace and truth of ***In the beginning God*** with our God who is the beginning and the end!

Reflections – Responses – Challenges – Encouragements – God-breathing Thoughts

Do I believe it?
And if I do, what am I going to do about it?

Lord, please let me hear your voice, your love, your wisdom, your grace and truth.

CHOOSE LIFE!

Yes! It really is all about choice!

True life – living a deep, real, purposeful, peace-filled, love-knowing life – is all about choosing what God wants for us. And God wants all that is truly for our best! God, the Creator, Savior and Lord of our lives, deeply wants to give us His true life. Yet, God leaves the decision to us as to whether we will choose life or death.

Tragically, in so many different ways, we continually choose death. We choose death through every one of our selfish thoughts, words, actions and interactions. We choose death through our arrogance and self-righteous judgment. We choose death through our complacency and hate. We choose death through our unforgiveness and lack of compassion.

As we make these choices, we bring death in some way – mentally, physically, emotionally, spiritually and relationally – to our own lives, to the lives of those around us and, far too often, to those precious ones we are supposed to love most dearly. These death choices only serve to kill our hope and our trust in God, increase our fear and worry, shred all sense of peace and destroy our very closest relationships.

Still, our God continually offers to give us His true life. The choice is ours.

> *I have set before you life and death, blessings and curses.*
> *Now choose life, so that you and your children may live*
> *and that you may love the LORD your God, listen to his voice,*
> *and hold fast to him. For the LORD is your life...*
> Deuteronomy 30:19-20

> *Jesus answered, "I am the way and the truth and the life.*
> *No one comes to the Father except through me."*
> John 14:6

> *"The thief comes only to steal and kill and destroy;*
> *I have come that they may have life, and have it to the full."*
> John 10:10

With Christ as our life – as our giver of life to the full – we have been given the power to bring life to ourselves, to our dearest ones, to our friends, to our co-workers, to our neighbors and to strangers. Choosing true life – and bringing true life to others – happens with every word we speak, with every attitude we exude, with every action we take and with every interaction we have that come from us with true love, patience, kindness, unselfishness, understanding, compassion, gentleness, helpfulness, encouragement, forgiveness and thankfulness.

Choose life, precious ones – intentionally, actively, constantly and tenaciously. Choose God's true life for yourself. Bring God's true life to all those around you.

Reflections – Responses – Challenges – Encouragements – God-breathing Thoughts

Do I believe it?
And if I do, what am I going to do about it?

Lord, please let me hear your voice, your love, your wisdom, your grace and truth.

AGREEING WITH GOD

There is nothing that God says or promises that God is not able to accomplish.

The transforming of our lives happens when we believe that God is faithful to His Word and that God and His Word are good, true, powerful and purposeful. Transformation happens as we humbly and willingly, actively and intentionally, trust in our Eternal God – in His love and goodness – more than in our own limited perspective about our circumstances.

Agreeing with God – taking God at His Word – absolutely requires a leap of faith from each and every one of us. Yet, even in this leap of faith, we are never alone. Our God is with us always. Our God loves us beyond our comprehension and wants us to know Him and trust Him. Our God wants us to agree with Him, with His words and His ways as to what He declares and reveals is the very best for our lives. Our God is present to help carry us through that leap of faith. We just have to be willing to make it.

As we choose to agree with our God, taking Him at His Word, we open ourselves up to the power of God's love that brings salvation, healing, freedom, renewal and restoration into our lives, into our minds and hearts and into our relationships.

> *"As the rain and the snow come down from heaven, and do not return to it*
> *without watering the earth and making it bud and flourish,*
> *so that it yields seed for the sower and bread for the eater,*
> *so is my word that goes out from my mouth: It will not return to me empty,*
> *but will accomplish what I desire and achieve the purpose for which I sent it."*
> Isaiah 55:10-11

> *For the word of God is alive and active. Sharper than any double-edged sword,*
> *it penetrates even to dividing soul and spirit, joints and marrow;*
> *it judges the thoughts and attitudes of the heart.*
> Hebrews 4:12-13

> *We know that in all things God works for the good of those who love him, who have been*
> *called according to his purpose…to be conformed to the likeness of his Son...*
> Romans 8:28-29

> *Now the Lord is the Spirit, and where the Spirit of the Lord is, there is freedom.*
> *And we all…are being transformed into his image with ever-increasing glory…*
> 2 Corinthians 3:17-18

Our God purposes for each of us, as His followers and deeply loved children, to be continually conformed and transformed into the likeness of our Lord Jesus Christ. May we each invite God to help us to trust Him, help us to take Him at His Word – help us to agree with Him. May we each choose to let God's love and His Word of grace and truth have more and more influence over our every thought, perspective, word, action and interaction.

Beautiful, powerful and purposeful transformation happens when we agree with God.

Do I believe it?
And if I do, what am I going to do about it?

Lord, please let me hear your voice, your love, your wisdom, your grace and truth.

GOD'S HOLY POWER-TOOL

God's power is intimate and unlimited in its ability to transform lives. There is nothing too difficult for God! We often make God so much smaller and limited by the way we live and think. Yet, there is nothing small or limited about our Almighty God!

Our God gave His Holy – intimate and unlimited – Spirit to live within us and work through each of us who claim Jesus as Savior and Lord. Oh! What a power-tool of transformation God has given to us who believe!

> *God is able to do immeasurably more than all we ask or imagine,*
> *according to his power that is at work within us...*
> Ephesians 3:20

Think about it. What's the strongest tool or machine you have ever used or seen used?

I know it wasn't the world's most powerful tool, but not long ago I stopped to watch what looked like a gigantic, yellow, mechanized-metal version of a Tyrannosaurus Rex. It was taking mammoth bites out of an old building that was being removed in order to build something new in its place. Just like a little kid, I stood there totally mesmerized by the power of that machine to completely transform the area it worked on.

Now God doesn't *often* bite me, although He definitely has taken out a good number of chunks. This happens each time that the truth of God's Word confronts my self-centered thinking and actions. Even when God seems to bite, He always does it out of His love for us. God's purpose is to set us free and transform us from everything that truly would damage or destroy us.

God has given us His Holy Spirit to work within us and through us so that we may know and truly believe that our God is the Almighty God, who is far greater and more powerful than anything we could ever experience or imagine.

God's joy is more powerful than our deepest sadness.
God's peace is more powerful than our most crushing fear.
God's patience is more powerful than our fiercest frustration.
God's kindness is more powerful than our cruelest reality.
God's gentleness is more powerful than our rawest emotion.
God's hope is more powerful than our darkest discouragement.
God's strength is more powerful than our greatest weakness.
God's mercy is more powerful than our most evil sin.
God's love is more powerful than death!

God's Spirit is the intimate, unlimited power-tool that our God has placed within each of us – to accomplish His loving purpose to transform us.

So! Let's crank up the power, Darlin's, and let God's Spirit take a bite out of any and every thing in us that may be skewing our perspective of who our Almighty God is or hindering and limiting His transforming power within our lives!

Reflections – Responses – Challenges – Encouragements – God-breathing Thoughts

Do I believe it?
And if I do, what am I going to do about it?

Lord, please let me hear your voice, your love, your wisdom, your grace and truth.

_____

_____

_____

_____

_____

_____

_____

_____

_____

_____

_____

_____

_____

_____

_____

_____

_____

_____

_____

_____

_____

_____

_____

_____

_____

_____

GOD'S LOVE – NO MATTER WHAT!

"I know my mommy and daddy love me no matter what!"

Years ago when we were living in France, our precious, three-year-old Erin rhythmically repeated that phrase, "I know my mommy and daddy love me no matter what!" – over and over again during a three hour train trip from Chalon-sur-Saône to Paris. With her red, curly-haired head resting on my lap, she looked up at us, her mommy and daddy, with absolute trust shining in her green eyes. What an unbelievable and beautiful sing-songy declaration of trust she was expressing about our love for her!

And I know that even as crazy much as we love both of our beautiful daughters, Erin and Julia, we are still such frail, flawed and finite human beings and oh-so-imperfect as parents.

Still, we were given our little girl's unconditional trust that Tim and I would always have an unconditional love for her. Amazing and humbling. What an incredible statement of faith she made that day. "I know my mommy and daddy love me no matter what!"

If such a small child was able to put that much trust in her imperfect parents, believing they would always love her *no matter what,* how much more should each one of us choose to trust in our Heavenly Father's love with that same confidence and joy?

Our God's love for us is perfect. There is nothing frail, flawed or finite about our God or about the unfailing, everlasting love He has for each of us. There is absolutely nothing in all creation that will ever be able to separate us from our God's love. No matter what!

> *For I am convinced that neither death nor life,*
> *neither angels nor demons,*
> *neither the present nor the future,*
> *nor any powers,*
> *neither height nor depth,*
> *nor anything else in all creation,*
> *will be able to separate us from the love of God*
> *that is in Christ Jesus our Lord.*
> Romans 8:38-39

I am convinced of this!

God's love is greater than the very powers of hell.
God's love is greater than any damaging or destructive experiences we have here on earth.

I pray that every person in this world will come to know the *no matter what* love of our God! May each of us become convinced – and live as if we truly are convinced – that with Jesus as our Savior and Lord, there is absolutely nothing in all creation that could ever separate any of us from the perfect, unfailing and everlasting love of our God.

No matter what!

Reflections – Responses – Challenges – Encouragements – God-breathing Thoughts

Do I believe it?
And if I do, what am I going to do about it?

Lord, please let me hear your voice, your love, your wisdom, your grace and truth.

FAMILY RESEMBLANCE

Our God does things in big ways when it comes to His children! Right from creation, the Lord purposed that we would be made in God's image. We were intended to resemble our God.

Sadly, our sin and pride, our self-centered and selfish choices damaged that likeness and separated us from our intended, intimate relationship with our Creator. But! That didn't stop our God! Through Jesus – through His love, His humble life-sacrifice and His death-conquering resurrection – God's purpose for us is able to be fulfilled in us as we choose to let God conform us more and more to the likeness of His Holy Son.

In the beginning God created the heavens and the earth.

Then God said, "Let us make mankind in our image, in our likeness..."
So God created mankind in his own image,
in the image of God he created them;
male and female he created them."
Genesis 1:1, 26, 27

...to be conformed to the image of his Son...
Romans 8:29

My maiden name is Roberts. My dad comes from a large family in Mississippi, and although I've only seen some of my Southern relatives a few times in my life, they really are family. And ever since I was little, I've been told that I have "That Roberts Look!"

Several years ago, my dad gave me an old photograph of my great-grandmother. It was startling how much I looked like her – someone I had never known nor even met. The striking family resemblance of our images was undeniable. She, though family, was a stranger to me.

What about my family resemblance to my Heavenly Father? It is God who made me. It is God who really knows me and has made Himself known to me through His Word, His Spirit and His love. It is my Heavenly Father who came for me in my brokenness, who saved me and comforted me and transformed me from being a child of abuse to being a child of the King of kings.

Do I look like God? Are people able to tell whose family I belong to because I have "That Jesus Look?" Are God's features, God's characteristics – of love and compassion, grace and truth, wisdom and courage, peace and power – recognizable in me? I hope so. I pray so.

After all, that is God's plan for me and for all of us as God's children: To be conformed to think and speak, act and live and love more and more like our His holy Son Jesus. God is still working His family resemblance transformation out in all of us. And He's not going to stop on this side of heaven!

What a beautiful thing it will be when God welcomes us to our eternal home and we recognize all our family members – from every nation and generation since the creation of this world. Our family resemblance will be absolutely remarkable. We will all have "That Jesus Look!"

Do I believe it?
And if I do, what am I going to do about it?

Lord, please let me hear your voice, your love, your wisdom, your grace and truth.

WHAT KIND OF TREE WOULD YOU BE?

What kind of a tree would you be if you were a tree? I know on some days I feel and act like that scrawny, little tree from *A Charlie Brown's Christmas*. Yet, God's love is able to powerfully change all of our weakness, hurt and ugliness into beauty and strength. God heals our hearts and minds and forgives our sins.

God transforms us from brokenness and despair into oaks of righteousness – deeply rooting us in His Word and nurturing us by His Spirit. In Christ our characters can be transformed from one like a frail and scrawny, almost unidentifiable and seemingly useless tree, to a character that is like a strong and mighty oak providing a place of rest, shelter, safety and nourishment for others. God desires to grow each of us into oaks of righteousness and to use us to make known His love and majesty to those around us. How amazing is that!

The Spirit of the Sovereign LORD is on me,
because the LORD has anointed me to proclaim good news to the poor.
He has sent me to bind up the brokenhearted,
to proclaim freedom for the captives and release from darkness for the prisoners,
to proclaim the year of the LORD's favor and the day of vengeance of our God,
to comfort all who mourn, to provide for those who grieve in Zion –
to bestow on them a crown of beauty instead of ashes,
the oil of joy instead of mourning,
and a garment of praise instead of a spirit of despair.
They will be called oaks of righteousness,
a planting of the LORD for the display of his splendor.
Isaiah 61:1-3

I love this passage of Scripture so much. The Sovereignty of our God, His absolute raw power, the-nothing-can-stand-in-His-way-kind-of-power is so perfectly evident here. Our God has a task to accomplish – and it is about turning our world upside down by His intimate and powerful intervention in our lives.

Right in the midst of our loneliest and most destitute times, right in the midst of our most painful experiences and deepest heartbreaks, right in the midst of our darkest sin, our God announces His Good News:

I love you. I heal you. I free you. I forgive you. I have good things – the best things – for your life. I comfort you. I turn your grief and pain into beauty and joy. I turn your weakness into strength. I will transform you so that others may know My love and power as they shine through your life.

Jesus is able to do all of this for and through each one of us – no matter what we may have suffered or what suffering we may have caused. Our God takes our frailty and transforms us into His oaks of righteousness as we yield ourselves, and all of our experiences, over to Him! And as we yield to our Sovereign Lord, we will grow stronger, revealing to others – more fully and more freely – our God's eternal love and splendor!

Reflections – Responses – Challenges – Encouragements – God-breathing Thoughts

Do I believe it?
And if I do, what am I going to do about it?

Lord, please let me hear your voice, your love, your wisdom, your grace and truth.

DELIGHTFUL DESIRES

It seems that for all people born to this earth, there is something within each of us that desires and longs for something beyond ourselves. I believe that these desires for something more, something bigger and something better actually come from being created in the image of God.

I believe, as image bearers of our Creator, our innermost being deeply longs to be connected with, and more truly reflecting the likeness of, the One and Only who can truly, and delightfully, fulfill our heart's deepest desires.

> *Take delight in the LORD and he will give you the desires of your heart.*
> Psalm 37:4

Unfortunately, in this broken world – with all of its confusion, disappointment, hurt and our own sinful behavior – our heart's deepest desire to be in relationship with our God has gotten so twisted and thwarted, so hidden and hardened. In the darkness of this world, we end up trusting more in ourselves than we trust in our God. In our brokenness and blindness, we won't trust that God really loves us, if He loves us at all. In the deception of the twisted and thwarted truths about God, we won't really believe that God desires to be good to us, or that He cares about giving us the desires of our hearts.

Yet, we are called to take delight in the Lord, trusting that our God will give us the desires of our hearts. Here the Hebrew phrase for *take delight*, calls us *to be soft and pliable* before our God and to His working in our hearts.

As we choose to be soft and pliable in our God's hands, as we take delight in the Lord, we will give up our self-focused desires and sense of entitlement, our pride and stubbornness, our hurt and hate, our doubt and denial, our resentment and fear, our self-righteousness and self-reliance.

It is here, being soft, pliable and delighting in our Lord, that we will humbly and thankfully trust God's love for us and hold fast to believing that God is good – regardless of our circumstances. Believing that our God knows what is truly and eternally good for us – and that He wants to give these good things to us.

It is here, being soft, pliable and delighting in our Lord, that we will grow to be more like Jesus in His love, grace and truth, wisdom and mercy, courage and compassion, strength and hope, joy and peace, patience and kindness, gentleness and generosity.

It is here, being soft, pliable and delighting in our Lord, that our God is able to do His greatest work within us: Transforming us, in our innermost being and our most obvious self-expression, to reflect the beauty of God's likeness and character in all we are and in all we do. This was God's intent from our very creation. This will be the fulfillment of our heart's deepest desire.

It is here, being soft, pliable and delighting in our Lord, that the desires of our hearts will actually become the same desires that our God has for all of us who are His children by faith. And, oh! When the desires of our hearts line up with the holy and righteous, loving and good desires of our God, we can be absolutely certain that our God will take great delight in fulfilling these desires for each and every one of us!

Reflections – Responses – Challenges – Encouragements – God-breathing Thoughts

Do I believe it?
And if I do, what am I going to do about it?

Lord, please let me hear your voice, your love, your wisdom, your grace and truth.

HOW BIG IS YOUR GOD?

We often trust in our own abilities, experiences, reasoning, planning and sheer willpower to work things out for our lives. Yet, deep within us we know that even our best efforts are not always enough to give us clarity and wisdom for the multitude of life circumstances and decisions we face. They were never meant to. God wants us to trust Him. God alone has the eternal perspective to know exactly how to best lead and direct our lives!

> *Trust in the LORD with all your heart*
> *and lean not on your own understanding;*
> *in all your ways submit to God,*
> *and he will make your paths straight.*
> Proverbs 3:5-6

What is this trusting in God thing all about? Are we really supposed to trust God with all our heart? Trust God in all our ways? In a word: Yes.

To do this, we need to get real about who we really believe God is. Our personal perspective of God is the scale on which our trust in God is measured. So, how big is your God? How big is my God? Do I really believe that God is all He claims to be? Do I really believe that God is as big as the Bible says? Do I believe that my God is...

Creator of all, Wonderful Counselor, Mighty God, Everlasting Father, Prince of Peace,
Healer, Savior, Deliverer, Shelter, Strength, Anointed Messiah, Forgiver of Sins,
Destroyer of Death, Rescuer from the Dominon of Darkness, the Resurrection and the Life,
Transformer of Lives, Healer of Hearts, Renewer of Minds, Restorer of Souls,
Just, Wise, Perfect, Holy, Alpha and Omega – the Beginning and the End,
Immanuel – God with us, Unfailing Love, the Way and the Truth and the Life.

These are just a few of the names and claims of our God as revealed in Scripture.

So, what's not to trust? Still, when the stuff of life gets tough, frustrating, overwhelming, scary, out-of-control, maddening, lonely, dark or just plain stupid – my natural, first response is often to try to figure out a way to gain control of the situation as quickly as possible, and relieve the pain as much as possible.

Trusting God with all my heart is about being humble. Humble enough to trust God – even when I don't like, don't want or don't understand my circumstances.

Trusting God is about getting really honest not only about who I believe God is, but also about who I really am. I am not God. I am not the all-powerful, sovereign One of the universe. I am not perfect love. I am not transcending peace. I really don't have all the answers. This is not a news flash. This is the truth – and it really does set me free and make my paths straight.

So, how big is my God? Far bigger than my own understanding and absolutely worthy of all my trust for all of my life!

How big is your God?

STOP THE HAMSTER DANCE!

When worried, frustrated, stressed to the max or feeling out of control, many of us run around like crazy or, at the very least, let our minds run around in crazy circles trying to figure out all the things we need to do to put some semblance of order back into our lives. We can spend countless moments (hours, days) worrying about all of the *what ifs* of every possible scenario.

I call this the *Hamster Dance*. We allow our worried, frustrated and stressed-out thinking to run us ragged just as hamsters do when they run around furiously in their little caged wheel. Never going anywhere.

We need to step back and look at what all that crazy worry has done for us: Pretty much nothing! Except for maybe giving us some restless nights, ulcers, headaches, stiff necks and short nails. We need to admit that all the energy we pour into our crazy, worry-filled thoughts resolves absolutely nothing. Gets us absolutely nowhere. Just like that stupid, constantly spinning, held-in-one-place Hamster Dance wheel.

If we would each choose to seek God with that same energy and passion we put into our insane Hamster Dance thinking, our God could quiet our souls with His presence and reassure us that He knows exactly what's going on in our lives and that He does have plans for us. And they are good. Even in the midst of our most difficult and confusing circumstances, God is still God. God is still in control. God is still with us. We just need to be a bit more still before God.

"For I know the plans I have for you," declares the LORD,
"plans to prosper you and not to harm you, plans to give you hope and a future."
Jeremiah 29:11

"Be still, and know that I am God;
I will be exalted among the nations,
I will be exalted in the earth."

The LORD Almighty is with us,
the God of Jacob is our fortress.
Psalm 46:10-11

Stop the Hamster Dance! Take a deep breath. No matter what the circumstances of our lives are, we need to stop the Hamster Dance of worry (of anger, of bitterness, of pride...). We each need to choose and choose and choose to keep on trusting God.

Trust that God knows all you are experiencing. He does. Trust that God loves you. He does. Trust that God intends good for you. He does. Trust that God is a Truth Teller. He is.

Stop the Hamster Dance! Let's intentionally choose to change our thinking to trust God and His truths more than all those crazy scenarios we let run through our heads. Instead, let's continually choose to "keep in step with the Spirit" (Galatians 5:25), which, unlike the Hamster Dance, moves us forward by God's rhythm and pace of love, hope and peace. That's the dance, with God in the lead, that I want to dance every day of my life!

Reflections – Responses – Challenges – Encouragements – God-breathing Thoughts

Do I believe it?
And if I do, what am I going to do about it?

Lord, please let me hear your voice, your love, your wisdom, your grace and truth.

WHERE THE GOOD WAY IS

Why is doing what is best, what we know is from God's love and leading so very difficult to choose sometimes? We know what is good and right, but we just can't bring ourselves to do it, at least not right then.

Why is this so difficult? My deep theological answer: We don't want to.

> *This is what the LORD says: "Stand at the crossroads and look*
> *...ask where the good way is, and walk in it, and you will find rest for your souls.*
> *But you said, 'We will not walk in it.' "*
> Jeremiah 6:16

So, there it is. God's clear direction of what His good way is for us. God has answered our questions and shown us the good way (God's way!) to go. God tells us to walk in it – follow His path for our lives. And our God promises that when we do walk in obedience to Him, we will find rest for our souls. Why, then, when so many of us are so very restless in our souls and worn out by life, won't we choose to obey God? Again, from the school of cut-to-the-chase-theology: We don't want to.

God's Word reveals that our stubborn, self-magnifying response to His loving command to walk in His way is far too often: "We will not walk in it." I don't know about you, but when I respond to God with that kind of attitude and behavior, I have to face the very ugly truth that I'm pretty much flipping God off. In my self-centered thinking and acting, I am telling God that I want what I want when I want it...that what I want is what I'm going after. Even if He doesn't like it. I'm telling God to just stay out of my way as I go my own way. I have the right to decide for myself what I do with my life, my thoughts, my words, my actions and my relationships. I'm letting God know, in such a very mature fashion: You're not the boss of me!

I can decide to go my own way. That's true. I (and you) have been given freedom of choice. But! That doesn't change the fact that in the grand scheme of eternity, God is the boss of me. God is the giver and ruler of Life. God is the King of kings and Lord of lords. So, whether or not I choose to live in obedience to God's good, righteous and loving authority – this does not change the fact that God is the sovereign authority for all eternity. God never changes.

Yet, God, in His loving, sovereign authority, promises a change for each of us who choose to follow God's good way and walk in obedience to Him. That change: Rest for our souls.

Ahhhhh...rest and refreshment, quietness and strength...for my soul. I know for certain that kind of soul-rest has never been the result of any of my stubborn-go-my-own-way decisions. God really is a lot smarter than I am! So, with God's grace and strength, I'm asking God not only to show me His good way for my life-walk, I'm also asking God to grab me by the nape of my neck and drag me over to His good way – if He has to!

I don't want to forfeit any more rest for my soul by selfishly choosing something I want to do that has absolutely no eternal value and, most likely, has some pretty ugly temporal consequences. I want my life to be God's. And I sure as heck want some of that soul-rest that following God's good way alone offers!

Want to join me on that path? There's plenty of room. And plenty of loving, soul-rest to go around for all of us who choose to walk in God's good way!

Do I believe it?
And if I do, what am I going to do about it?

Lord, please let me hear your voice, your love, your wisdom, your grace and truth.

THE TERMS OF ACCEPTANCE

Our God offers us salvation and strength as we come to Him in repentance and in trust. Yet, we're often so full of ourselves that we have no room or willingness *to accept* the love and hope that God would give us.

This is what the Sovereign LORD, the Holy One of Israel says:
"In repentance and rest is your salvation, in quietness and trust is your strength,
but you would have none of it."
Isaiah 30:15

I really wish the last line of this verse didn't have to be written. How unbelievably tragic it is that when God offers us salvation and strength, we would actually choose to reject Him and His gifts. Each of us in some way, at some point in time – and maybe some of us for all eternity – actually chooses to "have none of it."

That truth just makes my heart hurt. How can any of us choose, or continue to choose for even one moment longer, to "have none of it" when we all need *all of it* so desperately?

Because we don't like the terms of acceptance.

The terms of Salvation:
To *repent*, I have to admit that I need to do things differently. That I have done things that are wrong. That I need forgiveness. This term of acceptance is the high cost of honesty.

To *rest*, I have to admit that I cannot earn my salvation by anything I do. That I have to stop doing things in my own power. That I need to receive the loving, sacrificial, completed gift of salvation that comes through Jesus alone. This term of acceptance is the high cost of humility.

The terms of Strength:
To be *quiet*, I have to admit that I need to be silent before God to hear His Spirit and recognize His Word of grace and truth. I have to admit that I fill my head with the noise of my own thinking, planning and justifications. That I'm afraid God won't answer me anyway. This term of acceptance is the high cost of discomfort in quietly listening for, and to, God.

To *trust*, I have to admit that I rely on my own wisdom and ways to work out the circumstances in my life rather than on God. That I have my doubts about how loving and almighty God really is. That I don't fully believe God will come through for me, so I'd best handle things on my own. This term of acceptance is the high cost of dependence on God.

The terms of acceptance on our part – honesty, humility, discomfort in quietness and dependence on God – are nothing compared to what our God has for us. God's perfect salvation and unfaltering strength are offered for all eternity. These holy gifts have the power to transform minds, lives and relationships in mighty ways, right now and for always.

May we each choose to accept God's terms and *have all of it* – all the days of our lives!

Reflections – Responses – Challenges – Encouragements – God-breathing Thoughts

Do I believe it?
And if I do, what am I going to do about it?

Lord, please let me hear your voice, your love, your wisdom, your grace and truth.

IF ONLY...LET GOD HOLD YOU!

"If only I had let God hold me when I wuz a younger man, I never would'uv done the things to y'all that I done" (*Convinced!*, p. 222).

My dad spoke those words of confession, in his very thick Mississippi accent, at age seventy-three, as he finally, humbly accepted Jesus as his Savior. God saw my dad's repentant heart, and received him as His child for all eternity – right then and there. The Lord had always been reaching out, always wanting to hold my dad and lead his life. But my dad had ignored God for far too many years, and forfeited his own peace and the peace of our family.

"Come near me and listen to this..."
This is what the LORD says – your Redeemer, the Holy One of Israel:
"I am the LORD your God, who teaches you what is best for you,
who directs you in the way you should go.
If only you had paid attention to my commands,
your peace would have been like a river..."
Isaiah 48:16-18

If only...if only...if only...

My dad had lived much of his life addicted to alcohol and narcotic drugs, abusing my mom, my four siblings and me in horrible ways – emotionally, physically and sexually.

Yet! Because of God's healing and hold on my life, I am free to let God's peace flow as a deep and mighty river in my life. My dad's choices to abuse cannot and do not hold any power over me any longer. Rather, I am held by my loving God, the Lord of all the universe – the Redeemer, the Holy One – who teaches me what is best: Love and forgive. I am held by my loving God who directs me in the way I should go: Follow Jesus.

I am so fully thankful for my Lord's transforming grace and unfailing love that healed my broken heart and renewed my shattered life. And I am thankful, beyond my ability to express it, for God's pursuing love that finally broke through to my dad's stubborn heart by His righteous conviction of sin and His eternal grace and truth that would set my dad free from all his bondages. Only by finally listening to the Lord, *and letting God hold him*, could my dad receive the salvation he so desperately, and eternally, needed.

Four years after my dad *let God hold him*, he died. As we gathered for a private memorial service, my sister, my brothers, our spouses and our children prayed and thanked God for who God is and for the power of our Lord Jesus to redeem and give peace to every life. Right now, and for all eternity, *if only we would let God hold us*. We released my dad's ashes into the river that ran through our childhood property. God had already welcomed my dad Home – to be held by, to listen to and walk with his Lord forever along the banks of the "river of the water of life" (Revelation 22:1) in unimaginable and unending peace.

May we each *let God hold us now* and crush every "*if only*" in our lives, so that God's perfect peace will flow to us and through us to each precious life that we touch.

Reflections – Responses – Challenges – Encouragements – God-breathing Thoughts

Do I believe it?
And if I do, what am I going to do about it?

Lord, please let me hear your voice, your love, your wisdom, your grace and truth.

KNOWLEDGE IS POWER – DIVINE POWER

There are days I can feel pretty powerless. Powerless to make things (even good and right things) happen for my family. Powerless to shield those I love from difficult and painful times. Powerless to accomplish the goals and dreams I have for my life and my work. Powerless to be fully healthy of body, mind and spirit. Powerless to make anyone trust God and follow the life-giving, peace-bringing way of our Lord Jesus. The truth is, in these ways, I am powerless.

Our God has a far different idea of what true power is, and what, through His divine power, He has already made available to us.

God's divine power has given us everything we need [for life and godliness]
for a godly life through our knowledge of him who called us
by his own glory and goodness.
2 Peter 1:3

This verse does not say that God's divine power has given us everything we need for wealth, health, luxury, ease, great influence and getting all our ducks in a row. Oh, no! Our God is more concerned about building our relationship with Him than ensuring our personal comfort, convenience, sense of control or self-sufficiency. Our God is more concerned about all things eternal, and giving us everything we need for what eternally matters: life and godliness.

"Very truly I tell you, whoever hears my word and believes him who sent me
has eternal life and will not be judged but has crossed over from death to life."
John 5:24

The fruit of the Spirit is love, joy, peace, patience, kindness,
goodness, faithfulness, gentleness and self-control...
Since we live by the Spirit, let us keep in step with the Spirit.
Galatians 5:22-23, 25

God's divine power has given everything we need for true *life* – a life lived in relationship with our Lord Jesus right now, right in the midst of our messes and masterpieces, and an eternal life with the Master of all Creation! And we have been given everything we need for *godliness* – for the complete renewing, healing and transforming of our innermost beings so we will more fully reflect the likeness of our Holy God in whose image we were originally created!

God's divine power has given us (notice this is already accomplished from God's perspective) everything we need for life and godliness! However, it is only received through our knowledge of Him who called us by His own glory and goodness. The more fully we get to know our God – through reading and trusting His living and active Word and seeking the Holy Spirit's guidance through prayer – the more open we will be to receive everything we need for life and godliness.

Do I, do you, believe our God has given us everything we need for life and godliness?
Will I, will you, choose to intentionally grow in the knowledge of our God and His Word?

My answers, with deep humility and thankfulness: Yes. Knowledge of my God and His Word is power – divine power – that gives me everything I need in all my most powerless of moments. Which is every moment of my life.

Do I believe it?
And if I do, what am I going to do about it?

Lord, please let me hear your voice, your love, your wisdom, your grace and truth.

TRUTH-THINKING WILL SET YOU FREE

Christianity is a thinking activity.

Every new day, every one of us as a follower of Jesus must make an intentional, thinking choice to trust our God and hold fast to God's truth. It is in this intentionality of our thought choices, and in our subsequent action choices birthed from this *truth-thinking*, that we are set free. God's loving, life-giving, head-clearing, action-directing truth offers freedom to our minds and our lives at the very deepest of levels. It is in holding fast to God's truth that we are set free for all eternity – one victorious thought, one victorious action, one victorious day at a time.

> **Jesus said, "If you hold to my teaching, you are really my disciples.**
> **Then you will know the truth, and the truth will set you free."**
> John 8:31-32

To know the freedom that God's truth brings us, we need to know God's Word and hold fast to what God teaches us through His Word. But, quite often God must first help us recognize the lies. I call them LFTPOHs – Lies From The Pit Of Hell – that hold us in freedom-destroying bondage. For me, there were many years that my mind was held captive by twisted thinking and damaged perceptions that had absolutely nothing to do with God's freeing truth.

The more I learned of God's truth, the more I recognized the lies – the LFTPOHs – that were crippling me and holding me captive. Oh! There were understandable reasons for how my mind got to be bound by those lies. My experiences of abuse, rape and rejection were horrendously crippling life events. As well, the captivity that came from the lies I told myself in order to justify my own sin, selfishness, pride and shame was just as crippling.

No matter what my reasons were (or are) for the LFTPOHs in my life, they do not change God's truth. Instead, God's truth changes me – and continues to change me by setting me free and keeping me free!

What are some of God's freeing truths that broke the powerful vise-grip of the LFTPOHs in my life? What are some of the *truth-thinking* choices I must make and trust each and every day of my life?

Some of the BIGGIES: *God loves me. God loves me so much more, and so much more perfectly, than any person ever could. God's love drives out all fear. Jesus died for my sins and my shame. I am completely forgiven. I am God's precious child. I am living now and will live forever in the loving presence of my God. God knows me intimately. God understands me completely. God is my protector and defender. God is my hope. God speaks. God wants me to listen. Peace and joy come by trusting and obeying God. I am never, ever alone. I am never without help. I am filled with the Spirit of the Living God. I am called to be Christ's ambassador of love and reconciliation in the lives of others. I am more than a conqueror through the love of Jesus. Nothing will ever separate me from God's love.*

I told you they were BIGGIES. So! Since Christianity is a thinking – a *truth-thinking* – activity, may we each choose to know, trust and hold fast to God's LFTPOH-killing, freedom-bringing truth with every thought, every action, every day of our lives!

Do I believe it?
And if I do, what am I going to do about it?

Lord, please let me hear your voice, your love, your wisdom, your grace and truth.

HEY! WHO CUT IN ON YOU?

Have you ever gone through a good period of time (even if it was a *very short* one) when things seemed to be going fairly smoothly and you were doing things pretty darn well in pretty much every way? Sweeeeet, right?

Then suddenly that good, easy, sweet flowing period came to a screeching halt and you're left wondering what the heck just happened?

That can happen in our Christian walk, too. Whenever I come to a screeching halt or face a major blunder or slow-down spiritually, I find myself wondering: *What happened? Where did my peace go? Where did my hope go? Where did my enthusiasm go? Where did my close walk with Jesus go? What got in my way? Who cut me off?*

At least that last question, *"Who cut me off?"* I can usually answer quite definitively: *That would be me.*

> ***You were running a good race.***
> ***Who cut in on you and kept you from obeying the truth?***
> Galatians 5:7

Did you ever hear this old spiritual hymn? It often plays in my head:
"It's me! It's me, it's me, O Lord, standing in the need of prayer!"
(Repeat! And get even more real!)
"Not my brother, not my sister, but it's me, O Lord! Standing in the need of prayer!"

And it's also me - standing in my own way, cutting in front of me. I was running a good race. I was feeling pretty peaceful, pretty loving, pretty much flowing with wisdom, joy and kindness! And then: *Who the heck allowed me to get all grumpy? Who the heck invited me to a full-blown pity party? Who gave me all those grandiose kudos and let my head just get too big for the rest of me? Who put my Bible out of my reach so I wasn't reaching for it? Who the heck started that darn hamster dance music - and left me spinning my wheels inside my own head?*

I was running a good race. Doggone it! Who cut in on me? *That would be me.*
It was my limited perspective. I lost God's eternal perspective or, at the very least, I put it aside for awhile. It was my pride. It was my yucky *I've-got-a-right-to-feel-and-act-that-way* attitude. I took up my own self-focused, self-importance instead of the power of the humility of Jesus.

It was me. I cut in on me.

But, look! There's my Abba! There's my Lord who never changes. God's Spirit. God's Word. True. Faithful. Loving. Pulling me back. (Sometimes with a bit of a snap to my head!) Pulling me, leading me back into the good race. Pulling me back into His grace and truth.

No matter what the circumstances or the *cutting in on me* experiences are in my life, Jesus is always there, willing and able, to get me back on His good course. Of course. Sweeeeet!

Do I believe it?
And if I do, what am I going to do about it?

Lord, please let me hear your voice, your love, your wisdom, your grace and truth.

FORGIVENESS IS THE FULLNESS OF FREEDOM!
(a teaching excerpt on Forgiveness © 2009)

Forgiveness is the fullness of God's gift of freedom for us.

Forgive whatever grievances you may have against one another.
Forgive as the Lord forgave you.
Colossians 3:13

Forgiveness is an intentional, mind and heart encompassing choice we must make in order to be truly set free. Forgiveness is a determined decision to trust and depend on – not our own feelings or natural responses to our painful experiences, but rather on – God, God's Word, God's love and God's power to move us and empower us to forgive even what we deem as unforgivable. True freedom requires us to do things God's way: Forgive everyone of everything every time. But! Let me assure you, forgiving others is not about denying the injustice or the ugliness of the sin done against you. Never. No matter how big or how small it was. Nor does true forgiveness stand in the way of the legal consequences that are right, necessary and in line with our earthly justice system for those who have wronged you.

Forgiving others is not about pretending that it didn't really hurt.
Forgiving others is not about somehow stuffing it to the back corner of our minds.
Forgiving others does not in any way diminish or deny the gravity of the sins done against us.
Forgiving others is definitely not about acting as if "It's okay."

Jesus did not die because sin is okay! Jesus died exactly because all sin is a deathblow to our souls. Jesus died because all sin is big, bad, ugly, relationship-destroying and life-killing. Jesus died a brutal death precisely because sin is so terribly destructive. Jesus Christ fully paid the price for my sins, for yours, and for everyone who has ever sinned against us. Jesus died because that was God's perfect plan, God's holy, loving choice, to completely eradicate and set us free from the bondage of sin in our lives. Whether that bondage is grown out of our own sins or from the sins that have come against us from others.

To live in freedom, to live in the power of God's healing and transformation, we must accept the truth that God forgives us completely through the sufficient and perfect sacrifice of Jesus. To live in freedom and to live in obedience to God, we must live out the truth that God demands that we forgive everyone of everything every time. Period.

Forgiving others is not conditional upon any action of those who have wronged us. We are to forgive everyone of everything every time regardless as to whether or not they have ever:
Asked for forgiveness.
Admitted the wrong done to us.
Acknowledged the validity of our hurt and anger.
Agreed with our perspective about their sins against us.

Forgiving others does not even require that they still be alive.

Forgiveness is never optional for the children of God. To live in the fullness of God's freedom, in the beauty and transforming power of God's freedom, we must follow Christ's example and command: Forgive. Forgive. Forgive. Ahhhhh! Freedom!

Do I believe it?
And if I do, what am I going to do about it?

Lord, please let me hear your voice, your love, your wisdom, your grace and truth.

READY. SET. GO!

Have you ever seen a little girl or boy run, dance, gallop or skip full force into the arms of her or his mommy or daddy? Seeing that child's freedom and confidence in the love of the parents is such a wonderful and joyful thing to witness!

As a mommy, oh my goodness! My heart would fill to overflowing as my precious daughters showed their trust in my love and in my arms. At times they would run full out, jumping into my arms for a big hug and kiss, for a crazy twirl in the air or for us to start our next silly dance!

Other times, my heart would overflow with thankfulness as my girls trusted my love and my arms to comfort and care for their hurt little knees, elbows, chins and broken toys.

And, later, as my beautiful girls grew older, my heart would overflow with thankfulness, even as my eyes filled and flowed with tears for them, each time they trusted me with their broken hearts, bruised egos, problems and pressures.

As crazy much as I love my daughters, I know I have not loved them perfectly. And so do they. My daughters have not always been able or willing to run to me with all things, at all times, in all their circumstances with the same freedom and confidence they did as young children. I know this is, in part, a normal phase of growing up – a normal and necessary step for my two precious daughters, and for most people, to grow into adulthood with confidence in their own ability to make their own decisions and deal with their own difficulties.

Sometimes, however, not trusting another person is also partly because we all are frail, flawed and finite. We just don't always want to share those things about ourselves that would reveal these truths to others, or even to ourselves. Sometimes, the person with whom we're sharing just isn't hearing our hearts or responding to us with the love, attention, understanding, support and compassion that we want from them. I have been on both sides of this trust-respond thing.

Thanks be to God for how different He is from us! How beyond compare and comprehension is the truth that we all may approach our Heavenly Father with full freedom and confidence – with all things, at all times, in all circumstances! And our Holy Abba will love us perfectly. Always.

In Christ and through faith in him
we may approach God with freedom and confidence.
Ephesians 3:12

Let us then approach God's throne of grace with confidence,
so that we may receive mercy and find grace to help us in our time of need.
Hebrews 4:16

Because of all that Jesus has done for us and through our faith in Him, we can trust our Holy God with full freedom and confidence! We are loved. We are forgiven. We are understood. We are strengthened. We are comforted. We are encouraged. We are safe. We are His.

So let's all run – with childlike faith, trust and hope – with full force into the arms and into the presence of our eternally loving, sovereign and intimate Heavenly Father!

Ready. Set. Go!

Reflections – Responses – Challenges – Encouragements – God-breathing Thoughts

Do I believe it?
And if I do, what am I going to do about it?

Lord, please let me hear your voice, your love, your wisdom, your grace and truth.

REMEMBER WHO YOU ARE!

I was shaken. I walked through the train station, fighting back tears and nausea. I had been horribly sick while away from home. Alone. These last few days had been rough. The last six months had been rougher – filled with way too many funerals. Way too much loss for me and for some dear friends. I was worn out. I just wanted to get home. I struggled down the station's stairs with two suitcases. The escalator only went up. And apparently I was invisible. No one helped me with my bags. No one. I rushed to the platform just in time to see the train blow right past me. I just stood there. Shaken. Sick. Crying. (I hope they don't keep the security videos. I was a real mess.) I called my husband Tim. He lovingly, powerfully prayed for me. I just couldn't pray for myself. Not right then. I was so worn out. So shaken.

While on the train (I finally caught one), Tim sent me a text message with the Scripture below. Tim used God's Word to call me to remember who I am in Jesus. And to remember the power and confidence that I have within me – to endure. Even when I am shaken.

> *Remember those earlier days after you had received the light,*
> *when you endured [stood your ground] in a great conflict full of suffering.*
> *So do not throw away your confidence; it will be richly rewarded.*
> *...we do not belong to those who shrink back and are destroyed,*
> *but to those who have faith and are saved.*
> Hebrews 10:32, 35, 39

I felt God's shouting out to me through His Word and from His love: *"Remember who you are! C'mon, girl! Get your head together. I Am with you! I have given you My Light! Do not allow the darkness to swallow you up! Remember all you and I have already conquered! You have gone through tougher times than these! Don't fall apart now! Stand your ground! Endure! Stand firm on My Truth! I know you're shaken! But fight! Fight for your peace! Fight for your perspective! Remember who you are! And, Remember who I Am! I Am your confidence! Remember that! Do not shrink back! I Am Greater than this! Do not be destroyed! I Am your very Life! I Am your very Strength! Remember who you are! Remember Who and What you believe! Remember you are Saved for all Eternity! Don't lose your confidence now! Not about these things that will not last! Remember you are Mine! Endure! Stand your ground! Fiercely! Powerfully! Tenaciously! Stand your ground with complete humility before Me and with complete confidence and faith in Me as you remember who I Am!"*

This Scripture. This specific message from God overwhelmed me with God's intimacy to me and the power of God's Word for me. Right then. Right there. I started to breathe deeply again even as the tears still rolled down my face. I was being quieted in my soul. I was being strengthened in my deepest core. I started to focus again on God's grace and truth, hope and strength, peace and courage. I started to focus again on Jesus. Really, really focus on Jesus.

God never asks us to deny our reality or pretend it isn't hard. Really hard at times. God is the Truth, and He certainly doesn't expect us to lie or to be falsely peaceful and or pretend to be strong in any way. At any time. What God does ask of us is to give Him our heads and hearts again and again. Fully. Continually. In the sweet times. In the rough times. And always remember who we are in Him!

Do I believe it?
And if I do, what am I going to do about it?

Lord, please let me hear your voice, your love, your wisdom, your grace and truth.

SHHHHH...THE BELOVED IS RESTING

You may have seen a picture of Jesus carrying a little lamb on His strong, powerful shoulders. We need to take that image as our own. And recognize the loving, protective care Jesus has for the little lamb who is carried. This is exactly how our Lord carries each one of us. In God we are safe. In God we may rest in His constant protection. In God we are carried in His love for us. Because we are His beloved.

Let the beloved of the LORD rest secure in him, for he shields the beloved all day long, and the one the LORD loves rests between his shoulders.
Deuteronomy 33:12

Isn't this an amazing image to grab hold of for ourselves? First of all, we are called the beloved. Oh, just stay there for a moment. Rest in that truth. Really sense the power, passion and intimate love that the One who calls you His beloved has for you. It's a great word. It's a great reality. We are powerfully, passionately and intimately loved by the Lord of all Creation, by our Almighty God. We are His beloved.

God knows His beloved so well. God knows we need quiet. We need stillness and rest. We need to rest right in the midst of our rushing and busyness and all of the noise and demands in our lives. Our God knows we need to feel secure and safe in order to rest. We need to know we are protected. We can't rest if we're worried or afraid, pressured or distracted. God promises us a rest that is secure in Him, shielded by His eternal, protective love every moment. All day long.

We, as the Lord's beloved, are picked up to rest on His shoulders. We can trust God. We can trust His shoulders. These are the same ones that Isaiah spoke of when he wrote:

...the government will be on his shoulders...
Isaiah 9:6.

Yes. All authority in all of Creation rests on our Lord's shoulders. So, I'm thinking that's a pretty safe place for each of us, as the Lord's beloved, to rest, too.

And just as our Erin and Julia did to me and to their daddy when they were little girls, I'm going to raise my hands up to Jesus – letting Him know I want, and desperately need, to be picked up and to be held in the safety of His loving arms. And I'm going to settle down and snuggle in for a good, refreshing, safety-giving rest. Rest as God's little lamb. Rest as the Lord's beloved.

Shhhhh...You rest, too.

Right in the midst of whatever this day brings to you. Rest as the beloved of your Lord!

Reflections – Responses – Challenges – Encouragements – God-breathing Thoughts

Do I believe it?
And if I do, what am I going to do about it?

Lord, please let me hear your voice, your love, your wisdom, your grace and truth.

RAISE THAT BABY TO BE AN ADULT!

"Raise that baby to be an adult!" These were some very strong and wise words spoken to me when our first-born daughter was only two weeks old. They were spoken by an older, wiser woman (who was actually, at that time, quite a bit younger than I am now). Spoken by a mom who knew that it is a great gift to love our children so fully that we would, from the very beginning of their days, choose to guide them towards adulthood. Guide these precious, tiny individuals towards wisdom and maturity, responsibility and compassion for others. And, for us as believers in Jesus, it also meant we were to raise up our babies in the knowledge and love of the Lord. With all that in mind, I added my own mantra: *And raise that baby on your knees!*

Since my husband and I knew God's Word declares that one day:
> *...at the name of Jesus every knee should bow,*
> *in heaven and on earth and under the earth,*
> *and every tongue acknowledge that Jesus Christ is Lord...*
> Philippians 2:10-11

We knew that humility before our God was essential to do any of this baby-raising thing! We knew that, whether or not our babies would ever choose to be God's babies, we still had a call on our lives to do it God's Way – to raise them with lots and lots of God's love, wisdom and help!

> *Love the LORD your God with all your heart and with all your soul and with all your strength. These commandments that I give you today are to be upon your hearts. Impress them on your children. Talk about them when you sit at home and when you walk along the road, when you lie down and when you get up.*
> Deuteronomy 6:5-7

Just as we are to raise up our own babies this way, it is *the way* God wants all of us to grow up as His followers, as His children – as the Body of Christ.

> *When I was a child, I talked like a child, I thought like a child.*
> *When I became [an adult], I put the ways of childhood behind me.*
> I Corinthians 13:11

Grow up. Set aside childish things. God's greatest purpose for all of us is to grow up to be more like Jesus. God desires, and transforms, His children "to be conformed to the image of his Son" (Romans 8:29).

To be like Jesus is pretty grown up. To be like Jesus requires a *child-like* trust in our loving Abba and a willing, obedient heart to set aside all things *childish*. Our choices and actions should reflect our humility before God, our love for God, our Christ-likeness in wisdom, maturity, responsibility and compassion for others. As God's babies on the way to adulthood – on the way to being more like Jesus – we should: *Love others. Forgive others. Strengthen and heal our families. Respect and protect others. Give to others. Share what we have. Share what we know of God's love and salvation. Provide for the hungry. Care for the hurting. Sacrifice our self-centered actions and attitudes for the sake of others. Live out God's love, grace and truth, justice and peace, mercy and compassion in every way possible with everyone!*

May we each choose, as God's babies, to let God raise us to be adults. His Way.

Reflections – Responses – Challenges – Encouragements – God-breathing Thoughts

Do I believe it?
And if I do, what am I going to do about it?

Lord, please let me hear your voice, your love, your wisdom, your grace and truth.

GOD'S GOOD AND TRANSFORMING INTENTIONS

We might not always understand why we experience hard and hurtful circumstances and relationships in life. I certainly don't. At least not in their entirety as to the timing or duration or frequency or who or what is involved. Yet, one of the things that helps me to stop asking why – even when my heart is breaking over the hard and hurtful experiences in my life or in the lives of those I love – is to remember that we live in a broken world.

Most of us would agree that, of course, this world is not perfect. Yet, when we experience the reality of this broken world – in the form of betrayal, abuse, illness, death, job loss, status loss, unfair or cruel treatment, disappointment over unmet hopes and dreams – we often react with a certain measure of shock and spend much of our energy asking why. And sometimes the only answer to "the why" we may ever get on this side of heaven is that this is a broken world. Filled with broken people (like me) who, because of our sins, can cause deep brokenness in the lives of others. But! That is not where God intends to leave any of us! Ever.

Whatever our hard and hurtful experiences or circumstances or relationships may have been, or are right now, we need to let God have the last Word! We need to allow God's good and transforming intentions have more power over us than the meanness and evil, sadness and injustice of this broken world and all of its broken people.

We need to trust and embrace – and be embraced by – God's love and peace, grace and truth as the authoritative power over our minds, our hearts, our actions, our talk and our self-talk. God will never ask us to deny how hurtful and hard our experiences and circumstances are, but He asks us to let Him give us His power and perspective to transform them into something that will reveal God's goodness and transforming love.

I have no doubt that God hates sin and that He always hated the abuse I experienced because of the sin choices made against me within my family. No matter what my abusers' intentions were, God never intended to leave me in a state of brokenness. Instead, through the love and forgiveness of Jesus, every shred of power has been ripped away from the abuse and from my abusers. God's good and transforming intentions were, and are, to take away the power (not necessarily the experiences) of all things hard and hurtful so that they would no longer destroy or diminish me. In any way. In Christ all is forgiven. And I am set free.

> *You intended to harm me,*
> *but God intended it for good*
> *to accomplish what is now being done,*
> *the saving of many lives.*
> Genesis 50:20

Our God is able to take all our hard and hurtful, ugly and evil experiences – even if we don't understand "the why" – and use them to unveil His amazing beauty. God is able to fully transform all things that others intended for evil into uncompromising evidence of God's good intentions and unfailing love for us. And we are set free to let others know about the truth of God's eternal love, the power of forgiveness, the gift of salvation and the fullness of healing and life offered through our Lord Jesus Christ!

Do I believe it?
And if I do, what am I going to do about it?

Lord, please let me hear your voice, your love, your wisdom, your grace and truth.

EACH NEW DAY...EACH NEW MOMENT...I NEED JESUS

Each day. Each Moment. I need Jesus.
The realization of this simply stated, but eternally desperate, need for my Lord's love and presence in my life seems to grow stronger within me each passing day. Maybe it's age. Maybe it's God's wisdom speaking to my soul. I need Jesus.

I know that as God's child by faith, I am sealed for all eternity by His Holy Spirit for the day of redemption (Ephesians 4:30)! In Jesus I am *Signed, Sealed, Delivered! I'm yours!* (Yeah, go ahead, break into that Stevie Wonder song! I always do!)

I know that in my Lord Jesus there is nothing
> *...In all creation that will be able to separate us*
> *From the love of god that is in Christ Jesus our Lord.*
> Romans 8:39

And still, each new day, each new moment, I need to intentionally acknowledge that I need Jesus. I need to intentionally choose to breathe in the truths of my eternally present, infinitely, unfailingly loving God. I am not God. I am His child. I am loved deeply – far beyond my ability to comprehend. I am intimately cared for by the Sovereign Lord of all that exists. I am transformed by His love in my innermost being, in the depths of my mind, heart and soul. I am empowered by the grace and truth that come in all their fullness through my Lord Jesus Christ.

Each day. Each Moment. I need Jesus. And our God lavishly and continually pours out His love and presence, peace and power to all of His children. Each new day. Each new moment.

> *See what great love the Father has lavished on us,*
> *that we should be called children of God! And that is what we are!*
> 1 John 3:1

May God help each of us to continually choose to *receive all* that Christ offers (and constantly get over ourselves) so that we will know His love in deeper, more tangible, more healing and transforming ways each new day, each new moment of our lives.

And in this way, may God continually grow each of us to be a *reflection* of, and offer, His love in deeper, more tangible, more healing and transforming ways each new day, each new moment, with each and every person in our lives.

We all need Jesus. And our God meets all of our needs, through the filling of our lives with His love and presence, His peace and power in ways that go far beyond our understanding and expectations – and last far beyond our earthly life.

> *And my God will meet all your needs*
> *according to the riches of his glory in Christ Jesus.*
> Philippians 4:19

We all need Jesus. More desperately than we really know. Each new day. Each new moment. For all of eternity.

Do I believe it?
And if I do, what am I going to do about it?

Lord, please let me hear your voice, your love, your wisdom, your grace and truth.

THE PEACE POSSIBILITY

When there is strain, brokenness and even outright hatred and animosity between people, it seems that the possibility of peace is impossible. This would be true if the only peace we would be willing to recognize as true peace was the absolute ending of all tensions by all the people involved.

God's way of peace begins with One. Himself. His life. His sacrifice for our peace. God does it all. We, then, have the choice as to whether or not we will live at peace with Him.

...*the punishment that brought us peace was upon him...*
Isaiah 53:5

Yet, for us, when our relationships with others are seething – even under the surface – with bitterness, judgment, misjudgment, hurt and anger, we will often wait for the other person to make the first move towards restoring the relationship. *After all, their wrongs have been so very wrong – and certainly more wrong than ours. They owe us an apology first – and it darn well better be a good one. They are the ones who need to change first. And certainly more than we do. They are the ones who really need to prove themselves as ready to be different if there is ever going to be any peace in any way in this relationship.*

Oh! We so very much need to get over ourselves! We need to recognize the responsibility that we each have to live at peace with others. We need to choose to follow Christ's example and allow humility and courage to mingle within our hearts and minds so that peace will flow from our mouths and actions. In all of our interactions.

If it is possible, as far as it depends on you, live at peace with everyone.
Romans 12:18

I know that peace with certain people will not always be possible, and certainly not all of the time. With other people, peace may never be possible, at any time. You and I have no power to change anyone, in any way. However, each of us does have the power to choose to give up our own stubborn pride and self-centered, self-focused attitudes and behaviors. We can choose to seek God's wisdom and way of peace to show us what we can, and should do – how we are to think and speak and act with others – in order *to live at peace with everyone as far as it depends on us.*

As we raised our daughters, we tried to teach them that each person within our family has the same power to either be a Peace-Maker or a Peace-Breaker. How they used their power to make or break the peace was their own choice. It depended on them. They couldn't make that choice for anyone else in the family.

Living at peace with others, God's Way, depends on one. One person humbly, courageously choosing to do the right thing, even if no one else does.

Our Lord Jesus, the Prince of Peace, gave up His life to bring us peace. What might you need to give up in order for the possibility of peace to flow through your own heart and soul and into the lives of others?

Do I believe it?
And if I do, what am I going to do about it?

Lord, please let me hear your voice, your love, your wisdom, your grace and truth.

OVERCOME EVIL WITH GOOD!

Do you ever just feel absolutely overwhelmed or overcome by the evil in the world? Or by the evil that comes at you from the people or the circumstances in your own life?

I do. And when that is the case, we must remember that we have not been left powerless or without choice. Sometimes our choice is much simpler than we realize or remember. God directs us and enables us to do things God's way. To overcome evil with good.

Do not be overcome by evil, but overcome evil with good.
Romans 12:21

I am humbled beyond explanation by God's call on my life to enter so intimately into the lives of others as I speak, write, counsel and teach from God's Word about His love, grace and truth. Humbled and thankful. In awe of God. In awe of what God can do in our lives.

Yet, I have a confession: *There are times I just want to run away and hide. There are times I want to just stop listening and talking to anyone and everyone. There are times I want to stop trying. There are times I feel overcome by all of the meanness and evil and pain and ugliness and poverty and injustice and brokenness and cruelty and selfishness there is in this world. There is in me. There is in us. There is in the way we treat others. There is in the way we live.*

And, then, there it is. There it comes again. Unfailingly. God's powerful, sweet whoosh of goodness and love. God's good love.

And God quiets me.
God offers Himself as my hiding place.
God gives my mind His Sabbath rest.
And there, God renews me with His eternal perspective.
God reminds me, tenderly and strongly, that Jesus Christ has already overcome all the power of evil for all eternity with His good love.
God overcomes. God wins.

It does not, therefore, depend on human desire or effort, but on God's mercy.
Romans 9:16

And I can breathe again.

I can listen and speak and stay in the moment – even in the midst of the unleashed fury of ugly and evil – to love people again with, and only because of, the power of God's good love that overcomes evil. It never depends on me. Not ever. It all depends on God and His good love and mercy. Always.

We are not to be overcome by evil. Not ever. We are to overcome evil with good. Always.

May we each choose to listen, to trust and obey and to be empowered by the truth of God's good love for all of us. May we each choose to overcome evil with good. With that one person. In that one situation. With one good thought. With one good word. With one good action. One day at a time. Each day of our lives.

Do I believe it?
And if I do, what am I going to do about it?

Lord, please let me hear your voice, your love, your wisdom, your grace and truth.

January 26

ONE OUTSTANDING DEBT TO CARRY

Many of us have dealt with, or may be in the midst of dealing with even now, the far-reaching consequences of carrying excessive personal financial debt. At times this debt comes to us through no fault of our own, but rather as the result of overwhelming personal crises in our lives such as unexpected unemployment, a flood, a fire, an accident, a severe and debilitating illness or a death of a family member. Or our debt may be the result of our own poor planning and the unwise financial decisions we've made. Either way, this debt can be a crushing and humiliating experience.

Our God cares so much about all the details of our lives, including our financial and material circumstances. God desires us to become wise stewards with all of our resources – whether they are meager or abundant.

Yet, there is *one debt* that God desires us to keep as an outstanding account and carry it indefinitely, all the days of our lives: *the debt of loving others.* This is the one account that we must never consider as paid in full – or even as possible to pay it fully.

> *Let no debt remain outstanding,*
> *except the continuing debt to love one another...*
> Romans 13:8

As believers and followers of Christ, we are His ambassadors, and in Him and by His Spirit we have been given unlimited, over-flowing resources to pay towards this debt of love into the lives of others. "God is love" (1 John 4:8). And God calls each of us to share His love with others – actively, intentionally, constantly, practically, tangibly, sincerely, sacrificially, humbly. The Word of God clearly tells us that when it comes to loving one another, we must consider this as the *one debt* that will always remain outstanding.

What Christ has done for us through the holy sacrifice of His life – for the forgiveness of our sins and the promise of eternal life – can never be repaid. Nor is it meant to be. Christ's sacrifice is a pure, passionate gift of love from our Holy God, and it is to be fully and freely received by us.

Our response to this amazing love from our Holy God ought to be to love others. Really love others. The need for love in this world and in the lives of every person around us will always remain outstanding on this side of heaven.

> *May the Lord make your love increase and overflow*
> *for each other and for everyone else...*
> 1 Thessalonians 3:12

May each of us choose, over and over again, to pay towards our outstanding debt of love through the limitless resources of our God who loves us unfailing and constantly! May we each allow God's love, Spirit, power, passion and compassion to flow through each of us so that we may love others in practical and spiritual, temporal and eternal ways! Today and every day of our lives.

Do I believe it?
And if I do, what am I going to do about it?

Lord, please let me hear your voice, your love, your wisdom, your grace and truth.

DO YOU WANT TO GET WELL?

I am absolutely convinced that God is able to fully heal and restore any life and completely transform each of us by the renewing of our minds. What I am not so convinced of is our own willingness to let God do His powerful work in us. Fully. His Way.

God had to really challenge me to look deeply inside myself and decide not only if I truly *believed* God could heal my heart after so much abuse in my life, but also if I truly *wanted* God to heal my heart. I had already forgiven my family as a teenager. This had brought enormous freedom and healing to my life. But, Oh! There was much more work to be done.

During the first year of our marriage, with my Timmy's help, God made it very clear that He needed to take me deeper in order to make me freer. My Tim, who loved me better than anyone, understood me better than anyone, was also the sweet, sharp sword that God used to help cut away the crippling power of victimhood I was holding onto as part of my identity (and hadn't even realized it). One day after an especially difficult and ugly call with my parents, I broke into a fit of self-pity and anger. *How could they still be this way when all I did was try to love them and be a reflection of Jesus' love for them? When were they ever going to get it? When were they ever going to change?*

In the midst of my ranting, Tim asked me, tenderly and gently (and quite courageously), "Sylane, do you want to be happy?" That cut me so deeply. I had a right to vent. At least with him! Arrrgghh! But that cutting was actually from my Lord who had spoken very similar words to another cripple whose path He had crossed.

> *At the pool of Bethesda...a great number of disabled people used to lie – the blind, the lame, the paralyzed. One who was there had been an invalid for thirty-eight years. When Jesus saw him lying there and learned that he had been in this condition for a long time, Jesus asked him, "Do you want to get well?"*
> John 5:2-6

Oh, my! God used this passage of Scripture in an all-up-in-my-face-because-God-loves-me way to show me that there was something still inside me that was refusing to fully *want* God's full healing and power instead of my full right to self-pity. Ouch! *God wanted me to want Him* to fully heal me and take away every last vestige of victimhood from my life! Because of His Love for me. God wanted me free, and reminded me of His Word of Truth that declares:

> *In all these things we are more than conquerors through him who loved us.*
> Romans 8:37

Just as Jesus had challenged that man at the pool of Bethesda, He challenged me: *Do you want to get well?* My answer so many years ago was, and still is: *Yes! No more victimhood. Jesus, You call me more than a conqueror. Lord, I want to be well! Help me let You intervene and interrupt my patterns of thinking and speaking, acting, interacting and reacting in every way with everyone so that I may walk with You in the freedom of the full healing You offer!*

What about you: *Do you want to get well?* Do you want our God who loves you so much to bring His full healing into your life? I am convinced this is what God wants!

Do I believe it?
And if I do, what am I going to do about it?

Lord, please let me hear your voice, your love, your wisdom, your grace and truth.

GOD'S CUTTING EDGE OF LOVE

God's Word is alive. It's living and active. It is not dead, dull or dormant! God's Word is meant to penetrate our minds, permeate our actions and purify our innermost beings so that we will become more like Jesus, the living Word of God, in all we do and in all we are.

For the word of God is alive and active. Sharper than any double-edged sword,
it penetrates even to dividing soul and spirit, joints and marrow;
it judges the thoughts and attitudes of the heart.
Hebrews 4:12

Have you ever heard the phrase: "Well, he certainly isn't the sharpest tool in the shed"? He (whoever he, or she, is) may seem a little clueless or a bit oblivious about what's going on around him. Or maybe he lacks the knowledge level or skill required to accomplish a specific task.

Well, I am certain that there is nothing clueless or oblivious, in any way, about the living and active Word of God. God's Word is absolutely the sharpest tool in God's shed. God is fully aware, fully knowledgeable of what is going on in every circumstance, in every relationship, in every individual. Nothing is hidden from the eyes of our loving and omniscient God. And our God is the true master swordsman, the master surgeon, who wields His Word – His living, active, double-edged sword – with perfect precision and with the precise purpose of transforming each of His children to be more and more like Jesus.

God does indeed have His work cut out for Him! But in His love for us, God is tireless and relentless in penetrating our innermost being, our thoughts, motivations and attitudes. God cuts through our self-focused perspective in order to free us to live – really live – in a trusting and intimate relationship with our God and with others. For this to be accomplished, we have to hear and honestly allow God's Word to point out where we are motivated by our own personal versions of truth, by our own twisted thinking or by LFTPOHs (Lies From The Pit Of Hell) as we interact and respond to others and, even, to God Himself.

God must continually divide and separate out from us anything and everything that does not line up with God's Word of grace and truth. This is a lifetime process. We must continually submit to God's living and active Word so that He may reveal our flawed thinking and heal our bruised hearts. And transform us beautifully and continually into the likeness of Christ.

Sometimes this cutting away, separating and dividing work within our innermost being can be a very painful process. So, too, is physical surgery. Yet, most of us would be willing to submit ourselves to a human surgeon's skills if we were faced with a diseased organ or a deadly growth of cancer within our bodies. We would submit so that we may live.

How much more should we trust ourselves over to our God, who not only has the perfect skill to cut away any and all things that are unhealthy and deadly for our mental, emotional and spiritual well-being, but does it all completely out of His perfect love for us! So that we may live!

To be more like Jesus is God's great and loving purpose for each of us. And to fulfill it, God places us on His cutting edge of love. The very safest place we could ever be.

Reflections – Responses – Challenges – Encouragements – God-breathing Thoughts

Do I believe it?
And if I do, what am I going to do about it?

Lord, please let me hear your voice, your love, your wisdom, your grace and truth.

NO FISHING ALLOWED

It is true that our God is a Holy God and God hates sin. That will never change. However, through the sacrifice of Jesus, we are completely pardoned of our guilt and forgiven of every sin. When we confess and repent – sincerely, with not even one shred of self-justification, nor any blaming of anyone else for the sinful choices we have made – our God delights to forgive us and show us the fullness of His mercy!

God actively and intentionally separates us from our sins. Our Lord Jesus completely crushes them under His nail-pierced feet. And with His nail-scarred hands, He flings them forever into the depths of the sea. Never to disrupt our relationship with our Holy God again.

Who is a God like you, who pardons sin and forgives the transgression of the remnant
of his inheritance? You do not stay angry forever but delight to show mercy.
You will again have compassion on us; you will tread our sins underfoot
and hurl our iniquities into the depths of the sea.
Micah 7:18-19

Our God compassionately chooses to completely forgive us of each of our sins and free us from all the power of shame and guilt-ridden entrapment those sins would hold over our lives. In Jesus Christ our sins have been thoroughly and eternally punished. On the cross, even in His agony, Jesus cried out in victory, "It is finished!" And He meant it.

When we confess and ask our Holy God to forgive us for all the stupid, ugly, dark, evil sins that we all have done – He does. In His unfathomable, unfailing love, God removes all of the blame and all of the shame of all our sins – taking them in His Holy Arms, those same Holy Arms that were once outstretched on the cross, and hurls them into the depths of the sea!

So, Darlin's, that means: No fishing allowed!

Do not go grabbing for your Shame-On-Me-Fishing-Pole to continually drag out your sins and beat yourself up over and over and over again for the sins you have sincerely confessed, and from which you have truly repented. (If you haven't, then, that's another matter altogether.)

That Shame-On-Me-Fishing-Pole is really built from pride, not humility. It is pride that keeps us entrapped in the pain, the embarrassment and the shock over the fact that we could have sinned in such a way (whatever that way was). It is pride that keeps us from accepting the full truth that only in Jesus are we forgiven. The full truth that we cannot add anything to the work Jesus completed on the cross for our forgiveness. We cannot make ourselves any more forgiven by staying in a state of remorse. Our sins are ugly. The remorse we feel should only bring us, in full humility, to the foot of the cross so we will let the blood of Jesus completely cover all our sins. In humility, there is freedom. Our sins and our shame have been hurled into the depths of the sea, never to be seen again. In humility, we celebrate the grace and truth that it was Jesus who put up that sign: No fishing allowed!

So! Don't even go there! Don't go to that place where your heart is entrapped in pride and shame. No fishing allowed! Instead, take up your Freedom-Fishing-Pole, follow Jesus and become fishers of men and women!

Do I believe it?
And if I do, what am I going to do about it?

Lord, please let me hear your voice, your love, your wisdom, your grace and truth.

REMEMBER WHEN YOU SAID…?

God never forgets the promises He makes to those of us who put our trust in Him. And sometimes, especially in those hard and hurting times in our lives, we need to pray back to God His own words. We need to name the truths that we believe about God. We need to claim the hope that God gives us. For our sake. For God's glory.

God knows His Word is faithful and true. Because God is faithful and true. God knows what He has for us and who He wants to be to us – our full hope and our very life.

> *Remember your word to your servant,*
> *for you have given me hope.*
> *My comfort in my suffering is this:*
> *Your promise preserves my life.*
> Psalm 119:49-50

Have you ever prayed anything like this? Like I have, many times?

My God! Remember when You said that You are my Hope?
My Strength? My Joy? My Light?
My Defender? My Protector? My Shelter? My Shield?
My Provider? My Helper? My Healer? My Comfort?
My Shepherd? My Savior? My Hiding Place?
My Righteous Judge? My Redeemer from sin?
My Rescuer from the dominion of darkness?
My Wonderful Counselor? My Mighty God?
My Everlasting Father? My Prince of Peace?
My Way? My Truth? My Life?
God, those are Your words! Not mine!
And I need You to be all of those for me, right now!

Our God, in His love and mercy, in His grace and truth, answers each of us quietly and firmly.
I Am who I Am. I never change. My Word is True. I call you to trust Me.

God knows who He is. God always remembers. And God is faithful to His Word and what He promises to His children. It is we who forget. Or we, at least temporarily, do not keep in the forefront of our minds the truth of God's love for us, the peace of God's presence with us, and the hope of God's promises to us.

It is we who are shaken by what seems to be a delay or a dismissal to our cries out to God. Yet, our God is not shaken. And even in our hardest and most heart-breaking moments and seasons of our lives, we need to remember that God is God. And God's faithfulness and love for us and His Word to us are unfailing and eternal.

It is you and I who need to remember. Remember what God says. Remember who God is.

So, go ahead! Pray back to God His own words. God loves it when we know His Word! Then, choose to trust God at His Word. God remembers His promises. God remembers you.

Reflections – Responses – Challenges – Encouragements – God-breathing Thoughts

Do I believe it?
And if I do, what am I going to do about it?

Lord, please let me hear your voice, your love, your wisdom, your grace and truth.

WORDS TO TAKE TO HEART

In our corner of the world, we have such accessibility to the Bible. It's very easy to forget that there are many Christian sisters and brothers around the world who are desperate to own a Bible. Who are desperate to be able to freely read and openly study the Scriptures without fear of persecution or prosecution. There are, also, still so many others throughout our world who do not yet know and have never read for themselves about the grace and truth of God that is found in the Bible – the written, inspired, teaching, correcting, encouraging, transforming Word of our Living God. God's words that are our life.

Take to heart all the words I have solemnly declared to you this day
...They are not just idle words for you – they are your life.
Deuteronomy 32:46-47

I have to admit that I take my easy access to the Bible for granted way too often. Just as I do the air I breathe, the food I eat, the water I drink. Even though I desperately need each of these to live. It is the same with God's words. We are not to take any of God's words for granted. Rather, we are to take all of God's words to heart. Because they are our life.

God's words are not idle – like a vehicle going nowhere, just sitting, running its engine, with no movement, and just getting emptier and emptier of its source of power. No! God's words are living, active, powerful and purposeful. And they are to be taken to heart – taken to the very core of our innermost being – so that God's words may give each of us all the power we need to live. Truly live.

Here are just a very few of God's life-giving words that we so desperately need in our lives:
We need love. God is love. – 1 John 4:8,16
We need unfailing love. – Exodus 15:13, Romans 8:37-39
We need to love God and others and ourselves. – Deuteronomy 6:4-5; Leviticus 19:18;
Mark 12:30-31; Matthew 22:37-39; Luke 10:27
We need hope. God is our hope. – Psalm 25:5; Romans 15:13
We need to put our hope in God's word. – Psalm 119:24, Proverbs 3:5-6
We need peace. God is the Prince of Peace. – Isaiah 9:6, Isaiah 53:5, John 16:33
We need peace beyond our understanding. – Philippians 4:7
We need forgiveness. God offers forgiveness. – Psalm 130:4; Acts 2:38; 1 John 1:8-9
We need eternal salvation, fully and only given by Holy God through our Lord Jesus –
Psalm 62:7; John 3:16-18; Acts 4:12; Romans1:16; Romans 3:22-26; Ephesians 2:8-9;
Philippians 2:5-11
We need life. The Lord is our life. – Deuteronomy 30:19-20; John 10:10; John 11:25;
John 14:6; Romans 8:6; 2 Peter 1:3

No, God's words are not idle. They are powerful, saving, healing, filling, freeing, purposeful. God's words are our very life. Never to be taken for granted.

May each one of us choose to get to know God's words and take them to heart – in every area, in every relationship, in every circumstance and in every moment of our lives. May each of us also choose to share God's words of life more freely, lovingly and courageously with those whose hearts have not yet taken them in.

Reflections – Responses – Challenges – Encouragements – God-breathing Thoughts

Do I believe it?
And if I do, what am I going to do about it?

Lord, please let me hear your voice, your love, your wisdom, your grace and truth.

LOVING GOD – LOVING US

God is One. And God wants one thing from us more than anything else. To love Him.

God created us to be in an intimate love relationship with Him forever. It was broken by our sin. Yet, God's love for us would not allow it to end that way. God gave His One and Only Son to save us – to save all who would believe. All because of God's love for us. When we love God we are actually responding to the love that God has first poured out to us.

> *We love because he first loved us.*
> 1 John 4:19

Our active choice to love God needs to be a daily, intentional choice – an acknowledgement of and thankfulness for who our God is, for all that our God offers to us now and for eternity and for all that our God empowers us to do through His love.

Our God is the Creator of all the wonders and majesty of this universe – of all that we can see and know, of all that is yet unseen and unknown and of all that is far beyond our imagination. We live only by God's loving decision. Our God is absolutely the sovereign One over all that exists, the sovereign, eternal One of all space and time.

And our God is Immanuel – God with us. Our God is intimate in His love for us, intimate in His knowledge of us, intimate in His presence with us. Our sovereign and intimate God is worthy and deserving of all our love, devotion and thankfulness.

God's choice to sacrifice His Holy Son Jesus gives us an undeserved and unshakable eternal salvation. God's love for us brings hope, peace, courage and joy to our lives. Trusting and obeying God's Word – especially as we choose to actively and sincerely love others – are powerful, fruit-bearing, tangible demonstrations of our love for God.

> *"The most important commandment," answered Jesus, "is this:*
> *'Hear, O Israel: The Lord our God, the Lord is one.*
> *Love the Lord your God with all your heart and with all your soul*
> *and with all your mind and with all your strength.' "*
> Mark 12:29-30

Loving God in these ways is worshiping our God "in the Spirit and in truth" (John 4:24). When we love God *in the Spirit and in truth,* our lives are put into a deeper, sweeter, purer balance. We are given an increasingly mature and eternal perspective. We are held in God's unfailing hope. We are protected by God's transcending peace.

The act of loving our Holy God, to which all of us are called as His followers and children, actually brings God's deepest, eternal blessings to us – to our hearts and our souls and our minds and our strength.

Loving our God truly is the very best thing we could ever do to love ourselves.

Do I believe it?
And if I do, what am I going to do about it?

Lord, please let me hear your voice, your love, your wisdom, your grace and truth.

SHAKEN AND STIRRED

Even when we weren't looking for God's love, or didn't even know it existed, God poured out the full measure of His love for us through His Holy Son Jesus. Each one of us is so precious and valuable to our God that He shook our world by first entering among us and, then, by sacrificing His Son to pay for our sins. Through this love-sacrifice of Jesus, the sting of death and the power of sin have been shaken off from each of us who believe. For all eternity.

> *This is how God showed his love among us:*
> *God sent his one and only Son into the world that we might live through him.*
> *This is love: not that we loved God,*
> *but that he loved us and sent his Son as an atoning sacrifice for our sins.*
> 1 John 4:9-10

I would love to tell you that I fully understand this incredible, passionate, holding-back-nothing love of God. But I don't. I can't grasp it in its entirety. At least not on this side of heaven. Yet, in the deepest core of my being, my mind and my soul, I know this is truth. And this truth has totally shaken my world. And my heart has been stirred back to life!

To Christ's unlimited love and passion, I can only respond (and did and, by the grace of God, always will) with: *Yes, Lord, I believe You. I believe You love me. I believe that You, Lord Jesus, You died for me. You died for my every sin. You alone are my Savior. In You alone I am forgiven. In You I am set free from all the holds of evil and hurtful things in my life. In You alone I have life. And You chose to do all of this because You love me.*

Please don't read that too quickly. It's not meant to sound like *gag-me-with-a-spoon, Christianese* language that flows like well-rehearsed religious lines without any real power. No! The power behind these words of accepting God's love for me – even when I didn't, and still don't fully, understand God's incredible, shake-my-world-up and stir-my-heart kind of love – is the very same power of God that moves mountains, heals the brokenhearted, sets the captives free and raises the dead to life!

Jesus shook my life. Shook my thinking. In my world-view (which was far too well-established by age seven) I *knew* that I was not loved, and certainly not special enough for anybody to love me. I couldn't be. Not with all of the abuse, the screaming, the incest, the guns, the knives, the fear, the hatred, the hurt, the anger, the evil, the sickness that came at me. Even as a very young child, I had clear and well-founded evidence that I was not, and probably never would be, loved. But! Jesus Christ, the Lord of heaven and earth, the Sovereign God over everything that exists, moved the mountain of my fear, hurt and hate to shake my world and stir my heart! The Eternal God loves me so much that He gave up all His comfort to comfort me.

The Holy One of God loves us all so much that He gave up His life to give us a new life. Beginning immediately and lasting for all eternity! Jesus Christ chose to be taken captive by the cruelty of this world in order to set us free from its power. Our God enters right into our messy lives to shake our worlds and stir our hearts with His love, grace and truth!

May we each let God's love shake us up and stir our hearts so that we will live in His love and share His love – His outrageous, unfailing, unfathomable love – with others!

Do I believe it?
And if I do, what am I going to do about it?

Lord, please let me hear your voice, your love, your wisdom, your grace and truth.

IT JUST MAKES SENSE

Some things just make sense. There is what would seem to be a natural response and order to certain things. The sun rises and the earth is warmed. The rain falls and waters the earth. So it is supposed to be with God's love. We receive it freely from God. Our response should be to share God's love freely with others.

> **Dear friends, since God so loved us,**
> **we also ought to love one another.**
> 1 John 4:11

We complicate things so much. We ego-tize (I'm making words up again!) things so often.

Truth is, it isn't so complicated. And it isn't about us. It's about God reaching out to each and every one of us in this world with His perfect, life-giving, all-powerful love. Since God loves us so outrageously, persistently, unfailingly, passionately much, we ought to – we should, we must, we need to – love others! It just makes sense.

So, let's de-complicate things. De-egotize them.

Our best and most perfect way of responding to the love of our Holy God is to love the people around us. This is what Jesus did. And for us who are true followers of Christ, it is what we ought to do. Without making it more complicated. By setting aside our ego. Loving others – all others and even, and maybe especially, those who hurt us, frustrate us, disappoint us, fail us, or just plain make us crazy – is what we are called to do.

It isn't about us. It's about Jesus.

It's all about becoming more and more like Jesus and letting His transforming love take greater power over everything that we are and every way that we interact with others. It's all about letting Christ's love teach us and lead us, intimately and powerfully, to love others more and more like He does. Loving someone not for what we can get out of it. But loving someone because it is the right thing – the God thing – to do. Loving others because of God's love for us just makes sense. Anything less, anything more complicated or ego-tized, just doesn't.

Oh, this kind of love might not make sense to people who don't yet know the love of Jesus for themselves. This kind of love may even look downright foolish at times. (Oh, my goodness! God has written a number of *foolish-love* stories into my life. Often when I'm traveling on planes, trains, subways or have entirely different plans for my day. I think this comes with the territory for all of us who follow Jesus!)

We are called to love full out and foolishly, if necessary. It's okay if it doesn't make sense to others. God's love still brings His unfathomable grace, truth, freedom and life to all who would receive His love. Always. All the more reason for us to choose to love those who have not yet received God's love and salvation for themselves. Loving others because of Christ's love for us is able to break the power of hell and soften the hardest of hearts! Starting with our own.

So, let's not complicate or ego-tize our interactions with others so much. God loves us. Let's love others. It just makes sense.

Do I believe it?
And if I do, what am I going to do about it?

Lord, please let me hear your voice, your love, your wisdom, your grace and truth.

MIGHTY AND TENDER LOVE

Our Holy God, the maker of heaven and earth, is mighty and sovereign. And our mighty and sovereign God is also tender and compassionate towards us. Our Lord intimately knows our circumstances and our hearts. And during those times when we feel most vulnerable and weak, our God's mighty and tender love will protect us.

> **A bruised reed he will not break,**
> **and a smoldering wick he will not snuff out.**
> Isaiah 42:3

God knows when we are feeling frail and at our breaking point. God knows when our energy is depleted and we are feeling burned out. God knows us. God loves us.

It's so important for us to remember that no matter how awful, frightened and fragile we may feel in the midst of our messy times, nothing changes the might and tenderness of our God in any way. God doesn't change. God does not grow weak or worn out. God's love does not fail. God is our safe and strong place. God can always be trusted. We need to choose to believe these truths and trust our God during those times and in those circumstances when we are feeling most weak and unprotected.

God, unlike some people we may know or experiences we have had, does not "kick us when we're down." God doesn't take advantage of us when we are weak. Rather, when we choose to turn to God – recognizing and admitting that we really do need Him to help us, heal us, hold us, comfort us, lead us, fill us, forgive us, refresh us and renew us – God will use *this* to our advantage. To know Him better. To move us closer to Him. To make us stronger in Him. To experience God's mighty and tender love more powerfully and intimately.

We really are so safe in God's loving hands. They are the mighty and sovereign hands that fashioned every detail of this creation. They are the tender and compassionate hands that are eternally marked with the nail-driven scars of His crucifixion.

> **Show me the wonders of your great love,**
> **you who save by your right hand...**
> Psalm 17:7

> **I cling to you; your right hand upholds me.**
> Psalm 63:8

Our Lord Jesus Christ reaches out to take us by the hand as we walk through each day, each circumstance, each relationship, each responsibility and each moment. Reaching out to give us His mighty and tender love in all we are, in all we do.

May we each choose to reach back and take hold of the hand of our Lord Jesus so that we will know and experience the mighty and tender love of His good grip.

Do I believe it?
And if I do, what am I going to do about it?

Lord, please let me hear your voice, your love, your wisdom, your grace and truth.

BELONG AND BE LOVED

We all want to belong. We all want to be loved.

We want to belong to something bigger than ourselves where we are truly loved, deeply understood and fully accepted. We want to belong where we are completely loved, sincerely respected and intimately known and, therefore, safe enough to be lovingly and truthfully corrected and guided. We want to belong where our mistakes and our sins will be fully forgiven and never used against us, because we are so deeply loved.

Yet, in all these ways, at some level, all people fail us. Families fail us. Friends fail us. The faithful fail us. We fail all others and, even, ourselves.

This sense of true belonging – of being truly, perfectly, completely loved – is offered only from our Eternal Abba, who has compellingly revealed His unfailing, incomprehensible love for us through the sacrifice and resurrection of His Son, our Savior Jesus Christ – to whom, by faith, we belong forever!

> *For this reason I kneel before the Father,*
> *from whom every family in heaven and on earth derives its name!*
> *I pray that out of his glorious riches he may strengthen you*
> *with power through his Spirit in your inner being,*
> *so that Christ may dwell in your hearts by faith.*
> *And I pray that you, being rooted and established in love,*
> *may have power, together with all the Lord's holy people,*
> *to grasp how wide and long and high and deep is the love of Christ,*
> *and to know this love that surpasses knowledge –*
> *that you may be filled to the measure of all the fullness of God.*
> Ephesians 3:14-19

We belong! Our Holy Abba, our Eternal Father has claimed us fully as His own through the sacrifice of His beloved Son Jesus. We belong to God. We're part of His family. Just think about that. We are God's chosen and outrageously loved children, belonging together with all of the Lord's holy people, for all eternity!

We are loved! We are loved by our Holy God with a love that is wider and longer, higher and deeper and more powerful than we will ever fully be able to grasp on this side of heaven! We are loved by our God with a love that surpasses all knowledge and fills us with the very Spirit and nature of our Heavenly Abba, our God who is love!

May each of us choose to trust and live in these freeing and empowering truths: That we are unfailingly loved by our God! That we belong, now and forever, to God's family!

And because of these transforming truths, may each of us choose to actively and intentionally offer Christ's love more fully, more quickly, more continually, more compassionately and more mercifully to all those around us. To all those precious ones who desperately desire to *belong and be loved*. Just like us.

Reflections – Responses – Challenges – Encouragements – God-breathing Thoughts

Do I believe it?
And if I do, what am I going to do about it?

Lord, please let me hear your voice, your love, your wisdom, your grace and truth.

GOD'S LOVE-WATCH

God is actively watching us. And that is a very good thing. However, I know some of us have a hard time not imagining God as playing some sort of cosmic game of Whack-A-Mole with a big hammer in His hand and His eyes moving all over, watching every detail of our lives, ready to bring down a mighty blow on our heads the minute we pop out of our hole.

Our God is watching us. But! His purpose, for those of us whose lives belong to Him, is to strengthen our hearts. And that is a very good thing.

> *For the eyes of the LORD range throughout the earth*
> *to strengthen those whose hearts are fully committed to him.*
> 2 Chronicles 16:9

Our God does a Love-Watch over us. Our God watches us, His people, to strengthen our hearts. Not to crush us. Not to bruise us. Not to break us. Not to smack us down. God watches us to strengthen us.

Our God sees our hearts. He sees clearly the places where we are hurting or confused, struggling or disappointed, frustrated or burned out, angry or sad. And our God comforts us intimately and powerfully, giving us His strength for our hearts.

And our God also sees our sin. Far more clearly than we do. God will confront us and correct us when He sees that we are doing wrong. Yet, this, too, is for the purpose of strengthening our hearts. Sin weakens us. Twists us. Hardens us. Destroys us. God's choice to intervene and interrupt us with His grace and truth, right in the midst of our sins, is for the holy purpose of purifying us – which always strengthens us.

Both God's comfort and correction come purely from God's intimate love for us and His desire to strengthen our hearts. Our God wants all of His people to be strong. Really strong.

We are under God's Love-Watch. And that is a very good thing.

Would the same be true of the way we watch others? Would our husbands, wives, children, sisters, brothers, mothers, fathers, boyfriends, girlfriends, close friends, pastors, elders, church friends, neighbors say they are under *our Love-Watch*?

Do those who are in our world, who are our people, sense that our eyes are watching them to strengthen their hearts? To encourage them? To guide them in God's loving, best ways? To give them comfort? To give them understanding and compassion? Or do our watchful eyes – and our subsequent words and actions – hurt them and weaken them? Put them on the defensive? Do we shut them down or help bring them out? Do our people feel braver and stronger having been under our gaze? Or do they just want to run for cover because we're playing Whack-A-Mole with their hearts?

As God's people, let's do life God's way. Let's purposefully choose to do a *Love-Watch* today. Let's comfort, protect, encourage and strengthen the hearts of our people. I know God will be watching us, and our hearts will be strengthened as He does.

Do I believe it?
And if I do, what am I going to do about it?

Lord, please let me hear your voice, your love, your wisdom, your grace and truth.

NOTHING HIDDEN

The Lord is able to see and know all of our pretenses and fears, all of our thankfulness and joy. God sees and knows all of our prejudices and criticisms, all of our kindnesses and encouragements. God sees and knows all of our limited thinking and all of our wisdom-infused thinking. The Lord clearly sees and fully knows what we think of ourselves, of others, of our circumstances and of Him.

Our God looks intimately and intensely into the deepest recesses of our hearts – seeing all of who we truly are. There is absolutely nothing hidden from the eyes of our God – God's eyes of love and grace and truth.

> *The LORD does not look at the things people look at.*
> *People look at the outward appearance,*
> *but the LORD looks at the heart.*
> 1 Samuel 16:7

Nothing hidden. Nothing at all.

The Lord sees everything within our hearts, within our minds, within our motivations. This might seem a little bit scary. But it is actually a wonderful freedom. Because our God sees and knows us so completely, we don't have to put any energy at all into trying to be someone or something we are not.

As we learn to trust our God's unfailing love for us, we realize what a beautiful, deep-breath kind of freedom it is for our Lord to see and know us so completely. A freedom, before our God and people, because we don't have to pretend or justify or try to cover up any of our thinking, speaking, acting and interacting with others that reveal just how frail, flawed and finite we are.

We all do wrong. We all do wrong blatantly, subtly, intentionally and unintentionally. God knows this full well. Christ died to forgive us, not by pretending or trying to deny our sins but by taking on the full force of their agonizing consequences through His death. God's judgment against our sins and the punishment for them is completed in Christ. We are free not to hide.

May we trust God's love enough for us, that we will be able to accept and trust the truth of this. Our God does look intensely into us, and always will out of His intimate love for us.

Our God knows that the more we willingly yield and open our hearts intentionally to Him, the more freely and powerfully He is able to move to strengthen and transform our hearts. Our God will strengthen our hearts with His love, His grace and His truth, His thoughts, His ways and His eternal perspective. To have a heart that is continually strengthened and transformed to reflect the likeness of our Lord Jesus Christ is the greatest freedom we will ever know!

So, let's choose to be uncovered, without any falsehood or façade before our God who loves us so much. Let's choose to be redirected and renewed in the deepest areas of our lives, our minds and our hearts. How beautiful and freeing it is that nothing is hidden to our God!

Reflections – Responses – Challenges – Encouragements – God-breathing Thoughts

Do I believe it?
And if I do, what am I going to do about it?

Lord, please let me hear your voice, your love, your wisdom, your grace and truth.

February 8

GUARD YOUR HEART

Our hearts are so very important to God. He tells us to make guarding our hearts a top priority. That our hearts are the very wellspring of our lives.

> ***Above all else, guard your heart,***
> ***[for it is the wellspring of life]***
> ***everything you do flows from it.***
> Proverbs 4:23

If our hearts are this *above all else* so important to God, then, we need to seriously think about just how seriously we need to guard them. The word "heart" in Scripture refers to far more than what we often realize. In biblical language our heart is the very center of the human spirit from which all our emotions, thoughts, motivations and actions flow.

God's Word, God's loving, wise, holy intention and righteous direction to each of us is to: Guard our hearts. Guard our emotions. Don't allow frustration, sadness, anger, fear, pride, hurt, lust, jealousy, self-pity, exhaustion, excitement, boredom, numbness or selfishness in any way have control over our hearts. Rather, we are to seek our God and trust Him to give us the love and peace, grace and truth of Jesus Christ to be the deep, balancing, healing, and transforming power that rules over, and flows through, each of our hearts – the very wellspring of our lives.

Guard our hearts. Guard against allowing our unhealthy emotions and reactive responses to our difficult circumstances to become our patterned thoughts and imprisoning perspectives. These can too easily become raging torrents of twisted thought scenarios played out in our hearts that damage and destroy the life-giving flow of our wellsprings.

Those twisted thought patterns can keep our hearts trapped with:
What if I had? What if I had not? Why me? Why not me?
I should have said. I should have done.
I can't believe I did that. I can't believe that was done to me.
This will never get better. I will never get better.
I can't forgive that. God will never forgive me...and on and on and on.

These unhealthy thought patterns and imprisoning perspectives turn our hearts – turn our emotions, thoughts, motivations and actions – away from our God. They block our wellspring and the flow of God's eternal love and perspective that strengthens us, calms us, encourages us and empowers us.

As we choose humility and honesty before God, our hearts will be guarded and our wellsprings made well. May we each guard our hearts. Guard our emotions, thoughts, motivations and actions. Guard every word – spoken, written and thought. Guard every look. Every way we look at others. Everything we look at. Every touch. Every move. Every facial expression. Every gesture. Everything we do. Every way we do it. Everywhere. Every time. With every person.

From out of our hearts flows the deepest essence of who we are. From out of our hearts all that we think, feel, say and do is formed and expressed. How loving and wise of our God to tell us to guard our hearts above all else! God wants our wellsprings well!

Reflections – Responses – Challenges – Encouragements – God-breathing Thoughts

Do I believe it?
And if I do, what am I going to do about it?

Lord, please let me hear your voice, your love, your wisdom, your grace and truth.

GOD'S GRACE POSITIONED SALVATION – GOD'S GPS

Most of us have used some kind of a GPS, Global Positioning System, to help us find our way when traveling along a new or unknown route to an unfamiliar destination. By means of an intricate (and totally beyond my grasp) satellite communication system, we can be guided to almost any place in the world. Very cool.

However, even the most sophisticated technology can fail us. Our GPS can be rendered insufficient or incapable of directing us to exactly where we need and want to go. Unexpected circumstances can hinder our way. Road work. Road blocks. Detours. Sudden accidents. Water main breaks. A parade. For me, recently, it was an ice storm with downed wires and downed trees. All kinds of situations can keep us from getting to our destination – in the expected way and within the expected time frame – even with access to the latest and greatest high-tech devices.

Ahhhhh…not so with our God. Our God promises to lead us, His redeemed people, by His unfailing love and to guide us by His strength to the place where our hearts long to be and need to be: In the presence of our Holy God. Our God's unfailing love and strength can lead and guide us there right now – right in the midst of this world, right in the midst of this life with all of its detours and unexpected circumstances. And, then, one day our God's unfailing love and strength will lead and guide us fully into His holy dwelling. For all eternity.

> ***In your unfailing love you will lead the people you have redeemed.***
> ***In your strength you will guide them to your holy dwelling.***
> Exodus 15:13

Yes! Our God has His own GPS for us – His *Grace Positioned Salvation* – offered through our Lord Jesus Christ. God's unfailing love led Jesus to the cross. And positioning Himself there, our Jesus cleared the way of any and every sin and shame obstacle, detour and unexpected circumstance that would keep us from becoming the redeemed people of our Holy God. And in God's strength, Jesus was triumphantly raised to life and promises to lead and guide us to our final and forever destination – the holy dwelling of our Heavenly Father.

Our God's *Grace Positioned Salvation* will lead and guide us to become more and more like Jesus while we are still on this side of heaven. When unexpected circumstances or our own sin or pride or fear or stubbornness cause our lives and our faith journeys to be detoured, re-routed or blocked for a time, our Lord will direct us back to His way and His truth and His life. Our God will lead and guide us with His unfailing love and strength. We have been redeemed. We can never be too far off course that our Holy God cannot reach us and bring us back.

And our Holy God will lead and guide each one of us, His redeemed people, to the full and final realization and destination of God's *Grace Positioned Salvation*. Our God's unfailing love and strength will bring us home to live with our Abba in His holy dwelling. Forever. Never to be lost or detoured again.

Ahhhhh…God's GPS will never fail. May we each choose to follow closely as our God leads and guides us by His unfailing love and strength. Every day of our lives.

Do I believe it?
And if I do, what am I going to do about it?

Lord, please let me hear your voice, your love, your wisdom, your grace and truth.

COMPLETELY AND UTTERLY DEPENDENT

God alone is the One who truly loves us and knows us and understands us. God alone is the One who saves us. God alone is the One who determines our true honor. Neither people nor our circumstances should ever be given more authority and power over our peace and our perspective of who we are than our Holy God.

My salvation and my honor depend on God
Psalm 62:7

We really are completely and utterly dependent on God. I know the truth of this may make some of us very uncomfortable and questioning, if not downright dismissive and annoyed. Being completely and utterly dependent on anyone or anything, other than ourselves, is not how we usually go about our daily lives. Yet, when we begin to grasp the wild, passionate, perfect, faithful and unfailing love God has for each of us, we will realize that being completely and utterly dependent on God is a very good thing. And a very freeing truth.

The Scripture above tells us that "My salvation...depends on God." Most of us who have accepted Jesus Christ as our Savior would agree with that statement. We have come to understand that we cannot save ourselves. Not by anything we do. Not by our most kind and generous acts. Not by our most pious habits of attending church, praying, fasting, serving. We understand that no one else, not even the most faithful believer, can bring us salvation. Neither can our greatest mocker nor harshest critic ever take away our salvation. We are completely and utterly dependent on Jesus' death on the cross to give us salvation, to forgive our sins and to redeem our lives by His blood. Your salvation – "my salvation...depends on God." Hallelujah! Our salvation does not depend on us, or on anyone else!

But! That is not all the above Scripture says. It says, "My salvation *and my honor* depend on God." We need to let this truth of God – that our honor is just as dependent on God as is our salvation – completely transform us so that we will know how incredibly valued, honored and loved we truly are by our God. Many of us work so hard to make sure we attain certain goals, achieve certain titles, receive appropriate compensation or rightful recognition for our efforts. Yet, our true eternal honor is not dependent on us, no more than is our eternal salvation. Nothing we do will ever be able to make us any more honored than we are right now because of the honor God has already bestowed on us. God honors – loves and values – us beyond what we could ever imagine, beyond what we could ever earn in our own strength. Neither our very best efforts nor our very worst failings will ever change, ever increase or decrease, the honor that God has already imparted on us by His perfect love. Our true eternal honor is not dependent in any way on whether or not people treat us as honorable, valuable and loved. Oh, we want to be treated in those ways. Very much. I know. I want this, too. But recognizing God's truth that He alone has the authority to determine our honor is absolute freedom and peace for us. Hallelujah! Our honor does not depend on us, or on anyone else!

God has made it clear that He alone is the source of both our salvation and our honor. No one but God has the authority or the perfect love to give these to us. And God has given them. They are eternally immutable gifts from our Holy God. May we each choose to fully trust God at His Word, and live in the truth and freedom that our salvation and our honor, completely and utterly, depend on God!

Reflections – Responses – Challenges – Encouragements – God-breathing Thoughts

Do I believe it?
And if I do, what am I going to do about it?

Lord, please let me hear your voice, your love, your wisdom, your grace and truth.

GOD'S ONE WAY TO LOVE

God is One. And God has one over-arching purpose to be worked out in the lives of His children. We are...

...to be conformed to the image of his Son...
Romans 8:29

As we allow God's conforming, transforming work to be done within our lives, each one of us will become more and more one person. One with God. One person – whether we are alone or with those we love or with those we find difficult to love, whether we are with a few or with many, whether we are at work, at play, at church, on vacation or in an unexpected circumstance or location – becoming more and more like Jesus. Becoming more and more one authentic, loving, sincere person.

God is One. God is Love.

God refines us so that any duplicity of character can no longer easily exist within us. To become more like Jesus, we are to be transformed by God's Spirit and God's Word so we may love others as our One God loves us. And that requires sincerity.

Love must be sincere.
Romans 12:9

I am so thankful for every time God *schmushes* down (expresses succinctly and right to the point – in case you weren't sure of my meaning) what He is asking of us. What God requires us to do. Well, God got right to the point here. God *schmushed* it all right down for us on this one: Love must be sincere.

There is nothing to question. Nothing to debate. No great theological-philosophical rhetoric to work through in order to gain clarity of understanding. There is nothing to dispute, discuss or deliberate. Love must be sincere.
No pretenses.
No prejudices.
No pre-conditions.
No arguments.
No excuses.
No games.
No ulterior motives.
No manipulations.
No hypocrisy.
Just a wide-opened willingness to let the transforming grace and truth of Jesus Christ heal us, strengthen us, purify us and grow us up so that we will love others – all others – as God loves us. In sincerity. In truth.

Love must be sincere. This is God's one way to love.

Reflections – Responses – Challenges – Encouragements – God-breathing Thoughts

Do I believe it?
And if I do, what am I going to do about it?

Lord, please let me hear your voice, your love, your wisdom, your grace and truth.

BREATH-TAKING, BREATH-GIVING GOD

When I slow down enough to really let the Word of God and the character of God grab hold of my heart, it takes my breath away. The love and faithfulness, the righteousness and justice of our Lord are real. They are eternal and available to us, every breathing moment of our lives. We all need to slow down and let our eternal God take our breath away. When we do, God will give it right back again. Restoring and refreshing not only our breathing, but also our very lives.

> **Your love, LORD, reaches to the heavens, your faithfulness to the skies.**
> **Your righteousness is like the highest mountains, your justice like the great deep.**
> Psalm 36:5-6

Breathe. Just Breathe. Stop rushing, working, planning, doing. Breathe in the truth that you are more than what you do. Breathe in the truth that you are loved passionately, unfailingly by the eternal God of all creation, of all time and space. Pretty breath-taking to think about, isn't it?

Let this take your breath away: *God's love reaches to the heavens. God's faithfulness reaches to the skies.* Think about the immeasurable expanse of the heavens and skies. No expert astronomer has yet been able to define their true limits. The vast, unending beauty and wonder of the sun, the moon, the stars, the galaxies, the universe cannot be fully captured or accurately measured by any human means. So it is with God's love for you and God's faithfulness to you. They have no limits. No boundary lines exist. God's love and faithfulness are eternal, unfailing and absolutely indescribable in their beauty, wonder and expanse.

Let this take your breath away: *God's righteousness is like the highest mountains.* God's righteousness is majestic, unwavering, immovable, clearly seen and known for what it is – for all who will look upon it. God's righteousness is truth. Just because someone has never seen the Himalayas, Alps or Andes does not mean they do not exist. When they are seen, these high and mighty mountains absolutely dominate the panorama. So it is with God's righteousness. Our standards for, and perspectives on, what is right and good are completely dwarfed in the presence of the high and mighty mountain of God's righteousness. It is upon God's righteousness that we must set our eyes; and allow God's righteousness to stand firm and powerful in our lives.

Let this take your breath away: *God's justice is like the great deep.* Our very existence is intricately tied to the great deep, to the waters of this world. The waters bring nourishment and healing to many. Our harvests depend on the rains. The waters unite and divide us – bringing together peoples and nations within the continents while separating others by enormous, watery distances. The great deep is filled with life and mysteries that we have not even begun to understand. So it is with God's justice. God's justice nourishes and heals us as we seek His ruling and ways. God's justice brings a harvest of true followers as we humble ourselves before Him. God's justice will either unite us or divide us. We will either be God's people standing with Him, acknowledging His just judgment, or we will not be God's people, and will be separated from Him, by God's same just judgment. God's justice is far deeper than our thoughts can comprehend. God's justice is full of life and mystery, able to see beneath the surface and circumstances of our lives. God always sees us clearly, always judges us rightly, because God's justice is always based on His love, faithfulness and righteousness.

Let that take your breath away. And give it right back again with wonder. Now breathe.

Do I believe it?
And if I do, what am I going to do about it?

Lord, please let me hear your voice, your love, your wisdom, your grace and truth.

February 13

GOD'S LOVING, DEMANDING DIRECTIVES

God knows how much we need Him and His loving, demanding directives in our lives. Even when we don't want either. God gets right to the point about how we should live, act and interact with others. Our God does this plain talking all for our very best, all out of His love for us.

> *"Do not seek revenge or bear a grudge against anyone among your people,*
> *but love your neighbor as yourself. I am the LORD."*
> Leviticus 19:18

God's love takes us deep. *We are not to seek revenge.* Not even a little bit of revenge? Even if they really deserve it? No. None.

Only God is able see everything and everyone involved with perfect clarity and discernment. We can't. Only God is able to justly judge the actual sin and the deep thoughts, motivations and circumstances of the one who wronged us. We can't. We don't even want to. We just want revenge. Vengeance is God's. Not ours.

Our God chose to impose all judgment against, and all punishment for, all sin onto His holy Son Jesus. For us to mete out vengeance based on our own very limited, self-focused perspective is a dangerous game of playing God. It is out of God's love that He tells us not to seek revenge. Payback isn't sweet. It's a bitter mockery of the sacrifice Jesus made as the full punishment for all sin – for all time, for all people.

God's love takes us deeper. *We are not to bear a grudge against another person.* Even if we hold the grudge silently inside our own heads? Even if nobody else knows about the grudge? No. Never.

Bearing a grudge is like bearing a heavy, stone wall cemented together by unforgiveness. We think we are entitled to this attitude because of the evil, hurtful things that were done to us. But that kind of thinking, that we think we're entitled to, is actually absolute entrapment. If we keep bearing this grudge, the weight of it will crush us. Leaving us in a crumbled mess of bitterness and resentment. It is out of God's love for us that He tells us not to bear a grudge. We cannot bear a grudge and, at the same time, bear witness to the forgiveness we have freely received through Jesus Christ.

God's love takes us deeper still. *Love your neighbor as yourself.* God loves us. All of us. Out of that love for all His children, God wants us to love others. All others. We are to love our neighbors as we love ourselves. And we should love ourselves in truthful, health-bringing, caring, wise ways. It is out of God's love for us that He tells us to love our neighbors as ourselves. It is for our very best that God wants us to choose thoughts, words, actions and interactions that reflect and reveal Christ's love for all.

God's directives are loving and demanding – in the deepest, most freeing ways possible.

Reflections – Responses – Challenges – Encouragements – God-breathing Thoughts

Do I believe it?
And if I do, what am I going to do about it?

Lord, please let me hear your voice, your love, your wisdom, your grace and truth.

LOVE COUNTS

What really matters to God? What really counts as God's top priority for us as His children, as His people of faith? God gets right to it. God *schmushes* (There's that word again!) everything down for us.

God's Word speaks so clearly and concisely that we cannot deny or doubt God's meaning. What matters, what really counts to God? That we love!

> **The only thing that counts is faith expressing itself through love.**
> Galatians 5:6

Happy Valentine's Day! I know for some of you this is just a schmaltzy day that the card, candy, flower, restaurant and jewelry industries have infused with advertising-steroids to make it a bigger deal for us. Not going to argue that point. But, let's put all that aside.

Happy Valentine's Day! What is going to make this day count for you?
Whether or not you have that someone special in your life right now.
Whether or not you've been acting all that special to your someone special.
Whether or not that someone special has been acting all that special to you.

As a child of God, we are given the answer for how to make Valentine's Day count. Actually, God has given us the answer for how to make every day and every moment count.

It's not convoluted or complicated. To live out our lives as a child of God, to live out our relationship with Jesus Christ, *the only thing that counts is faith expressing itself through love.*

Real love. Really given. God has given us His perfect, sacrificial, passionate, compassionate and everlasting love. God has given this to each of His children. And each one of us is to draw from God's love, constantly and continually, as we interact with others. All others.
Our special ones.
Our not so special ones.
And all those especially challenging ones in our lives.

We are called to love. Really love. *The only thing that counts is faith expressing itself through love.* We shouldn't waste any more time. We need to stop doing any and every thing else that isn't a true expression of love. No matter how entrenched in our not-so-loving habits we have become. We need to get over ourselves and love those around us.

Happy Valentine's Day!

Make this day and every day count for God. For yourself. For others. Love!

Do I believe it?
And if I do, what am I going to do about it?

Lord, please let me hear your voice, your love, your wisdom, your grace and truth.

LOVE IS... – PART 1 – GOD'S OVERVIEW

What does real love look like? God is passionate and purposeful in making that very clear to us. Our God gives us a very comprehensive overview of His view of love.

Love is patient, Love is kind.
Love does not envy,
Love does not boast, Love is not proud.
Love does not dishonor others [Love is not rude],
Love is not self-seeking,
Love is not easily angered,
Love keeps no record of wrongs.
Love does not delight in evil but rejoices with the truth.
Love always protects, Love always trusts,
Love always hopes, Love always perseveres.
Love never fails.
1 Corinthians 13:4-8

This beautiful passage has been quoted by many, many people over the years, by believers and by not-yet-believers, as a moving description of the deepest essence and fullest expression of love. This is what love is. This is what love looks like. But not always what *our love* looks like.

This is what God's love looks like. This is how God loves us. Recognize this truth first. This is how God loves us. Let this powerful, life-changing truth of the unfailing love God has for us completely renew and fill, heal and transform our minds, our hearts, our souls, our spirits.

God wants His children to know the depths of His love for us. And as we grasp this truth more fully, we will be more and more conformed to the likeness of Jesus. God's plan is to transform us within our deepest core so that we will know His love for us and love others the way He loves them and us.

We need to let God change us. Deeply and daily. We need to actively and intentionally make choices in our words and actions that are truly lined up with, and empowered by, God's transforming love.

In these few short verses, God has given us the characteristics of His love, the actions of His love and the promises of His love. And God promises to empower each of us, His children, with the full measure of His unfailing love.

Read this passage again – God's overview of what love Is. Get a good view of what God's love for you – what God's love for each of us – looks like. And what we will look like…and speak like…and act like…as we love others more and more the way our God loves them and our God loves us.

Reflections – Responses – Challenges – Encouragements – God-breathing Thoughts

Do I believe it?
And if I do, what am I going to do about it?

Lord, please let me hear your voice, your love, your wisdom, your grace and truth.

LOVE IS...PATIENT and KIND – part 2

Love is...the very power and nature of the Living God. And God's love is patient and kind. It is for us to fully receive. It is for us to fully give.

Love is patient, Love is kind...
1 Corinthians 13:4

God's love is so real. God knows exactly what we need for our own hearts to be strengthened, encouraged, protected, healed and transformed. We need God's full and perfect love. We need God's patient and kind love.

It is God's love that offers us the patient understanding and gentle kindness that our hearts cry out to receive. God's patient and kind love holds us tenderly and securely in ways that soothe our souls and offer us a place of rest and sanctuary for our minds, our bodies, our souls and our spirits.

I didn't know much about patience or kindness growing up. Snap judgments, a hard smack across the face, cruel criticisms, ugly words – and far uglier, abusive actions were what I knew most, and most often.

But what I lived and experienced – what you may have lived or experienced – does not change who God is. Our past experiences and circumstances – no matter how soul-diminishing they may have been – do not limit the power of God to transform our lives. Our past experiences and circumstances – no matter how ugly and awful – do not change the eternal, beautiful gift God has for us. God loves us. And our God's love is patient and kind. Always.

God's Word is true. God's love is true. God's patient and kind love is full of understanding and compassion for who we truly are. Our God loves us, patiently and kindly, in the midst of all our foibles and in the mess of all our frailties and flaws.

God's patient and kind love quiets us, slows us down, holds us safely, gently reaches into our souls, massages our hearts and refreshes our spirits.

God's patient and kind love embraces and encourages us with the pure love that comes from our true Father, our Heavenly Abba. Each one of us is a very beloved child – a very beloved woman or a very beloved man – of our Holy God.

And our Holy God commands and empowers us to offer His patient and kind love to all those in our lives. Yes, all. No matter what we may have known or experienced from others.

God calls every one of us to love others in such a way that they will know the strengthening, encouraging, protecting, healing, transforming grace and truth of God's patient and kind love in their own lives. Today.

Reflections – Responses – Challenges – Encouragements – God-breathing Thoughts

Do I believe it?
And if I do, what am I going to do about it?

Lord, please let me hear your voice, your love, your wisdom, your grace and truth.

LOVE IS...LOVE DOES NOT ENVY – part 3

God's love is able to fill the very deepest needs and most persistent longings of our hearts and lives. God's love is not only able to fill these deep needs and longings, but it is only God's love that ever will fill them completely. Seeking to have them met from any source other than God's love will fill us instead with disappointment, bitterness and resentment. Fill us with envy.

> ***Love does not envy.***
> 1 Corinthians 13:4

In the presence and fullness of God's love, there is nothing to envy. Sadly, we don't always allow God's love, and the good gifts God has provided through His love, to really do what they were meant to do: Fill us with deep satisfaction, contentment and thankfulness. Fulfill the deepest longings of our very souls.

Envy takes a firm claw-like hold on us whenever we look to other people, other things or other circumstances, anything other than God, to be the source for our happiness and our reasons for thankfulness. Whenever we crave what else there is out there, that we think we should have, we become jealous and envious and lose all sight of the truth of God's love.

Envy feeds on twisted lies of dissatisfaction and ungratefulness. We want that something else. We want that something that somebody else has. That different circumstance, that different job, that different title, that different home, that different car, that different personality, that different ability, that different body, that different family, that different spouse, that different life!

Envy shuts us away from God, and we no longer can see the truth of His love for us. Too many disappointments and resentments over what we don't have cloud our view. But others can clearly view the ugly, greedy, jealous, satisfied-with-nothing attitudes that envy spews from us. That is not the way love does it! Love does not envy.

Envy keeps us from truly acknowledging and thanking God as the One who has given us all we need to satisfy our souls. As the One who has given us our very breath. As the One who cut off the breath of His Son Jesus in order to forgive our sins and give us eternal life. That is the way love does it! Love does not envy.

We need to look around. Not at anyone else. Just look around at our own circumstances and our own relationships. We need to love the way true love does: Take nothing and no one for granted. Find a reason (even if it's a small one) to thank God for all the circumstances in your life, for all the people in your life. And thank them, too. Give God thanks for who He is. Give God thanks for all you have. Give up and get rid of all envy and bitterness.

Be grateful. You will love more greatly. Love does not envy.

Do I believe it?
And if I do, what am I going to do about it?

Lord, please let me hear your voice, your love, your wisdom, your grace and truth.

LOVE IS...WITHOUT BOASTING OR PRIDE – part 4

God's love is powerful beyond our comprehension. God's love has no limits. It has no bounds. Yet in the fullness of its strength, God's love is humble – reaching into the lives and hearts of His children. True love has no need to boast or act in prideful ways. True love's amazing power is self-evident, not self-aggrandizing.

Love does not boast, Love is not proud.
1 Corinthians 13:4

God's love does not ask us to put ourselves down. God actually calls us to love ourselves according to God's good way: We are to love God and others as we love ourselves. And true love is to be completely void of any and all self-important boasting and self-focused or self-righteous pride. Love does not boast, Love is not proud.

Several years ago Tim and I were first asked to speak at *The Marriage Course* offered by our (East Coast) home church. We were happy to share what God has done, is doing and will continue to do in our marriage. This opportunity made us step back and analyze: What is it that makes our marriage what it is? Absolutely, the over-arching answer is love. God's love is the all-encompassing foundation and fortress for our marriage, for us living out our lives as lovers, partners, parents and friends.

As we dug down deeper into what makes our marriage work in the midst of all that comes at us in life, the answer we both came up with is this: Humility. Huh!? Yes, humility. Not boasting. Not pride. Not self-focused thinking or selfishly-demanding behaviors.

True love knows that humility is a powerful and strengthening force in any relationship. There is nothing weak in true humility. It is one of God's most powerful weapons against everything that would destroy relationships. True love lifts up the other. Builds up the other. Encourages the other. Strengthens the other. Love does not boast, Love is not proud.

Doesn't it make sense that humility – not boasting, not prideful actions – is what truly builds any relationship in amazing ways? Think about it: God's fullest revelation of love came through the absolute, extravagant humility of Jesus Christ. Jesus humbled Himself and submitted His will to do what the Father, whom He loved so much, wanted Him to do. Jesus humbled Himself so that all the children of God would know the boundless love of their Heavenly Father. Through the humility of Jesus, our enslavement to sin and the power of death were crushed and conquered for all eternity. There is no weakness in humility.

All forms of boasting, all expressions of selfish pride are deadly to all relationships. Humility is the expression of true love that is strong enough to be fully authentic without any puffed-up presentation of self. It just isn't necessary. The extravagant humility and self-sacrificing love of Jesus prove this. God offers us this same power to love as He loves. True love is strong enough to be humble. Love does not boast, Love is not proud.

Reflections – Responses – Challenges – Encouragements – God-breathing Thoughts

Do I believe it?
And if I do, what am I going to do about it?

Lord, please let me hear your voice, your love, your wisdom, your grace and truth.

LOVE IS...DOES NOT DISHONOR OTHERS, LOVE IS NOT RUDE,
LOVE IS NOT SELF-SEEKING – part 5

God's love absolutely amazes me. The fact that God speaks to us in the first place is absolutely mind-boggling. But, then, to think that God speaks to us frail, flawed and finite human beings in loving, honoring, respectful ways is really beyond my grasp. Out of His love for us, God constantly seeks us out, even when we continually turn away. God knows that the very best thing for every one of us is to be in a love relationship with Him.

Love does not dishonor others [Love is not rude],
Love is not self-seeking.
1 Corinthians 13:5

God's loving ways and thoughts are far higher and deeper than ours. God is the Sovereign Authority over all there is, and certainly our Superior. Yet, our God speaks to us intimately and with great respect through His Holy Scriptures and Holy Spirit. Even when God must confront us in clear, strong ways about our wrong behavior and tell us hard truths about ourselves, God is never rude. Love does not dishonor others, Love is not rude, Love is not self-seeking.

But what about my tone? My words? My attitude? How do I come across when crossed? Dishonoring others in any way comes from an attitude of ugly, self-deluding over-importance and entitlement. We can get all rude, nasty and uppity (and sometimes dangerous) when someone dares to cut in front us – in a line, in a car, in our lives – in any way. Our tone, words and attitudes can turn sarcastic, biting, dismissive, destructive and dishonoring when others in our world dare to turn their attention to things other than meeting our very important needs. (Even if they have no idea what those needs of ours are in the first place – because we didn't tell them!) This is not love. Love does not dishonor others, Love is not rude, Love is not self-seeking.

Self-seeking attitudes and behaviors have nothing to do with love! Ego-warped thinking – *What have you done for me lately? What will I get out of you that will be good for me?* – is a poisonous, self-centered attitude that gives birth to all kinds of relationship-killing behaviors. Manipulation. Shaming. Using. Abusing. Disregarding. Disrespecting. Dishonoring. When we are stuck in our self-seeking attitudes, there is no seeking for the other's very best. There is no seeking for the other one to truly know love and truly feel loved. Lust and covetousness are the real names for a self-seeking attitude – *I want what I want, when I want it, how I want it, from where I want it and from whom I want it. There is only me. There is no other.* This is not love. Love does not dishonor others, Love is not rude, Love is not self-seeking.

God's love always seeks the other out. God's love seeks us out, even when we are only seeking for ourselves. God does not need us to fulfill something that He lacks. There is nothing lacking in God. But, oh, God wants us! And God wants to give us the fullness of His joy as we grow in an intimate love relationship with Him! God always seeks us. God always seeks to give us His very best. Love does not dishonor others, Love is not rude, Love is not self-seeking.

May we each choose to speak and act in loving, honoring and respectful ways. May we each seek to give to others our very best as we consider what is truly best for them. This is love.

Reflections – Responses – Challenges – Encouragements – God-breathing Thoughts

Do I believe it?
And if I do, what am I going to do about it?

Lord, please let me hear your voice, your love, your wisdom, your grace and truth.

LOVE IS...NOT EASILY ANGERED – part 6

God's love flows powerfully with peace, grace, truth and tenderness. And in God's perfect and holy love, God also gets angry. Angry at our evil. Angry at our prejudice. Angry at our pride. Angry at our meanness and cruelty towards others. Angry at our ignoring the needs of the needy around us. Angry at our selfishness. Angry at our greed. Angry at our lust. Angry at our lies. Angry at our sins.

Yet in His love, God is never short-tempered, cranky or mean-spirited. God's anger is never based on changing seasons, circumstances or moods. God's anger against all sin and all evil is based, as it always has been, on God's truth, righteousness and love.

Love is not easily angered
1 Corinthians 13:5

God doesn't snap at us. God doesn't snap under pressure. God doesn't respond defensively. God's anger is never based on feeling hurt or ignored, frustrated or tired, busy or annoyed, frail or frazzled, sick or moody. God desires each of us to be more like Jesus in our character, thinking, speaking and behavior – including in our reactions to anything and anyone that could make us angry. To be like Jesus, we have to do it God's way. Love is not easily angered.

Confession: Anger is one area – in my frail, flawed and finite state – that God has to work on constantly. God must continually redirect my often-too-self-focused perspective so that I will respond more slowly, more maturely, more lovingly. Which, of course, is a lot more like Jesus than smacking people upside their fool heads! Most of the time (But not always!) when I feel the anger stirring up in me, I'm able to keep it as an inside-my-head-only-storm. However, my anger is still very real, and the stuff screaming around inside my head can be very ugly. Even if no one else ever sees it or hears it. And God reminds me: Love is not easily angered.

By God's love and grace, I have learned to invite God right into my anger. Right into its ferocity. Right into its nastiness. And God is not afraid to come in! By inviting God into my anger, He lovingly leads me into the eye of my own storm. Into the calmer place of thought and focus. By inviting God into my anger, I am letting God know: *I want to do things Your way, God! I need Your help! Get in here, God! Take control of my head! Take control of my thoughts! Arrrrgggghhh! Take control of my mouth! Help me be more like Jesus!* Yep! That's pretty much the script of my dialogue (okay, monologue at that point) with God.

By inviting God into my anger, I get over myself much more quickly. I can view the people with whom I'm angry with what I call *mercy-eyes*. I stop looking at myself and all the reasons I'm angry. The mercy-eyes that God gives me are able to see others with love and compassion. With mercy-eyes I can view and understand the people and the circumstances from a truer, calmer, more eternal perspective. Love is not easily angered.

May we each invite God right into the midst of our storms to do His deep, loving, calming and transforming work within us. That is the way of God's love. Love is not easily angered.

Do I believe it?
And if I do, what am I going to do about it?

Lord, please let me hear your voice, your love, your wisdom, your grace and truth.

LOVE IS...LOVE KEEPS NO RECORD OF WRONGS – *part 7*

God loves us perfectly and outrageously. God loves us in such a thoroughly renewing and cleansing way. The love of Jesus that took Him to the cross also brought us into the presence of our Holy God. And we can only enter there with no trace of sin. The records of all our wrongs, of all our sins, of all our shame have been completely obliterated by the blood of Jesus. We are innocent before our Holy Abba.

Love keeps no record of wrongs
1 Corinthians 13:5

To love as our Lord Jesus loves, we must love in intentional, active and transforming ways. We must get rid of all our mental (and written) lists of every wrong that has ever been done to us by any and everyone throughout our entire lives. We have no righteous authority to hold onto the wrongs by which other people have injured us. No matter how horrendous those wrongs were. Love and bitterness cannot exist together. Love and accusation cannot exist together. Not ever. Love keeps no record of wrongs.

The death of Jesus paid for all the sins of all who wronged us. His death also paid the full price for all of our stubborn, bitter, judgmental, unforgiving attitudes. We cannot stay justified in our blaming, accusing, shaming ways of thinking when it comes to the wrongs of others. Jesus' death sentence fulfilled all punishment for all sins. We must forgive. Our unforgiving posture holds us captive to its deadly, destructive power over our lives. We must shred, burn, bury and totally destroy the record of wrongs we keep against others. All others. For all sins. Love keeps no record of wrongs.

It was God's love, God's grace and truth that brought me to this transforming knowledge. And it was the very power of the Living God that moved me to choose to forgive my abusers of all the emotional, physical and sexual abuse I suffered. All of it. That all seemed so unforgiveable.

And it was this same love of God, His grace, truth and transforming power that moved me to finally release myself from the shame that I had held onto, and been a prisoner of, because of some of my own very ugly sins. Sins committed even well after I had committed my life to Jesus. Love keeps no record of wrongs.

Because of the freeing love-truth of Jesus, we are not to keep a record of the wrongs of others or of our own wrongs either. We are to humbly and completely yield at the foot of the cross. We are to accept fully the truth and transformation, the freedom and forgiveness that the blood of Jesus offers to us. Jesus' blood covers all sin and all shame, for all others and for each one of us. For all time.

To live in an intimate love relationship with Jesus, we must do things His way. And our God radically eradicates the record of all sin and all shame for all time. We must choose to be humble, courageous and obedient and offer this same kind of love to others and to ourselves. Love keeps no record of wrongs.

Reflections – Responses – Challenges – Encouragements – God-breathing Thoughts

Do I believe it?
And if I do, what am I going to do about it?

Lord, please let me hear your voice, your love, your wisdom, your grace and truth.

LOVE IS...LOVE DOES NOT DELIGHT IN EVIL – part 8

Love and evil do not dance together.

There can be no partnership between love and evil on any level. At any time.

All sin – all evil – has nothing to do with love.

Love does not delight in evil
1 Corinthians 13:6

As humans, in our frail, flawed and finite state, we sometimes have a hard time recognizing or maybe – if we were to be really honest – we have a hard time admitting that we do things that are evil. Especially if we enjoyed doing those things.

We enjoyed our selfish, private, hidden sins – from pigging out to pornography.
We enjoyed our more public sins – from putting someone down to piercing someone's heart, from getting drunk to getting involved in an affair.
We enjoyed proving our point to the point of destroying someone else in some way.
We enjoyed getting back at someone.
We enjoyed getting away with something – that lie, that cheating, that stealing, that sin.

Love does not delight in evil.

No matter how we classify and justify our sinful actions, they are still evil.
We may view our sins as just small mistakes or as something that isn't really all that bad.
We may view our sins as our own private business alone.
We may even view our sins as willful and blatant acts, that we know are completely counter and displeasing to our Holy God, but we just don't care.

Love cannot and love will not delight in anything for which the Holy Son of God, our Lord Jesus Christ, had to suffer and die.

Love sees evil, clearly and completely, for what it evil is: life-deceiving, life-diminishing, life-damaging, life-destroying.

Love does not delight in evil.

Reflections – Responses – Challenges – Encouragements – God-breathing Thoughts

Do I believe it?
And if I do, what am I going to do about it?

Lord, please let me hear your voice, your love, your wisdom, your grace and truth.

LOVE IS...LOVE REJOICES WITH THE TRUTH – part 9

Oh! The dance of love and truth is inseparable and beautiful. Their partnership is one of unstoppable power. Their relationship is one of indescribable intimacy and perfect unity. And this is something to seriously celebrate!

Love rejoices with the truth.
1 Corinthians 13:6

God's love and God's truth are eternally bound – eternally One. As is our One God. Love and truth flow from, and make up, the absolute essence and very nature of our God.

God is love
1 John 4:8

Jesus answered, "I am...the truth..."
John 14:6

Love and truth can never be divided. No wedge can ever come between them. The unfailing strength of God's love and truth together will hold us tightly in our daily days and in our darkest hours. Giving us hope, peace and joy. Love rejoices with the truth.

Love can only, and will always, rejoice and celebrate with the truth. Because of love, Jesus took the punishment for everything that would separate us from our God. This is God's loving truth that sets His people free.

Free from every shred and tentacle of deception.
Free from every form of fear.
Free from every damaging wound to our hearts, souls, minds and strength.
Free from every accusation.
Free from every shame.
Free from the power of sin.
Free from the power of death.
Free to keep in step with the Spirit.
Free to live forever with our Abba – the One God of love and truth.

Love rejoices with the truth.

It was God's love that reached out to me and filled me when I didn't know, and didn't trust, that I could ever be truly loved. It was God's truth that turned my mind and my world completely upside-right – after being so horribly upside-down! God's love and truth have transformed me, and will keep on transforming me every day of my life while I'm still on this side of heaven.

There is no separation between God's love and truth. God's love and truth are always in full agreement. Their purpose is always the same. Their redeeming and renewing might in our lives is unstoppable. We who are in Christ can never be separated from Him. We are held intimately and powerfully by God's love and truth. We have an eternal reason to celebrate!

Love rejoices with the truth!

Reflections – Responses – Challenges – Encouragements – God-breathing Thoughts

Do I believe it?
And if I do, what am I going to do about it?

Lord, please let me hear your voice, your love, your wisdom, your grace and truth.

LOVE IS...LOVE ALWAYS PROTECTS, LOVE ALWAYS TRUSTS – part 10

God loves His children in passionately protective ways. He guards our very souls in His almighty care. No matter what our circumstances are, God never leaves us alone. As God's children we can never be separated from His love. Never. No matter how insane or sad, broken or frightening our experiences may be (were or will be), God is absolutely faithful to us. God's love always protects. Always.

God will need to gently, strongly grow us up in our trust of Him so that we may understand His loving protection from an eternal perspective. When we experience hard and ugly times – cruel attacks to our bodies, our reputations, our relationships, our expectations – we usually react with feeling completely unprotected and unable to trust. Still, these eternal truths remain:

> ***Love always protects, Love always trusts***
> 1 Corinthians 13:7

God is our protector. And God calls us to intentionally love others through protecting them – especially those in our most intimate relationships. In practical terms, it's easy to see how this protective love should be expressed as parents towards our children. Love's protection is to be offered in each of our relationships. First, and foremost, we are to tenaciously protect our relationship with our Lord Jesus. We are to lovingly, passionately protect our marriages, our unity and intimacy as a couple. We are to protectively love our families, friends, co-workers, neighbors and ourselves. This isn't about agreeing with everything individuals may choose to do. It's about honoring others as fellow image bearers of the Living God, so that we do not cause anyone to feel unprotected or unable to trust us in any way.

Do our family members, friends, co-workers, neighbors feel lovingly safe in their relationships with us? In a world that offers so little protection to our hearts, minds, bodies and souls, do our most precious people know they can trust us and run into our protective arms of love? Or do they run for cover? Are we a safe harbor, a refreshing place of rest for others? Or do they feel like they're walking on eggshells or shards of glass around us? Are they unable to trust how we will react to them? Do they feel unprotected because they're not even sure which *me*...which *you*...they may meet up with today? Love always protects. Love always trusts.

Our highest and deepest way to demonstrate our love for God is to trust Him. Trust His Word. Trust His Spirit. Trust His Grace. Trust His Truth. Trust His Love. Trusting God is eternally bound up in how we live and in how we relate to others – right here and now. Right in the midst of our hardest and ugliest of times. Right in the midst of crushing and broken trust in our human relationships. God wants us to know and live in His protective, trustworthy love every day, every night – in every circumstance, in every experience, in every relationship.

As we grow in allowing God to truly be our first love, we will grow in our understanding of how love can, and does, always protect and always trust. The more we love and trust God – who is the only, completely and constantly, protective and trustworthy One – the more we will be able to risk ourselves to love, to protect and to trust others.

Love always protects, Love always trusts.

Reflections – Responses – Challenges – Encouragements – God-breathing Thoughts

Do I believe it?
And if I do, what am I going to do about it?

Lord, please let me hear your voice, your love, your wisdom, your grace and truth.

LOVE IS...LOVE ALWAYS HOPES,
LOVE ALWAYS PERSEVERES – part 11

Love intentionally chooses to hope even when our circumstances seem hopeless – when loss pierces our souls and destruction comes at our bodies, our families, our sense of security.

Love intentionally chooses to persevere through our most difficult, confusing, drudgery-filled, frustrating and painful times of life.

Love always hopes, Love always perseveres.
1 Corinthians 13:7

How can love always hope? How can love always persevere? Because of Who Love is! Because of Who the source of all true love, hope and perseverance is in our lives!

Our God is Love. And our God is the God of hope. And our God is the Almighty Lord for whom nothing is impossible. God will accomplish and achieve His plans and purposes. And these are always birthed and always fulfilled through God's love. God's hope-filled, persevering love.

There is nothing and no one that God's love cannot transform. There is no life that God's love cannot redeem, restore and renew. There is no experience we will ever have that God's love will not be able to work out for our good, according to our God's good, loving and eternal purposes.

Love always hopes, Love always perseveres.

Our God is strong enough to walk with us through the darkest, loneliest, most confusing days of our lives. God's love is mighty enough to carry us when we're not sure we can take another step. Ever again. God's love lifts our spirits with His hope and strengthens us to persevere victoriously in ways we never could have imagined.

Love always hopes, Love always perseveres.

As we come to more fully grasp the truth of God's hope-filled, persevering love for ourselves, we will be able to love others better – even those hard-to-love others – with love's hope and in love's perseverance. And we will be able to more fully offer God's hope and perseverance to those precious ones who, like us, so desperately need God's encouraging and powerful love.

Love always hopes, Love always perseveres.

Reflections – Responses – Challenges – Encouragements – God-breathing Thoughts

Do I believe it?
And if I do, what am I going to do about it?

Lord, please let me hear your voice, your love, your wisdom, your grace and truth.

LOVE IS...LOVE NEVER FAILS – part 12

There is nothing weak about love. There is nothing frail, flawed or finite about love. There is nothing weak about our God. There are no frailties or flaws in our all-powerful, eternal God.

God cannot fail. God will not fail. God is love. And God's love will never fail.

> ### *Love never fails.*
> 1 Corinthians 13:8

We each must decide if we really believe this. As individuals, we each need to answer:

Do I really believe that God's love has never and will never fail me?
Do I believe...?
That God's love really is big enough to heal all of my wounds?
To drive away all of my fears?
To crush all of my doubts, confront all of my pride?
That God's love is big enough to strengthen me in every way and in every circumstance – whenever, wherever and however I need to be strengthened?
That God's love is big enough to forgive me of all of my sins and take away all of my shame? That God's love is big enough to hold me tightly and gently during those times I can't love God, anybody else or even myself?
That God's love is big enough to renew me, restore me and transform me to be more and more like Jesus – no matter what I've done, said and thought?

If you and I are able to answer, "Yes, I do believe!" – even if we have to, honestly and quickly, add, "Help me overcome my unbelief!" (as did the man in Mark 9:24) – then, you and I each need to answer this:

What am I going to do about it?
How will I think differently?
Speak differently?
Act differently?
Interact differently?
What will I do if I truly believe that God's love will never fail?

Love never fails. And this eternal truth from our Almighty God should make a difference in the way we live our lives in every possible way.

> ### *In all these things we are more than conquerors*
> ### *through him who loved us.*
> Romans 8:37

God's love does indeed have the final, unfailing word over all our heartaches and hard times, our sin and shame, our falsehood and failures, our loss and loneliness, our suffering and sadness. And that word through Jesus is: Victory!

Love never fails.

Reflections – Responses – Challenges – Encouragements – God-breathing Thoughts

Do I believe it?
And if I do, what am I going to do about it?

Lord, please let me hear your voice, your love, your wisdom, your grace and truth.

SEARCH ME, GOD...AND BE GENTLE

God knows everything about us. God knows our actions, our reactions, our words, our deepest impulses and our hidden thoughts. And although God knows all of this about us, we are still to intentionally and regularly invite God in to search our hearts. I believe God's RSVP to that invitation will always be, "Yes!"

> *Search me, God, and know my heart;*
> *test me and know my anxious thoughts.*
> *See if there is any offensive way in me,*
> *and lead me in the way everlasting.*
> Psalm 139:23-24

God calls us to invite Him into every portion of our thinking and acting. God is to have full access – top security clearance (okay, maybe the show "24" has had a bit too much influence on my thought process) – to review our lives and our behaviors to the minutest of details. Since God already knows everything about us, why do we have to invite Him in to look at us in such an intense way?

When we invite God in to review, inspect and interrogate our hearts, thoughts and ways, we are, first, agreeing with God that He has the authority to do so. God blesses our authentic humility by giving us a fuller, deeper sense of His loving intimacy with us even as He searches and purifies our hearts.

Through humility we place ourselves in the *right relational position* with our Almighty Lord, who takes our hand and leads us in His eternal, life-cleansing and life-freeing way.

As we continually choose to walk humbly with our God, according to His everlasting way, we place ourselves in the *right transformational position* to know and live in God's power to heal, restore and completely renew our lives in ways beyond our highest hopes or imaginations.

I desperately want to experience the fullness of God's authority and intimacy in my life. But, oh! The cleansing, correcting and redirecting process that must take place continually within my heart, thoughts, words and actions can be pretty rough. So! Whenever I pray this prayer, and it is necessarily often, I always add just a little bit more: *Search my heart, O God...and be gentle!*

I have honestly found that the more often I invite God in to really search, reveal and cleanse me of all my anxious thoughts and all my offensive ways, the more gentle God is able to be with me. Oh, sometimes I need (and I get) the full sandblasting power of God's correction to get through to me, so that I will see myself as God sees me. At other times, and I hope these will become more and more the norm, God is able to use a polishing cloth to remove the spiritual dullness, dimness and disobedience from my heart and my ways.

God loves us all so much. So, be courageous! Invite God in to truly search your heart and to lead you in His everlasting way. And if you need to add *"and be gentle"* like I always do, I'm pretty sure God will understand!

Reflections – Responses – Challenges – Encouragements – God-breathing Thoughts

Do I believe it?
And if I do, what am I going to do about it?

Lord, please let me hear your voice, your love, your wisdom, your grace and truth.

THE NEW HAS COME!

Whenever anyone accepts Jesus Christ as Savior, our Mighty God seals him or her with His Holy Spirit. This precious one is now a newborn baby, a beloved child of our Holy God, of our Eternal Abba. This precious one, this saved soul has been rescued from the dominion of darkness, from the power of death and from the destiny of hell.

All glory and thanks be to our Lord Jesus Christ who through His death and resurrection has made a way for everyone who believes to enter into an intimate and eternal relationship with our Holy God!

Still, here on earth we will be in a struggle with our own sin nature, and with the sin nature of others, every day on this side of eternity. But! Our saved souls are no longer held captive by the power and bondage of sin and death. Not anymore. Not in any way. That was the old order. The new has come!

> *If anyone is in Christ, the new creation has come:*
> *The old has gone, the new is here!*
> 2 Corinthians 5:17

In Christ there is freedom. There is power. There is renewal and transformation that are fully available to us every moment of every day, in every circumstance and in every season of our lives. Our God is with us. And God's Spirit is within us.

We have been given the very same power, the very same Spirit that raised Jesus Christ from the dead! God is able and passionately wants to empower each of us to live in and reveal, with ever-growing fullness, the new lives we have been given in Jesus!

Who needs to know you as this new child of God?
In what ways do you especially need to let God's love and power make you new?
Will you trust God's love to know what *old* must be gone from your life?
Will you trust God's love to know how to bring the *new* to its fullness in you?

Will you let God help you today, and in each new day, to live out the truth that our Lord has set you free and made you new?

Let's embrace this amazing and eternal truth: That in Christ, our God makes us His new creation. And God's joy is to make each one of us more and more like Jesus. Sin and death could not conquer Jesus. Sin and death are to have no more power over our new life in Him!

May we each allow God's loving and powerful renewal to be made known fully in and through us – in all that we are and in all we do. Let the old be gone! The new has come!

Do I believe it?
And if I do, what am I going to do about it?

Lord, please let me hear your voice, your love, your wisdom, your grace and truth.

LET'S TAKE A LEAP OF FAITH

Happy Leap Year! First, let me just get my *learning nerd* stuff out there. For those of us who follow the Gregorian calendar, a *leap year* is a year containing one additional day every fourth year in order to keep the calendar year synchronized with the astronomical or seasonal year. Calendars that have a fixed number of days each year will tend to drift over time with respect to the astronomical or seasonal event with which the year is supposed to correspond. By adding one day into the leap year, the drift can be corrected, and our earthly days and those measured in the cosmos and the seasons will be synchronized once again.

The heavenly bodies and the seasons move at their own set rhythm and pace. And it is we, and our pattern of counting days, that must adjust if we are to be synchronized. Our tendency to drift away from the rhythm and pace that God established in creation requires that a *leap* be made by us in order to catch up.

And so it is for us in the spiritual realm as well. We drift away from our God. We get out of sync with our Lord's intended plan set for us at Creation: To live as image bearers of our God. Outside of an intimate relationship with God, the rhythm and pace of our lives become erratic and independent – and eventually meaningless as we move farther and farther away from God's purposeful, eternal rhythm and pace.

Our God continually beckons us back to Himself. God reaches out to us to stop our drifting. God urges us to follow Him, love Him, walk with Him. God calls us to synchronize our lives with His Spirit and walk in obedience to our God, just as Jesus did. And God does all of this for our own good and out of His unfailing love for us!

And now, Israel, what does the LORD your God ask of you but to fear the LORD your God, to walk in obedience to him, to love him, to serve the LORD your God with all your heart and with all your soul, and to observe the LORD's commands and decrees that I am giving you today for your own good?
Deuteronomy 10:12-13

If we walk in the light, as he is in the light, we have fellowship with one another, and the blood of Jesus, his Son, purifies us from all sin.
1 John 1:7

If anyone obeys his word, love for God is truly made complete in them. This is how we know we are in him: Whoever claims to live in him must live [must walk] as Jesus did.
1 John 2:5-6

Since we live by the Spirit, let us keep in step with the Spirit.
Galatians 5:25

Let's each take a leap of faith – right over ourselves – right into God's loving arms, back into God's good and right, life-giving and eternal plans, rhythm and pace for our lives. Let's each take a leap of faith and let God stop all of our drifting. Let's each take a leap of faith and keep in step, in intimate synchronization, with the Spirit! What a leap of joy that will be!

Do I believe it?
And if I do, what am I going to do about it?

Lord, please let me hear your voice, your love, your wisdom, your grace and truth.

SOVEREIGN AUTHORITY – INTIMATE ABBA

The power and tenderness of our Holy God are inseparable manifestations of the way our Lord leads, protects and cares for us as His children. God reveals Himself to us as both the absolute Sovereign Authority over our lives and as our gentle, compassionate Intimate Abba whose love for us is beyond our comprehension and imagination. Our God's Sovereignty and Intimacy are intricately interwoven to bring all of us the fullness of God's guardianship and presence.

To experience God's fullest love for us, we must acknowledge and trust both His Sovereignty and His Intimacy. We must yield to God's rule and be cradled in God's care.

> *See, the Sovereign LORD comes with power, and he rules with a mighty arm...*
> *He tends his flock like a shepherd:*
> *He gathers the lambs in his arms and carries them close to his heart;*
> *he gently leads those that have young.*
> Isaiah 40:10-11

Being under the Sovereign Authority of our Holy God and in a deeply trusting relationship with our Intimate Abba is the safest, most beautiful place any of us could ever be! And we need to rest there...live there...in our hearts, in our minds, in our souls and – *Yes!* – even in our practical, taking-care-of-business, tangible, daily-day lives here on this earth.

As a child, the authority I knew was most often cruel or cold, attacking or absent. And any intimacy I knew was false, forced, dangerous and deceptive. But! What I knew as a child does not in any way reflect the grace and truth of our Sovereign and Intimate God! No! In Jesus Christ I have found not only safety and beauty but, also, my greatest freedom and most powerful strength as I let God be God in my life.

To let God be God, I must choose to acknowledge that my Lord Jesus does, indeed, have the right to be and, in the eternal reality of all things, is my Sovereign Authority. I must acknowledge that God's Authority is good and faithful, wise and wonderful. To let God be God, I must choose to trust, over and over and over again, that the One True God of all that exists truly loves me as my Intimate Abba, my Heavenly Father. And I must trust, outrageously and wholeheartedly, that my Intimate Abba always and only wants the very best for me, wants to know me deeply, wants me to know Him deeply, wants to spend time with me (every moment, actually), promises He will never leave me, passionately declares that there is nothing in all creation that could ever separate me from my Intimate Abba and His unfailing love.

Letting God be God brings such love, wisdom, strength, peace, hope, joy and freedom into our lives – right now, right here, and right until we are fully gathered in our Lord's arms on the other side of eternity!

I pray that each of us will choose to acknowledge and trust God as our Sovereign Authority and Intimate Abba in an ever-growing way, every day of our lives!

Do I believe it?
And if I do, what am I going to do about it?

Lord, please let me hear your voice, your love, your wisdom, your grace and truth.

UPSIDE RIGHT LIFE

Our God wants to turn our lives upside down.

When we realize, and choose to live in the truth, that the Lord really is our life – our Creator, our Savior and the Lover of our souls – we will want the Lord to fully lead our lives, sharpen our focus, deepen our passion, give us our purpose and guard our peace!

Oh! But to live in the truth that our Lord Jesus Christ truly is our life will mean that our lives will be turned upside down. We will need to let go of life as we've known it. We will need to hold onto all things loosely, except for the One who holds us tightly by His eternal love.

One of the very first things we will need to let go of is the perceived sense of control we have over our lives. It's a LFTPOH – a Lie From The Pit Of Hell!

The sooner and more fully we grasp that God alone is in control over our lives, over all lives, and over the grand scheme of all eternity, the sooner and more fully we will be set free to live our lives as they were meant to be lived. In the powerful, purposeful and eternally significant way that God intended for us!

> *Then Jesus said to his disciples, "…whoever wants to save their life will lose it,*
> *but whoever loses their life for me will find it."*
> Matthew 16:25

> *…For the LORD is your life…*
> Deuteronomy 30:20

Our God wants to turn our lives upside down.

Well, actually, our God wants to turn our lives upside right! And that's a very good thing!

What needs to be turned upside right in your life?
Your faith journey with Jesus?
Your relationship with your family?
Your attitudes about pretty much everyone and everything?
Your ways of spending your time, energy and resources?
Your hidden habits and secret sins?
What are you holding onto so tightly that it's holding you down from living fully in Christ?

Our God is the One who holds our lives and who is our life.

May we each let our God take us in His arms of love, of grace and of truth – turning us so we will see more clearly the eternal value and worth of our lives from our God's upright position. Only in losing our lives through following and loving our God will we ever hold onto our lives.

May we each let God turn our lives fully upside right so we will fully fix our eyes on Jesus, who is the resurrection and the life!

Reflections – Responses – Challenges – Encouragements – God-breathing Thoughts

Do I believe it?
And if I do, what am I going to do about it?

Lord, please let me hear your voice, your love, your wisdom, your grace and truth.

IGNORANCE IS NOT BLISS

Our Sovereign and Intimate God lovingly, passionately and continually reaches out to us so that we may know Him and know and receive His holy, freedom-bringing gifts of forgiveness, salvation and eternal life with Him. Yet, so many precious souls still do not know our God and His Love for them. So many still do not know God's Word of truth that sets us free from the power of sin and death, and sets us free to live a life filled with God's love, hope and peace.

> *"My people are destroyed from lack of knowledge."*
> Hosea 4:6

> *...God our Savior, who wants all people to be saved*
> *and to come to a knowledge of the truth.*
> *For there is one God and one mediator between God and mankind,*
> *the man Christ Jesus, who gave himself as a ransom for all people...*
> 1 Timothy 2:3-6

> *And being found in appearance as a man,*
> *Jesus humbled himself*
> *and became obedient to death –*
> *even to death on a cross!*
> *Therefore God exalted him to the highest place*
> *and gave him the name that is above every name,*
> *that at the name of Jesus every knee should bow,*
> *in heaven and on earth and under the earth,*
> *and every tongue acknowledge that Jesus Christ is Lord,*
> *to the glory of God the Father.*
> Philippians 2:8-11

One day everyone *will know* – and no longer be ignorant – that Jesus Christ is Lord.

One day everyone *will know* – and every tongue will acknowledge – that through the humble and sacrificial death of Jesus and through His glorious resurrection, our God offered His love gifts of salvation and eternal life to all who would believe.

One day everyone *will know*. But for many precious souls it will be too late. For some their ignorance is self-imposed by their own pride, self-sufficiency and stubbornness of heart that refuses to listen and learn of Jesus and, therefore, they reject Him as Savior and Lord. For others their ignorance is caused by a lack of compassion and courage from us, as believers in Jesus, to share the gospel of God's grace with them. For others their ignorance is fueled and fed by darkness, twisted truths and idolatry. The result is still the same: *My people are destroyed from lack of knowledge.*

Ignorance is not bliss. Knowing Jesus Christ as Savior and Lord, now and for all eternity, is!

What will you choose to do today to offer the love and saving knowledge of Jesus Christ to those precious souls around you? May our Sovereign and Intimate God give each of us His compassion and courage to bring His light that dispels all the darkness of ignorance and brings truth and life – now and for all eternity – to all who believe!

Do I believe it?
And if I do, what am I going to do about it?

Lord, please let me hear your voice, your love, your wisdom, your grace and truth.

SELF-JUSTIFICATION JUST DOESN'T WORK

Our efforts to justify our own wrong actions destroy the peace within all our relationships.

How wonderfully different is our justification in Christ! Through Jesus we are proclaimed as righteous in God's sight. Our justification is fully based on Jesus' death on the cross, all out of His pure and perfect love for us. And peace with our Holy God is the eternal result.

> *Therefore, since we have been justified by faith,*
> *we have peace with God through our Lord Jesus Christ*
> Romans 5:1

Self-justification is really just selfish. All time, energy, excuses, explanations or defensive posturing that we put forth in order to justify any of our own bad behavior is selfish and self-focused. Whenever we justify and defend our hurtful words and wrong actions (even if we think they're hidden), by pointing to how we have suffered in the past or by focusing on how hurt or angry someone else has made us feel, we're really held prisoner to our pride.

Self-justification is a deflective, defensive, sin-denying, self-protective behavior that doesn't have anything to do with the peace, freedom, forgiveness and righteousness that Jesus Christ gives to us through His sacrificial death. Self-justification just doesn't work!

People do hurt us. People do things that make us angry. Still, we always have the choice to do things God's ways. Always. We do not have to be bitter just because the situation is, or the other person is. We do not have to prove that we are right just because we think the other person is wrong. Any behavior in thought, word, action or reaction that comes from a desire to put someone else down or to punish them in some way or to seek retribution for their bad behavior towards us is just plain wrong. And self-justification will never make it right.

We who are followers of Jesus have been given the Spirit of the Living God to guide us, direct us and teach us how to be more like Jesus. And I am absolutely convinced that Jesus – the Holy One of God who never sinned, yet, became "sin for us so that we might become the righteousness of God" (2 Corinthians 5:21) – doesn't have anything to do with self-justification. Not one little bit. Not one little word. Not one nasty look. Not one unkind action. We who are in Christ have been given the great gift of being justified before our Holy God for all of our own ugly sins (including self-justification) so that we may receive the very peace of God, and have peace with God.

Let us, by God's loving power, truly forgive others. Let us, in honesty and humility, admit that we have done wrong and sincerely ask to be forgiven – without hanging onto even one single shred of self-justification. When we accept the gift of life-sacrificing justification given through Jesus we recognize that any attempt on our part to self-justify our own wrong behavior (no matter how provoked we may feel) is a complete denial and rejection of all that Jesus has done for us!

Self-justification just doesn't work. It's a waste of time and it's destructive. May we each choose, instead, to more fully receive and more freely give to others the love, forgiveness, grace and peace of our Holy God that come only through our Lord Jesus Christ!

Reflections – Responses – Challenges – Encouragements – God-breathing Thoughts

Do I believe it?
And if I do, what am I going to do about it?

Lord, please let me hear your voice, your love, your wisdom, your grace and truth.

COVENANT OF MIND AND HEART

God has done a new thing for His people. Through His eternally present Spirit, God's words and ways have now been put within our minds and hearts. They are intimately and powerfully available to shape us, guide us, heal us, renew us and transform us as the people of God!

Will we let them?

> *"This is the covenant I will make with the people of Israel after that time,"*
> *declares the LORD. "I will put my law in their minds and write it on their hearts.*
> *I will be their God, and they will be my people."*
> Jeremiah 31:33

Will we quiet ourselves enough to listen for the incredible truth God is telling us? He is ours. We are His. Through God's Spirit and the power of His Word, our Holy God takes up residence in our minds and hearts. He is not only with us – our God is within us!

Think about this, really quiet yourself and breathe in deeply this amazing truth. God makes this covenant, this beautiful, holy, eternal promise to us: We belong to Him and He to us. Our God promises that His law – His life-giving, peace-bringing, strength-empowering words and ways – will be placed purposefully within our minds and hearts. Revealing us to be His people.

Our God desires, and has made Himself outrageously available, to be in relationship with us. We were created to find, know and live in an intimate and powerful relationship with our Eternal Abba, experiencing our deepest fulfillment, strength, hope, purpose, peace, joy and love in His presence. And our God has placed His very presence, His Holy Spirit, within us.

How are you letting God's law of love, grace and truth – made intimately known to us by the indwelling of His Spirit – fill and rule over your mind and heart?

How are you letting all that God has put on your mind and written on your heart be known and experienced by others in your life?

With the Lord as your God and you as His child, how are you letting this incredible, mystical relationship – this beautiful, life-transforming covenant between God and you – make a renewing, inward and outward difference in you?

With the Lord as your God and you as His child, how are you letting this incredible, mystical relationship – this beautiful, life-transforming covenant between God and you – be made known in tangible, observable, living and loving ways to those around you?

> *Know therefore that the LORD your God is God;*
> *he is the faithful God, keeping his covenant of love to a thousand generations*
> *of those who love him and keep his commandments.*
> Deuteronomy 7:9

Our God is faithful to His covenant of love given to us! May all of us be faithful in keeping God's covenant and His law, put on our minds and written on our hearts, so that we will be powerfully transformed, revealing to all around us the Mind and Heart of our Holy God!

Do I believe it?
And if I do, what am I going to do about it?

Lord, please let me hear your voice, your love, your wisdom, your grace and truth.

THE SPIRIT OF POWER, LOVE AND SELF-DISCIPLINE

Each of us who has received Jesus as our Savior has been given so much more than we often realize – and so much more than we often choose to let empower, lead and calm our lives. We have been given the very Spirit of our Holy God to live within us, drawing us ever closer to our God and keeping our walk ever more in sync with our God's will and ways.

God's Spirit given to us is all about transforming us to think and act, to react and even to feel, more and more like our Lord Jesus Christ. This is freedom, healing and renewal!

God's Spirit is able to transform our every weakness, our every frailty, our every insecurity by His Spirit's gift of power poured into our spirit. We will be given a courage and a strength that are fully based on God's truths that "with God all things are possible" (Matthew 19:26) and that we "can do all things through Him who gives [us] strength" (Philippians 4:13).

God's Spirit is able to transform all of our thoughts and feelings of being unloved, unworthy, rejected, hurt and embittered by His Spirit's gift of love poured into our spirit. We will be given the deep and eternal assurance that we are loved by the Lord of all eternity – by "God [who] is love" (1 John 4:8) – with His unfailing, incomprehensible, inseparable, unchangeable love.

God's Spirit is able to transform all of our habitual and fleeting behaviors that come out from us through thoughts, words and acts of pride, anger, fear, worry, stubbornness, selfishness, lust, laziness, gluttony, judgment, arrogance (Go ahead! You can name some for yourself!) by His Spirit's gift of self-discipline and a sound mind poured into our spirit.

> *For the Spirit God gave us does not make us timid,*
> *but gives us power, love and self-discipline.*
> 2 Timothy 1:7

In Christ there is nothing timid, weak, unloving, sinful, out of sorts or out of control! Our holy, loving Lord wants to widen and deepen His Spirit's reign over and within our lives – over and within our hearts, minds, bodies and spirits.

God does this through what He has already given to those of us who have put our faith in Jesus Christ as our Savior and Lord. We have been given the eternal gift, of incalculable worth, by the giving of God's Holy Spirit to live within us. It is, then, up to us to acknowledge the Spirit's gifts that have already been given to us – have already been poured into our spirits – so that we will choose to put them into practice in our thoughts, in our words, in our actions, in our reactions, in every relationship and in every circumstance we encounter.

God is with us. God's Spirit is within us. God's good gifts – God's good transforming gifts – are poured into us! And our holy, loving Lord will help us to release the Spirit's gifts into our lives, and into the lives of all those around us. We just need to release our lives more and more fully to the Spirit's control, to the Spirit's leading us by God's gifts of power, love and self-discipline!

Do I believe it?
And if I do, what am I going to do about it?

Lord, please let me hear your voice, your love, your wisdom, your grace and truth.

KEEP YOUR HEAD!

I have to admit there are times when I just want to knock people upside their heads – hoping it would knock some sense into them so they would think right, speak right, act right, react right and interact right! Yep! Those very prideful, social-guru-of-the-world thoughts really do bounce around inside my head. And more times than I'd like to admit. Only by God's good grace, can I thankfully say that I haven't carried through by knocking any people upside their heads. Yet. (Giving a flick on the forehead doesn't count, right?)

Instead, I have learned (And God keeps me in His continual remediation lessons!) that I must invite God to, first, knock me upside my own fool head! There, God can teach me and lead me with His far wiser, far kinder, more balanced and more loving ways for my thoughts, words, actions, reactions and interactions.

And, oh! It is always so much better when we do things God's ways! So much better for ourselves and for all others involved. Instead of knocking people upside their heads out of my own frustration and pride, I'm called to take God's Word to heart – and into my head – and choose His ways in all situations. Always.

But you, keep your head in all situations...
2 Timothy 4:5

In Christ, and through His Spirit, we are given deep and unfailing gifts of love, wisdom, grace, truth, peace, patience, maturity and compassion. These gifts are able to empower us to choose God's eternal perspective and remain calm and thoughtful, humble and strong, kind and compassionate, balanced and wise even in the midst of the most difficult situations.

Right in the midst of a sudden crisis.
Right in the midst of facing cruel misjudgment.
Right in the midst of harsh and unjustified confrontation.
Right in the midst of devastating news.
Right in the midst of betrayal.
Right in the midst of ridicule.
Right in the midst of crushing loss.
Right in the midst of confusion.
Right in the midst of watching those we care about make sinful, stubborn, hurtful and harmful choices that deeply affect themselves and others in their lives.

Our God calls us *to keep our heads in all situations*.

The very best way – the only way – for us to do this is to actively and intentionally (and with a lot of deep, calming breaths) choose to –

...keep in step with the Spirit!
Galatians 5:25

May we each invite our Lord to rule our every thought, word, action, reaction and interaction so that we may *keep our heads in all situations* – and, thereby, lovingly and wisely protect the heads and hearts of all those around us!

Reflections – Responses – Challenges – Encouragements – God-breathing Thoughts

Do I believe it?
And if I do, what am I going to do about it?

Lord, please let me hear your voice, your love, your wisdom, your grace and truth.

KNOWING WHO YOU ARE – IN GOD AND TO GOD

Do you know who you are *in* God? Do you know who you are *to* God? Jesus did. Jesus knew who He was *in* and *to* God, and Jesus knew all that the Father had given Him.

> *Jesus knew that the Father had put all things under his power,*
> *and that he had come from God and was returning to God;*
> *so he got up from the meal, took off his outer clothing,*
> *and wrapped a towel around his waist.*
> *After that, he poured water into a basin*
> *and began to wash his disciples' feet,*
> *drying them with the towel that was wrapped around him.*
> John 13:3-5

This knowledge of who Jesus truly was – who Jesus is and will be forever – in relationship to His God gave Jesus the absolute power to be completely and outrageously humble. No act of loving servanthood – no matter how lowly or behind the scenes – could ever deny the truth of Jesus' eternal authority, power and position in His Holy God and Eternal Father.

It is in knowing and believing that we are loved perfectly, fully and unfailingly by our Holy God that we can more fully risk being rejected. Jesus did.

It is in knowing and believing that our God is absolutely faithful to us that we can more fully risk offering true love, forgiveness, kindness and compassion to those who are unfaithful and cruel to us. Jesus did.

It is in knowing and believing that our God is victorious over all that would break our hearts, weaken our bodies, crush our spirits and end our earthly lives that we can more fully risk giving thanks and trusting God during *the shadow of death times* in our lives. Jesus did.

It is in knowing and believing that we are children of the Most High God who "has rescued us from the dominion of darkness and brought us into the kingdom of the Son He loves" (Colossians 1:13), that we can more fully risk living in the incredible joy and hope of our promised resurrection and eternal life with our Heavenly Abba. Jesus did.

It is in knowing and believing that we have been given eternal and immutable honor as a child of the Living God, that we can more fully risk loving and serving others in the most humble, unappreciated and unacknowledged ways to make known the love of our God. Jesus did.

Knowing who we are *in* God and knowing who we are *to* God – believing these truths, holding onto these truths and living in these truths – brings blessings of peace and power to us for fulfilling God's loving, healing and transforming purpose in our lives. And through us into the lives of others! Just as Jesus did!

Reflections – Responses – Challenges – Encouragements – God-breathing Thoughts

Do I believe it?
And if I do, what am I going to do about it?

Lord, please let me hear your voice, your love, your wisdom, your grace and truth.

LIVE A LIFE WORTHY

Through our Lord Jesus Christ, we have been called by God to be redeemed, forgiven and given the great hope and sure promise of eternal life with our Holy God! In Christ we are called to live out our lives – right now, right here – in ways that will more and more fully reflect and express our renewed lives as children of God.

...I urge you to live a life worthy of the calling you have received.
Ephesians 4:1

Only by living in an intimate, dynamic relationship with the Worthy One, our Lord Jesus, is it even possible for us to *live a life worthy of the calling we have received.* Ahhhhh! But what a powerful, meaningful, legacy-leaving, adventurous, beautiful and, yes, challenging life it is to which we have been called! I, personally, would have it no other way.

When we accept our calling in Christ to be His redeemed people, we are also called to new identities as we live out our renewed and *worthy life*!

We are called God's beloved.
We are called the children of God.
We are called the light and salt of this world.
We are called more than conquerors.
We are called the church.
We are called a chosen people.
We are called the body of Christ.
We are called ambassadors of Christ.
We are called living stones.
We are called a royal priesthood.
We are called a holy nation.
We are called a people belonging to God.
We are called Christ's followers.
We are called Christ's servants.
We are called Christ's friends.

So, let us live our lives reaching out to others in the name of Jesus with His message of salvation, forgiveness and eternal life. Let us live our lives reaching out to others with Christ's loving heart, grace-and-truth speaking mouth, healing hands, open arms, compassionate eyes, listening ears and feet ready to go and help those around us.

This would be *living a life worthy of the calling we have received* from the Worthy One who has called us by His unfailing, all-powerful and sacrificial love!

Reflections – Responses – Challenges – Encouragements – God-breathing Thoughts

Do I believe it?
And if I do, what am I going to do about it?

Lord, please let me hear your voice, your love, your wisdom, your grace and truth.

LIMBO IS NOT A GOD REALITY

We don't always understand what is happening to us or around us – at least not right here, right now. We don't always understand why we're going through such frustrating and painful struggles and stresses in our present circumstances. We don't often know what we should plan for or what we should do as we face the certainty of uncertainties in our lives now and in our future. We just have so many questions and worries about the decisions we need to make and about the best options we should choose. We may often feel confused, fearful and out of control over our present experiences and our future uncertainties. Many times we speak about feeling like we're in a state of limbo. And we really don't like limbo.

Well, good news! Limbo is only a limited, human perception. Limbo is not a God reality.

My times are in your hands...
Psalm 31:15

God always knows every detail of every moment of our lives. God always knows everything about who we are, how we are, what we are going through and what we will experience in our future. Our Sovereign and Intimate Lord holds each of us, every day of our lives in His faithful and loving hands. There is never a moment that God leaves us or leaves the room!

There will be many things that are so very difficult, painful and confusing for us to deal with on this side of heaven. Our God knows this and promises to be with us. God asks us to trust Him. Trust that God sees what we cannot. Trust that God is good, faithful and loving. Trust that God reaches out His hands to us continually – to hold us, to calm us, to comfort us, to confront and to quiet our fears and doubts, to lead us, to empower us, to walk with us. And it is our Lord Jesus who allowed His holy hands to be pierced by crude and cruel nails on the cross so that we would know God's unfailing love, His mercy-drenched gift of salvation and His firm promise of eternal life with Him.

Our times – every moment of our lives, every experience in our past, present and future – are all in God's holy, powerful, tender, compassionate, redeeming, transforming and faithful hands! For all of us who by faith are in Christ, *this* is where we are and will always be – *here* in this eternal truth of being in God's eternal hands!

Limbo is not a God reality.

Do I believe it?
And if I do, what am I going to do about it?

Lord, please let me hear your voice, your love, your wisdom, your grace and truth.

FAITH IS NOT A FEELING

God requires faith from us. Faith in who our Lord claims to be. Faith in God's salvation plan through Jesus Christ alone. Faith that God will never leave us or forsake us. It is through the humility and courageousness of our faith that God honors us as His children. It is through the humility and courageousness of our faith that God establishes an intimate and eternal relationship with us and lavishes us with His unfailing love

For we live by faith, not by sight.
2 Corinthians 5:7

Faith is not a feeling. Faith is not about *feeling* that God is who God claims to be. Faith is not about *feeling* that I am saved. Faith is not about never *feeling* alone or abandoned, confused or frustrated, worn down or burned out during the hard times of our lives.

Faith is not a feeling. Faith is a conscious decision to take God and to trust God at God's Word. Faith often involves risk and uncertainty. Faith can sometimes involve long periods of waiting (from our perspective) to hear from God, or to sense any leading from God. Or to recognize the evidence that God really is – and has been – answering our heartfelt prayers.

So why should we live by faith and not by sight? Because it will only be by humbly and courageously trusting God that we will intimately know that God *is* who God claims to be: loving, holy, righteous, just, wise, compassionate, eternal, intimate, sovereign, faithful, true. It will only be by humbly and courageously trusting God that we will know Jesus Christ as our Savior, the one and only true "mediator between God and mankind" (1 Timothy 2:5).

But! Don't take my word for it. Take God's! God actually encourages us to seek Him and call out to Him. God promises to reveal Himself to those who would risk checking God out for who God claims to be.

Faith humbly and courageously agrees with God and the Truth of God's Word:
That we have been purposefully, wonderfully and fearfully, made in God's image, and through the redemption and salvation of Jesus Christ, we will yet be transformed into His likeness with ever-increasing glory. (Genesis 1:27; Psalm 139:1-14; Romans 8:29; 1 Corinthians 15:49; 2 Corinthians 3:18)
That God has a plan and a purpose for each of us. (Jeremiah 29:11, Ephesians 2:10)
That God has an everlasting love for us, and calls us to love Him and love others. (Jeremiah 31:3; Deuteronomy 6:4-5; Mark 12:29-31; 1 John 4:7-21)
That God intended us to have eternal life with Him, and through the sacrifice and resurrection of Jesus, the power of sin and death was fully conquered. (Genesis 2:9; Isaiah 53; Daniel 12:2, John 3:14-17; Romans 8:37-39; 1 Corinthians 15: 52-57)
That Jesus is the fullness of God's grace and truth. (John 1:14,17)
That Jesus is the way and the truth and the life...the only way to the Father. (John 14:6)

Faith is not a feeling. It is a decision, humbly and courageously, made to trust God at His Word – every day of our lives!

Living by faith is so much more than anything sight, or any feeling, could ever offer us. Our faith causes us to be embraced with the fullness of God's love and life, hope and peace for which our very souls crave. Our faith in Jesus as our Savior and Lord is something to live by, something to walk by, to run and jump, sing and dance by – now and for all eternity!

Reflections – Responses – Challenges – Encouragements – God-breathing Thoughts

Do I believe it?
And if I do, what am I going to do about it?

Lord, please let me hear your voice, your love, your wisdom, your grace and truth.

LET OUR FEELINGS CATCH UP WITH OUR FAITH

Years ago my precious friend Eddie was killed by a drunk driver. He had a beautiful wife and four young children. He had been ripped away from them suddenly and tragically. And Eddie had been ripped away from me.

When Eddie died I absolutely believed and had full faith that he was now in the loving arms of God. I knew that Eddie loved Jesus. Eddie trusted and followed Jesus as his Savior and Lord. Eddie lived out his faith in such gentle and powerful, humble and compassionate ways. When Eddie died I absolutely believed and had full faith that the Lord would intimately care for and provide for his beautiful family. I absolutely believed and had full faith that my God is sovereign and loving. Even in this devastating loss.

This was, and is, my determined faith in the One True God. And it was, and is, only through the intimate love of God that I have any faith at all.

But that's not how I felt at that painful time. Even though my faith was not shaken, my heart was completely broken.

Sometimes we have to *let our feelings catch up with our faith.*

Our Lord will hold us and tenderly love us with His compassion and mercy throughout every moment of that *catch up* time. God did this for me. I know God will do this for you.

Be merciful to me, LORD, for I am in distress;
my eyes grow weak with sorrow, my soul and my body with grief.
Psalm 31:9

Because of the LORD's great love we are not consumed,
for his compassions never fail.
They are new every morning;
great is your faithfulness.
I say to myself, "The LORD is my portion;
therefore I will wait for him."

The LORD is good to those whose hope is in him,
to the one who seeks him;
it is good to wait quietly
for the salvation of the LORD.
Lamentations 3:22-26

How loving and good is our Holy God! He holds us and comforts us with His great love, compassion and faithfulness. In the everlasting arms of our Heavenly Abba, we can rest and cry, breathe and be strengthened while our loving Lord tenderly and faithfully heals us and helps our feelings catch up with our faith.

Reflections – Responses – Challenges – Encouragements – God-breathing Thoughts

Do I believe it?
And if I do, what am I going to do about it?

Lord, please let me hear your voice, your love, your wisdom, your grace and truth.

GOD HIMSELF IS OUR HIDING PLACE

When I was a little girl, I spent a lot of time curled up, hiding in the upper shelf of a closet. I didn't want to be found. I didn't want to be hurt or touched any more by any one. To my little kid thinking, that closet seemed liked a really good idea, with me curled up into the tightest, tiniest ball I could possibly force my body. But the security of that hiding place was an illusion and temporary. I still remember the day when my hiding place was taken away from me. And I was, once again, taken by the abuse that crushed my innocence.

That self-made hiding place was not sufficient for my safety or my freedom. God alone is.

Any and all other security measures we take *to hide us away* from the very real, heartbreaking problems and pain of this world are just illusions and temporary. All the things we, in our own strength, put in place to give us a sense of ultimate protection and a secure hiding place away from hard times – whether physical, material, financial, intellectual, professional or relational security measures – are still just illusions and temporary. Helpful, sure. Practical, yes. Wise, absolutely. Yet, like my closet, these earthly hiding places are unable to entirely and eternally protect us when the brokenness of this world rears its ugly head.

Ahhhhh! But our God does things in such a much bigger way than we could ever even begin to imagine! Even when our self-determined security systems, our protective plans and our human-made hiding places fail, our God never will. Even in the midst of our most massive mess-up, our deepest sorrow, our sudden shock or ongoing pain, *our God Himself is our hiding place*. And God is True and Eternal.

> *You are my hiding place;*
> *you will protect me from trouble*
> *and surround me with songs of deliverance.*
> Psalm 32:7

God Himself is our hiding place. But not by hiding us away from the problems that are part of this broken world. No! God Himself is our hiding place in the midst of all our trouble. Protecting us with His eternal love from which we can never be separated. Filling us with His eternal peace that transcends all understanding. Revealing His eternal perspective that shatters all the lies of all illusions and temporary security. God Himself is our hiding place right in the center of every crisis, cruelty and confusion we experience. God Himself is our hiding place – the eternal calm that exists in the midst of life's storms that whirl and whip us around here on earth. And there, as our hiding place, our God surrounds us with His sweet and powerful songs of deliverance that flood our inner-most being – reminding us who our God is and renewing our trust in God's love and His absolute victory over all the power of sin and death through our Lord Jesus Christ!

There, hidden in our God, surrounded by His love, listening to His Spirit sing over us, our own songs of trust and thanksgiving begin to pour out to our God for the mighty hiding place He is!

Reflections – Responses – Challenges – Encouragements – God-breathing Thoughts

Do I believe it?
And if I do, what am I going to do about it?

Lord, please let me hear your voice, your love, your wisdom, your grace and truth.

STIRRED NESTS – GOD'S FLIGHT PLAN

God wants us to trust Him and, like an eagle, learn to fly with Him. Oftentimes, however, we'd rather stay in our nests – in our own comfort zones. We want to maintain and protect our known ways of doing things. It's just easier that way. Leaving our nests is risky business. Flying is riskier still.

> *[The LORD is] like an eagle that stirs up its nest and hovers over its young,*
> *that spreads its wings to catch them and carries them aloft.*
> Deuteronomy 32:11

God stirs up our nests out of His love for us to move us to greater strength, truth and freedom. Just as baby eagles don't get it when they're first stirred up and pushed out of their nests, we don't often realize we were created to soar! And our God hovers over us, catches us and carries us as we learn to match our flight plans to His.

It doesn't make sense for little eaglets – all comfy, warm and perfectly content – to suddenly be stirred up and pushed out of the comfort of their nests. But it is the only way for them to fly and attain the fullness of their created purpose.

For me, it didn't make sense to forgive the unforgivable and choose to love those who had treated me hatefully. Jesus sacrificing His holy life to die for the forgiveness of all the sins of all of us sinners doesn't make a whole lot of sense either. Yet, it is the very wisdom and power of God! God's soaring proclamation of love!

It didn't make sense for us to pack up a 2 year old and a 3 month old (born with a hole in her heart) and move to France when we didn't even speak the language. But God used this crazy, nonsensical move to intensify our understanding of God as the God of all creation, all nations and all peoples in deep, lasting and tangible ways. And what fabulous, and sometimes very uncomfortable, adventures we had during this stirred up time! It didn't make sense to stir up our lives again and move away from our comfortable home, good friends, good schools, established jobs and our loving church family when our girls were teenagers (What!?). But! God's crazy, nonsensical stirrings led to great growth, deeper faith and life paths that none of us could ever have imagined before God's hard, loving push out of our comfort zones.

God's stirrings for you may never entail learning a foreign language or changing your address (several times). God's Spirit may be urging you to share the love of Jesus with someone in your family, in your neighborhood, at work or school. Maybe God is stirring you to reach out to someone who is lonely or in need – that forgotten grandmother in a nursing home, that little boy who plays outside all by himself, that single, tired and frazzled mom, that newly widowed man who seems numbed to his soul, that living-on-the-edge teenager (who scares you a little bit), that soldier who could use a care package to know someone cares, that friend who just needs a listening heart.

God's stirrings will come in different ways to each of us as He calls us out of our comfort zones. Leaving the comfort of our nests is risky, I know. But, I am convinced that ignoring the stirrings of God's heart and will for our lives is far riskier to our well-being and the quality of our lives on every level – mentally, physically, relationally and spiritually.

So, fly, Darlin's, fly! The views and adventures while soaring with God are spectacular!

REST! IT DOES A BODY, AND A SOUL, GOOD!

We were created with a need for physical and spiritual rest. Our bodies, and everything else in our lives, can suffer some pretty serious consequences when we don't get proper rest.

Several years ago, after over two months of averaging only 2 to 2 ½ hours of sleep each night because of a very intense and full ministry schedule (and ridiculous stupidity on my part), I actually fell asleep while standing up, and broke my nose on the window frame on the way down!

Some people get a "Wake up call." I got a very strong, and a pretty painful, "Go to sleep call!" Which I have seriously heeded since that day. Many thanks go to some very loving and wise "watch-dog" people in my life.

How much more serious the consequences are for us when we do not rest our souls in God!

Everything breaks, not just our noses! Our peace, our hope, our perspective, our courage, our kindness, our patience, our joy, our love. Giving ourselves over to *soul rest* acknowledges our need for God to be our strength and our salvation. Our God who loves us and watches over us every moment of every day and every night continually offers His rest to all who come to Him.

> *Truly my soul finds rest in God;*
> *my salvation comes from him.*
> Psalm 62:1

> *This is what the Sovereign LORD, the Holy One of Israel, says:*
> *"In repentance and rest is your salvation,*
> *in quietness and trust is your strength,*
> *but you would have none of it."*
> Isaiah 30:15

Ignoring our God-created need to rest our bodies and our souls as we keep pushing ourselves physically, mentally and emotionally is really ignoring God. Ignoring God's love for us. Ignoring God's wisdom in giving us the need – and the gift – to quiet ourselves, quiet our thinking and quiet our activities. Ignoring God is body and soul damaging and depleting in every possible way. We each need to embrace and be refreshed by our God's holy rest, our God's holy Sabbath, for our bodies and our souls.

May we each choose to yield to our God's loving wisdom in creating us with a need to rest. May we choose to slow down, breathe more deeply and allow God to hold, restore, renew and refresh us – giving us deep rest for our bodies and souls. Take time for Sabbath moments each day with the Lord. Take a Sabbath day each week. Take extended times of Sabbath as often as you are able. We will come out of those Sabbath moments, days and times more in tune with our Loving God, with ourselves and more loving towards all those around us.

Rest! It does a body, and a soul, good!

Do I believe it?
And if I do, what am I going to do about it?

Lord, please let me hear your voice, your love, your wisdom, your grace and truth.

BE KIND!

Just before I went to first grade, my family moved away from our home in the very small, rural town of Mexico, New York (for just two years) to the much bigger city area of East Hartford, Connecticut. The morning of my first day of first grade was filled with so much frenzied activity as four of the five children in my family all had to get situated in our new classrooms in an unfamiliar building with unfamiliar faces.

I'm not exactly sure how it happened, but apparently I had settled myself into the wrong classroom. Just as all the craziness was turning to calm and all the children found their places, I suddenly found a very pretty woman with gentle eyes and a sweet smile kneeling down in front of my desk so that we were at eye level. She asked me my name. I told her. She then told me she would really like to be my teacher because I had such beautiful blue eyes. Then she held out her hand to me and asked if I would like to come over and be a student in her class. I said, "Yes, Ma'am," took her hand and walked – well, kind of skipped – with her across the hall where she had a very special desk waiting just for me, where she could always see my beautiful blue eyes.

Kindness. Extra, gentle, thoughtful, loving kindness. It wasn't required. It wasn't expected. That morning sitting in the wrong desk in the wrong classroom, there could have been very different words, attitudes and actions that came at me. But I'm pretty sure you wouldn't be reading about them right now. This kindness from this precious teacher, that took only a moment from her, has been one of my most treasured, happy and repeated memories of my entire, and mostly very painful, childhood. That precious woman made me feel special and wanted.

She gave the same kind of kindness that our God has for us. He comes to us – Immanuel, God with us – and calls us by name. He tells us we are beautiful to Him. He tells us He wants us with Him and holds out His Holy Hand to lead us to where we should go.

Kindness makes such a difference and it costs us so little. Yet, God's ultimate kindness to us cost Jesus His life. God chose this way to let us know how very special and wanted we are.

...whoever is kind to the needy honors God.
Proverbs 14:31

Be kind and compassionate to one another,
forgiving each other,
just as in Christ God forgave you.
Ephesians 4:32

Love is kind
1 Corinthians 13:4

Today...and tomorrow...and the next day...and the next, choose to be kind.
Kinder than you may feel.
Kinder than is expected.
Kinder than is necessary.
Kinder than you think someone deserves.

Reflections – Responses – Challenges – Encouragements – God-breathing Thoughts

Do I believe it?
And if I do, what am I going to do about it?

Lord, please let me hear your voice, your love, your wisdom, your grace and truth.

IT'S NOT ABOUT LUCK

Top o' the morning to ye!

Yes! It's St. Patrick's Day! And, like so many others, I'm enjoying a wee bit o' fun, wearing some green and claiming every ounce of Irish heritage that's within me! What about that "luck o' the Irish?" Oh! It's a fun thought, but luck is all about chance. Not certainty.

We as followers of Jesus Christ will, instead, depend on the certainty of our God's faithfulness, on His Word of grace and truth, on His unfailing love and on His transcending peace to lead and hold our lives now and for all eternity.

> *Let us draw near to God with a sincere heart*
> *and with the full assurance that faith brings...*
> *Let us hold unswervingly to the hope we profess,*
> *for he who promised is faithful.*
> Hebrews 10:22-23

Our God draws us near to Himself through our Lord Jesus. By faith in Christ's death and resurrection, we are reconciled fully to our Holy God and held tenderly and tenaciously every moment of our lives. Nothing can separate us from God's love. We do not know what each day will hold for us – or what circumstances or relationships will bring us joy and peace or sorrow and pain. No matter what our days hold, we can bring – right into God's throne room of grace – everything we are and everything we experience to our loving God, our Eternal Abba.

It's not about luck! Luck is fickle, fragile and faithful to no one.

It's about faith in our faithful God! Our God is the faithful One – the omnipotent, omniscient and omnipresent God, the sovereign, intimate and unchanging God, the Ancient of Days and the Alpha and the Omega – who loves us unfailingly!

It is through faith that we draw near to our faithful God *with a sincere heart and with full assurance* that we are loved and held by Him every moment of every day of our lives! It is our faithful Lord Jesus, the Resurrection and the Life, who will draw us near to Himself for all time!

Draw near to God. That's where our Abba wants each and every one of us.

May each of us hold unswervingly to the hope God has promised! Our God desires to give each of us a deeper, fuller assurance of who He is, how deeply He loves us and how faithfully He will care for us, hold us and walk with us every day of our lives.

Our Heavenly Abba will absolutely draw us to Himself with love and joy! And it's not about luck! It's all about our faithful God!

Do I believe it?
And if I do, what am I going to do about it?

Lord, please let me hear your voice, your love, your wisdom, your grace and truth.

GOD IS GOD. UNDERSTAND THAT.

We can get so very full of ourselves at times that we forget that God is God.

> ***Then the LORD answered Job out of the storm...***
> ***"Where were you when I laid the earth's foundation?***
> ***Tell me, if you understand."***
> Job 38:1, 4

There are so many things in this life that we can't understand. So many things we want to understand why they happen to us. Why they happen to our loved ones, to the innocent, to the helpless. But, if we were to be really honest with ourselves, we know we only ask God *the why* about the hard things in life. We want to be given answers and demand explanations for all the hatefulness in this world, for the difficult and challenging times, for the ugly and evil things, for the painful and devastating experiences and the sudden tragedies in our lives. Yet, we don't ever ask God *the why* about – or even feel a need to understand the reasons for – the loving and faithful relationships we have, the sweet times we enjoy, the beautiful and good things, the peaceful experiences and the unexpected joys in our lives.

We want to understand – often while shaking our fists and stomping our feet at God or while closing off our hearts to Him – *why*, if God loved us...*why*, if God was really good...*why* would all of these hateful, hard, ugly, evil, painful, devastating and tragic things happen to us and to others.

God understands our hurt and our anger. God understands our heartbreak. God understands the brokenness of this world. And God understands that even in this broken, sin-infested, pride-twisted world, there is much of His original intention for creation that still shines through to us. God still pours out His love, sweetness, beauty, goodness, peace and joy to us and to others in some way every day. Yet, we don't shake our fists or stomp our feet about this. Instead, we act as if we understand that these good times, provisions and experiences are our rightful entitlements, rather than gracious and holy gifts from our loving God.

We each need to understand – even in our very limited capacity to understand – how very much greater and how very different God is from us. We each need to understand, or at least acknowledge in some way, that God is God and we are not.

When we don't understand the circumstances and times of our lives, we can still choose to humbly and courageously embrace the truths that God has revealed to us through His Spirit, through His Word and through our Lord Jesus Christ. God reveals patiently, persistently and passionately His eternal nature as Creator, Redeemer, Deliverer, Savior and Lord. Our God reveals His eternal character as Loving, Faithful, Good, Patient, Kind, Wise, Righteous, Holy, Just, Merciful and Compassionate. And God in His goodness reveals to us that one day we will understand. One day we will know in full what we can only know in part on this side heaven.

> ***For now we see only a reflection as in a mirror; then we shall see face to face.***
> ***Now I know in part; then I shall know fully, even as I am fully known.***
> 1 Corinthians 13:12

While we wait for the fullness of understanding to be ours, may we each choose to understand, humbly and courageously, that God is God and we are not!

Reflections – Responses – Challenges – Encouragements – God-breathing Thoughts

Do I believe it?
And if I do, what am I going to do about it?

Lord, please let me hear your voice, your love, your wisdom, your grace and truth.

ABBA'S ARMS

The first thing I did as each of my daughters was birthed was to take my precious little baby girl in my arms, hold her tightly, kiss her all over, over and over again, and tell her how very much I loved her and promised her that I always, always would. And I did. And I do. And I will. Even in my imperfection. Each of my precious babies (now grown women) are loved by me forever. Loved beyond explanation. Loved no matter what.

Ahhhhh! How beautiful it is that we can trust our Heavenly Abba to love us perfectly! Beyond explanation. No matter what. How good it is for us to know that we always have a safe place for our souls, for all that we are – in all of our frailty and in all our of fierceness – to be loved generously and held tightly for all eternity!

Our Abba opens His holy arms to us offering His powerful and protective love for us and the reassurance of His constant and faithful presence with us. There is nothing that can limit the reach of our Abba's arms as He reaches out to us. There is nothing that can tire Abba's arms while He is holding us. His arms are the everlasting arms. So, too, are the everlasting love, shelter, peace, protection, salvation and strength that our Abba holds out for us to receive and to be held by – right here, right now and forever.

> *The eternal God is your refuge,*
> *and underneath are the everlasting arms.*
> Deuteronomy 33:27

We get tired. We're limited in our power to fix and control all of the hard and unwanted stuff that comes at us in our lives. We throw up our arms in frustration and disgust. We give up on our circumstances. We give up on people. We keep people at arms' length. Maybe because we're afraid of being hurt or rejected. Maybe because we're just too prideful to let anyone know what's really going on inside us and inside our own private, imperfect worlds. Maybe because we're just too self-centered to really care about others.

Our Abba really cares. Instead of throwing up His arms in frustration and disgust at the hardness of our hearts or the depth of our hurts, our Lord Jesus stretched His everlasting arms along the length of a wooden beam to die for our sins and our sorrows. The exact and perfect length to fully reach from heaven to earth and bring us fully and forever into our Abba's arms.

Abba's everlasting arms are always open wide with His love that will never fail us, with His grace that will never reject us and with His strength that can never be destroyed!

So snuggle in, Darlin's, and be held, healed and given hope in the everlasting arms of our Holy God! And, while you're there, offer your own growing-in-Christ-likeness arms to others who need to know just how very far the reach of God's everlasting arms can reach. No matter what.

Do I believe it?
And if I do, what am I going to do about it?

Lord, please let me hear your voice, your love, your wisdom, your grace and truth.

A NEW DAY! A NEW SONG OF THANKS!

We have been given a new day! May a new song of thanks flow from our hearts!

Sing to the LORD a new song; sing to the LORD, all the earth.
Sing to the LORD, praise His name; proclaim His salvation day after day.
Psalm 96:1-2

Come, let us sing for joy to the LORD;
let us shout aloud to the Rock of our salvation.
Let us come before him with thanksgiving
and extol him with music and song.
Psalm 95:1-2

Sing to the Lord! Sing out a new song of thanksgiving to our Almighty God! Here's just a very little bit of my thanksgiving heart song to our Lord. Feel free to join in or, even better, sing your own new song to our Holy Lord!

Thank You for YOU, Lord! Thank You for Jesus, my Savior and Lord, who gave His all for me! Thank you for this new day! Thank You for the gift of life on this earth! Thank You for the gift of eternal life with You! Life is Yours alone to give, and You have given it to me! You fill me with hope, joy, purpose and oh-so-much love! Thank You, Lord, for the people I love! Thank You for the people who love me! And, yes, thank You, too, Lord, for all the people who have hurt, hated and rejected me! Each one was given life and breath by You through Your holy love, purpose and power! Thank you for the sweet and easy times in my life, Lord, when my heart can easily sing thanksgiving to You! Thank You for the bitter and hard times in my life, Lord, when my heart is breaking – yet You keep me absolutely assured of Your love, presence and goodness as You sing over me (Zephaniah 3:17)! Thank You for the clear evidence You give me of Your order and wisdom, beauty and love in the wonder of Your creation! Thank You for the lengthening days of sunlight and the signs of renewed life and color that come with spring! And, Lord, thank You that people just smile a little bit more, and a little more freely, when the promise and hope of life are evident to them!

Thankfulness is one of the most powerful, mind-quieting, frustration-and-anger-diminishing and healing activities we could ever choose. Expending our energy, our efforts, our thoughts, our talk and even (or maybe especially) our self-talk on being thankful is truly perspective-renewing and life-transforming. Looking for, recognizing and giving thanks for the evidence of God's caring, compassionate love for us and His continual presence with us softens our hearts and refreshes our hope. Looking for, recognizing and giving thanks for the evidence of the kindness, help and encouragement that other people give us strengthens our relationships and refreshes our peace.

Holy Lord, please open our eyes to see Your love and power at work all around us – in creation, in others and in ourselves. Open our hearts and spirits to accept Your truest evidence of the promise and hope of life given through the salvation that comes through Jesus Christ. Open our minds and mouths to sing a new song of thankfulness to You continually in this new day, this new season and every new day of our lives. You alone are God. You alone are the giver of life. Thank You, Lord, for being You!

Do I believe it?
And if I do, what am I going to do about it?

Lord, please let me hear your voice, your love, your wisdom, your grace and truth.

CONTINUE TO LIVE!

We are never to get complacent or take for granted the amazing love gift of life we have received through Jesus. We are never to miss the opportunity to grow stronger by living in the power of God's Spirit and Word available to us. We are always to turn our attitudes towards thankfulness, recognizing that we are always held in God's unfailing love.

> *Just as you received Christ Jesus as Lord, continue to live in him,*
> *rooted and built up in him, strengthened in the faith as you were taught,*
> *and overflowing with thankfulness.*
> Colossians 2:6-7

We have received the wonderful, eternal gift of life through Jesus! And we need to remember to live this new life – to choose to *continue to live* this new life in a day-by-day way. Life in Jesus is not just a one day special. Salvation is an eternal gift of life. Eternal life with Jesus doesn't just begin on the other side of heaven when our earthly life is over. We're not to just bide our time, just making it through – and, maybe, just barely at that – while here on this earth.

Oh, no! That's not part of God's plan, and it doesn't reflect God's unlimited love and power given to all who belong to Jesus. Our eternal life with Jesus is part of our living reality right now. Our eternal life began the moment we trusted that Jesus died to forgive our sins and to give us life now and eternally. By God's Spirit and Word, we are brought to life and are called to *continue to live* each and every one of our days in Jesus – in His grace and truth.

Sometimes I forget this. Sometimes I get sad, discouraged, angry, prideful, pitiful, selfish, sinful, sick, tired, sick-and-tired, lazy, apathetic and just plain uppity! Whenever I forget all that God has for me – for all of us – so that I may *continue to live* in the love, the power, the grace and the truth of Jesus Christ, my Holy Abba reminds me that:

Continuing to live in Christ Jesus is about making the choice daily – moment by moment – to be active and intentional about growing deeper, closer and stronger in our intimacy with Jesus. So much of this will happen as we choose to consistently read, meditate on and apply God's Word – God's good, living, active and transforming Word – to our lives.

Continuing to live in Christ Jesus is about trusting God, His loving goodness and eternal plan – even if we don't feel the love or see any good reason for what we may be dealing with right at any given moment or season in our lives.

Continuing to live in Christ Jesus is about being teachable and willing to have our attitudes, perspectives and paradigms of reality shaken up as we grow more and more convinced of who God is and how greatly we are loved – beyond our imagination – by our good and faithful God.

Continuing to live in Christ Jesus is about choosing to commit ourselves to being more and more conformed to His likeness in every thing we are, in every word we speak, in every relationship we have, in every action, interaction and reaction that comes from us. We are to love God, love others and love ourselves in good, true, life-bringing and life-affirming ways.

May each of us choose every day day of our lives to *continue to live* in Christ Jesus! Live the truest, fullest lives we could ever have!

Do I believe it?
And if I do, what am I going to do about it?

Lord, please let me hear your voice, your love, your wisdom, your grace and truth.

THE LORD OF ALL CREATION TELLS US THAT...

God's constant and full presence with us is perfectly matched by His unlimited might to ultimately and eternally save us from all that would shatter our worlds and destroy our lives. God's deep and intimate care for us is revealed through His heart that takes great delight in us, by His love that quiets our greatest fears, our deepest doubts and our fiercest LFTPOHs (Lies From The Pit of Hell), and by the strong, gentle, rejoicing songs that our God sings over us as His precious and deeply loved children.

> *"The LORD your God is with you,*
> *the Mighty Warrior who saves.*
> *He will take great delight in you,*
> *[he will quiet you with his love]*
> *in his love he will no longer rebuke you,*
> *he will rejoice over you with singing."*
> Zephaniah 3:17

All that our God is and everything that our God offers to us reveal His sovereign authority and His intimate love for us!

The Lord of all creation tells us that He is with us! God is with you. With me. God is with His people – each one, everywhere, in every way, at every moment. The Lord our God is with us!

The Lord of all creation tells us that He is mighty to save! Able to save us from ourselves and our sins. Able to save us from others and the sins that come at us. Able to save us ultimately and eternally from all the wounds, wars and woes of living in this broken, mortal world. Our God is able to save us for that time when we will live fully and freely in our God's perfect and eternal kingdom.

The Lord of all creation tells us that He takes great delight in us as His precious children! Our Heavenly Abba is greatly delighted with us and with the joy we take in life. Our Abba is delighted with our playfulness and with our purposefulness, with living out our human lives as fully as possible and living them out in close relationship with Him. And our Heavenly Abba takes great delight when we show our love for Him and for His other children.

The Lord of all creation tells us that He quiets us with His love! Quiets us and calms us, holds us close and reassures us that nothing in all creation – nothing we have experienced, nothing that we have done, nothing that is in or out of our control, nothing in the earthly realms or in the heavenly realms – can ever separate us from the love of God that is in Christ Jesus our Lord (Romans 8:38-39)! Ahhhhh...the quieting, powerful love of our Abba!

The Lord of all creation tells us all this as He puts His living, loving, saving, transforming Words into song and joyfully sings them over us as His outrageously loved little ones!

Amazing God! Amazing Truths! May we each choose to more and more fully trust the Lord of all creation at His Word and in the songs He sings over us!

Reflections – Responses – Challenges – Encouragements – God-breathing Thoughts

Do I believe it?
And if I do, what am I going to do about it?

Lord, please let me hear your voice, your love, your wisdom, your grace and truth.

RISING LIKE THE SUN WITH THE SON!

I hate the idea of judgment. But it is God's truth. I hate the idea that there are people who are enemies of God, just as I was without Jesus, and that they will perish if they remain God's enemies. This, too, is God's truth.

God loves every person He created. God passionately and sacrificially gave His only Son to show us His love. And upon Jesus, God placed His entire righteous and holy judgment and full punishment for sin. For every sin. Ever committed. By everyone. There is no need for any of us to remain as enemies of God. Jesus already perished in our place. In Jesus we, who trust in God's Way for salvation – we who love God – will rise up with Him like the sun in its strength!

So may all your enemies perish, LORD!
But may all who love you be like the sun when it rises in its strength.
Judges 5:31

Is it time for you to say, "Yes!" to the salvation that is offered freely, fully and eternally through Jesus Christ and through God's unfailing, unrelenting love for you?

This is how God showed his love among us: He sent his one and only Son into the world that we might live through him. This is love: not that we loved God, but that he loved us, and sent his Son as an atoning sacrifice for our sins.
1 John 4:9-10

If you do not, yet, have this assurance of God's full forgiveness and eternal salvation, ask God to show you His love and truth revealed through Jesus. Please don't wait another day. You don't know if you will have another day. I'm not trying to be melodramatic. And my big signboard proclaiming: "Eternal judgment is at hand!" is out for repainting, so I'm not currently wearing it. However, Christ's love compels me to tell God's truth – not mine – of how very much God loves you, every one of you, and that Jesus is God's Only Way to eternal salvation.

Jesus answered, "I am the way and the truth and the life.
No one comes to the Father except through me."
John 14:6

I am so thankful that Alvin, my brother in Christ, knew that. Because on March 23, 2009 Alvin suddenly died in his driveway on his way to his car. No warning. No preparation. Just gone to this earth. But Alvin's life is secure! Alvin wasn't an enemy of God. Years before, he had put his faith in Jesus as Savior and enjoyed an intimate love relationship with his Lord who loves him immeasurably and eternally! In the Son of God, Alvin will rise like the sun in its strength!

Will that be true of you? And if it is, thank our Holy Living Lord! Then, ask yourself: Is there anyone that I love enough to tell them about the grace and truth of Jesus? God's grace and truth is this: Although there is judgment against God's enemies, our Lord has loved us by giving His own life for us so that we may become His children and His friends!

I pray that each of you will know the joy of loving God, who loves us so much that He did not spare His Son Jesus and promises that one day we will rise like the sun with His Son!

Reflections – Responses – Challenges – Encouragements – God-breathing Thoughts

Do I believe it?
And if I do, what am I going to do about it?

Lord, please let me hear your voice, your love, your wisdom, your grace and truth.

OPEN THE EYES OF MY HEART, LORD!

When our little Julia was born (Okay, not so little since she was just under eleven pounds at birth!), her eyes were squeezed shut by her cute and very round, chubby cheeks. I had to gently pry her eyelids open so I could see her eyes and she could begin to see me. I opened Julia's eyes lovingly and tenderly. My love for my baby daughter(s) was overwhelming. I just wanted that time of us seeing each other – even through her very unfocused, cheek closed-up, newborn eyes – to begin as soon as possible.

In the movie "Avatar" when the indigenous Na'vis people from the planet Pandora intimately understood and connected with the essence and nature – connected with the heart and soul – of another, they would declare, "I see you." The eyes of their hearts were opened to another.

Our Holy God intimately understands and is connected to us as our Creator and Lord. God sees us, knows us and loves us beyond our comprehension. And God desires to open up the eyes of our hearts so that we may see Him, know Him, trust Him and love Him.

> *I pray that the eyes of your heart may be enlightened*
> *in order that you may know the hope to which he has called you,*
> *the riches of his glorious inheritance in his holy people,*
> *and his incomparably great power for us who believe.*
> Ephesians 1:18-19

With Jesus as our Savior and Lord, we have been given a new life through Him as the Light of the world. Our Lord wants us to see – as His True Light opens and fills the eyes of our hearts – all the abundance of God's love and goodness given to us. In Christ's True Light, our hearts and our lives on every level, will be opened so that we may live as God's people with a clear, eternal and purposeful calling, with an unlimited hope, with spiritual riches and resources beyond measure and overflowing with the Spirit's power.

May we each invite God to gently, lovingly, tenderly (suddenly and strongly, if necessary) pry open the eyes of our hearts. May we choose to not stay blinded any longer in any way by any hardness or coldness or apathy filling our hearts. May we choose to not stay visually impaired because of our sins, doubts, fears, pride, hypocrisy, self-righteousness or judgment.

Lord, let us see You! Open the eyes of our hearts and move each of us to trust and love You more fully! Fill us and flow through us so that we may live and love with your True Light shining though our hearts into the lives of others who are still held captive by the darkness!

Reflections – Responses – Challenges – Encouragements – God-breathing Thoughts

Do I believe it?
And if I do, what am I going to do about it?

Lord, please let me hear your voice, your love, your wisdom, your grace and truth.

GOD CAN WHEN I CAN'T.
GOD UNDERSTANDS WHEN I DON'T.

There are so many things I cannot do. There are so many things I do not understand.

The truth of this is not meant to worry me or disturb me. It is meant, however, to keep me humble before our Lord. Always. And even as I'm humbled, this truth doesn't weaken me or diminish me in any way. It's God's truth. And God's truth never does that.

Rather, accepting this truth helps me to choose to trust my God, my Abba, even more with every part of my life.

> *Great is our LORD and mighty in power;*
> *his understanding has no limit.*
> Psalm 147:5

What I cannot do in my own strength, I can completely trust over to God. Because I know if it lines up with God's holy and loving plans and His perfect timing, then nothing can stop the Lord Almighty from bringing it to pass.

We all are called to remain in Jesus, and be filled with the strength that He gives us to do all that we could not possibly do on our own. And, oh! The fruit that grows from doing things in the strength of Jesus is beautiful, life-giving, life-transforming and eternal!

> *"I am the vine; you are the branches.*
> *If you remain in me and I in you, you will bear much fruit;*
> *apart from me you can do nothing."*
> John 15:5

> *I can do all things through him who gives me strength.*
> Philippians 4:13

While there is much that I am too limited to fully comprehend in my own thinking, I can still stand strong and have peace because I know that there is no limit to my Abba's understanding. And, even though none of us will ever have full understanding of so very many things on this side of heaven, our Holy God still desires us to ask for His wisdom – which He promises to give to us generously.

> *If any of you lacks wisdom, you should ask God,*
> *who gives generously to all without finding fault,*
> *and it will be given to you.*
> James 1:5

Yes, there are many things we cannot do in our own strength. There are many things we do not understand in our own limited perception and perspective. May the truth of this free us up, and grow us up, to depend on and trust more and more fully in our Holy God's unfailing love, mighty power and unlimited wisdom!

Reflections – Responses – Challenges – Encouragements – God-breathing Thoughts

Do I believe it?
And if I do, what am I going to do about it?

Lord, please let me hear your voice, your love, your wisdom, your grace and truth.

REJOICE! AND REJOICE AGAIN!

Whenever I'm working on a project alone, I can often get intensely focused – entering and deeply submerging into my own private head zone – no matter what else may be going on around me. I can get this way, so much so, that if someone is trying to talk to me, whether a family member, a friend or a co-worker, they will likely have to work hard to get my attention and pull me back into the interactive world of human communication. Calling out to me and repeating their words will eventually break through to my consciousness, and my focus can be redirected to the present moment and the person who is present with me.

In my relationship with our ever-present God, I know I will always need to focus just a little more fully, listen just a little more quietly, direct my attention just a little more intentionally and obey just a little more quickly and willingly. (Okay! On most days, that would be: a lot more!) And I need to do this with the right attitude. An attitude of joy and thankfulness in my God.

Our God is good enough, and lovingly insistent enough, that He will be sure to get our attention. And when it comes to our attitude and our perspective – no matter what our circumstances may be, or wherever we may have allowed our private head zones to be focused upon – our God is more than happy to repeat Himself!

> *Rejoice in the Lord always. I will say it again: Rejoice!*
> Philippians 4:4

Rejoice! In the Lord. Always. Rejoice!

God calls out to us through His Word and through His Spirit to choose, and then choose again, to rejoice! In Him. Always. God calls out to us to break through our self-focused thinking and our self-focused living. God calls out to us to choose, and then choose again, to take on an attitude of joy and thankfulness. In Him. Always.

May we each rejoice –
In who our God is.
In God's presence that is with us.
In God's love that pursues us.
In God's sacrifice that saves us.
In God's grace that transforms us.
In God's truth that frees us.
In God's power that heals us.
In God's wisdom that leads us.
In God's hope that encourages us.
In God's strength that revives us.
In God's promises that assure us of who we are to Him.

May God's good, and lovingly insistent, call to us break through to each of us – wherever we are and whatever we're doing – so that we will choose, and then choose again, *to rejoice in our Lord always. I will say it again: Rejoice!*

Reflections – Responses – Challenges – Encouragements – God-breathing Thoughts

Do I believe it?
And if I do, what am I going to do about it?

Lord, please let me hear your voice, your love, your wisdom, your grace and truth.

GOD'S STRENGTH-BRINGING JOY

Our God knows that our circumstances can sometimes be hard, horrible, heart-breaking or just plain annoying and crazy-making at times. Yet, in every moment and in every experience of our lives, our God wants to be our strength.

Don't rush past that thought too quickly. Our God wants to be our strength. And our God wants to give us His strength-bringing joy!

> *The LORD is my strength [and my song] and my defense.*
> Exodus 15:2

> *The LORD is my strength and my shield.*
> Psalm 28:7

> *God is our refuge and strength.*
> Psalm 46:1

> *God is the strength of my heart.*
> Psalm 73:26

> *The Sovereign LORD is my strength.*
> Habakkuk 3:19

> *...for the joy of the LORD is your strength.*
> Nehemiah 8:10

Truly, our God is our strength. In our frail, flawed and finite selves, our God is our strength! Our God never ceases to reach out to us in His strong and eternal love. Our God never tires. And our God never tires of us. Our God – our God's joy – is our strength. And God wants us to choose His strength-bringing joy for our own lives, right in the midst of our most maddening, unimaginable and unexpected struggles.

God calls out to each one of us to let Him and His joy be our strength. God calls us to look beyond our own limited perceptions of our particular circumstances. We can't understand all things fully. Not here. Not now. God calls us to look beyond our own limited mental, physical and spiritual capacities and resources. We don't have the unlimited reserves to manage all things on our own. We were never meant to.

God knows that our strength will come, and be renewed, as we focus our minds and hearts on Him – on our loving, eternal, almighty Lord – and receive the blessings of His strength and His strength-bringing joy!

Reflections – Responses – Challenges – Encouragements – God-breathing Thoughts

Do I believe it?
And if I do, what am I going to do about it?

Lord, please let me hear your voice, your love, your wisdom, your grace and truth.

SATISFIED AND SINGING

There's a famous (and old) rock song that the Rolling Stones released in 1965 which echoes the cry of far too many of our hearts: "I Can't Get No Satisfaction!"

The truth of that depends on what it is that we're seeking to satisfy us. Stuff never will. People fully can't. Power, prestige and position just won't. All are too fragile, too flawed and too fleeting.

And then there's God. Eternal. Sovereign. Intimate. Faithful. Just. Almighty. Merciful. Compassionate. Loving God.

When what we are seeking is really a *Who*, we will know and find our God. We will know and experience His love for us. When we choose to seek God, sincerely and with all our hearts, we will be fully and eternally satisfied. We will be filled to over-flowing with what our hearts cry out for most loudly and most desperately: the unfailing love of our God.

Satisfy us in the morning with your unfailing love,
that we may sing for joy and be glad all our days.
Psalm 90:14

"You will seek me and find me when you seek me with all your heart.
I will be found by you," declares the LORD...
Jeremiah 29:13-14

"Then young women will dance and be glad, young men and old as well.
I will turn their mourning into gladness;
I will give them comfort and joy instead of sorrow.
I will satisfy the priests with abundance,
and my people will be filled with my bounty," declares the LORD.
Jeremiah 31:13-14

Our satisfaction is not, nor can it ever be, found in our circumstances – even the sweetest and best of them. Our true and lasting soul satisfaction is found only in our God, in His unfailing love for us and in His gifts of peace, joy and hope that are fully available to us. Our God wants to fully fill us and freely flow through us so that we and others will know God's unfailing love – and be satisfied!

May we each choose to turn our eyes and our hearts away from all that is fragile, flawed and fleeting as the source to satisfy our longings. May we, instead, lift our eyes and turn our hearts (over and over and over again) to the One who loves us more than we could ever begin to imagine – to the One who is eternal and satisfies us with His unfailing love!

Now *that* will satisfy our souls! *That* really is worth singing about!

Do I believe it?
And if I do, what am I going to do about it?

Lord, please let me hear your voice, your love, your wisdom, your grace and truth.

BEAUTIFUL IN ITS TIME

Our seasons change. The earth keeps revolving around the sun. We move from winter to spring to summer to fall. It's natural. It's expected. The cycle of seasons continues. So, too, do the seasons in our own lives. We experience times of accomplishments and achievements, of foibles and failures, times of great celebration and times of deep mourning. These changes, these seasons, are also expected, natural and continuous throughout our entire lives.

We often long to prolong the sweet and easy times. We want those good moments and days to last for every bit of lengthening time we could possibly stretch them. On the other hand, we would be very happy to rush, as quickly as possible and with the fewest negative effects as possible, through each of those painful, ugly and difficult times we experience.

Scripture tells us that everything – each experience, each circumstance – has its rightful time and season in our lives and, no matter what that season may bring to us, whether we want it or want to run from it, God will make everything beautiful in its time.

> *There is a time for everything,*
> *and a season for every activity under the heavens...*
> *God has made everything beautiful in its time.*
> Ecclesiastes 3:1, 11

Deep within our very souls we yearn for a time when we would be fully free of all that would break our hearts and cause us pain. We yearn for a time when all that has covered us in shame would be blown away. We yearn for a time when all the ugly and sinful things that have been done to us, and all the ugly and sinful things that we have done to others, would no longer cause one more moment of pain or regret for us or for those we have hurt. Our souls yearn deeply (and sometimes with only a vague and tiny trembling consciousness of it) for true and eternal beauty.

The fulfillment of these soul yearnings is offered to us fully in our beautiful God. Although their fulfillment is shrouded somewhat for now on this side of heaven, the fulfillment of God making everything beautiful is offered to us through our Savior and Lord Jesus Christ. Through one of the cruelest, most painful and darkest days of all time and space, our Sovereign God accepted the suffering and death of Jesus as the fulfillment of His holy justice – for the required punishment for our own sins. Beautiful.

And more beautiful still is the promise and hope we have been given of life eternal – right here, right now and forever – with our holy and beautiful God who raised Jesus Christ from death to life! It is this beautiful truth that we hold onto during each and every change and season of our lives. We can trust that whatever is hard, painful or ugly will be transformed by the eternally redeeming beauty of our Lord Jesus Christ. And it is through this same beautiful truth that we are able to see a glimpse and a reflection of our beautiful God in all that is good and beautiful in nature, in people and in our experiences.

May we each choose to trust our Sovereign God so that our eyes will see and hearts will know that there is purpose and beauty in each day and in each season of our lives!

Reflections – Responses – Challenges – Encouragements – God-breathing Thoughts

Do I believe it?
And if I do, what am I going to do about it?

Lord, please let me hear your voice, your love, your wisdom, your grace and truth.

IN A CLEAR, STRONG VOICE

In a clear, strong voice. That's how it began. That's how God speaks. God spoke and all that exists came into being. The first recorded words of God, "Let there be light," were spoken in a clear, strong voice. There was no confusion. God spoke and light sprang forth. Like God's Word so, too, is God's Light that breaks into our darkness. Clear and strong.

God speaks and things happen. Light and life are called into being. God speaks and, as David wrote, we may hear the voice of God's creation telling us something of the glory and wonder of who God is and what God is able to do.

> *The heavens declare the glory of God;*
> *the skies proclaim the work of his hands.*
> *Day after day they pour forth speech;*
> *night after night they display knowledge.*
> *They have no speech, they use no words;*
> *no sound is heard from them.*
> *Yet their voice goes out into all the earth,*
> *their words to the ends of the world.*
> Psalm 19:1-4

God's creation seems to be constantly speaking to us, revealing to us that God is real, that God is present and that God is powerful. Creation speaks of a God of wonder that has an eye and a heart for beauty. Why beauty? Why Wonder? Because the God who gave us breath in the first place wants to get our attention by taking our breath away!

Will we hear what is being said? Will we take time to listen for God's clear, strong voice? Oh, I know our lives are often busy and hassled. Our lives can be filled, even over-stuffed, with the needs and noises coming from other people, from our responsibilities at work, home and outside the home. We may not take time to listen for God's clear, strong voice because we're so intensely focused on listening to our own personal needs and the noises coming from inside our own heads. For some of us, our lives are seriously hurting with real physical, emotional and spiritual pain. We may feel trapped or crushed, unable to listen to anything beyond our own pain. Because of this, it is that much more important, with our hurried and hurting lives, to take time to listen to creation's declaration of a God who speaks to us in a clear, strong voice.

When was the last time you slowed down enough to look at, to listen to, the morning sky or the evening sky? To listen to that little stream, or river, or lake, or ocean? Stopped to listen to the hills, the mountains, the valleys, the open fields? And for you more urban dwellers, when was the last time you listened to that tree and patch of pretty flowers planted right there on that busy, crowded, gum-sticking-to-your-shoes sidewalk? Stopped to listen to that cool evening breeze that came after a hot, humid, sweaty day in the city?

May we each choose to listen and believe that God is God and that God is speaking to us! God wants us to hear Him, and through hearing Him to know Him. God speaks through His creation, through His Scriptures and through His Spirit. And God speaks His ultimate revelation of Himself through His Son Jesus, the Word made flesh, in a clear, strong voice!

Do I believe it?
And if I do, what am I going to do about it?

Lord, please let me hear your voice, your love, your wisdom, your grace and truth.

March 31

NOTHING AND NOBODY PUSHES GOD AROUND

Have you ever felt absolutely pushed to the very limits of your spiritual, emotional, mental and physical strength? I have. Many times. For different reasons, in different circumstances, with different people.

The freeing truth is that I really don't have enough strength on my own to take all the pushes and pulls that circumstances and people can bring into my life. I was never meant to do life or relationships in my own strength. None of us were.

No matter how strong (or right or wise or justified) we may think we are, we all need God to be our help and our strength. All the time. This isn't an easy truth for many of us to embrace. We don't like thinking we're out of control or unable to handle certain situations or relationships on our own. Often, we will only come to accept the truth of our need for God's help when we're absolutely pushed to our limits by unwanted and unexpected circumstances and by frustrating and difficult people that seem to invade our lives.

> *I was pushed back and about to fall,*
> *but the LORD helped me.*
> *The LORD is my strength [and my song] and my defense;*
> *he has become my salvation.*
> Psalm 118:13-14

It is a good thing – a very good thing – to deeply grasp this freeing truth (and live in it) of how desperate each one of us is for God's help and strength to keep us from falling. God wants us to rely on Him and on His unfailing love and unlimited strength. All the time. In all situations. Those times when we think we're strong enough to handle everything just fine on our own. Those times when we know we just can't handle one thing more.

Personally, during those times when I haven't relied on God's strength, I have done some very serious falling. And, unfortunately, it wasn't just me who got hurt on my way down. Feeling pushed, I have often pushed back in ego-centric, angry, selfish, self-justifying and just plain stupid ways.

Ahhhhh…how very different are those times when I have felt pushed to my very limits and have chosen, instead, to raise my head and my heart to trust and receive God's strength and listen for God's song to calm my thoughts, shape my words and direct my behaviors!

God is our only true help. God is our only true strength. Our only song. Our only salvation. Being honest about our very real need for, and our absolute dependence on, God's help and strength – at all times, in all circumstances, with all people – gives us an undeniable, uncontainable freedom! And nothing and nobody pushes our God around!

Instead of falling, may each of us fall more and more in love with our God - our eternal help, strength, song and salvation!

Reflections – Responses – Challenges – Encouragements – God-breathing Thoughts

Do I believe it?
And if I do, what am I going to do about it?

Lord, please let me hear your voice, your love, your wisdom, your grace and truth.

GOD'S FOOLISH WISDOM

Oh! We can all be so foolish at times! Thankfully, most of our foolishness leaves only a temporary mark or fleeting memory – with maybe just a bit of embarrassment thrown in. But the greatest act of foolishness we could ever commit, with eternal consequences, is to *not* put our faith in Jesus Christ as our Savior and Lord!

In perfect wisdom and boundless love, our Heavenly Father allowed Jesus – the sinless One, His perfect Son – to die for our sins so that we could be brought before our God as righteous, holy and redeemed. And God did this all out of His love!

> *For God so loved the world that he gave his one and only Son,*
> *that whoever believes in him shall not perish but have eternal life.*
> *For God did not send his Son into the world to condemn the world,*
> *but to save the world through him.*
> John 3:16-17

To those who do not *yet* know the love of God and the power of His great and total sacrifice in giving His Son Jesus for our forgiveness, salvation and eternal life, this seems like absolute foolishness! It's just too outrageous! It's just too simple!

Questions arise about such foolishness – and they should:
Is it really true that Jesus chose to die for me? To die for the forgiveness of all my sins?
Is it really true that through the resurrection of Jesus, all the power that sin and death had over me is completely broken and defeated forever?
Is it really true that because of my faith in Jesus, I can live now and forever in an intimately and eternally secure love relationship with my Heavenly Father?

The answer to each of these questions – from the very Word and Wisdom of God – is *Yes!*

> *...the message concerning the faith we proclaim: That if you declare with your mouth,*
> *"Jesus is Lord," and believe in your heart that God raised him from the dead,*
> *you will be saved. For it is with your heart that you believe and are justified,*
> *and it is with your mouth that you profess your faith and are saved.*
> Romans 10:8-10

How could this be? It doesn't make sense.

Oh, but it does. To our God. Jesus – through His death and resurrection – is the very power and wisdom of God! By God's will. In God's way.

> *...to those whom God has called, both Jews and Greeks,*
> *Christ is the power of God and the wisdom of God.*
> *For the foolishness of God is wiser than human wisdom...*
> *...Christ Jesus, who has become for us the wisdom of God –*
> *that is, our righteousness, holiness and redemption.*
> 1 Corinthians 1:24-25,30

May we each fully believe and trust God's foolish wisdom in giving His Son Jesus to save us and transform our lives – right now in this moment and for all eternity!

Do I believe it?
And if I do, what am I going to do about it?

Lord, please let me hear your voice, your love, your wisdom, your grace and truth.

WHAT'S IN A (NICK)NAME?

His name wasn't really Barnabas. It was Joseph.

It was the way Joseph (a Levite from Cyprus) lived out his relationship with his Lord Jesus and with his brothers and sisters in Christ that caused the apostles to nickname him Barnabas – which means Son of Encouragement. (Acts 4:36).

When Barnabas arrived and saw what the grace of God had done,
he was glad and encouraged them all
to remain true to the Lord with all their hearts.
Acts 11:23

I wonder what each of us would be nicknamed based on the way we live out our faith in Jesus. Based on how we live out our relationships with other people, and particularly, with our brothers and sisters in Christ.

Would our nicknames refer to the love we give freely and the faithfulness that shines deeply and consistently in our lives? Or would our nicknames refer to the hate that simmers in us and spews from us? Would our nicknames refer to the fear that grips us so tightly that we deny God's love and presence? Would our nicknames refer to the way we bring life or bring death to our relationships and to all we do? Would our nicknames refer to the forgiveness we offer or the judgment we hold against another?

Would our nicknames refer…
To our self-control or our need to control others?
To our righteousness or our self-righteousness?
To our thankfulness or our complaining?
To our living in freedom or in captivity?
To our encouragement or our criticism?
To our wisdom or our recklessness?
To our victory or our victimhood?
To our kindness or our cruelty?
To our joy or our bitterness?
To our peace or our panic?
To our truth or our lies?

Let love and faithfulness never leave you;
bind them around your neck,
write them on the tablet of your heart.
Then you will win favor and a good name
in the sight of God and man.
Proverbs 3:3-4

May each of us allow God's love and faithfulness to shape everything we are and everything we do! May we each be more and more transformed to the likeness of Jesus so that we would be named and nicknamed after the One whose Name is above all names!

Do I believe it?
And if I do, what am I going to do about it?

Lord, please let me hear your voice, your love, your wisdom, your grace and truth.

GOD'S LASTING WORD – GRASP THAT!

This world, this life, as we know it is temporary and transient.

How great is our God who has given us His eternal Word in which to place our trust!

> *"Heaven and earth will pass away,*
> *but my words will never pass away."*
> Mark 13:31

Does the thought that this world – this life we can see, hear, smell, taste and touch – will one day be completely gone scare you? Or do you already know the hope and promise of the deeper, eternal reality of God's everlasting, life-transforming Word? Oh! I pray you do!

God's Word, from Genesis 1:1 to Revelation 22:21, reveals our God to be mystical, holy, loving, all-powerful and purposeful. God's Word is revealed as eternal. It will not only never pass away, but God's Word is also revealed to be, right now and for all eternity, "alive and active" (Hebrews 4:12). God's Word reaches out to save us from everything that would keep us separated from our Holy Abba. God's Word reaches out to transform us into being more like Christ, even in this transient world, and to ultimately transform us into our eternal characters and bodies – set free forever from all that is frail, flawed and finite!

God's Word is love, grace, truth, salvation and transformation. God's Word is named Jesus! Jesus is our eternal hope, peace and joy. Jesus promises to be with us as we walk through this temporary, and often challenging and confusing, life. Jesus promises to bring each of us, who has trusted in the power and authority of His Word, into our eternal home with Him.

A bit hard to grasp, right? Ask God to help you grasp His Word – His eternal reality. God wants to answer you!

> *"This is what the LORD says, he who made the earth,*
> *the LORD who formed it and established it – the LORD is his name:*
> *'Call to me and I will answer you*
> *and tell you great and unsearchable things you do not know.' "*
> Jeremiah 33:2-3

The truth of God's mystical, holy, loving, all-powerful and purposeful Word shakes our senses and our sensibilities, our logic and our perception of tangible reality. The truth of God's alive and active Word, Jesus Christ, shakes us – and saves us – from all that will pass away in a flickering moment. The truth of God's alive and active Word brings us into God's everlasting realm of reality that will never pass away.

Jesus is the Word of God who spoke everything into existence. Jesus is the lasting Word of God who will call His people into everlasting life with Him. Grasp that. Be grasped by it.

Reflections – Responses – Challenges – Encouragements – God-breathing Thoughts

Do I believe it?
And if I do, what am I going to do about it?

Lord, please let me hear your voice, your love, your wisdom, your grace and truth.

THINGS WE CAN'T KNOW – THINGS WE DO KNOW

A number of years ago when Tim and I were caring for our friends' son for the weekend, we learned a fabulous lesson. This little four year old boy spoke great words of wisdom when I asked him a question. He didn't answer me with the often-heard, and more usual, response: "I don't know." Instead, this little guy answered me with a far more honest and humble response: "I can't know."

There are things on this side of heaven that we just can't know.

We've just got to be willing to humbly accept the truth of this. We can't know all that God knows. God is God. Only God is almighty and all-knowing. We are not. Yet, at the same time, there is so much that we do know. Because our almighty and all-knowing God has chosen to reveal these things to us.

> *The secret things belong to the LORD our God,*
> *but the things revealed belong to us and to our children forever,*
> *that we may know and follow all the words of this law.*
> Deuteronomy 29:29

God calls us to actively and intentionally respond to all those things that we *do know* – to all those things that our Lord has clearly revealed to us in His Word and by His Spirit.

With knowledge there comes a responsibility. With all that God has revealed to us, we must make a choice about whether or not we will trust what God's Word and Spirit have revealed. And if we do trust what God has made known, we need to choose to follow our Lord and follow His revealed ways for how we are to live as His children and followers.

God calls each one of us to fully trust and obey Him, to fully believe and follow Him in all that He has revealed to us in His Word and by His Spirit. And God, out of His incredible love for us, calls us to this deep, challenging and freedom-bringing place of trust and obedience to Him because our Lord fully knows what is for our very best.

> *"Father, I have revealed you to those whom you gave me out of the world.*
> *They were yours; you gave them to me and they have obeyed your word."*
> John 17:6

> *Jesus replied, "Anyone who loves me will obey my teaching.*
> *My Father will love them, and we will come to them and make our home with them."*
> John 14:23

Even when we *can't know* all the details surrounding our lives and circumstances, *we do know* that the very best thing we could ever do for ourselves is to trust and obey, to believe and follow our loving God – who knows us and all things fully! There will come a day of God's great and full revelation when we, too, will know in full, just as we are fully known.

> *Now I know in part; then I shall know fully even as I am fully known.*
> 1 Corinthians 13:12

Until that day, let's trust our God for all we can't know and follow Him in all we do know!

Reflections – Responses – Challenges – Encouragements – God-breathing Thoughts

Do I believe it?
And if I do, what am I going to do about it?

Lord, please let me hear your voice, your love, your wisdom, your grace and truth.

GOD SPEAKS. LISTEN! BELIEVE! LIVE!

Although we *can't know* everything on this side of heaven, God has been actively speaking to us and continually reaching out to us in very clear and powerful ways throughout the centuries.

God interrupts our lives – and our comfort-complacency zone of ignoring Him – in order to speak His powerful, eternal message of grace and truth to us. Through the death and resurrection of Jesus Christ, God's Holy Son, our Lord has spoken the full message of His everlasting love and purifying forgiveness for each of us who will listen and believe.

In the past God spoke to our ancestors
through the prophets at many times and in various ways,
but in these last days he has spoken to us by his Son,
whom he appointed heir of all things, and through whom he made the universe.
The Son is the radiance of God's glory and the exact representation of his being,
sustaining all things by his powerful word.
After he had provided purification for sins,
he sat down at the right hand of the Majesty in heaven.
Hebrews 1:1-3

God chose, out of His passionate, persistent, chasing-us-down love, to speak over and over again to His people through His prophets. Many times. In various ways. Yet, so many of those who heard did not and would not choose to believe God's message of love and life.

But God's love for us never stops. God's speaking His message to us never stopped either. It just got fuller, clearer and beyond our imagination. And the fullness of God's message, and the fullest reflection of His image, came to us in Jesus. God became man and died for us.

The Son is the image of the invisible God, the firstborn over all creation.
For in him all things were created: things in heaven and on earth, visible and invisible,
whether thrones or powers or rulers or authorities; all things have been created through
him and for him. He is before all things, and in him all things hold together.
For God was pleased to have all his fullness dwell in him,
and through him to reconcile to himself all things,
whether things on earth or things in heaven,
by making peace through his blood, shed on the cross.
Colossians 1:15-17

God spoke His definitive and ultimate message of love for all peoples of the world, His message of outrageous love for you and me, through giving us Jesus – and giving Jesus over to die for the forgiveness of our sins so that we might live.

God never stops speaking to us. God never stops pursuing us with His love.

Our choice is to listen and believe. And live.

Reflections – Responses – Challenges – Encouragements – God-breathing Thoughts

Do I believe it?
And if I do, what am I going to do about it?

Lord, please let me hear your voice, your love, your wisdom, your grace and truth.

WHERE DO WE APPLY?

We each need to think about where we really expend our energy, time and effort. Where is it that we apply ourselves? Where is it that we apply our hearts, our ears, our emotions, our thoughts, our motivations and our actions?

There are many people whose future is uncertain when it comes to their employment status. Some are currently unemployed. Some are under-employed. Some know that their jobs are on the line and may be gone soon. Some just desperately need to find a different job that better fits their skills and interests. These precious ones will be putting a great deal of energy, time and effort into applying for the kind of job that will provide for their financial needs – for their earthly survival needs. To apply energy, time and effort in this way is absolutely necessary and right for them to do. It is a good thing.

Others will be putting their energy, time and effort into applying for admittance into all sorts of educational programs, universities and specialized training courses. And once accepted into those programs, their energy, time and effort will be applied to further developing their abilities and talents within a variety of fields of study – from art to business, from language to math, from music to ministry, from salon services to carpentry, from plumbing to social work, from athletics to technology and oh-so-many other fields of expertise. To apply energy, time and effort to develop a greater knowledge level and stronger skills is also a very good thing. And for most people, it is a necessary requirement for getting and/or keeping their jobs.

Right in the midst of everything else that would – for good and necessary reasons – pull on our energy, time and efforts, our God wants us to apply our attention to Him, to His Word and His loving plan for our lives.

> **Apply your heart to instruction and your ears to words of knowledge.**
> Proverbs 23:12

God calls us to the very best and most necessary thing to which we should apply our hearts and our ears: To knowing and listening to – and following – God's Word and God's purposeful directions and good desires for our lives.

Yes, of course, we need to apply our energy, time and effort into our education and into our employment situations. This is good and necessary. And, yet, it is still only temporary.

Applying our hearts and our ears to God's eternal Word gives us a depth of peace and security, hope and perspective that no job, degree or certification in this world ever could. When we apply our hearts and ears to God's loving instruction and the knowledge of His truth, we can be absolutely certain that this will be one application – of our energy, time and effort – that will be fully accepted and bring great blessings to our lives, and to the lives of those around us!

Do I believe it?
And if I do, what am I going to do about it?

Lord, please let me hear your voice, your love, your wisdom, your grace and truth.

WHEN WORDS ARE MANY...WATCH OUT!

Communicating through words is such a fabulous gift that we humans have been given! But, oh! Like everything else, we must use this gift wisely. Our words, if not guarded by God's grace and truth, can twist reality in outrageous ways, or send a cutting blow to both our adversaries and our loved ones.

> *Sin is not ended by multiplying words*
> *[When words are many sin is not absent],*
> *but the prudent [the wise] hold their tongue.*
> Proverbs 10:19

When words are many, they can just be too many. And we need to: *Watch Out!*

I have never been viewed as a person of few words. I probably never will be. However, I do pray that God will continually and vigorously (That's how I need God to do it!) rule my head, my heart and my mouth so that my words, whether few or many, will be words that are wise, motivated from love and balanced with the grace and truth of our Lord Jesus Christ.

That's what I want. That's not always what I let happen.

I need God's strong and pure Spirit to direct and limit my words so that I do not exaggerate and/or "spin" the telling of anything that would not match with the way Jesus would tell it. Otherwise, that would be telling lies. *Watch Out!*

I need God's strong and sovereign Spirit to direct and stop my words so that I do not keep talking – thinking that if I say just the right (or enough) words to someone that they will get it. Get me. Or get my point – and do things my way! The truth is: I am called to humbly listen to and follow God's Word for myself. And to trust God to speak into the heart and life of the other person. In God's time. In God's Way. All my talking in the world does not make me anyone's Holy Spirit! *Watch Out!*

I need God's strong and loving Spirit to direct and form my words so that I speak words that are as full of the grace of Christ as they are full of the truth of Christ. Even when I am called to speak hard truths into someone's life, I need to be doing this only out of a grace-filled, sincere and compassionate love for them. And that comes only from Jesus. Otherwise, this truth-telling would be self-serving – coming from frustration, hurt, anger, self-righteousness or pride – rather than from a servant's heart, and mouth, of love. *Watch Out!*

So, although I probably will never be known as a person of few words, I do want my Lord to grow me, more and more, so that I will be a vessel of God's Words and obedient to God's Ways in speaking those words. At all times. With all people.

And if I can't-won't (ca-won't) do that, may God help me to choose, once again, what I call the "Wisdom of Silence!" This is God's ultimate, loving, *Watch Out!* weapon to protect all of us – speakers and listeners alike – from too many words.

Reflections – Responses – Challenges – Encouragements – God-breathing Thoughts

Do I believe it?
And if I do, what am I going to do about it?

Lord, please let me hear your voice, your love, your wisdom, your grace and truth.

April 8

BALANCE BETWEEN THE BOOKENDS

Balance in all things comes to us as we allow God to hold our lives in His love, grace and truth so that all of our thinking, speaking, acting and interacting will honor God and be a blessing to others and ourselves.

This balance is based on living in God's truths that remind us that:
We are absolutely dependent on God for everything.
God's inexhaustible power is fully available to us at all times, in every season, in every experience and in every circumstance of our lives – as we choose to trust God.

Within this balance – of choosing sincere humility before our holy, loving God and trusting in the unfailing strength that comes to us from our almighty God – is where we need to keep our minds, attitudes, perspectives, words and actions, reactions and interactions. Always.

We each need to determine – we each need to intentionally choose – to live continually between, what I call, *The Bookends of Faith*:

> *"...apart from me you can do nothing..."*
> John 15:5

> *I can do all things through him who gives me strength.*
> Philippians 4:13

Living between the *Bookends of Faith* is the safest, truest and strongest place we could ever choose to live. This is the place of greatest balance for our lives, for our relationships with others and with our Holy God!

In sincere humility before our Lord, we have the true and right perspective that all that we are, all that we have, all that we are able to do – everything about us, our lives, and even our very breath – comes from our Creator God. It is humbling and freeing all at the same time. We are called to believe this truth and live like we truly believe that *apart from Jesus Christ we can do nothing.* Ultimate humility.

Ahhhhh! And the other *Bookend of Faith* is just as true. In our Lord Jesus Christ, the truth of our dependence on God is exactly what leaves us open to receive the full power of God. In our Lord's strength we have been given the power to deal with *all things in His strength* – every person, every detail, every circumstance, every joy, every tragedy and every moment that comes into our lives. Ultimate power.

Nothing apart from Jesus – all things in His strength. Holy Balance.

This is God's perfect, loving and powerful balance in which we each are meant to live – in between the *Bookends of Faith* – so that we may live in true freedom, receiving unfailing strength as we live in humble dependence on our Lord Jesus Christ!

Reflections – Responses – Challenges – Encouragements – God-breathing Thoughts

Do I believe it?
And if I do, what am I going to do about it?

Lord, please let me hear your voice, your love, your wisdom, your grace and truth.

_____

_____

_____

_____

_____

_____

_____

_____

_____

_____

_____

_____

_____

_____

_____

_____

_____

_____

_____

_____

_____

_____

_____

_____

_____

GOD'S STRENGTH FOR MY FEET

God's strength offers us a power so far beyond ourselves that we have likely been astonished at (or maybe thankfully relieved and surprised at) the challenges we have been able to meet and the heights to which we have managed to climb when faced with tough, tiresome, terrible and terrifying circumstances.

I know that for me, when I look carefully and honestly at my life and the transforming journey God has taken me on, I can clearly see that it was God's Sovereign love, wisdom and strength that placed my feet on His path and held me tightly the entire way. Each step of the way. One step at a time.

The Sovereign LORD is my strength;
he makes my feet like the feet of a deer,
he enables me to tread on the heights.
Habakkuk 3:19

My God picked me up each time I fell down, and fell down again. God picked me up during those times when I stubbornly, pridefully, foolishly chose to go my own way instead of God's good way. God picked me up during those times when I allowed the hurt and frustration caused by others or the pain and confusion I felt over my circumstances to knock me off my feet. My sovereign, loving Lord picked me up, cleaned me off, forgave me, calmed me, encouraged me, comforted me, confronted me, corrected me and, once again, offered me the fullness of His strength to get my feet back to walking along the heights. With Him!

With all my heart, I believe our God wants each of us to be able to scale the heights of all that would seem too daunting to overcome, too painful to endure, too challenging to conquer and too dark to redeem. With all my heart, I believe that we are able – as we yield ourselves to humbly and honestly acknowledge that we need God to enable us through His strength – to mount the masses of challenges we face and the messes we make in our lives.

Now to him who is able to do immeasurably more
than all we ask or imagine,
according to his power that is at work within us,
to him be glory in the church and in Christ Jesus
throughout all generations, for ever and ever! Amen.
Ephesians 3:20-21

May each of us be awed at, and outrageously thankful for, the strength and the power that our Almighty God gives to us! Each step of the way. One step at a time. To climb to the heights. With Him!

Do I believe it?
And if I do, what am I going to do about it?

Lord, please let me hear your voice, your love, your wisdom, your grace and truth.

TO WHOM SHALL WE GO?

One heart-breaking day, after some soul-challenging teachings by Jesus, some of His disciples turned back and no longer followed Him.

Jesus continually reaches out to us. Yet, He forces no one to follow. He only invites. Jesus wants all those who would choose to follow Him to fully trust Him with their hearts and their lives. And so, on that heart-breaking day of hard teachings, Jesus asked His twelve apostles if they wanted to leave Him too.

May each one of us be able to choose – to believe and declare – as Simon Peter answered:

> *"Lord, to whom shall we go?*
> *You have the words of eternal life.*
> *We believe and know that you are the Holy One of God."*
> John 6:68-69

To whom shall we go? I just love that first, gut-honest response by Peter. It's not: To *where* shall we go? It's not: *What* shall we do? No. Peter's first response is: To *whom* shall we go?

That really is the foundational question at the core of each of our hearts. Our hearts cry out for an eternal and intimate relationship. Our hearts cry out for the eternal and intimate *Who*.

We want to know to *whom* do we belong. We want to know to *whom* will our hearts and souls respond and recognize as the One who answers our deepest cries for love and life.

It is only in the intimacy of an eternal relationship with Jesus that we will know true love. It is only in relationship with Jesus that we will know true life – now and forever. It is only in Jesus that we will know truth. Jesus is the Holy One of God – our Messiah, Savior, Redeemer, King.

It is as we recognize who Jesus is – through seeking to understand and know Him, through listening to His life-bringing, eternal words – that we will be moved to choose Him, to believe Him and to passionately follow Him as the One to *whom* we should go!

Jesus is the Holy One of God before *whom* every knee will bow and every tongue confess this eternal truth!

> *...at the name of Jesus every knee should bow,*
> *in heaven and on earth and under the earth,*
> *and every tongue acknowledge that Jesus Christ is Lord,*
> *to the glory of God the Father.*
> Philippians 2:10-11

May we each choose now to go to Jesus – so we may hear and know Him, believe and follow Him as He speaks His words of eternal life to us!

Reflections – Responses – Challenges – Encouragements – God-breathing Thoughts

Do I believe it?
And if I do, what am I going to do about it?

Lord, please let me hear your voice, your love, your wisdom, your grace and truth.

TO WHOM WILL YOU COMPARE ME?

"To whom will you compare me?
Or who is my equal?" says the Holy One.

Lift your eyes and look to the heavens:
Who created all these?
He who brings out the starry host one by one,
and calls forth each of them by name.
Because of his great power and mighty strength,
Not one of them is missing.
Isaiah 40:25-26

I am so thankful that God is so great. So big. So powerful. So intimate. So all-knowing. So strong. I am so thankful that no one and nothing is God's equal. Because I need – we all need – the deep soul-security that God alone is the Sovereign One over all that exists. That God is bigger than anyone and anything, any circumstance and situation that could discombobulate and disturb our lives.

To whom will we compare God? To no one. To nothing.

I need to know that my God intimately knows me and personally calls me by name, just as He does each one of the incalculable number of stars in the vast universe He created.

To whom will we compare God? To no one. To nothing.

I need to know that my God is great in power and mighty in strength, because there are moments and days and seasons when I feel (and truly am) completely powerless and unable to keep the discombobulating, disturbing stuff of life away from me and from those I love. God is never discombobulated. God is never disturbed. God is always great in power and mighty in strength.

To whom will we compare God? To no one. To nothing.

I need to know that my God always sees me, always cares about where I am – literally and figuratively – in the minutiae of my life and in the grand scheme of eternity for my life. I need to know that to my God I am never missed, and I could never go missing.

To whom will we compare God? To no one. To nothing.

Our God is the Sovereign God over all creation. Unimaginably intimate with us, His beloved creations. Our God is great in power. Mighty in strength. Our God is all-knowing.

Our God is absolutely incomparable. And I am so thankful.

Do I believe it?
And if I do, what am I going to do about it?

Lord, please let me hear your voice, your love, your wisdom, your grace and truth.

OH! THE BALANCE OF SHINING AND DOING!

Jesus spoke both of these very clear messages about our good and righteous acts:

> *"You are the light of the world…*
> *let your light shine before others,*
> *that they may see your good deeds*
> *and glorify your Father in heaven."*
> Matthew 5:14,16

> *"Be careful not to practice your righteousness*
> *in front of others to be seen by them."*
> Matthew 6:1

Taken one at a time, these messages are very clear about our good and righteous acts. Yet, taken together, we really have to pull out the truth of them for what they mean for us. We have to figure out what the balance truly is between *shining our light before others* and *not practicing our righteousness in front of others.*

As followers of Jesus, the Light of the world, we are meant to reflect His light, His love, His generosity, His justice, His kindness and His compassion in deeply spiritual ways and in absolutely practical and tangible ways as we serve our God and do good deeds. We are meant to shine. A light is not to be hidden. But! The light, though clearly seen, is not the object intended to be seen. The light is to shine so that something else or – in our case, as followers of Christ – Someone Else is seen. God is to be revealed. God is to be made known. God is to be acknowledged and given praise by those who have benefitted from the works of light and love, generosity and justice, kindness and compassion that we have done.

The balance here: We, in shining our light before others, intimately and clearly know and acknowledge who the True Light is, and from whom our ability and power to shine has come, and for what eternal purpose we've been given to shine in the first place – for the praise and glory of our Father in heaven.

And, yet, as we go about the practicing of righteousness, our Lord Jesus strictly warns us to be careful not to do these acts of righteousness before others just to be seen by them. Yes, we are to do acts of righteousness. And in some way, on some level, at some time, they will be seen by others. However, it will always come down to answering ourselves honestly about: For whom are we doing what we do? In what manner and attitude do we go about doing our acts of righteousness? And for whose praise and glory are we doing them?

The balance here: Our reasons, our motivations and our purposes for doing what is good and loving, generous and just, kind and compassionate are not to be birthed from our pride or from our desire to be elevated in the eyes of others in any way. If our acts of righteousness are true acts of righteousness, then we will, with joy and thankfulness, give praise and glory to our Father in heaven. And so will the other people who have witnessed and been blessed by our actions.

Oh, Balance! May we each shine and do great good works of righteousness with a right heart and the right motivations so that the Righteous One will receive all the praise and glory!

Reflections – Responses – Challenges – Encouragements – God-breathing Thoughts

Do I believe it?
And if I do, what am I going to do about it?

Lord, please let me hear your voice, your love, your wisdom, your grace and truth.

NEW EVERY MORNING!

Our Lord's great love, compassions and faithfulness are offered new to us every new morning of our lives. No matter what our yesterday was like.

> *Because of the LORD's great love we are not consumed,*
> *for his compassions never fail.*
> *They are new every morning; great is your faithfulness.*
> Lamentations 3:22-23

Our moods, our behavior, our circumstances, our health, our hope, our families, our friends, our jobs, our bank accounts, our perspectives – all can change, and sometimes quite radically, from one day to the next. There are many things we can't rely on to remain the same over the course of our days. We don't have absolute certainty or control in any situation or relationship.

Yet, we can be absolutely certain that the Lord's great love for us is as present with us today as it was yesterday. And we can be absolutely certain that our Lord's great love for us will be just as present with us in the new morning that will greet us tomorrow.

We can be absolutely certain that our Lord's compassions and mercies will flow constantly, consistently and unfailingly to all of us as His children. Each new morning of each new day.

We can be absolutely certain that our Lord's great faithfulness to us is based on who He is. Not on who we are. Not on what we do. Not on what we say. Not on what we think. Our Lord is the same sovereign, holy, faithful God yesterday, today and tomorrow.

Our Lord's great love, compassion and faithfulness are newly offered to us every new morning. If we will receive them, we will be renewed every new morning by them. And in our renewal, our Lord empowers each one of us to offer His great love, compassion and faithfulness to all those around us – to those who have broken hearts or broken bodies, broken relationships or broken dreams. As we are renewed, we are given power to also offer the Lord's great love, compassion and faithfulness to those who have broken our own hearts, have hurt our bodies and have betrayed our trust and dismantled our dreams.

Is there someone in your life that needs this renewed offering of the Lord's love, compassion and faithfulness from you? By the Lord's powerful Spirit working in and through us, it is always possible to do this. Not necessarily easily. But it is always possible.

It is the through the very same power that raised Jesus from the dead that our Lord will work to renew us and work through us to offer *new every morning* love, compassion and faithfulness to all those around us, including, and maybe especially, to those who have disappointed us or who have hurt us the very most!

Do I believe it?
And if I do, what am I going to do about it?

Lord, please let me hear your voice, your love, your wisdom, your grace and truth.

UNFAIR! WHAT TO DO?

Sometimes we can feel that life is unfair. And most of those times – not always, but most of those times – it really isn't even our fault. Still, we find ourselves in what seems like an unfair circumstance. Or we're in a situation with unfair (and maybe, even, with very mean and evil) people. And we just can't do a darn thing to make it better or change the situation or bring about justice. At least not justice according to our own perspective of what justice should look like. And we definitely don't have the power to bring about justice according our to own *hurry up and make it right, right now* timeline.

We are not only left powerless in these unfair, unjust circumstances, but we may actually find ourselves in the situation where no one else sees the truth from our perspective. That can be a devastating and faith-shaking place to be. But it doesn't shake God. God is the God of Justice. God is the God who sees – and sees far more clearly than we are able.

What does God ask of us when our situation is so unfair, so unjust?

> *Commit your way to the LORD;*
> *trust in him and he will do this:*
> *He will make your righteous reward shine like the dawn,*
> *[the justice of your cause] your vindication like the noonday sun.*
> *Be still before the LORD and wait patiently for him;*
> *do not fret when people succeed in their ways,*
> *when they carry out their wicked schemes.*
> *Refrain from anger and turn from wrath;*
> *do not fret – it leads only to evil.*
> *For those who are evil will be destroyed,*
> *but those who hope in the LORD will inherit the land.*
> Psalm 37:5-9

What has God asked of me, when I've found myself in these unjust, unfair circumstances with unjust, unfair people? Well, it definitely wasn't to continue stomping my feet or slamming my cupboards or yelling all sorts of ugly stuff, really, really loudly! Even if the yelling was, only and usually, just inside my head. God has made it pretty clear that the inside-my-head-yelling still counts as yelling to God. And it's really not all that helpful in the big scheme of things.

No. Instead, God has asked, *told*, me to do this: To trust God and be still. To commit my way to God. To wait for God's justice. I am to commit to God all of my circumstances – no matter how unjust they are, or how unfair they seem. I am to commit to God all of my ways – all of my circumstances, my perspective, my planning, my desires, my frustration, my thinking, my speaking, my acting, my facial expressions, my tone of voice, my stomping, my slamming and my yelling – over to God.

My everything is to be consciously, intentionally, actively, immediately and continually entrusted over and committed to my God. God, not I, is in control. God, not I, sees fully. I am to be quiet and wait. I am to put my hope in the Lord. God is just. Justice is God's to work out. Not mine. And my God can be fully trusted. Righteousness and justice will shine for all eternity!

Reflections – Responses – Challenges – Encouragements – God-breathing Thoughts

Do I believe it?
And if I do, what am I going to do about it?

Lord, please let me hear your voice, your love, your wisdom, your grace and truth.

DEBT FREE LIVING

Today is April 15th. This is tax day in the United States. We have a debt to pay. All of our taxes for the previous year come due today. Some of us may be getting a refund because our tax debt was already paid. Many, maybe even most of us, however, still have a tax debt that we need to pay out to our government.

Some of us may try to finagle or, at least, creatively fill out our tax forms to ensure that the amount we owe is doing some version of what I call: "The Tax Limbo Dance." You know: "How Low Can You Owe?" Some of us may even choose to completely ignore our debt owed – ignore our responsibility to pay our government-determined tax amount. Determining in our own minds that it is we – not the government, nor anyone else – who decide what we do with our money and everything else that belongs to us.

Well, maybe some people will get away with the creative finagling in figuring the amount of tax debt they owe. Others may seemingly get away with disregarding their debt all together. Whatever our attitudes and our subsequent actions are regarding the payment of our taxes, our Lord Jesus has something to say to us not only about what we need to give to our governments, but something much more important about what we need to give to God.

> *"So give back to Caesar what is Caesar's,*
> *and give to God what is God's."*
> Matthew 22:21

Jesus is telling us here that we each need to fulfill our responsibilities to the governments under which we live. And yet far beyond that, Jesus is challenging us to really think about what actually belongs to God. And Jesus is calling us to act faithfully in giving back to God all that belongs to God.

You and your accountant (or maybe Turbo Tax) will figure out the debt you owe in taxes. As for figuring out what belongs to God, God makes that perfectly clear.

> *The earth is the LORD's,*
> *and everything in it,*
> *the world, and all who live in it!*
> Psalm 24:1

All that exists, all people everywhere, all that we have, all that we are, all of our very lives truly belong to God! No figuring out deductions here. No finagling at all. Everything belongs to God.

And, Oh! Our God really does want us to live, knowing and believing, the truth that we belong to Him! Our loving God desires the very best for our lives. And that comes to us when we give our lives fully back to the One, our Lord Jesus Christ, who gave His life for us! Jesus accepted the full responsibility of paying the full price of our full debt owed to God. Believing this truth, living in this truth, is our way to "give to God what is God's." This is truly debt free living!

Do I believe it?
And if I do, what am I going to do about it?

Lord, please let me hear your voice, your love, your wisdom, your grace and truth.

IT IS NOT TOO DIFFICULT

We can often make things so much more difficult than they really are. So much more complicated than they need to be. Sadly, this thinking – that things are too difficult for us – can be especially pervasive when it comes to living out our lives as believers and followers of Jesus Christ. We forget, we ignore or we don't really believe God's beautiful Word of grace and truth that tells us clearly:

> *"...with God all things are possible."*
> Matthew 19:26

Emphasis on *with God.* Not on our own. Not in our own strength. Not in our own wisdom. Not in our own righteousness. *With God.* All things are possible.

God tells us, just as He told His people wandering in the Sinai desert for forty years, that it is not too difficult to live out our faith relationship with Him. It is not too difficult to trust God. It is not too difficult to obey God.

> *Now what I am commanding you today*
> *is not too difficult for you or beyond your reach.*
> *...No, the word is very near you;*
> *it is in your mouth and in your heart so you may obey it.*
> Deuteronomy 30:11,14

God has not left us alone to live as His people in our own strength. Oh, no! That would be too difficult. Rather, our God, in His love and perfect provision, has given us the intimacy of His very present Holy Spirit and the power of His Word to surround us, fill us, strengthen us, heal us and transform us.

God may, and often does, take us out of our comfort zones in order to transform us more and more into the likeness of our Lord Jesus. Even as God does this, He is always, always very near to us offering His comfort. And in His presence and through His love and power, we are confident that nothing is too difficult.

God never said that our lives and our circumstances would always be easy. They're not. But following God's commands, that bring peace to our souls and hope to our lives, is not, and never will be, too difficult for us...*with God.* When we choose to remember that God declares His unfailing love for us and promises His constant presence with us, then following God's commands is not too difficult for us. When we choose to speak God's Word of grace and truth to ourselves so that God's Word fills our minds and takes root in our hearts, then following God's commands is not too difficult for us. When we choose to trust in God's power rather than in our own strength and ability to obey our God, then following God's commands is not too difficult for us.

God is near. God's Word is near.

Let God's Word flow from your mouth and fill your heart. Speak God's Word of grace and truth, first, to yourself, and watch God prove that it is not too difficult to live out your faith, it is not too difficult to trust and obey God's commands *with God*!

Reflections – Responses – Challenges – Encouragements – God-breathing Thoughts

Do I believe it?
And if I do, what am I going to do about it?

Lord, please let me hear your voice, your love, your wisdom, your grace and truth.

UNEXPLAINABLE GRACE AND COMPASSION

I'm not sure I'll ever really be able to grasp how passionately our Lord loves me. How passionately our God loves each and every one of us. Yet, that's what the Bible tells us over and over again. And God tells us this so clearly through the willing, sacrificial death of Jesus for the forgiveness of our sins. Not His. For the gift of our eternal life. Through His.

I'm not sure I'll ever really be able comprehend the idea that our Lord actually longs to pour out His grace and goodness onto us and into us, and through us to others.

I'm not sure I'll ever really be able to fully understand how it is that our Lord chooses to come close to us and to rise up, showing us His compassion for us. Yet, that's what the Bible tells us. Our God is a God who wants good for us. Our God is a God who wants to show us His grace and compassion.

> *Yet the LORD longs to be gracious to you;*
> *therefore he will rise up to show you compassion.*
> *For the LORD is a God of justice.*
> *Blessed are all who wait on the LORD.*
> Isaiah 30:18

No, I'm not sure about how or why our Lord – the God of justice – loves us in the outrageous, unexplainable ways that He does. But! I am convinced that this is true because my life has been irrevocably transformed by my Lord's unexplainable grace and compassion. It was through trusting that Jesus paid the full price for my own ugly sins, and for all the sins of all others, that I understood that God's justice had been fully met through the death of Jesus Christ.

It was in trusting God at God's Word, in trusting in Jesus' death and resurrection for my own forgiveness, that I was able to open myself up to receive God's grace and compassion – receive God's longing and God's power – to forgive all those who had ever caused me harm or hurt of any kind, at any time.

And I am convinced that the Lord wants, and is more able than you could ever imagine, to transform your life, too, with His unexplainable grace and compassion! Will you let Him?

Will you allow the truth of God's Word – His gracious, compassionate and just Word – to break through to you?
In the places you want to stay in control?
In the places you want to stay angry or bitter or self-righteous or self-sufficient?
In the places you refuse to believe that Jesus' death was really enough for your forgiveness?
In the places you refuse to believe that Jesus' death was really enough for the forgiveness of all others? Even for those most evil of others? Even when this isn't your sense of justice?

Our Lord is the God of justice who longs to pour out His grace and compassion to each of us. And I am so thankful He does! My life depends on God's amazing, unexplainable grace and compassion – right now and for all eternity. And so does yours.

Do I believe it?
And if I do, what am I going to do about it?

Lord, please let me hear your voice, your love, your wisdom, your grace and truth.

EXAMINATION PROCESS

God tells us to examine ourselves, to examine our ways. Those ways that we are to examine include every way that we think, perceive, speak, stay silent, respond, act, react, interact, spend our time, spend our money, roll our eyes and all other forms of body language.

If we take the time to look, really look, at ourselves – examine and test our ways – we will know deep in our souls that we need the Lord. I know I do. At all times. In all ways.

> **Let us examine our ways and test them,**
> **and let us return to the LORD.**
> Lamentations 3:40

To tell you the truth, I would much rather have it be God and I together scrutinizing all of my ways, rather than having to be corrected (challenged, convicted or embarrassed) by someone else. Although that has happened several times before in my life, and I know it will keep on happening too! God uses believers and not-yet-believers to correct His people. I'd just rather have it be God who's getting all up in my face instead of other people. Not because I'm so holy. It's really because I'm a wimp. God's correction, challenge and conviction of my ways come only, and always, out of His love for me. God has no other agenda than that He wants His very best for me, and He wants the purest possible reflection of His Son Jesus to come through me. God wants to build me up, even when He has to humble me because of my pride, stubbornness and every wrong behavior (seen or unseen by others) that I do. Correction, challenge, conviction – and examination of all my ways – are much easier to take from my God, and with my God, because He is the One who loves me the very most!

Our God is so good. No matter what our ways have been, our loving, holy God always calls us back to Himself. Our Lord always wants us to return to Him. To stay with Him. And to follow His ways very, very closely.

The reality is that we are being scrutinized by those around us – just as we scrutinize others. It is so important and so urgent that we, as followers of Christ, reflect our Lord more purely, beautifully and fully so that all those around us will see and know the love, grace and truth that our God offers to all people. At all times.

May each of us be courageous enough to invite God into the examination process of all of our ways. May we each take to heart our God's loving, righteous, stern and tender correction, challenge and conviction for our own behaviors. May each of us, who claim to be followers of Christ, truly follow Him so that the Body of Christ will look, think, speak and act like the Body of Christ! When we do, we will be true ambassadors of our God. It is then that those around us will be drawn to Jesus as Savior and Lord.

Oh! What an eternal impact our willingness to undergo God's examination process can have in our own lives and in the lives of those with whom we interact!

Reflections – Responses – Challenges – Encouragements – God-breathing Thoughts

Do I believe it?
And if I do, what am I going to do about it?

Lord, please let me hear your voice, your love, your wisdom, your grace and truth.

THAT QUIET, DARK, CONFUSING DAY – THIS IS SATURDAY

Two days ago a Maundy Thursday service was offered where we remembered that during His last Passover meal with His apostles, Jesus gave us a new command: "Love one another as I have loved you." This was the same night that Jesus knelt down as a lowly servant to wash the feet of His followers to show them that His love is truly about humbly caring for and cleaning even the roughest, dirtiest areas of our lives. Yet, we are cut to our souls to know that this new command of love was given on the very same night that Jesus was left alone by all His closest friends as He poured out His heart in agonizing prayer to His Father. It was the same night that Jesus was betrayed by Judas, one of His closest followers, who with a kiss brought a crowd carrying clubs and swords to seize and arrest the Prince of Peace. It was the same night that the one Jesus had named Peter, *the Rock*, would crumble and choose to lie about Him and three times deny even knowing Jesus. How could this outrageous denial happen? Wasn't it Peter who had once boldly proclaimed, "You are the Christ! The Son of the Living God!"?

And the next day, the Good Friday service had each of us look full in the face of our Jesus as He suffered a horribly cruel, shameful, unjust, undeserved death on the cross. He was falsely accused. Jesus was mocked, slapped, beaten with fists, whipped with the flesh-ripping lashes. His holy head was punctured and bloodied by the fierce push of the crown of thorns. His feet that walked so many miles to preach good news to the poor and His healing hands that had healed all manner of illness, cast out demons and gave life back to the dead, were now brutally forced to stop as nails were hammered into them, pushing His flesh and blood into the wood of the cross. And even after Jesus committed His spirit into the hands of His Father and gave up His last breath, His side was pierced by the cruel and scrutinizing stabbing of the soldier's sword. On Friday Jesus died in an agony of spirit and body that none of us will ever fully comprehend. He suffered the physical torment of outrageous brutality while bearing the weight of every sin ever committed by every person throughout all of human history. Jesus died for me. For my sin. For you. For your sin. For the sins of every person who has ever hurt you, has ever hurt anyone, in any way. And as Jesus bore the crushing, killing weight of all our sins, the spiritual torture that he suffered was far worse than any physical cruelty could ever inflict. "Jesus became sin for us so that we might become the righteousness of God" (2 Corinthians 5:21) – and in so doing Jesus, the Son of God, was condemned, rejected, alienated, separated and abandoned by His God and His Father. The ripping of His holy, yet now, sin-blackened soul away from the eternal and beautiful unity He had shared with His Abba was an agony inflicted on Jesus that shuddered and shocked all of creation. On Friday Jesus died. His dead, disfigured body was taken down from the cross, and Jesus was buried in a tomb meant for someone else.

And now it's Saturday. No more lies. No more betrayal. No more denial. No more brutality. Just death. And quiet. And darkness. And confusion.

This is Saturday. The Sabbath. But rest comes only as shock. Only as numbness. Only from exhaustion of body, mind and spirit. This is Saturday. We wait. There is something we are holding onto. But right now, that something is indistinguishable. Shock and numbness that are far more real and far more tangible than anything else right now on this quiet, dark and confusing day. Too many questions. Too much unknown. And so we wait.

Surely he took up our pain and bore our suffering, yet we considered him punished by God, stricken by him, and afflicted. But he was pierced for our transgressions, he was crushed for our iniquities; the punishment that brought us peace was on him, and by his wounds we are healed. We all, like sheep, have gone astray, each of us has turned to our own way; and the LORD has laid on him the iniquity of us all.
Isaiah 53:4-6

Do I believe it?
And if I do, what am I going to do about it?

Lord, please let me hear your voice, your love, your wisdom, your grace and truth.

JESUS HAS RISEN! ALWAYS REMEMBER!

On the first day of the week, very early in the morning, the women took the spices they had prepared and went to the tomb. They found the stone rolled away from the tomb, but when they entered, they did not find the body of the Lord Jesus. While they were wondering about this, suddenly two men in clothes that gleamed like lightning stood beside them. In their fright the women bowed down with their faces to the ground, but the men said to them, "Why do you look for the living among the dead?
He is not here; he has risen!
Remember how he told you, while he was still with you in Galilee:
'The Son of Man must be delivered over to the hands of sinners,
be crucified, and on the third day be raised again.' "
Then they remembered his words.
Luke 24:1-8

Jesus has risen! Always remember! This truth changes everything! This truth changes every one of us who would ever believe!

Jesus has conquered the power of sin! Jesus laid down His pure life to purify us by His own blood shed on the cross for the forgiveness of our sins. And through this act of ultimate love, Jesus bore the full punishment of our condemnation and separation from our Holy, Creator God. And now we who trust in Jesus as our Messiah, as our eternal Savior, may approach our Heavenly Father as His holy and dearly loved children!

Jesus has risen! Always remember! Jesus has conquered the power of death! Our Lord Jesus could not be bound by the cords of death. He is the Lord of Life – the One who holds all power and authority to eternally conquer death and to grant eternal life to all who believe. Jesus Himself assured us of this great hope and this great victory over death:

"Very truly I tell you, whoever hears my word and believes him who sent me has eternal life and will not be judged but has crossed over from death to life."
John 5:24

Jesus has risen! Always remember!

Jesus desires each one of us to hear and believe His Words of grace and truth:
I died for your sins. I alone could do this. You are forgiven. You are set free of all blame and all shame. I bore all sin for all time, all for your freedom!
I have eternal life to give you. I alone could do this. You need never fear death again. I swallowed it up in full victory. Death cannot hold my children. I have already rescued you from death and brought you into the promised eternal life with me!

Jesus has risen! Always remember! You have a decision to make. We all have a decision to make about Jesus. Believe the message of Jesus and receive the salvation and eternal life that come through Jesus Christ alone. Ask Jesus, even now, to be your Savior. Let God know that you believe that Jesus is His Son who died for your sins and rose from the dead to give you eternal life. God loves you so much. Your Heavenly Father wants you to hear and believe. God wants you to be set free from the power of sin and the punishment of death. God wants you to know the total forgiveness that Jesus alone offers and the hope and joy of eternal life with Him – the Holy God over all creation! Believe. And thank God for loving you so very much that He gave His Son for your salvation. Thank God for hearing your heart and accepting your belief in Jesus as your Savior. Tell someone about your life-saving, life-transforming decision to trust in Jesus!

Jesus has risen! Always remember! And always live like you remember!

Reflections – Responses – Challenges – Encouragements – God-breathing Thoughts

Do I believe it?
And if I do, what am I going to do about it?

Lord, please let me hear your voice, your love, your wisdom, your grace and truth.

_____

_____

_____

_____

_____

_____

_____

_____

_____

_____

_____

_____

_____

_____

_____

_____

_____

_____

_____

_____

_____

_____

_____

April 21

LOVE. REALLY LOVE.

There is a roar in my spirit – loud and fierce, urgent and loving – beyond what I can explain. Touch of God? God's Spirit speaking? Roar of God? I think so. "Lord, what message for your people do I tell?" I ask.

Therefore, I urge you brothers and sisters, in view of God's mercy,
to offer your bodies as living sacrifices,
holy and pleasing to God – this is your true and proper worship.
Do not conform [any longer] to the pattern of this world,
but be transformed by the renewing of your mind.
Romans 12:1-2

And God speaks to my soul – over and over again – for all of us:
Love. Really love. I gave My all on the cross for you, my beloved. Give yourself over to Me and be transformed.

Stop what you're doing. Quiet your own soul. Rest your mind from your own scenarios filled with fears and anger, frustration and resentment, shame and pride. Stop trying to control the people and circumstances in your life. I am the Sovereign God of unfailing love. I am intimately present with you to quiet you, to renew and transform your mind and to lead you in My good and purpose-filled ways for your life.

Love. Really love. I gave My all on the cross for you, my beloved. Give yourself over to Me and be transformed.

Stop the judgment. Your self-focus, your self-pity and your self-righteousness leave you blind to the hurt of others, leave you deaf to their heart cries, leave you incapable of true and wise discernment (even about yourself), and they leave you unwilling to offer any true compassion and mercy to those you judge as undeserving. I am the God of compassion and mercy and I alone am the only Righteous Judge. No one deserves my compassion and mercy. But! Out of my love, I give them freely to all who believe that Jesus, My One and Only Son, has already received all the punishment for all sin for all time so that all may be forgiven and given eternal life with Me.

Love. Really love. I gave My all on the cross for you, my beloved. Give yourself over to Me and be transformed.

Stop all your ways of wounding of others. Stop and recognize you will not have all the answers you want. Stop and accept that you will not have all the admissions of guilt or apologies you demand. Stop and understand that only I see truth clearly. And it is truth that I desire in you and from you. Stop your twisted stories, manipulative words and outright lies – they are futile and foolish before Me. They are dangerous and destructive for you and for those you around you.

Love. Really love. I gave My all on the cross for you, my beloved. Give yourself over to Me and be transformed.

Love. Really love. Humbly love. Patiently love. Kindly love. Tangibly love. Thoughtfully love. Generously love. Maturely love. Sacrificially love. I urge you, be transformed by My love to love. Really love. Because I really love you. I always have. I always will.

Do I believe it?
And if I do, what am I going to do about it?

Lord, please let me hear your voice, your love, your wisdom, your grace and truth.

GOD'S VERY GOOD WORK OF COMPLETION

Today is Earth Day. I well remember the original Earth Day held on April 22, 1970! Wearing my tie-dyed shirt, bell-bottom jeans with big, bright flowers embroidered on each leg, I could match the passion and zeal of any true (and much older) flower-child as I helped my fifth grade class clean up around our school and nearby neighborhoods. We were taking care of our earth. We were raising awareness of its delicate environmental balance that we all needed to respect in order to keep our earth beautiful and healthy for us and for generations yet to come. We were on a mission! And, oh-so-many years later, we realize that we didn't keep our focus, our passion or our purpose to care for our earth. We didn't complete the work.

God's behavior throughout the biblical account of creation challenges me to really look around and appreciate this magnificent earth – this precious gift – God gave us to care for, even as it supplies every need we have for the sustenance of our lives. God took time to look at, enjoy and assess His completed work in creation.

> *God saw all that he had made, and it was very good.*
> *And there was evening, and there was morning – the sixth day.*
> *Thus the heavens and the earth were completed in all their vast array.*
> Genesis 1:31-2:1

God saw all the vast array of the heavens and the earth He had made. His work in creation was completed. It was beautiful. Wonderful. God saw the tangible evidence produced by His spoken Word and Spirit throughout His creation. And God proclaimed the completion of all that He had done as *very good*.

God, by His passionate and sacrificial love for us and by His Word and Spirit given to us, will also see the good work He began in us brought to its full completion. And, as we enter fully into the eternal kingdom of our Lord Jesus Christ, that completed work in us will also be *very good*!

> *...being confident of this, that he who began a good work in you*
> *will carry it on to completion until the day of Christ Jesus.*
> Philippians 1:6

While we're still on this side of heaven, our God calls us to be aware of and take care of our earth – the *very good* place our God created for us to live. And, as children by faith, our God calls us to be aware of and take care of our innermost being – where God has placed His *very good* work within us.

I pray that, as stewards of this earth, we will each take a little more time and spend a little more energy in caring for our earth. This is a simple way to acknowledge our responsibility for the condition of our earth, and to thank our God for giving us this *very good* gift.

I pray that, as children of our Holy God, we will each take a little more time and spend a little more energy on allowing God's Word and Spirit more and more freedom and power to continue God's transforming work in our lives. On that day of Christ Jesus, may our God see, assess and proclaim that His work within each of us is fully complete and *very good*!

Reflections – Responses – Challenges – Encouragements – God-breathing Thoughts

Do I believe it?
And if I do, what am I going to do about it?

Lord, please let me hear your voice, your love, your wisdom, your grace and truth.

TAKE A WALK FOR LIFE

When Enoch had lived 65 years, he became the father of Methuselah.
After he became the father of Methuselah, Enoch walked with God 300 years
and had other sons and daughters.
Altogether, Enoch lived 365 years. Enoch walked faithfully with God;
then he was no more, because God took him away.
Genesis 5:21-24

By faith Enoch was taken from this life, so that he did not experience death:
"He could not be found, because God had taken him away."
For before he was taken, he was commended as one who pleased God.
And without faith it is impossible to please God,
because anyone who comes to him must believe that he exists
and that he rewards those who earnestly seek him.
Hebrews 11:5-6

Enoch walked with God. Such a simple statement. Such an amazing and powerful statement to be said about anyone. Even more incomprehensible to my mind is that our holy, almighty and sovereign God makes Himself intimately available to us and wants to walk with us.

What was going on with Enoch that he became known for walking with God? We don't know a great deal of details about Enoch, but in these couple of Scripture passages, much can be gleaned. Personally, I wonder if Enoch may have experienced some deep turning point of faith when he became a daddy to Methuselah since the Scripture reads: "...after he became the father of Methuselah, Enoch walked with God for 300 years..." Something life-changing, perspective-changing and priority-changing may have happened to Enoch at the birth of his child. Maybe some awakening of awe and thankfulness for the gift of life he saw so clearly, and held so closely, in his newborn baby. Maybe some powerful pull on his mind and soul made Enoch realize that the Giver of Life was near, and He wanted Enoch to know Him and walk with Him as his Eternal Father.

Enoch walked with God. He sought God earnestly. And God was found because God is always near and is always found by all who earnestly seek Him. Enoch wanted to be in an intimate relationship with God, to walk with Him, to share his life with Him. This wasn't just a short-lived emotional response that moved Enoch to seek and walk intimately with God only for a little while, as so often accompanies a life-changing event – whether that is a birth or a death or any other human experience in between these two extremes. No. Enoch was moved by an earnest faith that acknowledges the truth of God as the Giver of Life and as the God who is Ever Present with us. Enoch grabbed hold of God's hand to take a walk with Him and he didn't let go. And God never let go of Enoch. God and Enoch took a walk for life – right into eternity.

God is always faithful. God is always near. God wants to walk with us. God will intimately keep walking with us throughout every experience and every moment of our lives. God will, and wants to, walk with us every day of our lives and lead us to live our lives with eternal purpose, deep meaning, unexpected adventure, full hope and unfailing love. When we choose to walk, and keep walking, with God, we will live lives like nothing we could even begin to imagine! Let's reach out in faith. Let's seek God earnestly. And let go of anything and everything else that may be holding us back. Let's take hold of God's holy, loving hand and take a walk for life!

Reflections – Responses – Challenges – Encouragements – God-breathing Thoughts

Do I believe it?
And if I do, what am I going to do about it?

Lord, please let me hear your voice, your love, your wisdom, your grace and truth.

THE WAY OUT IS THE WAY IN

Do you remember Flip Wilson? He starred in a comedy TV show back in the early 1970s. On his show, Flip Wilson often played a character named Geraldine Jones who, whenever her wrongs were exposed, would adamantly and vociferously declare, "The devil made me do it!"

To this, I respond with a deep theological truth: Baloney! Yes, I know that one of Satan's manipulative and evil roles is as tempter. And tempted we will be. Yet, God has given each one of us the freedom to choose whether or not we will give in to temptation. I alone am responsible for my sin. You alone are responsible for your sin. But! We are not alone in our experience of temptation.

God's Word tells us that the seizing grip of temptation is common to all. Temptation grabs at all of us and rears its ugly and enticing head to every one of us. Still, we can often feel like we are all alone, even desperately so, in our struggle against the power of temptation. This sense of aloneness that can overtake us is a LFTPOH – a Lie From The Pit Of Hell. Not only do others wrestle in their minds, bodies and spirits with similar temptations, but God also promises us that we are never left alone in our struggles. Our God is with us. And He has the power to lead us out of, and away from, the crush of temptation – if we will choose to be led by Him, in His way.

> *No temptation has overtaken you except what is common to mankind.*
> *And God is faithful; he will not let you be tempted beyond what you can bear.*
> *But when you are tempted, God will also provide a way out*
> *so that you can endure [stand up under] it.*
> 1 Corinthians 10:13

Even when we are facing our most fierce, gripping and crushing temptations, we will always have a choice about whether to sin or not to sin. We are not left alone in the battle against temptation. Never. Our God is with us. Always. Our God always provides a way out from giving in to our sinful cravings. God always gives us the choice to say, "No!" to sin by the power of His Love, Word and Spirit.

The way out is to say, "Yes!" to standing up in obedience to God. To say, "Yes!" to standing up in trusting God's love. To say, "Yes!" to standing up in God's freedom and power. God Himself provides the way out from our giving in to the gripping, life-crushing influence of temptation. Always. The way out, of all temptation, is for each of us to choose God and His good ways for our lives.

I know that those (all too often) times when I choose my own way – when I choose to give in to temptation and choose to give in to the lure and the selfish-satisfaction of sin – it is not because I have no choice. It is not because someone else or, even, "the devil made me do it." It is not because I can't do anything other than sin in that moment. Rather, it is because I won't do anything other than sin in that moment. I ignore and reject God's way out.

Standing up in God's love and power is *the way out* that God always provides for us to conquer the crush of temptation. This is also *the way in* to being filled with God's peace, joy and freedom as we say, "Yes!" to obeying God's loving and protective ways.

Do I believe it?
And if I do, what am I going to do about it?

Lord, please let me hear your voice, your love, your wisdom, your grace and truth.

STEP BY STEP BY STEP – IN LOVE

Life requires energy. To be alive, certainly, we need physical energy and strength to keep us going. We were never meant to go from birth to death sensing that we're just barely surviving. Just barely making it through. We were never meant to let all of our life's energy be depleted, wasted or destroyed.

To truly *live* life – to do far more than just survive – requires far more than physical energy. We need God's love and Spirit in our lives to live a life with an energized purpose.

We are created in the image of God. And we are meant to live out our lives in relationship with our God – intimately, intentionally and courageously. We are meant to purposefully live in such a life-confirming, purposeful way that the image and likeness of our Lord Jesus within us will be reflected in the fullest way possible – even in the most fleeting of moments, in the most challenging of circumstances and in the most difficult of relationships.

How can we live like that? Step by step by step as we keep in step with the Spirit of God and walk as Jesus walked.

Since we live by the Spirit, let us keep in step with Spirit.
Galatians 5:25

If anyone obeys his word, God's love is truly made complete in him.
This is how we know we are in him:
Whoever claims to live in him must live [walk] as Jesus did.
1 John 2:5-6

And this is love: that we walk in obedience to his commands.
As you have heard from the beginning, his command is that you walk in love.
2 John 1:6

Life here on this earth is outrageously brief – even if we live to a fabulous old age. And I know that I do not want my life's energy to be depleted, wasted or destroyed because I choose to walk in my own strength, in my pride, in my selfishness, in my self-pity, in my apathy, in my worry or in my busyness. We all need to choose how we are going to live each moment of each day that we are given. Step by step by step!

I want to spend my life's energy purposefully walking in an intimate relationship with my God. Step by step by step!

I want to spend my life's energy purposefully walking as Jesus walked, keeping in step with the Spirit of the Living God, by loving others – in brief encounters and in each of my *for a lifetime* relationships – intentionally, sincerely, deeply, generously, tangibly, sacrificially and joyfully! Step by step by step!

What's your next step? Our God will give you the energy and purpose for which He created you – to live and walk in His unfailing love! Step by step by step!

Reflections – Responses – Challenges – Encouragements – God-breathing Thoughts

Do I believe it?
And if I do, what am I going to do about it?

Lord, please let me hear your voice, your love, your wisdom, your grace and truth.

"KNOCK! KNOCK!"
"WHO'S THERE?"

You've probably heard and told a few "Knock! Knock!" jokes over the years. In Scripture, God makes it very clear to us, just as he did to Cain, that we need to be aware of who or what is at our door.

The LORD said to Cain, "Why are you angry? Why is your face downcast?
If you do what is right, will you not be accepted?
But if you do not do what is right, sin is crouching at your door;
it desires to have you, but you must rule over [master] it.
Genesis 4:6-7

After the fall of man, God didn't just pick up and walk away from us. God has wanted, and will always want, us to choose to be in an intimate relationship with Him, to trust Him and obey His Word. Our God wants us to know the depth of the love, acceptance and peace that comes to us when we choose to live in a right and intimate relationship with Him.

The Lord asks us to examine ourselves and our motives so that we will not let any sin or any of our emotions – anger, hurt, fear, stress, arrogance, sadness, self-pity, self-sufficiency – rule over us more than our God. The Lord speaks warnings to us to tell us that sin is crouching at our door (Knock! Knock!). That sin desires to have us. To devour us and destroy us. And that is no joking matter. The Lord tells us that we must master sin. In saying this, God reminds us and empowers us with the knowledge that we always have a choice when it comes to sin. And I am absolutely convinced that our Lord never asks us to do anything for which He will not also equip us to accomplish it.

Sadly, you and I all choose sin, one way or another, with varying consequences for ourselves and for others. No matter what our sin is – sin always devours and always destroys. In this fallen world, sin will always be crouching at each of our doors. This isn't a surprise.

So, how do we master sin? How do we avoid being devoured and destroyed by sin?

First, we have to *want* to master sin. We have to be willing to depend on God as our Lord, and not on ourselves. And certainly we cannot allow our emotions, our knee-jerk reactions, our self-focused sense of justice and our life-warping habits to rule us. Then, we need to *choose* to master sin. We need to run into the loving arms of our Lord Jesus Christ – who has fully mastered the power of sin and its deadly destruction over us for all eternity. We must go *Knock, Knocking* on our Lord's door for protection, self-control and the strength we need to be able to master the onslaught of temptation and the destruction of sin. Our God promises to open His door to us.

"knock and the door will be opened to you"
Matthew 7:7

Our God has lovingly and powerfully given us all we need to master sin as we stay in His care and live in obedience to His Word. Let's each choose to knock on our Lord's door, instead of being knocked over by sin! It's our choice. Knock! Knock!

Reflections – Responses – Challenges – Encouragements – God-breathing Thoughts

Do I believe it?
And if I do, what am I going to do about it?

Lord, please let me hear your voice, your love, your wisdom, your grace and truth.

TAKE TIME TO BE HOLY!

***The LORD said to Moses, "Speak to the entire assembly of Israel and say to them:
'Be holy because I, the LORD your God, am holy.' "***
Leviticus 19:1-2

There is an old hymn named, "Take Time To Be Holy." When I looked up the lyrics online, two men with two different dates were listed: William D. Longstaff, 1882, as the lyricist and George C. Stebbins, 1890, as the composer. Not much more information was given about them except that the reference to the Leviticus Scripture passage above was cited as the inspirational verse for the writing of this hymn. Thank You, God, for continuing to speak to us through your *living and active Word* (Hebrews 4:12)!

This old hymn just keeps going through my mind – as does the truth about our very real need to take time to be holy, and to offer true and sincere heart worship to our Holy God through the way we live our lives. Our Holy God is the One who has given us life and breath and eternal life through our Savior and Lord Jesus. It is only right (Oh, that it would also be natural!) for us to respond to our Holy God's love by taking time to be holy and living our lives in a holy, thankful, and worshipful way! Read, pray, reflect on and sing the words of this beautiful old hymn:

> Take time to be holy, speak oft with thy Lord;
> Abide in Him always, and feed on His Word.
> Make friends of God's children, help those who are weak,
> Forgetting in nothing His blessing to seek.
>
> Take time to be holy, the world rushes on;
> Spend much time in secret, with Jesus alone.
> By looking to Jesus, like Him thou shalt be;
> Thy friends in thy conduct His likeness shall see.
>
> Take time to be holy, let Him be thy Guide;
> And run not before Him, whatever betide.
> In joy or in sorrow, still follow the Lord,
> And, looking to Jesus, still trust in His Word.
>
> Take time to be holy, be calm in thy soul,
> Each thought and each motive beneath His control.
> Thus led by His Spirit to fountains of love,
> Thou soon shalt be fitted for service above.

Read, pray, reflect on and sing the words of this beautiful old hymn, again! Do you believe these words have a message of truth for you? Then, do something about it.

May we each choose to take time to be holy! May we each take time – and thought and energy and action – to be holy! Take time to be like our Holy, Almighty Lord who loves us in unfailing, sacrificial, transforming and everlasting ways!

Reflections – Responses – Challenges – Encouragements – God-breathing Thoughts

Do I believe it?
And if I do, what am I going to do about it?

Lord, please let me hear your voice, your love, your wisdom, your grace and truth.

WHAT ARE YOU LIVING ON?

Jesus, the Living Word of God, answered the tempter's every push, plea, pressure and twisted persuasion with the true, eternal Word of God. How much more should we get to know, trust, depend on and live on the grace and truth, the love and power of God's Word to feed us, lead us and strengthen us every moment of every day of our lives?

Jesus answered, "It is written: 'Man does not live on bread alone,
but on every word that comes from the mouth of God.' "
Matthew 4:4

We need God to live. Bread is good – even very good (especially warm and fresh from the oven). But we don't actually live on bread, or fruits or vegetables or meats or even our favorite comfort foods. At least not in the deepest part of our souls. And certainly not for all eternity. We need God to give us life and sustain our lives. Now and for all eternity. Without God there is no life. As a matter of fact, God's Word even tells us that:

...the LORD is your life...
Deuteronomy 30:20

Jesus made it clear that our lives depend on every word that comes from the mouth of God. As we get to know, trust and live on God's Word, our minds and souls will be fed with the absolute assurance that in Christ alone our deepest needs are met – our deepest, most desperate needs – for unfailing love and eternal life with our God.

These truly are what our souls hunger for even if we act, temporarily, as if something less than these will satisfy and fill us. No man-made bread, no man-made pleasure, no man-made success, could ever fulfill the deepest soul needs we each have. No. We live – and live most fully and freely – on God's Word.

As we live on God's Word, in our daily-day lives right here and now, our minds and souls will be fed the strength, courage, peace and self-control of Christ that are able to empower us to be victorious over the trappings of any and every temptation that come our way. I know that whenever I give in to temptation (Darn it!), it is not because of any lack of nourishment or strength that God's Word provides for me. No, it is because I choose, at those times, not to go back home to my Abba's table where His living, active and powerful Word is always available to feed and fill me. And had I gone to *Abba's Word Buffet*, I would have received all I needed to deal with all of the pushes, pleas, pressures and twisted persuasions that life presents to me.

As we choose to feed on and live on God's Word, we will be shaped by it, just as we are shaped by our physical food. God's Word will shape and transform each one of us to be more and more like Jesus – more loving, more patient, more forgiving, more humble, more powerful, more kind, more wise.

For myself, I am absolutely convinced that God's Word is absolutely essential for my life and for every aspect of my mental, spiritual, emotional, relational and, yes, even for my physical well-being. I must feed on and live on God's Word in order to truly live – and live fully and freely! Oh! How delicious God's Word is!

What are you living on?

Do I believe it?
And if I do, what am I going to do about it?

Lord, please let me hear your voice, your love, your wisdom, your grace and truth.

TRUSTING THE INVISIBLE – VISIBLY

The Son is the image of the invisible God, the firstborn over all creation...
For God was pleased to have all his fullness dwell in him,
and through him to reconcile to himself all things,
whether things on earth or things in heaven,
by making peace through his blood shed on the cross.
Colossians 1:15, 19-20

For we live by faith, not by sight.
2 Corinthians 5:7

"Let your light so shine before others,
that they may see your good deeds and glorify your Father in heaven."
Matthew 5:16

We, who have put our faith in Jesus as Messiah, have put our trust in the Invisible. Not exactly a natural, practical or success-driven choice, is it? Nope. It goes against our more natural inclinations of *let me see, hear, touch, taste and smell something* to know that it's real. It goes against our sense of practicality that tells us that we must do Step A, B and C in order to manage our lives. It goes against our need to be the one in control of our lives (and of the lives of all those around us) in order to be successful in this life, in our work, in our family, in our fame and in our fate.

We, who have put our trust in the Invisible God through His Son Jesus – who died a cruel and ugly death for the forgiveness of our sins and who conquered the power of death fully through His resurrection – are called to trust in the Invisible and do so visibly. Yes, although we are called to live by faith and not by sight, we are also called to let our light, given by the Light of the world, shine so radiantly that others will visibly *see our good deeds*. Visibly see that Jesus has made a very real, tangible, eternal, right-here-and-now difference in our lives. The Invisible God intends to make Himself visible – make His love, grace, truth, peace and hope known – to others by how we visibly live our lives.

Yes, this is a big job for us as God's children. Remember, though, that all we need to visibly live out our trust in the Invisible God has all been given to us already through our God's sovereign and intimate love, God's ever-present Spirit and God's eternal Word. Are you taking time to be filled up deeply in your own mind, body, spirit and soul to sense God's invisible presence so that your burdens are lightened and your whole being is enlightened by the light of Jesus?

Do this, and you will not be able to hide the light of Jesus to those around you! You will love more sincerely, forgive more freely, speak more truthfully, act more kindly, show more mercy, help more willingly, offer your gifts more generously and fill those around you more fully with the hope that flows from the very heart of our Invisible God to visibly save and transform lives!

Trusting in the Invisible visibly is a grand and glorious call from our God and a heart-pumping, adventurous, powerful way to live!

Do I believe it?
And if I do, what am I going to do about it?

Lord, please let me hear your voice, your love, your wisdom, your grace and truth.

PERSPECTIVE. PEACE. POWER.

Perspective. Peace. Power. How do we get these (and keep these) in the midst of turmoil, frustration or personal assaults to our bodies, minds, emotions, relationships, reputations or finances? How do we share these as we watch, and walk with, our loved ones as they go through hard and hurting times?

First, we've got to be real. God never asks us to deny the hurt and brokenness, the shock and disappointment and the *just plain hard stuff* of life we experience. Denial is not some warped kind of proof that our faith is steadfast and we are strong. Sometimes the very denial of our hurt, anger, doubt, fear and frustration may actually be more tightly linked to our pride than to our real and humble trust in, and dependence on, our Eternal Abba.

Second, we've got to let God be God. Not us. Not in our limited understanding. Certainly not in our own limited power. It is a great freedom to admit the truth that we are each frail, flawed and finite. And it is a great hope to know that there is nothing frail, flawed or finite about the Sovereign Lord of all Creation who loves us far more than what we could ever imagine!

Third, we've got to choose to believe and receive what God offers to us. In His way. In His time. God always offers us His perspective, peace and power to strengthen, transform and renew our hearts and minds right in the very midst of all our messes. God's fullest offer comes to us through the sacrifice and resurrection of our Savior Jesus Christ! And He has declared:

"I am with you always to the very end of the age."
Matthew 28:20

Jesus is ours to believe and receive – as are our God's ever-present Holy Spirit and our God's living and active Word. Be encouraged as you reflect on who our God is and the perspective, peace and power He offers:

He will be called Wonderful Counselor, Mighty God, Everlasting Father, Prince of Peace.
Isaiah 9:6

"Though the mountains be shaken and the hills be removed,
yet my unfailing love for you will not be shaken nor my covenant of peace be removed,"
says the LORD, who has compassion on you.
Isaiah 54:10

...the mind governed by the Spirit is life and peace.
Romans 8:6

God's divine power has given us everything we need for a godly life [life and godliness]
through our knowledge of him who called us by his own glory and goodness.
2 Peter 1:3

For the Spirit God gave us does not make us timid,
but gives us power, love and self-discipline [a sound mind].
2 Timothy 1:7

May the God of hope fill you with all joy and peace as you trust in him,
so that you may overflow with hope by the power of the Holy Spirit.
Romans 15:13

Breathe. Believe. Receive. Be held by our Sovereign God's perspective, peace and power!

Do I believe it?
And if I do, what am I going to do about it?

Lord, please let me hear your voice, your love, your wisdom, your grace and truth.

RUNNING WITH PERSEVERANCE. SHARING THE JOY!

We have a continual choice to make about whether or not we will walk with our God – about whether or not we will run with perseverance the race of faith, *the true amazing race*, marked out for us. And we each have to make this choice intentionally and actively every single day of our lives.

> *...let us throw off everything that hinders and the sin that so easily entangles.*
> *And let us run with perseverance the race marked out for us.*
> *fixing our eyes on Jesus, [the author] the pioneer and perfecter of faith.*
> *For the joy set before him he endured the cross, scorning its shame,*
> *and sat down at the right hand of the throne of God.*
> Hebrews 12:1-2

To run this amazing race, we need to get rid of all of the junk – all of the sin and all of the empty, self-focused thinking, speaking and acting – that holds us back, weighs us down and trips us up. If we're honest with ourselves, we can easily recognize the *entangling sin* in our lives that needs to be thrown out and thrown off! We're also to throw off *everything that hinders* us from running our faith race with perseverance. Sometimes these hindering things are harder to recognize because they are not always, and not necessarily, sin. Rather, they are often the things we let run our lives, even unintentionally. And these hindering things can definitely run us ragged with our overbooked schedules, our attempts to please everyone (family members, friends, bosses, coworkers, teachers, peers, fellow believers), our lack of sleep, our lack of healthy eating patterns and, especially, by our lack of time spent resting in God's love and presence and meditating on His Word.

Let's get on with really living like God's children and being the people of faith we have been saved and called to be. Let's choose to run our race of faith with determined and deliberate perseverance as we follow our Lord Jesus. Let's run (grow, mature, think, speak and act) our faith race with our eyes firmly fixed and focused on Jesus and on His way of doing things, according to the pace that He sets for us.

We can trust our God who runs (crawls, walks, leaps and dances) with us every step of the way. Our God will continually pour out His love, peace, strength and courage so that we may be able to endure and conquer all the hardships, frustrations and barriers that could ever come at us. Even if some of these had been put there by us!

Let's put our faith in Jesus, the author and perfecter of our faith, and allow Him to mark out and plan the course of our race. Jesus is the One, the Only One, who is able to give us His deep and eternal joy no matter what our day – no matter what our faith race – may bring. Jesus already ran straight into hell for us in order to secure our place in heaven with Him!

Because of all that Jesus has already accomplished for us, may we each choose to be a bucket and be filled with God's unfailing love that gives us the power to run our faith race with perseverance! May we each choose to share, even now, in the conquering, victorious joy that our Lord Jesus offers to us! And may we share His joy with all those around us – who may be running themselves ragged – as we run the race marked out for each of us!

Do I believe it?
And if I do, what am I going to do about it?

Lord, please let me hear your voice, your love, your wisdom, your grace and truth.

BE THANKFUL AND WORSHIP!

Therefore, since we are receiving a kingdom that cannot be shaken,
let us be thankful, and so worship God acceptably with reverence and awe,
for our "God is a consuming fire."
Hebrews 12:28-29

How much more humbly, honestly and intentionally our worship would flow from us if we were to truly step back, recognize, acknowledge and live in the truth that everything in our world – our homes, our jobs, our finances, our possessions and even our physical bodies – everything we know and experience in this tangible, temporal world can and will be shaken! Everything can and will pass away! None of these is eternal. Not one.

But! Our God is a consuming fire who, even as everything temporal is shaken and passes away, will give to us His eternal kingdom that can never be shaken! We will receive our God's eternal kingdom that will never pass away! Our God's eternal kingdom, which holds everything of true beauty and eternal value, will also hold each one of us who has put our faith in Jesus Christ as our Savior and Lord, as our One and Only Eternal King!

That should shake us up and shake us out of offering to our Eternal God – our Creator, Mighty God, Wonderful Counselor, Everlasting Father, Prince of Peace, Redeemer, Deliverer, King of kings and Lord of lords – any form of worship that has become complacent, compromised, rote or weary! Our God's kingdom cannot be shaken, nor can those who belong to Him!

So! Let's get our worship on! Worship that is true and acceptable to our God who is a consuming fire! Worship that is thankful! Worship that steps into the throne room of our God's grace with reverence and awe!

Let our worship shake our hearts to the very core with thankfulness!
Thankful for our God's gift of life and breath, every new day, every single moment.
Thankful for God's unfailing, inseparable love and constant presence with us (Romans 8:39; Matthew 28:20).
Thankful for God's Word who reveals the fullness of God's grace and truth to us in living and active ways (John 1:14,17; Hebrews 4:12).
Thankful for "the God and Father of our Lord Jesus Christ who has blessed us in the heavenly realms with every spiritual blessing" (Ephesians 1:3).
Thankful for God's Spirit who feeds us, fills us and flows through us with the life and mind-transforming "fruit of the Spirit" (Galatians 5:22-23).
Thankful for everyone, every experience, every circumstance, every season of life – the beautiful and the ugly, the pleasant and the painful, the righteous and the wicked – that God allows in our lives because "we know that in all things God works for the good of those who love him, who have been called according to his purpose"…"to be conformed to the image of his Son" (Romans 8:28-29).

Let our true worship reach up to the heart of God as we reach out to the hearts of others with God's unfailing, compassionate, forgiving, tender, strong and tangible love! This is the purest, most powerful form of worship we could ever offer to our God! Let our worship shake us up so that we will actively, intentionally, practically and continually love others with thankfulness. Love others with reverence and respect. Love others with awe because they, like we, are image bearers of the One True God, who is a consuming fire!

Reflections – Responses – Challenges – Encouragements – God-breathing Thoughts

Do I believe it?
And if I do, what am I going to do about it?

Lord, please let me hear your voice, your love, your wisdom, your grace and truth.

_____

_____

_____

_____

_____

_____

_____

_____

_____

_____

_____

_____

_____

_____

_____

_____

_____

_____

_____

_____

_____

_____

_____

COMMANDING STRENGTH AND COURAGE

God's Word often challenges us right to our very core. God commands us to trust and obey Him even when the circumstances around us seem absolutely overwhelming. Out of God's love for us, He demands our trust and promises to be with us wherever we go.

"Have I not commanded you? Be strong and courageous. Do not be afraid;
do not be discouraged, for the LORD your God will be with you wherever you go. "
Joshua 1:9

I lost it. I totally lost it. I was okay right until that moment. God had held me together through His amazing and powerful grip on my spirit, on my mind and on my words for over the past week. I had been able to share my faith openly and honestly with my family – who usually didn't want to hear about Jesus. Not again. Not from me.

It was May 1981. My Oldest Brother was dead at twenty-four. His funeral wouldn't be for at least a week due numerous logistical details. I lived about two hours away. No need to rush back. Tim was away on business. I was alone. And God used that week powerfully. I took calls from my different family members, without the others knowing. Each had deep, real, heart-broken, soul-searching, God-searching questions. I was the *Jesus-freak* in the family. So they called me. With God's love, presence, strength and courage, I quietly shared from Scripture and from my heart the hope I have in Jesus. God was using even My Oldest Brother's death to open up ways for God's Word and love to be poured into my family's life. I had been praying for each of them for years. Witnessing to them for years. Ridicule was often their response. At best, I was blown-off and ignored. Yet, during that painful, and amazing, week before My Oldest Brother's funeral, God gave me time to share Christ's eternal love and salvation with different members of my family!

Then, I lost it. Totally lost it. Driving back from the funeral home, we hit a bunny. And with the death of that little bunny, I was flooded with my own grief and shock over My Oldest Brother's sudden death. I was overcome with passionate urgency for each one in my family to accept the salvation of Jesus. I desperately wanted them to know and accept the love of God. I ached in my deepest soul, calling for each one to, "Turn around! Run into the arms of Jesus! Right now, before it's too late!" But it wasn't happening. I wasn't seeing it. I was blinded with grief and fear. Death comes so suddenly. For people. For bunnies. I was blinded from hope. I was afraid and discouraged. *When would my family turn to God? When would the twistedness and sickness within my family be ended? How was I going to keep going in my relationship with them? How was I going to keep sharing Jesus with them? They had wanted some of Jesus from me, privately on the phone. But now they were all back to keeping me, and my faith, at a distance. Keeping me shut out. Even from loving them. When would they ever be saved and healed?*

As Tim drove, I sobbed hysterically, out-of-control. Tim yelled at me. Just once. Very loudly. He needed to command my attention, so that I could remember the command of God. I am not to be afraid or discouraged by my fear or pain. I am to open my eyes and heart to God's powerful, peace-giving truth: God is with me and will be with me wherever I go. Yes! My God of commanding strength and courage is with me. I can, and I am commanded to, trust Him.

I do. And, eventually, so did each precious member of my family. Thanks be to Jesus!

Do I believe it?
And if I do, what am I going to do about it?

Lord, please let me hear your voice, your love, your wisdom, your grace and truth.

I'M TOO LITTLE TO BE SO BIG!

Oh, Abba! I'm too little to be so big! That's what I call out (cry out, shout out, whimper out, sigh out) to my God whenever I feel like life is just a little too much for me to handle.

I care so much about so many people – those dearest ones in our family of six, our two Compassion Children, our extended family members on all sides, including all the family members of our two sons-in-love, our closest friends who truly are family to us, and all those with whom, and to whom, I minister. I want God's very best for each one – for their physical, mental, emotional, relational and spiritual health. I want so very much, and pray so very much, for them all. *Oh, Jesus! You know they all need You! You know all else they need, too! But! I'll be happy to remind You! Oh, Abba! I'm too little to be so big!*

I can get physically worn down from wearing so many hats while ministering. I absolutely love my job, and could never imagine doing anything else. Still, sometimes trying to lovingly serve-lead the ministry and manage the constant, varied and traveling demands on me is just plain, well, demanding. I find myself trying to maintain some bizarre kind of balance which, on certain days, lies somewhere in the midst of intense multi-tasking, multiple time zones and multiple personalities! *Oh, Abba! I'm too little to be so big!*

You know what? Sometimes I just get really tired of having to be mature or, at least, act as if I'm mature regardless of how I may be feeling at that moment. *Thank you, God, for being ever-present to snap the stupidity and immaturity right out of me, if I let you!* But, Ouch! It's just so tiring and hard to constantly choose God's maturity when I just want to stomp my feet, yell really loudly, punch something or someone! *Oh, Abba! I'm too little to be so big!*

Well, you know what I hear right back from my God when I call out (cry out, shout out, whimper out, sigh out) *Oh, Abba! I'm too little to be so big!* I hear God agreeing with me:

You are too little to be so big! Stop trying to be so big, so balanced and mature on your own. You can't do it! Get over yourself! Seek Me. Look to Me. I Am Bigger. I am bigger than any concern you may have for your family, friends and all those to whom you minister. I am able to meet the biggest needs any of them could ever have. (And thanks for the offer to remind Me, but I've got it covered!) I am bigger than any balance you may try to find on your own. I am bigger than any of your feelings, and will give you deep peace and true maturity as you rely on Me, My Word and My Way. Let your perspective of Me get bigger. As you do, the demands you sense to be on you alone will get smaller. As I get bigger in your perspective, My strength and power will renew you even when you are most weak, weary and worn out.

Do you not know? Have you not heard? The LORD is the everlasting God,
the Creator of the ends of the earth. He will not grow tired or weary and
his understanding no one can fathom. He gives strength to the weary
and increases the power of the weak. Even youths grow tired and weary,
and young men stumble and fall;
but those who hope in the LORD
will renew their strength like eagles;
they will run and not grow weary,
they will walk and not be faint.
Isaiah 40:28-31

Oh, Abba! It's so good to be so little because You are so BIG!

Reflections – Responses – Challenges – Encouragements – God-breathing Thoughts

Do I believe it?
And if I do, what am I going to do about it?

Lord, please let me hear your voice, your love, your wisdom, your grace and truth.

WALK THIS WAY!

When our youngest daughter Julia was just a toddler and learning the fine art of walking like a Big Girl (You know, without falling smack on her forehead every four or five steps!), she would often imitate the walk of our dear Italian friend Claudio. She loved him. And rightly so. Claudio showered her with loving adoration, speaking to her in his sing-songy, oh-so-fabulous Italian accent, with an incredibly animated face and equally expressive hands. And almost every phrase Claudio spoke to her ended in "*Julia-tina-piccolina.*" Yes, Claudio held a very special place in his heart for Julia. And Julia held a very special place in her heart for him. One of the most obvious and consistent ways that Julia would show her love and adoration for Claudio was to imitate and, to the very best of her ability, try to master the way Claudio walked.

So, Claudio – dark skinned, with dark hair and dark eyes – standing erect and taking very long strides with both hands clasped firmly behind his back, would lead as Julia followed. And, oh! She followed him! Our little Julia – our little red-headed, curly-haired toddler, with bright blue eyes – would follow very closely behind Claudio, imitating him as precisely as possible, with her chubby little hands clasped behind her back and taking the longest strides her chubby little legs would allow. And off they'd go! Leader and follower – walking in love and taking great joy in just how very similar their walks were!

Our God takes great joy in us! Our God celebrates with us every moment we choose to walk as Jesus walked! Every moment we choose to obey our Abba's Word just as Jesus obeyed! Every moment we choose to be imitators of our God as His dearly loved, and absolutely adored, children!

> *If anyone obeys his word, love for God is truly made complete in them.*
> *This is how we know we are in him:*
> *Whoever claims to live in him must [walk] live as Jesus did.*
> 1 John 2:5-6

> *Follow God's example, therefore, as dearly loved children and walk in the way of love,*
> *just as Christ loved us and gave himself up for us*
> *as a fragrant offering and sacrifice to God.*
> Ephesians 5:1-2

Will we stumble and fall? Will we take a misstep or a wrong turn – even several times – in our walk as we attempt to live our lives following Jesus? Yes, of course, we will. Yet, our Abba is here with His outstretched, everlasting arms to pick us up, as His dearly loved children, and set us back on our feet. With His promised presence, unfailing love, and unlimited power, our God encourages us to keep on walking – keep on imitating Him. We are His. He is ours.

When we choose to walk as Jesus walked, to be an imitator of our God – Oh! – the beauty of Jesus, His love, grace and truth will flow from us and be released into the lives of all those around us! What a fabulous power-walk of love it is to walk as Jesus walked!

Will you walk this way?

Reflections – Responses – Challenges – Encouragements – God-breathing Thoughts

Do I believe it?
And if I do, what am I going to do about it?

Lord, please let me hear your voice, your love, your wisdom, your grace and truth.

SPIRITUAL DWARFS – part 1 –
WHO'S TAKING UP RESIDENCE
IN YOUR HEART, MIND AND SOUL?

When we believe and accept Jesus – as the only way to our Creator, our Heavenly Father, and as our Savior from the death-sentence of sin, and as the Resurrection and the Life for our promised eternal life – some really big changes take place for us and within us!

Therefore, if anyone is in Christ, the new creation has come:
The old has gone, the new is here! All this is from God...
2 Corinthians 5:17-18

But wait a minute! I'm not entirely new yet. I'm a long way from perfect. There's still too much of the old me showing up, way too often. However, our God is perfect! And our God is calling, urging and supplying everything that every one of us needs to be conformed and transformed, with ever-increasing glory, into the likeness of God's Perfect Son, our Lord Jesus Christ, (Romans 12:2; 2 Peter 1:3; Romans 8:29; 2 Corinthians 3:17-18).

So what's our problem? Why are we not letting the big changes take place within us? Why isn't the old all gone and the new fully here? Well, my take on it, personally, is this: When we do not make full use of, and embrace God's life-transforming power through all that God has done for us and has put within us – His Spirit and His Word – we leave room for some very ugly, old self patterns of thinking, speaking, acting and interacting to continue taking up residency, and control, within our hearts, minds and souls.

These old patterns are not only characteristics of my old self (Which is supposed to be gone! Darn it!), but these old patterns actually seem to take on a life all their own as very yucky, destructive, bondage-making, life-twisting characters. I call them the *Spiritual Dwarfs*.

Let me introduce you to just seven of my own Spiritual Dwarfs. They are: *Prideful, Fearful, Sinful, Shameful, Whiny, Grumpy, and Dopey.* Yeah, I'm pretty sure you can picture them! Over the next few days, I'll let you get to know each one in a little more detail and the truths of God that each of these Spiritual Dwarfs deny.

You may even recognize a few of these Spiritual Dwarfs from personal experience. They may not live as full-time residents in your own hearts, minds and souls right now. But! You may be allowing these Spiritual Dwarfs, your old self characters, to come by and visit you way too frequently, and stay way too long!

Our Spiritual Dwarfs are not planning to leave politely. Just as Jesus was crucified so that the old self would be gone from within us, our actions need to be just as fierce, focused and with finality as God's actions are against sin! To live in the fullness and freedom of the new life given to us through the love, sacrifice and resurrection of our Lord Jesus Christ, we have only one, non-negotiable choice to make: Kill the dwarfs!

The sole resident of our souls is to be the Holy Spirit of our Loving, Mighty and Eternal God! Kill the dwarfs! *The old has gone, the new has come! All this is from God!*

Do I believe it?
And if I do, what am I going to do about it?

Lord, please let me hear your voice, your love, your wisdom, your grace and truth.

SPIRITUAL DWARFS – part 2 – PRIDEFUL

Every Spiritual Dwarf is a liar. Each of them denies some truth of God.

Hear Prideful as he speaks his lies: "I don't need anyone else but me. I am in control. I am always right. I am wise enough to decide my fate. I am strong enough on my own to get through all situations without anything from anyone else. I am able to get what I want. And whatever I get is mine – deserved and obtained by my own power, efforts and intellect. Not only do I not need anyone else to help me in my life, it would do everyone else a great deal of good to listen to me tell them how to run their lives!"

Prideful denies the very need of God. Prideful is so self-focused in his outrageous lies, that the Holy, Sovereign God is dismissed entirely or, at the very least, considered unnecessary for Prideful to live as Prideful determines is best for himself.

Oh, my goodness! Does this Spiritual Dwarf need to be killed in your life? He does in mine. Over and over and over again! Allowing Prideful to live out his destructive lies in our lives is very dangerous for us and for everyone with whom we interact.

> *Pride[ful] goes before destruction, a haughty spirit before a fall.*
> Proverbs 16:18

Prideful is a powerful, ugly and persistent Spiritual Dwarf who speaks the most and, often, speaks the loudest of all the other Dwarfs. Yet, Prideful can, at the same time, hide insidiously behind the façade of the other Spiritual Dwarfs. Prideful is not only a liar, Prideful boasts of self and temporal things from a very skewed and limited perspective. His boasts focus on nothing of eternal substance or value and are completely lacking in any true godly wisdom.

God tells us His truth: Understanding and knowing Him is what really gives anyone any real wisdom and any true source of pride. And that godly pride comes from a place of sincere humility before the Sovereign Lord.

> *This is what the LORD says: "Let not the wise boast of their wisdom*
> *or the strong boast of their strength or the rich boast of their riches,*
> *but let the one who boasts boast about this: that they understand and know me,*
> *that I am the LORD, who exercises kindness, justice and righteousness on earth,*
> *for in these I delight," declares the LORD.*
> Jeremiah 9:23-24

> *When pride[ful] comes, then comes disgrace,*
> *but with humility comes wisdom.*
> Proverbs 11:2

God loves us and wants the very best for each of us. Killing the Spiritual Dwarf of Prideful is the very best thing we could do in order to live in true wisdom and power, by humbly holding fast to our Sovereign Lord's eternal truth: We all need God!

Reflections – Responses – Challenges – Encouragements – God-breathing Thoughts

Do I believe it?
And if I do, what am I going to do about it?

Lord, please let me hear your voice, your love, your wisdom, your grace and truth.

SPIRITUAL DWARFS – part 3 – FEARFUL

Every Spiritual Dwarf is a liar. Each of them denies some truth of God.

Hear Fearful as he speaks his lies: "I am so worried! I don't know how I'm ever going to be able to get through this. I don't know if I even can! I'm really scared about what might happen! There are just too many things that I am facing right now that are so difficult. I don't see an end in sight! I am so stressed! Everything is so out of control. My heart's racing! My thoughts are all over the place! I just want to run away from all the people and all the circumstances that are causing me pain, worry and stress! I just want to get everything and everybody to be all right and doing the right thing – then I wouldn't be so worried. This is too awful! I'm just not going to survive all this!"

Fearful denies the perfect love and transcending peace of God. Fearful speaks the outrageous lie that God cannot be trusted! Fearful does not, will not, trust God's absolute and inseparable love and God's promise of peace from Himself, the very Prince of Peace.

Fearful's thinking and speaking patterns are like a hamster (On crack!) running as fast as possible in his little ball inside his cage. I call this the Hamster Dance. And it is absolutely futile and leads only to fatigue of body, mind and spirit. Fearful's thoughts go over and over the problems, the possible outcomes, and, of course, all the worst case scenarios. Potentially helpful and calming solutions are quickly met with the word, "But!" And the Hamster Dance begins again. Fearful needs to be killed completely! And all the lies that are spun in that Hamster Dance God-denying-thought-ball must be completely crushed!

God tells us His truth: He is in control. God's love destroys and drives out all fear. God's love is able to quiet us and pour out the transcending peace of our Lord Jesus Christ to guard our hearts and minds – in even our most disturbing and unsettling circumstances.

> *God is love...There is no fear in love. But perfect love drives out fear,*
> *because fear has to do with punishment.*
> *The one who fears is not made perfect in love.*
> 1 John 4:16, 18

> *"The LORD your God is with you, the Mighty Warrior who saves.*
> *He will take great delight in you, in his love he will no longer rebuke you*
> *[he will quiet you with his love], he will rejoice over you with singing."*
> Zephaniah 3:17

> *Do not be anxious about anything, but in every situation,*
> *by prayer and petition, with thanksgiving, present your requests to God.*
> *And the peace of God, which transcends all understanding,*
> *will guard your hearts and your minds in Christ Jesus.*
> Philippians 4:6-7

God loves us and wants the very best for each of us. Killing the Spiritual Dwarf of Fearful will set us free to trust that our Sovereign God really is in control and that His powerful, quieting Love and transcending Peace are always available to us!

Reflections – Responses – Challenges – Encouragements – God-breathing Thoughts

Do I believe it?
And if I do, what am I going to do about it?

Lord, please let me hear your voice, your love, your wisdom, your grace and truth.

SPIRITUAL DWARFS – part 4 – SINFUL

Every Spiritual Dwarf is a liar. Each of them denies some truth of God.

Hear Sinful as he speaks his lies: "You're not the boss of me! Nobody is! I am the final and only authority for my life! I decide what is right or wrong for me. No one has the right to impose judgment on me! I can do whatever I want. When I want. Where I want. How I want. With whom I want. To whom I want. And as often as I want. This is my life! And I will live it the way I want! I don't have to answer to anybody!"

Sinful denies the Sovereign Authority and Holy Rule of God. Sinful speaks the destructive, dangerously narcissistic, self-elevating lies against God, the One who holds complete and final authority and holy rule over every life, now and eternally! Sinful twists his God-given gift of freedom of choice into the ugly lie that he is in control. And not God. Sinful is blind, deaf and dismissive to God's truth that one day Sinful will have to answer for everything he chooses to do before our Holy God. Sinful rebels against every claim of authority over his life. Except for his own. All Sinful does to bring himself comfort, control and pleasure, whether fleetingly or habitually, will, in the end, bring only eternally tragic and deadly consequences to him.

God tells us His truth: God is the Sovereign Authority who has set His Holy Rule over every life. It is out of God's deep love for us that He set His holy, protective, righteous standards and boundaries for the way we should live. Our God also set death as the deserved punishment for all our Sinful, selfish, hurtful, evil, rebellious, God-opposing behaviors. In outrageous love for us, Jesus sacrificed His holy life to fulfill God's righteous judgment against sin so that our sins could be forgiven and we could be reconciled with our Sovereign and Holy God.

> *"There is no one holy like the LORD; there is no one besides you;*
> *there is no Rock like our God...those who oppose the LORD will be broken.*
> *The Most High will thunder from heaven; the LORD will judge the ends of the earth."*
> 1 Samuel 2:2, 10

> *Do not be deceived: God cannot be mocked. A man reaps what he sows. Whoever sows to*
> *please their flesh [their Sinful nature], from the flesh will reap destruction;*
> *Whoever sows to please the Spirit, from the Spirit will reap eternal life.*
> Galatians 6:7-8

> *The mind governed by flesh [Sinful man] is hostile to God,*
> *but the mind governed by the Spirit is life and peace.*
> Romans 8:6

> *For the wages of Sin[ful] is death,*
> *but the gift of God is eternal life in Christ Jesus our Lord.*
> Romans 6:23

> *God demonstrates his own love for us in this:*
> *While we were still sinners, Christ died for us.*
> Romans 5:8

God loves us and wants the very best for each of us. Killing the Spiritual Dwarf of Sinful will set us free to live fully reconciled lives as dearly loved children of our Sovereign and Holy God and as true followers of our Lord Jesus Christ!

Reflections – Responses – Challenges – Encouragements – God-breathing Thoughts

Do I believe it?
And if I do, what am I going to do about it?

Lord, please let me hear your voice, your love, your wisdom, your grace and truth.

SPIRITUAL DWARFS – part 5 – SHAMEFUL

Every Spiritual Dwarf is a liar. Each of them denies some truth of God.

Hear Shameful as he speaks his lies: "God cannot possibly forgive me for what I've done. It is too awful. Too evil. Too embarrassing. What I've done goes against everything I know is right. But I still did it. And I did it even after I had truly accepted and professed Jesus as my Savior. How could I have made such a sinful choice? I deserve to feel this pain. I knew better! I knew Jesus! I will never be free from this shame. Nor should I be. I must bear this shame forever."

Shameful denies the Unlimited Mercy of God and the Power of the Cross. Shameful denies that Jesus' death on the cross is the full atoning sacrifice for our sins and our shame.

Shameful twists our thinking to believe that we are, and deserve to be, miserably held captive by the shame of our sins. Shameful denies that the blood Jesus shed for us through His brutal and cruel crucifixion was enough to pay for our sins and our shame. Shameful speaks lies that come directly from Prideful: "Although *I* am forgiven, *I* still must carry the weight and sharp pain of shame for *my* Shameful sins." Shameful keeps Jesus nailed to the cross, rejecting the resurrection power of Jesus as the mighty conqueror over sin and shame!

God tells us His truth: God does demand that we come to Him in sincere confession and repentance for our sins. And, then, believe and fully trust that through the Unlimited Mercy of God and the Power of the Cross, we are fully forgiven and set free from every bit of Shameful's life-crushing weight. We can add nothing to what Jesus has already done for us! Thinking and acting in any other Shameful way spits in the face of our Holy God and His sacrificial love!

> *Godly sorrow brings repentance that leads to salvation and leaves no regret,*
> *but worldly [Shameful] sorrow brings death.*
> 2 Corinthians 7:10

> *If we confess our sins, God is faithful and just and will forgive us our sins*
> *and purify us from all unrighteousness.*
> 1 John 1:9

> *But now God has reconciled you by Christ's physical body through death*
> *to present you holy in his sight without blemish and free from accusation!*
> Colossians 1:22

> *God made him who had no sin to be sin for us,*
> *so that in him we might become the righteousness of God.*
> 2 Corinthians 5:21

> *It is for freedom that Christ has set us free. Stand firm, then,*
> *and do not let yourselves be burdened again by a yoke of slavery.*
> Galatians 5:1

God loves us and wants the very best for each of us. Killing the Spiritual Dwarf of Shameful will set us free to live in the beautiful truth of the transforming grace that our Lord Jesus offers to us – with His heart full of love and His victoriously lifted, nail-scarred hands!

Do I believe it?
And if I do, what am I going to do about it?

Lord, please let me hear your voice, your love, your wisdom, your grace and truth.

SPIRITUAL DWARFS – part 6 – WHINY

Every Spiritual Dwarf is a liar. Each of them denies some truth of God.

Hear Whiny as he speaks his lies: "I can't believe everything keeps going wrong for me. Life is so unfair! What did I do to deserve all these troubles, illnesses and complications? All these family issues? All this misjudgment? How long am I going to have to put up with all these hard times? All these hard people? Why does my computer always crash? Why does my car keep breaking down? Why do bad things always happen to me? Whyyyyy Me?"

Whiny denies the Hope of God and God's Eternal Perspective. Whiny lays down a heavy, smelly, dark blanket over our hearts and our minds so that we begin to suffocate on our own self-focused, self-pitying attitudes. Whiny blinds our vision from the Hope of God so completely that we lose all ability to see beyond our own dim, depressing, circumstantial, temporal and warped perspectives. Whiny keeps our eyes focused so inwardly on our limited interpretation of our problems that the freeing truth found in God's Eternal Perspective is diminished, distrusted and discarded. God's Hope goes unseen, unknown, unacknowledged and inexperienced.

God tells us His truth: We are not alone. God is with us. God offers us courage and peace even in the midst of the most horrendous, troubling times of our lives! We have a Savior who endured horrendous opposition and conquered! In Christ we have Hope now and forever. Our God is able to shift our self-pitying perspective to His Eternal Perspective so that we may trust Him to help us overcome all that life would throw at us!

"Have I not commanded you? Be strong and courageous. Do not be afraid;
do not be discouraged, for the LORD your God will be with you wherever you go."
Joshua 1:9

...[Fix] our eyes on Jesus, [the author] the pioneer and perfecter of faith.
For the joy set before him he endured the cross, scorning its shame, and sat down at the
right hand of the throne of God. Consider him who endured such opposition from sinners,
so that you will not grow weary and lose heart.
Hebrews 12:2-3

We are hard pressed on every side, but not crushed; perplexed, but not in despair;
persecuted, but not abandoned; struck down, but not destroyed...because we know that the
one who raised the Lord Jesus from the dead will also raise us with Jesus and present us
with you to himself...Therefore we do not lose heart. Though outwardly we are wasting
away, yet inwardly we are being renewed day by day. For our light and momentary
troubles are achieving for us an eternal glory that far outweighs them all!
2 Corinthians 4:8-9, 14, 16-17

May the God of hope fill you with all joy and peace as you trust in him,
so that you may overflow with hope by the power of the Holy Spirit!
Romans 15:13

God loves us and wants the very best for each of us. Killing the Spiritual Dwarf of Whiny will set us free from the darkness of self-pity to live in the very present, conquering Hope of our God and His Eternal Perspective!

Do I believe it?
And if I do, what am I going to do about it?

Lord, please let me hear your voice, your love, your wisdom, your grace and truth.

SPIRITUAL DWARFS – part 7 – GRUMPY

Every Spiritual Dwarf is a liar. Each of them denies some truth of God.

Hear Grumpy as he speaks his lies: "I am so angry! Who does she think she is? I am so tired of all the crud that keeps getting dumped on me! I am flippin' done with having to pick up the slack for others! I never get a break! All these stupid people are making me crazy! Somebody's about to get a verbal smack down! Arrrgghh! All these stupid drivers! And my stupid, stupid computer! I just want to slap somebody!"

Grumpy denies the Kindness, Patience and Joy of God. Grumpy snarls and shouts inside our heads, stomps around in our brains and spills out of us in ugly, self-centered, cruel, defensive and destructive ways! Grumpy storms away, turns his back, stomps around, slams cupboards and car doors, punches walls, curses everything that gets in his way or doesn't meet his specifications! Crossed arms, hateful expressions, clinched jaws, defensive-offensive posturing and those judgmental, death-stare-giving eyes are just a few of Grumpy's special trademarks! Grumpy's words are cruel and attacking. Grumpy's silence is cold and hard. Both wield great power to inflict pain, guilt, shock and break the hearts of those around us – especially those closest to us.

God tells us His truth: As dearly loved children, God desires to pour His Kindness, Patience and Joy into us, and through us, to others. In Christ we are changed. God makes us new – right to the very core of our innermost being, right to our deepest emotions, thoughts, motivations and actions! God does all this through His love!

Therefore, as God's chosen people, holy and dearly loved, clothe yourselves with compassion, kindness, humility, gentleness and patience. Bear with each other and forgive one another if any of you has a grievance against someone. Forgive as the Lord forgave you. And over all these virtues put on love, which binds them all together in perfect unity. Let the peace of Christ rule in your hearts…
Colossians 3:12-17

…to be made new in the attitude of your minds; and to put on the new self, created to be like God in true righteousness and holiness…"In your anger do not sin"…Do not let any unwholesome talk come out of your mouths, but only what is helpful for building others up according to their needs, that it may benefit those who listen. And do not grieve the Holy Spirit of God…Get rid of all bitterness, rage and anger, brawling and slander, along with every form of malice. Be kind and compassionate to one another, forgiving each other, just as in Christ God forgave you.
Ephesians 4:23-24, 26, 29-32

The fruit of the Spirit is love, joy, peace, patience, kindness, goodness, faithfulness, gentleness and self-control.
Galatians 5:22-23

God loves us and wants the very best for each of us. Killing the Spiritual Dwarf of Grumpy will set us free from the tyranny of being a tyrant! God desires to fill us and transform us with His Kindness, Patience and Joy – all freely given to us so that we may freely give them to others!

Reflections – Responses – Challenges – Encouragements – God-breathing Thoughts

Do I believe it?
And if I do, what am I going to do about it?

Lord, please let me hear your voice, your love, your wisdom, your grace and truth.

SPIRITUAL DWARFS – part 8 – DOPEY

Every Spiritual Dwarf is a liar. Each of them denies some truth of God.

Hear Dopey as he speaks his lies: "I just don't know nothin'. I don't know what to say. I'll never be able to talk real good to nobody 'bout Jesus. So, I'll just say nothin' at all. 'Cuz if peoples really wants to hear 'bout Jesus, they'd ask a pastor or a priest or somebody smart like that. I don't want to bother nobody. I just want to be liked. Yep, I'll be really, really nice, dance around and smile a lot. I'll shine my light that way! Stayin' quiet, 'sted of talkin' 'bout Jesus."

Dopey denies the Promise and Power of God to give us the Words, Ways and Wisdom to share our faith in Jesus. Dopey may seem harmless enough, even cute, and oh-so-likeable! But his lies are insidious and dangerous. Dopey's lies of not knowing nothin' or not wanting to bother nobody are falsely humble and insecure at best, and completely untrue for someone who has accepted Jesus' gift of salvation for himself. At worst, Dopey's lying influence leads us to a place of apathy, lacking true compassion for the precious people around us – all who desperately need to hear about and believe in Jesus as the One through whom God's gifts of love, salvation, healing, freedom and transformation come to us.

God tells us His truth: God calls each of us to be ambassadors of Christ. All of us, who have accepted God's gifts of forgiveness and eternal life through Jesus, are called to share in the ministry of reconciliation with people who do not *yet* know the love of God. Our God gives us everything we need, His Promise and Power, His Words, Ways and Wisdom, to share our hope and faith in Jesus – even as frail, flawed, finite and Dopey as we are, or think we are!

All this is from God, who reconciled us to himself through Christ and gave us the ministry of reconciliation: that God was reconciling the world to himself in Christ, not counting people's sins against them. And God has committed to us the message of reconciliation. We are, therefore, Christ's ambassadors, as though God were making his appeal through us.
2 Corinthians 5:18-20

"...do not worry about how you will defend yourselves or what you will say, for the Holy Spirit will teach you at that time what you should say."
Luke 12:11-12

"You will receive power when the Holy Spirit comes on you; and you will be my witnesses in Jerusalem, and in all Judea and Samaria, and to the ends of the earth."
Acts 1:8

In your hearts revere Christ as Lord. Always be prepared to give an answer to everyone who asks you to give the reason for the hope that you have. But do this with gentleness and respect.
1 Peter 3:15

God loves us and wants the very best for each of us. Killing the Spiritual Dwarf of Dopey will set us free to know the joy of living as Christ's ambassadors, sharing in God's glorious ministry of reconciliation as we tell others of the great hope we have in Jesus! Now, that's something to smile and dance about!

Reflections – Responses – Challenges – Encouragements – God-breathing Thoughts

Do I believe it?
And if I do, what am I going to do about it?

Lord, please let me hear your voice, your love, your wisdom, your grace and truth.

SPIRITUAL DWARFS – part 9 – WHAT TO DO?

Oh! Those Spiritual Dwarfs: Prideful, Fearful, Sinful, Shameful, Whiny, Grumpy and Dopey! And all their evil friends, of so many other names: Lustful, Forceful, Two-Face-ful, Disgraceful, Sneaky, Meany, Nasty, Crabby, Lazy, Busy...and on and on! They all wreak horrible havoc within our hearts, souls, minds, bodies and relationships.

What are we ever going to do? Those Spiritual Dwarfs just keep yapping, shouting and telling us that we have a right to choose to think what we think, do what we do, and live how we live. Quite honestly, the Spiritual Dwarfs are right in this *one* way: We do have a choice. Always.

It was God's loving, sovereign choice to give each of us the gift of freedom of choice. But! We must be wise with this precious gift! Choosing anything other than God's way is no freedom at all. Turning our backs on God, and our focus on ourselves, is an ugly, vicious, evil, lying trap. This LFTPOH (Lie From The Pit Of Hell) would have us believe that the ultimate way to assert our independence, freedom and control over our own lives is to create our own standards for right and wrong – according to what we think and what we do and how we live.

This is a deadly lie. Our God wants us to live! The battle for our hearts, souls, minds, bodies and relationships has always been about life and death. Right from the beginning, in the Garden of Eden we were each given a choice: Believe our Loving Creator-Eternal God, take God at God's Word, and live *or* ignore and disobey God's Word and die. God made this gift of choice so clear to His people as He led them out of slavery and into the Promised Land.

> *...I have set before you life and death, blessings and curses.*
> *Now choose life, so that you and your children may live and that*
> *you may love the LORD your God, listen to his voice, and hold fast to him.*
> *For the LORD is your life...*
> Deuteronomy 30:19-20

It has always been about choice. We need to realize that everything we think, say and do is either bringing more life or more death to our minds, bodies, souls and relationships. It is in choosing to listen to, obey and "hold fast to" the loving, life-giving Word of God that we are able to kill the Spiritual Dwarfs and live! Our God is our life! Our God is our freedom!

> *It is for freedom that Christ has set us free. Stand firm, then,*
> *and do not let yourselves be burdened again by a yoke of slavery!*
> Galatians 5:1

I am convinced that God and God's Word are life and freedom to me. They are my song. They are my breath. They are the guardians of my heart, soul, mind, body and relationships.

Jesus has already died and risen to conquer the influence and lies of all that is evil – from outside of us and within us – that would hold us in bondage and kill us!

The choice is still, and always will be, about life and death: Ours or the Spiritual Dwarfs. What to do? Kill the Dwarfs!

Reflections – Responses – Challenges – Encouragements – God-breathing Thoughts

Do I believe it?
And if I do, what am I going to do about it?

Lord, please let me hear your voice, your love, your wisdom, your grace and truth.

SARDINES, ANYONE?

Sometimes some things are just not in our control. Okay! That really should say: Most of the time most things are not even close to being in our control! Good thing God is!

Oh! It's those extra special reminders of how very much not in control we are that can either make us cry, make us angry or, hopefully more often, they can make laugh out loud! Well, I have done a bit of all three over the years! Sometimes over very serious circumstances and sometimes over absolutely absurd circumstances! Either way, I have learned that attitude and perspective are what matter most in every circumstance.

Let me share one of those extra special reminders – this one falls into the absolutely absurd category – of how very much not in control I am. A few years back, I ordered a lovely basket of delicious goodies for my daughter's birthday. It was to be filled with gourmet cheeses and crackers, fabulous mustards, shortbread cookies, chocolate dipped cookies, French-twists, select teas, hot chocolates, coffees and (Oh, yes!) Godiva chocolates. The basket itself was a beautifully crafted masterpiece. And just to assure me the well-deserved title of Super Mom, I asked that a brightly colored *Happy Birthday!* balloon be attached to this fabulous feast in a basket! It was to be delivered to my daughter's NYC office a little after 9:30 am on the morning of her birthday.

Sometimes some things are just not in our control. My extra special reminder of just how very much not in control I am looked like this: The basket arrived after 5 pm; there was no balloon; the fabulous feast in a basket consisted of some plastic wrapped American cheese, some yellow mustard and a can of sardines.

Let me assure you that my daughter was able to laugh much more quickly than I! She even gave me credit for being clever and funny by sending a very un-gourmet basket as a joke for her birthday! Now if that isn't grace, I don't know what is! But. No. I had other Super Mom intentions! It didn't happen the way I planned it at all! And I just had to laugh!

Sometimes some things are just not in our control. Are you okay with that reality? Am I?

For the moment, I can say, "Yes!" This attitude is made by an intentional choice to intentionally believe the truth perspective that declares: God is in control. Now and always. God is in control when my life and my times are completely insane, absurd, annoying or confusing. God is in control when my life and my times are horribly shocking, sad, lonely, painful or scary. God is in control when my life and my times are powerfully effective, amazingly adventurous, magnificently sweet, fabulously easy or ridiculously funny.

My times are in your hands...
Psalm 31:15

God is in control at all times, in all places, in all circumstances.

And sometimes we just have to laugh! Sardines, anyone?

Our mouths were filled with laughter,
our tongues with songs of joy!
Psalm 126:2

Do I believe it?
And if I do, what am I going to do about it?

Lord, please let me hear your voice, your love, your wisdom, your grace and truth.

NEAR – FAR: POWERFUL WORDS, POWERFUL CHOICE!

Do you remember Grover, that cute and furry monster from Sesame Street? He often taught about prepositions of location. What? You know, words like: over, under, near, far!

These words have great power to help us know where things are. They change our whole understanding of where something or someone is actually positioned. They're basically our linguistic GPS.

The words *Near* and *Far* have especially powerful, eternal life consequences when it comes to us and our Lord. Throughout Scripture, our God is calling out to us: *Come near to Me. Come know My love for you. Come listen to Me. Come put your faith in Me. Come trust in Me. Come near to Me now. Come be with Me forever.*

Just as Grover encouraged the little children to run up to the television screen in order to come near, so we must run into the arms of our Lord Jesus Christ in order to come near to our Heavenly Father, our Holy Abba.

> *Those who are far from you will perish;*
> *you destroy all who are unfaithful to you.*
> *But as for me, it is good to be near God.*
> *I have made the Sovereign LORD my refuge;*
> *I will tell of your deeds.*
> Psalm 73:27-28

> *Jesus said to them, "Let the little children come [near] to me,*
> *and do not hinder them, for the kingdom of God belongs to such as these.*
> *Truly I tell you, anyone who will not receive the kingdom of God*
> *like a little child will never enter it."*
> Mark 10:14-15

> *Come near to God and he will come near to you.*
> James 4:8

> *Seek the LORD while he may be found; call on him while he is near.*
> *Let the wicked forsake their ways and the unrighteous their thoughts.*
> *Let them turn to the LORD, and he will have mercy on them,*
> *and to our God, for he will freely pardon.*
> Isaiah 55:6-7

Come on, let's run near to our Lord! Let's come near to our God in faith and receive His promised love and mercy! Let's come near to our Lord and stay in His presence! Our Lord is near, and always has been, waiting with outstretched, loving arms. The very same arms that were once stretched out on a cross for us, in the fullness of His love as He came near to us.

Our God is very near. He is Immanuel – God with us. May we each turn to God and choose to be very near to Him. *It is good to be near God*! Really good! Now and for all eternity!

Reflections – Responses – Challenges – Encouragements – God-breathing Thoughts

Do I believe it?
And if I do, what am I going to do about it?

Lord, please let me hear your voice, your love, your wisdom, your grace and truth.

STILL STORMING OR STILLED STORMS?

Storms hit.

Some storms physically attack and hit our lives in the forms of the geological giants and meteorological monsters – earthquakes, mudslides, avalanches, tsunamis, hurricanes, tornadoes, flooding, ice and snow storms and fire storms. Even if we have warning of their arrival, we have little to no power to stop the devastation they may cause us, our loved ones or our belongings.

Some storms are the terrible and terrifying tempests that come and attack our health, the life of a loved one, our plans and intentions for the present and our hopes for the future. These storms often hit with little or no warning. They come at us as part of the hard reality that we are living in a frail, flawed and finite world.

Some storms that we get caught in come at us as consequences of our own unwise or immoral choices in behavior, in words and in relationships. These storms may come subtly at first, but soon grow in force and ferocity, taking us down in ugly and destructive ways. They come because we refused to heed the warning signs and remove ourselves from the danger zones.

Some storms are "headwinds" only. These storms wreak havoc with our emotions and our perspectives, but are actually formed (and kept stirred-up) by our own self-focused pride and sense of entitlement rather than by anything of real substance attacking us. It's more likely that someone or something rained on our parade, and we've refused to let it go and get over ourselves.

Whatever the cause of the storm or the circumstance that puts us in it or the mind-set that keeps us in it, we can be sure that God is with us! As we truly seek our Lord's help, we can be sure that the power of the storm is no match for the power of our God, His unfailing love and His wonderful actions in our lives.

> *Then they cried out to the LORD in their trouble,*
> *and he brought them out of their distress.*
> *He stilled the storm to a whisper; the waves of the sea were hushed.*
> *They were glad when it grew calm, and he guided them to their desired haven.*
> *Let them give thanks to the LORD for his unfailing love*
> *and his wonderful deeds for mankind.*
> Psalm 107:28-31

Since the storms are still going to come at us – or come because of us – we need to run into our Lord's storm-stilling, compassionate, and forgiving arms. We need to fully turn to our Lord and trust in our God's unfailing love that is present with us even when we are in one of life's most crushing storms. By God's unfailing love, the most dangerous of storms are stilled to a whisper. By God's constant presence and wonderful deeds in our lives, the most frightening and destructive forces formed by life's storms cannot overtake us!

> *"...in me you may have peace. In this world you will have trouble.*
> *But take heart! I have overcome the world!"*
> John 16:33

Reflections – Responses – Challenges – Encouragements – God-breathing Thoughts

Do I believe it?
And if I do, what am I going to do about it?

Lord, please let me hear your voice, your love, your wisdom, your grace and truth.

GOD IS NOT LIMITED BY OUR LIMITATIONS!

Have you ever thought...
That you've come to the absolute end of your ability to deal with things?
That you've come to the absolute end of your strength and hope?
That the circumstances seem absolutely monstrous and insurmountable?
That the other people involved seem absolutely monstrous and unmovable?
That you just don't believe that anyone or anything else is going to change? Ever!

You're tired of the battle. You're tired of the hardship. You're tired of your limitations.

I get it. I understand all about insurmountable circumstances and monstrous people. I have compassion for you.

Our God offers far more than His perfect understanding and unfailing compassion for us when we're dealing with monstrously insurmountable circumstances and monstrously unmovable people! However, our God does so by, first, dealing with us! God's love, grace and truth come to us most fully and freely as we, first, let God search us. Change us. Cleanse us. Lead us in His life-healing, life-renewing, life-transforming ways. In order to overcome my limitations in dealing with anything and anyone, I must, first, invite God to search, change, cleanse and lead me! Because sometimes that insurmountable circumstance came from my own wrong thinking, speaking and acting. And sometimes that monstrously unmovable person is I.

> *Search me, God, and know my heart; test me and know my anxious thoughts.*
> *See if there is any offensive way in me, and lead me in the way everlasting.*
> Psalm 139:23-24

God offers us His strength, courage, and constant presence so that we may follow His leading – even when it's scary, humbling, uncertain and a little crazy!

> *"Have I not commanded you? Be strong and courageous. Do not be afraid;*
> *do not be discouraged, for the LORD your God will be with you wherever you go."*
> Joshua 1:9

God offers us His Spirit to empower us to conquer the most monstrous and insurmountable circumstances we may face. God offers us His Spirit to empower us to love and forgive the most monstrous and unmovable persons in our lives.

> *In all these things we are more than conquerors through him who loved us.*
> Romans 8:37

> *"I tell you, love your enemies and pray for those who persecute you."*
> Matthew 5:44

> *God is able to do immeasurably more than all we ask or imagine,*
> *according to his power that is at work within us...*
> Ephesians 3:20

God is not limited by our limitations! And in Christ, with the power of His love, grace and truth, we don't have to be limited either!

Reflections – Responses – Challenges – Encouragements – God-breathing Thoughts

Do I believe it?
And if I do, what am I going to do about it?

Lord, please let me hear your voice, your love, your wisdom, your grace and truth.

LOVE MUST BE SINCERE! DUH!

I love God's Word. It reveals grace. It speaks truth.

Love must be sincere.
Romans 12:9

I have to admit, and I may sound a little irreverent here, but when I first read that verse: "Love must be sincere," my initial reaction was: *Well, Duh! Of course, love must be sincere! Isn't that obvious? How else would we love? Duh!*

Okay, that was my first reaction. Then, I stopped to think and asked myself: How differently would I love if I always chose to think about loving in absolute sincerity? How differently would I love if I invited God to fill me and lead me to love others with His full, perfect and sincere love? What would this mean? What would that kind of love be like?

It would be pretty darn radical, extravagant, outrageous, and seem downright crazy at times!

Loving others sincerely would not be conditional on anyone meeting a certain standard of behavior or following certain values in order for us to love them.
Loving others sincerely would mean that we send out no hidden messages. That we would love others with no falsehood at any level, at any time – with no hook and no hiding.
Loving others sincerely would mean that we love with no pride and no prejudice.
Loving others sincerely would not be dependent on them loving us first or loving us back or loving us according to our expectations, demands and desires.
Loving others sincerely would not require or demand anything from them – not even an apology – in order for us to deem them worthy of our love.

Now, this is not about foolishly or fearfully setting ourselves up to be hurt, nor is it to encourage anyone to stay in any kind of an abusive, destructive relationship. This is about loving another person, including ourselves, sincerely – God's way! Loving others with God's heart for them, and accepting God's love for ourselves, means that we would no longer be controlled by our experiences of being hurt, rejected, abused or hatefully treated by others. We would be able to love others sincerely in, and only because of, the power of God's love, grace and truth!

To be able to love others sincerely, we must, first, believe and hold onto the incredible truth of God's perfect, unfailing, sincere love for us – the eternal love of our Holy God – for which our souls desperately crave! As we trust God's love for us, we are set free to love others sincerely. We can be sincerely compassionate towards the failings of others – forgiving everything from their casual thoughtlessness towards us to their ugliest and cruelest sins inflicted upon us. This is exactly how the sincere love of Jesus loves us, and empowers us to sincerely love others!

So, maybe, "Love must be sincere" is not such a *Duh!* kind of statement after all. Rather, it is a high calling, a Jesus-like way to love another person that can only be done as we allow our God, who is Love, to transform our thinking, our words, our actions, our all!

To love as God calls us to love: "Love must be sincere," we must be fully dependent on God's powerful, faithful, forgiving, unchanging, unconditional, extravagant, outrageous and crazy love for ourselves and everyone else! Now that statement deserves a *Duh!*

Reflections – Responses – Challenges – Encouragements – God-breathing Thoughts

Do I believe it?
And if I do, what am I going to do about it?

Lord, please let me hear your voice, your love, your wisdom, your grace and truth.

CHOOSING QUIET. KNOWING GOD.

As a teacher and a speaker who talks a great deal (and maybe especially because that's how I often serve), I deeply value and desperately need quiet time alone with God. Purposefully taking time, choosing to be quiet – consciously and intentionally quiet – is so good for my soul, my head, my heart and my body. Choosing to be quiet – consciously and intentionally quiet – is so healing. So refreshing. So powerful. So humbling.

So much noise comes from our high-tech world of constant and instantaneous contact and information. We are inundated with distractions that come at us – and we seek out – from the TV and radio, from iPods and iPads, from all things cyberspace and social media, from smart phones and stupid phones!

So much noise comes from our rushing, busy, and on-the-go world filled with cars, trucks, subways, taxis, buses, trains and planes. And all those sirens! (No, Toto, I don't live in Kansas. I live in Princeton, between New York City and Philadelphia, *and* in Los Gatos, smack dab in the heart of Silicon Valley!)

Then there's the noise that comes from all the talking around us. Much of that noise comes from other people. Much of the noise being made comes from us as we interact and converse (teach and speak) with others in real time. Much more of the noise, however, comes from within our own heads. We create, and listen to, the noise of so many of our own imagined interactions, conversations, rebuttals, worries, full blown stage and screen productions about what we want to happen in our lives or what we are fearful may happen in our lives! There are full color commentaries and play-by-play interpretations about everyone and everything going on perpetually inside our minds! Oh, we need some quiet!

Everything and everyone with whom we want to (or maybe don't want to) interact will still be there in a few moments. So, shhhhh...Let's each, for just a few moments, choose to be quiet and listen to our God.

"Be still, and know that I Am God..."
Psalm 46:10

Be still. Be silent. Be strengthened. Be healed. Be refreshed. Be Quiet.

Be still, and know God's presence. God is with us. God will never leave us or forsake us.
Be still, and know God's unfailing love. God's love fills our souls' greatest needs and answers our hearts' deepest cries. We are loved. We are cherished. We belong to our God.
Be still, and know God's unlimited power and transcending peace that shatters all darkness.
Be still, and know God's transforming grace that changes our mourning into joy, our hate into love, our bondage into freedom, our cruelest injustice into unconditional forgiveness, our deepest shame into untarnished purity, our weakness into strength and our death into a resurrected and eternal life!

So, shhhhh...Take a deep breath. Choose to Be Quiet. Choose to Know God.

Reflections – Responses – Challenges – Encouragements – God-breathing Thoughts

Do I believe it?
And if I do, what am I going to do about it?

Lord, please let me hear your voice, your love, your wisdom, your grace and truth.

WAKE UP WITH AWARENESS!

What goes through your mind when you first wake up? Okay, maybe, it's not when you first get out of bed – got to give grace to all who are not morning people! (Give me grace for being one of those odd creatures!) Once your brain is functioning (after a cup of coffee or four), what are some of your first thoughts as you begin the new day? Do you immediately start thinking about all you have to get done? Do you just start *doing* the day by getting yourself on – on the phone, on-line, on email, on Facebook, on Twitter? Do you just start *doing* your day by getting yourself up and out? Up and out to care for little ones, to go to the gym, office, school, church, doctor's appointment, or an early morning get-together with a friend or co-worker? Do your first waking thoughts immediately go into that Hamster Dance, circling over all the things and people that had filled your consciousness right up until you finally (and, maybe, fitfully) fell asleep last night?

Whatever our usual first waking thoughts are, our God reminds us of some of His fabulous truths for us to be aware of as we begin each new morning – and, even, every new moment!

> *...when I awake, I am still with you.*
> Psalm 139:18

> *In the morning, LORD, you hear my voice;*
> *in the morning I lay my requests before you*
> *and wait expectantly.*
> Psalm 5:3

> *The LORD has done it this very day; let us rejoice today and be glad.*
> *[This is the day the LORD has made; let us rejoice and be glad in it.]*
> Psalm 118:24

> *Whatever is true, whatever is noble, whatever is right,*
> *whatever is pure, whatever is lovely, whatever is admirable –*
> *if anything is excellent or praiseworthy – think about such things.*
> Philippians 4:8

> *Because of the LORD's great love we are not consumed,*
> *for his compassions never fail.*
> *They are new every morning;*
> *great is your faithfulness.*
> Lamentations 3:22-23

Let's choose to wake up – and wake up our minds – with awareness of these amazing and eternal truths from our God:
God is with us!
We are with God! We will never be left alone!
God hears us!
We can wait in expectant trust that God answers our prayers! In His good way!
This new day is a gift! That awareness should fill our hearts and minds with joy!
God is true, noble, right, pure, lovely, admirable, excellent and praiseworthy!
God's love for us is great!
God's compassions for us never fail! They are new every morning!

Wake up with awareness of God's love, presence, peace, power and perspective! God and God's truths will carry you through all that today brings!

Reflections – Responses – Challenges – Encouragements – God-breathing Thoughts

Do I believe it?
And if I do, what am I going to do about it?

Lord, please let me hear your voice, your love, your wisdom, your grace and truth.

GOD'S SWEET, FULL, SOUL-SATISFYING FRUIT
OF RIGHTEOUSNESS

Our Holy God has made a way – through the love and sacrifice of our Lord Jesus – to impart His own righteousness on us. This is so beyond my full comprehension. Yet, it is God's Word and the reality for all of us who have trusted in Jesus as our Savior.

As you read the Scriptures below, take time to reflect on God's loving and sacrificial gift of righteousness given to you. Let it become more deeply rooted in your soul and in your understanding. Let God's sweet, full and soul-satisfying fruit of righteousness be made more vibrantly alive and more amazingly abundant in you as you generously share it with others.

All this is from God…God made him who had no sin to be sin for us,
so that in him we might become the righteousness of God.
2 Corinthians 5:18, 21

Jesus taught, "I am the vine; you are the branches. If you remain in me and I in you,
you will bear much fruit; apart from me you can do nothing."
John 15:5

The fruit of that righteousness will be peace;
its effect will be quietness and confidence forever.
Isaiah 32:17

"Blessed is the one who trusts in the LORD, whose confidence is in him.
They will be like a tree planted by the water that sends out its roots by the stream.
It does not fear when the heat comes; its leaves are always green.
It has no worries in the year of drought and never fails to bear fruit."
Jeremiah 17:7-8

The fruit of the righteous is a tree of life, and one who is wise saves lives.
Proverbs 11:30

They will be called oaks of righteousness,
a planting of the LORD for the display of his splendor.
Isaiah 61:3

All this – all of our being made righteous and fruitful, peaceful and confident, wise and strong – *is from God*. All this is *for the display of God's splendor* so that we will be filled and, then, generously nourish and bless all those around us with God's righteous fruit that is being grown up in us! As we do, may we, first and always, remember to nourish and bless those precious ones closest to us – our own families and those we claim to care about the very most. These precious ones, all too often, end up getting our leftover fruit or our most rotten, spoiled or dried-up fruit, rather than getting the very sweetest, fullest, most soul-satisfying fruit of righteousness that cost our Heavenly Father so much to give it to us!

Reflections – Responses – Challenges – Encouragements – God-breathing Thoughts

Do I believe it?
And if I do, what am I going to do about it?

Lord, please let me hear your voice, your love, your wisdom, your grace and truth.

_____

_____

_____

_____

_____

_____

_____

_____

_____

_____

_____

_____

_____

_____

_____

_____

_____

_____

_____

_____

_____

_____

_____

_____

_____

LIVING THE TRUTH OF PSALM 23 – part 1

For the next few days, I want us to read, reflectively read, the words of Psalm 23 a few verses at a time. I want God to show us more of what living the truth of His Word via Psalm 23 means. Let's take this journey together, seeking our Lord, our Shepherd, to lead us.

> *The LORD is my shepherd, [I shall not be in want] I lack nothing.*
> *He makes me lie down in green pastures,*
> *he leads me beside quiet waters,*
> *he [restores] refreshes my soul.*
> Psalm 23:1-3

The words from Psalm 23 are some of the most familiar, best-known words from the entire Bible – familiar to believers and not-yet-believers around the world. This Psalm is often read during times of deep crises in our lives or at the bedside of the sick and dying or later read at their funerals. The words of Psalm 23 are powerful and soul-refreshing. And they are true.

These words are just as true, powerful and soul-refreshing during the routine times of our daily-day lives and during those sweet, peaceful periods of time (that really do come from time to time). The words from Psalm 23 are meant to be read and known as true, powerful and soul-refreshing even during our most joyful times of celebration.

Because…
We always need our Lord, our Shepherd. Not just when we are aware of our great need.
We always need our Lord, our Shepherd, to lead us. Not just when we are confused as to where we should go.
We always need our Lord, our Shepherd, to provide for us. Not just when we are insecure about our ability to provide for ourselves.
We always need our Lord, our Shepherd, to show us where and how to rest. Not just when we are burned out and worn down by life.
We always need our Lord, our Shepherd, to lead us to the quiet waters where He restores our souls. Not just when we realize that the flow of life and hope and peace in our inner-most beings is dry and shriveled or bitter and rancid.

Read, again, those first few beginning verses from Psalm 23:

> *The LORD is my shepherd, [I shall not be in want] I lack nothing.*
> *He makes me lie down in green pastures,*
> *he leads me beside quiet waters,*
> *he [restores] refreshes my soul.*
> Psalm 23:1-3

Our daily, desperate and, even, delightful need for our Lord, our Shepherd, never changes. Our God never changes. But, oh! Our God wants to change us with His true, powerful and soul-refreshing Word! May God's truth be lived out in our consciousness, in our choices, and in our ever-growing intimacy with our Shepherd as we allow Him to lead us every moment, every day – whatever our days may bring.

Reflections – Responses – Challenges – Encouragements – God-breathing Thoughts

Do I believe it?
And if I do, what am I going to do about it?

Lord, please let me hear your voice, your love, your wisdom, your grace and truth.

LIVING THE TRUTH OF PSALM 23 – part 2

As we read reflectively through Psalm 23, I'm asking God to show us what living the truth of His Word means for each of our days. Whether it is a day of sadness, surprises, simplicity or celebration.

The LORD guides me [in paths of righteousness]
along the right paths for his name's sake.
Psalm 23:3

Within these few words there is so much revealed about our Lord – His truth, power and soul-refreshing intimacy and purpose. So, let's do the rap-thing: Break it down!

Who: *The Lord, our Shepherd* – the Holy One, the Creator of all that is seen and unseen, the Great One – enters into our world. The Lord, who is beyond our full grasp of understanding, reaches out to us to intervene in our lives. Into our mortal, needy, frail, flawed and finite lives. And the Lord, our Shepherd, comes to us with His unlimited, unfailing love!

What: *Guides me.* How extravagantly intimate the Holy One, the Sovereign Lord, our Shepherd, is with each of us! Our Shepherd walks with us. Lives with us. Our Shepherd desires to lead us, teach us, nurture us and guide us. If I would take more time to honestly think about and reflect on Who is actually guiding me, instead of asserting my independence (aka: willfulness and stubbornness) to determine my own direction, I would, more often and more immediately, respond with the rightful attitudes of awe, humility and thankfulness. And I would, more often and more immediately, actively and intentionally, seek the Lord, my Shepherd, to guide me every single day. Every single moment. With every single breath.

Where: *In paths of righteousness.* Our Lord, our Shepherd, guides us (and passionately invites us, but does not force us) to walk on and live on His holy ground – on His paths of righteousness. Yet, too often, we choose to go our own way. And it isn't pretty. When I choose to stay on my own me-centered path, I am ego-focused. It is then that I lose my focus. It is then that I lose my way. As we choose to walk with our Lord on His paths of righteousness, we will receive the fullness of our Lord's eternal gifts of life, love, grace, truth, peace and purpose. No matter what temporal obstacles may be in our way.

Why: *For His name's sake.* Our Lord, our Shepherd, purposes for each of us to know who He is – who He truly is! Our Lord, our Shepherd, purposes to reveal Himself and His love, salvation, sovereignty, power, intimacy and purpose to the world – to each precious individual ever born to this world. And our Lord, our Shepherd, chooses to use us to reveal Himself to others, as we choose to walk on His paths of righteousness. For His name's sake!

What an amazing and humbling intimacy we've been given with our Lord, our Shepherd, as He guides us! What an amazing and humbling purpose we've been given by our Lord, our Shepherd, to share with others about God's life-guiding, life-transforming love, grace, truth, righteousness, intimacy and purpose that He offers to each and every one of us!

Read, again, today's verse:
The LORD guides me [in paths of righteousness]
along the right paths for his name's sake.
Psalm 23:3

Let's take a walk on the Righteous Side with our Lord, our Shepherd!

Do I believe it?
And if I do, what am I going to do about it?

Lord, please let me hear your voice, your love, your wisdom, your grace and truth.

LIVING THE TRUTH OF PSALM 23 – part 3

As we read reflectively through Psalm 23, a few verses at a time, I pray that our God will lead each of us to know what living the truth of His Word means for each of our days. Whether it is a day of sadness, surprises, simplicity or celebration.

> *Even though I walk through the darkest valley [of the shadow of death],*
> *I will fear no evil, for you are with me...*
> Psalm 23:4

This verse is often clung to most tightly during the most frightening, overwhelming and tragedy-filled times of our lives. Those times when we can no longer deny the truth of our own mortality or the mortality of someone we love deeply. Maybe we've received a diagnosis or suffered an injury that completely uncovers the truth that has always been there: We are indeed frail, flawed and finite human beings.

And so we find ourselves walking in the valley of the shadow of death. This can be so scary. It can feel so lonely. On this side of heaven, we must face the unchanging truth that tragedy, loss and death do indeed come to us, and we have no choice but to walk through these times.

Yet! When we choose to walk with our Lord, our Shepherd, His eternal unchanging truth changes us. With our Lord, our Shepherd, there is no need to fear evil. There is no need to fear death. There is no need to fear that we are not prepared for or strong enough to make it through the valley of the shadow of death. Because we don't have to be strong enough. At least not on our own.

Our Lord, our Shepherd, is with us! This is the unchanging truth that has the power to change us. This is the unchanging truth that changes our hearts, our minds and our spirits – right on this side of heaven – even as we walk through the valley of the shadow of death. This is the unchanging truth that changes our present perspective and our eternal destiny. We understand that because we belong to, and are with, our Lord and Shepherd, everything that we could possibly face here on this earth is only a shadow. It is not made of anything substantive. It is not made of anything eternal. It is temporal and passing. Hard and painful, awful and ugly – Yes. But it is still, and only, temporal and passing. As we choose to stay close to our Lord and Shepherd, we will not only pass through the valley of the shadow of death, but we will overcome it in full victory and walk in inexplicable and unfailing love, joy and peace with our Lord and Shepherd for all of eternity! The days of the shadow will come. But they will come to nothing. They are only shadow. Our God is eternal!

Read, again, today's verse:

> *Even though I walk through the darkest valley [of the shadow of death],*
> *I will fear no evil, for you are with me...*
> Psalm 23:4

May this unchanging truth, that our Lord and Shepherd is with us in all circumstances, at all times, change us! May God's eternal presence give comfort to our souls and courage to our hearts as we walk with Him every step of the way through our days of sadness, surprises, simplicity, celebration and shadow!

Do I believe it?
And if I do, what am I going to do about it?

Lord, please let me hear your voice, your love, your wisdom, your grace and truth.

LIVING THE TRUTH OF PSALM 23 – part 4

As we read reflectively through Psalm 23, a few verses at a time, I pray that our God will lead each of us to know what living the truth of His Word means for each of our days. Whether it is a day of sadness, surprises, simplicity or celebration.

...your rod and your staff, they comfort me.
Psalm 23:4

The Lord's rod and staff are means of bringing comfort to us? How can that be? My personal idea of comfort is taking a long walk by the ocean or taking some quiet time, drinking strong coffee and eating natural peanut butter mixed with dark chocolate chips. But! The Lord's rod and staff? These are not the first things I think of when I need comfort. Yet, here it is for each of us to understand and believe. Our Shepherd's rod and staff are signs and instruments of His authority and leadership over His sheep, and their purpose is to bring us comfort.

Our Shepherd uses His rod and staff in *gentle* ways to show His authority and leadership over our lives – and always, and only, out of His deep love for us:
To show us the way to go. His rod, an extension of His mighty arm, points out the path we are to follow as our Shepherd walks with us, staff in hand.
To count us. Our Shepherd uses His rod to be sure that not one of us is missing or lost.
To guide us to walk closely with Him and closer to each other – with a gentle tap from His rod or a gentle pull from the hook of His staff.
To rescue us from a fall we inadvertently took. The hook of His staff pulls us back to safety.

Our Shepherd uses His rod and staff, in *strong* ways, to show His authority and leadership over our lives – and always, and only, out of His deep love for us:
To discipline us. A whack from His rod or a tug from His staff brings our focus back to Him.
To show us that we are in imminent and serious danger. His rod and staff may be used roughly to turn us around immediately and move us out of harm's way.
To stop our continual wandering away. Our Shepherd may use His rod and staff to break our legs. Our Shepherd would, then, pick us up, carry us on His shoulders, keeping us close to His heart as we heal, strengthen and learn to stay close to the One who loves us most.
To fight off our enemies. Our Shepherd uses His rod and staff as weapons to fiercely fight for us, passionately defend us and completely defeat all who would harm and destroy us.

Read, again, today's verse:

...your rod and your staff, they comfort me.
Psalm 23:4

There is peace, provision and passionate protection and correction as we walk with our Lord and Shepherd. Out of His great love for us, our Shepherd will, *gently and strongly*, use His rod and staff to keep us very close to Himself. This is the very best place we could ever be. Here we are held tightly by His love, led fully by His authority – guided and grown by His rod and His staff – and given the greatest comfort we could ever know!

Do I believe it?
And if I do, what am I going to do about it?

Lord, please let me hear your voice, your love, your wisdom, your grace and truth.

LIVING THE TRUTH OF PSALM 23 – part 5

As we read reflectively through Psalm 23, a few verses at a time, I pray that our God will lead each of us to know what living the truth of His Word means for each of our days. Whether it is a day of sadness, surprises, simplicity or celebration.

You prepare a table before me in the presence of my enemies.
Psalm 23:5

I have to admit that I am getting more and more blown away by what our Lord and Shepherd does for each of us as we allow Him to have His rightful, loving place of sovereign authority in our lives.

Our Lord prepares a table, prepares a banquet, for us His people. His doors are thrown open and we are lovingly and enthusiastically invited to dine with our King. His warm and generous welcome and all the abundant provisions for a feast that will replenish, restore and refresh us are all there. All for us.

Our Lord's plans, preparations and provisions to bring us to the table He has set before us cannot be hindered in any way by anything our adversaries do to us. Nor can our Lord's plans, preparations and provisions be hindered by any adverse circumstances or situations we may be experiencing. No. The intimate fellowship with our Lord, and the magnificent banquet He has prepared for us, will go on just as He plans. The offer to fellowship and feast with our Lord, right in the presence of our enemies, will never cease. Our enemies' presence around us and our enemies' persecution towards us do not hold any power to destroy or deter what our mighty Lord, our loving Shepherd, offers us as we dine and commune with Him.

And I do know that just one of the many dishes that is lavishly offered at our Lord's banquet table is the Fruit of the Spirit. The components of this dish alone – Love, Joy, Peace, Patience, Kindness, Goodness, Faithfulness, Gentleness and Self-control (Galatians 5:22-23) – fill our lives with replenishing, restoring, refreshing power beyond our imagination. Power against which no enemy can stand.

Our Lord, our Great Shepherd Jesus Christ, when faced with the full force of His enemy's temptations and taunts, declared that we live, not on bread made by human hands alone, "but on every word that comes from the mouth of God" (Matthew 4:4). Fill up on God's Word! It is our very life source.

Our Lord's table, prepared for us, is where our Lord offers Himself to us in unimaginably intimate fellowship and lavishly provides us with His life-filling, life-transforming fare. No matter what state of affairs our lives may be in.

Read, again, today's verse:
You prepare a table before me in the presence of my enemies.
Psalm 23:5

Come to the table. The welcome is given. All is prepared. Come to the table prepared by our loving, almighty Lord and Shepherd. His provisions are unlimited. His plans never fail. His banquet never ends. Here, we will be replenished, restored and refreshed, right in the presence of our enemies – because our King is present with us!

Do I believe it?
And if I do, what am I going to do about it?

Lord, please let me hear your voice, your love, your wisdom, your grace and truth.

LIVING THE TRUTH OF PSALM 23 – part 6

As we read reflectively through Psalm 23, a few verses at a time, I pray that our God will lead each of us to know what living the truth of His Word means for each of our days. Whether it is a day of sadness, surprises, simplicity or celebration.

You anoint my head with oil; my cup overflows.
Psalm 23:5

The outrageous love and honor, the abundant overflowing blessings given by our Lord and Shepherd to each of us, absolutely astounds and humbles me. This is God, the Lord Almighty, the Holy One, the Creator of all that exists. This is the Alpha and the Omega. And it is He who anoints *our* heads as His honored ones!

This isn't about us. This isn't about us earning this anointing. And this, certainly, is not about us deserving this anointing. This is all about our Lord. It is He who chooses to anoint each of us who trusts in Him as our Savior and King. It is our Lord who anoints each of His followers as His honored guest, His beloved child and His intimate friend. It is our Lord who chooses to anoint His followers to be His ambassadors – setting us apart to carry His message of love and grace and truth to all those around us.

Our Lord pours out His oil – His anointing Holy Spirit – over our heads, rubbing it in with His almighty hands that formed all that exists in all of creation. His anointing heals our minds and soothes our souls with the touch of His humble, nail-scarred hands that reveals His unfailing love and eternal salvation. That we are anointed by the Lord Most High as His honored ones, is more than I can fully grasp. But! Our God of love and kindness does not stop there!

No. Our Lord and Shepherd makes our cups – our lives – to overflow. He, Himself, is the freely offered and abundantly flowing water of life that cleanses us, fills us and wells up in us to overflow with God's love and blessings into our own lives, and into the lives of those around us. Our Lord chose to sacrificially pour out His own life for us. And He invites each one of us to put our cups – our lives – into His hands so that He may fill them, and us, to overflowing!

As our cups – our lives – are held in the hands of our Lord and Shepherd (Give Him your cup!), He pours out His love, His life, His grace, His truth, His forgiveness, His freedom, His wisdom, His peace, His courage, His hope, His power...and on and on and on...into our lives. These abundantly-flowing, life-transforming blessings are given by our Lord and Shepherd. By His loving choice. Again, not because we have earned or deserved any of these blessings. This is all about our Lord making His love, and the gift of His own sacrificed life, very real in our lives.

Read, again, today's verse:

You anoint my head with oil; my cup overflows.
Psalm 23:5

Be soothed. Be honored. Be set apart. Be anointed by our Lord and Shepherd. Be blessed. Be refreshed. Be filled to overflowing to bless the lives of others with the love, grace and truth of our Lord and Shepherd!

Do I believe it?
And if I do, what am I going to do about it?

Lord, please let me hear your voice, your love, your wisdom, your grace and truth.

LIVING THE TRUTH OF PSALM 23 – part 7

As we read reflectively through Psalm 23, a few verses at a time, I pray that our God will lead each of us to know what living the truth of His Word means for each of our days. Whether it is a day of sadness, surprises, simplicity or celebration.

Surely your goodness and love will follow me all the days of my life...
Psalm 23:6

The perfect, passionate Goodness and the undeniable, unfailing Love of our Lord and Shepherd will follow us – literally, pursue us – all of the days of our lives. Can you even imagine this? Our Lord's Goodness and Love follow and pursue us so that He may attend to us and care for us in deep and daily ways.

When I, intentionally and actively, choose to walk with my Lord and Shepherd, seeking to follow Him, yielding to His loving authority over my life, it is very easy to know, see and sense God's Goodness and Love following and pursuing me, attending to me and caring for me. Even in the most challenging, devastating or sad circumstances.

When I do not, intentionally and actively, choose to walk with my Lord and Shepherd, not seeking to follow Him, not yielding to His loving authority over my life, it is so very hard to know, see and sense His Goodness and Love following and pursuing me, attending to me and caring for me. I'm going my own way. And in those moments, I am not attending to His way nor caring about it, for that matter.

But! No matter what I may be choosing or what I may be sensing, our Lord's Goodness and Love are continually following and pursuing me, attending to me and caring for me! And this is true for each and every one of us! Our God never changes! It is we who choose to change focus. It is we who choose to change directions. Not God!

And it is each one of us who needs to turn around and run into the outstretched arms of our Lord and Shepherd. We each need to know, see and sense our Lord and Shepherd's perfect, passionate Goodness and His undeniable, unfailing Love all the days of our lives. We all are desperate for Him and for all that His Goodness and Love bring into our lives.

We each need to view and review our life-walks from God's perspective, and trust in God's unchanging truth: His Goodness and Love follow us all the days of our lives. When we do, it is then that we will know, see and sense God's Goodness and Love in deeper, tangible, healing and hope-filled ways all the days of our lives. Even in the most challenging, devastating or sad circumstances. It is, also, then, as we walk a life-path marked by our Lord's Goodness and Love, that we will be God's vessels to bring His healing and hope to others in our lives.

Read, again, today's verse:
Surely your goodness and love will follow me all the days of my life...
Psalm 23:6

Let's take a walk! May our whole life-walk be one where we know, see, sense *and* share our Lord's Goodness and Love which continually follow and pursue, attend to and care for every person in this world – all the days of our lives!

Reflections – Responses – Challenges – Encouragements – God-breathing Thoughts

Do I believe it?
And if I do, what am I going to do about it?

Lord, please let me hear your voice, your love, your wisdom, your grace and truth.

LIVING THE TRUTH OF PSALM 23 – part 8

As we read reflectively through Psalm 23, a few verses at a time, I pray that our God will lead each of us to know what living the truth of His Word means for each of our days. Whether it is a day of sadness, surprises, simplicity or celebration.

...and I will dwell in the house of the LORD forever.
Psalm 23:6

Wow! A permanent address! We are welcomed to enter in and take up permanent residence in our Abba's house as His very beloved children. For me, as one who has lived a very nomadic life (living in at least fourteen homes since 1980, and currently living bi-coastally), the idea of settling into a forever home is deeply meaningful and beautifully hope-filled.

The Living God, our eternal Lord and Shepherd, invites us to dwell with Him forever. God wants us to know how deeply He loves us and how fully we belong to Him. God wants us home. God wants us to know the transforming truth that we are eternally part of His family.

Ahhhhh…home. Home is where the heart is. And God's heart, filled with unfailing love for us, beckons each and every one of us to come home to Him. Come home to His love, His grace, His truth. Come home – for all eternity – to the only place where our burdens are gone, our lives are fully set free and we are our truest, purest selves. Forever.

Home. We, whose hearts hold Jesus as our Savior, have moved our dwelling place to be, now and forever, with our Lord and Shepherd. We, whose hearts hold Jesus as our Savior, have been given God's Holy Spirit to live within us – assuring us that we are His and He is ours. Assuring us that God Himself is our home. Assuring us that one day we each will be fully and finally home. All of us, whose hearts hold Jesus as our Savior, are given the absolute promise that death does not have the final word. Rather, through the resurrection power of our Almighty God, we will enter into the fullness of our Lord and Shepherd's unveiled, perfect, beautiful and loving presence. We will arrive safely, joyfully home! Ahhhhh…home.

What about you? Do you know where your eternal dwelling place will be? Do you know how to get home to Abba, to the Lord and Shepherd? Is your heart at home with Jesus? If not, today is a very good day for you to move. For you to change your permanent dwelling place to God's home. Invite Jesus to be your Savior. Acknowledge that you need to be forgiven for all your sins. Believe that Jesus, who is "the way and the truth and the life" (John 14:6), has made a way home for you through His death and resurrection! Trust Jesus. You will be welcomed home by our Lord and our Shepherd with love, forgiveness, freedom and joy!

Read, again, today's verse:

...and I will dwell in the house of the LORD forever.
Psalm 23:6

Ahhhhh…home. Forever.

Do I believe it?
And if I do, what am I going to do about it?

Lord, please let me hear your voice, your love, your wisdom, your grace and truth.

LIVING THE TRUTH OF PSALM 23 – part 9

We have just spent the last few days reading through Psalm 23, a few verses at a time, and praying that our God will lead each of us to know what living the truth of His Word means for each of our days. Whether it is a day of sadness, surprises, simplicity or celebration.

Read Psalm 23, yet again, in its entirety, listening for God's living and active truth in His holy and eternal Word.

> *The LORD is my shepherd, [I shall not be in want] I lack nothing.*
> *He makes me lie down in green pastures,*
> *he leads me beside quiet waters,*
> *he [restores] refreshes my soul.*
> *The LORD guides me [in paths of righteousness]*
> *along the right paths for his name's sake.*
> *Even though I walk through the darkest valley [of the shadow of death],*
> *I will fear no evil, for you are with me;*
> *your rod and your staff, they comfort me.*
> *You prepare a table before me*
> *in the presence of my enemies.*
> *You anoint my head with oil;*
> *my cup overflows.*
> *Surely your goodness and love will follow me*
> *all the days of my life,*
> *and I will dwell in the house of the LORD forever.*

Take time to listen, really listen, to God. Take time to hear and know the power of God's grace and truth found here in Psalm 23. Take time to breathe deeply and be quiet before your Lord and Shepherd.

You see, God's Word is not meant to be merely read or heard. No. God's Word is living and active. And God's Word is meant to be actively and intentionally lived out in each of our lives, for each of our days. Because we always need our Lord and Shepherd…
To lead us continually in His sovereign and intimate love.
To know and fulfill the deepest desires of our souls, the deepest wants of our hearts.
To show us where and how to rest fully and freely in the safety of His love.
To restore and refresh our souls with His tender care and beauty.
To guide us in His righteousness so we may shine with His likeness.
To walk with us here in the dark shadow lands of this broken world.
To calm our every fear with His loving and constant presence.
To comfort, correct and protect us by His gentle and strong ways.
To give us His lavish sustenance and full victory, right in the midst of our enemies.
To soothe us and honor us, set us apart and anoint us with His overflowing Spirit.
To follow us and pursue us, to attend to us and care for us passionately and persistently.
To assure us that He will bring us home to the fullness of His love and joy for all eternity.

May each of us live in and be led by the truth of God's Word every day of our lives! Amen!

Do I believe it?
And if I do, what am I going to do about it?

Lord, please let me hear your voice, your love, your wisdom, your grace and truth.

DON'T MISS THE MESSAGE!

Have you ever received a letter, a card, a notice, an invitation (evite, Facebook invitations included), and you didn't really take the time to read it right away? You knew you needed to read it. Needed to check out what it had to say. You even knew who sent it to you. But, you still just put it aside, over and over again. You just never got back to it, at least not until it was too late for the relevant information or invitation within the message to make any difference in your life. Maybe that letter, card or invitation got stuck between some pages in your overflowing mass of messages, and you just missed knowing it was ever even there for you. You hadn't taken the time to sort the real messages from the junk messages carefully enough. And you missed something very important, something very special.

Years ago, I inadvertently recycled (after meticulously tearing it into bits and pieces) a fairly sizeable check. The message I thought was junk mail was actually a very kind and tangible gift for me that I had not expected. I hadn't taken the time to look at it carefully enough to recognize it for what it truly was!

In the same way, we can so easily miss the messages from our God if we do not, will not, take the time to look, listen, acknowledge and receive all that our God offers to us through His Word and His Spirit. And we really do not want to miss those messages! They are life and love messages to us from the very heart of our Sovereign God. Through God's revealed Word and by the power of God's Spirit, we are given knowledge that is life-saving and life-transforming. Through God's revealed Word and by the power of God's Spirit, we receive the love, wisdom, encouragement, guidance, joy, peace and power to know, trust and follow the Living God!

We will never be able to fully know and understand our God on this side of heaven. But! All that God does reveal to us is ours forever! We need to receive it! We need to live it!

> *The secret things belong to the LORD our God, but the things revealed belong to us and to our children forever, that we may follow all the words of this law.*
> Deuteronomy 29:29

The Lord of all creation even invites us frail, flawed and finite people into an intimate dialogue with Him so He may tell us things we could not possibly know without His holy revelation.

> *"This is what the LORD says, he who made the earth, the LORD who formed it and established it – the LORD is his name: 'Call to me and I will answer you and tell you great and unsearchable things you do not know.' "*
> Jeremiah 33:2-3

Our God has already revealed to us, and shared with us, His ultimate message: His Son Jesus laid down His life for us so that we could be reconciled fully to our Heavenly Father through the forgiveness of our sins and the gift of eternal life! This message, this knowledge, given and revealed by our Holy God holds divine power – offering us everything we need for life and godliness.

> *God's divine power has given us everything we need for [life and godliness] a godly life through our knowledge of him who called us by his own glory and goodness.*
> 2 Peter 1:3

Let's not miss the messages of God! Let's listen! Let's learn! Let's be open to God's revelation! Let's know, trust and follow the Living God – living as God's people with the divine power of God's Word and God's Spirit fully available to all of us, at all times!

Reflections – Responses – Challenges – Encouragements – God-breathing Thoughts

Do I believe it?
And if I do, what am I going to do about it?

Lord, please let me hear your voice, your love, your wisdom, your grace and truth.

WHAT'S YOUR SAMUEL?

Hannah wanted a baby so much. Her years of longing bubbled up and out of control on one particular trip to Shiloh when she attended a festival of worship and sacrifice to the Lord Almighty. At that time in Israel's history, Shiloh was where the Central Sanctuary and the Ark of the Covenant were located. This was holy ground for a holy celebration.

This was also the place and the time that...

> *In deep anguish [bitterness of soul] Hannah prayed to the LORD, weeping bitterly.*
> 1 Samuel 1:10

Hannah's entire being – her head, heart, soul and body – cried out to her God, begging Him to hear and answer her prayers for a son. Hannah knew that only the Lord, as the Giver of Life, could give her a child. Hannah made a solemn vow in that holy place as she poured her whole self before her God. If God would give her a child, she would give her child – her future son – back to the Lord to serve Him all the days of his life. God heard and honored Hannah's prayer. And Hannah honored her promise to the Lord.

And at just the right time, according to our God's perfect plans and perfect timing, the Lord answered Hannah's desperately longing prayers for a son.

> *She named him Samuel, saying, "Because I asked the LORD for him."*
> 1 Samuel 1:20

Samuel sounds very much like the Hebrew word for "heard of God." Hannah knew that Samuel was the tangible, living proof that the Lord Almighty, the God she worshipped, truly is the God who hears. And Hannah bubbled up, once again, in thanksgiving, awe and praise to the Lord Almighty. To the God who hears, she proclaimed:

> *"There is no one holy like the LORD; there is no one besides you;*
> *there is no Rock like our God."*
> 1 Samuel 2:2

What's your Samuel? What do you acknowledge and give thanks for in your life as tangible, living proof for how the Lord Almighty, the God who hears, has heard and answered you?

What's your Samuel? Are you willing to hold your *Samuel* loosely – whether it is a person you love deeply or a goal you've attained – because you know that your *Samuel* came to you completely out of the unfailing love and perfect will of our Holy God?

What's your Samuel? Are you willing to truly give your *Samuel* back to the Lord by trusting God and His ways completely with the ones you love and the sense of security that came with the goals you attained?

Whatever our *Samuels* may be, may we each trust the heart of our Holy God as our *Samuels* come into, and change, and go out of our lives – knowing full well that our *Samuels* have always belonged to our God who hears our hearts.

Do I believe it?
And if I do, what am I going to do about it?

Lord, please let me hear your voice, your love, your wisdom, your grace and truth.

GOD'S WISDOM IS WAITING

There are so many times that I am so clearly aware that my own thinking is just not enough. No matter how perceptive, discerning and analytical I may be – or think I may be!

My thinking, on its own, just isn't always broad enough or deep enough or visionary enough or objective enough to give me the insight and wisdom that I need. I need more than my own insight and wisdom when an on-the-spot interpretation of a critical situation must be made which requires immediate action and sudden intervention. I need more than my own insight and wisdom when a longer view interpretation of a complex situation must be made which requires broad-scoping actions and far-reaching plans to be put into place. And, quite honestly, I realize more and more that even for those seemingly simple situations, I need more than my own insight and wisdom.

My thinking, on its own, just isn't always enough.

This is actually a very good and freeing realization to come to. Because, this is absolute truth for me, and for pretty much every other person on this planet. Or, at least, it will be at some point in each life, in some situation. Whether we admit it or not.

How great is our God! And how well our God knows us and knows our needs! God invites us to seek His wisdom. This requires humility on our parts (which is not exactly the core character trait in too many of us human beings) as we acknowledge that we really do need God's wisdom – since there is a lack of it in our own thinking!

When we do ask, our God is so good, so kind and so faithful in giving out His wisdom to us. Our God gives us His wisdom without ever giving us any sense of blame or guilt or shame for not being wise enough on our own in the first place! How great is our merciful God who loves us and knows that we desperately need all the wisdom He would give us.

> ***If any of you lacks wisdom, you should ask God,***
> ***who gives generously to all without finding fault,***
> ***and it will be given to you.***
> James 1:5

How great is our God! How good and loving our God wants to be to us. God knows our every need. And God knows we need His wisdom. There will always be those critical and complex (and those seemingly simple) situations in our lives where our own, even brilliant, thinking is not – nor will it ever be – enough. We need to be humble enough to agree with God about what we lack. We need to be humble and trusting enough to ask for God's wisdom, believing He will give it to us just as He has said. Generously!

With all the different situations, circumstances and relationships that are part of our lives, and that swirl around continually in our thinking, isn't it time for each of us to ask our God for His insight and wisdom? We were never meant to do life – or figure it out – on our own!

God's wisdom is waiting! What are we waiting for?

Reflections – Responses – Challenges – Encouragements – God-breathing Thoughts

Do I believe it?
And if I do, what am I going to do about it?

Lord, please let me hear your voice, your love, your wisdom, your grace and truth.

BE PREPARED!

I thought I was prepared. I wasn't. The news that brought great sadness and far-reaching consequences came suddenly. It came hard. It came with hurt. It came with unanswerable questions. And as it came, it changed a great many things for a great many people. And I was not fully prepared.

But! Our God is never taken by surprise. Our God never changes – no matter what changes come at us. Our God is always and fully aware of all things, of all people, at all times, in all circumstances and, therefore, our God is fully prepared. Always. Because of God's deep love for us and His transforming work within us, our God purposes to make each one of us more and more like Jesus. And that means we are to be prepared!

> *Therefore, with minds that are alert and fully sober*
> *[prepare your minds for action and be self-controlled],*
> *set your hope fully on the grace to be brought to you*
> *when Jesus Christ is revealed at his coming.*
> 1 Peter 1:13

Our God calls us to *prepare our minds for action.* This doesn't mean that we should live under a constant burden of stress as we try to figure everything out ahead of time or worry about circumstances and events that may never happen. However, we are to recognize the truth that we live in a broken world, and that reality – and the experiences it brings into our lives – can break our hearts, shatter our trust, rip away our peace and confuse our minds.

Our God calls us to *be self-controlled.* We, who are followers of Christ, never have to rely on our own powers of self-control. We never have to believe the lie that we are alone in handling the difficult, trying and tempting situations that come at all of us in this broken world. This is a Lie From The Pit Of Hell. (Yes, a LFTPOH!) Our God is with us. The Spirit of the Living God is within us – giving us full access to God's holy fruit of self-control. And our God gives us faithful brothers and sisters, His Body, to support, correct and encourage and guide us. For our own sakes and for the sakes of others, we need to daily ask our God to take greater and greater control of our thinking, reacting and responding to every situation and circumstance we face.

Our God calls us to *set our hope fully on the grace to be given us when Jesus Christ is revealed.* As children of the risen King, believing in His imminent return, we look forward to the day when our Lord Jesus Christ will be fully and finally revealed as the Sovereign God over all that exists. As we set our hopes fully on our God and trust the truth of His ultimate victory over all that is sin-scarred and death-touched in this broken world, we will be held safely – even in our most turbulent, unsettling times. Setting our hope fully, intentionally and actively, on our Lord Jesus Christ will bring great healing to our hearts, restoration to our trust, depth to our peace and calmness to our minds.

Our God is with us. Our God's Spirit is within us. May we each choose to allow God's transforming grace and truth to have full rule over our minds and our lives right in the midst of every unexpected, yet-to-be-expected circumstance we face in this broken world. "God's divine power has given us everything we need for life and godliness" (2 Peter 3:1). In Christ, and with the help of our faithful brothers and sisters, we will be able to rise up to meet every difficult, trying and tempting situation with a mind that is well-prepared for Christ-like action, held tightly by God's gift of self-control and overflowing with the full hope that comes in trusting God's unfailing love and eternal promises! Be Prepared!

Do I believe it?
And if I do, what am I going to do about it?

Lord, please let me hear your voice, your love, your wisdom, your grace and truth.

GOT GRACE? GOT GRACE EFFECTS?

Not long ago a Scripture really jumped out at me, and I thought to myself, what a great inscription for my epitaph. No, I am not being morbid, nor am I making an announcement about my impending death. However, I will say that the freedom of living without the fear of death because of our Lord Jesus Christ, does make dealing with the reality of my future death a whole heck of a lot easier to accept!

The Scripture for my possible epitaph?

By the grace of God I am what I am,
and his grace to me was not without effect.
1 Corinthians 15:10

By the grace of God I am what I am. And what I know *I am* is:
a forgiven sinner.
a new creation.
a temple for God's Spirit.
a servant of God.
a child of God.
a friend of God.
a citizen of heaven.
an ambassador of Christ.
an oak of righteousness.
a warrior.
a sheep.
a member of the Body of Christ and His royal priesthood and His holy nation.
a work in progress that God will bring to completion.

God's grace to me was not without effect. God's grace, God's eternally effective, powerfully transforming grace, is the deep and all-consuming truth of which I am convinced. God's grace changed everything in my life. God's grace changed me.
I was broken – I am healed.
I was in bondage – I am set free.
I was fearful – I am courageous.
I planned death – God planned life.
I was hatefully treated – I forgave.
I hated – I love.

So, in my life (and possibly on my epitaph) I want it known and I want to proclaim – all for the praise and glory of our Lord Jesus Christ:

By the grace of God I am what I am,
and his grace to me was not without effect.
1 Corinthians 15:10

How about you? Got Grace? Got Grace Effects? Got an idea for your living epitaph?

Reflections – Responses – Challenges – Encouragements – God-breathing Thoughts

Do I believe it?
And if I do, what am I going to do about it?

Lord, please let me hear your voice, your love, your wisdom, your grace and truth.

TRANSFORMED BY GRACE!

Transformed by grace! For each of us who has placed our trust in Jesus Christ as our Savior, that's what we are. Transformed by grace! Well, that's what we are from the eternal plane and perspective, from God's view of us, anyway.

> *For God has rescued us from the dominion of darkness*
> *and brought us into the kingdom of the Son he loves,*
> *in whom we have redemption, the forgiveness of sins.*
> Colossians 1:13-14

Wow! Take a minute. Now take a few more, and think about what this means. Really means.

Through the love and sacrifice of our Lord Jesus Christ, we have been rescued out of the captivity and condemnation of the dominion of darkness. We have been brought fully and safely into the presence of, and into a restored and reconciled relationship with, our Eternal Holy King. We are fully forgiven. We are brought fully to life as a child of the Living God – for now and for all eternity. We are transformed by grace!

Does this rescue, does this eternal transformation, really change anything for me in the here and now? Does it change how I think? How I speak? How I act? How I interact with others – with all others? Does it change how and what I do in public? Does it change how and what I do in private? Would anyone be able to see that I've been rescued and transformed by grace?

Does Jesus really make a difference in who I am? Does who I am in Jesus make a difference to those around me? Do I look and act transformed? How deep is this transformation in my life? Does it only go to my superficial level? To my comfort level? To my go to church, offer my tithe, say some prayers, read my Bible level? Or does this radical, outrageous act of Jesus dying on the cross to rescue me from the dominion of darkness transform me in radical, outrageous ways?

> *I urge you, brothers and sisters, in view of God's mercy,*
> *to offer your bodies as a living sacrifice,*
> *holy and pleasing to God – this is your true and proper worship.*
> *Do not conform [any longer] to the pattern of this world,*
> *but be transformed by the renewing of your mind.*
> Romans 12:1-2

We each have a choice to make as to how we will respond to the mercy of God – how we will respond to the radical, outrageous love of Jesus Christ that rescued us from the dominion of darkness in order to bring us to Himself and His eternal kingdom. And we have to make these mercy-of-God response choices every single day, and many times throughout the day. Will we let the truth that we have been transformed – and will continually be transformed – by grace make any true and living difference in the way we live our lives?

What choices are you making in your thoughts, words and actions and in your relationships that are keeping you from living out the full truth that you have been rescued from the dominion of darkness? Let God assure you of His radical, outrageous love for you. God only and always wants the very best for you. And being transformed by grace is God's most radical, outrageous work of love in our lives!

Reflections – Responses – Challenges – Encouragements – God-breathing Thoughts

Do I believe it?
And if I do, what am I going to do about it?

Lord, please let me hear your voice, your love, your wisdom, your grace and truth.

IT DOESN'T HAVE TO BE BIG. OUR GOD IS!

A tangible act of love and kindness – no matter how small it may seem to you – can be used in a big way by our very big God!

> *"The King will reply, 'Truly I tell you, whatever you did*
> *for one of the least of these brothers and sisters of mine,*
> *you did for me.' "*
> Matthew 25:40

It doesn't have to be big. Our God is! God is able to take every gesture, word and action that reflect His character of love and kindness and touch the hearts of others in immeasurable ways. Think of some of those ways that God has touched you in big ways through the small, loving, kind acts of another. I cannot even begin to tell all the ways that I have been touched by the loving, kind acts of others over my lifetime. But! Here are just a few:

The simple, spoken and written, encouragements that some of my teachers gave me as they saw something in me that no one in my family saw or was willing to acknowledge.

The friend and her family who shared the love of Jesus, great afternoon snacks and so much of their precious time with me.

The Pastor who met with me after school, to go through the required lessons, so that I could walk myself down the church aisle to be baptized at age 13.

The two older couples at church who always made an effort to speak and laugh with me, and make me feel loved as a young teenager who came to church on my own.

The woman who was courageous enough to challenge me to obey God's command to forgive all who had caused me horrendous pain and warped my early life.

The boy who befriended me (a crazy, hurting, Jesus-loving girl) and trusted God enough to marry me. Okay. Maybe this one's not so small. Happy Anniversary, my Timmy!

The friends who traveled for hours to visit and pray with my mom when she was dying, even though they had never met her.

The friends who made chocolate-chip brownies for my daughter's kindergarten birthday party so I could stay a little longer with my mom during one of her last days on this earth.

The friend who walked with me for hours while I sobbed over a deeply painful rejection.

The friends who talked me into keeping a manicure appointment I couldn't afford, then sneakily went and paid for it so I could "feel like me" for a speaking engagement I had.

The friend who created special music CDs to remind me of deep times of ministry.

Every meal ever made for my family during hard times of mourning, illness and injury.

Each note, email, text, call, visit, smile and hug that came to me at just the right time.

Each prayer ever prayed for me by another.

Small gestures, maybe. Small cost to the giver, probably. But, these and so many other small gifts of love and kindness given by so many precious people have had a big impact on me and on the direction my life has taken. I was "one of the least of these." But, not to God. And God used each of these seemingly small gifts of love and kindness to assure me of just how big He is, and how big His love for me is! What was done for me was done for Jesus. And I am so very, very thankful. And so is Jesus.

May we each be ever more aware of those around us and choose to touch their lives, and the heart of Jesus, with tangible acts of love and kindness. It doesn't have to be big. Our God is!

Do I believe it?
And if I do, what am I going to do about it?

Lord, please let me hear your voice, your love, your wisdom, your grace and truth.

SHOUT! PSALM 100 – part 1

What makes you shout? Your kids? Your spouse? Your job? Your co-workers? Watching your favorite team blow the game? Driving alongside all those crazy people on the road?

Most of us probably need to change up the things that make us shout! We need to get focused on shouting about what, and shouting in the way, our Lord wants us to shout!

Shout for joy to the LORD, all the earth!
Psalm 100:1

Our Lord wants us to shout for joy to Him! Unfortunately, we all too quickly, and way too often, think about all the things and people that make us angry, frustrated, sad and hurt. All those things and people that make us shout (or growl, or groan or curse or...)!

Oh! We so need to get over ourselves! (And, yes! I am speaking directly to myself!) Because the Lord is good. And the Lord loves us with an unimaginable and eternal love. Our Lord offers us a life of peace, strength, courage and hope – right now on this side of heaven – as we trust Him with our lives and choose to love and obey Him.

So, how can we get ourselves to the mind-focused, heart-held place where we will honestly and more freely choose to shout for joy to our Lord?

Choose to think about the wonders of life and all that we have been given by our God!
Choose to think about everyone and everything that brings us joy – even in small ways!
Choose to think about our Lord's ultimate sacrifice of His Son Jesus to forgive our sins!
Choose to think about our Lord's boundless power through the resurrection of Jesus that promises eternal life to all who believe!
Choose to think about who our Lord is!
Choose to think about who we are in Him – holy and dearly loved children, redeemed, rescued, transformed, ambassadors, and co-heirs with Jesus Christ!
Choose to think about all those times when the Lord was weaving together circumstances, people and events in your life – all for your very best, and for His good and eternal purposes.
Choose to think about our Lord's unfailing, inseparable love and constant presence with all of us, at all times!

As we think about our Lord's love, kindness, mercy, grace and outrageous generosity to us, we should each be filled with wonder, with awe, with thankfulness and with joy! Offering sincere, joy-filled thanks to our Lord is just one simple way – though powerful and mind-transforming – to show our love to our Lord and Heavenly Abba!

Our joy, our love and our thanks to our Lord should flow more and more freely and naturally from us as we grow in the knowledge of who our Lord truly is and how greatly He loves us! In spite of who we truly are. Our Lord is the Almighty God! Our Lord is the Eternal God of all of life! Our Lord is the Holy One over all of creation! We are here, we breathe, and we live only because of the love, each life-breath and every provision given to us by our Lord!

Now, that's something to shout about! So! Go ahead! *Shout for joy to the Lord, all the earth!* And that goes for all of us on this earth! *Shout!* With a whole lot of thankfulness!

Reflections – Responses – Challenges – Encouragements – God-breathing Thoughts

Do I believe it?
And if I do, what am I going to do about it?

Lord, please let me hear your voice, your love, your wisdom, your grace and truth.

WORSHIP! PSALM 100 – part 2

What comes to your mind when you think of the word worship?

Does going to a church service come to mind? Does a favorite hymn or a modern-day praise song? Does reading and receiving a teaching on a Scripture passage, or a liturgical reading, come to mind? Does bowing your head in solemn prayer or lifting your hands in praise? Does giving your tithe or taking communion come to mind?

What is worship to you? To me? What we really need to ask and understand – and live out – is: What is worship to our God? What kind of worship from us is meaningful to our Lord? After all, it is our Lord who is receiving our worship.

> *Worship the LORD with gladness; come before him with joyful songs.*
> Psalm 100:2

Our Lord is the One True God, Creator, Life-Giver, Sovereign, Eternal, Holy, Perfect, Provider, Wonderful Counselor, Mighty God, Everlasting Father and Prince of Peace. Our Lord is our Help, Healer, Hope, Shepherd and Savior. Our Lord is the Way and the Truth and the Life. Our Lord is Love. Our Lord cannot be put into a box or kept on a shelf where we can pull Him out once a week – or even two or three times each week – to worship Him.

Our Lord broke through all barriers and boundaries of time and space. He broke through all of our limited abilities to comprehend what is incomprehensible: That our Holy God entered into our time and space to reveal His love for us – His outrageous, all-encompassing, saving, transforming love. Our Lord shatters all concepts of what love is. Jesus Christ is absolutely radical, passionate, persistent, self-sacrificing and death-conquering in His love for us!

Oh! May our eyes, hearts, minds and spirits respond to our Lord's love in such a way that we will worship Him as He desires and deserves! Jesus told us what our Heavenly Father truly desires from His children as we worship Him:

> *"...a time is coming and has now come when the true worshipers will worship the Father*
> *in the Spirit and in truth, for they are the kind of worshipers the Father seeks.*
> *God is spirit, and his worshipers must worship in the Spirit and in truth."*
> John 4:23-24

As we worship our Lord in the Spirit and in truth, we will be moved to love Him and love those around us by choosing to:

> *...stop doing wrong. Learn to do right; seek justice. Defend the oppressed.*
> *Take up the cause of the fatherless; plead the case of the widow.*
> Isaiah 1:16, 17

So, come, and worship the Lord! And sing with your whole life as you live for Him!

> *Worship the LORD with gladness; come before him with joyful songs.*
> Psalm 100:2

Reflections – Responses – Challenges – Encouragements – God-breathing Thoughts

Do I believe it?
And if I do, what am I going to do about it?

Lord, please let me hear your voice, your love, your wisdom, your grace and truth.

_____

_____

_____

_____

_____

_____

_____

_____

_____

_____

_____

_____

_____

_____

_____

_____

_____

_____

_____

_____

_____

_____

_____

KNOW! PSALM 100 – part 3

So, what do you *know*?

Growing up I often heard my Grandpa greet his friends and customers (he sold Watkins Products in his later years) with that phrase, "So, what do you *know*?" instead of the more usual, "Hello! How are you?"

I thought it was a pretty funny way to greet somebody, but I was always curious to hear how his friends and customers, especially the old-timers, would answer that question. Some did so seriously, some with a bit of news, some with a bit of humor:
"The old arthritis is kickin' up a bit." "Fishin's good right now." "I'm still alive, and that's darn good to know!" "Spectin' more rain soon." "Hazel's feeling better now after doin' so poorly all winter." "I'm still better lookin' than you. Always will be."

So, what do you *know*? What do I *know*? Whatever it is – whether it is knowledge we have gained from earning a PhD in Nuclear Physics or knowledge we have gained through years of playing rip-roaring games of Tic-Tac-Toe – it pales in comparison to what our God wants us to know. And what we need to know.

> *Know that the LORD is God.*
> *It is he who made us, and we are his;*
> *we are his people, the sheep of his pasture.*
> Psalm 100:3

Amazing. God wants us to know Him and know who we are to Him. The Lord our God is so completely sovereign over us and yet so incredibly intimate with us, all at the same time.

Do we live like we know that the Lord is God – the Holy One over all creation?
Do we live like we know that our very breath, our very life – and everything that we are as human beings – was given to us and made for us by the Lord our God?
Do we live like we know that we are the Lord's precious, deeply and eternally loved people?
Do we live like we know that we are not alone?
Do we live like we know that we truly belong to the Lord our God?
Do we live like we know that we have a place forever in the heart of our Heavenly Abba?
Do we live like we know that we are His sheep – and were made to follow Him?
Do we live like we know that He is our Shepherd, Savior, Leader, King, Provider, Protector?
Do we live like we know that living in the truth that our God is always with us, always loving us – no matter what we may be experiencing – is our safe pasture?

Knowledge truly is power, divine power, when it comes to knowing that the Lord is God!

> *God's divine power has given us everything we need for [life and godliness] a godly life*
> *through our knowledge of him who called us by his own glory and goodness.*
> 2 Peter 1:3

May the Lord our God reveal to each of us – through His Word and by His Holy Spirit – a fuller, deeper knowledge of who He is and who we are to Him! And may each of us choose to live our lives empowered and led by this God-given, life-transforming knowledge!

Reflections – Responses – Challenges – Encouragements – God-breathing Thoughts

Do I believe it?
And if I do, what am I going to do about it?

Lord, please let me hear your voice, your love, your wisdom, your grace and truth.

ENTER! PSALM 100 – part 4

Enter Here! Have you seen those helpful signs in parking lots or on business and private doors that clearly mark the entrance? My doctor's office now takes up one whole side of a building that had once been several different offices. On my first visit to her newly renovated office space, I was immediately confronted with a dilemma. I needed to make a decision: Through which of the five doors should I enter? It was so confusing! Nothing marked the entryway.

I am so thankful that when it comes to our God, He not only tells us where to enter, He also tells us how to enter!

Enter his gates with thanksgiving and his courts with praise;
give thanks to him and praise his name.
Psalm 100:4

Our Lord is saying to us, *"Come right on in! Come into My holy presence! Enter right through the front door – through the front gates – of My temple, the temple of the Lord Most High! Enter into My courts! Come on in! Enter here! I want you with Me!"*

What an unfathomable invitation and welcome we have been given by the Lord our God! Our Lord is calling us to enter into His intimate presence. Enter here!

Yet, we must always remember that our Lord is not only intimate with us, but He is also, and forever, the Sovereign Lord over all creation, over all eternity. And in His sovereignty, our Lord calls us to enter into His intimacy with our hearts, minds and spirits full of praise and thanksgiving for who He is as the Lord our God!

Each time that we choose to enter into the presence of our Holy God with thanksgiving and praise, it is actually our God who lifts us up from all that may be weighing us down and weighing heavily on our hearts, minds and spirits. Our God does not need us to give Him thanks and praise. God knows who He is. There is absolutely no insecurity or any egotistical motive behind our God asking us to enter into His sovereign and intimate presence with thanksgiving and praise. Rather, our God is fully and only motivated by His deep and unfailing love for us. Our God knows that there is great power and deep hope, full healing and renewed perspective for each of us as we take the time to give our Lord our thanks and praise – even in our times of pain and confusion, frustration and fear.

As we lift our eyes off our own self-absorbed, problem-focused thinking and onto our Lord with thanksgiving and praise, we are lifted away from everything that would consume us and diminish us. We are lifted high and held lovingly and safely in the Everlasting Arms of Abba – our Sovereign and Intimate God! Each and every thing that the Lord asks of us, and every way that the Lord asks us to do anything, always flows from His incomprehensible love for us. Our God wants our very best for us at all times. Our God loves us perfectly, and this will never change.

Enter where? Right through the gates and into the holy presence of our Intimate Lord!
Enter how? With hearts full of thanksgiving and praise for who our Sovereign Lord is!

Enter here! Enter now! And we will enter into a greater joy, a deeper trust and a sweeter peace as we enter into the loving presence of our Sovereign and Intimate Lord!

Do I believe it?
And if I do, what am I going to do about it?

Lord, please let me hear your voice, your love, your wisdom, your grace and truth.

THE LORD IS…! PSALM 100 – part 5

Do you believe the Lord is good? Do you believe that God's love and faithfulness are infinite and eternal? These are not questions to be asked, or answered, lightly, or in an unexamined way. Take some time to think about what you honestly believe about the Lord our God.

What each of us really thinks, what each of us really believes about God – or doesn't think or doesn't believe about God – is probably the single, greatest influence over all of our lives. Over our attitudes, our words, our actions, our interactions and our relationships.

> *For the LORD is good and his love endures forever;*
> *his faithfulness continues through all generations.*
> Psalm 100:5

Does our perspective about the Lord's goodness, love and faithfulness change based on our differing moods on any given day? Do our beliefs about the Lord's character fluctuate with all the different circumstances and experiences we go through on this side of heaven?

There may be many of us who are able to say with our mouths, and maybe even with our minds, that the Lord is good, loving and faithful. Yet, within our innermost beings, within the depths of our hearts, we cannot truly latch on to this God-proclaimed truth as a personal reality. At least not fully.

God understands our struggles to see Him with the eyes of our hearts as the good, loving and faithful God He is, when the realities of this world too easily and too often break our hearts. God gives us both whispers and shouts of His goodness, love and faithfulness all around us. We need to look around, yes, even in the midst of our most troubling times – to know Him and His character. Come hear and see God's goodness, love and faithfulness:
The sun rose this morning.
The beauty and life seen in the sky both day and night.
The provision from the earth and the beauty and sustenance that spring from it.
The power and life that flow through the waters – the oceans, lakes, rivers and streams.
The diverse majesty of earth's landscape – the mountains, hills, plains, canyons and deserts.
The magnificence and wonder of every living being – human, animal and plant.
The smile of a stranger.
The greeting of a friend.
The kindness of a neighbor.
The belly-laugh you just couldn't contain.
The music that lifts your heart and makes your feet dance.
The prayers and comfort, encouragement and support of those who care.
The very breath you are now breathing.

And revelation after revelation of God's unchanging character and eternal nature are made known to us through the entirety of His Word! Either God is true or He is not. Either God's Word revealed to us is true or it is not. A choice needs to be made about what we really believe about our Lord. God, tenderly and compassionately, understands our struggles in this broken world, and how our limited, temporal-bound view and self-focused thinking make it difficult to know and trust Him. Our God also knows that it is when we let our hearts and minds together take the leap of faith and choose to trust God at His Word, that we will know that our Lord truly is good, loving and faithful! Trust that! Believe that! And watch the truth of our God powerfully transform our attitudes, our words, our actions, our interactions, our relationships – and all of our lives!

Do I believe it?
And if I do, what am I going to do about it?

Lord, please let me hear your voice, your love, your wisdom, your grace and truth.

GOD'S ULTIMATE FASHION MAKEOVER

Do you have any clothes in your closet or dresser drawers that you've had for a really long time? And that you still wear regularly? Maybe these clothes have some special significance or comfort for you. Maybe they've just weathered the passing of time exceptionally well. Maybe they've never gone out of fashion or, at least, not out of your sense of fashion!

I have a few long-lasting favorites of my own. A silk blouse and a dressy sweater – both of these I've had since 1987 from when we lived in France. Another favorite is my Mickey Mouse sweatshirt I got on our first trip to Disney Land after moving from France to Southern California in 1988. (I didn't realize then that we'd be back to Disney Land for a total of seven times over the next two years with our two little girls and lots of guests!)

As amazingly well as these three articles of clothing have stood the test of time (and some very major life-changes), there is nothing more lasting than the eternally-enduring clothing – our Spiritual Wardrobe – that our Holy God and Heavenly Father has designed for us who have put our lives into His loving hands.

> *Therefore, as God's chosen people, holy and dearly loved,*
> *clothe yourselves with compassion, kindness,*
> *humility, gentleness and patience.*
> *Bear with each other and forgive one another*
> *if any of you have a grievance against someone.*
> *Forgive as the Lord forgave you.*
> *And over all these virtues put on love,*
> *which binds them all together in perfect unity.*
> Colossians 3:12-14

You've probably heard it said, "The clothing makes the man." Well, our God has beautifully fashioned the perfect clothing, the perfect holy covering, that will *re-make* every man, woman and child who belong to Him. God has perfectly and powerfully designed the Ultimate Fashion Makeover for each of us who are His children!

Our God begins our Ultimate Fashion Makeover from the inside out. And it lasts for all eternity. We just have to be willing to stay in God's hands and hold still long enough to let God fully dress our minds, hearts, spirits and characters – each and every day – in His powerfully transforming, holy and eternal clothing.

God's fashions are meant to fashion each of us into the very likeness and beautiful reflection of His Son, our Lord and Savior Jesus Christ. Clothed with the very character of our Holy Lord – clothed in His compassion, kindness, humility, gentleness, patience, forgiveness and love – we will reflect Christ's beauty, and assure all those around us that our God is present with us, passionate about us and powerful through us!

So, what are you wearing? Is it time for you to invite our God to do an Ultimate Fashion Makeover in your life – right from your innermost being out? Our Lord has just the perfect outfit for each of us. And over the years, the fabric God uses for our eternal, Jesus-like makeover will only become stronger and more beautiful! What a statement His clothing will make on us!

COME ON! WE DO KNOW!

Have you ever wondered what God is asking you to do as His follower, as His child, and as His ambassador in this world? Have you ever thrown your arms up in confusion or exasperation with the people around you because you're just not sure how you're supposed to act around them? How you're supposed to interact with them? Some of these people are easy to interact with and we feel comfortable, and even confident, around them. Then there are those other people who are so much more challenging or annoying to us. And still others whose habits and lifestyles we can't even begin to fathom or feel comfortable around. What does God want from us then?

Come on! We do know! In absolute clarity, and in a fabulously sword-to-the-heart-of-the-matter directive, our God does not in any way cloud or hide His greatest command and call on our lives when it comes to what we are to do as His followers and how we are to interact with others – all others! Our God has made it perfectly clear throughout His Word!

Love the LORD your God with all your heart
and with all your soul and with all your strength.
Deuteronomy 6:5

"...love your neighbor as yourself. I am the LORD."
Leviticus 19:18

"...love your enemies, do good to them."
Luke 6:35

"My command is this: Love each other as I have loved you."
John 15:12

"This is my command: Love each other."
John 15:17

Follow God's example, therefore, as dearly loved children
and walk in the way of love [live a life of love], just as Christ loved us
and gave himself up for us as a fragrant offering and sacrifice to God.
Ephesians 5:1-2

Dear friends, since God so loved us, we also ought to love one another.
1 John 4:11

Love must be sincere.
Romans 12:9

So, come on! We do know! Our God has made it perfectly clear throughout His Word!

Let's each choose to actively and intentionally love others, even our enemies, with the grace and the truth, the compassion and the forgiveness, the power and the possibilities that come only through the love of our Lord and Savior Jesus Christ!

Do I believe it?
And if I do, what am I going to do about it?

Lord, please let me hear your voice, your love, your wisdom, your grace and truth.

KNOWING LIFE! KNOWING JOY!

We come to know and believe something or someone because someone has told us, taught us or testified to us about that something or someone. Or we come to know and believe something or someone because we have had direct experience with that something or someone for ourselves.

The Apostle John really knew Jesus. And John had a passion to tell us about Jesus, His Lord! He knew the flesh-and-blood man Jesus. He knew Jesus the Risen Lord. He knew that Jesus was One with the Eternal God, One as the Living Word, One as the Son with the Father and the Spirit. And John wanted everyone to know Jesus, and to know the life and the joy that Jesus is, and that Jesus alone offers.

> *That which was from the beginning, which we have heard,*
> *which we have seen with our eyes, which we have looked at*
> *and our hands have touched – this we proclaim*
> *concerning the Word of life.*
> *The life appeared; we have seen it and testify to it,*
> *and we proclaim to you the eternal life,*
> *which was with the Father and has appeared to us.*
> *We proclaim to you what we have seen and heard,*
> *so that you also may have fellowship with us.*
> *And our fellowship is with the Father and with his Son, Jesus Christ.*
> *We write this to make our joy complete.*
> 1 John 1:1-4

For John, knowing Jesus was knowing life and knowing joy! John had such joy in knowing Jesus, and his passionate heart would not be completely full of joy until others also knew – and believed – that Jesus is the Eternal God, the Eternal Life and the Living Word.

Although we cannot physically see, hear or touch Jesus as John did, we can know the truth of who Jesus is. He is the Living, Eternal Word of God – present with us now and for all eternity. Our Lord Jesus makes Himself known to us through the testimony of His Word, through the testimony of His Holy Spirit and through the testimony of others.

We can know the truth of Jesus for ourselves in deep and life-transforming, hope and peace-bringing, very real ways as we see, hear and touch the testimony that Jesus gives to each of us as we trust our lives over to His care. As we grow in trusting Jesus with our daily-day experiences and with all the highs and lows we experience in the different seasons of our lives, we will get to know Jesus personally and intimately and know the joy that He brings.

John tells us that his joy will be complete when we know Jesus as the Life. And! I can assure you that knowing Jesus for who He is for yourself will bring more joy – deeper, higher, truer joy – to you than you can possibly imagine!

If you know Jesus already as the Living Word of God and as the Eternal Life given for you – Give Thanks! And share with others the joy you know in knowing Jesus – so that your joy and their joy may be complete!

Do I believe it?
And if I do, what am I going to do about it?

Lord, please let me hear your voice, your love, your wisdom, your grace and truth.

BEING EFFECTIVE AND PRODUCTIVE

Being Effective and Productive. Hmmmmm? Those aren't exactly the first words that jump to the top of my mind when I think about the transformation that takes place in each of our lives because of God's astounding act of love on our behalf – the death and resurrection of our Lord Jesus Christ.

Yet, in our relationship and in our fellowship with Jesus, in our knowledge of Him and in what He has given to us through His Spirit and His Word, this is exactly what we are to become. Effective and productive. We were created in the image of the Lord Most High to be people of purpose – and our God intends for each of us to become effective and productive in the deepest, truest, most constantly increasing and most eternal way possible as we…

> ***…participate in the divine nature*** [of Jesus Christ].
> 2 Peter 1:4

> ***For this very reason, make every effort to add to your faith goodness;***
> ***and to goodness, knowledge;***
> ***and to knowledge, self-control;***
> ***and to self-control, perseverance;***
> ***and to perseverance, godliness;***
> ***and to godliness, mutual affection [kindness];***
> ***and to mutual affection [kindness], love.***
> ***For if you possess these qualities in increasing measure,***
> ***they will keep you from being ineffective and unproductive***
> ***in your knowledge of our Lord Jesus Christ.***
> ***But whoever does not have them***
> ***is nearsighted and blind,***
> ***forgetting that they have been cleansed from their past sins.***
> 2 Peter 1:5-9

There is no limitation to how Jesus is able to transform us, with ever increasing measure, to be more like Him in our nature, in our thoughts, words, actions and interactions.

The divine nature of Christ called us into existence – into life – in the first place.

The divine nature of Christ declares to us, and reminds us of, all our Lord Jesus has done for us through His love, His merciful forgiveness of our sins and His gift of eternal life.

The divine nature of Christ gives us everything we need to live out this life, right here and right now, as His effective and productive followers (2 Peter 1:3).

The divine nature of Christ gives us the purpose and the power to be effective and productive ambassadors of Christ (2 Corinthians 5:20; Ephesians 3:20-21).

The divine nature of Christ continually fills us, increases in us and flows through us with His eternally effective and productive qualities of faith, goodness, knowledge, self-control, perseverance, godliness, kindness and love.

May each of us seek to reflect the divine nature of Christ in all circumstances, with all people – as His transformed people, effective and productive, now and for all eternity!

Reflections – Responses – Challenges – Encouragements – God-breathing Thoughts

Do I believe it?
And if I do, what am I going to do about it?

Lord, please let me hear your voice, your love, your wisdom, your grace and truth.

DON'T FORFEIT THE GRACE!

Those who cling to worthless idols [forfeit the grace that could be theirs]
turn away from God's love for them.
...Salvation comes from the LORD.
Jonah 2:8-9

What might you, what might I, be clinging to as worthless idols? What is that something that we may be clinging to on which we base our identity or our security or our happiness or our purpose?

For most of us, in our current times, our idols probably do not look like the idols of ancient pagan worship or superstitious practices. Although, they certainly could.

More likely, our idol may be our need to gain wealth for wealth's sake, well beyond our need and well beyond our giving. Our idol may be our desire to gather material evidence (things and stuff), from cars to collectibles, as a display of our financial strength or our depth of focused interest and expertise. Our idol may be having, and making others aware of, the various experiences we've had or the higher educational degrees we've earned. Our idol may be the need to exert our power over others – blatantly or subtly, cruelly or manipulatively – to keep our identity as the one to be respected, as the one in authority. Our idols may not even be clearly recognized by us, but we still cling to them. These idols are often held onto as unhealthy, imbalanced identities of ourselves such as: seeing ourselves always as a victim of hurts and handicaps, circumstances and choices (made by others, of course); or as a martyr, constantly sacrificing our personal wants and needs (but without the joy in the giving); or as the smart one or the beautiful one, as the cool one or the popular one; or as the ever-happy talker who needs to be the life of the party, the center of attention; or as the introverted recluse who chooses to hide in his own thoughts and solo-activities, not engaging with others – partly out of timidity, partly out of apathy; or as the wise and wonderful super-hero who always has just the right words and right ways to help others, but is unwilling to show any personal vulnerability.

We each need to invite God into our hearts and minds to help us recognize and acknowledge any and every idol to which we may be clinging. We need to ask God for His loving, purifying, strength-giving help to tear down and rip away these idols that truly bring nothing to our lives. All idols only warp and ruin, diminish and destroy – in our own eyes and in the eyes of others – our true identity as a child of God and the eternal security we have in Jesus Christ our Lord.

If we are clinging to anything other than the Lord our God who loves us, if we are clinging to anything other than the salvation that comes through Jesus Christ alone, then we are clinging to worthless idols. And it just isn't worth it!

Nothing is worth forfeiting the grace of our Lord. Nothing. It is our Holy, Loving Lord who alone gives us life, now and for all eternity. It is our Holy, Loving Lord who alone gives us our true identity, true love, true joy, true peace, true wisdom, true healing, true strength, true security, true riches and true honor.

Clinging onto our Lord, and allowing our Lord to cling onto us, is the only way to know and live in God's loving, transforming grace! Don't ever forfeit that! God's grace is life itself!

Do I believe it?
And if I do, what am I going to do about it?

Lord, please let me hear your voice, your love, your wisdom, your grace and truth.

unlimited

June 18

HERE COMES TROUBLE!

"Uh, oh! Here comes trouble!"

Have you ever had anyone say that about you as you were approaching? I have, and possibly many more have thought it! A number of times I heard it humorously from my Grandpa or from one of his old-timer friends when I came to visit him at his assisted living apartment and, then, later when visiting him at the nursing home. "Uh, oh! Here comes trouble!" Grandpa and his buddies would say it to see if they could get a bit of a rise out of me. Or they would say it to tease me about how fast I *might* have driven during the two-hour trip (which often took me significantly less time) from my home to Grandpa's place.

However, there have been a number of occasions for me, and probably for many of you, when, because of our faith in the Almighty God and as a servant of Jesus, we have been called to disturb the peace – to be a *troubler* – for the sake of God's love, grace and truth to be known to the people around us.

This was true for the prophet Elijah. King Ahab of Israel had tried to hunt down Elijah for some time, without any success. Elijah had courageously spoken out against the wrongs committed by the people of Israel and their leaders, all who were supposed to be the people of God. So, King Ahab wasn't exactly a big fan of Elijah. Ahab wanted to put a stop to all the trouble that Elijah was causing. Then one day, according to God's perfect timing and perfect plan, the Lord directed Elijah to go and present himself to his adversary King Ahab. (Yes! God can ask some pretty outrageous things of His followers!) The meeting and greeting between Ahab and Elijah went like this:

> **When Ahab saw Elijah, he said to him, "Is that you, you troubler of Israel?"**
>
> **"I have not made trouble for Israel," Elijah replied.**
> **"But you and your father's family have.**
> **You have abandoned the LORD's commands**
> **and have followed the Baals** *[false gods and idols].*"
> 1 Kings 18:17-18

God wants us to be His people. To be His light in this dark and broken world. And sometimes, God needs to send a *troubler* to shake us up. To wake us up spiritually so that we will follow our God, keep His commands and reflect God's love, grace and truth to others. Our Lord does all this *troubling* in our lives out of His incomprehensible love for us. Out of His deep desire to be in an intimately growing relationship with each one of us.

And sometimes, you or I may be the one called by God to approach others as the Lord's *troubler* – aka ambassador of Christ! Out of compassion for others and so that they would know the true love, salvation, hope, healing, peace, freedom and transformation that come from obeying the commands of our Almighty God, would we be willing to trust God enough to disturb the peace – to become a *troubler* – for the Lord? Even if it's uncomfortable? Even if the timing is not our timing? Even if we're likely to be ignored or misjudged by, at least, some of those with whom we are called to share God's words and ways?

So be it! *Here Comes Trouble!* When being a *troubler* comes from our Lord's call on us as His ambassadors, we need to follow and obey. And we can trust that *troubling* others with God's love, grace and truth is all for God's good, right and loving purposes in their lives.

Reflections – Responses – Challenges – Encouragements – God-breathing Thoughts

Do I believe it?
And if I do, what am I going to do about it?

Lord, please let me hear your voice, your love, your wisdom, your grace and truth.

ANONYMOUS LOVE

Some time ago I got some *Anonymous Love* sent to me. It came in the form of a card – a message mailed to my home. Not voice-mailed, not emailed, not texted, not facebooked, not tweeted, not blogged. (Although, love in each of these forms – through any delivery system, food and hugs included – is still fabulous and deeply appreciated love!)

The Anonymous Love Card was signed by "a servant and messenger of God" – and began with this phrase: "Your life shows what your words tell – that daily walking with God really makes all the difference."

It made me just stop. Really Stop. I was thankful. I was blessed by this gift of Anonymous Love. The message was such a kind and timely encouragement to me – as it was meant to be. (If the sender is reading this: *Thank you for taking the time to speak to my heart with such loving and powerful words from your heart and God's!)*

What also made me just stop – Really Stop – was that I was absolutely humbled by the reality that my open faith walk is being openly reviewed, openly watched, openly critiqued and openly tested by others for its authenticity. Of course, at one level, I know this – and have for a long time. I also know that this is exactly what should happen. We are "to test the spirits" (1 John 4:1). Still, it caught my attention. Not so much about being judged as authentic or not, but realizing that my words, actions and interactions may influence the way other precious people view God. That is a very humbling and challenging (and a little bit daunting) reality for me.

Oh! I am so thankful that *it is God* who is perfect love. *It is God* who is perfect goodness. Perfect presence. Perfect hope, joy and peace. Therefore, whenever and however God chooses to use me – in my brokenness, in my quirkiness, and in spite of the fact that I am frail, flawed and finite – I can be fully confident that *it will be God* who is seen and made known, and *it will be God* who makes every real and lasting difference in anyone's life! I just need to trust my God and point to Jesus! Just as others have done, and do, so for me – with their faithful words and ways and through their faithful lives.

So, yes, I am humbled and challenged as I think about the influence my faith walk can have on others. Yet, more than anything, I am thankful for the walk that Jesus chose to walk for each of us. Jesus walks with us as Immanuel – God with us, as the Holy Lamb of God – giving His life for the forgiveness of our sins, and as the Risen, Conquering King – giving us eternal life!

With all my heart, energy and life, I want everyone to know the love of Jesus and the very real and eternal difference He is able to make in each of our lives! There is nothing anonymous about the love of Jesus! He has given His all, for all to know, for all to receive. And our Lord wants us, as His ambassadors, to reflect the glory of His love to all those around us, and to be united, loving each other deeply, as we do this!

> *May the God who gives endurance and encouragement give you [a spirit of unity]*
> *the same attitude of mind toward each other that Christ Jesus had, so that with*
> *one mind and one voice you may glorify the God and Father of our Lord Jesus Christ.*
> Romans 15:5-6

Be encouraged! Be an encourager for Jesus! Anonymously or obviously, share His love!

Reflections – Responses – Challenges – Encouragements – God-breathing Thoughts

Do I believe it?
And if I do, what am I going to do about it?

Lord, please let me hear your voice, your love, your wisdom, your grace and truth.

GOD'S THUMBPRINT ON OUR HEARTS

...God has set eternity in the human heart;
yet no one can fathom what God has done from beginning to end.
Ecclesiastes 3:11

Amazing. Just think about that for a minute: *God has set eternity in each of our hearts*.

God purposefully, fearfully and wonderfully, formed each one of us with His thumbprint in our hearts. That *setting of eternity in our hearts* is experienced by us as a deep longing for *The Eternal*. That *setting of eternity in our hearts* is a persistent, inner awareness that life is meant to be lived for an eternity – to be lived far beyond this fleeting, mortal life we now experience. God's Thumbprint, God's *setting of eternity in our hearts,* is experienced by us as a profound yearning and a soul-level sensing – sometimes strong and clear, other times quiet and fleeting – that we belong to God, that we are loved by our Creator and we are not alone.

God made each one of us as His special creation. We each were created as loved and unique – right down to having our own unique set of fingerprints, thumbprints included, that match no one else who has ever lived, or ever will live, on this earth. And it is God's own unique Thumbprint on our hearts – that deep imprint of yearning within our innermost beings for eternity and for our God – that will only be matched by, and fulfilled through, the saving, transforming, eternal-life-giving love of our Lord Jesus Christ!

We cannot even begin to fathom what our God has planned and done from the beginning of time and, already counts as accomplished, for the end of time, as we know it. Our God is awesome and beyond comprehension in His wonder. Our God is eternal, and eternity is found only in Him!

Although we cannot fully comprehend or even begin to imagine what our eternal lives will look like or be like with our God, we do know the *way* and the *truth* about eternal *life*. Our Lord and Savior Jesus speaks it right into our hearts, where God has set eternity:

"Do not let your hearts be troubled. You believe in God; believe also in me.
My Father's house has many rooms; if that were not so,
would I have told you that I am going there to prepare a place for you?
And if I go and prepare a place for you, I will come back
and take you to be with me that you also may be where I am.
...I am the way and the truth and the life.
No one comes to the Father except through me."
John 14:1-4, 6

God made each one of us out of His inexplicable, unfathomable love. Our God sealed our formation with His own Thumbprint imprinted on our hearts so that we would always yearn for and, therefore, seek eternity and eternal life with our God. And our God not only set eternity in our hearts, our God also fully gave us His way and His truth by giving His life for our salvation. Our hearts, and all of our longings, are able to be fulfilled – beyond our imagination and our ability to fathom – through the eternal, life-giving love of our Lord Jesus Christ, who reaches out His own nail-scarred, holy hands to take us home for all eternity!

Reflections – Responses – Challenges – Encouragements – God-breathing Thoughts

Do I believe it?
And if I do, what am I going to do about it?

Lord, please let me hear your voice, your love, your wisdom, your grace and truth.

ASK! PASSIONATELY AND PERSISTENTLY!

Then Jesus said to them, "Suppose you have a friend, and you go to him at midnight and say, 'Friend, lend me three loaves of bread; a friend of mine on a journey has come to me, and I have no food to offer him.' And suppose the one inside answers, 'Don't bother me. The door is already locked, and my children and I are in bed. I can't get up and give you anything.' I tell you, even though he will not get up and give you the bread because of friendship, yet because of your shameless audacity he will surely get up and give you as much as you need. So I say to you: Ask and it will be given to you...For everyone who asks receives..."
Luke 11:5-10

Ask God. Ask God with faith and fervency, with passion and persistence. If what you are asking for comes from a heart that is seeking to offer love or welcome, kindness or compassion, help or hope, rest or refreshment to another – then what you are asking for lines up fully with the loving, welcoming, kind, compassionate, helpful, hope-filled, rest and refreshment-giving heart of our Holy Living Lord. Ask. And keep on asking. These prayers, this kind of asking, God loves to answer.

Are you coming to God on behalf of others? Asking God to woo them to Himself with His deep, unfailing and incomprehensible love? Asking God to open their hearts to His salvation and transformation? Are you asking God to let them know and experience His full freedom, deep peace, great joy, amazing wisdom and complete healing that come through an intimate love relationship with Jesus Christ? Are you coming to God asking for these same deep, life-renewing and transforming gifts for yourself?

Ask God. Ask God with faith and fervency, with passion and persistence. Our God, our Abba, knows that we are just like little children. We can't always (or hardly ever) see the full picture of what is truly best for us or lines up most perfectly with God's perfect and eternal perspective of our lives and the lives of those we love. Our God does not reject our sincere and heartfelt prayers. He knows we are little and unable to know all that He knows. The very act of asking our Abba for anything is showing Him that we know and believe He's the One who hears us and is able to answer us. When we come to God with that childlike faith, I absolutely believe our Abba is well pleased and looks on us with tenderness. We, like the little ones we are – even if we can't understand God's answers or seeming silence – must yield and trust that God will answer us, His beloved children, in the way He knows is absolutely best at the absolutely best time.

I have seen the gates of hell and the strongholds of sin stormed and destroyed in my own life and in the lives of many whom I love so very much. I, along with others, have relentlessly gone before our Holy God to plead for their salvation, healing, transformation and restoration. And God has shown Himself Mighty! God passionately and persistently loves us. God wants us to love others and love ourselves in such a way that we would be moved to ask God passionately and persistently to fully release His love and power of transforming grace and freeing truth into their lives and into ours.

So! Ask passionately and persistently for everything that would bring God's unfailing love, grace, truth and perfect will into your life and into the lives of others. Ask! And it will be given. That is God's Word. That is God's promise.

Do I believe it?
And if I do, what am I going to do about it?

Lord, please let me hear your voice, your love, your wisdom, your grace and truth.

WISDOM FROM GOD – AS TOLD BY A TRUCK

The other morning as I drove to work (always one of my special quiet times to pray), I was behind a large truck for quite some time. Within a bright yellow background across the back panel of this truck was written one word in big, bold, black letters: THINK.

THINK. Nothing else was written. Just THINK. And so I did. And as I started thinking, I was first reminded of what God tells us about His own thoughts and ways:

> *"For my thoughts are not your thoughts,*
> *neither are your ways my ways," declares the LORD.*
> *"As the heavens are higher than the earth,*
> *so are my ways higher than your ways*
> *and my thoughts than your thoughts."*
> Isaiah 55:8-9

And through the Apostle Paul, our God tells us what we should put our time, energy and effort into thinking about:

> *Finally, brothers and sisters,*
> *whatever is true,*
> *whatever is noble,*
> *whatever is right,*
> *whatever is pure,*
> *whatever is lovely,*
> *whatever is admirable*
> *– if anything is excellent or praiseworthy –*
> *think about such things.*
> Philippians 4:8

As we choose, intentionally and actively, to *think about such things*, our thoughts, attitudes and perspective will be lifted out of, and away from, our own worry and hurt, our busyness and frustration, our sense of entitlement and our self-centered focus. When we make an effort to think about whatever is true, noble, right, pure, lovely, admirable, excellent and praiseworthy, our thoughts are lifted higher and closer to the thoughts of our God. It is then that we, more quickly and more often, will have our minds filled with the things that really matter in the grand scheme of eternity: Life itself. Every breath we are given. The people we love. The people who love us. Every moment and experience, every encounter and revelation we have that give us a sense of God's love and peace, God's hope and kindness, God's goodness and mercy, God's beauty and magnificence – with us and around us.

As we choose, intentionally and actively, to *think about such things*, so, too, will our ways – our words, actions, reactions and interactions – be lifted higher and closer to the ways of our God. All that we spend more and more of our time, energy and effort thinking about will be clearly reflected in all that we do.

Let's THINK! Let's be deeply transformed into the likeness of our Lord and Savior Jesus – in our innermost being and in our outermost expression.

Ahhhhh! Such wisdom from God – as told by a truck!

Reflections – Responses – Challenges – Encouragements – God-breathing Thoughts

Do I believe it?
And if I do, what am I going to do about it?

Lord, please let me hear your voice, your love, your wisdom, your grace and truth.

LET ALL BLINDNESS FALL AWAY!

Do you know anyone who is blind or seriously visually impaired? They may function amazingly well and live quite independently in spite of the significant challenges and limitations they must deal with every day. Still, the fact remains: They are not able to see clearly, if they're able to see anything at all.

That fact puts those who are blind and seriously visually impaired in a far greater risk of danger if something or someone were to come unexpectedly into their presence or onto their path that they cannot see, or that they are ill-equipped to avoid or even recognize. Likewise, those without clear vision could also be a serious danger to others if they were to choose to ignore the presence of the people around them, pushing right through on their own determined paths in a self-focused, sightless, insensitive way. And there are certain activities, like driving a car, that those without sight should never do at any time. (At least not until a robotics or self-driving car is perfected!) There is neither any excuse for acting in such wrongful and foolish ways, nor is it possible to avoid the pain and suffering that would affect all involved when the inevitable crash comes.

We, too, can be blind or, at least, seriously visually impaired – spiritually, emotionally and relationally – when it comes to having a clear perspective on how our self-focused, sightless, and insensitive words and actions can cause serious damage to the lives of those around us, and to our own lives. It is, sadly and most often, upon those with whom our lives are most closely bound, those we claim to love the very most – our husbands, wives, children, parents, siblings and friends – that our blinded perspective wields its greatest chaos and destructive damage. Our God does not want us to be blind any longer, in any way – not spiritually, emotionally or relationally – to Him, to others or to ourselves!

"I will lead the blind by ways they have not known,
along unfamiliar paths I will guide them;
I will turn the darkness into light before them
And make the rough places smooth.
These are the things I will do;
I will not forsake them."
Isaiah 42:16

Our God reaches out to lead us and guide us on new, unknown and unfamiliar paths. Oh! But we don't have to fear! These paths are fully known to and planned by our Holy God! These paths bring healing and freedom, wisdom and peace to our lives – and clearer sight to our spiritual, emotional and relational eyes. God will bring the light of His grace and truth to us – washing away the darkness of our sin and shame. God will make our rough places smooth (those rough places in life where we cannot bear to take another step) as we trust Him and His promise to walk with us and to never forsake us. And God will make the rough places within us smooth – by exposing our self-centered seeing and behaving to His light so that our own inner darkness will be burned away, and we will be set free. Walking on God's paths will open our eyes and our hearts more and more fully to our God's unfailing love for us. As we see and know God's great love for us more clearly, we will more readily open our eyes to those around us and offer greater love, kindness, mercy and compassion to them.

Ahhhhh! Let all blindness fall away as we trust our God to lead us in His light and love!

Do I believe it?
And if I do, what am I going to do about it?

Lord, please let me hear your voice, your love, your wisdom, your grace and truth.

THE WHO AND THE WHAT OF GOD – WISDOM

The more I get to know God through His Word and His Spirit, the more I understand and experience that *The Who of God* and *The What of God* are absolutely bound together and inseparable. Entering into, and remaining in, a living and active relationship with our God, not only brings God and His children into deeper intimacy with each other, it also fills God's children with His very nature in amazingly transforming ways.

The Who our God is – Wisdom:

> ### And he will be called...Wonderful Counselor
> Isaiah 9:6

The *What our God* gives – His Very Self – transforms our nature to be more like our God and flows through us so that God's nature is made known to others around us:

> ### Counsel and judgment are mine; I have insight, I have power.
> Proverbs 8:14

> ### The fear of the LORD is the beginning of wisdom;
> ### all who follow his precepts have good understanding. To him belongs eternal praise.
> Psalm 111:10

> ### If any of you lacks wisdom, you should ask God,
> ### who gives generously to all without finding fault, and it will be given to you.
> James 1:5

> ### Who is wise and understanding among you?
> ### Let him show it by their good life, by deeds done in humility that comes from wisdom.
> James 3:13

> ### ...with humility comes wisdom.
> ### ...and the one who is wise saves lives.
> Proverbs 11:2, 30

> ### ...that they may have the full riches of complete understanding,
> ### in order that they may know the mystery of God, namely, Christ,
> ### in whom are hidden all the treasures of wisdom and knowledge.
> Colossians 2:2-3

> ### Those who are wise will shine like the brightness of the heavens,
> ### and those who lead many to righteousness, like the stars for ever and ever.
> Daniel 12:3

The Who of God and *The What of God* are inextricably interwoven and mysteriously given to us to bring us into a deeper, living oneness with our Holy God as He gives His own Spirit to live within us, transforming us to be more and more like Him in character, in thoughts, words, actions, interactions and reactions.

Our God is the Wonderful Counselor, giver of all true, righteous and eternal wisdom! May we each of us come to know our God more intimately, be filled more powerfully and shine more fully with God's wisdom in all we are, in all we do and in all of our encounters with everyone!

Do I believe it?
And if I do, what am I going to do about it?

Lord, please let me hear your voice, your love, your wisdom, your grace and truth.

WHAT'CHA WATCHIN' FOR?

What are you watching for? What are you looking for? An easier day? A promotion? A vacation? An encouragement? An achievement? An award? A quick answer? A plan that all comes together? A cure? A new relationship? A healed and renewed long-term relationship? An easier time with a cantankerous family member, boss, co-worker or neighbor? An easier life? All of the above?

What we watch for depends on where our eyes are focused – physically, emotionally, mentally, relationally and spiritually. What we watch for reflects what we expect to see and experience. God's Word tells us, and His Spirit confirms it: We can watch for, and expect to see and experience, the mighty strength and unfailing love of God as our protective, enduring, non-destructible fortress!

> *You are my strength, I watch for you;*
> *you, God, are my fortress,*
> *[my loving God] my God on whom I can rely.*
> Psalm 59:9-10

Our God wants us to lift up our eyes and watch for Him – His love, His strength, His protection. And as we do, what we will see, more clearly and transformingly, is that our God is watching us with His eyes of love, grace and truth. Our God is – at every moment of every day – watching out for us, and watching over us! We just need to watch for our God!

> *I lift up my eyes to the [hills] mountains –*
> *where does my help come from?*
> *My help comes from the LORD,*
> *the Maker of heaven and earth.*
>
> *He will not let your foot slip –*
> *he who watches over you will not slumber;*
> *indeed, he who watches over Israel*
> *will neither slumber nor sleep.*
>
> *The LORD watches over you –*
> *the LORD is your shade at your right hand;*
> *the sun will not harm you by day,*
> *nor the moon by night.*
>
> *The LORD will keep you from all harm –*
> *he will watch over your life;*
> *the LORD will watch over your coming and your going*
> *both now and forevermore.*
> Psalm 121

Even if we don't fully understand God, or see things God's way, the truth is that our God is always awake and watching over us as His precious, beloved children. May we each choose to trust God's promises of love, strength, presence and protection and His watchful love over our lives. May we each choose to lift up our eyes and watch for – and expect – that our God will show up in powerful, help-bringing, peace-giving and loving ways!

What'cha Watchin' for?

Reflections – Responses – Challenges – Encouragements – God-breathing Thoughts

Do I believe it?
And if I do, what am I going to do about it?

Lord, please let me hear your voice, your love, your wisdom, your grace and truth.

IF YOU LOVE ME...

Maybe you've said this to someone. Maybe someone has said it to you. "If you love me..." Go ahead. Fill in the blank. How would you have finished that line when speaking to someone? How would someone else have finished that line when speaking to you?

God's love for us is not conditional. It can't be. Because the condition of God – the essence of God's very nature – is love.

> **God is love.**
> 1 John 4:8,16

God does ask us, however, to show our love and live out our love for Him by obeying His commands. And even in this, our Lord does not leave us alone. Our God never requires anything of us for which He will not also supply the help and the power we need to accomplish it. We just have to ask for His help – which we desperately and honestly need, even on our easiest of days, whether we acknowledge this truth or not! Our God gives us His omnipresent Holy Spirit to lovingly and truthfully lead us, to counsel us and empower us to obey our God.

> **"If you love me, keep my commands.**
> **And I will ask the Father,**
> **and he will give you another advocate [Counselor]**
> **to be with you forever – the Spirit of truth."**
> John 14:15-17

Jesus is finishing the line, "If you love me..." far differently than many of us would with our loved ones. We often expect our loved ones to figure out, all on their own, what we want or need in order to feel loved. You know, *if you really loved me...you would just know what would be special or important to me...you would just know what would be significant and memorable for me... you would just know what would make me feel loved. If you really loved me...you should darn-well-better be able to figure out just how I need you to show me! I certainly shouldn't have to tell you!* Apparently, *knowing – and then, of course, doing –* what would be most loving, special, important or significant for our loved ones, without ever being clearly told what that is, really says, "I love you" to the people in our lives. Really?

As a counselor of individuals, couples and families, may I just say that this is immature, egocentric and totally ridiculous thinking? Was that blunt enough? And! Let me also say that I've been personally guilty of this same kind of thinking myself.

Full of grace and truth, Jesus speaks to us clearly and honestly. No games. No manipulation. Jesus just tells us directly how He wants us to show our love for Him: *Keep My commands.* Even as Jesus tells us how to show our love for Him, He lets us know that He will give us everything we need to accomplish this. Our Holy God fills us with His very Presence through the giving of the Wonderful Counselor, the Spirit of truth, to live in us and be with us forever. Our God loves us so much that He never leaves us. Nor does God expect us to have the power or the knowledge on our own to love Him perfectly. Giving us His Holy Spirit to empower us to love and obey Him more fully is really God's way of fully loving us.

God has given us His life and His Spirit to show His love for us. Let's give our Lord Jesus back some love, just the way He likes it: Let's choose to intimately know and tenaciously keep His loving, truth-filled, life-transforming commands!

Do I believe it?
And if I do, what am I going to do about it?

Lord, please let me hear your voice, your love, your wisdom, your grace and truth.

A SIMPLE TRUST – AN OUTRAGEOUS CLAIM

I have a simple trust in an outrageous claim. Jesus said:

> *"Because I live, you also will live."*
> John 14:19

I am convinced that Jesus is the Lord of Life. I am convinced that He sacrificed His own life for mine so that I could be forgiven completely of each and every one of my sins and be made Holy in God's sight. Outrageous. I am convinced that Jesus rose to life again, conquering and obliterating the power of death over me. Outrageous. I am convinced that through faith in Jesus I have eternal life with Him, right now on this earth and will be living with Him in heaven for ever and ever. Outrageous.

I trust Jesus. In all of His outrageous claims. In all of the outrageous claims that the Bible makes about Jesus. I trust Jesus. Period. It's not a blind or naïve trust. It's not an ignorant or anti-intellectual trust. It's not a trust that is afraid to wrestle with God about…well, just about everything…at one time or another.

My trust comes from being in relationship with Jesus. Opening myself up enough to allow His love to enter – at first, very gently and tenderly – into my broken life and messed up mind. Opening my life and my mind – intellectually and spiritually – to search and know the Word of God. And I have come to – been brought to, by my loving God – this place of simple trust in the outrageous claims of Jesus.

I am convinced that God's love is unfailing, ever-present and inseparable from me. I am convinced that God's Word is truth, is living, is active, was "made flesh" (became fully human) in Jesus, and is revealed to me and brought to my mind by the Holy Spirit, who now lives within me. I am convinced – simply and completely – that because Jesus lives, I live – now and will for all eternity. Outrageous.

In relationship with Jesus, I live more fully, more freely, more healed, more whole, more transformed – even in the midst of this broken and sin-ugly world. I am more alive and more joy-filled, and more aware of God's beauty and His gift of life than I could ever be without the truth that Jesus lives and the relationship with Him that gives me a life that is full beyond measure – and will last far beyond the measure of time!

Because Jesus lives and because Jesus loves me, my simple trust in His outrageous claims moves me to take risks to live in courageous ways and love others in crazy ways. To be more and more transformed to be like Jesus. He washed feet. He went without sleep, without food, without a settled home. He dealt with people plotting against Him, misunderstanding Him, completely rejecting Him. Hating Him. And still Jesus loved us enough to do the outrageous, the courageous, the crazy way of showing us His love. Jesus took on God's full and righteous judgment and punishment against sin and was killed in our place. And we were set free, we were made righteous in our Holy God's sight. Outrageous.

So, yes. I have a simple trust in Jesus' outrageous claim: *Because I live, you also will live.* And I want to live every day I have *for* Jesus and live every day I have in close relationship *with* Jesus.

What about you? Do you believe this outrageous claim? Do live, because Jesus lives?

Reflections – Responses – Challenges – Encouragements – God-breathing Thoughts

Do I believe it?
And if I do, what am I going to do about it?

Lord, please let me hear your voice, your love, your wisdom, your grace and truth.

POWERFUL PURPOSE – MAGNIFICENT MYSTERY

My purpose is that they may be encouraged in heart and united in love,
so that they may have the full riches of complete understanding,
in order that they may know the mystery of God, namely, Christ,
in whom are hidden all the treasures of wisdom and knowledge.
I tell you this so that no one may deceive you by fine-sounding arguments.
Colossians 2:2-4

Our God speaks through the Apostle Paul as His vessel to reveal God's own passionate and powerful purpose for all of us who have put our trust in Jesus Christ as Savior and Lord.

God purposes us to be encouraged in heart – given strength, hope, confidence and courage at the very core of who we are. The heart, in biblical language, has a broad and deep meaning. The heart is understood to be the very center – the innermost being – of the human spirit. And from the heart flows all of our emotions, our thoughts, our motivations and our actions. Our Mighty God purposes that we should each be encouraged in our hearts. Encouraged in all that we are, in all that we feel, in all that we think, in all that we are moved by, and in all that we choose to do. Our God wants to encourage us from the inside out and all around us.

God purposes us to be united in love, by the love of our Lord Jesus Christ. God purposes for us to truly understand that we belong to each other as God's children, as brothers and sisters in faith. God purposes for us to intentionally and actively love, care, protect and support one another because of our oneness in Christ. We are to show our unity in love with each other in deep and spiritual ways and in practical and tangible ways. We are to be known by our love for one another because of the love of God we now know for ourselves. We are to lead with love in all we do as we follow our Lord Jesus.

God purposes us to have, and to be eternally and immeasurably blessed by, the full riches of complete understanding – by all the treasures of wisdom and knowledge – found in God's eternal truth and purpose that were once kept as a mystery, until God's chosen and perfect timing for these treasures to be revealed:
Jesus Christ is the Living God in human form!
Jesus died for us to forgive our sins!
Jesus rose from the dead to conquer death!
Jesus will come again!

God purposes that each of us should fully know and understand, believe and live in His revealed truth and freeing grace – His holy mystery of how our Lord and Savior Jesus Christ accomplished the fullness of God's eternal purposes to rescue and redeem His lost children!

Hold fast to all of God's life-giving, transforming grace and freeing truth so that no one and nothing will ever be able to deceive you! Hold fast so that no LFTPOH – Lie From The Pit Of Hell – could ever warp the love, hope and freedom that Jesus Christ alone brings to our lives, for today and for all eternity!

Be encouraged! Love each other powerfully and unselfishly. Be filled with God's lavish gifts of understanding, wisdom and knowledge that have all been made known and given to us through our Lord Jesus Christ!

Do I believe it?
And if I do, what am I going to do about it?

Lord, please let me hear your voice, your love, your wisdom, your grace and truth.

SO THEN, WHAT?

Have you ever started something new – maybe a new job, a new course of study, a new career, a new hobby, a new relationship, a new move out of your old neighborhood, or a new direction out of your old comfort zone?

At first, you felt excited, maybe even passionate, about these new changes in your life. You knew they were right for you, on oh-so-many levels. You may even have felt clearly, strongly and peacefully led by our God to make these changes in your life. And so you did. Then – with the new things in place, with the changes made – you hit some kind of challenge or confusion, some distraction or frustration, some doubt or disappointment. Maybe these were minor challenges. Maybe they were absolutely shocking, unexpected and painful. Either way, you were left wondering: So then, what? What should I do? How do I deal with this?

In order to live out our faith in Jesus Christ – whether we are fairly new to a faith relationship with Jesus or we have been living out our faith relationship with Jesus for a very long time – our God, who never changes even if everything changes in our lives, gives us all the same clear, full answer to the question: So then, what?

> *So then, just as you received Christ Jesus as Lord,*
> *continue to live in him,*
> *rooted and built up in him,*
> *strengthened in the faith as you were taught,*
> *and overflowing with thankfulness!*
> Colossians 2:6-7

No matter what challenge, confusion, distraction or frustration, doubt or disappointment we may face in our lives – including within our faith journey with Jesus – our loving, living, fully present, powerful Lord lets us know exactly what we need to do. Our God encourages us to focus our minds on Jesus, and on the reasons and the way we received Him as Lord of our lives in the first place.

Think about this for yourself. What drew you to Christ as your Lord? For me, as a seven year old who felt so utterly unloved, angry and afraid, Jesus entered into my life with His love – through God's Word, God's Spirit and the love of His servants who shared the grace and truth of Christ's salvation with me at a summer camp. I understood that only in God, in my Heavenly Abba, would I ever know, and be able to trust, the eternal, unchanging love that my soul, mind, heart – my very life – needed so desperately. And then, those beautiful summer camp servants gave me a Bible of my very own.

Our God calls us to continue to live in Him – just as we did when God first brought us to life in Christ. Our relationship with our Lord is for all eternity – and it is to be a living and active, deeply intimate and continually growing relationship. As God's children, we are to hold firm and be transformed – rooted and built up – by God's love, Word and Spirit. And we are to learn (be taught) and know God's Word – His grace and His truth – through the reading, studying and trusting of God's Word. As we do, our faith will become increasingly strong, and our thankfulness for our God, who never changes and loves us beyond measure, will overflow!

So then, no matter what new things, and all the changes that come with them, may come into our lives, let us each choose to continue to live in our Lord Jesus Christ, who is our Life!

Reflections – Responses – Challenges – Encouragements – God-breathing Thoughts

Do I believe it?
And if I do, what am I going to do about it?

Lord, please let me hear your voice, your love, your wisdom, your grace and truth.

A TIME TO TRUST

There is a time for everything, and a season for every activity under the heavens.
Ecclesiastes 3:1

Everything that we have ever experienced, and everything that we will yet experience at some point in the future, has its own time and its own season in our lives. But! That doesn't mean we are going to like everything, or even understand everything, that happens in our lives or the timing of when everything happens. Still, we are called to trust in the One True God whose sovereign purpose and unfailing love will one day reveal to us that...

He has made everything beautiful in its time.
Ecclesiastes 3:11

Until that time – whether our seasons bring birth or death, weeping or laughing, mourning or dancing, scattering or gathering, silence or speaking, war or peace – it is always the time for each one of us to choose to trust in the Lord. With all our hearts. In all our ways.

Trust in the LORD with all your heart
and lean not on your own understanding;
in all your ways [acknowledge] submit to God,
and he will direct your paths.
Proverbs 3:5-6

Our God is loving and faithful and good in all His ways. I know that's not how many of us will automatically respond to, or naturally feel about, the different times and seasons we experience in our lives. Some times and seasons are just so very hard, so very sad, so very confusing. Still, we are to trust our God. Always. With all our heart. In all our ways.

We are to trust our God when it is easy for us to trust Him – in those times and seasons of our lives that bring birth and laughter, dancing and peace.

We are to trust our God when it is so very difficult for us to trust Him – in those times and seasons of our lives that bring death and weeping, mourning and war.

Our God, who is eternally, sovereignly and intimately loving, faithful and good in all His ways, sees and knows and understands far more than we could ever even begin to see, know and understand about the times and seasons of our lives.

And so, we are called to trust in the One who promises to make everything beautiful in its time. We are called to trust in the One who will direct our paths – even when our view is clouded by the darkness of this broken world or overshadowed by fears or we are blinded by our own tears.

One day we will each be astounded by the beauty that will shine through everything we have ever experienced – everything will be fully redeemed and transformed by our Lord Jesus Christ – from every time and every season of our lives!

Until that time, may we choose to let this day and every day be a time to trust our Lord! With all our hearts. In all our ways. Always.

Do I believe it?
And if I do, what am I going to do about it?

Lord, please let me hear your voice, your love, your wisdom, your grace and truth.

MOUTH MANAGEMENT

Throughout scripture, God addresses the need for each of us to be aware of our words and all that comes from our mouths, through our lips and our tongues. King David knew that he could not trust his own power or wisdom to keep from sinning with his words. He was a "man after God's own heart," yet David desperately needed God to make him a man whose mouth also honored Him. I, too, am so very aware of my real and constant need for God's mouth management over my words. And as did David, so I pray fervently for God to…

> *Set a guard over my mouth, LORD; keep watch over the door of my lips.*
> Psalm 141:3

This is such a great, and a rightly humble and oh-so-very necessary, prayer for me to pray. For all who are followers of Christ. We need to invite God to guard our words, our tongues, our lips, and every single thought that motivated our speech in the first place! As followers of Jesus, we're supposed to be ambassadors – message bringers – of God's love and His words of grace and truth. Passionately, I want this to be true of me at every moment of every day. Sadly and humbly, I admit that it is not. Other words and other tones of voice come from me that do nothing to show the beauty and love of Jesus that has transformed my life.

The prophet Isaiah was given a magnificent and mysterious vision of the Lord seated on His throne surrounded and worshiped by angelic beings. When confronted with the holiness and majesty of the glory of God, Isaiah immediately confessed his sin. And what would this man of God, this prophet of the Most High God, need to confess? Sins of the mouth.

> *"Woe to me!" I cried. "I am ruined! For I am a man of unclean lips,*
> *and I live among a people of unclean lips,*
> *and my eyes have seen the King, the LORD Almighty."*
> Isaiah 6:5

This problem of unclean lips is something that each of us honestly needs to address. It's not just about having a "potty mouth." So, if that's not your particular sin of choice, good for you! However, whether our words and tones of voice come out in hateful ways, lying ways, gossiping ways, condemning ways, shameful ways, manipulative ways or prideful ways, we all need our God to intervene and interrupt us. This needs to happen even before our thoughts can be formed into words and spew out from our mouths. This intervention and interruption needs to happen inside our hearts. Remember: the heart in biblical language encompasses all of our emotions, thoughts, motivations and actions. So, once our words – that have not been, first, filtered through God's holy and loving mouth management – are out, it isn't going to be pretty.

> *Sin is not ended by multiplying words [When words are many sin is not absent]*
> Proverbs 10:19

We each need God to infuse our mouths, and our hearts, with His love, grace, truth, wisdom, peace, purity, humility, kindness, thankfulness and compassion. Our Lord Jesus, who is the Word of God, wants to guard our words and guard others who would hear our words.

Will you invite God to manage your mouth today? And continually?

I will. And I'll ask God to just keep me quiet altogether – just shut me up, when necessary!

Reflections – Responses – Challenges – Encouragements – God-breathing Thoughts

Do I believe it?
And if I do, what am I going to do about it?

Lord, please let me hear your voice, your love, your wisdom, your grace and truth.

A BRAVE INVITATION FOR A TRANSFORMING PURPOSE

Let a righteous man strike me – it is a kindness;
let him rebuke me – it is oil on my head.
My head will not refuse it…
Psalm 141:5

Now just so you know, I'm not running right out and eagerly inviting the most righteous man or woman I know to take their best shot at me. Having someone take a strike at me is definitely not my preferred means of being corrected or rebuked! Yes, I do know that the righteous "strike" is metaphorical. Although, I have to admit that there have been a few times (in my self-righteous mode) that I've thought about knocking a few people upside their heads, thinking it just might knock some sense into them!

Being corrected and rebuked in any manner isn't exactly what I really want to happen. No matter who does it. It also isn't exactly a natural thing to invite another person, no matter how righteous he or she may be, to get all up in my face to confront me about my sins – my wrong thinking, my wrong speaking, my wrong acting, my wrong reacting. No. Not natural at all. Not comfortable at all.

However, if you're in a relationship with God, you probably already know that our supernatural God doesn't concern Himself with working only in the realms of what is natural or comfortable for us. Especially if what we're considering as natural is still part of our sin nature, rather than part of God's good and beautiful work within us to transform our natures to be fully alive, fully free and fully loving. Just like Jesus.

I had to stop and think about this challenge. Or rather, my supernatural God, who loves me so much and wants the very best for me, made me stop and think about this – about being willing to be confronted about any of my sins and habits that would mar and diminish my life in – and my witness for – my Lord Jesus Christ. So…I first asked myself: *Why not? Why not intentionally invite someone I trust – someone who is seeking God's love, grace and truth – to keep me accountable, keep me humble, keep me teachable, keep me growing, keep me sharp and wise, keep me transforming more and more into the likeness of Jesus?*

No. This is not natural. Not comfortable. But! It is right and good, loving and transforming!

So, a number of years ago I purposefully asked a few of the most trusted and godly people in my life to watch me, and watch out for me. I invited them to be aware of my actions, my words and my attitudes. To be aware of how I'm taking care of myself, taking care of the people in my life and how I am fulfilling the call to be an ambassador of Christ. To get all up in my face – to *strike me righteously* (Although only with their words!) – about anything they see in me that needs to be purged or purified, reshaped or reshuffled, extinguished or extended in order for God's love, wisdom, grace and truth to shine most brightly in my life and through my life.

No. This is not natural. This is not comfortable. It is a brave invitation for a transforming purpose. So! *Why Not?* This *righteous strike* comes out of God's deep and unfailing love for us. God will use everything – His Word, His Spirit, our experiences and members of the Body of Christ – to help grow each of us to be more and more like Jesus. Our God wants us fully alive, fully free and fully loving. All for God's glory and joy!

Reflections – Responses – Challenges – Encouragements – God-breathing Thoughts

Do I believe it?
And if I do, what am I going to do about it?

Lord, please let me hear your voice, your love, your wisdom, your grace and truth.

_____

_____

_____

_____

_____

_____

_____

_____

_____

_____

_____

_____

_____

_____

_____

_____

_____

_____

_____

_____

_____

_____

_____

THINKING AND THANKING

We always thank God for all of you and continually mention you in our prayers.
We remember before our God and Father your work produced by faith, your labor
prompted by love, and your endurance inspired by hope in our Lord Jesus Christ.
1 Thessalonians 1:2-3

So many people flow in and out of our lives.

Some people, even in the briefest of encounters, may impact our lives in profound ways because they act as, and are, vessels of God's love, grace and truth. Right then. Right for that particular moment and for a specific purpose.

Other people, over the course of many years, may have been (and still are) beautiful and powerful reflections of Christ to us because of their long-lasting faithfulness, loving service and patient, hope-filled endurance. These precious ones continually choose to ask God to lead their lives so that they may be vessels of His love, grace and truth – each and every day, in each and every encounter and relationship they have.

Take time to think about these people – even if you can't quite pull up their names or even their faces from your memory bank. Think about those people who God used in a particular moment and for a specific reason in your life. Think about those people who God used over and over again, over many, many seasons of your life in many, many ways.

Take time to thank God for these people. Thank God for how He powerfully and deeply – gently or sternly, surprisingly or expectedly – used each of them in your life. All because He loves you! Lift these people in prayer. Be encouraged by them. Be challenged by them.

Take time to ask God to transform you to be more and more like Jesus. Take time to ask God to increase *your works produced by faith, your labor prompted by love and your endurance flowing from the inspired hope you have in our Lord Jesus Christ!*

Then, be sure to take time to *let God* do His good work in you, knowing you can be...

...confident of this, that he who began a good work in you
will carry it on to completion until the day of Christ Jesus.
Philippians 1:6

May each of us allow God to make us always ready to impact and influence the lives of others – whether for a brief and fleeting moment or over the course of many years – with the love, grace and truth of our Lord Jesus Christ!

As we do, our God will be moving the hearts and minds of those whose lives He has allowed us to impact, to lift their voices in thanksgiving to Him, glorifying and blessing the God and Father of our Lord Jesus Christ for the blessings we have been in their lives.

How beautiful is that! So, think about and thank God for the people who have blessed your life in oh-so-many different ways! And be blessed with the very real possibility that you will also be on someone else's *thinking and thanking* list!

Do I believe it?
And if I do, what am I going to do about it?

Lord, please let me hear your voice, your love, your wisdom, your grace and truth.

DECLARATION OF DEPENDENCE

Today is the celebration of Independence Day in the United States. A day when we commemorate the adoption of the Declaration of Independence on July 4, 1776 – which announced to the world that our thirteen colonies were no longer part of the British Empire. They were now declared to be thirteen sovereign states, which together formed the new nation of the United States of America.

That declaration – no matter how strongly presented were the grievances against the empire to which we belonged or the justifications given for separating ourselves from it – did not automatically bring the freedom and independence to us as a nation, nor to us as individual citizens of this new nation. All out war ensued. Struggle, suffering and sacrifices were required of all, in various ways, to different degrees, in the fight for freedom. A tenacious, unrelenting determination to be fully free and independent pushed a rag-tag, ill-equipped, inexperienced, newly formed fighting force to fight against – and ultimately defeat – one of the world's most organized, highly trained and experienced military forces.

For we who are followers of Jesus Christ, it is our *Declaration of Dependence* on our Holy God that sets us free! Our Lord Jesus struggled, suffered and sacrificed His All to fight and defeat the authority and power that sin and death held over our lives. It is in holding to these truths: That our God, by the sacrifice of Jesus' life and the victory of His resurrection, has set us free from the dominion of darkness that rules over this temporal world. In placing our faith fully in, and acknowledging our complete dependence on, all that Jesus has accomplished on our behalf is where our true and eternal freedom stands!

"...apart from me you can do nothing."
John 15:5

For he has rescued us from the dominion of darkness and brought us into the kingdom of the Son he loves, in whom we have redemption, the forgiveness of sins.
Colossians 1:13-14

It is for freedom that Christ has set us free!
Stand firm, then, and do not let yourselves be burdened again by a yoke of slavery.
Galatians 5:1

In all these things we are more than conquerors through him who loved us.
Romans 8:37

"If you hold to my teaching, you are really my disciples.
Then you will know the truth, and the truth will set you free."
John 8:31-32

The truth is our very breath, our very life and our eternal freedom depend solely on our Lord Jesus Christ! May we each celebrate and live out this *Declaration of Dependence* every day of our lives – standing firm, tenaciously and determinedly, in the freedom that our Holy God has given to us as His children and as eternal citizens of Heaven!

Do I believe it?
And if I do, what am I going to do about it?

Lord, please let me hear your voice, your love, your wisdom, your grace and truth.

THE UNFOLDING OF GOD'S WORD

Was there ever a time when some portion of Scripture just seemed to come alive for you? Or, maybe I should say, that you came more alive by it? As you read or as you listened, your world and your thinking got a little bit brighter with the revelation, the opening up – the unfolding of God's words – to you. God's Word is meant to do exactly that!

The unfolding of your words gives light; it gives understanding to the simple.
Psalm 119:130

Light is essential for life. Even the very first recorded words of God that we have, when He spoke all of creation into being, were, *"Let there be light!"* – Genesis 1:3

The words of God are powerful beyond our *simple* comprehension – bringing light to our lives in this dark world and bringing us into fellowship with our *God in whose light we see light* (Psalm 36). Our God sent His Son Jesus Christ, *the Eternal Word of God made flesh, as the True Light of the world* (John 1). And it is through Jesus that *we* are *rescued from the dominion of darkness and brought into God's eternal kingdom of light* (Colossians 1). God's Word, God's True Light, breaks through our darkness to expose not only our need for forgiveness because of our sins, but also to expose the unfailing, uncompromising, life-giving love that our Eternal Abba has for each one of us! This unfolding of the words of God is an understanding that each one of us *simple ones* desperately needs. This is an understanding that has the power to radically transform our lives right now and for all eternity, as our minds and hearts are enlightened by the unfolding of the words of God.

...my God turns my darkness into light.
Psalm 18:28

The precepts of the LORD are right, giving joy to the heart.
The commands of the LORD are radiant, giving light to the eyes.
Psalm 19:8-9

The LORD is my light and my salvation – whom shall I fear?
Psalm 27:1

Your word is a lamp for my feet, and a light on my path.
Psalm 119:105

"I am the light of the world.
Whoever follows me will never walk in darkness, but will have the light of life."
John 8:12

For God, who said, "Let light shine out of the darkness,"
made his light shine in our hearts to give us the light
of the knowledge of God's glory displayed in the face of Christ.
2 Corinthians 4:6

May the words of God be fully unfolded and shine brightly in and through each of us *simple ones* so that we may share the light of Christ with deep understanding to all those around us!

Do I believe it?
And if I do, what am I going to do about it?

Lord, please let me hear your voice, your love, your wisdom, your grace and truth.

RESTED? OR WEAKENED AND WARPED?

***This is what the LORD says: "Stand at the crossroads and look;
ask for the ancient paths, ask where the good way is,
and walk in it, and you will find rest for your souls.
But you said, 'We will not walk in it.' "***
Jeremiah 6:16

So, there we are facing another life-decision, wondering what to do. Wondering which way to go. The Lord tells us to stand and look – and recognize – that we are at a decision point in our lives. We are to be stable and alert at these crossroads. We are not to be pushed around nor blind-sided by anyone or anything while we are assessing our circumstances and the decisions we need to make. We are to stand and look, be stable and alert, as we seek God's good way.

Maybe those decision-demanding crossroads are about a major life change for you – a relationship, a move, a job, a total career change, a change in your physical or mental health.

We also need to recognize that we are standing at those decision-demanding crossroads every time we choose to think, speak or act. Yes, every time. Whether in our daily-day lives and our long-lasting relationships or in the more obvious crossroads during the major life changes we experience, we have choices to make about whether we will choose to walk in God's good way or in our self-focused, self-centered way.

No matter what decision-demanding crossroads we are at, the Lord tells us to ask for the ancient paths, to ask where the good way is. In other words, we are to ask our Lord – who is the Ancient of Days, the Eternal One – what His righteous, good direction would be for us.

Then, the Lord tells us clearly (Because apparently the Lord knows He needs to be very specific and concrete with us!) to walk in that good way – to walk in His way. The Lord loves us powerfully and passionately and wants the very best for each and every one of us. Our God knows that His good way *is* the very best for us. And our Lord promises that we will find rest for our souls – we will find peace, restoration, security, strength, joy – when we do choose to walk in God's good way!

Oh! It would be so fabulous *if* that were where this Scripture verse ended. You know: *We stood, we looked, we asked God, we obeyed God, and we received the Lord's strong and loving rest for our souls!* But, sadly, that's not the end of this verse. Instead, God makes it clear that our tendency towards stubbornness and rebellion against our Lord's holy, loving authority is revealed in our choices at the crossroads of our lives. Way too often, we – in our thoughts, words, actions, reactions and interactions – stomp our feet, shake our fists, and turn our faces away from where the Lord wants to lead us. We make it clear, one way or another, that when it comes to following the Lord's good way: *We will not walk in it!*

Living our lives really is all about choice. Choices about everything we think, say and do, about every way we speak to and treat others in our lives. Our God, out of His unfailing love for us, calls out to us to seek Him, trust His love, and walk in His good way – as we make each and every choice at each and every decision-demanding crossroad of our lives. Choosing to walk in our Lord's good way is the only way for souls to be given our God's life-restoring, life-blessing rest. Any and every other choice weakens and warps us. So, watch where you walk!

Do I believe it?
And if I do, what am I going to do about it?

Lord, please let me hear your voice, your love, your wisdom, your grace and truth.

IT'S BEEN RAINING! SO WHAT?

Not too long ago we went through a few days in a row when the rain just kept pouring down. At times, the rainstorms took the power down. And we brought the candles out. The rain forced us to change a number of our plans for our usual summertime outdoors and at-the-shore activities. Some of us had to force ourselves not to let the *grumpies* take over our attitudes, words and actions. Not gonna mention any names!

I could almost sense God smiling, shaking His head at us and thinking:
Yes. It's raining. It's dark. It's gloomy. And it's not exactly what you wanted or expected this season to be like. So what? You're still alive. And I am still God! (Don't you love it when God just tells it like it is?!) *You have so many reasons to be thankful! The rain shouldn't make a difference. Focus on what is true, eternal, bright and beautiful always! I am still God! I love you! I am with you! I give you life and breath – and oh-so-much-more! I do not change. My loving, hope-filled purposes will still be accomplished even if your plans are subject to change!*

And God's Word – a fabulous, get-over-yourself-about-the-rain passage – filled my head and my heart:

> *"As the rain and snow come down from heaven,*
> *and do not return to it without watering the earth*
> *and making it bud and flourish,*
> *so that it yields seed for the sower and bread for the eater,*
> *so is my word that goes out from my mouth:*
> *It will not return to me empty,*
> *but will accomplish what I desire and*
> *achieve the purpose for which I sent it.*
> *You will go out in joy and be led forth in peace..."*
> Isaiah 55:10-12

So, yes, it was raining a lot lately. So what?

God is still God. God's desires and purposes will still be achieved and accomplished. And with God leading us, we can still go out in joy and be led forth in peace. No matter what desires of ours are denied. No matter what purposes of ours have to be put off.

This will happen for each of us every time we choose to keep our ears open to God's purpose-accomplishing Word of love, grace and truth. This will happen for each of us every time we choose to keep our eyes open to the joy and peace that is around us and available to us every single day – even on the gloomiest of rain-drenched days!

Even on our gloomy days that have nothing to do with the weather, but rather have everything to do with the storms of life we experience, these truths are still true. God is still God. God is still in control. God still loves us. God's desires and purposes, which are perfect and eternally the very best for us, will still be achieved and accomplished.

We might not have any choice about the rainy days and the storms of life we experience. However, we always have a choice about trusting our God, His Word, His desires and His purposes – and knowing that His joy and peace are always available to fill us and lead us! No matter what!

Do I believe it?
And if I do, what am I going to do about it?

Lord, please let me hear your voice, your love, your wisdom, your grace and truth.

A REMINDER...

I am reminded of your sincere faith...
2 Timothy 1:5

Sometimes we just need someone else to remind us of who we are in Christ. To remind us of the faith that we truly do have in our Lord Jesus Christ...and the faith that has been witnessed by others in the way we live our lives. These reminders of our sincere faith, that others have seen and experienced, can be powerful and timely encouragements to our souls.

Reaching out to others, encouraging them in the faith they have shown and lived out as they follow Christ, might be just what they need, right now. This acknowledgement and reminder of their faith can be such a loving and tangible way to bless our brothers and sisters in Christ – and bring glory to our God, who gives each of us the strength to live out our faith.

And maybe part of the encouragement we are to give to our brothers and sisters in Christ, is to help them to remember what they have been given by God through their faith in Christ. And what they have not been given!

For this reason I remind you to fan into flames the gift of God...
For the Spirit God gave us does not make us timid,
but gives us power, love and self-discipline.
2 Timothy 1:6-7

Our God has given us amazing, unlimited resources – power, love, self-discipline and oh-so-much-more – within our spirits, by the gift of His Holy Spirit that we each received when we accepted Jesus Christ as our Savior and Lord. All that our God has given to us, we are to fan into flames. God placed His Holy Spirit, His Holy Fire, within each of us as a follower of Christ. It is up to each of us to yield more and more – actively and intentionally – to the Spirit's desire to purify us, consume us, and burn brightly within us and through us. And through God's Spirit within our spirits, we are to reflect the likeness of Jesus to all those around us.

We need to remember who our God is and what the characteristics of His eternal nature are that have been placed within our spirits...and what have not been. Our God did not give any of us a spirit timidity or fear, of pride or anger, of judgment or condescension, of selfishness or self-righteousness. Our God has instead given us His Spirit of power and filled us with all of the fruit of His Holy Spirit, His "love, joy, peace, patience, kindness, goodness, faithfulness, gentleness and self-control" (Galatians 5:22-23).

All that God has placed within us through His Spirit is always available to us at all times. It is for each of us to remember to purposefully and persistently fan into flames all that our God has given us. As we do, everything that comes from our old nature – our fears and pride, and anything else that would weaken and warp, damage and destroy, our reflection and experience of Christ within us – will be fully burned away in the strength and brilliance of God's Holy Fire!

Remember: Live out your faith in sincere ways! Encourage others whose sincere faith has blessed you! Fan into flames – day-by-day – all that the Spirit of God has placed within you to powerfully live out your faith in our Lord Jesus Christ! Encourage others to do the same!

Reflections – Responses – Challenges – Encouragements – God-breathing Thoughts

Do I believe it?
And if I do, what am I going to do about it?

Lord, please let me hear your voice, your love, your wisdom, your grace and truth.

FROM HUMILITY TO ETERNITY

Six weeks can fly by so quickly or six weeks can seem like an eternity. Six weeks, back in 1992, was the time it took to bring my mom to a much-needed, freedom-bringing humility so that she would be brought into the amazing and beautiful eternity she would share with Jesus. Before this, many years of heartbreak *for* my parents because of their own brokenness and "lostness", and continued hurt *from* my parents because of their abusive behaviors, had been my reality. From the time I was thirteen years old, many tears and many prayers were passionately offered up for both my mom and dad – praying that they would each turn hearts to Jesus. I desperately wanted them and all of my family to recognize how desperate they are – how desperate we all are – for our holy, eternal, loving God. How desperate we all are for Jesus – our only Savior.

And then, those six weeks came. Six weeks of horrendous suffering for my mom as she was put in the hospital with ovarian cancer, already fully metastasized throughout all of her organs, brain and blood. My mom was fifty-nine years old and her death certificate would soon be written. But not before our loving, holy, forgiving, saving Lord Jesus would write my mom's name in His Book of Life with His blood offered for the forgiveness of her sins! The same blood that Jesus shed for the forgiveness of my sins. And for yours.

My mom had to humbly come face-to-face with her desperate need for forgiveness and eternal salvation. Those six weeks were a time of deep physical suffering and incredible vulnerability for my mom. But it saved her life for all eternity!

My guilt has overwhelmed me like a burden too heavy to bear. My wounds fester and are loathsome because of my sinful folly. I am bowed down and brought very low; all day long I go about mourning. My back is filled with searing pain; there is no health in my body. I am feeble and utterly crushed; I groan in anguish of heart. All my longings lie open before you, LORD; my sighing is not hidden from you. I confess my iniquity; I am troubled by my sin.
Psalm 38:4-8, 18

Three days before my mom died, while with the Jesus-serving Hospital Chaplain, my mom asked for the forgiveness of her sins and accepted the gift of eternal salvation that Jesus alone can give! Hallelujah! My mom is free. Her humility before God brought her into eternity with Him. Through the love of Jesus, my mom and I will not be eternally separated. We will be together. We will share in a love relationship we never knew here on earth. All this is because of who Jesus Christ is and what He has done for us. We all need the same blood and sacrifice of Jesus. We all need the same death-defying, resurrection power to bring us to our heavenly, eternal home with Jesus Christ our Lord, our Holy God.

Once you were alienated from God and were enemies in your minds because of your evil behavior. But now he has reconciled you by Christ's physical body through death to present you holy in his sight, without blemish and free from accusation...
Colossians 1:21-22

How great is our God! How unlimited God is in love, mercy and power! From humility before our God, we are moved into eternity with Him!

Do you know where and with whom you'll be for all eternity? Jesus is here. He gave His life out of love for you! Ask Him to forgive you. Ask Him to be your Savior. His answer to you is already, "Yes!" You just need to ask and believe.

Reflections – Responses – Challenges – Encouragements – God-breathing Thoughts

Do I believe it?
And if I do, what am I going to do about it?

Lord, please let me hear your voice, your love, your wisdom, your grace and truth.

WHOSE SIDE AM I ON?

Often when we are in some kind of conflict with another person, or with a group of people, or when nations rage against nations – and especially when this conflict is public knowledge and being fought out in the public arena – we want to know: *Who is on our side? Who is against us? Who is our ally? Who is our enemy? Who supports us? Who opposes us? Who will fight with us?*

Joshua son of Nun, after living through, and following Moses, for the full forty years of wandering in the desert, was anointed as the one by whom God would lead the Israelites across the Jordan and into the Promised Land. Once the Jordan was crossed, Joshua had the task of leading the Israelite army to conquer and claim the land in the Name of the Lord and for His people to settle. Before going into battle against Jericho, Joshua encountered a man. And Joshua had these same kind of *Whose side are you on?* questions running through his mind. That man, however, was no ordinary man. His side had already been determined. That man's side was not up for grabs. That man's side was not up for discussion or debate.

> *Joshua looked up and saw a man standing in front of him with a drawn sword*
> *in his hand. Joshua went up to him and asked, "Are you for us or for our enemies?"*
> *"Neither," he replied, "but as commander of the army of the LORD I have now come."*
> *Then Joshua fell facedown to the ground in reverence, and asked him,*
> *"What message does my LORD have for his servant?"*
> Joshua 5:13-14

This experience humbled Joshua. He learned that day that he was not to concern himself so much with determining whose side those around him are on. These alliances are often self-focused, self-seeking and can be temporally fleeting and fickle. Rather, Joshua understood that he must align himself only and always with the Lord, his Eternal Leader, who takes no human side and is always faithful to fulfilling His own righteous and holy purposes.

What about you? What about me? What do we need to learn from this? Personally, I need to continually keep myself in check as Joshua learned to do. I need to ask myself:
Am I trying to line others up on my side in order to justify my perspectives on issues? In order to justify my actions in various circumstances? Am I fighting only for myself? For my own ego or reputation? For my rights as I see them? Or, am I honestly and actively seeking to line myself up with the Lord's will, ways and righteousness?

The question for me, and for each of us, is not: "Who's on my side?" Rather, the right and righteous question truly is: "Whose side am I on?"

May each one of us be able to answer this question with humility and sincerity, with courage and conviction: "I am on the side of the Lord!"

May we each thank God for the battle that Jesus fought and won for our very souls, through His shed blood on the cross!

May we each keep our eyes, minds and hearts focused on Jesus – focused on where He is leading us and the spiritual battles that rage against His love and authority that we are called to fight. May we each, by God's mighty power, stand firmly on the side of our Lord today, tomorrow and forever!

Do I believe it?
And if I do, what am I going to do about it?

Lord, please let me hear your voice, your love, your wisdom, your grace and truth.

JUST SHOW UP!

"I don't think I'm going to get to hear the speaker today. I'm the only one here to set up for lunch. So, thanks for coming in! I really appreciate that you two just showed up to help me get things done. By the way, what brought you here today?" asked a woman from an inner-city Philadelphia church, who was apparently in charge of (and totally on her own) preparing the lunch for her church's Spiritual Renewal Day.

I smiled, kept cutting up tomatoes and getting sandwich platters ready and said, "We're happy to help! It'll go much faster if we work together, then, we can all go upstairs when the first session begins." DeAnne, my sister in Christ and Administrative Angel, who was ministering with me that day, agreed, and kept cutting her own boatload of tomatoes and filling the platters with all sorts of food. DeAnne also identified me as the speaker for this Spiritual Renewal Day.

The woman was completely surprised. She never expected that the guest ministry team would just show up in the kitchen and start working with her when we saw her need for help. But! If we're supposed to become more and more like Jesus, isn't that exactly where Jesus would have been? And isn't that exactly where we should have just showed up?

Jesus just showed up – and kept showing up. Just where He was supposed to be. Just with whom He was supposed to be. And every time, Jesus did His Father's work. Sometimes Jesus showed up to heal the hurting and the helpless. Sometimes Jesus showed up to set people free from demons. Sometimes Jesus showed up to teach parables and lessons about the Kingdom of God. Sometimes Jesus showed up to give out lunch to thousands. Sometimes Jesus showed up to calm the sea. Sometimes Jesus showed up to challenge people's sense of religious righteousness. Sometimes Jesus showed up to ask people who they think He is.

Sometimes Jesus showed up to clearly tell who He is. That happened one day when Jesus showed up at a well in Samaria – a place hated by the Jews. There, Jesus spoke to a woman who was most likely hated or, at least, held in contempt by her neighbors. She had had five husbands and was now with a man who wasn't her husband. Yet, it was to her, at that well, at that moment in time, that Jesus showed up to speak. Part of their dialogue went like this:

> *Jesus replied, "believe me, a time is coming when you will worship*
> *the Father neither on this mountain nor in Jerusalem...*
> *God is spirit, and his worshipers must worship him in the Spirit and in truth."*
> *The woman said, "I know that Messiah (called Christ) is coming.*
> *When he comes he will explain everything to us."*
> *Then Jesus declared, "I, the one who is speaking to you – I am he."*
> John 4:21, 24-26

Jesus just showed up. Just where He was supposed to be. Just with whom He was supposed to be. And every time, Jesus did His Father's work. And that day Jesus took His time to speak with a woman alone at a well – in a hated region, living a broken life – and to her, Jesus announced Himself as the Lord's Messiah! And she believed. And through this transformed woman's testimony, "many of the Samaritans from that town believed in him" (John 4:39).

Think about where our Lord may be asking you to just show up to touch a life with the love and kindness, the grace and truth of our Lord Jesus Christ. Then, go! Just show up!

Reflections – Responses – Challenges – Encouragements – God-breathing Thoughts

Do I believe it?
And if I do, what am I going to do about it?

Lord, please let me hear your voice, your love, your wisdom, your grace and truth.

NO LEASH! KNOW BALANCE!

Do you ever feel out of balance? Emotionally, mentally, physically, relationally, spiritually? I do. And I don't like it. Not one little bit.

A long time ago, I asked God (naively, albeit sincerely) to hold me tightly. I told God that I didn't want Him to give me even a short leash. I told God I didn't want any leash, no slack – in the connection between Him and me – at all. I asked God to hold me tightly, firmly and constantly so that I would know and sense His love, His leading and His correction continually and immediately in my life. Like I said, that was a naïve, albeit sincere prayer. God, who is never naïve and always sincere, answered my prayer. Happily. Quickly. Strongly. I believe it was God who moved me to pray that prayer in the first place. It lines up so fully with what God wants for each of us. It is in full agreement with "God's good, pleasing and perfect will" (Romans 12:2).

> *I am the LORD your God; consecrate yourselves and be holy,*
> *because I am holy.*
> Leviticus 11:44

> *...to those sanctified in Christ and called to be his holy people...*
> 1 Corinthians 1:2

> *Since we live by the Spirit, let us keep in step with the Spirit.*
> Galatians 5:25

Yes, God answered my naïve, sincere prayer just as I had asked. (You've heard: *Be careful for what you ask!*) The hold God has on me almost feels like a heavy, strong, metal ring, that is invisible to the eye but pierces right into my chest, right through my heart and into my innermost being. And, there, I am held tightly by the nail-scarred and fully loving hands of my Lord Jesus Christ.

Having God answer my prayer that clearly, fully (and strangely) really is great. Really. Yet, one of the biggest effects of being held so tightly is that I am highly sensitive to being out of balance – out of shalom – with my God. Out of balance – out of love – towards others. Out of balance – out of care – for myself.

Whenever I'm thinking, saying or doing things that aren't following God's leading, *God's good, pleasing and perfect will* (And that is still way too often! Darn it!), I feel so out of balance – so out of God's shalom. It is then that I feel God giving me a good hard yank on the ring attached to my heart. Yanking me back to God's perspective, to God's purpose and plan for my life. Yanking me back so that I will get God's point and get myself back on His path very quickly, following Him very closely. No leash! No leeway!

God's yank on my heart is actually God's passionate, protective, incredible love for me and His faithfulness to hold me tightly, just as I asked Him to do! God is my balance. God gives me my truest life, my greatest freedom, my deepest shalom. And, yes, sometimes God gives it to me through a good hard yank!

May God's powerful, unfailing love always give each of us a good hard yank on our hearts so that we will walk and live – emotionally, mentally, physically, relationally and spiritually – in God's loving and perfect balance! No leash! Know balance!

Reflections – Responses – Challenges – Encouragements – God-breathing Thoughts

Do I believe it?
And if I do, what am I going to do about it?

Lord, please let me hear your voice, your love, your wisdom, your grace and truth.

MY HEART YELLED AT ME!

That whole balance thing – shalom with my God – really is essential to my emotional, mental, physical, relational and spiritual well-being! Yours, too! Did I just hear somebody just say, "Duh!"? Oh! Wait a minute, that was my heart! Because of God's yank!

A couple of mornings ago I got up crazy early, ready to just jump right into what I needed to do because I had a lot to do before leaving my home to get to where I needed to go, to do what I needed to do! I had a full day of ministry – counseling and mentoring appointments, visiting with precious people who are hurting, face-to-face meetings with ministry leaders, making phone calls, answering emails, an international Skype call, and some very necessary writing time.

I love what I do, and I needed to get myself ready so I would be fully ready to do what I do!

So, I got up crazy early because I needed to take some time to stretch and exercise. I needed to take some time to go through the mail that had piled up for over a week. I needed to take a shower. And wash my hair. And style my hair. And put on make-up. And put on some clothes other than just my shorts and a tee shirt. None of which I had done for a number of days while super-focused in my writer's zone. I hadn't had any face-to-face get-togethers with anyone over the last several days, other than with my very kind and gracious family. All who have seen me in my unwashed state and my unkempt writer's zone regalia, with my crazy-sticking-up-all-over writer's zone hair. Quite often. And they still love me!

So, I thought God and I could just start our morning out by chatting while I took some time to stretch and exercise. I thought God and I could chat while I took some time to go through the mail that had piled up over the last week. I thought God and I could chat while I got my shower. And washed my hair. And styled my hair. I thought God and I could chat while I put on my make-up. And put on some clothes other than my shorts and a tee shirt.

But! That was not God's plan! That wasn't what my heart was telling me either. And I felt God's good hard yank on my heart. I needed God's balance – God's shalom. That day was going to require real time with God if I was going to give anything of His love and grace and truth to any of the people with whom I would be ministering and meeting. I needed to really seek God. And my heart knew that. My heart knew it wasn't enough to lightly chat with God while I did other things. Not then. Not ever.

So! My heart was yanked, and did what any smart heart would do. My heart yelled at me!

> ***My heart says of you, "Seek His face!"***
> ***Your face, LORD, I will seek!***
> Psalm 27:8

My heart knew that balance and shalom would come to me only by stopping all other things. Stopping all other thoughts and agendas. Stopping all other activities. I needed to fully and earnestly seek my God's face – which is attached to my God's heart – which is filled and flowing with my God's love and balance and shalom for me!

How about you? Is your heart yelling at you, or maybe just whispering, "Seek His Face!"? Either way, will you answer, "Your face, Lord, I will seek!"?

Do I believe it?
And if I do, what am I going to do about it?

Lord, please let me hear your voice, your love, your wisdom, your grace and truth.

GOD'S JUST RULE, GUIDANCE and CHOCOLATE CROISSANTS!

Happy Bastille Day! C'est le quatorze juillet. (It's the 14th of July!) One of the major national holidays of France. It may not make a bit of difference in your life. And that's okay. I'm planning to start my day with some good strong French-pressed coffee and at least one pain au chocolat (chocolate croissant). We had lived in France for two years, and I feel it's only right that I should join in the celebration! Actually, I'll use any excuse to drink great coffee and eat chocolate croissants!

On the more historically relevant and serious side, Bastille Day, as is our own Independence Day, is a time when we recognize and honor the courageous people who were willing to turn their countries upside-down and sacrifice their own lives in order to turn the rule of justice upside-right. These days are celebrated with songs, parades and all kinds of fanfare.

We people still don't have the whole ruling justly thing down perfectly. Not by a long shot.

But our God does! And God's just rule guides us in holy and righteous ways! This is something for all of us – for all peoples of every nation – to celebrate and sing about!

> *May the peoples praise you, God;*
> *may all the peoples praise you.*
> *May the nations be glad and sing for joy,*
> *for you rule the peoples with equity*
> *and guide the nations of the earth!*
> Psalm 67:3-4

Let us thank God for His just rule and guidance that is available to each of us, even now, as individuals, as groups and as whole nations. Let us trust in God's just rule and guidance always. Especially in these current days when we are so keenly aware of the many and evil injustices done in this dark world. Injustices done by individuals against individuals, groups against groups and nations against nations.

May each of us seek to follow God's just rule and guidance in our everyday lives. May we each yield to God's love and choose to be vessels of His justice and peace. Even with people and in places where it may seem impossible.

> *Blessed are those who act justly,*
> *who always do what is right.*
> Psalm 106:3

> *If it is possible, as far as it depends on you, live at peace with everyone.*
> Romans 12:18

No matter what is happening in our personal or global worlds, we can and should thank our Sovereign Lord always because He promises to make known His just rule and guidance in all their fullness as we join Him in His Eternal Kingdom! Eternity starts now.

So! Be glad and sing for joy, and maybe even eat a chocolate croissant or two just to add to the celebration of God's unshakable, eternal, just rule and guidance!

Reflections – Responses – Challenges – Encouragements – God-breathing Thoughts

Do I believe it?
And if I do, what am I going to do about it?

Lord, please let me hear your voice, your love, your wisdom, your grace and truth.

WHOLEHEARTEDLY – WHOLE HEARTS

We don't like to think of God as getting angry. At least not at us. We like to think of God as our kind and caring Heavenly Father, as our friend, as someone who will put up with pretty much anything because He's such a nice and loving God.

It is true that the Lord is loving. As a matter of fact, "God is love" (1 John 4:8,16).

It is equally true that the Lord is the sovereign, holy, righteous, almighty authority over all that exists – over all that God has called into being. Our Lord has the right to rule over us.

But we don't always want God to rule us. We don't really want God to tell us what to do. What we do want is to be loved. We like that part of God. But this whole obedience thing – and following the will and ways of the Lord – is a whole other matter. At least we think so.

The Israelites, on their journey out of captivity from slavery in Egypt to the Promised Land, kept rebelling against the Lord's will and ways. They refused to yield to and trust the Lord's authority. They could not – would not (That's a *ca-won't!*) trust that the Lord's leadership of them and His authority over them came only out of His love and desire to be their Eternal Protector. Sadly, their rebellion caused significant consequences.

> *The LORD's anger was aroused that day and He swore this oath:*
> *"Because they have not followed me wholeheartedly,*
> *not one of those who were twenty years old or more when they came up out of Egypt*
> *will see the land I promised on oath to Abraham, Isaac and Jacob –*
> *not one except Caleb son of Jephunneh the Kenizzite and Joshua son of Nun,*
> *for they followed the LORD wholeheartedly."*
> Numbers 32:10-12

When we go, and keep on going, in our own selfishly-determined ways and doing things based on our own limited perspectives and self-absorbed pride, we always end up hurting ourselves and, quite often, hurting those around us. Especially those we claim to love the very most.

The Lord wants us to obey and follow Him. The Lord wants us to trust Him wholeheartedly. This desire comes only and always out of God's eternal and unfailing love for us. Our Lord knows that it is only in following and trusting Him wholeheartedly that our hearts and our lives will be wholly filled with His love, His peace, His purpose, His hope and the joy of knowing His good and faithful promises as realities in our lives. Caleb and Joshua knew this. And they followed and trusted the Lord wholeheartedly.

God knows our hearts. Don't be afraid to be honest with God about the blatant and hidden ways you rebel against His authority over you – about the blatant and hidden ways you rebel against His love for you. God will forgive you. God will lead you in love. Our God, who is the Sovereign Lord and Eternal Love, wants each of us to choose, actively and intentionally, to follow and trust Him wholeheartedly so that our hearts will be made whole!

Do I believe it?
And if I do, what am I going to do about it?

Lord, please let me hear your voice, your love, your wisdom, your grace and truth.

IS JESUS ABLE?

We call out and cry out to the Lord to help us, to heal us, to hear us. To forgive us, to save us. To rescue us and deliver us from death, from our sins and from the sins of others. We call out and cry out to the Lord to give us His love, give us peace, give us hope, give us a sense of belonging, give us clear direction. Make us new.

As we call out and cry out to Jesus, do we really believe He is able to do these incredible life-changing things for us, in us and through us? Jesus asked others this same question.

> *As Jesus went on from there, two blind men followed him, calling out,*
> *"Have mercy on us, Son of David!"*
> *When he had gone indoors, the blind men came to him, and he asked them,*
> *"Do you believe that I am able to do this?"*
> *"Yes, Lord," they replied.*
> *Then he touched their eyes and said, "According to your faith let it be done to you."*
> Matthew 9:27-29

Do we believe and trust Jesus for who He is – the Lord's Messiah, the "Son of David" promised to rule forever? Do we trust Jesus at His Word? Do we believe that Jesus is able to do what we cannot possibly do for ourselves? Heal our lives. Transform our minds. And of greatest importance to Jesus – to forgive us and save us from our sins so that we may live in an intimate relationship with our God – now and for all eternity as His very loved children.

Jesus asked the two blind men if they believed He was able to heal their blindness. These blind men had undoubtedly heard about Jesus – heard about the many miraculous healings Jesus had been doing in their region. These blind men may have even heard Jesus speaking directly – heard, for themselves, His astonishing, authoritative teachings about the kingdom of God. They had heard about Jesus. They had heard Jesus. Now they wanted to see.

And these two blind men called out to Jesus, acknowledging Him – one they had not yet seen with their own eyes – as the promised Messiah. They were willing to tenaciously pursue Jesus, in spite of the darkness of their personal worlds, right into someone else's house. Because they believed Jesus was able!

Jesus asks each of us, even now, "Do you believe that I am able to do this?" Whatever your *this* is? Do you believe that Jesus is able to do what needs to be done in your life to set you free? Free from the guilt of your sin? Free from the brokenness you have known in your mind, body, spirit and relationships? Free from the demons and destructive habits that have plagued you and trapped you? Is Jesus – the Jesus you have heard about, the Jesus you have heard speak into your mind and heart through His Word and Spirit – able to do *this*?

We each need to answer this question for ourselves. And we may need to answer it many times throughout our lives as the darkness of our personal experiences, the darkness of our personal sins and the darkness of this dark and broken world blind us.

May our God give each of us the faith to acknowledge Jesus as the One who sets us free! May our God give each of us the tenacity to pursue Him and trust Him to do – for us, in us and through us – what we cannot possibly do for ourselves! Jesus is able!

Reflections – Responses – Challenges – Encouragements – God-breathing Thoughts

Do I believe it?
And if I do, what am I going to do about it?

Lord, please let me hear your voice, your love, your wisdom, your grace and truth.

WHAT DOES GOD WANT FROM US?

There may be times in our lives when we just throw our arms up in the air, shake our heads and feel absolutely confused and confounded about what God wants from us.

Maybe we've gotten to this point of bewilderment because we strayed from God for a period of time. Or we chose to put God on a shelf. And now, when we feel the Spirit tugging on our hearts to call us back home – back into a real, intimate and committed walk with Jesus – we're a little defensive and stubborn as we ask, "What do you want from me, God?"

Maybe we've gotten to this point of bewilderment because of all the hurt and hardship we've been going through, which has become absolutely unbearable and burdensome beyond what we could ever have imagined. And now, when we feel the Spirit tugging on our hearts to call us to keep trusting Jesus, even in our pain, we just feel it is too much, and we ask God, "What more could you possibly want from me, God?"

Maybe we've gotten to this point of bewilderment because of all the pressures and pulls, distractions and disruptions from so many sources – our families, our work, our school, our social life, our social networking, our church. And now, when we feel the Spirit tugging on our hearts to call us to rest our souls and reset our priorities, we respond with a bit of indignation, and we ask God, "What do you expect me to give up in order to do something for you, God?"

No matter what our circumstances are – no matter whether we have walked away from our relationship with Jesus or we have been overwhelmed by the hard times in our lives or we have been too busy to keep our relationship with Jesus as our first priority – our God lets us know what He wants from each of us.

> *He has shown you, O mortal, what is good. And what does the LORD require of you?*
> *To act justly and to love mercy and to walk humbly with your God.*
> Micah 6:8

All that the Lord requires of us, all that the Lord wants from us, is actually a blessing for us.

When we act justly, our hearts are filled with purpose. Acting justly means we reach out to people with respect, recognizing and validating their worth as fellow image-bearers of God. This can be done in such simple everyday ways. Other times, we may be called to act justly by giving our voice, our time, our energy and our finances to help secure justice for some of the least, the last and the lost of this world. Acting justly brings us into deeper intimacy with God, puts our burdens into perspective and places our priorities into God's eternal realm.

When we love mercy, our hearts are set free from every shred of victimhood and every selfish desire for vindication. As we love mercy, we offer true forgiveness to all who have hurt us. We begin to understand the breadth, length, height and depth of the love of Jesus and the price He paid for the forgiveness of our sins. As we love mercy, *we love God, we love others and we love ourselves* – God's greatest commandment of all. (Mark 12:30-31)

When we walk humbly with our God, our hearts are filled with awe that we, who are frail, flawed and finite, have even been invited by the Sovereign Lord of all eternity to walk with Him! We have been invited to walk with, to live with, our God in an intimate, freeing and soul-refreshing relationship! Our God just wants us to do it humbly.

Do I believe it?
And if I do, what am I going to do about it?

Lord, please let me hear your voice, your love, your wisdom, your grace and truth.

DON'T BE STUPID!

God speaks to us through His Word and by His Spirit in so many different ways. Sometimes God's Word speaks to us about historical events. Sometimes God's Word speaks to us in prophecies – some of which are already fulfilled, others are yet to be fulfilled. Sometimes God's Word speaks to us in commands, corrections, cautions and encouragements. Sometimes God's Word speaks to us in parables and metaphors. Sometimes God's Word speaks to us in emotionally charged poetry and songs.

And sometimes God's Word speaks to us bluntly and blatantly in extreme, cut-to-the-chase, get-to-the-point ways. That's exactly how many of the passages from Proverbs impact me. Bluntly.

> *Whoever loves discipline loves knowledge,*
> *but whoever hates correction is stupid.*
> Proverbs 12:1

It really says that? That way? Yes! God's Word speaks this bluntly to get His point across. God wants us to clearly, and without a lot of room for differing interpretations, understand that there are consequences for all our attitudes and behaviors. God wants us to understand that this *all up in our face* Proverb is meant to bring us life-giving, life-freeing truth.

When we *love discipline* – when we love to learn how we should live and act, speak and respond – we will love the knowledge and understanding it brings into our lives. And when we reject and hate the wise and godly correction, teaching and discipling-discipline that come to us, from God's love for us, we're just being stupid! And pride is the root-feeding material for that kind of stupidity.

We are told, as followers of Christ, that we should…

> *have the same mindset as that of Christ Jesus…he humbled himself*
> *by becoming obedient to death – even death on a cross!*
> Philippians 2:5,8

Our pride blocks us from humbly and open-mindedly accepting and learning lessons about ourselves that would actually free us and deepen us to grow in strength, wisdom and love. We may not like the manner in which the discipline and correction comes into our lives. We may not even like the person from whom the discipline and correction comes into our lives.

Yet, it would be *stupid* of us not to check our pride at the door, and prayerfully ask God: *What truth-filled discipline from God's heart and mind do I need to accept and learn from? What correction in my thinking, speaking, acting, reacting and interacting needs to happen?*

We need to trust God's love for us so much that we will love His discipline and correction that come to us – even if it sometimes comes to us in harsh ways – teaching us hard truths about ourselves. We need to trust God's love for us so much that we will love to grow, mature and become more like Jesus.

May we each choose the attitude of our Lord Jesus Christ, who brings truth, freedom and transformation into our lives! Choose humility and, thereby, choose wisdom! In other words: *Don't Be Stupid!*

Reflections – Responses – Challenges – Encouragements – God-breathing Thoughts

Do I believe it?
And if I do, what am I going to do about it?

Lord, please let me hear your voice, your love, your wisdom, your grace and truth.

_____

_____

_____

_____

_____

_____

_____

_____

_____

_____

_____

_____

_____

_____

_____

_____

_____

_____

_____

_____

_____

_____

IT DOES A BODY – MIND AND SPIRIT – GOOD!

We hear so much about the need for good nutrition and regular exercise in order to be healthy and strong. We may hear all about it. We may even believe it. But! In order for good nutrition and regular exercise to do us any good, we still have to do something about it!

Within Scripture there are some great guidelines about being healthy as well. As a counselor and a minister of God's Word for many years, I have witnessed the deeply interwoven connection between our spiritual health and that of our physical and mental health. This connection is absolutely incredible and undeniable. And it should not be ignored.

However, this is a broken world, and I want to make it clear that there is not always a perfect alignment with our spiritual health and our physical and mental health. I have known many individuals who have suffered from crippling and devastating illnesses and pain in their bodies and minds – none of which reveal the depth and breadth of their spiritual health and their intimate relationship with God. Likewise, I have known others whose physical strength and mental prowess reveal nothing of the dark and destitute state of their spiritual health and their non-existent relationship with God.

Choosing to live in a humble and teachable way before our God will always bring us greater spiritual health and bring us into a more mature, intimate relationship with our Lord. And, as God's Word assures us, there is a deep connection between our spiritual health and our physical and mental well-being. When looking at issues that bring us ill health and physical and mental imbalance, we need to seriously consider and sincerely assess the state of our spiritual relationship with God. Our spiritual health can absolutely affect our whole body.

Do not be wise in your own eyes; fear the LORD and shun evil.
This will bring health to your body and nourishment to your bones.
Proverbs 3:7-8

Do not let [Wisdom's words] out of your sight,
keep them within your heart;
for they are life to those who find them
and health to one's whole body.
Proverbs 4:21-22

Light in a messenger's eyes brings joy to the heart,
and good news gives health to the bones.
Proverbs 15:30

But for you who revere my name,
the sun of righteousness will rise with healing in its rays.
And you will go out and frolic like well-fed calves.
Malachi 4:2

We may hear about the spiritual-physical-mental health connection. We may even be avid believers of this connection. But! We still have to do something about it! May each of us choose to be humble and teachable before our God! It does a body – mind and spirit – good!

Do I believe it?
And if I do, what am I going to do about it?

Lord, please let me hear your voice, your love, your wisdom, your grace and truth.

ONE GIANT LEAP FOR EVERY ONE OF US

Do you remember where you were on July 20, 1969? Maybe you don't. But I do. This was the day Apollo 11 landed on the Moon. And I, along with countless Americans and many others around the world, watched this out-of-our-world experience while glued to my television set. As Walter Cronkite brought us the news of this amazing, unfathomable feat made possible by a driven passion, a strong competitive streak and scientific knowledge, we celebrated and marveled at the success of this magnificent step that humans had taken!

Neil Armstrong, the first man to ever walk on the Moon, uttered his now world famous words when taking his first step on the Lunar surface, "That's one small step for man – one giant leap for mankind."

In honor of Apollo 11's anniversary, these words are being reiterated on every news source available - TV, radio, newspapers, magazines and via incalculable cyberspace communication sources never even imagined back in 1969 by the brilliant scientists who made this adventure on the Moon possible.

God not only imagined this amazing feat by men and women of science and courage, God gave them and us – the people created by His love and will – the intellect, the insight and the ability to do many, amazingly great things!

> *In their hearts humans plan their course,*
> *but the LORD establishes their steps.*
> Proverbs 16:9

God Himself as the Lord of all creation has given us our very life, our very breath and every ability to think, plan, attempt and accomplish any and everything we do. Oh, that we all would, as individuals and as people of the earth, plan our course and choose our steps to do great things – in small ways and in big ways – to care for other people and for the good of our world!

Think about where and how you're walking today. Think about what steps you are taking as you journey through your life. Think about what steps you are taking as your life intertwines with others. Will your steps reflect and use – well, wisely and generously – the life, the breath, the intellect, the insight and the ability to do amazing things that God has given to you? Or will your steps crush the spirits, hopes and dreams of someone else around you – maybe even the littlest ones around you? Will you step on somebody's toes by thoughtless words and actions? Will your steps put your foot in your own mouth? Will your steps take you into places of shameful and sinful thoughts, words and actions?

Our God has given us every ability to plan our course. Yet, our God alone holds and reserves the sovereign authority to determine our steps, and which of our steps will be of eternal value. As we acknowledge our Holy God as our life-giver, may each of us choose to walk closely with Him, in each of our steps.

> *Since we live by the Spirit, let us keep in step with the Spirit.*
> Galatians 5:25

Let's each think honestly and carefully about our steps and the impact they have for our own lives and for the lives of every person into whose life we step. May we each choose to walk in God's loving, good ways! That would be a giant leap for each and every one of us!

Do I believe it?
And if I do, what am I going to do about it?

Lord, please let me hear your voice, your love, your wisdom, your grace and truth.

WITH WHOLEHEARTED DEVOTION AND A WILLING MIND

As the aged King David prepared his son Solomon to take up the throne as a servant of God and as the King of Israel, David had strong and wise counsel for his son.

> *"And you, my son Solomon, acknowledge the God of your father,*
> *and serve Him with wholehearted devotion and with a willing mind,*
> *for the LORD searches every heart*
> *and understands every desire and every thought.*
> *If you seek him, he will be found by you;*
> *but if you forsake him, he will reject you forever."*
> 1 Chronicles 28:9

David's counsel to Solomon is counsel that we, too, should take for ourselves. As children, servants and ambassadors of the Most High God, we need to fully embrace the wisdom of serving our God with a wholehearted devotion and a willing mind as we live out the details of our daily-day lives...during our days of great joy and peace...and during our days of great turmoil and sadness.

God knows us full well. And our Lord wants our hearts and minds to be wholeheartedly and willingly devoted to Him. Our God wants us to actively and intentionally seek to love and follow Him with all that we are and with all that we think, say and do.

Our great blessing in serving and seeking our Lord with wholehearted devotion and a willing mind – and our God's loving and faithful promise to us – is that as we seek the Lord, *He will be found* by us! Our God has promised that as we seek Him, we will find and know Him. As we seek Him, we will know God's loving and intimate presence with us forever. We will know God's strong and holy leading. We will know God's wise and protective guidance for us all the days of our lives. Through our Lord Jesus Christ coming to us in order to rescue us from God's righteous judgment against our sins, it is actually we who have been found!

Is there anything stopping you from serving and seeking the Lord with wholehearted devotion and a willing mind? Nothing this world has to offer – nothing you may be holding onto – is worth the cost of keeping you from an intimate, powerful and eternal relationship with the Lord.

Ask the Lord to reveal to you, and take away from you, any and all obstacles of pride, self-focused living and hidden or blatant sins that you have put up in your life that stop you from serving and seeking the Lord with wholehearted devotion and a willing mind.

Ask the Lord to reveal to you, and take away from you, any and all obstacles of hurt, bitterness and resentment that have grown up in you from your painful experiences with other people and from disappointing and difficult circumstances that stop you from serving and seeking the Lord with wholehearted devotion and a willing mind.

Let nothing rule over you except the love and leadership of the Lord our God! Our Lord Jesus gave Himself with wholehearted devotion and a willing mind as He chose to die for our salvation! Let us choose to live in His resurrection power – living in His joy and freedom, peace and purpose, truth and transformation – as we choose to serve and seek the Lord our God with wholehearted devotion and a willing mind! Every day of our lives!

Do I believe it?
And if I do, what am I going to do about it?

Lord, please let me hear your voice, your love, your wisdom, your grace and truth.

COVENANT OF LOVE

At the dedication of the temple in Jerusalem, King Solomon took time to acknowledge God and His faithfulness to those who choose to serve and follow the Lord wholeheartedly.

"LORD, the God of Israel, there is no God like you in heaven or on earth – you who keep your covenant of love with your servants who continue wholeheartedly in your way."
2 Chronicles 6:14

I love that phrase about God: *"...You who keep your covenant of love..."* Wow.

We are given a promise of love. More than that. This is a holy assurance of faithful love from the eternal, sovereign Lord of all creation. God is the keeper of His covenant of love to us who are frail, flawed and finite. Again, I repeat: Wow.

Coming from a childhood where love – protective, faithful, tender, caring and compassionate love – was almost entirely unknown and twisted by ugly, destructive abuse, it took some serious, supernatural convincing by God's Word and Spirit for me to come to the place where I absolutely trusted that God is good and is truly faithful to His covenant of love. And I am convinced! Awed, humbled, thankful and convinced!

God's covenant of love is a certain thing. No matter the uncertainties of our lives. God doesn't change. God's love for us, with a passion and a faithfulness that knows no bounds, does not change either. But we do. We turn away from our loving God, way too often, and choose to go our own way instead of choosing to continue wholeheartedly in following our God's way.

Oh, choices! Next time you have to make a decision about what you will think, say and do (and that's hundreds of times each day), choose to: Stop first. Ask yourself: Will your decision take you farther away from living in, and living out, the truth of the Lord's faithful covenant of love made to you as you choose to go your own self-focused way? Or will your thoughts, words and actions reveal your choice to continue wholeheartedly to live in, and live out, God's good and holy way – which is formed by and filled with God's faithful covenant of love made to you?

This decision should be a no-brainer, right? Yeah. Should be. But I know that I can, and too often still do, choose to turn my brain off from listening to God about continuing wholeheartedly in His good and holy way. Sometimes I just want to go my way. I'm listening to me. Not to God. In those moments, I'm feeling and being selfish, self-pitying, self-righteous, prideful or just plain grumpy – and I'm not in a hurry to get over myself. So, I just shut my brain off from listening to God. In those moments, I ignore God. And trust me, when I do that, it just isn't pretty.

Our God loves us so much. And for those of us who trust in God's fullest revelation of His covenant of love – the death and resurrection of our Lord Jesus Christ – we need to continue wholeheartedly in following God's good and holy way. Every day of our lives. With our every thought, word and action. With every choice and decision we make. It is here, in those moments of choices and decisions (that come to us constantly), that God's covenant of love to us may be lived out through us in tangible and powerful ways, touching the lives of all those around us – all who desperately need to know God's covenant of love for themselves.

Reflections – Responses – Challenges – Encouragements – God-breathing Thoughts

Do I believe it?
And if I do, what am I going to do about it?

Lord, please let me hear your voice, your love, your wisdom, your grace and truth.

DO YOU WANT TO BE IMMORTAL?

Do you want to live forever? Do you want to be immortal?

I do. But not here on this earth. I want to live forever with my God in His eternal Kingdom, where sin and shame, pain and death, war and destruction have no place and no power. I want to be immortal and live eternally in the presence of my loving and holy Abba.

There is a way to be an immortal and live in the presence of the Eternal God. This way is found only in Jesus.

In the way of righteousness there is life; along that path is immortality.
Proverbs 12:28

Jesus answered, "I am the way and the truth and the life.
No one comes to the Father except through me."
John 14:6

...then know this, you and all the people of Israel: It is by the name of Jesus Christ
of Nazareth, whom you crucified but whom God raised from the dead...
Salvation is found in no one else for there is no other name under heaven
given to mankind by which we must be saved.
Acts 4:10, 12

Jesus said to her, "I am the resurrection and the life. The one who believes in me
will live, even though they die; and whoever lives by believing in me will never die.
Do you believe this?"
John 11:25-26

We each need to answer some questions honestly for ourselves: *Do we believe Jesus is the resurrection and the life?* Do we believe that Jesus is the way to be immortal? That Jesus is way to live eternally with our God?

For all of us who have put our faith in Jesus Christ as our Savior, we have already been birthed into eternal life – into immortality. Our immortal, eternal life with our Holy God began the moment we *declared with our mouths and believed in our hearts that Jesus is Lord* (Romans 10:9). Sin has been fully forgiven. The power of death has been fully conquered. And God calls us to live in these eternal, immortal truths – right now!

Each of us, as the rescued and redeemed people of God, are called to live our new and resurrected – our eternal and immortal – lives by following God's greatest commandment. To live our lives as God had always intended us to live them from the birth of creation:

"Love the Lord your God with all your heart and with all your soul and with all your mind
and with all your strength [and]...Love your neighbor as yourself."
Mark 12:30-31

May God open each of our hearts and minds to trust Jesus fully as our one and only way to live eternally with our Heavenly Abba, as our one and only way to be immortal! And may we live our lives – our immortal lives – with the full flow and power of Christ's love for our God, for others and for ourselves!

Do I believe it?
And if I do, what am I going to do about it?

Lord, please let me hear your voice, your love, your wisdom, your grace and truth.

STONES AND ROCKS – POLISHED TO BRILLIANCE

Stones and rocks have been part of so many stories in the Bible – the stones that Noah, Abraham, Isaac, Jacob, Moses, Joshua, and so many others set up as altars to the Lord. The twelve stones, engraved like a seal with the names of each of the twelve tribes of Israel, that were mounted in the ceremonial breastplate of the priests who served the Lord. The twelve stones that were taken from the middle of the Jordan as a memorial sign of the Lord's faithful leading of Israel into the Promised Land. The five stones (Although he only needed one!) that the shepherd boy David, later to be Israel's king, took up to conquer Goliath and the Philistines who had defied the armies of the Living God. The Lord Himself is referred to as the Rock and my Rock over and over again. Jesus Christ, our Messiah, is the Cornerstone and the Living Stone. And we ourselves, as followers of Jesus Christ, are called to be living stones, built together with other believers to love, serve and represent our Lord.

As you come to him, the Living Stone – rejected by humans but chosen by God and precious to him – you also, like living stones, are being built into a spiritual house to be a holy priesthood, offering spiritual sacrifices acceptable to God through Jesus Christ.
1 Peter 2:4-5

Over the years, I have collected all kinds of stones and rocks from many places, under many circumstances, as a tangible way to remember the journey and thank my God for leading me faithfully – even when I didn't know how or where or why I was going or what I would encounter when I got there. These stones and rocks helped me to remember and acknowledge that God was not only leading me, but that God was also actively and intentionally shaping me with His eternal purpose in mind. That, no matter where I went, whom I was with or what I did, I was...

...to be conformed to the image of His Son...
Romans 8:29

Most of the time that shaping and conforming has not come easily. Need brought it. Pain brought it. Loss brought it. Loneliness brought it. Rejection brought it. Confession and repentance of sin brought it. Frustration brought it. Disappointment brought it. Helplessness brought it. Annoying, arrogant, difficult and cruel people brought it. God took all that was hard in my life, and softened me. God took all that revealed my weaknesses, and strengthened me.

A card I received awhile back expressed that exact sentiment. It read: *"The most beautiful stones have been tossed by the wind and washed by the water and polished to brilliance by life's strongest storms."*

Our Lord has collected His people, His living stones, by His unfailing, conquering love. And in Jesus and through His unlimited grace and eternal truth, we each are to be shaped, conformed and transformed more and more into His likeness – the beautiful and eternal Living Stone. We are each to be *"polished to brilliance!"*

May we each give ourselves over, more fully and freely, more actively and intentionally, to our Lord's shaping and conforming labor of love to be done in our lives. In this way, each of us will become a sign, an altar, a memorial stone – a brilliantly polished stone – pointing others to our Lord Jesus Christ, to His love, salvation and transforming power.

Reflections – Responses – Challenges – Encouragements – God-breathing Thoughts

Do I believe it?
And if I do, what am I going to do about it?

Lord, please let me hear your voice, your love, your wisdom, your grace and truth.

DOES GOD LIVE IN YOUR HOUSE?

Does God live in your house? Or is God just a neighbor of yours?

You know, maybe you see each other when you come out your door to go to work or to school? Or when you bring your mail in or take your trash out? Or on a really beautiful day – when you just have to be outside – you run into God walking around your neighborhood? Maybe you're even a good neighbor to God. You always keep your yard mowed, leaves raked or sidewalk shoveled as the seasons demand. You even toss His newspaper up closer to His front step if you're the first one out in the morning. As far as you can tell, you never do anything to really bother God. And by golly! Anytime your paths cross you always smile, wave and say, "Hello!" to God. So you're obviously a pretty darn good neighbor. Some people never say, "Hello!" to their neighbors after all. There have even been times when the two of you worked on some pretty meaningful projects together for the benefit of others.

Yet, somehow you know that every time you have a brief – and even polite – encounter with God, He wants something more. It seems like God would love for the two of you to really get to know each other. But, you just don't have the time. You just don't want God in your life in any real way. Not in any actual face-to-face, intimate, involved-with-your-life kind of way. Being God's neighbor is just fine with you.

It's not fine with God. God doesn't want to be our neighbor. God is not Mr. Rogers.

God is our Creator, Sustainer, Savior, Mighty God, Wonderful Counselor, Everlasting Father, Prince of Peace, Sovereign and Intimate Lord, our Abba! And our God, who loves us beyond what we could ever imagine, wants to live with us and live in us.

> *"Because I live, you also will live.*
> *On that day you will realize that I am in my Father*
> *and you are in me, and I am in you."*
> John 14:19-20

> *Jesus replied, "Anyone who loves me will obey my teaching.*
> *My Father will love them, and we will come to them and make our home with them."*
> John 14:23

God wants so much more for each one of us. Even if we have put our faith in Jesus as Savior, we may still very much need to fully open up our houses – fully open up our hearts – to honestly, intimately and powerfully let God, His Word and His Spirit take up permanent residence with us. Is God's Name on the deed to your life? Do you know that God is your life? Do you know God loves you as your Eternal Abba – your Heavenly Daddy? Do you know God's heart for you? Do you love and trust and obey God because you are His precious child?

God will never be satisfied, and we will never know the sweet joy of intimacy with God, if we keep God only as our neighbor, never letting Him fully into our houses, our hearts and our lives.

I pray that each of us will courageously open up the door to our hearts in a radical way to truly let God live with us, in us and through us – so that we will be God's messengers of love and peace, grace and truth to all of our other neighbors!

Do I believe it?
And if I do, what am I going to do about it?

Lord, please let me hear your voice, your love, your wisdom, your grace and truth.

TAKE HOLD OF MY HEAD, GOD! I WANT TO SLAP SOMEBODY!

There are days that I have to, loudly, clearly and a bit forcefully, make myself keep repeating what I call my *Take Hold of My Head, God! – Jesus Refrain.* Which, at times, is the only thing keeping me refrained from slapping somebody!

Grace and Truth...Grace and Truth...Grace and Truth...Grace and Truth...

> **The Word became flesh and made his dwelling among us. We have seen his glory,**
> **the glory of the one and only Son, who came from the Father, full of grace and truth.**
> **...grace and truth came through Jesus Christ.**
> John 1:14, 17

Grace and Truth...Grace and Truth...Grace and Truth...Grace and Truth...

Sometimes the evil in this world – the evil within us as individuals, the wars and rapes, the murder and brutality, the evil we inflict right within our own families, within our closest, most trusted relationships, and even within the Body of Christ – just overwhelms me. I shouldn't be surprised. I'm not. Not really. I've counseled people for many years, and am intimately and personally aware of the ugly evil that comes from and pervades every life to some extent. So, no, the evil I am confronted with, from others and myself, is not a surprise to me. But I hate it!

> **The LORD looks down from heaven on all mankind to see if there are any who**
> **understand, any who seek God. All have turned away, all have become corrupt;**
> **there is no one who does good, not even one. Do all these evildoers know nothing?**
> **They devour my people as though eating bread; they never call on the LORD.**
> Psalm 14:2-4

I know that the evil in this world – the prideful, ugly, lying, devouring, truth-twisting, cruel, adulterous, idolatrous, greedy, rebellious, self-centered, controlling, manipulative, dangerous, life-destroying evil – is not a surprise to God! This evil is exactly why Jesus – the One and Only, holy, righteous, pure Son of God – had to sacrifice His own life in order that we might be forgiven and become children of God. Jesus died for what is killing us: Sin. Jesus died for the sin that is killing our families, our relationships, our neighbors, our nations, our world.

That is the *Grace and Truth...Grace and Truth...Grace and Truth...Grace and Truth...*of Jesus Christ that is holding my head and keeping me from slapping somebody right now! Because the truth is, I am the one that somebody else may want to slap because of my sin – because of my own evil. And the grace is, Jesus has already died for my sins, and has set me free from the power of both sin and shame in my life!

That is the G*race and Truth...Grace and Truth...Grace and Truth...Grace and Truth...*of Jesus Christ that is giving me peace, perspective, balance, willingness and strength to keep loving, to keep forgiving, to keep teaching, writing and counseling, to keep living in and sharing the love, salvation, freedom, power, healing and transformation that come through Jesus Christ alone!

May the *Grace and Truth...Grace and Truth...Grace and Truth...Grace and Truth...*of Jesus Christ take hold of each of our heads! And rule in each of our lives!

Reflections – Responses – Challenges – Encouragements – God-breathing Thoughts

Do I believe it?
And if I do, what am I going to do about it?

Lord, please let me hear your voice, your love, your wisdom, your grace and truth.

SALVATION – DONE! TRANSFORMATION – CONTINUING!

When we believe, and put our faith in, the truth that Jesus is the Son of God who died for the forgiveness of our sins and rose from the dead to give us eternal life with our Heavenly Father, our salvation for all of eternity is accomplished. Done! Finished! Complete!

Isn't that fabulous? It truly is the Good News – the Gospel from our Holy God. We need never to fear damnation or death again. Jesus bore all the punishment for our sins. We are forgiven completely. Jesus conquered death through His eternal resurrection. We have been given the promise of eternal life from the Life Giver Himself.

Our salvation is absolutely sure from the day, from the very moment, we accept Jesus as God's Messiah, as the Savior of our lives. A work fully completed through the death and resurrection of Jesus.

Our transformation, however, requires us to make day by day, moment by moment choices as we yield to God's renewing work within us to make us more like Him.

Jesus Christ saves us from the power of sin and death. Jesus, just as passionately, desires to transform us and put an end to all of our habits and patterns of thinking, speaking, acting, reacting and interacting that limit us from living in the full grace, truth, freedom, power and love He has made available to us right now on this side of heaven.

So, then, just as you received Christ Jesus as Lord,
continue to live your lives in him, rooted and built up in him,
strengthened in the faith as you were taught,
and overflowing with thankfulness.
Colossians 2:6-7

We should overflow with thankfulness for our eternal salvation! Its promise of eternal life with our Holy God is beyond hope, beyond joy – and I believe heaven is well beyond anything I could ever, ever imagine. We should overflow with thankfulness for the unlimited resurrection power of our Lord Jesus, who is able to bring true and amazing transformation into our lives – into our minds, mouths, hearts and souls. And we can be…

…confident of this, that he who began a good work in you
will carry it on to completion until the day of Christ Jesus.
Philippians 1:6

Our Lord desires to continually free us from every twisted lie and destructive pattern we have. Our Lord desires to continually transform us to reflect His life and glory through each of our lives.

…we are being transformed into his image with ever-increasing glory…
2 Corinthians 3:18

God's salvation has given us forgiveness and life for all eternity. Let our thanksgiving overflow! God's transformation works lovingly and continually within us to give us a life of freedom, peace, purpose and power – right here and now. Let our thanksgiving overflow!

Reflections – Responses – Challenges – Encouragements – God-breathing Thoughts

Do I believe it?
And if I do, what am I going to do about it?

Lord, please let me hear your voice, your love, your wisdom, your grace and truth.

IT IS A BEAUTIFUL THING!

For just as each of us has one body with many members, and these members
do not all have the same function, so in Christ we, though many,
form one body, and each member belongs to all the others.
Romans 12:4-5

The Body of Christ, on this side of heaven, is so very far from perfect. Still, when even a few sisters and brothers come together in love, prayer and service, and the Body of Christ acts like the Body of Christ, it is a beautiful thing! When the Body of Christ acts like the Body of Christ, the whole Body is blessed by its diversity and its unity. Our God is blessed as we, together and using our different gifts and abilities, bless others in Jesus' Name! And it is a beautiful thing.

When the Body of Christ acts like the Body of Christ, differences in the gifts, abilities, talents, passions, perspectives and energy levels among the individual members are embraced and understood as given creatively, purposefully and lovingly – as well as with a good bit of humor – from the One and Only God, who alone is able to make us one with the Father, Son and Holy Spirit. Because we all belong to the one Body of Christ, we come to appreciate and give thanks for God's truth that "each member belongs to all the others." And it is a beautiful thing.

There will be Body blessings for each of us as we accept and celebrate the diversity of gifts that our sisters and brothers in Christ bring to our lives. Their presence and perspectives will sharpen us, encourage us and challenge us to be more like Jesus. Their diversity of gifts and abilities will fill in gaping holes where we ourselves are most lacking. There will be Body blessings for each of us as we continually, passionately and tenaciously guard and build up the unity given to us through the Spirit of God. This unity is transforming, humbling, healing, maturing and empowering for the Body of Christ as we yield to the grace and truth of God, who calls us to love each other as Jesus has loved us! And it is a beautiful thing.

Yet, since we who make up the Body are still so very far from perfect, we need to inquire of our God and look honestly and inwardly at ourselves, and ask:
Is there any way that I am diminishing or destroying the unity of the Body of Christ?
How and when and why do I not use the gifts and abilities God gave me to bless the Body?
How and when and who do I self-righteously judge, pridefully criticize and disdainfully dismiss within the Body of Christ?
How and when and who do I not love as Christ loves His Body?
How do I take the beautiful thing that the Body of Christ is meant to be and make it ugly?

Over the years I have been powerfully and tangibly loved, challenged and grown up by the Body of Christ acting like the Body of Christ. I have received intimate care during times of crisis, illness and loss. I have received sharp, yet loving and necessary, blows of correction. I have been encouraged, prayed for, and supported personally and in the transforming ministry call that God has placed on my life. I am so thankful for the Body! And it is a beautiful thing.

May each of us yield to our Lord and Savior Jesus as the true Head of the Body! For when the Body of Christ acts like the Body of Christ – when we love, honor, encourage, care for, support, gently and strongly correct our members, and tenaciously guard and protect our unity with our God and with each other – it is a beautiful thing!

Reflections – Responses – Challenges – Encouragements – God-breathing Thoughts

Do I believe it?
And if I do, what am I going to do about it?

Lord, please let me hear your voice, your love, your wisdom, your grace and truth.

GOD'S COMFORT, CHALLENGE AND AWE – ALL GOOD THINGS!

"Am I only a God nearby," declares the LORD, "and not a God far away?
Who can hide in secret places so that I cannot see him?" declares the LORD.
"Do not I fill heaven and earth?" declares the LORD.
Jeremiah 23:23-24

Comfort, challenge and awe are all found in our holy God! They are all good things!

Comfort. Our God is nearby no matter where we are, no matter what our circumstances, no matter what we are feeling, no matter how difficult, sad, frustrating or fear-bringing our lives may be at any moment in time. Our God is omnipresent for all of us. Our God is intimate with each of us as individuals. God's Word declares His truth: *I am nearby. I am with you always.* Take a moment and be comforted. It is a good thing.

Challenge. Our God sees everything. Our God knows everything. Our God sees and knows each one of us – in every place, in every relationship, in our every thought, in our every word, in our every action – in every moment of our lives. God's Word declares His truth: *There is no secret place away from Me. You can never hide from Me.* Take a moment and be challenged. It is a good thing.

Awe. God's sovereign and holy presence fills all of creation – all that is seen and unseen. God's sovereign and holy presence fills all that exists. God's Word declares His truth: *I am sovereign. I fill and rule over all things in all ways at all times.* Take a moment and be filled with awe. It is a good thing.

As we allow God to lead our lives, to truly be our Savior and our Lord, God's comfort, challenge and awe all become, more and more, very good things in our lives. Because our God is nearby, because our God sees and knows everything, because our God is the sovereign ruler of all that exists, we cannot hide any of our sins from Him. Because our God is nearby, because our God sees and knows everything, because our God is the sovereign ruler of all that exists, we cannot keep any bitterness or unforgiveness towards anyone hidden from our God. And that's a good thing because both sin and unforgiveness destroy us - destroy our peace, our hope, our relationship with God and with other people in our lives.

As we acknowledge that our God truly is nearby, sees and knows everything, and is the sovereign ruler of all that exists, God's Spirit calls us to humbly and sincerely confess our sins. And in that confession, we are given the full-measure of God's loving forgiveness. Our Lord Jesus Christ has already conquered the power and pull of sin through His death on the cross and through His eternal resurrection! And that is a good thing!

As we acknowledge that our God truly is nearby, sees and knows everything, and is the sovereign ruler of all that exists, we are set free from every bondage that has kept us captive to our bitterness, unforgiveness, shame, pride and fear. Jesus Christ has come to set us free – free to live a life of love, mercy, compassion, courage, strength, peace and trust in Him! And that is a good thing!

May we all be comforted, challenged and filled with awe at these truths declared by our Lord! They are all very good things!

Reflections – Responses – Challenges – Encouragements – God-breathing Thoughts

Do I believe it?
And if I do, what am I going to do about it?

Lord, please let me hear your voice, your love, your wisdom, your grace and truth.

NOT A WHOLE LOT OF SIMPLE! BUT A WHOLE LOT OF PEACE!

We are told to trust God. We are told to have a simple trust – a childlike trust – in our God.

Simple trust? I'm thinking there's really not a whole lot of simple when it comes to trusting our God.

To trust God – to really trust God – takes a bold and courageous determination of our minds. To trust God – to really trust God – we must constantly and continually, actively and intentionally, choose to invite and allow God's Word and Spirit to rule over our hearts, our minds, our thoughts, our feelings, our fears, our stresses, our anxieties, our need for some semblance of control in circumstances that may be very much out of our control. (Which really is the truth about pretty much everything and every circumstance!)

To trust God is no simple matter. To trust God – to really trust God – is a conscious, effort-filled, energy-directed choice.

God gives us a blueprint for this not-so-simple choice of trust: Prayer and Thanksgiving. God gives us a promised blessing as we follow His blueprint of trust: Transcending Peace.

> *Do not be anxious about anything, but in every situation, by prayer and petition,*
> *with thanksgiving, present your requests to God.*
> *And the peace of God, which transcends all understanding,*
> *will guard your hearts and your minds in Christ Jesus.*
> Philippians 4:6-7

Trusting God does not mean – nor does it promise – that each of our circumstances will always end up just as we hope, diligently plan and work for, and, even, desperately, heart-wrenchingly desire. Trusting God is not some kind of flippant fairy tale solution to the pain, brokenness and difficult challenges that we all face in our lives.

However, trusting God does mean – and always promises – that we will be given God's transcending peace right in the midst of each of our circumstances. Trusting God does mean – and always promises – that God's transcending peace will be at work in us, over us and through us – guarding our hearts, our minds, our thoughts and our emotions from every Lie From The Pit Of Hell (LFTPOH) that would ravage and rob us of the truth and power of the transcending peace of our Lord Jesus Christ.

So, no, there's not a whole lot of simple when it comes to trusting God. We have to give everything over to Him. Over and over and over again. And that's not done simply. That's done by tenaciously remembering and acknowledging who our God is and who He is to us –

> *Wonderful Counselor, Mighty God, Everlasting Father, Prince of Peace*
> Isaiah 9:6

The childlike part of trust – that our God wants from us and for us – does come to us when we choose to get very honest in recognizing how very much we need God. How very much not in control we are. Not so simple for most of us. But, oh! When we choose to trust who our God is and who He is to us, when we choose to go to our God in prayer and with thanksgiving, there is a whole lot of peace for us – a whole lot of transcending peace!

Do I believe it?
And if I do, what am I going to do about it?

Lord, please let me hear your voice, your love, your wisdom, your grace and truth.

JOY AND GLADNESS, THANKSGIVING AND SINGING!
AND A BIT OF DANCING, TOO!

The LORD will surely comfort Zion
and will look with compassion on all her ruins;
He will make her deserts like Eden,
her wastelands like the garden of the LORD.
Joy and gladness will be found in her,
thanksgiving and the sound of singing.
Isaiah 51:3

This passage speaks of a time when the Lord's great comfort and compassion for Zion – for the people of Zion – will be both historically and eternally realized. It will be a time when destruction will be completely transformed into abundant life and unfailing resources of beauty and nourishment. This is God's ultimate fulfillment of His promise to His people – to those who are part of His true kingdom, to those who will be living with Him in the true and eternal Zion.

I can only barely begin to imagine the incredible, beautiful, holy and free from all sin, death and decay place to which our Lord will bring us home! When God's promise is fulfilled in its entirety, we will know true joy and gladness! When God's promise is fulfilled in its entirety, thanksgiving and singing will be heard! And I'm thinking there will probably be a bit of dancing going on, too!

Although we, as the redeemed people of God's eternal Zion, must wait in hope for the fullness of God's kingdom to be revealed, we need to remember that God's comfort and compassion, renewal and transforming power are available to each of us – right here and right now on this side of heaven! The love of Jesus Christ, His eternal salvation and His powerful transformation should make all the difference in each of our lives right now.

God's comfort and compassion, renewal and transforming power should radically change each one of us as individuals. God's comfort and compassion, renewal and transforming power should radically change each and every one of us in every relationship we have and in every circumstance we experience in our lives.

In Jesus Christ we are given full hope, freedom and transformation!
What was condemned is now forgiven!
What was dead is now alive!
What was broken is now healed!
What was in bondage is now set free!
What was bitter is now sweet!
What was weak is now strong!
What was poor is now rich!
What was lost is now found!
What was dark is now light!

Yes, we do have to wait for the fullness of God's eternal kingdom – His heavenly Zion – to be revealed. But! In the meantime, let's celebrate that our Lord and Savior Jesus Christ changes everything!

May we each invite and allow Jesus to change everything in us. Right now. And as we do, there will be joy and gladness within our hearts, thanksgiving and singing will be heard! And I'm thinking there will probably be a bit of dancing going on, too!

Reflections – Responses – Challenges – Encouragements – God-breathing Thoughts

Do I believe it?
And if I do, what am I going to do about it?

Lord, please let me hear your voice, your love, your wisdom, your grace and truth.

GOD'S KIND OF KINDNESS

At one time we too were foolish, disobedient, deceived
and enslaved by all kinds of passions and pleasures.
We lived in malice and envy, being hated and hating one another.
But when the kindness and love of God our Savior appeared, he saved us,
not because of righteous things we had done, but because of his mercy.
He saved us through the washing of rebirth and renewal by the Holy Spirit,
whom He poured out on us generously through Jesus Christ our Savior.
Titus 3:3-6

Ouch. Tough words, hard words about our sins. About my sins. Don't like to read them, hear them or acknowledge them. Yet, they are true words from God's Word about us – about you, about me – before we put our faith in the salvation and renewal offered to us by the blood of Jesus, by the forgiveness and cleansing of our sins. Sadly, this struggle for my mind, heart, words, actions, reactions and interactions goes on, and will go on, on this side of heaven. And it will for you, too. Thanks be to God for His kindness and love that have forever set His children free from the bondage of this struggle!

God's kind of kindness is so different from what we offer to others. God's kind of kindness is so different from what others have offered to us. And it makes all the difference for us right now and for all of eternity!

God's kind of kindness to us is not based on anything we have done. It cannot be earned. It is not deserved. God's kind of kindness is not conditional. God is unchangeable. God's kind of kindness is based on who God is and not on who we are. God's kind of kindness is not limited by our own perceptions of self or by how others view us. God's kind of kindness is not limited by how we have been wounded, treated or twisted by others or by our circumstances. God's kind of kindness is not weakened by the ways we have been hurt by others, nor by the ways we have been hurtful towards others. God's kind of kindness is not altered because we have been hated or hateful.

God's kind of kindness comes to us through His unfailing, unlimited love and unleashed mercy – offering us full forgiveness for our sins, healing for our minds, renewal for our lives and eternal life with our Holy God – through the sacrificial death and conquering resurrection of our Lord Jesus Christ. Jesus' death and resurrection have destroyed the power that sin and death had held over our lives. Through the blood of Christ, this bondage is broken. We are set free.

Each of us is given the choice to accept and fully receive the salvation, kindness, love and mercy offered to us by our Lord Jesus Christ. And as we accept and receive salvation, God's Holy Spirit – who has been generously and powerfully given to us, to live within us – is able to fully cleanse us and fully renew us for all eternity. We each also have a choice to make about continually giving ourselves over to the Spirit's washing and renewal work within us. We have a choice to make about giving the Spirit more elbow room so that God's freeing, powerful purpose of transforming us to be more like Jesus will be done every day of our lives. Moment by moment. Thought by thought. Word by word. Action by action.

May we each allow the freedom and power of God's kind of kindness – that cost Jesus His life – to rule over and lead our lives completely!

Do I believe it?
And if I do, what am I going to do about it?

Lord, please let me hear your voice, your love, your wisdom, your grace and truth.

GOD'S KIND OF KINDNESS – GOD'S FOLLOW-UP PLAN

"But to you who are listening I say:
Love your enemies, do good to those who hate you,
bless those who curse you, pray for those who mistreat you.
...love your enemies, do good to them,
and lend to them without expecting to get anything back.
Then your reward will be great, and you will be children of the Most High,
because he is kind to the ungrateful and wicked.
Be merciful just as your Father is merciful."
Luke 6:27-28, 35-36

As we hear about and accept for ourselves God's kind of kindness offered to us through the salvation that comes through Jesus Christ, God's kind of kindness will have a follow-up plan for each one of us – to be carried out in and through each one of our lives.

God's follow-up plan is for a radical transformation, so real and so deep, to take place in each of our lives – in each of our minds, attitudes and actions – that we, as children of the Most High, will reflect God's kind of kindness to others.

God's follow-up plan intends and purposes that God's kind of kindness will, with increasing power and evidence, change absolutely everything within us – everything within the way we think, speak, act and react in every one of our circumstances and in every one of our relationships. Including with our God and with ourselves.

Through God's kind of kindness we, as children of the Most High, are supernaturally empowered by God's Spirit and commanded by God's mercy to do outrageous things! Things that don't make any kind of sense on this side of heaven. Things exactly like Jesus has done for us. Through God's kind of kindness we are empowered and commanded –
To love our enemies.
To do good to those who hate us.
To bless those who curse us.
To pray for those who mistreat us.
To give generously to others without any expectation of return.

We are supernaturally empowered by God's Spirit and commanded by God's mercy to give, and live out, God's radical, real and deep kind of kindness with even the most ungrateful and wicked people in our lives.

God's kind of kindness is outrageous and extravagant, generous and compassionate, active and intentional! This is the same kind of kindness that our Holy God has given to each of us!

God's kind of kindness is no small thing! It spreads its arms on a cross, goes to hell in our place and reaches to heaven on our behalf!

God's follow-up plan for us, as children of the Most High, is to give to others that same kind of kindness! Giving it in all of its outrageous and extravagant, generous and compassionate, active and intentional ways! Just as we have been supernaturally empowered by God's Spirit and commanded by God's mercy to do!

Reflections – Responses – Challenges – Encouragements – God-breathing Thoughts

Do I believe it?
And if I do, what am I going to do about it?

Lord, please let me hear your voice, your love, your wisdom, your grace and truth.

ABSOLUTELY PERFECT AND FAR HIGHER

"For my thoughts are not your thoughts,
neither are your ways my ways.
As the heavens are higher than the earth,
so are my ways higher than your ways
and my thoughts than your thoughts..." declares the LORD.
Isaiah 55:8-9

God's thoughts are not our thoughts. God's ways are not our ways.

I have come to accept these truths about my own thoughts and ways. Not necessarily easily at first. Now I humbly, peacefully and with full confidence trust in God's absolutely perfect and far higher thoughts and ways. Through God's Word and God's Spirit and through many countless experiences in my own life, I've clearly and powerfully sensed God's love, presence, peace, intervention and transformation. I've clearly and powerfully come to accept that God's thoughts and ways are not my ways. They are absolutely perfect and far higher than mine.

God is God. God can be trusted. God is eternally unchangeable and good. God is love.

It is not only in knowing and believing these truths about God, but it is also in honestly and vulnerably admitting the truth about myself, that I have come to fully trust that God's thoughts and ways really are absolutely perfect and far higher than mine.

I'm not God. I'm little. I'm frail. I'm flawed. I'm finite. And I'm far too often fickle – loving God and serving God with all of my heart, my soul, my mind, my strength, my words and my actions in one moment and, then, moved to impatience and impulsivity, meanness and moodiness the next. I'm not God. And I certainly wouldn't want, or trust, a god like me!

In admitting my earthly, temporal state – of being little, frail, flawed, finite and fickle – I am set free to more fully trust that God, who is God, can be trusted. I am set free to trust that God's thoughts and ways are absolutely perfect and far higher than mine. Even if I don't understand them. Even if I don't like them. Even if I want God's thoughts and ways – and timing – to be different. To be more like mine. Especially when I want all the sin and suffering, all the brokenness and badness within us as individuals and all around us in the world, to be ended once and for all. Right now. I will still trust God, who is God, for His thoughts and ways – and timing – when it comes to the people I love. Even when I want these precious ones to receive the fullness of God's healing, the fullness of God's peace, the fullness of God's provision. Right now. I will still trust God, who is God, for His thoughts and ways – and timing – when there are precious ones I want desperately to put their full faith in Jesus as their Savior. To fully trust Jesus as their Lord. Right now.

God is God. God can be trusted. God is eternally unchangeable and good. God is love.

We never could have imagined that God's thoughts of love and mercy towards us would have placed His holy Son Jesus on the cross as His way to rescue and redeem us and bring us to Himself fully and forever!

God's thoughts and ways are absolutely perfect and far higher than ours. Thanks be to God!

Reflections – Responses – Challenges – Encouragements – God-breathing Thoughts

Do I believe it?
And if I do, what am I going to do about it?

Lord, please let me hear your voice, your love, your wisdom, your grace and truth.

STORAGE TALK

Tim and I have moved many times since we were first married in 1980. We've moved to several different homes, to four different states (to two of them twice over the years), to several different towns, and even to France when our daughters were very small. We've packed, unpacked, sorted and purged. We've put things in storage and brought things back out of storage with each and every one of our moves.

Every time we've brought things out of storage, we've been blessed by the life-stories that most of our things hold for us and for our family. As we unpacked these good, useful, wanted and memory-laden things, we would tell stories, laugh a bit, and maybe tear up just a little bit (okay, I would anyway). And we would be thankful for these things that we had put in storage, and were now bringing back out. They would be part of our lives in our new home. These things that we brought out of storage were, to a certain extent, obvious ways for us to be known, and experienced, by others. Our storage says a lot about who we are.

On the other hand, there have been times when we've been surprised, disappointed, and even a little dumbfounded, when something we had intended to get rid of, something that should have been put out with the trash – because it was no longer useful, or it was broken, or it had been ruined by the elements and was warped, rusted or totally worn out – was found among our good, useful, wanted and memory-laden storage items. Oh, these things would be conversation starters, too – mostly making us ask ourselves, *"What on earth made us think that was okay to keep? What were we possibly thinking to have allowed that thing to be put in storage with all of our other things?"*

And so it is with our hearts. We need to be honestly aware of what we have stored up inside of our hearts – inside of our emotions, thoughts, motivations, perceptions, attitudes, actions and habits. Because what we have stored up inside of our hearts says a great deal about us – and flows out from us. And most often, our hearts will flow out through our mouths.

> *"A good man brings good things out of the good stored up in his heart,*
> *and an evil man brings evil things out of the evil stored up in his heart.*
> *For the mouth speaks what the heart is full of."*
> Luke 6:45

Whatever we store up in our hearts – whether it is hate or love, bitterness or forgiveness, selfishness or kindness, pride or humility, fear or courage, woundedness or healing, judgment or compassion, jealousy or thankfulness – all of it will find a way to be expressed out through our mouths. Our hearts will be known, and experienced by others, through our words. And not just through the words we actually speak, but much of what is stored up in our hearts will be known, and experienced by others, through how – when, to whom, where and why – we choose to speak these words.

So, what's your storage talk like? What's your heart filled with? Are there perceptions and attitudes and overflow that are warped and broken, dangerous and damaging? Let God purge and unpack these, and fill your heart and your storage talk with the fruit of the Spirit: "love, joy, peace, patience, kindness, goodness, faithfulness, gentleness and self-control" (Galatians 5:22-23). This is how we should be known, and experienced by others as we speak and live out our lives as followers of Christ!

Do I believe it?
And if I do, what am I going to do about it?

Lord, please let me hear your voice, your love, your wisdom, your grace and truth.

BREATHE DEEPLY, PRAISE OFTEN, REFRESH OTHERS!

Then the LORD God...breathed into his nostrils the breath of life,
and the man became a living being.
Genesis 2:7

Breathe. Take a moment to breathe. Really. Right now. Breathe in God's life-giving, life-sustaining and life-transforming breath. Breathe. Deeply. Slowly. Quietly. Intentionally. Let God's breath of life clear your head. Let God's breath of life lift your heart and free your soul from the worries in your life. Even for just a moment. Breathe.

God's breath of life breathed into us and we were created. It only makes sense that in order for us to live with any real sense of balance, hope and peace – because too often our focus is on the busyness and bother, the brokenness and bad experiences in our lives and in our world – we would need to take some real and deliberate time to breathe. Really breathe. And be renewed and refreshed. God's breath of life has no limits to its love and power!

God's breath of life breathed into the beaten, scarred, pierced, crucified, dead body of Jesus and brought Him to life again as the glorious Conqueror King who shattered the power of sin and death for all eternity! Breathe in God's gift of forgiveness and His sure promise to resurrect your life. God's breath of life has no limits to its love and power!

Our lives on this earth and our eternal lives are given and guarded by God's breath of life! That is something to celebrate!

Let everything that has breath praise the LORD. Praise the LORD.
Psalm 150:6

Every breath we have been given is a gift! And we're meant to live out our every breath with thanksgiving to God. Our lives and breath are not meant to be controlled by the busyness of our days, nor by the bothersome circumstances we face. Our lives and breath are not meant to be crushed by the brokenness and bad experiences of this world. No! We have been made in the image of God – made by the Eternal One who gave us His breath of life so that we would have life! It is our Lord Jesus Christ who gave up His own life breath so that we would live eternally with Him! God's breath of life has no limits to its love and power! Praise the Lord!

How are you using those breaths you've been given by the life breath of God? Are you taking time to let God take your breath away by His love for you? Are you taking time to let God's beauty and majesty revealed through nature – in the mountains and oceans, in the hills and lakes, in the forests and deserts, in the flowers and fruit, in the stars, the sun and the moon, in the flight of the birds, in the jump of a whale, in the roar of a lion, in the wiggles of a puppy, in the purr of a kitten – refresh you and reconnect you with the life breath you've been given?

Are you taking time to refresh others? Do those around you breathe a little easier, a little more deeply because of the way you listen to them, help them, encourage them and love them? Do they breathe a word of praise to God because of you?

God's breath of life has no limits to its love and power! So, take the time to breathe deeply, praise often and refresh others!

Do I believe it?
And if I do, what am I going to do about it?

Lord, please let me hear your voice, your love, your wisdom, your grace and truth.

BREATHE DEEPLY, LEARN CONTINUALLY, BE PREPARED!

Our lives on this earth and our eternal lives are given and guarded by God's breath of life! God's breath of life has no limits to its love and power!

And it is by God's Word – God's God-breathed Word – that we learn continually how to live in God's good and righteous ways. It is by God's God-breathed Word that we are prepared and fully equipped for every good work on this side of heaven!

> *All Scripture is God-breathed and is useful for teaching,*
> *rebuking, correcting and training in righteousness,*
> *so that the servant of God*
> *may be thoroughly equipped for every good work.*
> 2 Timothy 3:16-17

> *For the word of God is alive and active.*
> Hebrews 4:12

God's Word is living and active and is meant to impact every area of our lives and direct every activity of our every day. All Scripture is infused with the very life breath of our God who has given us life, and who works to transform our lives here and now, so that we will reflect the love, beauty, grace and truth of our Lord Jesus Christ to all those around us. This is God's very good work. This is exactly what the Word of God prepares and equips us to do!

And we are to breathe deeply and learn continually and be prepared by God's God-breathed Word – that has no limit to its love and power – to do God's good work!

To live our lives as followers and disciples, as ambassadors and servants of our Lord Jesus Christ requires that we embrace the truth that we must always keep a humble attitude and remain fully teachable to our Lord. Our learning from God's God-breathed Word is meant to be a continual process in our lives. Over the years, I have definitely found that most of my lessons from God's Word are not only continually taking me deeper in my understanding of who God is and how I am to follow Christ, but most of my lessons are actually remedial in nature – necessarily repeated lessons! Maybe that's the truth for you too.

There are so many times that I must take time to breathe deeply and remember who I am in Christ. Remember all that God has done for me. Remember who holds my life breath – now and for all eternity – in His good and holy, loving and beautiful hands. There are times I must remember and hold onto all the truths of God's God-breathed Word that have set me free from every Lie From The Pit Of Hell (LFTPOH) and continually set me free from my stubborn pride.

Continual and remedial teaching, rebuking, correcting and training in righteousness come from God's God-breathed Word with a very clear purpose: We are to be prepared, thoroughly equipped, for every good work our God calls us to do. Still, some of those lessons, especially the rebuking and correcting ones, can be pretty painful and definitely not a lot of fun as we go through them. But! They are freeing. They all come from God's good and perfect love for us!

God's greatest good work is that we love like He loves. So, breathe deeply, learn continually and be prepared to be the heart, hands and feet of Jesus to all those around you!

Reflections – Responses – Challenges – Encouragements – God-breathing Thoughts

Do I believe it?
And if I do, what am I going to do about it?

Lord, please let me hear your voice, your love, your wisdom, your grace and truth.

THE WHO AND THE WHAT OF GOD – MIGHTY GOD!

The Who of God and *The What of God* are absolutely bound together and inseparable. A living, active relationship with our God brings us into a deeper intimacy and greater knowledge of *Who* our God is. Through this relationship, our God pours out His very nature – His Holy Spirit – into our innermost beings so that we will then pour out to others *The What* our God has given to us. As we are filled and flowing with both *The Who of God* and *The What of God,* we are renewed, we are set free, and we become a blessing and a tangible reflection of the Living Christ to others in amazingly transforming ways.

The Who our God is – Mighty God:

> **And he will be called...Mighty God**
> Isaiah 9:6

> **"I am God Almighty"**
> Genesis 35:11

> **Sovereign LORD, you have begun to show to your servant your greatness**
> **and your strong hand. For what god is there in heaven or on earth**
> **who can do the deeds and mighty works you do?**
> Deuteronomy 3:24

The What our God gives – His strength – transforms our nature to be more like Him and flows through us so that God's nature is revealed and made known to those around us:

> **It is God who arms me with strength and keeps my way secure.**
> 2 Samuel 22:33

> **Splendor and majesty are before him;**
> **strength and joy are in his dwelling place.**
> 1 Chronicles 16:27

> **Do not grieve, for the joy of the LORD is your strength.**
> Nehemiah 8:10

> **I can do all things through him who gives me strength.**
> Philippians 4:13

Our God is the Mighty God who gives us His strength. *The Who of God* and *The What of God* are inextricably interwoven and mysteriously given to us to bring us into a deeper, living oneness with our Holy God as He gives His own Spirit to live within us, transforming us to be more and more like Him in character, in thoughts, words, actions, interactions and reactions.

Our God is the Mighty God – the giver of all true strength. Strength that is unlimited by our weakness. Strength that is not bound or broken, damaged or destroyed by our circumstances. Strength that brings an inexpressible, supernatural sense of security, joy and power to our minds, hearts and souls. Strength that allows us to be ambassadors of our Mighty God, offering His eternal security, joy and power to those who need Him and His strength – to those who need *The Who of God* and *The What of God* for themselves, just as we do!

Reflections – Responses – Challenges – Encouragements – God-breathing Thoughts

Do I believe it?
And if I do, what am I going to do about it?

Lord, please let me hear your voice, your love, your wisdom, your grace and truth.

MEEK IS AMAZING

Meekness sometimes gets a bad rap. If someone is described as meek, we too quickly and too often imagine a person whose strength of character more closely resembles cooked spaghetti rather than a mighty tower. We assign a certain sense of wimpiness, timidity and maybe even a bit of naiveté to those we view as meek.

This kind of meekness is not the meekness of the people of God who receive blessings and promises from the Lord for being meek – His way.

> *...the meek will inherit the land and enjoy peace and prosperity.*
> Psalm 37:11

> *...I will remove from you your arrogant boasters...*
> *But I will leave within you the meek and humble.*
> *The remnant of Israel will trust in the name of the LORD.*
> Zephaniah 3:11-12

> *"Blessed are the meek, for they will inherit the earth."*
> Matthew 5:5

To be meek – God's way – is to live a life that is marked by sincere humility, powered by gentleness, and courageously chooses to trust in and obey God as the Sovereign Lord over all that exists and over all that happens.

To be meek – God's way – comes with deep blessings and promises for us:
We will be given a place – a land, a city, the earth – as an inheritance for us, that belongs to us. A home where we will belong. Because we belong to God. Forever.
We will know the joy of God's great and full peace in this land.

Our Lord Jesus Christ lived a life of outrageous meekness. From his lowly birth in a stable to His brutal death on a cross, the life of Jesus was marked with humility. A humility that was far beyond sincere. The humility of Jesus was extravagant and extreme. And His holy head, face, back, hands, feet and side were marked by the scars of His extravagant and extreme humility – marked by the beatings, the fists, the floggings, the thorns, the nails and the sword.

The meekness, the powerful gentleness of Jesus ministered to and transformed the lives of all who believed Him as He declared the nearness of God's Kingdom and preached the good news of God's unfailing love, grace and truth. The powerful gentleness of Jesus touched the lives of the least, the last and the lost as they were healed of all their illnesses, delivered from all their demons, and raised from death back to life.

In meekness, Jesus courageously trusted and obeyed His Father, even when it meant He would be tempted at His weakest moments, betrayed by one of His closest followers, denied by one of His closest friends, be mocked, rejected, punished and killed for the sins of the world – though He was the Only innocent and righteous One. Jesus did all this so we would know the great blessings and promises of our God – to enjoy our land, our eternal home with Him, our Holy God for ever and ever.

Meek is amazing! And it looks just like Jesus.

Reflections – Responses – Challenges – Encouragements – God-breathing Thoughts

Do I believe it?
And if I do, what am I going to do about it?

Lord, please let me hear your voice, your love, your wisdom, your grace and truth.

AB-SOUL-UTELY WORTH IT!

Then he called the crowd to him along with his disciples and said:
"Whoever wants to be my disciple must deny themselves and take up their cross
and follow me. For whoever wants to save their life will lose it,
but whoever loses their life for me and for the gospel will save it.
What good is it for someone to gain the whole world, yet forfeit their soul?
Or what can anyone give in exchange for their soul?"
Mark 8:34-37

I love that Jesus called the crowd to come up close to Him. Jesus wanted everyone – those who knew Him personally and followed Him in some very real and regular ways, as well as every person who seemed to be looking in Jesus' direction and was within earshot of His speaking – to come close, gather right up near Him and listen closely.

Imagine you were in the crowd that day. Imagine the thrill of being invited to gather in close – to be called to come right up near this amazing, healing, preaching, demon-conquering, food-multiplying, life-restoring, growing-in-fame, maybe-the-Messiah Rabbi! Jesus had something important and wonderful to tell us. We knew His words would bless us and change our lives.

But, this? This didn't sound like blessing. This didn't sound like the kind of life change I had in mind. Deny myself? Take up my cross? Lose my life? That's what following Jesus means? Lose my soul if I don't do this? I think Jesus has lost His mind!

Then I see His eyes. I hear His heart. His heart for me – not wanting me to lose my soul. Not wanting me to be lost and empty because of what I hold onto in this life. Jesus is speaking to my very soul about how to save my soul. Jesus is wanting, with everything in Him – and oh, there is so much within Him – for me to live my fullest, freest, most purposeful and powerful life possible. But it comes at a cost. An unexpectedly deep and tangible cost. Is it worth it?

And the love of Jesus opens my ears. Opens my heart. I hear and understand. Losing my life for Jesus – who gave up His life for me – and losing my life to make His gospel known, is the most beautiful, life-transforming, soul-saving life I could ever know. So, I choose to –

Deny myself. Deny my selfishness. Deny my self-centeredness. Deny my self-focus, and live focused on Jesus and loving Him and loving others.

Take up my cross and follow Jesus. Take up my cross – remembering the total submission to His Father's will and His outrageous love that moved Jesus to die for me, for the forgiveness of my sins. Take up my cross – knowing that there will be days and seasons of pain, frustration, rejection and suffering that come with following Jesus. Take up my cross – yielding to my God completely, trusting His goodness always, being convinced fully of His eternal victory and filled with the love, peace and hope Jesus gives me right in the midst of the mess. Jesus is with me. He knows the weight of my cross. And He knows the immeasurable, incalculable joy that I will know fully as I follow Him right into eternity and lay my cross down at His beautiful feet forever.

Lose my life. Lose my life for Jesus to become His child, His ambassador, His follower, His friend. Lose my life for Jesus and be given the most powerful, purpose-filled life imaginable – to declare the gospel of Jesus who forgives and saves the lives of all who believe and follow.

Is it worth it? Yes! It is *ab-soul-utely* worth it!

Reflections – Responses – Challenges – Encouragements – God-breathing Thoughts

Do I believe it?
And if I do, what am I going to do about it?

Lord, please let me hear your voice, your love, your wisdom, your grace and truth.

THE TRUTH, THE WHOLE TRUTH, AND NOTHING BUT THE TRUTH

For we cannot do anything against the truth, but only for the truth.
2 Corinthians 13:8

What an audacious, incredible concept this is: *To not be able to do anything against the truth. To only be able to do what is for the truth.* Can you imagine a world where we could not do anything in contradiction to the truth? A world where everything we did lined up with and was in agreement with the truth? What would that mean for you? For me?

Jesus declares, "I am the truth" (John 14:6). So, we need to start there. Humbly. Continuing from there, courageously, in God's truth found in His Word and revealed by His Spirit.

We each need to accept God's transforming truths fully, intimately and personally:

I am loved. Out of God's love, He created me. God's love is unfailing, abounding, everlasting, patient, kind, protective, faithful, righteous. God's love endures forever.
I am a sinner. I am forgiven. Jesus died to set me free from the power and bondage of sin.
I am frail. My body is mortal, subject to illness and death. There is nothing frail about God. Jesus rose from the dead to set me free from the power and bondage of death. One day, God will give me my eternal, imperishable, *unfrail* body and I will live with my Lord forever.
I am flawed. I still sin. I still act and react selfishly, foolishly, defensively, offensively and pridefully – far too quickly and far too often. There is nothing flawed about our God who is full of grace and truth. Our God is holy, righteous and just. Our God is perfect love whose mercies and compassions never fail.
I am finite. I am limited in wisdom, in strength, in power, in peace and in love. There is nothing finite about our God. He is the Eternal One. The Alpha and the Omega. There is nothing limited about our God. With God all things are possible.

God's transforming truths are meant to guide us, fill us and protect us. God wants us to line up and agree with, to stand and live in, His transforming truths in every area of our lives:

In Wisdom – Wisdom first comes when we fear the Lord (Psalm 111:10, Proverbs 9:10).
We need to humbly acknowledge our lack of wisdom, asking God to give it to us – and God will give His wisdom to us generously (James 1:5).
In Strength – We can do all things through the strength Christ gives us (Philippians 4:13).
In Power – God is able to do immeasurably more than all we ask or imagine, according to His power that is at work within us (Ephesians 3:21).
In Peace – As we give God all of our anxieties, worries, fears and frustrations – in prayer and with thanksgiving – we will be given God's transcending peace to guard our hearts and our minds in our Lord Jesus Christ (Philippians 3:6-7).
In Love – God is love (1 John 4:8,16). *God loves us so much that He sent His One and Only Son into the world that we might live through Him* (John 3:16; 1 John 4:9-10). *Since God so loved us – who were once His enemies – we are to love our enemies also* (Colossians 1:21; Luke 6:27, 35). *We are to love others the way Jesus loves us* (John 15:17; 1 John 4:11-12). *The only thing that counts is faith expressing itself through love* (Galatians 5:6).

May each of us line up with and live in God's truths and be so transformed that we offer God's love, grace and truth to others. To all others. May God help us to *not be able to do anything against God's truth.* May God help us to live in and live for God's truth, God's whole and holy truth – and nothing but God's truth.

Do I believe it?
And if I do, what am I going to do about it?

Lord, please let me hear your voice, your love, your wisdom, your grace and truth.

SERVANT-LISTENING

The LORD came and stood there,
calling as at the other times, "Samuel! Samuel!"
Then Samuel said, "Speak, for your servant is listening."
1 Samuel 3:10

The night had almost passed. Three other times before this dialogue with God, the young Samuel (probably around 12 years old) had heard his name called out. This intimate approach by God happened at a time when Scripture tells us:

In those days the word of the LORD was rare;
there were not many visions.
1 Samuel 3:1

So, of course, it's understandable that this young, inexperienced Samuel thought it was Eli, the high priest and judge of Israel and Samuel's mentor-master, who he had heard calling out to him in the middle of the night. But it wasn't. Samuel's sleep was being disturbed by God. Samuel's name was being called out by the Lord Most High Himself.

After the third time of Samuel running into where Eli was sleeping to find out why his master had summoned him and how he could possibly serve him, Eli finally understood what was happening. It was the Lord's voice Samuel had heard. Eli then counseled the young Samuel on how to respond to the Lord's call. This true counsel came from a man who himself had failed miserably at listening to and obeying the Lord, specifically when it came to correcting his own sons. Eli's sons, Hophni and Phinehas, also served as priests, but were known as "scoundrels; they had no regard for the LORD" (1 Samuel 2:12).

Samuel, however, listened to Eli's instructions and did as he was told. He went back to listen for the Lord's voice – to listen to the Lord's words – as a humble, willing and obedient servant. And the Lord came and stood near Samuel and spoke to him. That night, an intimate, life-long conversation and relationship began with the Lord leading and Samuel following.

How simple Samuel's response to the Lord was, *"Speak, for your servant is listening."* That righteous humility, courageous willingness and ready obedience before the Lord made all the difference in this one young person's life. Samuel's life was powerfully transformed through his simple act of listening to the Lord. And the Lord honored and blessed Samuel's servant-listening.

The LORD was with Samuel as he grew up,
and he let none of Samuel's words fall to the ground.
And all of Israel from Dan to Beersheba recognized
that Samuel was attested as a prophet of the LORD.
1 Samuel 3:19-20

Will we choose as Samuel did, no matter what our age? No matter what our circumstance or position in life is? Will we choose to humbly, willingly and obediently listen to the Lord? Will we choose to let the Lord into our lives in such an intimate and powerful way through the simple act of listening? It will make all the difference in our lives, if we do. And God will use us to make a difference in the lives of others.

Speak, Lord, for your servant is listening!

Do I believe it?
And if I do, what am I going to do about it?

Lord, please let me hear your voice, your love, your wisdom, your grace and truth.

IT IS. BUT IT ISN'T. BUT IT IS!

LORD, our LORD, how majestic is your name in all the earth!
Psalm 8:1

When I read these words from Scripture, one of the praise song tunes to which this passage was put to music goes through my head. It just makes me want to get up and start singing and dancing a little bit! It's so upbeat, happy, hope-filled and powerful. I know and believe that *the Lord's name is majestic in all of the earth!* It is true.

But it isn't true. Not really. Not all the time. At least not for me. Not in the way I live out my life and make each of my moment-by-moment choices on this earth. Is the Lord's name majestic to me? Yes. Most of the time. But there are still too many times when I think, speak and act as if I never knew the Lord's name. During those times, I regard myself as the majestic one. Denying, in my own little corner of the earth – wherever that happens to be at the time – that the Lord's name is majestic in *all* of the earth. So, no. It isn't true that the Lord's name is majestic in all of the earth. Because I, for one – as one of God's created children of this earth – have far too often, in far too many ways, diminished and dismissed the Lord's majestic name.

But it is true! God's Spirit and God's Word declare that *the Lord's name is majestic in all of the earth!* God doesn't change. And nothing I do or anyone else does – has done or will ever do – could possibly change the majestic name of the Lord! Not in this earthly temporal realm. Not in the eternal realm. Not ever. Not by our kindest, most compassionate, most loving ways. Not by our most selfish, most evil, most hateful ways. Neither our very best nor our very worst ways can change the unchangeable truth that *the Lord's name is majestic in all of the earth!*

Our Lord's name – after name after name – by which He has revealed Himself, is majestic!
El Shaddai – The Lord God Almighty
El Elyon – The Most High God
El Olam – The Everlasting God
Elohim – God, Judge, Creator
El Roi – The God who Sees
Adonai – Lord, Master
Yahweh – Lord Jehovah
Jehovah Nissi – The Lord my Banner
Jehovah Raah – The Lord my Shepherd
Jehovah Rapha – The Lord who Heals
Jehovah Shamma – The Lord is There
Jehovah Tsidkenu – The Lord our Righteousness
Jehovah Mekoddishkem – The Lord who Sanctifies you
Jehovah Jireh – The Lord will Provide
Jehovah Shalom – The Lord is Peace
Jehovah Sabaoth – The Lord of Hosts
Jesus – The Lord Saves

...at the name of Jesus every knee should bow, in heaven and on earth and under the earth, and every tongue acknowledge that Jesus Christ is Lord, to the glory of God the Father.
Philippians 2:10-11

O Lord, our Lord, how majestic is your name in all of the earth! It is true!

Do I believe it?
And if I do, what am I going to do about it?

Lord, please let me hear your voice, your love, your wisdom, your grace and truth.

QUESTIONS AND ANSWERS AND INTIMACY

Have you and God had a question and answer session lately? Our God created us to be in communion and community – in intimate relationship with Him. To grow in this relationship with our God, we need to be in conversation with Him. So, again, I ask: Have you and God had a question and answer session lately?

Our God actually invites us into this intimate conversation with Him. Amazing.

> *This is what the LORD says, he who made the earth,*
> *the LORD who formed it and established it – the LORD is his name:*
> *"Call to me and I will answer you*
> *and tell you great and unsearchable things you do not know."*
> Jeremiah 33:2-3

So, ask away! Yes, and ask with a certain humility acknowledging that God is God, the holy and sovereign One over all that exists. And we are not. Ask with a certain understanding that we won't understand everything on this side of heaven. Still, ask away! Our God invites us, and wants us, to know Him deeply and to know all that He reveals to us through His Word and His Spirit. As we're asking our God questions, we need to be open to answering some questions that God asks us, too.

> *"I am the LORD, the God of all mankind. Is anything too hard for me?"*
> Jeremiah 32:26-27

> *"But what about you?" he asked. "Who do you say I am?"*
> Matthew 16:15

> *Jesus said to [Martha], "I am the resurrection and the life. The one who believes in me*
> *will live, even though they die; and whoever lives by believing in me will never die.*
> *Do you believe this?"*
> John 11:25-26

> *"Who of you by worrying can add a single hour to your life?*
> *Since you cannot do this very little thing, why do you worry about the rest?"*
> Luke 12:25-26

Sometimes both the question and the answer are found within the same passage of Scripture.

> *He has shown you, O mortal, what is good. And what does the LORD require of you?*
> *To act justly and to love mercy and to walk humbly with your God.*
> Micah 6:8

> *Who shall separate us from the love of Christ? Shall trouble or hardship or persecution or*
> *famine or nakedness or danger or sword?…No, in all these things we are more than*
> *conquerors through him who loved us. For I am convinced that neither death nor life,*
> *neither angels nor demons, neither the present nor the future, nor any powers,*
> *neither height nor depth, nor anything else in all creation,*
> *will be able to separate us from the love of God that is in Christ Jesus our Lord.*
> Romans 8:35, 37-39

Let's each have ongoing question and answer sessions with our God. Expect God to answer. Expect God to ask us questions. Be blessed and challenged by all our God reveals to us and by all He doesn't reveal to us on this side of heaven – knowing and trusting that there is absolutely nothing in all creation could ever separate us from the intimacy of His love!

Reflections – Responses – Challenges – Encouragements – God-breathing Thoughts

Do I believe it?
And if I do, what am I going to do about it?

Lord, please let me hear your voice, your love, your wisdom, your grace and truth.

FLIGHT OR FIGHT? – part 1 – FLIGHT TIME

Flight or Fight? Those are two big generalizations on how we as individuals (or as a group) may respond to conflicts and crises. How we may respond to the battles we are in - battles for our spirits, minds, hearts and bodies on this side of heaven.

We often choose flight in the midst of these battles because we want to avoid the uncomfortable situations, tough conversations and pretty much every circumstance that might put us in, what we perceive to be, an embarrassing, vulnerable, tense or awkward position with other people. We act as though our worth and our honor are in our own hands or are in danger of being changed by the words and actions of someone else. So we choose flight to avoid that from happening. Our honor, like our salvation, is only and eternally dependent on God. Period.

> *My salvation and my honor depend on God.*
> Psalm 62:7

When we choose flight, we close ourselves down to God's unlimited power that is available to work in us and through us – no matter what or who we may be facing.

> *Now to him who is able to do immeasurably more than all we ask or imagine,*
> *according to his power that is at work within us...*
> Ephesians 3:20

When we choose to be less concerned about protecting our own image and comfort level, when we choose to not let fear rule us and push us to choose flight, we'll be far more free to truly love others, God and ourselves. Because it is love that drives out all fear. And it is love through which we become more than conquerors in all things. As more than conquerors, we never have to run away in fear. We never have to choose flight – from anyone or any circumstance because we are constantly held by God's perfect love.

> *There is no fear in love. But perfect love drives out fear...*
> 1 John 4:18

> *...we are more than conquerors through Him who loved us...[nothing] in all creation,*
> *will be able to separate us from the love of God that is in Christ Jesus our Lord.*
> Romans 8:37, 39

There is, however, an absolutely right time for flight. Every time we're tempted. We need to take flight right away, in every way – mind, body and spirit – from every hook of temptation and evil pull that comes into our lives. Even if we put it there in the first place!

> *Flee from sexual immorality...*
> 1 Corinthians 6:18

> *But you, man [and woman] of God, flee from all this [evil], and pursue righteousness,*
> *godliness, faith, love, endurance and gentleness.*
> 1 Timothy 6:11

Whatever our battle, may we each allow God to lead us into victory, holding us steady, as we depend on God to guard our honor, guide us away from temptation and give us His love, power and full transforming grace – in each of our circumstances, in each of our relationships, for each of our days. Allowing God to lead us His way will cause our hearts, minds and spirits to soar. Now, that's the way we should take flight!

Do I believe it?
And if I do, what am I going to do about it?

Lord, please let me hear your voice, your love, your wisdom, your grace and truth.

FLIGHT OR FIGHT? – part 2 – FREEDOM FIGHT

Flight or Fight? Those are two big generalizations on how we as individuals (or as a group) may respond to conflicts and crises. How we may respond to the battles we are in – battles for our spirits, minds, hearts and bodies on this side of heaven.

We often choose to fight in the midst of these battles because we are trying to defend ourselves, our reputation and our self-image from the judgments and misjudgments that come from other people. We want to manage how others view us. We fight against being told who we are, how we are or what our weaknesses are. We fight against every criticism. We might not say it aloud or fight in physical and verbal ways (although that certainly happens), but, at the very least, the fight is seething inside of us and we are consumed with bitterness and hate toward those who would attack our ego, our image, our actions, our motivations. *How dare they judge me! How dare they tell me what I should do! Who do they think they are?!*

We need to understand that our self-worth can never be changed by what another person thinks of us or even by how we are treated by others. It is a waste of our energy, effort, thought, action and time to fight against misjudgments in order for others to know us as we want to be known.

Instead, we need to receive and focus our energy, effort, thought, action and time on the divine power that God has given us through our knowledge of Him. Knowing God and being equipped and filled with God's divine power provides us with weapons that are far superior and eternally victorious in the fight for our spirits, minds, hearts and bodies than any of our self-focused, self-justifying and self-defending ways.

> *His divine power has given us everything we need for a godly life*
> *through our knowledge of him who called us by his own glory and goodness.*
> 2 Peter 1:3

We need to recognize that with God as the protector and defender of our lives and our honor, we do not have to fight against the attacks of another. These have no eternal significance.

> *What, then, shall we say in response to these things?*
> *If God is for us, who can be against us?*
> Romans 8:31

Far too often we choose to fight against the people who have wounded us in the same way that we have suffered. We fight back through our words and actions with the same kind of weapons that came against us – hurt, mistreatment, rejection, lies, abuse, betrayal, manipulation, selfishness, thoughtlessness, coldness, cruelty and evil. These only diminish us and keep us bound as captives to hate and anger, depression and deceit.

We have been set free to live and fight in the power of our Lord Jesus Christ, our conquering Savior. Not in the power of hurt and sin.

> *It is for freedom that Christ has set us free. Stand firm, then,*
> *and do not let yourselves be burdened again by a yoke of slavery.*
> Galatians 5:1

Let our fight be truly a freedom fight so that we will stand more strongly, live more fully and love more freely as the redeemed and beloved people of God!

Do I believe it?
And if I do, what am I going to do about it?

Lord, please let me hear your voice, your love, your wisdom, your grace and truth.

FLIGHT OR FIGHT? – part 3 – TAKE FLIGHT AND FIGHT THE RIGHT FIGHT

Flight or Fight? God's Word and Spirit empower us with divine power to know when and how we should take flight or stand our ground and fight.

His divine power has given us everything we need for a godly life
through our knowledge of him who called us by his own glory and goodness.
2 Peter 1:3

Our Lord Jesus knows every temptation that pulls at us and deceitfully lies to us, enticing us to sin and to justify our sins. God has provided a way for us to take flight from temptation.

No temptation has overtaken you except what is common to mankind.
And God is faithful; he will not let you be tempted beyond what you can bear.
But when you are tempted, he will also provide a way out so that you can endure it.
1 Corinthians 10:13

Our Lord Jesus knows every abuse, misjudgment, cruelty and outrageous evil that would make us want to fight in the same way and with the same weapons that this broken world fights. But! We are to fight with the weapons given to us by our God and infused with His divine power.

For though we live in the world, we do not wage war as the world does.
The weapons we fight with are not the weapons of the world.
On the contrary, they have divine power to demolish strongholds.
2 Corinthians 10:3-4

Our God's greatest divine weapon is for us to know our God and learn from Him humbly and willingly so that God's divine purpose will be accomplished within each of us –

...to be conformed to the image of His Son...
Romans 8:29

The more transformed into the image of Jesus we are, the more we'll be able to take flight from every temptation and fight the right fight as Jesus did – using God's Word and His divine weapons to conquer temptation and evil. Christ's weapons: love, prayer, forgiveness, sacrifice, obedience to God, compassion, kindness, humility, gentleness and patience.

"Love your enemies and pray for those who persecute you." – Matthew 5:44
Bear with each other and forgive one another if any of you has a grievance against someone. Forgive as the Lord forgave you. – Colossians 3:13
I urge you, brothers and sisters, in view of God's mercy, to offer your bodies as a living sacrifice, holy and pleasing to God...Do not conform to the pattern of this world, but be transformed by the renewing of your mind. – Romans 12:1-2
This is love: that we walk in obedience to his commands. As you heard from the beginning, his command is that you walk in love. – 2 John 1:6
As God's chosen people, holy and dearly loved, clothe yourselves with compassion, kindness, humility, gentleness and patience. – Colossians 3:12
Fight the good fight of the faith... – 1 Timothy 6:12

We are called to fight. But! We must be certain we are fighting the right fight that will conform us to be more like Jesus. Then we will be vessels of God's love, healing and transformation in the lives of others. All others. To our closest family and friends and to our cruelest enemies. This is the divine power and knowledge of our Lord Jesus that will change us for all eternity!

Reflections – Responses – Challenges – Encouragements – God-breathing Thoughts

Do I believe it?
And if I do, what am I going to do about it?

Lord, please let me hear your voice, your love, your wisdom, your grace and truth.

SIMPLE BETRAYALS

Jesus asked him, "Judas, are you betraying the Son of Man with a kiss?"
Luke 22:48

I don't know if Judas understood the full consequences of his betrayal. Or that this simple, everyday cultural greeting in their Middle-Eastern world – his simple kiss on the cheek of Jesus – would be forever recognized as a horrendous act of betrayal. I don't know if Judas had any real sense of how his simple, everyday action would become one of the world's most infamous betrayals – with cruel and killing consequences. For him. And for Jesus.

But it did make me start to question where and how easily do I betray Jesus as my Lord through my simple, everyday thoughts, words and actions? Where and how easily do I betray my intimate relationship with Jesus?

Do I betray Jesus in the way I use and prioritize my time? In my busyness? In my seeking to accomplish certain goals? Do I betray Jesus by rushing right into and through my day – giving Him only a fleeting moment or just a small measured portion of my time? Do I betray Jesus in my multi-tasking and to-do lists? Do I betray Jesus in my down time? In the way I spend my time when I don't have to answer to anyone for how I use it? Do I betray Jesus by giving Him very little of my fully focused attention? Simple everyday behavior that can become a betrayal of Jesus as the Lord of my life. A betrayal of the intimacy of our relationship.

Do I betray Jesus in my thoughts, words and actions? Where, how and how often do I betray Jesus and betray His love and sacrifice when I think, speak and act in prideful, self-centered, ugly and mean ways? Do I betray Jesus in my facial expressions, in my body language, in my tone of voice? In my driving? In my eating? Simple everyday behavior that can become a betrayal of Jesus as the Lord of my life. A betrayal of the intimacy of our relationship.

Do I betray Jesus in my relationships? Do I get angry too quickly? Do I blow people off? Do I write people off? Do I betray Jesus by becoming critical, arrogant, dismissive, defensive or offensive? Do I demand my own way? Do I forgive others? Or do I betray the cost of my own forgiveness, paid for by the blood of Jesus, by holding onto bitterness and resentment for the wrongs done to me? Do I betray Jesus by not loving as He loved – sincerely, intentionally, actively and continually? Not loving even those I claim are most precious to me as Jesus loved? Simple everyday behavior that can become a betrayal of Jesus as the Lord of my life. A betrayal of the intimacy of our relationship.

How simply, far too easily and even more thoughtlessly, I can betray the love and lordship of Jesus through my simple, everyday – and even culturally accepted – thoughts, words and actions. And I know the consequences of those simple betrayals. They cost Jesus His life.

We, the rescued, redeemed and renewed children of God, need to ask our God to help us to stay intimate with, mindful of and thankful for Jesus – every moment of our every day. This is God's good idea as well – keeping us from even simple, everyday betrayals.

Devote yourselves to prayer [listening and talking with God],
being watchful [of all we think, say and do],
and thankful [for God's unfailing love, continual presence and unlimited power].
Colossians 4:2

Do I believe it?
And if I do, what am I going to do about it?

Lord, please let me hear your voice, your love, your wisdom, your grace and truth.

EXTOL AWAY!

I will extol the LORD at all times;
his praise will always be on my lips.
I will glory in the LORD;
let the afflicted hear and rejoice.
Glorify the LORD with me;
let us exalt his name together.
Psalm 34:1-3

David was one happy psalmist when he wrote these words! God had once again answered David's prayers for deliverance from his enemies. And David was filled with overwhelming joy and thanksgiving for God's love, mercies and goodness. David was extolling the Lord!

What does that mean? Extol is not a word I often use in my daily vocabulary. I understand the basic sense of it. And I like the sound of it. Extol is even kind of fun to say. So, being a word nerd, I wanted to know more precisely what the definition of extol is. Got out my dictionary and happily looked it up. Because that's what a word nerd does!

Extol: to praise somebody or something with great enthusiasm and admiration. Yep. I had the right understanding of the word. Now, it's time to make sure I'm doing it!

Make sure I'm extolling my Lord at all times. When I take time to consciously get out of my own limited mindset – get out of my own way and, definitely, get over myself – and think about who my Lord truly is, the extolling flows freely.

For the LORD is [my] life...
Deuteronomy 30:20

And over the years I have come to know the Lord or, rather, the Lord has revealed Himself to me as – my Creator, Savior, Rescuer, Forgiver, Renewer, Restorer, Protector, Defender, Healer, Help, Hope, Joy, Peace, Strength, Courage, Conqueror, Calm, Wisdom, Anchor, Abba, Light, Shepherd, Grace-giver, Truth-bringer, my balance – my Life. And, oh, so very much more!

And as I extol my Lord for who He is and for the ways He has made Himself known, I want my lips to be praising Him always. I want my soul to be boasting in my Lord at all times. I want the afflicted to hear and rejoice, because I have been one of the afflicted – through abuse and rejection, through hard times and illness, through loss and sadness. Yet! I have heard of and experienced the Lord's love, mercies and goodness for myself. And I am rejoicing so thankfully!

You also have been one of the afflicted – at some time, in some way because we live in a broken and imperfect world among broken and imperfect people. My prayer is that you, too, have heard of and experienced for yourself our Lord's love, mercies and goodness, and that, even today, you are rejoicing in our Lord!

No matter what our days may bring, since we know who our Lord is, let's take time – with our thoughts, with our lips and with our souls – to extol, praise, boast in, glorify and exalt our Lord's name forever! Let's extol away!

Reflections – Responses – Challenges – Encouragements – God-breathing Thoughts

Do I believe it?
And if I do, what am I going to do about it?

Lord, please let me hear your voice, your love, your wisdom, your grace and truth.

SOUL FOOD

Meanwhile his disciples urged him, "Rabbi, eat something."
But he said to them, "I have food to eat that you know nothing about."
Then his disciples said to each other, "Could someone have brought him food?"
"My food," said Jesus, "is to do the will of him who sent me and to finish his work."
John 4:31-34

We are physical people, absolutely. We need physical food from this earth's resources to feed us, nourish us, grow us, strengthen us, keep us going and keep us alive. No question. No doubt. For many of us, we also have special meals and delicious, favorite foods – our go-to-comfort foods – that feed something deep within us.

Jesus felt hunger just as we do. His disciples cared about Him and His well-being. They were worried that Jesus hadn't eaten anything recently or, at least, hadn't eaten enough. Yet, Jesus was still going strong in ministering to the needy ones around Him. And He let his beloved disciples know that He had something more nourishing than physical food and even more delicious than comfort food. Jesus was being filled directly by His Abba. Jesus was being fed through the communion and the commitment of being in continual communication with His Abba and willingly, happily, and thankfully doing Abba's kingdom work here on earth. Jesus was being fed and filled with the richest, most satisfying, eternally significant *soul food*.

What's your soul food source?

Where am I, where are you, getting the deepest nourishment for our souls? Where do we find the source of our energy? Our strength? Our refreshment? Our purpose?

Jesus got His soul food from His Abba – from knowing and doing His Abba's will. Jesus was in constant intimate communication with His Abba. This communion and connection gave Jesus the full knowledge of His Abba's will and the desire to lovingly obey Him. Here, in this very intimate relationship with His Abba, Jesus continually received His energy, His strength, His refreshment and His glorious, eternal purpose for all He was called to do in this life. Here, in this very intimate relationship with His Abba, Jesus was filled beyond our comprehension with His Abba's soul food!

Since all of us, as God's children, are to become more and more like Jesus, I'm thinking we need to be sure we go to and receive from the same soul food source as Jesus did. We need to be in the same kind of continual communion and communication with our Holy Abba. Like Jesus, we need to commit to knowing and doing our Heavenly Father's will – and do it willingly, happily and thankfully! Ahhhhh...soul food.

Yes, let's take care of our bodies. Let's eat the physical food that will feed us, nourish us, grow us, strengthen us, keep us going and keep us alive. Let's give thanks for all that our Lord and Creator has provided for our physical needs...and even for our comfort.

And let's each always seek to be continually filled with our Abba's soul food! It's delicious!

Taste and see that the LORD is good!
Psalm 34:8

Reflections – Responses – Challenges – Encouragements – God-breathing Thoughts

Do I believe it?
And if I do, what am I going to do about it?

Lord, please let me hear your voice, your love, your wisdom, your grace and truth.

UNCHANGING, UNSHAKABLE CONFIDENCE

But blessed is the one who trusts in the LORD,
whose confidence is in him.
Jeremiah 17:7

This verse is so bottom-line basic to our faith. We are called to place our deepest, truest trust fully in our Lord who loves us eternally. We are called to place our deepest, truest confidence completely and only in the Lord our God as our Savior, our Strength, our Hope, our Peace and our Life.

When we allow ourselves to trust our God like that – taking God at His Word – believing that our God is who Scripture declares Him to be, we are empowered with a strong and peace-filled confidence. And this confidence in our Lord does not necessarily, or even very often, have to match the tangible, objective realities of the circumstances and the challenges that come into our lives.

Still, as we are held in this trusting, full-out confidence in our Lord, we are blessed. There we are held by our Lord's love, hope and peace. There we are able to take a deep, soul-quieting breath. Even through our tears, confusions, hurts and frustrations.

Our deepest, truest confidence is not to be based on anything about ourselves. Our confidence is not to be found in our strength or our health, our intellect or our bank account, our talents or our education, our job or social status, nor in any of our personal or professional relationships.

All of these tangible, objective realities in our lives can change in an instant. And if not in an instant – every one of them will change over time, in some way. Not one of them will last forever. And when these tangible, objective realities do change, if our confidence was found in them, we can be horribly changed and shaken to our very core.

Our God never changes. This truth makes all the difference for us now and for all eternity. The confidence that fills us and blesses us as we trust in our Lord is unchanging and unshakable. Oh, we will still be changed. We will still be shaken to our very core. But in amazing and eternal ways! As we put our full confidence in our Lord, in His love for us, in His constant presence with us and in His eternal and good purposes for our lives – even when we aren't able to understand those purposes at the time – we are changed and shaken to be more and more like our Lord and Savior Jesus. Beautifully. Powerfully. Peacefully. Thankfully.

Trust and confidence in our Lord may seem absolutely outrageous at times.

The LORD is my light and my salvation – whom shall I fear?
The LORD is the stronghold of my life – of whom shall I be afraid?
When the wicked advance against me to devour me,
it is my enemies and my foes who will stumble and fall.
Though an army besiege me, my heart will not fear;
though war break out against me, even then I will be confident!
Psalm 27:3

May each of us be fully and outrageously blessed – in every circumstance and challenge of our lives – by an unchanging, unshakable confidence in our Lord!

Reflections – Responses – Challenges – Encouragements – God-breathing Thoughts

Do I believe it?
And if I do, what am I going to do about it?

Lord, please let me hear your voice, your love, your wisdom, your grace and truth.

GOD WANTS TO KNOW – GOD WANTS IT TO SHOW

Jesus had to ask Peter three times:

"Do you love me?"
Peter answered, "Lord, you know all things; you know that I love you."
John 21:17

What if Jesus were right here, right in front of me – right in front of you – asking, "Do you love me?" Would I be able to say to Jesus, "Lord, you know that I love you?" Does my God, who absolutely knows all things, know that I love Him? Does it show?

How would it show? What would let Jesus know that I really love Him? Immediately my mind jumps to Him and His love. I know deep in my soul that Jesus loves me. I look back on my life and I see such clear and intimate evidence of God's love for me. It was His love that made me love Him.

Jesus' gift of salvation, the sacrifice of His life for the forgiveness of my sins, is the resounding and absolute assurance to me – intellectually, emotionally and spiritually – that I am deeply and eternally loved by the Holy One, the Lord of all Creation. I was only seven, a very hurting little girl, when Jesus interrupted my life with His salvation. I learned that my Heavenly Father loves me beyond what I could ever imagine and would love me for all time. And always and only in good and right ways. And it made me love Him.

As a saved seven-year-old little girl, I was given a Bible and sensed the presence of Jesus – God's Word made flesh – with me every time I read His Word. Jesus interrupted the truth of my painful world, by opening His Word of Truth to me. Each time I opened and read my Bible, I sensed Jesus sitting with me, talking to me, teaching me, helping me, growing me. Loving me. And it made me love Him.

That I'm even alive today is the most tangible evidence of all that Jesus loves me. Jesus interrupted my plan to kill myself when the abuse in my family and being raped by a stranger absolutely ripped away the very last shred of any hope that life was worth living. I planned suicide as my only way to escape this ugly, evil, broken, hateful world. God had a much better – death-interrupting, life-transforming – loving plan. And it made me love Him.

It is the love of Jesus – the Living Messiah, God's beloved Son, my Savior and Lord – that has completely transformed my life. It is Jesus who, out of His full and outrageous love for me, passionately and persistently keeps interrupting me to bring about His deep and oh-so-necessary transforming work in me – in my thoughts, in my words, in my actions, in my reactions, in my relationships – every day of my life! And it makes me love Him even more.

So, if Jesus were right here, right in front of me asking, "Do you love me?" My answer would be, "Lord, You know all things; You know that I love you. But only because You first loved me!"

We love because he first loved us.
1 John 4:19

Jesus interrupts my life to make me love others, and want to love others, as He has loved me. This is how I show Jesus my love. This is how Jesus wants my love for Him to show.

The only thing that counts is faith expressing itself through love.
Galatians 5:6

Reflections – Responses – Challenges – Encouragements – God-breathing Thoughts

Do I believe it?
And if I do, what am I going to do about it?

Lord, please let me hear your voice, your love, your wisdom, your grace and truth.

CHOSEN WITNESSES

Think of some of the most amazing events and experiences that you have ever been privileged enough to witness. Maybe you witnessed sincere and deep lasting love between a husband and wife – maybe even between your own mom and dad. Maybe you witnessed the birth of a precious child. Maybe you witnessed someone you loved, who was very sick, getting well. Maybe you witnessed someone you loved going home to be with Jesus.

Maybe you witnessed the beauty and majesty of God's creation while at the ocean...or in the mountains...or along the rivers...or in endless, open fields...or at a canyon's edge...or while watching a sunrise...or a sunset. Maybe you witnessed the amazing creatures of God in many places, in many activities – from your beloved pet to wild animals in their natural habitat. Maybe you witnessed the beauty and bounty of growing fruit and flowers, vegetation and trees. Maybe you witnessed (Finally!) your favorite team winning a championship game. Maybe you witnessed and experienced a really great meal with a really great friend.

From the life-changing to the life-gratifying, we are privileged to be witnesses to many amazing events and experiences over the course of our lifetimes. Yet, our Lord calls us to give witness to something far more amazing than anything else we could ever imagine: The Lord Himself!

"You are my witnesses," declares the LORD,
"and my servant whom I have chosen,
so that you may know and believe me and understand that I am he.
Before me no god was formed, nor will there be one after me.
I, even I, am the LORD, and apart from me there is no savior."
Isaiah 43:10-11

To be the Lord's chosen witness is a deep and personal invitation for each one of us to know and believe God. To know and understand that the Lord alone is our Savior. To be the Lord's witness is to experience His love, His presence, His grace and His truth. We have been given the opportunity to witness and know God's fullest revelation of Himself – His Son Jesus Christ.

The Son is the image of the invisible God, the firstborn over all creation. For in him all things were created: things in heaven and on earth, visible and invisible, whether thrones or powers or rulers or authorities; all things have been created through him and for him. He is before all things, and in him all things hold together. And he is the head of the body, the church; he is the beginning and the firstborn from among the dead, so that in everything he might have the supremacy. For God was pleased to have all his fullness dwell in him, and through him to reconcile to himself all things, whether things on earth or things in heaven, by making peace through his blood, shed on the cross.
Colossians 1:15-20

It is Jesus Himself who, just before returning to heaven, gave this promise and commission.

"But you will receive power when the Holy Spirit comes on you; and you will be my witnesses in Jerusalem, and in all Judea and Samaria, and to the ends of the earth."
Acts 1:8

We are called to know our God – our only Savior – and live as His chosen witnesses today!

Reflections – Responses – Challenges – Encouragements – God-breathing Thoughts

Do I believe it?
And if I do, what am I going to do about it?

Lord, please let me hear your voice, your love, your wisdom, your grace and truth.

THINK ABOUT THAT! CAREFULLY!

Now this is what the LORD Almighty says:
"Give careful thought to your ways."
Haggai 1:5, 7

The Lord speaks these same words twice within just a very short passage of Scripture. So, I'm thinking God wants us to pay really close attention to what He's saying. Here, the Lord is telling us to pay attention, to be aware of, to *give careful thought* to what we are doing.

These words of God's challenge and encouragement, correction and direction were given to His people who, after years of exile, had been allowed to return to Jerusalem. God called them – and even made it possible for them – to rebuild the temple. And His people accepted this task and did indeed start their God-given, purposeful project. After two years of committed work, the foundation of the new temple was completed. And there was great celebration.

But, then, the work on the temple just stopped. People got busy with their own lives, with their own homes, with their own schedules, with their own priorities. With their own everything. They focused away from God's priorities, even that soon after everything they had suffered as a people exiled because of disobedience to their God. Even that soon after God had made a way for them to come back to their homeland.

What about me? How quickly, if I am not careful, do I get back into my own ways of doing things? How soon do I get back into my own patterns of behaviors and thoughts that ignore and dismiss God and, even, outrightly disobey Him? How often do I put my priorities and perspectives above the Lord's call on, and His desire for, my life? How easy is it for me to just focus on myself and on what I want, if I do not consciously and carefully take the time to think about the fact that my entire life belongs to God?

My honest answer to each of these questions: far too quickly, far too often and far too easily.

It is out of God's love for us that He calls us to *give careful thought to our ways.* Our God knows that setting Him and His will above our own is what will truly bring us the greatest peace, the greatest security, the greatest joy and the greatest fulfillment our lives could ever know. We were made to be in relationship with our God. We were made to trust God's love for us and follow His ways for our lives, which are always the way to life – true life. But we get out of balance with this truth. We get deceived, and stop trusting God and His love for us. We get busy, and focus on our own plans and priorities. We get selfish, and want what we want when we want it and how we want it. We get prideful, and think and act as if our own ways and self-set purposes are of utmost importance and the ultimate truth for our lives.

Jesus answered, "I am the way and the truth and the life."
John 14:6

As we recognize our tendencies to go our own ways, I pray that each of us, with trusting in God's unfailing love and His ever-willing heart to help us and lead us, will return to doing things God's ways. Far more quickly, far more often and far more easily!

God's ways are always for our very best and come only from His passionate, unfailing love. Think about that! Carefully!

Do I believe it?
And if I do, what am I going to do about it?

Lord, please let me hear your voice, your love, your wisdom, your grace and truth.

THE GLORY OF THE LORD REVEALED – BEFORE US AND IN US

A voice of one calling:
"In the wilderness prepare the way for the LORD;
make straight in the desert a highway for our God.
Every valley shall be raised up,
every mountain and hill made low;
the rough ground shall become level,
the rugged places a plain.
And the glory of the LORD will be revealed,
and all the people will together see it.
For the mouth of the LORD has spoken."
Isaiah 40:3-5

Have you had someone call to you, talk with you, lovingly share the Word of the Lord with you? Share the Word of the Lord's power to transform your life? Have you listened?

Have you taken God's Word into your desert? Into those places of endless struggle, searing pressure and the shifting sands of insecurity? Have you taken God's Word into exactly where you need the Lord's truth to touch your heart, renew your mind and refresh your spirit so that you may know the sweet and filling, freely flowing life that springs from His Word?

Have you taken God's Word into your wilderness? Into your places of thoughts, words, actions and reactions where you still tend to wander and rebel? Have you taken God's Word into your wilderness places so that you may know and live the adventure and fulfillment of walking with the Almighty, Living God in amazing intimacy and with astounding power?

Have you taken God's Word into your deep valleys of loneliness, rejection, disappointment, hurt, loss and sadness so that God's Spirit may lift you up with His unfailing love, hold you in His eternal presence, comfort you with His transcending peace and fill you with His perfect hope?

Have you taken God's Word into the mountains and hills of your life, into those places where it seems that you face insurmountable obstacles? Those places where you believe you are not able to forgive that hateful person, where you're not able to heal from that addiction, not able to be set free from victimhood and self-inflicted failure, not able to be filled with peace in the midst of turmoil and chaos in your family or at work? Have you taken God's Word into those places where it is by His Word and Spirit that both your mind and your life may be transformed by His love to make you more and more like Jesus? Have you taken God's Word into those places where His power is made perfect in your weakness? And you are made into more than a conqueror?

Have you taken God's Word into your own rugged and rough places that are formed by and filled with pride and prejudice, selfishness and self-righteousness, lust and lying? Have you taken God's Word into these places so that God may transform you, refine you, smooth you, balance you, strengthen you and make you safe and level ground for the other people in your life to be around?

Let us listen. Let us allow the Word of God to enter fully into all of our thoughts and ways. And together we will see the glory of our Lord Jesus Christ revealed before us and in us!

Reflections – Responses – Challenges – Encouragements – God-breathing Thoughts

Do I believe it?
And if I do, what am I going to do about it?

Lord, please let me hear your voice, your love, your wisdom, your grace and truth.

WEARING AND WRITING FOR THE LORD

A lot of people, both men and women, wear crosses around their necks. Some of these crosses are simple, some ornate, some delicate, some heavy, some hold deep or sentimental meaning for the wearer. But all of these crosses, whether intentionally done by the wearer or not, point to the place of sacrifice where our Lord Jesus wore and bore the weight of our sins. Jesus wore and bore this weight on the cross so that we may be forgiven and have eternal life.

Other people will have Scripture verses written out in their homes, on stationery, on screen-savers, on bumper stickers, on tee shirts, on key chains and, even, on candy wrappers.

This is all fine and good. And all these *wearing and writing* ways can absolutely be ways to express our faith. These can be tangible and visible ways for us to live as God's children and witness to others of our faith in Jesus as Savior and Lord. But! We must be sure that these kind of tangible and visible – *wearing and writing* – expressions are not the only ways we give witness to the faith we have in Jesus. It must be through our thoughts, words, actions and reactions – through our everyday lives every day – that we truly wear and write out our testimony to our Holy God.

> *Let love and faithfulness never leave you;*
> *bind them around your neck,*
> *write them on the tablet of your heart.*
> Proverbs 3:3

What are you – what am I – wearing and writing for the Lord?

Do people see that I'm wearing love and faithfulness as my permanent attire? Or are love and faithfulness just part of my accessories – like a belt or a tie, like cufflinks or a pocket square, like heels or a purse, like a necklace or earrings? Do I change up my love and faithfulness – the amount I show and the amount I wear – depending on where I am, whom I'm with and what I'm doing?

Are love and faithfulness so deeply written on my heart that my very life is keeping the rhythm and pace of love and faithfulness with each thought I have, with each word I speak, with each action I choose? Or does the beat of my heart easily change when I'm tired and frustrated, self-focused and busy? Does my heart beat instead, and far too often, with the rhythm and pace of anger and judgment, dismissal and criticism, pride and selfishness?

Will I choose to wear God's love and faithfulness more consistently? Will wearing active and authentic love and faithfulness – living out my faith in God in very real ways – ever become as sweetly comfortable and natural as wearing my favorite sweatshirt?

Will I let God's love and faithfulness be fully written on my heart and fully engraved into the very core of my being? So much so that people would be able to read my life – my words, my actions and my reactions – as a love letter from God to them?

May we each choose to wear and write, in all their fullness, the love and faithfulness of our Lord Jesus Christ – through our everyday lives every day!

Do I believe it?
And if I do, what am I going to do about it?

Lord, please let me hear your voice, your love, your wisdom, your grace and truth.

WORDS AND WAYS THAT WEARY GOD

I don't often think of God getting weary. But He does. He gets weary of our sins and of our words that don't line up with His truth. God is never weakened by anything. Yet, God does get tired of us continuing in our self-focused, prideful ways and creating God in our own image, rather than accepting God's revelation of Himself as the truth.

> *You have wearied the LORD with your words.*
> *"How have we wearied him?" you ask.*
> *By saying, "All who do evil are good in the eyes of the LORD,*
> *and he is pleased with them" or "Where is the God of justice?"*
> Malachi 2:17

Neither of these thinking patterns line up with God's truth. Not only do they weary God, but they are eternally, deadly lies for us.

Evil is never good in the eyes of the Lord. Sin is sin and it is always deadly and destructive. God is never pleased with sin or with any of us buying into the twisted lies that declare: Because God is so loving, kind and forgiving, there cannot possibly be any eternal judgment against sin. God is too loving to have anyone go to hell. These lies lead to the absolute denial of the necessity for Jesus Christ to die on the cross for the forgiveness of our sins and as God's reconciling way for us to receive the gift of eternal life with Him.

God's truth: God loves us so much, beyond what we could ever imagine, that God gave His Holy Son Jesus to take the death punishment we deserved for our sins. God's Truth: This outrageous, passionate, sacrifice is the true measure of God's love for us – not excusing sin or denying that the evil of sin is not deadly and destructive to every single one of us.

Questioning God's justice, which is His very nature, is questioning God's sovereignty, God's power and God's goodness. The lies that twist us: If God were truly just, then evil wouldn't happen in this world. Evil and greedy people wouldn't seem to win so much of the time. Evil wouldn't be done to hurt or kill the innocent. Children wouldn't get sick and die. There would be no tragedies. There would be no suffering if God were just, sovereign, powerful and good. These lies deny the responsibility of those who choose to hurt others spiritually, physically, emotionally and financially. These lies deny that we are living in a world that bears the brokenness caused by sin. And in this broken world, accidents do happen, innocents are hurt and killed, sickness and tragedies do come.

God's truth: God is just, sovereign, powerful and good. God sees all and knows all, and rightly judges all circumstances and people. God's truth: God is always in control, even as we live in a world that often seems out of control. God's truth: God has an eternal perspective and an eternal purpose that is always just, even if we cannot see it or understand it while on this side of heaven. God's truth: God is with us, even in our deepest hurt or most shocking tragedy. God's truth: God invites us into His love, into His care, into following His just and loving ways.

God's truth: Through God's Word and Spirit, we are empowered with His renewal, freedom and transformation to reveal and live out God's just, loving, right and good ways – in our actions and in our words. And living this way will never weary our God!

Do I believe it?
And if I do, what am I going to do about it?

Lord, please let me hear your voice, your love, your wisdom, your grace and truth.

INNERMOST INTEGRITY

Because of my integrity you uphold me
and set me in your presence forever.
Psalm 41:12

Integrity, according to the Encarta English Dictionary means, *the quality of possessing and steadfastly adhering to high moral principles or professional standards; completeness – the state of being complete or undivided; wholeness – the state of being sound or undamaged.*

A few of the synonyms for integrity are: *honesty, truthfulness, honor, uprightness, unity.*

God's Word tells us that in our integrity our Lord upholds us and sets us in His presence forever. Think about that. Our God absolutely honors the integrity – the unity, the oneness, the truthfulness, the moral strength, the uprightness – of our hearts and minds, of our characters and of our very lives. And our omnipresent God sets us, as people of integrity, in His presence forever.

And I have to ask:
In my integrity...Do I possess and steadfastly adhere to God's true and high moral principles and standards? Do I do this at home? At work? At leisure? In my closest relationships? In my professional relationships? With my neighbors? With strangers? In my car? When I control the remote? When I'm all by myself?

In my integrity...Am I one person, undivided, without duplicity or hypocrisy? At home? At work? At leisure? In my closest relationships? In my professional relationships? With my neighbors? With strangers? In my car? When I control the remote? When I'm all by myself?

In my integrity...Am I sound and reliable, pure and safe for others in my life and for myself? At home? At work? At leisure? In my closest relationships? In my professional relationships? With my neighbors? With strangers? In my car? When I control the remote? When I'm all by myself?

Oh, I want to act with innermost integrity in every circumstance and relationship! This really is my heart's desire. Yet, to answer honestly, and with integrity, I have to say: No. I am not a woman of innermost integrity at every moment of every day, in every thought, in every word and in every action. I am not a woman of innermost integrity with every person or even when I'm by myself.

And I cannot become a person of innermost integrity on my own. I need God. We all do. Thanks be to God, who desires, and is able, to uphold and shape each of us by the truth of His Word and the power of His Spirit to become more and more like Jesus – to reveal the presence of God's own innermost integrity, truth, honor and oneness within ourselves.

Hear, O Israel: The LORD our God, the LORD is one.
Deuteronomy 6:4

May we each be powerfully upheld in innermost integrity as we humbly give ourselves over to God's transforming work, over and over again. As we are set in the presence of our Lord, who is one!

Reflections – Responses – Challenges – Encouragements – God-breathing Thoughts

Do I believe it?
And if I do, what am I going to do about it?

Lord, please let me hear your voice, your love, your wisdom, your grace and truth.

BEING A TRUE FRIEND

Being a true friend is far different than hanging out with someone. (Although taking time to just chill with someone can be a whole lot of fun and a really good way to let our minds and bodies decompress and de-stress.) Being a true friend requires more of us than just having fun and relaxing with someone.

Being a true friend is more than being a casual acquaintance to someone. Or being a good and respectful co-worker. Or even being a really good and thoughtful neighbor.

Being a true friend is a lot more than just being friendly. (Although we all could work just a little bit more on that! With all those around us. Starting right in our own homes, with our own families.)

God's Word has so much to say about the character and actions of a true friend. Here are just a few passages to think about, pray about, and do something about!

A friend loves at all times...
Proverbs 17:17

Whoever would foster love covers over an offense,
but whoever repeats the matter separates friends.
Proverbs 17:9

One who has unreliable friends soon comes to ruin,
but there is a friend who sticks closer than a brother.
Proverbs 18:24

Wounds from a friend can be trusted...
Proverbs 27:6

And from our Lord Jesus Christ, we learn what true love and true friendship really are.

"My command is this: Love each other as I have loved you.
Greater love has no one than this: to lay down one's life for one's friends.
You are my friends if you do what I command."
John 15:12-14

May we each accept the unfailing, powerful love and fullest act of intimate and outrageously sacrificial friendship that we could ever receive. Jesus laid down His perfect, sinless life for us, while we were still His enemies. Jesus didn't wait for us to change our attitudes or behaviors towards Him. Jesus didn't wait for us to be friendly and loving to Him. Jesus was a true friend, a true lover of our souls. And He doesn't want any of us to die without knowing the saving truth of His love and the power of His friendship.

As we follow Jesus, we are called by Him to: "Love each other as I have loved you." This is the fullest measure of what being a true friend is. May each of us choose to let God strengthen us and soften us so we will love others as Jesus has loved us – truly loving them in our thoughts, in our words, in our actions and in every circumstance. As we do, we will not only be true friends to those around us, we will be true friends of God!

Do I believe it?
And if I do, what am I going to do about it?

Lord, please let me hear your voice, your love, your wisdom, your grace and truth.

WHOSE BATTLE?

He reached down from on high and took hold of me;
he drew me out of deep waters.
he rescued me from my powerful enemy,
from my foes, who were too strong for me.
They confronted me in the day of my disaster,
but the LORD was my support.
He brought me out into a spacious place;
he rescued me because he delighted in me.
2 Samuel 22:17-20

Are you in the midst of a battle? At work? At home? With your husband? With your wife? With your ex? With your children? With anyone? In any place?

Do you feel like you are overwhelmed by the deep and crashing waters of these conflicts, of these problems, of these battles? Do you feel backed into a corner with no place to go?

If "Yes" is the way that any of us answer any of these questions, then we really need to ask ourselves some other questions, some deeply challenging and personal questions:

What part am I playing to keep the battle going?

In what ways have I gotten myself into these deep waters?

What have I done to back myself, or the other person, into a corner so that resolution no longer seems like a remote possibility?

On whose power, strength and support have I truly been depending? On God's or my own?

Do I really want to be rescued from this battle? Or does the conflict itself somehow bring justification to my wrong actions? Or bring satisfaction to my mean-streak?

If our battles are really for the cause of Jesus Christ, then, battle on in the mighty power, Word and Spirit of our Living God! We can be sure that these battles will be won by the Lord Himself – in His time and in His way. And the Lord's victory will stand for all eternity.

If, however, our battles have grown out of our pride, our fear, our lack of forgiveness, our stubborn, self-focused thinking and our lack of true Jesus-like sacrificial love, then we might as well just suck those deep waters right into our lungs, because we are not breathing or thinking, speaking or acting, living or loving or battling in the way that pleases – that delights – our Lord!

When our battles are truly the Lord's battles and our foes are the Lord's foes – the destructive force of sin and hate, of cruelty and unforgiveness, and of every fear that twists and cripples our minds and lives – then, we will be rescued. Then, we will be held in God's eternal safety. Then, we will be empowered, strengthened, supported and brought into the spacious place of our God's transcending peace. Then, we will know the intimate, victorious love of God who delights in us. Remember and trust: "the battle is the LORD's" (1 Samuel 17:47)! Now and forever.

Reflections – Responses – Challenges – Encouragements – God-breathing Thoughts

Do I believe it?
And if I do, what am I going to do about it?

Lord, please let me hear your voice, your love, your wisdom, your grace and truth.

LOVE'S TRANSFORMING POWER

Transformation through the love of Jesus can take us from pain to peace, from cringing to courage, from hurting to healing. And it always takes us to our fullest life possible - both here on earth and in heaven.

> *Do not conform [any longer] to the pattern of this world,*
> *but be transformed by the renewing of your mind.*
> Romans 12:2

> *"The thief comes only to steal and kill and destroy;*
> *I have come that they may have life, and have it to the full."*
> John 10:10

> *"...in me you may have peace. In this world you will have trouble.*
> *But take heart! I have overcome the world!"*
> John 16:33

> *"I am the resurrection and the life. The one who believes in me will live,*
> *even though they die; and whoever lives by believing in me will never die.*
> *Do you believe this?"*
> John 11:25

Do you believe that the love of Jesus that brings you salvation will also bring you resurrection? Until that resurrection, do you believe that the love of Jesus is able to transform and renew your mind and, therefore, transform and renew your life, right now, right here on earth? *Do you believe it?* Many of you already know what my next question is: *What are you going to do about it?*

If I believe that the love of Jesus is able to take me from pain to peace, then I must allow Jesus to enter into my deepest pain. I must open up myself to Him. In full vulnerability. In full trust. No matter what I have chosen that causes me pain or shame or regret. No matter what pain or shame or regret has come to me by the choices of other people, or by life's circumstances. I must let Jesus hold me and fill me with His transcending peace – His peace that permeates my soul far deeper than any pain ever could.

If I believe that the love of Jesus is able to take me from cringing to courage, then I must embrace the truth that my fear is foolish in view of the almighty power and eternal presence of my Holy God. I must let Jesus transform me by His Word and Spirit so I will recognize and crush every Lie From The Pit Of Hell (LFTPOH) that would diminish and destroy me. I must let Jesus fill me with the fullness of His courage that has already overcome this broken, fear-inducing, sinful, dying world! And I must allow Jesus to help me live as He lives today and for all eternity – victoriously!

If I believe that the love of Jesus is able to take me from hurting to healing, then I must allow the love of Jesus to transform all my perceptions, at every level, in every way, in every circumstance, in every relationship, that still identifies me or justifies me as being a victim. I must see myself – we all must see ourselves – from God's transforming perspective! We are made to be "oaks of righteousness, a planting of the LORD for the display of his splendor" (Isaiah 61:3).

This is love's transforming power.

Do I believe it?
And if I do, what am I going to do about it?

Lord, please let me hear your voice, your love, your wisdom, your grace and truth.

GOD'S SURE HOPE

God makes it so clear to us, because of who God is and what God has done, that we can have a sure hope in God's intimate, ever-present and unfailing love for us! Because of who God is and what God has done, we can have a sure hope of eternal life with our loving Lord. We can have a sure hope that all God plans and promises will come about. And we can have a sure hope that we will not be disappointed as we place our full trust in our Holy God for every aspect of our lives, in every moment of our lives – now and for all eternity.

Our hope is never to look like or feel like or behave like a fragile and false superstition. Our hope is not to be based on any superstitious acts that somehow, supposedly, help to make our desired outcomes become a reality. There is no truth, there is no substance or assurance, and there is no sure hope in anything superstitious.

We don't have to cross our fingers. We don't have to knock on wood. We need only to put our full hope, our full trust, in what was fully accomplished through Jesus Christ on that wooden cross at Calvary!

> *And hope does not put us to shame, because God's love*
> *has been poured out into our hearts through the Holy Spirit,*
> *who has been given to us. You see, at just the right time,*
> *when we were still powerless, Christ died for the ungodly.*
> *Very rarely will anyone die for a righteous person,*
> *though for a good person someone might possibly dare to die.*
> *But God demonstrates his own love for us in this:*
> *While we were still sinners, Christ died for us.*
> Romans 5:5-8

> *...those who hope in me will not be disappointed.*
> Isaiah 49:23

Not only is our hope never to be based in anything superstitious, but our hope is not and can never be self-achieved or self-dependent in any way.

Our hope comes solely from God's love for us. Not from our good works or most loving acts. Our hope comes solely from the unexpected, undeserved sacrifice of the life of Jesus Christ that brings us His beautiful and holy gifts of forgiveness, salvation, renewal, transformation and eternal life.

What a sweet freedom and amazing joy we have been given through the hope – the sure hope – that comes through our Lord Jesus Christ! We don't ever have to worry or wonder about whether we did enough to earn God's approval. We don't ever have to doubt God's love for us, from which we can never be separated. We don't have to calculate our goodness against our badness – tenuously, fearfully hoping that somehow we made the cut for salvation and eternal life with our Lord.

We have a sure hope in Christ. We have a faithful God. We have been promised life and love for all eternity.

Are you putting aside your superstitions and self-dependencies to enjoy God's sure hope – this sweet freedom and amazing joy that comes from our Lord? I sure hope so!

Reflections – Responses – Challenges – Encouragements – God-breathing Thoughts

Do I believe it?
And if I do, what am I going to do about it?

Lord, please let me hear your voice, your love, your wisdom, your grace and truth.

SCHOOL'S IN FOREVER

Many children and adults across our nation, and throughout the world, are beginning a new school year during this season. From our littlest ones, whose eyes are big and hopeful, and wondering what being in school is all about, to our older ones, who may be learning a trade and gaining skills to build and create, fix and develop a variety of things, to those who may be long-term students in their final year of a doctoral program (maybe even completing their second or third doctorate degree) – all of them will have a beginning and an end to their formal educational programs.

Not so for us as children of God and followers of Christ. For us, school's in forever. And it's a beautiful, protective, life-guiding and life-transforming thing! As children of God and followers of Christ, we are to give ourselves over to our loving, teaching God – who wants to teach us His good ways, every single day of our lives.

> *Only be careful, and watch yourselves closely*
> *so that you do not forget the things your eyes have seen*
> *or let them fade from your heart as long as you live.*
> *Teach them to your children and to their children after them.*
> Deuteronomy 4:9

> *I will instruct you and teach you in the way you should go;*
> *I will counsel you with my loving eye on you.*
> Psalm 32:8

> *You are good, and what you do is good; teach me your decrees.*
> Psalm 119:68

> *Jesus said…"If you hold to my teaching, you are really my disciples.*
> *Then you will know the truth, and the truth will set you free."*
> John 8:31-32

> *Jesus said…"the Advocate, the Holy Spirit, whom the Father will send in my name,*
> *will teach you all things and will remind you of everything I have said to you."*
> John 14:26

> *All Scripture is God-breathed, and is useful for teaching,*
> *rebuking, correcting and training in righteousness…*
> 2 Timothy 3:16

> *Instruct the wise and they will be wiser still;*
> *teach the righteous and they will add to their learning.*
> Proverbs 9:9

As children of God and followers of Christ, growing in the wisdom and knowledge of our Lord is meant to be an integral and continual part of our intimate and eternal relationship with our holy God. Unlike the song, "School's Out," made famous by rocker Alice Cooper (who I actually met in Stuttgart, Germany several years ago), for us, school's in forever! And that's a beautiful, protective, life-guiding and life-transforming thing!

Teach on, God, teach on!

Do I believe it?
And if I do, what am I going to do about it?

Lord, please let me hear your voice, your love, your wisdom, your grace and truth.

ENTRANCE EXAM. NEED A REFRESHER COURSE?

Over and over again in the Bible, especially in what are known as the Epistles (the letters written to teach, encourage, correct and mentor different churches and faith communities on how to live their lives as followers of Jesus), the authors of these letters took time to greet the people who would be reading or listening to their messages.

The authors gave thought to how they should make their entrance into the lives of others. They knew how very important it was for them to first, always and fully, point their readers and listeners to the loving grace and holy truth of our Lord Jesus Christ – before they continued on with the rest of their God-given message.

Some loving, wise and beautiful entrance examples are included here. Read them fully. Hear the depth of love and the humble hearts that continually pointed to our Lord. Sense the spirit and attitude of unity, encouragement and care from which these messages were written.

Grace and peace be yours in abundance
through our knowledge of God and of Jesus our Lord.
2 Peter 1:2

To all in Rome [to all everywhere] who are loved by God and called to be his holy people:
Grace and peace to you from God our Father
and from the Lord Jesus Christ.
Romans 1:7

To the church of God in Corinth, to those sanctified in Christ Jesus
and called to be his holy people, together with all those everywhere
who call on the name of our Lord Jesus Christ – their Lord and ours:
Grace and peace to you from God our Father and the Lord Jesus Christ.
1 Corinthians 1:2-3

Grace and peace to you from God our Father and the Lord Jesus Christ,
who gave himself for our sins, to rescue us from the present evil age,
according to the will of our God and Father,
to whom be glory for ever and ever. Amen.
Galatians 1:3-5

...To those who have been called,
who are loved in God the Father and kept for Jesus Christ:
Mercy, peace and love be yours in abundance.
Jude 1-2

When we enter into someone's life – whether for a fleeting moment in a chance encounter or more regularly in our neighborhoods, at work, at school, at church, at organized sports and activities or continually and daily within our family relationships – do we enter with love? Do we enter with humility that acknowledges Jesus as our Lord? Do we enter in a spirit and attitude of unity, encouragement and care?

How would you do? How would I do on an *Entrance Exam* into someone else's life? Is it time for a *Refresher Course* in the grace and truth and love of our Lord Jesus so that each of us will be refreshing to others as we enter into their lives – whether we enter for a moment or for a lifetime?

Do I believe it?
And if I do, what am I going to do about it?

Lord, please let me hear your voice, your love, your wisdom, your grace and truth.

PURE JOY. WHENEVER.

*Consider it pure joy, my brothers and sisters, whenever you face trials of many kinds,
because you know that the testing of your faith produces perseverance.*
James 1:2-3

I have to admit that I don't really jump up and down with joy whenever I'm facing, or being faced-down, by trials of many kinds. Or any kind, for that matter. Considering it pure joy has not exactly been my very first, nor my most natural, response to the evil and brokenness, problems and frustrations, disappointments and difficulties – the trials of many kinds – I've experienced in my life.

However, I do know that God's Word is true. And God's Word is living and active, powerful and transforming. So, there's got to be something to this "consider it pure joy" craziness, right? Even if considering it pure joy is outrageously challenging and completely unnatural, right?

Yes. To both of those questions.

Whenever we choose to do things according to God's way – or perceive and think about things in God's way – there is always something deep and beautiful, powerful and peaceful for us. Probably the deepest and most beautiful, powerful and peaceful thing we could ever receive, as we follow God's ways for our actions and thoughts, is a growing sense of intimacy in our relationship with our Lord. And, specifically, as we trust God and choose, albeit challenging and unnatural, to consider it pure joy whenever we face trials of many kinds, we will also be beautifully, powerfully and peacefully blessed as we grow in Christ-like perseverance.

It is so important that we understand that our God does not tell us to consider *our trials of many kinds* as pure joy. That would be ludicrous. Because "God is love" (1 John 4:8); and "Love does not delight in evil but rejoices with the truth" (1 Corinthians 13:6).

Rather, our loving, holy and sovereign God tells us to consider it pure joy *whenever* we face these trials of many kinds. It is because of *who* our God is that we can consider all of our "whenevers" as pure joy – always. Our God is "Immanuel – God with us" (Matthew 1:23). God's Word gives us this sure promise: "the LORD your God goes with you; he will never leave you nor forsake you" (Deuteronomy 31:6). And our risen, victorious Lord Jesus declares, out of His love for us and His authority over all that exists, "I am with you always, to the very end of the age" (Matthew 28:20).

Trusting that our God is *who* He claims to be – trusting that our God is with us right in the midst of the mess, and trusting that our God is able to conquer all the crushing blows of life as He intimately, lovingly transforms us into people of perseverance – enables us to consider all of our "whenevers" as pure joy. Even when our "whenevers" find us facing evil and brokenness, problems and frustrations, disappointments and difficulties.

No! Our God is not asking us to consider our trials of many kinds as pure joy. Our God is asking us to consider Him, consider our relationship with Him, and consider the transforming results in our lives that come through God's great love for us – in this case, a Christ-like perseverance – to always be considered as pure joy! Whenever!

Reflections – Responses – Challenges – Encouragements – God-breathing Thoughts

Do I believe it?
And if I do, what am I going to do about it?

Lord, please let me hear your voice, your love, your wisdom, your grace and truth.

PERSEVERE! GOD'S JUST NOT DONE WITH US YET!

Let perseverance finish its work
so that you may be mature and complete, not lacking anything.
James 1:4

I'm not fully mature. I'm not fully complete. I'm definitely lacking in many things God would like to see more fully developed in me. And I've got many things God would dearly like to work out of me. God's just not done with me yet. And, if you're reading this rather than living in the full presence of our Heavenly Abba, I'm pretty sure God's not done with you yet either!

Our Lord loves us and is with us. God calls us to trust that His work, His loving and powerful work of perseverance in our lives, is to grow us continually to be more like our Lord Jesus. More loving. More forgiving. More wise. More patient. More compassionate. More courageous. More peaceful. More thankful. This is maturity. This is completeness. This is lacking in nothing.

Choosing to faithfully persevere in each of life's circumstances is exactly what our Lord Jesus calls us to do. This isn't our most natural response to many of the challenging circumstances we face. Choosing to trust God, choosing to receive and grow in His powerful perseverance is a lifelong, day-by-day work. And this is God's lifelong, day-by-day work within us – to grow us to completeness. We are to be co-laborers with Christ by allowing Him full access to transform our minds and our lives in order to bring us to maturity. We need to recognize that it truly is God's job to do this. What a freeing truth that is! We can't do it on our own. It's God's work within us that makes us mature and complete, that makes sure we are not lacking in anything of eternal value. It isn't up to us to make this happen. Our job is to willingly invite and allow our God, His Word and His Spirit to do His good work within us day-by-day. And we can be...

...confident of this, that he who began a good work in you
will carry it on to completion until the day of Christ Jesus.
Philippians 1:6

Inviting God to do His good work within us is so much less painful and exhausting than is ignoring our God – ignoring God's love, ignoring God's good purposes for us – until we find ourselves in absolute confusion, frustration, disillusionment and utter brokenness.

Persevering in our own strength, in our own wisdom, in our own will power, and in our own way can get us pretty far. There will be some amazing things we can do, some amazing obstacles we can overcome. We were created as image bearers of our God, and God wants us to use the strengths and gifts He has given us, but never to the point of ignoring our God. Never to the point of denying God's love and power in our lives – since God gave us life in the first place! Allowing God to lovingly, powerfully work within us to grow us in perseverance, to completion and maturity, is far more amazing than we could ever imagine!

God...is able to do immeasurably more than all we ask or imagine,
according to his power that is at work within us...
Ephesians 3:20

Persevere! God's just not done with us yet! Let's each allow God to finish His good work within us. Day-by-day. Each day of our lives.

Reflections – Responses – Challenges – Encouragements – God-breathing Thoughts

Do I believe it?
And if I do, what am I going to do about it?

Lord, please let me hear your voice, your love, your wisdom, your grace and truth.

COMMON COMPASSION

Rich and poor have this in common:
The LORD is the Maker of them all.
Proverbs 22:2

If I truly, down deep in my mind and in my soul, embrace the truth that both the poor and the rich (and all people in between) have been made and have been given life by the Holy God of all creation, then this should make a difference in all of my choices.

All of my choices – in my attitudes, words, actions, interactions, reactions and, even, in all of my facial expressions – because of our human commonality as creations of the One Living God, should be ruled by compassion. And this compassion should show itself towards others in very real, tangible, practical and spiritual ways. Compassion should rule my ways and my wallet, my purposes and plans, my time and my talents, my efforts and my energy, my perspectives and prayers.

We are loved by our Holy God in ways that are beyond our comprehension. Yet, for far too many of us, we don't fully accept the truth of God's incredible, compassionate love for us. As we begin to trust God more and more as a Truth Teller, especially about His outrageous love and unfailing compassion for us, we will be more able to let the love and compassion we have received from our God pour more freely and fully from us into the lives of others. All others.

Because of the LORD's great love we are not consumed,
for his compassions never fail.
They are new every morning;
great is your faithfulness.
Lamentations 3:22-23

We have this in common with all people – poor, rich, kind, cruel, hurting, hurtful, maddening, marvelous, loving, lost – the Lord is Maker of us all and our Lord offers His same great love and unfailing compassion to every single one of us. As children of God and followers of Jesus Christ, we each are to deeply breathe in and believe these God-declared truths that we share in common with all people. And as children of God and followers of Christ, we are to do something about these truths.

Maybe for you, what you need to do is to really believe these are true for you. You are made in the image and likeness of the Maker of all that exists. You are loved greatly, outrageously and offered the fullness of God's compassion through our Lord and Savior Jesus Christ. Neither of these truths can ever change – no matter how you may change or your life circumstances may change. These are unchanging truths from our unchanging God.

Maybe for you, what you need to do about these truths is to view people – each person who crosses your path or who just crosses you – through the Cross of Christ. You need to lay down your hatred, your judgment, your unforgiveness and your self-righteous anger because Jesus Christ laid down His life for you, out of His great love and unfailing compassion.

May the uncommon compassion that our Lord Jesus Christ has for us become our common compassion for all people!

Reflections – Responses – Challenges – Encouragements – God-breathing Thoughts

Do I believe it?
And if I do, what am I going to do about it?

Lord, please let me hear your voice, your love, your wisdom, your grace and truth.

QUIET! BE STILL!

The Sea of Galilee is 680 feet below sea level and surrounded by hills. Because of this, the winds blowing down from these hills to the sea can often cause surprising and dangerous storms. This was true on at least one occasion when Jesus and his disciples were in a boat, crossing from one side of the Sea of Galilee to the other.

> *A furious squall came up, and the waves broke over the boat,*
> *so that it was nearly swamped. Jesus was in the stern, sleeping on a cushion.*
> *The disciples woke him and said to him, "Teacher, don't you care if we drown?"*
> *He got up, rebuked the wind and said to the waves, "Quiet! Be still!"*
> *Then the wind died down and it was completely calm.*
> *He said to his disciples, "Why are you so afraid? Do you still have no faith?"*
> *They were terrified and asked each other,*
> *"Who is this? Even the wind and the waves obey him!"*
> Mark 4:39-41

Jesus has the power to quiet the fiercest storms and calm the most overwhelming of waves – in the physical, mental, emotional and spiritual realms. Jesus is Lord of all. Yet, way too often, when chaotic storms and overwhelming waves come crashing into our lives – in the form of a relationship filled with pain and uncertainty, a body suffering with illness or a crippling disability, a death of a spouse or a child or a friend, the loss of a job or financial security – we fill our heads with all manner of worry, anxiety, fear, frustration, depression, self pity and anger at the unfairness and out-of-our-control of it all.

Too often we allow our own fear-fed thoughts to run rampant in our heads. And this is deadly. We need to be able to sincerely respond to the disciples' question, *"Who is this?"* with a firm and faithful, "Jesus, You are the Sovereign Lord over all that exists! Jesus, You are the Prince of Peace!"

The wind and the waves obeyed Jesus when He said to them, "Quiet! Be Still!" For us, we are to not only obey Jesus when He speaks, "Quiet! Be Still!" to the storms causing havoc in our hearts and minds, we are also to trust Him to do for us – within us, through us, and even in spite of us – what we could not possibly do on our own. We are to receive the transcending peace of Jesus Christ that will guard our hearts and minds right in the midst of our mayhem.

Only then, when we trust and obey our Lord to allow His shalom, His peace to rule over us and in us, will our churning thoughts of chaos and crises, panic and pressure die down and be completely calm. Only then, when we trust and obey our Lord to allow His shalom, His peace to rule over us and in us, will we recognize and receive the power that our Prince of Peace has for us. At all times. In all circumstances.

So, shhhhh...Rest your heart, your mind, and your life in Jesus' love and care for you.

Take some time with Jesus, even now, and choose to trust and obey Him and His words, spoken in full and eternal authority and unfailing love, over your most tumultuous thoughts and furious storms, "Quiet! Be Still!"

Jesus Christ is now and always in control.

Do I believe it?
And if I do, what am I going to do about it?

Lord, please let me hear your voice, your love, your wisdom, your grace and truth.

TAKE NOTE OF THIS!

My dear brothers and sisters, take note of this:
Everyone should be quick to listen,
slow to speak and slow to become angry...
James 1:19

Take note of this! I just love how God inspired James to get our attention right up front!

So, let's take note: *Be quick to listen.* Let's really choose to quickly focus and fully listen to the one who is speaking. Let's value and honor each person. Let's let each person know they are being heard by us. Let's ask the Lord to help us listen quickly and fully to others with His love, attention and patience. The same love, attention and patience that our Lord gives to each one of us – always.

So, let's take note: *Be slow to speak.* Let's answer only after we have really heard the other person. Only after we have first sought to truly understand that person's thoughts, that person's words. Let's choose to not pre-judge what we think that person may have to say. Let's choose to not interrupt (Oh-my-goodness! I really had to learn this one! Coming from a family with five children, all born within five years from the oldest to the youngest, interrupting was what I did!) Let's choose to not have an already fully formulated rebuttal or counterpoint prepared even before the other person has finished speaking. That isn't really listening. Let's ask the Lord for His love, wisdom and timing before we speak. The same love, wisdom and time that our Lord gives to us when we are speaking to Him.

So, let's take note: *Be slow to become angry.* Let's be willing to choose a mind and heart of openness towards the other person and what he or she is truly saying before we open our mouths with any kind of anger, judgment, criticism, coldness or cruelty. Let's ask the Lord for His love, kindness and compassion as we react to and interact with each person. The same love, kindness and compassion that our Lord shows to us – continually.

Our God hears our hearts even when we don't know how to fully put into words all that would express, and make clear, our innermost thoughts and feelings. Our God loves us and listens to us – each one of us – with infinite and intimate attention, patience, wisdom, kindness and compassion. And although none of us can hear another's heart perfectly or listen as lovingly as God listens to us, we are to follow our Lord Jesus in all things. And that includes the way we listen and respond to others.

Jesus said...
"My sheep listen to my voice; I know them, and they follow me."
John 10:27

Listening, really listening, to other people in order to hear their hearts, in order to know and understand their thoughts and perspectives, is one of the most powerful and tangible ways we could ever show our love. And as we listen to Jesus, He tells us...

"My command is this: Love each other as I have loved you."
John 15:12

Take note of this, and love all others in the way our Lord Jesus loves us: Be quick to listen, slow to speak and slow to anger!

Do I believe it?
And if I do, what am I going to do about it?

Lord, please let me hear your voice, your love, your wisdom, your grace and truth.

OUR ANGER – GOD'S RIGHTEOUS LIVING WAY

…human anger does not produce the righteousness that God desires.
James 1:20

I don't know about you, but for me this verse brings out a very gut-level response of *Duh!* Of course, our human anger does not bring about the righteous life that God desires! *Duh!*

But, then, even with believing that this Scripture speaks God's good and freeing truth to me, I still too easily dismiss God and God's truth when I get all focused on me and my own reasons for self-righteous anger. I have to stop and look at myself very honestly. And it just isn't always pretty.

How often do I let myself rant and rave in anger? Even if no one else sees me? Even if no one else hears me? Even if my angry tirade is happening only in the privacy of my own little head? How long do I let myself stay in that place of anger – entertaining, and increasing, my angry thoughts, and justifying myself with several very good reasons as to why I should be so angry, and why I should stay that way for a while longer?

There's not a whole lot of righteousness and righteous living coming out of my human anger. Only a whole lot of ugly, prideful, deadly self-righteousness. When I let myself get stuck in this ugly, angry place, there just isn't any room to let the righteous living, that God desires to bring about in me and through me, manifest itself. Instead I'm feasting on anger. And that's sin.

Our God desires us to live a righteous life. Many of us need to understand (and maybe even redefine) that living a righteous life is not about being bound up in some sort of religious or legalistic code of behavior. Living the righteous life that our God desires for each of His children is, first and foremost, about living in a loving, intimate, honest relationship with our God. Living the righteous life that our God desires will also bring us the greatest freedom we could ever know and experience. Letting our God conform us to think, speak and act (even inside of our own little heads) more and more like Jesus is exactly the freedom – the righteous living – our God desires for us. This is God's loving purpose for our lives: to free us from anything and everything that would entrap and enslave us. Including our own anger.

Our loving response, to God's loving desires and purpose for us when it comes to our human anger, would be to immediately ask for God's help to deal with our anger in God's righteous living way. God's way of dealing with our anger is never about having us deny it or stuff it. God's way of dealing with our anger is never about us imploding and, thereby, destroying our own peace and freedom as we hold our anger in. Nor are we to explode in angry, ugly ways that destroy the peace and freedom of others. God knows anger will rise in us. He doesn't fault us that. However, out of God's love for us – out of His desires for us to live a righteous life – our God does demand:

In your anger do not sin.
Ephesians 4:26

We have choices to make. Our God never leaves us alone to accomplish what He desires to do in us and through us. As we ask God to help us in our ugliest anger, we will be transformed to be more quickly quieted in our minds; to view our anger-making circumstances from God's eternal and loving perspective. We will be more like Jesus. Our anger will not so fully entrap us. And we will be more fully free to more fully live the righteous life God desires us to live!

Do I believe it?
And if I do, what am I going to do about it?

Lord, please let me hear your voice, your love, your wisdom, your grace and truth.

BE SET FREE FROM FAVORITISM

My brothers and sisters, believers in our glorious Lord Jesus Christ
must not show favoritism.
Suppose a man comes into your meeting wearing a gold ring and fine clothes,
and a poor man in filthy old clothes also comes in.
If you show special attention to the man wearing fine clothes...
and [dismiss and disrespect] the poor man...
have you not discriminated among yourselves
and become judges with evil thoughts?
...If you really keep the royal law found in Scripture,
"Love your neighbor as yourself," you are doing right.
But if you show favoritism, you sin...
James 2:1-4, 8-9

Don't show favoritism...if you show favoritism, you sin. Oh, my. Taking this Scripture really to heart, breaks my heart. It uncovers my sinful heart tendencies more than I really want to admit. Now, I'm not one to fawn all over somebody just because they're somebody special or, at least, I judge them as more special than someone else. Yet, when I take this teaching from God's Word seriously and look honestly into my own heart, I have to admit that I do treat different people differently. I do show favoritism. My favoritism pendulum may not swing too widely, or too obviously, when it comes to how I view and treat people differently. Maybe no one else would ever notice the subtle changes – the subtle swings – in my behavior due to my judgments of different people. But they're there. Lord, forgive me.

Not long ago, this truth was driven home in a very personal, all-up-in-my-face kind of way. Literally. I had just gone through an intensive surgery in my mouth. Over the next two weeks, my entire face was grotesquely swollen and disfigured with crazy and very colorful bruising. About the fifth day after surgery, with my face still looking quite hideous, I braved going out in public to accomplish a few necessary errands. Because life just doesn't stop for ugly. What I experienced went from feeling uncomfortable to feeling outright dismissal and disrespect from others. At one shop where I was the next in line, one man actually looked at me then stepped in front of me. After that, the man working the register looked at the woman behind me and said, "Hey, beautiful. What can I get for you today?" I don't share this example (and trust me, there were several more during my grotesque face phase) for any kind of sympathy. God used these experiences to make me more intimately aware of, and sincerely sorry for, even my most subtle of favoritism pendulum swings.

I, and probably you as well, tend to judge people by their outward appearance – whether we judge them by their color, their size, by evidence of their intelligence or wealth, by their occupational position or talent, or by what we consider to be beautiful. We show favoritism.

May each of us check our hearts and ask God to give us purer love for all others and set us free from every prejudice, every swing of favoritism, that would block us from seeing each person for who he or she truly is: An image-bearer of our Loving God, our Holy Creator.

So God created mankind in his own image, in the image of God
he created them; male and female God created them.
Genesis 1:27

Reflections – Responses – Challenges – Encouragements – God-breathing Thoughts

Do I believe it?
And if I do, what am I going to do about it?

Lord, please let me hear your voice, your love, your wisdom, your grace and truth.

PRAISE THE LORD, O MY SOUL, AND REMEMBER!

Praise the LORD, my soul; all my inmost being, praise his holy name.
Praise the LORD, my soul, and forget not all his benefits –
who forgives all your sins
and heals all your diseases,
who redeems your life from the pit
and crowns you with love and compassion,
who satisfies your desires with good things
so that your youth is renewed like the eagle's.
Psalm 103:1-5

Praise the Lord, O my soul! How good and right, how refreshing and renewing, how balancing and breathing it is to our souls – to our minds, to our hearts, and to our bodies – to praise our Lord. How good it is for us to remember – actively and intentionally, humbly and thankfully – all the gifts of love, life, mercy, and strength that our Lord pours out to us now and eternally!

I have a dear friend who when I asked him how he prayed for himself during a time of great crisis, answered by telling me that he prayed during these days just like he always prayed: "Lord, thank you for all of the blessings you have given to me and my family. Thank you, Jesus, for saving me. Please forgive me of all of my sins. Help me be the man I should be."

A simple, humble prayer. A prayer filled with sincere thanksgiving. A prayer where his only requests were for the forgiveness of his sins and for God to help him to be the man that God wanted him to be.

I know my prayers are often far more convoluted than those of my friend's. They are often too pleading. Often too hurried. Often too ungrateful. Often too focused on the need for others to change instead of on my need for continual forgiveness and transformation.

My friend's way of praying moved me and challenged me. And I take more time for simple, humble prayers. More time to remember and sincerely thank God for all of His goodness and blessings in my life. More time to thank Jesus for His gift of salvation and for His inexplicable love that compelled Him to die for me. More time to confess my sins and receive God's forgiveness with deep gratitude and a heart set free. More time to ask God to help me to be the woman He wants me to be. Praise the Lord, O my soul!

My friend passed through his time of crisis, but not in the way, or the timing, that we who loved him wanted. He passed from our presence on this earth. We mourn with deep, heart-aching loss. And we celebrate the joy we know he now has because he passed into the full, eternal, and beautiful presence of Jesus, his Savior and Lord. Praise the Lord, O my soul!

May we each take time to call our souls to praise the Lord and remember all of His blessings given so generously to us! Our God loves us. Our God forgives us. Our God redeems our lives from death and saves us to share in His joy for all eternity. Our God heals our every disease and every bit of brokenness in our lives. Our God honors us – crowns us – with His love and compassion. Our God satisfies the deepest desires of our hearts with His good things. Our God renews our strength and transforms us in deep and beautiful ways to be His people forever. *Praise the Lord, O my soul, and remember!*

Reflections – Responses – Challenges – Encouragements – God-breathing Thoughts

Do I believe it?
And if I do, what am I going to do about it?

Lord, please let me hear your voice, your love, your wisdom, your grace and truth.

September 11

OUR UNCHANGING GOD

Jesus Christ is the same yesterday and today and forever.
Hebrews 13:8

How thankful I am that our God, our Holy Lord, our King and Savior Jesus Christ is always the same. How thankful I am that our God, our Holy Lord, our King and Savior Jesus Christ never changes.

This is not true for me or for you. This is not true for my circumstances or yours. This is not true for my world or yours. Because our circumstances and our world do not stay the same. Our circumstances and our world change.

And sometimes we, and our circumstances, and our world change in wonderful, exciting, adventurous ways. And sometimes in shocking, frightening, helpless ways.

Today is September 11, a day marking one more anniversary, since 2001, of the horrendous acts of terrorism and the murder of thousands of innocent people in New York City, Pennsylvania and at the Pentagon in Washington, DC.

Many of us still feel the loss of loved ones whose lives were claimed that day. Many of us know and care for others whose lives and families, hopes and dreams were devastatingly affected by these evil acts. Others of us can clearly remember the shock and sadness this day brought as incomprehensible hatred and cruelty seemed to change our circumstances and our world instantaneously – without our foreknowledge and without our ability to stop it.

And for a while, many people throughout many nations and, certainly, here in the United States, experienced a deep and sudden change in our circumstances and in our world, and even in our immediate priorities and plans. Our sense of security in life as we knew it was destroyed. Our sense of hope and our expectations for what that beautiful, bright, sunny September day should have been, were completely shattered.

Our only lasting security, our only unfailing hope and our only true peace are found only in our unchanging and sovereign God. Only in our God's love. Only in our God's transcending peace. Only in the salvation offered to us as Jesus sacrificed His holy life for the forgiveness of our sins. Only in Christ's resurrection and His promised gift of eternal life with Him. Everything else changes.

Take a moment to remember September 11, 2001, if you can. And if you can't, remember the truth that everything, except our unchanging God, changes.

Maybe it's a good day for each of us to make some changes.
Take time to thank God for your life.
Take time to thank God for this day.
Take time to let others know how very much you love them.
Take time to let others know how thankful you are to have them in your lives.
Take time to be kind.
Take time to forgive.
Take time to live.
Take time to laugh.
Take time to love!

Do I believe it?
And if I do, what am I going to do about it?

Lord, please let me hear your voice, your love, your wisdom, your grace and truth.

OUR LITTLENESS – OUR BIG GOD

May our Lord Jesus Christ himself and God our Father,
who loved us and by his grace gave us eternal encouragement and good hope,
encourage your hearts and strengthen you in every good deed and word.
2 Thessalonians 2:16-17

There are some days that I am more keenly aware of the everyday truth of how very little I really am. And quite honestly, this intense awareness of my littleness seems to come to me, more and more often, at some point during each one of my days.

This clear awareness of my littleness does not come from a sense or a feeling of insignificance in any way. My God has more than shown me how very significant I am to Him – how very dearly and unfailingly loved I am by Him. Jesus gave up His life to give me eternal life. Christ's sacrifice is an undeniable and outrageous act of love, an amazing and indisputable revelation of my (and of our) significance to our Holy God.

This acute sense of my littleness is actually a very good thing. It keeps me so very aware that God is God and I am not. It keeps me held in the truth that God is so much bigger than I am. And, oh! I am so thankful for this truth! I need my Big God. Always. In all ways.

I need my Big God to give me His bigger, higher thoughts, His bigger higher ways and truth. They clear my head and quiet my soul.

I need my Big God to give me His *bigger, purer* love and grace. They hold me and lift me. They comfort and forgive me. They grow me and guide me.

I need my Big God to give me His *bigger, stronger* eternal encouragement and good hope. They give me inspiration and motivation to keep going. They give me strength and perspective, courage and purpose.

I need my *bigger, higher, purer, stronger* God.

Every moment of every single day I need God's full love, grace, eternal encouragement, good hope and strength. I need my Big God and all that He offers to give me so that I may live with my heart and mind secure and encouraged. I need my Big God every moment of every single day to give me the strength to follow His good and loving will and ways in all I am, in all that I think, in all I say and in all I do. Because in myself I don't have this strength. I'm just too little.

In my littleness – in my honest view of my position and power compared to my very Big God – I am humbled and safe. In my littleness, I am set free from every false sense of self and every wrong estimation of my own power and control. In my littleness, I can breathe more deeply, knowing that my Big God is in control. In my littleness, I can live more fully, knowing that my Big God loves me like crazy and gives me a significance – through His sacrifice – that I cannot even begin to fathom.

May each of us more fully trust the love and grace, eternal encouragement, good hope and strength from our Big God! Our lives are not limited by our littleness. We are called and empowered to impact the lives of others with the bigness of our Lord Jesus Christ!

Reflections – Responses – Challenges – Encouragements – God-breathing Thoughts

Do I believe it?
And if I do, what am I going to do about it?

Lord, please let me hear your voice, your love, your wisdom, your grace and truth.

PREPARED AND PRE-PRAYERED TO BE CHRIST'S AMBASSADORS

...brothers and sisters, pray for us that the message of the Lord
may spread rapidly and be honored, just as it was with you.
May the Lord direct your hearts into God's love and Christ's perseverance.
2 Thessalonians 3:1, 5

I am so thankful that the apostle Paul knew how much he constantly needed prayer in order to do what our Holy God had asked him to do. That honest and humble need for prayer is so true for all of us who follow Jesus Christ. I desperately need prayer. Always. I need to set aside time in prayer by myself with my Heavenly Abba. I need to be in a continual prayer conversation with my God throughout my entire day – for every thing I do and for every interaction I have with every other person. And I need, real and regular, prayer support, encouragement, and strength from my brothers and sisters in Christ.

None of us who are on this faith journey, who are called as ambassadors of Christ, are meant to be lone individuals acting alone to accomplish the task God has given us: To spread the message of Christ's love, grace and truth. For this we need God. And we need each other.

We have the sure promise that the Lord's presence, love, grace, eternal encouragement, good hope, and strength will be with us always (2 Thessalonians 2:16-17). We need to continually go before our Lord, humbly and in trust, to receive these. And we need others – our brothers, sisters, friends, mentors, and children in faith – to continually lift us and guard us in prayer.

Each of us at some point in our faith journey will experience days and nights when we will desperately need all the love, strength, and courage that the prayers of others can bring to us. We will find ourselves discouraged, worn out, and battle-weary – but never alone! Our God will use His people – the Body of Christ – to be His healing balm, His refreshing breath, His holy zeal, and His powerful encouragement to bring us back to balance and strength as we live our lives following our Lord Jesus Christ and spreading His message of love, salvation and transformation.

Each of us, also, has the privilege and responsibility to take on this prayer-lifting, prayer-guarding role in the lives of our brothers, sisters, friends, mentors, and children in faith. We are to help point them – their hearts, minds, souls, and spirits – always back to the truth of God's love, always back to the power of Christ's perseverance. Just as they are to do for us. Always.

When we do this – when we honestly, actively love and support one another in prayer – we are loving one another as Christ loves us. When we honestly, actively love and support one another in prayer, we are bringing greater unity to the Body of Christ. When we honestly, actively love and support one another in prayer, we are all more fully prepared to reflect the beauty of Christ's love and perseverance to all with whom we interact.

May each of us choose to be – and help our brothers and sisters on this faith journey to be – more fully prepared and pre-prayered as Christ's ambassadors to share, and live out, the good news of our Savior and Lord Jesus Christ!

May God's full message of His life-transforming love, grace and truth *spread rapidly and be honored by many*! Starting with me...starting with you.

Reflections – Responses – Challenges – Encouragements – God-breathing Thoughts

Do I believe it?
And if I do, what am I going to do about it?

Lord, please let me hear your voice, your love, your wisdom, your grace and truth.

BROKEN OPEN! BREAK THROUGH!

The One who breaks open the way will go up before them;
they will break through the gate and go out.
Their king will pass through before them, the LORD at their head.
Micah 2:13

I love this! The One – the King, the Lord, the Messiah, our God, our Savior Jesus Christ – breaks open the way so that we will break through and go out, following Him at our head! What freedom! What victory! What joy!

Our Mighty God has broken open for us the most destructive, life-threatening barrier that keeps us from knowing true peace and eternal life. Our Lord Jesus Christ has broken open the gates of captivity and condemnation. Our King has broken open the very gates of hell – whose doors, that close in on us, are named: sin and death.

Jesus Christ, through His death for our sins and His resurrection for our lives, has broken open these gates for us. And the power of sin and death has been conquered. For all eternity.

Now, it is our choice. Will we accept this life-giving, life-forgiving, life-transforming truth and follow Jesus as the King who goes before us, as the Head over all of our lives? Will we choose to accept the freedom and the power our Lord Jesus offers us so that we, too, may break through the gate and go out?

C.S. Lewis once wrote that, "The gates of hell are locked from the inside."

Think about where and how you may be keeping yourself locked inside your own personal hell. Think about where and how you may be keeping yourself from trusting and living in the great freedom and victory already secured for each of us through the love and sacrifice of Jesus.

It's up to us to choose to trust and live in the truth of God's Word that declares that our Lord Jesus has fully broken open these gates. It's up to us to choose to let God help us break through all of the lies and the hurts, the sin and the shame, the fear and the pride that keep us locked inside our own hell.

It is for freedom that Christ has set us free.
Stand firm, then, and do not let yourselves be burdened again
by a yoke of slavery.
Galatians 5:1

Freedom and victory, life and peace have already been fully and eternally opened to us by the One – the King, the Lord, the Messiah, our God, our Savior Jesus Christ! Jesus has broken the yokes of slavery created by all of our sin, shame, wounds, bitterness, fear, pride, pain and past. We don't have to stay locked in by anything we have done or by anything that has been done to us.

May we each recognize the power of this truth and put our trust in Jesus who opens the way for us to live in His freedom and victory – right now and in each new day yet to come. May each of us choose to follow the One who goes before us so that we will break through and go out with joy, purpose, and passion!

Reflections – Responses – Challenges – Encouragements – God-breathing Thoughts

Do I believe it?
And if I do, what am I going to do about it?

Lord, please let me hear your voice, your love, your wisdom, your grace and truth.

FOLLOW JESUS ON A PATH MARKED OUT BY MERCY

As Jesus went on, he saw a man named Matthew sitting at the tax collector's booth.
"Follow me," he told him, and Matthew got up and followed him.
While Jesus was having dinner at Matthew's house, many tax collectors and "sinners"
came and ate with him and his disciples. When the Pharisees saw this,
they asked his disciples, "Why does your teacher eat with tax collectors and 'sinners'?"
On hearing this, Jesus said, "It is not the healthy who need a doctor, but the sick.
But go and learn what this means: 'I desire mercy, not sacrifice.'
For I have not come to call the righteous, but sinners."
Matthew 9:9-13

Jesus gets right up in our faces. He has to, or we might not ever let Him get into our hearts.

Here, Matthew is seen and called by Jesus, and Matthew, in a faith-filled response, sees that Jesus has something he can't resist, something he desperately needs. And Matthew gets up, right there and then, and follows Jesus.

Matthew welcomes Jesus into his home, offering Him a meal. Matthew, as host, feasts not only on the food placed before him, but also on the deep spiritual food offered through Christ's life-changing, mercy-filled words. Many of Matthew's guests are known to be *sinners*. Others are known to be righteous – at least by their own self-evaluations. And all of Matthew's guests need the life-changing mercy that only Jesus can give. But not all of them knew this.

The self-righteous voices are raised. The condemning criticism is spewed. The life-changing mercy of God Most High is challenged. And the sad, and damning, truth is that these *healthy ones* do not even begin to see how desperate they themselves are for the mercy of God. Nor do these *healthy ones* even consider the possibility that others, who are not like them but rather are *sinners*, could ever be worthy of God's blessings and goodness.

And Jesus gets right up in their faces. They are blind to their own desperate need for God. They are blind and uncaring, judgmental and condemning of the needy ones in their midst. They are blind to their own sinfulness. They can't see what the *sinners* see: their need for the mercy of God.

May Jesus get in our faces and into our hearts so that we will see and follow the One who alone can give us the mercy we so desperately need.

May Jesus get in our faces and into our hearts so that we will see others as no more, and no less, needy than are we.

May Jesus get in our faces and into our hearts so that we will see others with (what I call) *mercy eyes*, and help us to offer real, tangible, relational and spiritual mercy to all with whom we interact as we follow Jesus – the One who looked on us with the full measure of His mercy.

Jesus calls to each of us, "Follow Me!" And He holds out His nail-marked hands to us, calling us to follow Him on a path marked out by mercy – God's life-changing mercy that is to be fully received into our own hearts and lives and fully offered from us to all others along our paths.

Reflections – Responses – Challenges – Encouragements – God-breathing Thoughts

Do I believe it?
And if I do, what am I going to do about it?

Lord, please let me hear your voice, your love, your wisdom, your grace and truth.

OUR LORD'S LEGACY OF LOVE

As a father has compassion on his children,
so the LORD has compassion on those who fear him;
for he knows how we are formed, he remembers that we are dust.
The life of mortals is like grass,
they flourish like a flower of the field;
the wind blows over it and it is gone,
and its place remembers it no more.
But from everlasting to everlasting the LORD's love is with those who fear him,
and his righteousness with their children's children –
with those who keep his covenant and remember to obey his precepts.
Psalm 103:13-18

Amazing. Who our God is, what our God's character is, and the hope of eternity we have in our God's love – in our Lord's legacy of love – are so succinctly, clearly and beautifully expressed here.

Our God is the compassionate Father for all those who fear Him – for all those who trust Him. Oh! I know I need this compassion from my Heavenly Abba. We all do. Most of us have experienced times, maybe far too many times, when we have been dismissed or disheartened, disrespected or demeaned by another. Our God is the Lord of compassion. Love is who our God is (1 John 4:8). Loving compassion is what our God offers to His children continually.

Our God is the perfect and eternal One who knows each of us intimately and loves each of us compassionately in our mortal state – understanding how very frail and fleeting our lives on this earth are. We will each die to this earth. We will each die to all that is temporary. But this is not the end of life for those who fear and trust the Lord.

Our God declares that His love is from everlasting to everlasting. If God's love for us is eternal – always present, never ending, transcending all time and space – then our God must transform us from our mortal state into our immortal state so that we may receive His promised love that is from everlasting to everlasting. Our God of love is our Lord Jesus Christ who declared Himself to be "the resurrection and the life" (John 11:25). For all those who fear and trust our God, we have been given the absolute assurance that our lives are eternal and will be set free from all that breaks and binds us on this earth. We will know the fullness of God's love as we live for all eternity – from everlasting to everlasting – filled with, flowing with, and surrounded by God's beautiful, holy, and loving presence.

Our God promises that He will give His righteousness to our children's children as they, too, choose to fear and trust the Lord – as they, too, choose to keep God's covenant and obey His commands. Our God's compassionate, eternal love, His tender understanding of our frail and fleeting mortal life, and His gift of resurrecting righteousness – bestowed on all of us by faith – are newly and fully offered to each individual, to each of our children, in this generation and the next generation and the next…and the next…

Our God offers each of us His compassionate, powerful, life-transforming love and eternal righteousness – right now and for all eternity. This is our Lord's legacy of love for all who will choose to fear and trust our God. Amazing.

Do I believe it?
And if I do, what am I going to do about it?

Lord, please let me hear your voice, your love, your wisdom, your grace and truth.

WILL AND MAY – THE LORD'S TRUTH, OUR CHOICE

Many nations will come and say,
"Come, let us go up to the mountain of the LORD,
to the temple of the God of Jacob.
He will teach us his ways, so that we may walk in his paths.
All the nations may walk in the name of their gods,
but we will walk in the name of the LORD."
Micah 4:2, 5

Will and May...

When it comes to the truth of what the Lord will do, according to His Word, we can be certain it will happen. The Lord will do it. In this passage we have the Lord's promise that for those who seek God, for those who seek His truth and His wisdom: *The Lord will teach us His ways.*

And then, that word "may" appears: *...so that we may walk in His paths.* This is where certainty isn't so certain. Because this is where we people have a choice to make.

We can *go up to the mountain and the house of the Lord.* We can go to church and read our Bibles. We can put ourselves in all kinds of places – in Christian counseling, in Christ-focused conferences and retreats, in Jesus-honoring prayer and study groups – where the Word of the Lord is taught, presented, honored, and explained in its amazing and powerful life-saving, life-transforming truth. But each one of us still has a choice to make.

Will we trust and believe the teachings of the Lord so that we will walk in His paths? Or will we choose to continue walking in our own paths that can too often be oblivious to God's will or too filled with our own prideful ways and self-focused plans? Will we choose to continue walking in our own paths filled with fear and shame – sometimes more subtle, yet, still deadly forms of pride – because we will not choose to trust and believe that our Lord's love, grace, truth, forgiveness, and strength are more than enough for us?

Will we choose, whether blatantly or subtly, to walk in the names of other gods? Will we choose to walk in the name of any other thing – including ourselves, our attitudes, actions, abilities, desires and other relationships – that we trust more than the Lord? We may do this. *All nations* – all individuals – *may walk in the name of their gods.*

We have a choice. The Lord doesn't make us robots. The Lord doesn't force us to follow His teachings or walk in His paths. Our Lord desires to be in an authentic, loving, and intimate relationship with us. And that can't be forced. The Lord doesn't want us to walk in His paths out of some kind of superficial, religious-duty obligation we have imposed on ourselves. That path really wouldn't be the Lord's. So, even when we put ourselves in all the right places to hear the truth of the Lord's Word, we still have a choice to make.

We still have to choose, intentionally and actively, to respond to our Lord's love and leadership in our lives. And we can absolutely trust that when we do, our Lord will teach us His ways and walk with us on His paths! May each of us choose to follow our Lord's teachings and paths so that we will live out a radical, beautiful and powerful transformation in our lives – all accomplished through an authentic, loving and intimate relationship with our holy Lord! What a great choice to make!

Reflections – Responses – Challenges – Encouragements – God-breathing Thoughts

Do I believe it?
And if I do, what am I going to do about it?

Lord, please let me hear your voice, your love, your wisdom, your grace and truth.

WHAT TO DO?

The disciples asked him, "What must we do to do the works God requires?"
Jesus answered, "The work of God is this: to believe in the one he has sent."
John 6:28-29

"What must we do to do the works God requires?" That was the question. The disciples wanted a clear answer. They didn't want to miss their chance to do the works necessary to please God. And Jesus answers them with such a twist from what they expected to hear. Jesus told them the work that God requires of them is to "believe in the one God has sent."

Foundational and essential to doing any work that God requires of us – to doing anything that connects us in a righteous and intimate relationship with God – is to believe what God has already done: He has sent Jesus into this world to do the work that only the Holy One of God could do for us. Our work is to believe God. Believe in the one He has sent. Believe all that God has done for us by sending Jesus. Believe Jesus has died for our sins. Believe Jesus offers us complete forgiveness. Believe Jesus has risen from the grave and offers the gift of eternal life. Believe that Jesus has accomplished the full work God requires of us.

In believing in Jesus, we will understand that any other works that God has for us to do are works that are not required for our salvation, but rather are evidence of our relationship with our Holy God. We cannot add anything to the sacrifice Jesus made in giving His life for us.

In His simple and profound statement, Jesus makes it clear that the only work that God requires of us is to honestly believe in Jesus as our Savior. Believe in Jesus as our Lord. From this place of sincere belief – from this place of an intimate, powerful, restored, and transformed relationship with God – all other works that we do, as we live out our faith in God, should flow from this foundational and essential *required* work of God. Believe!

Maybe you already believe in Jesus as your Savior. Thanks be to God! Maybe this message is just to be an encouragement, a remembrance and a re-focus for you. Life is not always easy. There's a lot of work, a lot of pressure...and Jesus wants to remind you that the most important work that could ever be done in all of eternity has already been fully done for you!

Maybe, though, you've never yet believed in the one God has sent. Maybe today, maybe this moment, is the time for you to make this "work" choice: to believe the message of Jesus and receive the salvation and eternal life that come through Jesus Christ alone. God loves you so much. Your Heavenly Father wants you to hear His truth and believe. God wants you to know the total forgiveness that Jesus alone offers and the hope and joy of eternal life with the Sovereign and Holy God of all creation!

What to do? Ask Jesus, even now, to be your Savior. Let God know that you believe Jesus is His Son who died for your sins and rose from the dead to give you eternal life.

What to do? Believe. And thank God for hearing your prayer of faith in Jesus, the one He has sent. Tell someone about your decision to trust in Jesus as your Savior. You have entered into a relationship with the Eternal God through this foundational and essential God-required work: Believe in the One God has sent.

Welcome Home, precious one, Welcome Home!

Reflections – Responses – Challenges – Encouragements – God-breathing Thoughts

Do I believe it?
And if I do, what am I going to do about it?

Lord, please let me hear your voice, your love, your wisdom, your grace and truth.

HARD TRUTH WITH THE FULLNESS OF GRACE

"...The harvest is the end of the age and the harvesters are angels...
The Son of Man will send out his angels, and they will weed out of his kingdom
everything that causes sin and all who do evil.
They will throw them into the blazing furnace,
where there will be weeping and gnashing of teeth.
Then the righteous will shine like the sun in the kingdom of their Father.
Whoever has ears, let them hear.

...Once again, the kingdom of heaven is like a net that was let down into the lake
and caught all kinds of fish. When it was full, the fishermen pulled it up on the shore.
Then they sat down and collected the good fish in baskets, but threw the bad away.
This is how it will be at the end of the age. The angels will come and separate the wicked
from the righteous and throw them into the blazing furnace, where there will be weeping
and gnashing of teeth. Have you understood all these things?" Jesus asked.
Matthew 13:39-43; 47-51

Jesus teaches so many parables revealing what the kingdom of heaven is like – seeds sown yielding different harvests or none at all; good seeds sown that are then surrounded by weeds; a mustard seed that grows into a tree to provide shelter and rest for birds; dough that rises as yeast works through it; great value recognized in a field with a hidden treasure and a pearl of great worth is found; fish caught in a net, some kept, some thrown out. In all of these parables, Jesus repeatedly lets us know the truth that not every person will enter into His kingdom – the kingdom of heaven.

And, quite honestly, this truth is a hard truth for me. As are others that Jesus spoke. Still, they are Word of God given truths. And Jesus, who is the "Word made flesh" (John 1:14), spoke the hard truth that God, in His righteous judgment, will separate those who will enter the kingdom of heaven from those who will not. It is not for me, or for any of us, to pick and choose which truths we'll accept from God because we like them and they make us feel loved, blessed or encouraged. It is not for me, or any of us, to pick and choose which truths we'll reject from God because we don't like them. Or don't think we need them. Or they're just too hard to accept.

God is God. God is one. God is love. God is good and God is just. God is holy and God is merciful. God is the righteous judge and the sacrificial lamb. It is in the very fullness of God's perfect and unchanging character that we must trust. It is the very fullness of God's grace and truth that we must hear, believe, honor, and embrace.

Jesus embraces us with His unfailing love and nail-scarred hands. Jesus is the one from whom the fullness of God's "grace and truth came" to us (John 1:17). All that is sin, all who are unrepentant and all who are unsaved sinners will be separated from God's goodness and righteousness. Such a very hard truth. Yet, God's truths, even His hardest truths, are never separated from the fullness of His grace.

May we each ask God to bring the fullness of His grace and truth to us and into everything we do – trusting God to be God in our lives, and in the lives of all others.

Reflections – Responses – Challenges – Encouragements – God-breathing Thoughts

Do I believe it?
And if I do, what am I going to do about it?

Lord, please let me hear your voice, your love, your wisdom, your grace and truth.

GOD'S SPIRIT WITHIN – GIVEN MORE ELBOW ROOM

I have been crucified with Christ and I no longer live,
but Christ lives in me.
Galatians 2:20

Let's make this personal. God did.

Because of His unfailing, pursuing, passionate love, Jesus – God's holy and perfect Son – gave His life for you. For me. Because of His absolute and extravagant humility, Jesus obeyed His Heavenly Abba even to the point of choosing to die a cruel and shameful death for you. For me. Because of His incomprehensible, almighty power, Jesus rose from the dead and conquered sin and death to give eternal life to you. To me. And the resurrected, eternally sovereign Lord Jesus chooses to live in you, and in me – through the person and presence of His Holy Spirit – so that neither sin nor death will ever have any more power to rule over, condemn or destroy you and your life or me and my life. Ever again.

Jesus has put the person and presence of His Holy Spirit within each of us who is His child by faith and His follower by choice. And the Spirit of our Lord Jesus wants to take up our entire beings and transform our entire lives so that we will more truly and authentically reflect the unfailing, pursuing, passionate love of Jesus. More truly and authentically reflect the absolute and extravagant humility of Jesus. More truly and authentically reflect the incomprehensible, almighty power of our resurrected, eternally sovereign Lord Jesus.

Each one of us who has accepted Jesus Christ by faith – who has trusted in His salvation for the forgiveness of our sins and His sure promise of eternal life – has been given the Spirit of the Living God to live within him and her, right now. This, then, should make all the difference in how we live, right now. The Spirit of the Living Christ living within us should make all the difference in how we are known. The Spirit of the Living Christ living within us should make all the difference in how we are perceived by other people – no matter how fleeting or long-lasting our interactions and relationships with them may be. The Holy Spirit of the Living God is alive. God's Spirit is never meant to lie dormant within us. Never meant to be diminished nor dismissed. God's Spirit is entitled and empowered to take up Christ's full loving, humble, and powerful rule over our thoughts, our words, and the tone of our words. The Spirit of the Living Christ is entitled and empowered to take up His full loving, humble, and powerful rule over our actions, reactions, interactions, and, even, over our body language and facial expressions.

The Spirit of the Living God is entitled and empowered to conform and transform each one of us – each of us who is God's child by faith and His follower by choice – into the likeness and image of our Lord Jesus Christ (Romans 8:29). Let's choose to give God's Spirit, the Christ who lives in us, more elbow room in each of our lives – in all that we are, in all that we think, in all that we say, in all that we do, in all that we express in any and every way.

May it be the living Christ who is more and more clearly known and perceived by others as they get to know and form their perceptions about each of us. May we each choose, actively and intentionally, to give the Spirit of the Living Christ more and more elbow room to fully live and love, celebrate and serve within us and through us and, even, in spite of us! All for the glory of our God and King!

Do I believe it?
And if I do, what am I going to do about it?

Lord, please let me hear your voice, your love, your wisdom, your grace and truth.

ABBA'S ARMS – OUR HIDING PLACE

You are my hiding place; you will protect me from trouble
and surround me with songs of deliverance.
Psalm 32:7

Do you ever just want to run away and hide? Hide from all the pressures of life? Hide from other people? Hide from all your responsibilities? I do. At least, sometimes.

And, then, God reminds me that often my feelings of wanting to run away and hide may come as a result of my own skewed thinking that believes (or at least acts as if) I'm more in control than I truly am. Or that I am somehow more important or more powerful than I truly am.

My feelings of wanting to run away and hide may also come because I think something that I am suffering is unjust and unfair. And, on this side of heaven, that just may be true. Maybe I want to run away and hide because I just plain don't want to deal with the awful reality of whatever I'm dealing with – whether it is an illness or a death of someone I love; whether it is the cruelty of abuse or a personal attack on my character; whether it is an attitude or addiction I can't seem to overcome or even want to overcome; whether it is a heart-breaking, confusing personal relationship or a relationship with someone that never should have happened; whether I am overwhelmed by the demands of my job or deflated by a cold and profit-driven job that offers no real security, very little financial stability, and no true enjoyment. Sometimes, I, and maybe you too, just want to run away and hide.

Many circumstances and relationships may make us want to run away and hide because of the amount of sheer pressure – or sadness or loss or frustration or anger or confusion or embarrassment or discouragement – that we feel. And, if it is possible, getting away from the stress – or, at least, from some of the stressors – for even a little bit of time, can be a very good and wise thing for the healing and restoration of our minds, bodies and souls.

But! How good and peaceful, strengthening and renewing is the truth that our God is our hiding place. Always and forever. No matter what trouble may surround us or come full force into our lives – unwanted and unexpected. God is with us. And as God's deeply loved and precious children, we don't ever need to run away and hide from the brokenness of this world. We just need to run into the arms of our Heavenly Abba and hide more fully in His quieting love, in His transcending peace, in His eternal perspective, and in His intimate presence in our lives.

There in our Abba's arms we are protected from all that would threaten, hurt, confuse, and destroy us. In our Abba's arms we can hide. In our Abba's arms we can rest quietly, right in the midst of turmoil, and listen to our Abba's songs of deliverance with awe, joy and thanksgiving. We can trust that the love we find in the everlasting arms of our Almighty Abba is more powerful, more lasting, and more true than anything that could come at us in this world.

No matter what you may be going through, or may want to run away from and hide, remember to run to the true source of love, peace, strength and renewal. We each need to choose to run into our Abba's arms. To run to our God, the sweet, safe, and holy hiding place for our minds, bodies, and souls. There in Abba's arms we can breathe life again.

Reflections – Responses – Challenges – Encouragements – God-breathing Thoughts

Do I believe it?
And if I do, what am I going to do about it?

Lord, please let me hear your voice, your love, your wisdom, your grace and truth.

SO, SING!

I will sing of your love and justice;
to you, LORD, I will sing praise.
Psalm 101:1

Let's give ourselves time to slow down our minds, hearts, bodies, and spirits so they can wrap themselves around these words of Scripture and begin to sing of these deep and eternally declared truths of our God. Let's give ourselves over to embracing these truths about who our God is and what God is like. Eternal truths that go far beyond our human understanding and experiences – especially when it comes to what love is and what is just.

Although stated succinctly, the power of God's Word that declares, "God is love" (1 John 4:8) and "God is just" (2 Thessalonians 1:6), should fill our hearts with a deep trust in our eternal God who never changes. And God will never change His character. God is love. And God's love for us is unfailing, always reaching out to us, and continually with us – even during those times we aren't feeling very loved by anyone or feeling very loving towards anyone. God is just. And God's justice is always right and holy, pure and unswayed by anything corrupt or by any temporary circumstances we may experience – even during those times we feel that everything we are going through is unjust and unfair, cruel and unkind. Our God is still love. Our God is still just.

Our God is one and, therefore, His justice is bound to His love and His love is bound to His justice – inseparably and eternally. And God's love and justice are good. These powerful, freeing truths should make our minds, hearts, bodies, and spirits sing to our Lord as we thank Him for His love that is unfailing and His justice that is pure!

May we each take time to lift up our spiritual eyes to see beyond our circumstances, and sense more deeply than our earthbound feelings, that our God is the God of love and justice. And as we see and sense these truths, may we each acknowledge, give thanks for, and sing about our Lord's eternally certain love and justice.

Sing to the Lord – in your brokenness or in your abundance, in your pain or in your peace, in your confusion or in your clarity. Sing to the Lord who loves you beyond all measure and beyond all human understanding. Sing to the Lord of His love that walked among us as a man, as our Messiah – breaking all boundaries of time and space, breaking all boundaries of every kind that would dare attempt to separate us from knowing God's love. Sing to the Lord who is just beyond all measure and beyond all human understanding. Sing to the Lord of His justice that accepted the poured out blood and death of His holy Son Jesus as the full payment for our every wrong thought, wrong word, wrong action, wrong response, and wrong relationship that we have ever had or will yet have.

Sing to the Lord that His justice was fully satisfied in Jesus' sacrifice! God's justice demands nothing more from us for the forgiveness of our sins. Sing to the Lord that we are now set free, through the power of Christ's resurrection, to know the fullness of God's unfailing love for us! No matter what your temporary reality might be or feel like right now, these are God's eternal, unchanging truths. And they are good. So, sing!

Do I believe it?
And if I do, what am I going to do about it?

Lord, please let me hear your voice, your love, your wisdom, your grace and truth.

LOVE OR NOTHING!

There are people in our world who are absolutely brilliant and greatly gifted in many different ways. Individuals can show great mastery and expertise knowledge of different specialties such as science, math, language, literature, music, art, philosophy, business, architecture, agriculture, and on and on. And there are some individuals who are gifted in an amazing and almost superhuman combination of many of these areas, all at the same time.

There are people in our world who serve other people in great and sacrificial ways. These people care for the homeless and the helpless, the hopeless and the sick in all kinds of ways as they serve individually or support ministries and organizations with their time, their talents, and their tithes. These individuals sacrifice, in one way or another, to help feed the hungry, clothe the poor, visit the prisoners, care for widows and orphans, supply clean water and healing medicines, build homes, schools and hospitals.

All of these incredible intellectual gifts that individuals possess, and all of these activities that individuals do for the good of another, can be wonderful things. Or they can be nothing. They can mean nothing.

> *I will show you the most excellent way.*
> *If I speak in the tongues of men or of angels,*
> *but do not have love, I am only a resounding gong or a clanging cymbal.*
> *If I have the gift of prophecy and can fathom all mysteries and all knowledge,*
> *and if I have a faith that can move mountains,*
> *but do not have love, I am nothing.*
> *If I give all I possess to the poor and*
> *give over my body to hardship that I may boast,*
> *but do not have love, I gain nothing.*
> 1 Corinthians 12:31, 13:1-3

Anything of any true and eternal value, of any true and eternal power, comes from love. Comes from authentic, God-given, God-transforming love.

Without God's love filling us, motivating us, grounding us, informing us, and serving through us, we are nothing. Nothing we know or possess, nothing we do, even in the most brilliant and astounding ways or in the most self-sacrificial ways, will ever have any true and eternal value if it does not come from God's love. For we know that "God is love" (1 John 4:8) and our God is true and eternal. Our God is all worthy and all powerful.

Only God's love is eternally true and transforming. Only God's love is able to make any circumstance, any activity, and any relationship matter – now and for all eternity. Only God's transforming love is able to bring true and eternal hope to the hopeless, peace to the fearful, healing to the sick, and life to the dead!

May God, our God who is love, free each one of us up from every shred of pride we have – in what we know and possess, in the temporary positions and perceived power we hold, and in our own earthbound, limited perspectives and plans – so that we may live and fully love as Jesus does, the One who gave His all out of His love for us!

It really is love or nothing!

Do I believe it?
And if I do, what am I going to do about it?

Lord, please let me hear your voice, your love, your wisdom, your grace and truth.

OVERTAKEN BY JOY!

There are times, sometimes seemingly unceasing, when the pressure and responsibility of our lives, family, work, and other commitments can completely overwhelm us. There are times when the deep sadness and crushing distress we walk through can absolutely overtake us. Our own inclination to sin seems to always be right there ready to consume us. Our hearts are broken, and we, too often, feel powerless to help those who suffer the ravages of poverty, hunger, natural disasters, abuse of every kind, and where the lives, homes and security of innocents are ripped apart by violence, greed, cruelty and evil. And the hard truth, whether we admit it or deny it, is that death will not be escaped by any of us on this side of heaven.

But! That is not the end of the story! That is not the end of this life's hope! That is not the end of life's path for those who trust in the Lord – for those who trust in our Mighty God who ransoms and redeems, renews and restores our lives!

> *Those the LORD has rescued will return.*
> *They will enter Zion with singing;*
> *everlasting joy will crown their heads.*
> *Gladness and joy will overtake them,*
> *and sorrow and sighing will flee away.*
> Isaiah 51:11

Even now, no matter what pressures or sadness, ugly realities or fears you may be facing, let your heart, head and spirit be filled with God's transcending peace and hope! Because we, who have put our faith in our Lord Jesus as the ransom for our lives, have received God's sure promise that we will enter into His presence with singing! Everlasting joy will crown our heads! Gladness and joy will overtake us! Sorrow and sighing will flee away!

Let everything, except God's absolute promise of your ransomed life in Christ, be set aside in your thinking right now.

> *For he has rescued us from the dominion of darkness*
> *and brought us into the kingdom of the Son he loves,*
> *in whom we have redemption, the forgiveness of sins...*
> *For God was pleased to have all his fullness dwell in him,*
> *and through him to reconcile to himself all things,*
> *whether things on earth or things in heaven*
> *by making peace through his blood, shed on the cross.*
> Colossians 1:13-14, 19-20

Let yourself breathe in God's love, God's renewing life breath. Let everything within your mind, body, heart and soul be overtaken by joy in the loving presence and sure promises of our "Wonderful Counselor, our Mighty God, our Everlasting Father, our Prince of Peace" (Isaiah 9:6).

God's promises are sure. Be overtaken by joy! And overtake the darkness of this broken world by sharing God's love, hope and joy with all those around you!

Reflections – Responses – Challenges – Encouragements – God-breathing Thoughts

Do I believe it?
And if I do, what am I going to do about it?

Lord, please let me hear your voice, your love, your wisdom, your grace and truth.

September 25

TO THE POINT: WHO'S THE FOOL?

Sometimes God's Word gets right to the point and quite sharply. These pointed and poignant Scripture passages require no dissecting. They need no special hermeneutical, interpretive studies to shed light on their meaning. They speak to us with all clarity. For example:

The fool says in his heart, "There is no God."
Psalm 53:1

Nope. There is absolutely no confusion about the meaning of this verse. *The fool denies the existence of God.*

Well! That's not me! I am a believer in the God of all creation! I have placed my faith in Jesus Christ as my Savior and my Lord!

Whoa! Before I get too smug about how my faith in God somehow excludes me from the *Fool Club*, I have to get real with myself, and ask some tough questions:

How much more of a fool am I, as a child of God saved by the blood of Jesus, when I ignore God's truth, discount God's grace, disobey God's Word and plug my ears and shut off my heart to the Spirit's prompting?

How much more of a fool am I, as a woman transformed by the love, grace and truth of Jesus, when I act in hateful, unforgiving, prideful, unmerciful, truth-twisting, selfish ways? (Yes, even if most of those hateful, unforgiving, prideful, unmerciful, truth-twisting, selfish ways occur only within the privacy of my own head, and no one else witnesses my foolish, ungodly ways! I am still a fool!)

How much more of a fool am I, as a lost and needy human being for whom God reached through time and space to be with, when I don't reach out to my neighbor who's overwhelmed with life as a single mom? Or when I don't take time to listen to the old man's stories about his wife who's been gone now for twelve years? Or don't reach out with smiles, kindness, playfulness and encouragement to the children who pass through my day?

How much more of a fool am I, as an ambassador of the Living Christ who has been given God's message of love, hope, forgiveness, freedom, and life to share with all who will hear, so that they, too, may believe, when I stay silent because I just really don't want to talk to that family member or friend or neighbor one more time about Jesus? Or when I won't take the time to build relationships with new people and be a vessel of God's love to them? Or when I refuse to listen to the Spirit urging me to engage that stranger in a conversation?

So, no, I won't be admitted into the *Fool Club* because I deny the existence of God. However, I will be a welcomed and regular guest every time I refuse to let my beliefs in God and in His holy Son Jesus Christ, my Savior and Lord, make any real and significant, obvious and transforming difference in my life.

Jesus gave His life to make all the difference in our lives. Now it's our choice, our joy, and our purpose to let Jesus make all the difference in us, so that through us He can make an eternal difference in the lives of all those around us! And He's not foolin'!

Reflections – Responses – Challenges – Encouragements – God-breathing Thoughts

Do I believe it?
And if I do, what am I going to do about it?

Lord, please let me hear your voice, your love, your wisdom, your grace and truth.

_____

_____

_____

_____

_____

_____

_____

_____

_____

_____

_____

_____

_____

_____

_____

_____

_____

_____

_____

_____

_____

_____

_____

_____

_____

_____

THE FULL JOY: LESS OF ME. MORE OF JESUS.

John, who came to be known as John the Baptist, had been faithfully fulfilling the mission that the Lord had placed on his life: John called people to "prepare the way of the Lord...to make the paths straight for the Lord" (Matthew 3:3, Mark 1:3). John raised his voice to teach people to acknowledge their sins, repent of those sins, and be baptized as a way to prepare themselves, their minds, hearts, and lives for the coming of the Lord, the long-awaited Messiah of God.

And Jesus did come. And, with His coming, there came a time for John's role as the preparer of the way to diminish. There came a time for the people to recognize that all that John did – all of the amazing, powerful, life-changing ministry that John had done – was all, and had always been, intended only to point people to Jesus. Never to himself.

John knew this. And he had the wise humility and holy passion to accomplish the purpose for which the Living God had chosen him: To direct people's attention, and bring honor and glory to Christ – the Messiah of the Lord. And in doing this, John knew great purpose and great joy.

> *John replied, "A person can receive only what is given them from heaven.*
> *You yourselves can testify that I said, 'I am not the Christ but am sent ahead of him.'*
> *The bride belongs to the bridegroom.*
> *The friend who attends the bridegroom waits and listens for him,*
> *and is full of joy when he hears the bridegroom's voice.*
> *...He must become greater: I must become less."*
> John 3:27-30

Every one of us, who has put our faith in Jesus as our Savior and Lord, has been sealed as a child of God for all eternity! This powerful, freeing, grace-filled truth should, in itself, bring us full joy! And every one of us, who has put our faith in Jesus as our Savior and Lord, has been given the task of being an ambassador of Christ in this world. We are given the task of living out and sharing the hope we have in Jesus. We are called to be living messages of the very real, tangible, unconditional, unselfish, and unfailing love of our Lord Jesus Christ to all those around us. This is what we have received. This is what we are to give.

May each one of us more fully receive, and remember, God's full message of love that came to us through the death and resurrection of our Lord Jesus Christ. There is nothing that kept Jesus back from receiving the punishment of the cross that should have been ours or from conquering the power of the grave and giving us eternal life! Jesus did all of this out of love - out of His crazy, outrageous, humble, and powerful love - for each one of us so that we could live lives that are transformed and set free by the fullness of His joy.

May each one of us know the same full joy that John did as we choose to let our lives humbly, wisely, and powerfully reflect less of us and more and more and more of Jesus – in every way we think, speak, act, react, and interact! Every day of our lives!

To Jesus Christ alone be all honor and glory! This is God's full joy. And ours. Amen!

Do I believe it?
And if I do, what am I going to do about it?

Lord, please let me hear your voice, your love, your wisdom, your grace and truth.

September 27

FAITH THAT AMAZES

Jesus was amazed by the faith that different people expressed – both faith that was lacking and dismissive of who He was and faith that was unquestioning, trusting and humble.

While in His own hometown of Nazareth, among some of those who knew Him best since He was a child – neighbors, fellow synagogue members, His own relatives – Jesus was amazed by their lack of faith. Not only did they express little to no faith in who He was and what miracles He could do, many of those in Nazareth also "took offense at him" (John 6:3).

> *Jesus said to them, "A prophet is not without honor*
> *except in his own town, among his relatives and in his own home."*
> *He could not do any miracles there,*
> *except lay his hands on a few sick people and heal them.*
> *He was amazed at their lack of faith.*
> Mark 6:4-6

Yet, it was in Capernaum, not far from where He grew up, that Jesus was amazed by the faith of a Gentile, a Roman centurion. Here was a man of authority who expressed great and humble faith in the power and authority that Jesus had to transform lives. The centurion's unquestioning faith moved him to believe that Jesus only had to proclaim the healing, only had to "say the word" – Jesus didn't even need to come to the centurion's home – and his "servant will be healed" (Luke 7:7).

> *When Jesus heard this, he was amazed at him,*
> *and turning to the crowd following him, he said,*
> *"I tell you, I have not found such great faith even in Israel."*
> Luke 7:9

Amazing faith. How will Jesus find my faith? How will He find yours?

Do we put the Jesus we think we know, the Jesus we have all figured out – maybe even knew since we were children – in a box that we're comfortable with? And we'd really like to keep Jesus right there within the boundaries of the box that we've set? After all, we believe He's a nice God. He's a good God. He's a good teacher. We even believe He's the Savior who forgives our sins, and will one day take us to heaven when we die.

But, will we believe and let Jesus step into our lives right now in powerful, unexpected, and unimaginable ways? Will we release Jesus from our perceived limitations of who He is and what He is able to do? Will we believe and let Jesus step into our world the way He wants to? As the Almighty God, the Sovereign King and Lord over all that exists? Will we believe and let Jesus turn our worlds upside-down or, rather, upside-right from His viewpoint? To truly move us from living in darkness to living in His light? Will we believe that Jesus is able to heal us spiritually, mentally and physically of our blindness, deafness, muteness and brokenness? Will we believe and let Jesus transform us to be more like Him? To truly be filled and flowing more and more with His Spirit's fruit and power of "love, joy, peace, patience, kindness, goodness, faithfulness, gentleness and self-control" (Galatians 5:22-23)?

May we each allow the true Jesus to shake up our faith until it is as amazing as He deserves!

Do I believe it?
And if I do, what am I going to do about it?

Lord, please let me hear your voice, your love, your wisdom, your grace and truth.

PRESENT IN THE MOMENT – PROMISE OF ETERNITY

I absolutely believe in the importance of being present in the moment. This moment, right now, is all any of us can be absolutely certain that we have on this side of heaven.

It's so important for each of us to completely embrace the life, the moment, we have been given. Whenever we choose to be thankful for all that is good in our lives, for all the beauty that is around us – even when we're in the midst of difficult, uncertain or sad times – it is life-affirming and life-healing for our souls. We are lifted in heart and head every time we choose to take on, and stay in, an attitude of joy and thankfulness for our lives and for the moment we're in right now.

It's so important for each of us to be present in the moment and choose to love and treat others kindly, to more deeply appreciate and fully enjoy, to more quickly forgive and honestly respect the people in our lives – our family members, friends, neighbors, co-workers, bosses, teachers, students, passing acquaintances, strangers, and, yes, even all those people who challenge us, disappoint us, hurt us, and just plain make us crazy.

It's so important to not take anyone, or any moment we have with them, for granted. We only know for sure that we have this time, right now, with them and we need to be present in it so we will not miss the moment. God strengthens and encourages our hearts and our heads, as we choose to take on, and stay in, an attitude of love and kindness, compassion and mercy towards the people that have been put into our lives. Towards each of them, whether we're in intimate, long-lasting relationships with them or we share just a few fleeting moments together.

Remember, O God, that my life is but a breath;
my eyes will never see happiness again.
Job 7:7

Yes, our lives are fleeting and far shorter than we can imagine – even if we live beyond one hundred years here on this earth. If we are in Christ, the brevity of our earthly lives should not give birth to fear or despair. Rather, this truth should encourage, inspire and challenge us to more fully live and more freely love. Our Heavenly Father has given us a living hope to be in the presence of our Resurrected King and Lord Jesus Christ for all eternity!

Praise be to the God and Father of our Lord Jesus Christ!
In his great mercy he has given us new birth into a living hope
through the resurrection of Jesus Christ from the dead.
1 Peter 1:3

Knowing that our future is already promised, may we each be set free to be more present in each moment in ways that reflect God's love in very real, tangible, and transforming ways!

Be present in the moment, offering these presents to all those around you:
Smile more.
Listen well. Respond respectfully.
Be gentle. Be kind. Be encouraging.
Be compassionate. Be patient. Be a peacemaker.
Give mercy. Give generously. Give grace. Speak truth.
Forgive everyone of everything.
Call your parents. Call your kids.
Get over yourself.
Love as Jesus loves!

Be present in the moment with the help of Him who is present with us now and forever!

Reflections – Responses – Challenges – Encouragements – God-breathing Thoughts

Do I believe it?
And if I do, what am I going to do about it?

Lord, please let me hear your voice, your love, your wisdom, your grace and truth.

GOD'S OWN GPS

Many of us use a GPS whenever we're traveling – on both unfamiliar and fairly familiar roads. We'll trust that little cyber-directional system to get us physically to where we need to go. How much more we should trust Jesus as the One who can show us the way to go in our lives and is, in Himself, the way and the path of life!

Jesus spoke it clearly when He said,
> *"I am the way and the truth and the life.*
> *No one comes to the Father except through me."*
> John 14:6

> *You make known to me the path of life,*
> *you will fill me with joy in your presence,*
> *with eternal pleasures at your right hand.*
> Psalm 16:11

We who trust in Jesus as our Savior have had our eternal destiny radically and fabulously changed. We have been rescued from "the dominion of darkness" and brought into the "kingdom of the Son God loves" (Colossians 1:13). We have been brought from death to life. From hell to heaven. From condemnation to righteousness. And because of this amazing eternal destination change, we have a peace and a joy and a sure hope that can only come from the Spirit of the Living God.

However, we don't always have those same feelings during our daily-day lives because of all the changing circumstances that can bump us around, confuse us, shake us, anger us, sadden us, and wear us down. This life can be hard. And our circumstances can go from one extreme to the other.

How thankful I am that our God doesn't change. God always loves us. God is always with us. God is good. God is mighty. God is kind. God is faithful. God is wise. God is righteous. God is love.

Our circumstances do not determine or alter who our God is, or what God's character is like, in any way. Even when, in our own perceptions, we determine that God is good because things are good for us. Even when we determine that God is distant, unhearing, unfair, uncaring, or unfaithful to His promises when things are hard for us.

As God's children through faith in Jesus, we have trusted God with our eternal destiny. How much more do we need to trust Jesus with our daily-day lives! Really trust the One who is the way and the truth and the life. Trust the One who is the path of life for now and all eternity! We need to stay with Jesus. We need to listen to His Word. We need to keep in step with His Spirit. We need to trust Jesus who fully and humbly trusted His Father who led Him to the cross, but didn't leave Him there! Jesus was brought from death to life and into the fullness of joy in the eternal, beautiful, and powerful presence of His God and Father! And one day we will be brought there, too, by God's very own GPS – our Lord and Savior Jesus Christ!

May we each travel this life with God's peace, joy, and sure hope because we know that, no matter what we experience along our earthly paths, we will reach our eternal destination and celebrate with our Lord Jesus who has been with us all along the way as God's only way!

WHO ARE YOUR WALKING BUDDIES?

Walk with the wise and become wise,
for a companion of fools suffers harm.
Proverbs 13:20

Who are your walking buddies? Who are the people you really let get into your head? Who are the people you listen to for their opinions, perspectives, and advice? Who do you learn from, even as you walk together through life's experiences – the big ones, the great ones, the awful ones, and the daily-day ones?

Are you and I getting wiser as we walk with those particular people? Are you and I becoming more like Jesus – more loving, more authentic, more whole, more balanced – because of what we're learning or, at least, what we're being reminded of by our life-walk walking buddies?

If our answer is "Yes!" to these questions, well, let's keep on walking together with these people! Let's keep sharing the wisdom, love, grace and truth of Jesus Christ.

If our answer is "No!" to these questions, then we've got to take a serious look at where we may be being foolish. Where we may be suffering harm. Or, even, where we may be causing harm, in any way at all, to others. We need to think about what is talked about or not talked about as we walk along. We need to be very aware of what activities are done or not done, with these particular walking companions.

Now, I'm not suggesting that we should put ourselves into some kind of ridiculously tight, self-protecting, self-righteous, bubble-wrapped "Christian" life-walk, surrounded only by friends who stand firm against this world's evils with a mind-set ruled by harsh judgments and condemnation rather than with love and compassion. That kind of life-walk, with those kind of walking buddies, is not going to do a whole lot of good towards fulfilling God's plan and purpose for us, as His children, to be His light and salt to this world. Nor will that kind of boarded-up, closed-off life-walk allow us to be authentic ambassadors of Christ to the people around us who do not, yet, know of the very real love, unfailing mercy, and eternal hope offered by our Lord Jesus Christ.

We are called to walk as Jesus walked, to live as Jesus lived (Ephesians 5:2). Jesus kept counsel continually with His Father and with the Spirit as He walked on this earth, trusting their love, wisdom and righteousness for every step of His life. Even as He entered lovingly and challengingly into the lives of all humanity – into all of our lives as the least, the last, the lost, the sinners. Even as He walked to Golgotha to be crucified (Mark 15:22). Even as He stepped out of the grave in absolute victory!

So, who are your walking buddies? As followers of Christ, we are to "keep in step with the Spirit" (Galatians 5:25) while walking through this life. May each of us choose the Spirit of the Living Christ as our primary walking buddy – as our primary companion for giving us wisdom, counsel and eternal perspective. If we do that, we can be more greatly confident that we will not walk with fools and suffer harm.

With the Spirit of God as our closest walking companion, we will more likely choose other walking buddies who will help us grow wise in God's good, loving, faithful, hope-filled and victorious ways!

Reflections – Responses – Challenges – Encouragements – God-breathing Thoughts

Do I believe it?
And if I do, what am I going to do about it?

Lord, please let me hear your voice, your love, your wisdom, your grace and truth.

October 1

WE NEED ONLY TO BE STILL

The Israelites were terrified. Pharaoh's army was closing in behind them and the sea was in front of them. They were scared – they could only see destruction coming at them wherever they turned. They were angry. Out of control. Helpless. And immediately they jumped to the worst conclusions, certain they were going to die. They saw no escape, no way out of this perilous position. Certain that it would have been far better for them to have remained slaves to a cruel master rather than go through these uncertain and overwhelming times now.

The people of Israel were unable to see any rescue, any relief, or any escape from their trouble because they looked only from their own point of view. They cried out only from their own frightened, limited perspective. They cried out to the Lord, but they weren't trusting the Lord. They allowed their panic to rise and take over their minds.

God in His mercy reassured His frightened, untrusting people through His servant Moses.

Moses answered the people, "Do not be afraid.
Stand firm and you will see the deliverance the LORD will bring you today...
The LORD will fight for you; you need only to be still."
Exodus 14:13-14

We need only to be still.

There are so many times and circumstances in life that are hard, that are frightening, that are frustrating, that are sad. That is the truth of this broken, imperfect world.

Yet, with God as our deliverer – with God as our help, our hope, our very life – we are able to choose His peace. We are able to not be afraid. With God's everlasting arms around us, we are able to stand firm on His promises. With the almighty God as our faithful God, we can trust that we will see and experience His deliverance. We will see how He fights for us and wins! We need only to be still.

In our stillness, we can breathe more deeply the very life breath of our Living God. We can breathe in God's love for us and presence with us – into our bodies, minds and spirits. In our stillness, we can trust our God. We can let God quiet our minds. We can let God quiet our own voices that are spinning our hearts, minds, bodies and spirits out of control.

We need only to be still. In our stillness, we can more fully trust the eternal truth that God is good. That God is in control. That God does love us. That God is with us. In our stillness, we can trust that even the most difficult and awful times of our lives can be times for us to see and know God's great care and intimate love for us in deeper, undeniable, unfathomable and powerful ways.

We need only to be still. In our stillness, we will be able to choose God's truth as the interpreter of our circumstances instead of listening to the consuming voices of our fear, anger, sadness or any Lie From The Pit Of Hell (LFTPOH). In our stillness, we will sense God's presence. We will see His deliverance. We will experience His transcending peace as the Lord fights for us and wins!

We need only to be still.

550

Reflections – Responses – Challenges – Encouragements – God-breathing Thoughts

Do I believe it?
And if I do, what am I going to do about it?

Lord, please let me hear your voice, your love, your wisdom, your grace and truth.

I NEED A DRINK!

I need a drink! A deep, long, thirst-quenching drink from the fountain of life!

The teaching of the wise is a fountain of life,
turning a person from the snares of death.
Proverbs 13:14

The greatest wisdom of all comes from our God and from God's living and active Word – our Lord Jesus Christ, who offers us His fountain of "living water" (John 4:10). And, oh! I need to drink from this fountain of life continually!

God's Word teaches us that we all have two basic, fundamental choices to make about how we live – about how we think, speak, act and react as we live out each day of our lives. In one way or another, through everything that we do, we will either be choosing life or we will be choosing death.

...I have set before you life and death, blessings and curses...Now choose life...
Deuteronomy 30:19

Everything we do, in every way we think, speak, act and react, either brings *more life* – brings more wholeness, strength and health to all those around us, including to our own bodies, minds, spirits and relationships or everything we do brings *more death* – brings more deterioration, weakness and pain to all those around us, including to our own bodies, minds, spirits and relationships.

So, what's my drinking source? Is it God's Word and wisdom – God's fountain of life? Or is it from my own well that just isn't so well? Or am I more often found drinking from the world's wisdom whose news, cyberspace chatter, gossip, brokenness and blindness can pollute and poison my thinking and behavior? Is the fountain from which I choose to drink pure and clear, fresh and clean – true and eternal?

If we are what we eat, we can reasonably extend that thought to include: we are what we drink. And our God calls us to life. Calls us to follow His ways. Calls us to be continually transforming to be more like Jesus – the One who offers living water for all eternity. So, let's choose God's wisdom and Word as our fountain of life. Let's choose to drink deeply so that everything within us and everything that comes from us will become in us "a spring of water welling up to eternal life" (John 4:14).

And as we drink from this fountain of life found in God's wisdom and Word, let's offer life to all those around us. All are thirsty. All are in desperate need of Christ's living water. Let's offer a life-giving drink to others in very real and tangible ways – as we share God's love, hope through the salvation of Jesus, and as we offer help by being present and serving those who need encouragement and peace – who need a friend, a listening ear, a toilet fixed, a gutter cleaned, a child watched, an errand done, a bill paid, a household moved. Let's drink deeply and offer drinks to others from Christ's fountain of living water – through choosing life in everything we do and in everything we are.

I'll have another round, please!

Do I believe it?
And if I do, what am I going to do about it?

Lord, please let me hear your voice, your love, your wisdom, your grace and truth.

IT'S ALL UP TO GOD – NOT ME

It does not, therefore, depend on human desire or effort, but on God's mercy.
Romans 9:16

Our salvation and our transformation depend on God's mercy. Completely. Unquestionably. It's all up to God.

There are so many precious people in my life that I want for them to take full hold of what God is holding out for them to receive – fully and freely. Jesus offers God's salvation and eternal life. There are so many precious ones that I love that are still without God's assurance and peace in their lives. Some reject Jesus completely. Some dismiss or diminish Jesus as just a good teacher, a good man. Some set Jesus off to the side until He fits into their rhythm of life and lifestyle, or until their lives are suddenly turned upside down and they take Jesus off the shelf for awhile – at least until the crisis is over. My heart breaks for each one because they don't know the absolutely all encompassing love and eternal hope Jesus offers – no matter what stage of life they're in, no matter what state of mind they're in. And I'm so thankful that their salvation does not depend on me. Not in any way. Not through any of my desires. Not through any of my efforts.

Oh, I am to desire salvation for each and every one of them. I am to desire that each would know God's very best. I am to desire that each would know the joy that flows from an intimate love relationship with Jesus. I am to desire that each would know the full freedom that comes through the forgiveness of their sins and the assurance of eternal life because of Christ's death and resurrection. And I am to make efforts – loving, sincere, compassionate, courageous, humble, vulnerable efforts – for others to know the fullness of God's love and salvation that come only through Jesus. God's Word declares that His enemy is defeated and His followers are triumphant "by the blood of the Lamb and by the word of their testimony" (Revelation 12:11). So, yes! I am, as an ambassador of Christ, to bring God's salvation message to the world. But! I am only a messenger. I am not the Master of the Message. Nor am I the one who gives life-saving mercy to those who will receive it.

Just as I want so many precious people in my life to know the salvation of Christ, so, too, do I want them to know the transformation Jesus offers – transformation and freedom, healing and power – to each of His followers right now, and not just on the other side of heaven. Many people, who have already accepted the eternal gift of Christ's salvation, are still without any real transformation in their lives – in their minds, hearts, habits or relationships – as they live out their daily lives. For them, Jesus is more of a side note rather than their powerful Savior. Jesus is more of a luxury instead of their living Lord. My heart breaks for them because they don't know the joy, hope, peace, power, passion and purpose that are fully and freely available to them. They do not know the sweetness and strength that come from being transformed into the likeness of Jesus more and more each day.

I am called to deeply desire and make efforts – loving, sincere, compassionate, courageous, humble, vulnerable efforts – for these precious ones, who are still bound and crippled, to know the amazing transformation that the living Christ offers them.

I am to celebrate and stand in the freedom and truth that each person's transformation, like their salvation, depends on God's mercy. It is all up to God. Not me. And this gives me great hope and peace because I know that "with God all things are possible" (Matthew 19:26).

Reflections – Responses – Challenges – Encouragements – God-breathing Thoughts

Do I believe it?
And if I do, what am I going to do about it?

Lord, please let me hear your voice, your love, your wisdom, your grace and truth.

SMOLDERING WICKS – FRAGRANT PRAYERS

...a smoldering wick he will not snuff out...
Isaiah 42:3

I love to burn candles, especially ones with deep, earthy, soul-quieting fragrances. The other night, just before I went to sleep, I blew out the candle that had been burning brightly by my bedside. But that candle didn't go out immediately, or entirely, for a long time. And I was so happy that it didn't.

From that smoldering wick, circling rings of smoke went up, filling my nose and filling the room with a fragrance that seemed even stronger than when the flame was fully burning. And it made me think of how God likens the burning of incense – with its rising, fragrance-filled smoke – to the prayers of His people.

It is often when we come nearly to the end of ourselves that we finally choose to turn our heads, hearts and habits to God. It is often when we are almost completely burned out that we will humbly and honestly lift our prayers, our concerns, our fears and our hopes to God.

In our circling – and often feebly formed – prayers, we are seeking God. Seeking God's help. Seeking God's forgiveness. Seeking God's love. Seeking God's mercies. Seeking God's hope. Seeking God's peace. Seeking God's will. Seeking God's way and truth and life. And our Holy, Sovereign God never turns us away when we seek Him sincerely. Our God never turns His back on us when we humbly and honestly seek Him with all our hearts.

"Then you will call on me and come and pray to me, and I will listen to you.
You will seek me and find me when you seek me with all your heart.
I will be found by you," declares the LORD...
Jeremiah 29:12-14

Our God will be found by us as our humble prayers circle up to Him. As our hearts seek Him. Our God will hear us and be with us. Our God will show us His love and compassion. Our God will forgive us. Our God will help us and give us His hope. Our God will reveal His way and truth and life to us. No matter how sinful or shameful we have been. No matter how broken or burned out we are. Our God will hear us. Our God will breathe in our fragrance-filled, humble and honest prayers. And our God will answer us.

Our God knows how frail, flawed and finite we are. There is no shame in those truths – unless we let them keep us from truly seeking God with all our hearts. It is in accepting the humble truth that we are each just smoldering wicks – each of us in need of our God who is the eternal light and consuming fire – that we are set free to offer our hearts' fragrance-filled prayers to our loving and holy God.

Our merciful and compassionate God will not snuff out the smoldering wicks of our lives or our prayers. Rather, our life-giving, life-saving, life-transforming God will rekindle, renew and reshape our lives with the light and fire of His Holy Spirit. Our God will take our circling prayers and answer them with His unfailing love, His resurrection power and His intimate knowledge of who we are and the deepest needs we have burning in our souls.

Our God will take the smoldering, fragrance-filled prayers of our hearts and answer them with eternity's joy.

Do I believe it?
And if I do, what am I going to do about it?

Lord, please let me hear your voice, your love, your wisdom, your grace and truth.

October 5

ALWAYS PRAY AND DON'T GIVE UP!

Then Jesus told his disciples a parable to show them
that they should always pray and not give up.
Luke 18:1

Jesus told his followers to determinedly, tenaciously, continuously pray. To never give up.

Amazing. Jesus makes it absolutely clear that the God of all creation wants to hear from us. Wants us to keep going to Him. Keep praying to Him. Keep trusting that our Heavenly Father will hear us and will answer us.

The parable that Jesus told is of a widow who is seeking justice against her adversary. She had somehow been unfairly, unjustly mistreated by another person. And she wasn't going to take it lying down. The widow kept going to the judge in her town "who neither feared God nor cared about men" (Luke 18:2). She kept *praying* and didn't give up. Finally, and only because the widow had nearly worn him down, the judge granted her justice.

Jesus went on to assure his disciples that God hears our prayers and He will "bring about justice for his chosen ones, who cry out to him day and night...he will see that they get justice, and quickly" (Luke 18:7-8).

Our God is the God of justice. He will be true to Himself. He will be faithful to His people.

Jesus also taught His followers to pray in this way:

"Our Father in heaven, hallowed be your name,
your kingdom come, your will be done,
on earth as it is in heaven.
Give us today our daily bread.
And forgive us our debts,
as we also have forgiven our debtors.
And lead us not into temptation,
but deliver us from the evil one."
Matthew 6:9-13

So, when we are praying for the things that God wants in our lives – praying for all that will bring about, and reveal, God's kingdom, praying for the holy will of God to be made known and accomplished on this earth – we can be sure that God will answer these prayers. God will never tire of listening to or answering our prayers that seek His truth and justice, that ask for His mercy and salvation, His freedom and transformation – whether for our lives or for the lives of those we care about or, even, for the lives of those we find it hard to care about. We are to keep on praying and not give up. Not ever!

What do I, what do you, need to bring before our just, faithful, loving and sovereign Lord in prayer? What do we need to keep on praying – for whom do we need to keep on praying – that will bring God's justice to light, establish God's kingdom on earth and reveal God's perfect will more fully?

Be encouraged! Always pray – determinedly, tenaciously, continuously – and don't give up!

Do I believe it?
And if I do, what am I going to do about it?

Lord, please let me hear your voice, your love, your wisdom, your grace and truth.

OUR PURPOSEFUL GOD

The LORD said, "Surely I will deliver you for a good purpose..."
Jeremiah 15:11

God purposes to do so much for us, in us and through us!

God purposes to save each one of His children through the salvation freely offered through the death and resurrection of our Lord Jesus Christ. We need only trust that God has purposed it, and by faith receive God's beautiful and merciful love gift of salvation.

God purposes to transform each one of His children through the renewing and cleansing, freeing and healing of our lives – our minds, hearts, thoughts, words and actions. God's great purpose for each of His children is to make every one us – conform every one of us – to be more like His Son Jesus in all that we are in our innermost being and in all that we do, say and express.

God purposes to use each one of His children as loving, reconciling, grace and truth sharing ambassadors of our Lord Jesus Christ. God purposes to equip each of us with the filling of the Holy Spirit and with the power of His living and active Word.

Our God purposes so much fullness of life, now and for all eternity, for each one of us as His children! We need to trust our God, whose purposes will be achieved!

"So is my word that goes out from my mouth:
It will not return to me empty, but will accomplish what I desire
and achieve the purpose for which I sent it."
Isaiah 55:11

Let's cry out! Let's shout out to our God Most High! And let us yield our lives completely over to our God – thanking Him for the very gift of life He has given us, and recognizing that God's purposes are always loving, good, holy and freeing purposes for us, in us and through us!

"I have come that they may have life, and have it to the full."
John 10:10

You are a chosen people, a royal priesthood, a holy nation,
God's special possession, that you may declare the praises of him
who called you out of darkness into his wonderful light.
1 Peter 2:9-10

God has committed to us the message of reconciliation.
We are therefore Christ's ambassadors,
as though God were making his appeal through us.
2 Corinthians 5:19-20

For we are God's handiwork, created in Christ Jesus to do good works,
which God prepared in advance for us to do.
Ephesians 2:10

Jesus said, "A new command I give you: Love one another.
As I have loved you, so you must love one another."
John 13:34

How purposeful is our God! How purposeful and loving our lives will be as we willingly let God fulfill His purposes for us, in us and through us!

MAKE A BREAK FOR IT!

Old habits that were part of us before we accepted Jesus as Savior, can still have far too much influence and power over us even now. Jesus may absolutely be our Savior. He intends to be our Lord – by renewing us with His unfailing love, His living truth and His transforming grace.

> *If anyone is in Christ, the new creation has come;*
> *the old has gone, the new is here! All this is from God...*
> 2 Corinthians 5:17-18

Yes, in Christ we are made new! We are signed, sealed, delivered! The condemnation that comes from our sins, Jesus took all upon Himself. We are forgiven! In Christ we are set free from the power of death and given the sure promise of eternal life. Jesus died and rose again! All this, Jesus accomplished in order to give us new life in every area of our lives.

Yet, we wonder where our "newness" is. Our old habits can be so hard to break. Our old habits can still infiltrate everything about our ways of thinking, of perceiving and drawing conclusions about people and circumstances, about God and God's character. Our old habits can linger in our ways of speaking – the words we choose, the tone we use, the interruptions we make. Our old habits can still spew poison into every possible area of how we behave – in what we do privately when no one else is around or seems to know what we're doing, in how we act within our families or around our friends, with co-workers or strangers, in formal or informal settings. Our old habits can be our go-to comfort mode of thinking, speaking and acting. Our old habits can be (even for those who are fairly mature in their faith journey) our knee-jerk reaction mode when people or circumstances are difficult, frustrating, heartbreaking, surprising or unwanted.

Yet, our God declares that the old is gone, the new has come! That all "this new" is from God! Why, then, do we go back to our old habits and their life-twisting, deceptive, destructive, ugly ways? Our old ways do not in any way line up with the truth and freedom that come from our Lord Jesus Christ! Our old habits are deadly, weakening, miserable and enslaving.

> *...now that you know God – or rather are known by God – how is it*
> *that you are turning back to those weak and miserable forces?*
> *Do you wish to be enslaved by them all over again?*
> Galatians 4:9

Our God knows us and, as His children by faith, we, too, know our God. We need to choose to hold onto all that we know is true about our Lord. We need to choose to live our lives in the freedom that Jesus' blood has bought for us.

> *It is for freedom that Christ has set us free.*
> *Stand firm, then, and do not let yourselves be burdened again by a yoke of slavery.*
> Galatians 5:1

Make a break for it! Break from all those old deadly, weak, miserable and enslaving habits! Break from them by choosing to stand fully in the love, grace, truth, power and freedom that come through, and come from, our Lord Jesus Christ alone!

Do I believe it?
And if I do, what am I going to do about it?

Lord, please let me hear your voice, your love, your wisdom, your grace and truth.

GOD, COME AND GET ME!

Have you ever been in the wrong place? You know, a time when you were supposed to be in one place but you ended up somewhere else? Twice in just the last week this has happened to me. The first time, I can happily blame it on my car's GPS system. It just could not direct me to the actual location I needed to be. The second time, I misinterpreted where I was to meet someone. My fault entirely. Both times, whether it was my fault or not, I needed help. I needed redirection. I needed to reset my plans.

This need for help, this need for redirection, this need to reset my plans is a constant truth within my inner life of mind and spirit, body and soul. I need God always. I need God to come and get me. I so often (Okay, constantly!) need God to take hold of my every thought, my every perspective, my every emotion, my every plan so that my mind and spirit will be filled with His light and calmed and matured with His truth.

> *Send me your light and your faithful care, let them lead me;*
> *let them bring me to your holy mountain, to the place where you dwell.*
> *Then I will go to the altar of God, to God, my joy and my delight.*
> *I will praise you with the lyre, O God, my God.*
> Psalm 43:3-4

God, come and get me! Come to me so that I may come to You! Shine Your light into my confused, clouded, lost, dense and dark places! Bring me Your truth so that I may know my way to You and may know Your best way for my life. Your best way for every one of my days, for every one of my moments!

God, come and get me! Come to me so that I may let You take full hold of my head, my heart, my whole being! God, come and get me! Guide me completely by Your Holy Spirit so that I may know Your head and heart! So that I may know Your thoughts and ways – and follow You!

God, come and get me! Bring me to Your Holy mountain! Bring me to Your dwelling place so that I may breathe in the life-giving, life-restoring truth of Your constant presence with me! God, come to me so that I may be filled with Your eternal perspective and transcending peace that will guard my heart and mind always.

God, come and get me! Come to me so that I may go to You, and go with You, in the fullness of the joy and delight that You are to my life – to my mind, my spirit, my entire being! Come to me so that my thankfulness for You may be more deeply and continually expressed!

God, come and get me! Come to me so that I may go to You with the music You have poured into my soul! Come to me so that I may go with You, my God, with all that You have given to me! Come to me so that I may go with You as You lead me by Your love, wisdom, courage, hope, strength, goodness and peace!

God, come and get me! Come to me with Your help, with Your redirection and with Your resetting of my plans so that I may live more fully in Your light and truth!

God, come and get me – over and over and over again!

Reflections – Responses – Challenges – Encouragements – God-breathing Thoughts

Do I believe it?
And if I do, what am I going to do about it?

Lord, please let me hear your voice, your love, your wisdom, your grace and truth.

October 9

START SPREADIN' THE NEWS!

"Start spreadin' the news!" That's how the song *"New York, New York"* begins. I love New York. It's near and dear to my heart. Between growing up in New York state and different moves back and forth, New York was my home state for more than thirty-five years of my life. Now we're just a quick and easy train ride away from NYC – a sweet gift to us since our grown children currently live there! Good news for us anyway!

Our God has given us some amazing, life-giving news to spread! Some news about which we should not keep silent.

I proclaim your saving acts in the great assembly;
I do not seal my lips, LORD, as you know.
I do not hide your righteousness in my heart;
I speak of your faithfulness and salvation.
I do not conceal your love and your faithfulness from the great assembly.
Psalm 40:9-10

Our God has given us news to spread to all people everywhere! We are to proclaim it! Open our lips and tell it! We are to shine with God's righteousness given to us! We are to speak of God's faithfulness and salvation, His love and His truth! We are to spread God's good news!

We are to be ambassadors of Christ, spreading God's powerful message of reconciliation, forgiveness and freedom offered to us through the death and resurrection of our Lord Jesus.

All this is from God, who reconciled us to himself through Christ
and gave us the ministry of reconciliation:
that God was reconciling the world to himself in Christ,
not counting men's sins against them.
And he has committed to us the message of reconciliation.
We are therefore Christ's ambassadors,
as though God were making his appeal through us.
We implore you on Christ's behalf: Be reconciled to God.
God made him who had no sin to be sin for us,
so that in him we might become the righteousness of God.
2 Corinthians 5:18-21

Preach the Word;
be prepared in season and out of season;
correct, rebuke and encourage
– with great patience and careful instruction.
2 Timothy 4:2

"Go, stand in the temple courts," [the angel of the Lord] said,
"and tell the people all [the full message] about this new life."
Acts 5:20

All people everywhere need to know the love, grace, truth, faithfulness, hope and salvation of our Holy God! Everyone everywhere needs to know the full message of this new life in Jesus – God's Holy Son, our Messiah, the King of kings and Lord of lords!

Start spreadin' the news!

Reflections – Responses – Challenges – Encouragements – God-breathing Thoughts

Do I believe it?
And if I do, what am I going to do about it?

Lord, please let me hear your voice, your love, your wisdom, your grace and truth.

IT IS TIME TO SEEK THE LORD

It is time to seek the Lord. To seek our God in the midst of this moment. To seek our God right now, right where we are, wherever we are, however we are feeling – especially if we're just not feeling like it. It's time to seek our God today in whatever the circumstances of our day may be. It's time to seek the Lord. And this will be true again tomorrow...and the next day...and the next day...and every day of our lives.

As we seek the Lord, we are inviting our God into our lives more fully, more intimately, more powerfully. We are asking God to make our lives His holy ground for His purposes and plans to be accomplished and achieved in us.

> *Sow righteousness for yourselves,*
> *reap the fruit of unfailing love,*
> *and break up your unplowed ground;*
> *for it is time to seek the LORD,*
> *until he comes and showers his righteousness on you.*
> Hosea 10:12

It is time to seek the Lord in all we are and in all we do. With God's grace and truth as our planting tools, we are called and empowered to sow – deep within our hearts and minds, our souls and spirits – a righteousness that reflects the righteous character of our God. And "what is sown will be what is reaped" (Galatians 6:7). And this will be true for us because our "God is love" (1 John 4:18). As we sow in accordance with God's righteousness, we will reap the fruit of, and be grown up in, God's unfailing love.

To allow God's righteousness to be sown more completely into our lives, we need to seek the Lord, allowing Him to break up any and all hardness within our lives, minds, hearts and habits that have not yet been deeply plowed up and turned over by His love. Maybe the hardness, the *unplowedness*, in our ground has come from feeling trampled on and sucked dry by life's hard, hateful and hurtful circumstances or by the hard, hateful and hurtful people we encounter.

Our God understands all that may have caused the hardness of our unplowed ground – all of the hardness that seems to keep us beaten down and unfruitful. Yet, our God does not intend to keep us in that unplowed, hardened state. Our God has always meant for each of us – as those who seek Him and follow Him – to live an abundant life in Him: "I have come that they may have life, and have it to the full" (John 10:10). In Christ, there is nothing so hard, hateful or hurtful that our God cannot turn over and transform by the touch of His righteousness and love that come from His nail-marked hands.

It is time to seek the Lord. "Seek and you will find" (Matthew 7:7). When we seek the Lord, we will find the Lord's righteousness – and it will be sown deeply within our lives. When we seek the Lord, we will find the Lord's unfailing love and it will be reaped and flourish within our own lives and be generously given to others around us. When we seek the Lord, our unplowed ground will be healed, transformed, nurtured and prepared to yield an ever-increasing harvest of God's righteousness and unfailing love.

It is time to seek the Lord today...and tomorrow...and the next day...and the next day...and every day of our lives. Because one day our Lord will shower us – transforming us completely and eternally – by the fullness of His righteousness and unfailing love!

Reflections – Responses – Challenges – Encouragements – God-breathing Thoughts

Do I believe it?
And if I do, what am I going to do about it?

Lord, please let me hear your voice, your love, your wisdom, your grace and truth.

GIVE GOD WHAT GOD WANTS!

Many of us may have a fairly long list of what we want and desire from God. God has wants, too. And everything that God wants is all and always for our very best, now and eternally.

For I desire mercy, not sacrifice,
and acknowledgment of God rather than burnt offerings.
Hosea 6:6

Our God desires that we would live out every one of our relationships and encounters with other people with mercy filling us and flowing through us. God wants our lives to be marked by sincere, tangible, life-transforming, life-renewing, life-restoring, life-forgiving mercy.

Our God desires that each one of us would "love mercy" (Micah 6:8). And love mercy towards others more than we love and desire to be justified for the actions, even wrong actions, we choose to do. We are to love mercy more than we love and desire vengeance to be paid for the wrongs done against us.

Doing our "religious" acts and activities – even if those are good and right things – will mean nothing to our God. They will bring Him no joy. They will bring Him no pleasure if we lack authentic and active mercy for the women, men and children that walk with us on this earth.

If our sacrifices and burnt offerings or, more contemporarily, our tithes and gifts, our prayers and fasting, our studying of God's Word and our acts of service do not come from a heart that humbly and honestly acknowledges our own desperate need for God's mercy in our lives, then all of our "religious" acts and activities are empty and worthless. Our God wants mercy from us to others.

And our God wants to be acknowledged. God wants to be rightly and humbly honored, known and trusted by each one of us as His children and His image-bearers. Our God wants each of us to know and believe Him for who He is as the Giver, Sustainer, Redeemer and Deliverer of our lives, as our Messiah, the Resurrection and the Life, as our Help, our Hope, our Savior and our Sovereign Lord. As we humbly, fearfully and thankfully acknowledge God, and as we put our faith and trust in Him alone, this fulfills the desires of God's heart, because "without faith it is impossible to please God" (Hebrews 11:6).

May each of us take a little more time today to actively and intentionally think about what our God wants and desires from us. May we each take time to focus on what pleases our God instead of pushing our wants and desires to the top of our *God-please-give-me-that* list. May each of us take time to lift our hearts and our minds to our God, acknowledging Him as the One who holds our very lives in His very loving and merciful nail-scarred hands.

May each of us take time to offer real, tangible, ongoing mercy to those who are desperate in their circumstances of poverty, of hunger, of loss, of broken minds and broken bodies. May each of us take time to offer real, tangible, ongoing mercy to those who are despicable in the ways they have caused our lives to be mired and muddied, broken and bleak.

May we live our lives filled and flowing with mercy towards all others. This is the best way we could ever acknowledge our God. This is the best way to give God what God wants!

Reflections – Responses – Challenges – Encouragements – God-breathing Thoughts

Do I believe it?
And if I do, what am I going to do about it?

Lord, please let me hear your voice, your love, your wisdom, your grace and truth.

October 12

PURE HEART, STEADFAST SPIRIT – GOD'S JOY

Create in me a pure heart, O God,
and renew a steadfast spirit within me.
Psalm 51:10

These words of Scripture may be so familiar to so many of you. They are to me. Even now, one of the worship tunes, to which these words have been put, is going through my head. And I'm praying and I'm singing. And I'm sure of the truth of these God-given words.

What I really need to be sure of, and desire, is that I am sincerely praying these words for myself. Then, I need to be prepared for my Abba, for my Holy God to do whatever He needs to do to purify and strengthen my heart, to do whatever He needs to do to renew and make my spirit unwaveringly resolute and devoted to following and trusting my Lord Jesus.

Our heart, in the biblical sense, is the source where all of our emotions, thoughts, motivations and actions are formed and founded. Our heart is the source from which all of these flow. It is through the flow and expression of our hearts – through our emotions, thoughts, motivations and actions – that I, and all others, are known, perceived, seen, heard and experienced.

And I can tell you with absolute certainty that my God needs to continually purify so many of my emotions, thoughts, motivations and actions! My God needs to purify my heart! My heart and its flow have all been mucked up with the yuck of this world and with my own mucky, yucky choices. Sin and brokenness from the world still come at me. Sin and brokenness still wrestle within me, and sometimes I just invite them in to be a guest and stay for awhile.

O God, create in me a pure heart! Do Your deep cleansing, Your pervasive and persistent purification in me. Holy One, I need You to shape and lead my every emotion, thought, motivation and action. O my God, create in me a heart that more purely, passionately, fully and freely reflects Your heart at all times, in all places, with all people!

And there are days when my spirit is absolutely shaken. Never are God's truths, never is God's love shaken. God is God. Unchangeable and faithful. But my spirit can be shaken by the hard and unwanted, the difficult and unexpected, the frustrating and evil circumstances of this world. My spirit needs to be steadied by my steadfast God because I am frail, flawed and finite.

O God, renew in me a steadfast spirit. I need Your holy balance to hold me continually. I need Your love to come fill me again and again. I need Your peace to calm my fears. I need Your grace and truth, Your Word and Your Spirit to rule completely over all of me, from my innermost being to every thought, word, action and reaction that comes from me. I need You to transform me to be more like You. I need You to renew my spirit to be more like Yours!

Our loving Abba knows our deep and desperate need for our hearts to be continually cleansed, forgiven and purified. Our loving Abba knows our deep and desperate need for our spirits to be steadied in this changing and uncertain world. And it is God's joy to create in us a pure heart and renew a steadfast spirit within us! It is God's joy to make us more like Him!

Reflections – Responses – Challenges – Encouragements – God-breathing Thoughts

Do I believe it?
And if I do, what am I going to do about it?

Lord, please let me hear your voice, your love, your wisdom, your grace and truth.

PROMISED PEACE – JUST LISTEN!

I will listen to what God the LORD says:
he promises peace to his people, his faithful servants –
but let them not turn to folly.
Psalm 85:8

"Come near me and listen to this…"
This is what the LORD says – your Redeemer, the Holy One of Israel:
"I am the LORD your God,
who teaches you what is best for you,
who directs you in the way you should go.
If only you had paid attention to my commands,
your peace would have been like a river,
your well-being like the waves of the sea."
Isaiah 48:16-18

Have you ever said or, at least, wanted to tell someone – maybe even someone you deeply love – something like this? *If only you would just listen to me! If you listen now, you will have so much more peace in the days ahead! If you listen now, you will save yourself from creating unwanted, unhealthy and unholy complications in your circumstances and in your relationships!*

But sadly, and maybe not unexpectedly, they did not listen. And, then, the truth of their choices breaks your heart for them as you see their broken lives. The words that were not listened to keep rolling around in your head. *If only you had listened, you would have known so much more peace. You wouldn't be going through the pain…the problems…the embarrassment…the loss of reputation…the loss of relationships…the loss of hope…the shame…the crisis. If only you had just listened, you wouldn't be experiencing all the trouble that you cannot escape now!*

Our God calls out to us continually through His Word and His Spirit, speaking intimately to our innermost being. Our God calls to us, from the depths of His love for us, to just listen to Him. Calling us to listen to His peace-bringing, life-protecting words and commands. Our God calls us to listen. And obey. And live in His peace.

Oh! There have been so many times, far too many times, that I've chosen, stubbornly and selfishly, ridiculously and rebelliously, to ignore God's passionate plea for me to just listen to Him. *To not choose to go my own way. To not go away from God's way. To stop now. To turn around now. To come back to God now. Come back to His truth, His ways and His peace.* Oh! Things could've been so different, for me and for others, if only I had listened.

There are enough hard things that will come at us in life, hard things that will disrupt our peace. Some of these will come to us by no fault of our own. Yet! Some hard things that come at us in life, some hard things that disrupt our peace, come at us because of our own sinful, foolish choices. How wise we would be if we would choose to listen to our God more attentively, more quickly, more fully! How much more peace and righteousness would mark our lives if we would choose to listen to and obey God's Word and God's Spirit!

May we hold onto God's Word and ways, and hold onto each other in sincere and accountable love, so that we will listen to our God and be filled and flowing with His promised peace!

Reflections – Responses – Challenges – Encouragements – God-breathing Thoughts

Do I believe it?
And if I do, what am I going to do about it?

Lord, please let me hear your voice, your love, your wisdom, your grace and truth.

BUT GOD!

In Scripture we see the harsh realities of life. People are overcome by evil – by their own sinful choices or the sinful choices others make against them. People are overcome by the frailty of life, by the hardship of life and by the finality of death.

But not so with God! Our God does not leave His people alone or without hope! Our God rescues and redeems, heals and holds, guards and guides, sets us free and transforms our lives with His unfailing love and unlimited power!

Take time to read these few *But God!* verses. Let God encourage your heart and lift your head to trust Him more fully with all the "buts" and doubts, fears and pain you have in your life. Because nothing is impossible for God!

> *You intended to harm me, but God intended it for good*
> *to accomplish what is now being done, the saving of many lives.*
> Genesis 50:20

> *My flesh and my heart may fail,*
> *but God is the strength of my heart and my portion forever.*
> Psalm 73:26

> *But God will never forget the needy;*
> *the hope of the afflicted will never perish.*
> Psalm 9:18

> *But God will redeem me from the realm of the dead;*
> *he will surely take me to himself.*
> Psalm 49:15

> *But God demonstrates his own love for us in this:*
> *While we were yet sinners, Christ died for us.*
> Romans 5:8

> *But God raised him from the dead,*
> *freeing him from the agony of death,*
> *because it was impossible for death to keep its hold on him.*
> Acts 2:24

> *So you are no longer a slave [to sin],*
> *but God's child; and since you are his child,*
> *God has made you also an heir.*
> Galatians 4:7

> *Jesus looked at them and said, "With man this is impossible,*
> *but with God all things are possible."*
> Matthew 19:26

Hallelujah to our God – the God for whom all things are possible! All the "buts" and doubts, fears and pain we have in our lives cannot keep God from transforming us with His unfailing love and unlimited power! No buts about it!

Reflections – Responses – Challenges – Encouragements – God-breathing Thoughts

Do I believe it?
And if I do, what am I going to do about it?

Lord, please let me hear your voice, your love, your wisdom, your grace and truth.

BUT GOD! – breaking it down just a little bit more

Oh, those *But God!* scriptures! They are powerful, perspective-changing challenges. They are life-transforming promises. Let's reflect on a few of these "But God!" verses just a little bit more.

> *You intended to harm me, but God intended it for good*
> *to accomplish what is now being done, the saving of many lives.*
> Genesis 50:20

This verse, in particular, fills my soul with such deep assurance of God's loving sovereignty, His intimate care and His ability to absolutely astound us with His goodness and power to transform lives in spite of the horrendous evil and brokenness they may have experienced. I experienced deep harm and abuse as a child. I planned suicide. *But God!*

But God made Himself known to me by His Word and His Spirit.
But God gave His Son Jesus to die for me and forgive all my sins.
But God gave me eternal life, and one day I'll live in the fullness of His presence.
But God empowered me to forgive my abusers because Jesus had already died for them, too.
But God renews me continually by His Word and Spirit.
But God holds me and transforms me by His grace and truth.
But God guards my mind and heart in His transcending peace.
But God gives me the joy and hope He intended me to have from the moment of my birth.
But God gives me courage to follow Him, love Him, love others and love myself.
But God convinced me of, and continually fills and strengthens me with, His unfailing love.

Ahhhhh! *But God* can make such a difference – such an eternal difference – in a life! And this is true even as I recognize and embrace the truth of my human mortality.

> *My flesh and my heart may fail,*
> *but God is the strength of my heart and my portion forever.*
> *Psalm 73:26*

My flesh and my heart not only *may* fail, they *will* fail. (And some parts are failing already!)

But God *is* the strength of my heart! But God *is* my portion forever! My flesh and my heart *may-will* fail. But God encourages me! But God fills all of my deepest, truest heart needs!
But God is always loving!
But God is always present!
But God is always forgiving!
But God is always faithful!
But God is always good!
But God is my wisdom!
But God is my peace!
But God is my hope!
But God is my joy!

But for God, I would be lost. All of us would be. But God wasn't about to let that happen! He gave His Son to give His life for us. To give us true life. Eternal life. No buts about it!

Reflections – Responses – Challenges – Encouragements – God-breathing Thoughts

Do I believe it?
And if I do, what am I going to do about it?

Lord, please let me hear your voice, your love, your wisdom, your grace and truth.

October 16

THE REAL KILLER UNCLEANNESS

Some Pharisees and teachers of the law challenged Jesus about why his disciples were eating with "unclean" hands, not doing the ceremonial washing before a meal. Jesus needed to set them straight on what really makes a person "unclean" before God. And it has nothing to do with soap and water.

(Commercial break. For your physical health and protection against disease, especially in the flu season: Yes! Wash your hands! Often and well!)

Now, back to the real killer uncleanness: Sin.

> *Jesus called the crowd to him and said, "Listen to me, everyone, and understand this. Nothing outside a person can defile them [make them unclean] by going into them. Rather, it is what comes out of a person that defiles them...For it is from within, out of a person's heart, that evil thoughts come – sexual immorality, theft, murder, adultery, greed, malice, deceit, lewdness, envy, slander, arrogance and folly. All these evils come from inside and defile a person."*
> Mark 7:14-15, 21-23

Sin. Deadly. Dangerous. Dirty. Sin comes from within us – to threaten, infect, destroy our peace, wreck our relationships with God and with each other and kill every single one of us. Sin is the true pandemic illness of this world that touches all of us. We must be humble enough to accept our only hope for cure: The blood sacrifice of our Lord Jesus Christ. Out of God's outrageous love for us, Jesus took our punishment in death so that we might be given His pure life through the forgiveness of our sins and the power of His resurrection!

> *God made him who had no sin to be sin for us,*
> *so that in him we might become the righteousness of God.*
> 2 Corinthians 5:21

> *But now he has reconciled you by Christ's physical body through death*
> *to present you holy in his sight, without blemish and free from accusation.*
> Colossians 1:22

To have Jesus as our Savior and Lord is the very power of God that conquers sin and death. The very power of God to cleanse, heal, free and transform our lives! Is it time for you to invite Jesus to be your Savior? He is here for you. He loves you unfailingly.

Maybe it's time you to…
Let Jesus know you need Him. We all do.
Ask for God's forgiveness. We all have sinned. We all need to be forgiven.
Choose to trust in Jesus – in His death and in Jesus' blood poured out on the cross to be the full payment for your sin debt before our Holy God. This is God's fullest act of love for us.
Invite Jesus to be your Savior. This is the greatest life-transforming decision we can make.
Accept and believe the loving, faithful promise of God's salvation for you and the promised gift of eternal life with our Lord in heaven! Thank Him! You are His child! Welcome Home!

May each of us let our holy God cleanse us with the power of His love and the gift of His salvation! May all of us, as His children by faith, live our lives in the beauty and power of His cleansing love!

Reflections – Responses – Challenges – Encouragements – God-breathing Thoughts

Do I believe it?
And if I do, what am I going to do about it?

Lord, please let me hear your voice, your love, your wisdom, your grace and truth.

GOD'S GLORY AND PRAISE ARE HIS – ALONE!

"I am the LORD; that is my name!
I will not yield my glory to another or my praise to idols."
Isaiah 42:8

God is God. And God will not share His glory or praise with anyone or anything else. Why is this so important for us to understand? Why is the Lord so adamant in telling us that He will not give His glory or praise to another? Because God loves us.

God's love for us is fiercely protective of us. Fiercely desiring us to live in relationship with Him, right now and for all eternity. God's love for us moves Him to speak His truth, which is always intertwined and perfectly balanced with His grace, so that we will know what will set us free and keep us free. And when we human beings glorify or honor or praise anyone or anything else above the Lord of all creation, we are in imminent danger of losing ourselves to a lesser god. We are in danger of being entrapped and enslaved by idols – whether people or things or wealth or beauty or power or possessions or activities or habits or even self-righteous works of service. These idols, whatever they are, have no true power to meet our deepest soul needs. Only God does. God knows this. And our God passionately wants us to know His deep love for us. But, to truly know and experience God's unfailing, eternal love for us, we must understand, and respond to, the truth that God alone deserves the fullness of our love. That God alone deserves to be glorified, honored and praised above everyone and everything else in our lives.

Only God is...
Love. Creator. Giver of Life. Eternal One. Beginning and End – Alpha and Omega. Holy. Rescuer. Redeemer. Deliverer. Healer. Hope of Nations. Ancient of Days. Sovereign One. Wonderful Counselor. Mighty God. Everlasting Father. Prince of Peace. Righteous Judge. Immanuel. The Father. The Son. The Spirit. Our only Savior. Messiah. The Word made flesh. The Way. The Truth. The Life. The Resurrection. King of kings and Lord of lords.

No one and nothing else deserve to be honored as we are to honor the Lord. Our God gave this loving and fiercely protective truth to us as the very first of the Ten Commandments:

"You shall have no other gods before me."
Exodus 20:3

This direct and seemingly simple – and certainly righteous and holy – command, that we put nothing else, glorify and honor and praise nothing else, before our God, is God's loving and fiercely protective Word to keep us safe, to save our lives – to save our minds and our hearts, to save our souls and our relationships.

Take time, reflective time, to think about what place God has in your life. Is God your first and your highest? Your first and highest love? Your first and highest One to trust? Your first and highest joy? Your first and highest peace? Your first and highest security? Your first and highest satisfaction for your soul? Do you give God your first and highest praise and honor? Or must God share all of these with someone or something else in your life?

God is God. Out of God's fiercely protective love for us, He will never give His glory and praise to anyone or anything else. And out of our love for Him, neither should we. Ever.

Reflections – Responses – Challenges – Encouragements – God-breathing Thoughts

Do I believe it?
And if I do, what am I going to do about it?

Lord, please let me hear your voice, your love, your wisdom, your grace and truth.

LET THE LORD TAKE HOLD OF YOU!

He reached down from on high and took hold of me;
he drew me out of deep waters.
Psalm 18:16

The Lord wants so much to take hold of each and every one of us. Our Lord wants to hold us fast and draw us to Himself. Our Lord opens His loving, everlasting arms to us so He may save us, protect us, lead us and transform us. Our God loves us beyond our comprehension, but not beyond His own willingness to sacrifice His righteous life for the forgiveness of our sins. Our Lord doesn't want anyone to be eternally separated from Him by rejecting the salvation He freely offers to us, yet which cost Him so much.

The Lord...is patient with you, not wanting anyone to perish,
but everyone to come to repentance.
2 Peter 3:9

The Lord patiently waits for us to choose to let Him take hold of us with His great gift of salvation. Even as we stay in our sins, our hate, our hateful ways and reject our holy God who passionately pursues us with His love – our Lord remains patient.

This day, October 18, marks the anniversary of the eternal birthday of my dad. In 2002, my dad, at age seventy-three, finally let God take hold of him after living most of his life in stubborn and cruel defiance of God and God's righteous and loving ways. And many more than just Dad suffered because of the evil choices he made.

Yet there was God. Waiting patiently and wanting passionately to take hold of my dad. Jesus had already died for Dad. Nothing more needed to be accomplished for Dad to be born as a child of God, to be fully forgiven, to be saved and given eternal life with the Father. Jesus had accomplished it all. There is no other sufficient, acceptable sacrifice, offering or action that could bring forgiveness and salvation to my dad – or to me or to anyone else – except for the blood of Jesus poured out on the cross.

God made him who had no sin to be sin for us,
so that in him we might become the righteousness of God.
2 Corinthians 5:21

Jesus had accomplished it all. God just needed Dad to finally acknowledge his need for the forgiveness that cost Jesus His life. Dad just needed to finally acknowledge his need for God to take hold of him. On October 18, 2002, my dad did just that. And God took hold of my dad and drew him out of the deep waters of chaos and condemnation. That day God took hold of my dad through the great gift of salvation that comes only through the righteous sacrifice of Jesus.

Four years later, God took hold of my dad and escorted him away from all the chaos and deep waters that exist on this side of heaven. God brought Dad into his eternal home to live and walk with Him in peace along the river of life that flows from the throne of God.

May each of us let the Lord take hold of us! And take hold of us tightly – for ourselves and for each of the precious people whose lives we affect, now and in future generations, by the choices we make!

OPEN THE DOORS!

Ahaz, king of Judah (735-719 BC), had turned away from God in depraved and evil ways. He defiled and robbed the Lord's temple, worshiped idols and false gods, and went so far in his idolatry that…

Ahaz gathered together the furnishings from the temple of God
and cut them in pieces. He shut the doors of the LORD's temple
and set up altars at every street corner in Jerusalem.
2 Chronicles 28:24

Through his vile actions and grotesque idolatry, Ahaz made every attempt to deny God His rightful rule in the hearts of His people. Yet, the power Ahaz wielded was unable to keep his own son and successor to the throne of Judah, King Hezekiah, from turning his heart fully to Lord Almighty.

Hezekiah trusted in the LORD, the God of Israel.
There was no one like him among all the kings of Judah,
either before him or after him.
He held fast to the LORD and did not stop following him;
he kept the commands the LORD had given Moses.
2 Kings 18:5-6

As king, Hezekiah was passionate and persistent in trusting and bringing honor to the Lord. He had all the idols, symbols and altars to the pagan gods torn down and destroyed throughout the land of Judah. And as one of his very first acts as king, Hezekiah made sure that the Lord would be worshiped, once again, at the temple in Jerusalem.

In the first month of the first year of his reign [715 BC],
he opened the doors of the temple of the LORD and repaired them.
2 Chronicles 29:3

In our own lives, we need to ask: What is the condition of the doors of our hearts when it comes to worshiping, living for, trusting and loving the One True God?
Have we, in any way, allowed others to block us, to shut the doors of our hearts and keep us from worshiping the Lord?
Have we allowed others to shut us away from trusting the Lord?
Have we allowed the actions and words of others to hurt us, disappoint us or frustrate us so much that we have shut our own hearts down and shut them away from the Lord because of the pain, anger, judgment and self-pity we're still holding?
Have we, in any way, allowed our own sin, pride, stubbornness, laziness or other priorities to shut the doors of our hearts to worshiping, living for, trusting and loving our Lord?

Let's ask the Lord to open the doors of our hearts – no matter what or who may have shut them – so we may worship Him as the One True God, the Eternal and Sovereign King over all creation. So we may live for our God, as His children and ambassadors, offering Christ's love, mercy, forgiveness, hope and courage to all those around us. So we may trust our God more fully in every way, in every circumstance, every day of our lives. Let's ask the Lord to open the doors of our hearts so we may love our God as He deserves – "with all our heart and with all our soul and with all our mind and with all our strength" (Mark 12:30).

Open the doors of our hearts, Lord, open the doors of your holy temple within us, and let no one and nothing keep us shut away from worshiping, living for, trusting and loving You!

Reflections – Responses – Challenges – Encouragements – God-breathing Thoughts

Do I believe it?
And if I do, what am I going to do about it?

Lord, please let me hear your voice, your love, your wisdom, your grace and truth.

October 20

WE KNOW! WE KNOW! SO?

We know that anyone born of God does not continue to sin;
the One who was born of God keeps them safe, and the evil one cannot harm them.
We know that we are children of God,
and that the whole world is under the control of the evil one.
We know also that the Son of God has come and has given us understanding,
so that we may know him who is true.
And we are in him who is true by being in his Son Jesus Christ.
He is the true God and eternal life.
Dear children, keep yourselves from idols.
1 John 5:18-21

We know that because of our faith in Jesus Christ, we have become children of God. And as children born into eternal life through the sacrifice of Jesus and His victorious resurrection, *we know* that the power of the evil one no longer has control over us. Nor can the evil one harm us in any soul damaging or damning way. *We know* that as children of God, our true and eternal lives are sealed and kept safe forever in our Heavenly Abba's love and care.

We know that we have been given the Spirit of the Living Christ to lead us away from deliberately choosing to stay in the habit and lifestyle of sin. *We know* that the Spirit empowers us and renews us so that we may choose God's good and loving, beautiful and freeing ways.

We know that Jesus came to us so we could understand the Father's great love for us and intimately know Him as the One who is true. *We know* that our lives are now secure in our God, through our Lord Jesus Christ – the true God and eternal life.

We know that as God's children we are to keep ourselves from any and everything that would become an idol for us. *We know* that we are to turn away from any and every influence and activity that would become more important to us than our Lord Jesus Christ.

We know all of this because Jesus, the Eternal Word made flesh, has humbly and sacrificially revealed the incredible and unfailing love and power, grace and truth that our Heavenly Father has for each and every one of us!

So? If *we know* these eternal truths, how will we live out the truth of them now?
In what ways will we choose to think, speak, act and interact more like who we truly are in our Lord Jesus Christ – children born of the Most High God?
What sins are we still deliberately choosing and, thereby, silencing God's Spirit as we do?
In what areas of our lives do we need to trust God more fully as the One who loves us and is able to keep us safe from all things that would destroy our eternal hope, peace and joy?
Who or what has become an idol to us? Who or what do we need to release, and be released, from ruling over our desires, energy, time and resources?

We know that in Jesus we are children born of the Spirit and loved for all eternity! *We know* that "not anything in all creation will be able to separate us from the love of God that is in Christ Jesus our Lord" (Romans 8:39).

So? Let's live like we know! And through us, others will come to know the One who is true!

Do I believe it?
And if I do, what am I going to do about it?

Lord, please let me hear your voice, your love, your wisdom, your grace and truth.

REST – A HOLY SABBATH, A LOVING INVITATION

Rest. So essential for our physical, mental, emotional, relational and spiritual well-being.
Rest. So elusive, and the very real need for it is often ignored, dismissed and denied.

Yet, the Lord of all creation set aside time for Himself to rest.

> **Thus the heavens and the earth were completed in all their vast array.**
> **By the seventh day God had finished the work he had been doing;**
> **so on the seventh day he rested from all his work.**
> **Then God blessed the seventh day and made it holy,**
> **because on it he rested from all the work of creating that he had done.**
> Genesis 2:1-2

God set aside this holy time to rest, although our God Himself "will not grow tired or weary" (Isaiah 40:28). God established the practice and importance for us to stop all our work, *taking a day of rest, a holy Sabbath to the Lord* right from the time He provided manna to His people (Exodus 16). God feels so strongly about us *taking a holy Sabbath to the Lord,* that it made His top ten list:

> **Remember the Sabbath day by keeping it holy.**
> **Six days you shall labor and do all your work,**
> **but the seventh day is a sabbath to the LORD your God.**
> **On it you shall not do any work…For in six days the LORD made the heavens**
> **and the earth, the sea, and all that is in them, but he rested on the seventh day.**
> **Therefore the LORD blessed the Sabbath day and made it holy.**
> Exodus 20:8-11

Out of God's love for us, and out of His understanding our deepest soul and body needs, our God set aside the Sabbath day for us to keep as a holy day of rest, a holy day to worship our God without the busyness of life crowding in. How's that going for you?

I hate to admit it, but a full day of rest each week, as a holy Sabbath to the Lord, has not made my top ten list very often. Convicted. Ouch. I do believe, and try to live out, the truth that every day is a holy day to worship, seek and live for the Lord. But to come to a screeching halt for a full day each week – putting aside all my work, putting aside all I want to accomplish, putting down my lap-top, unplugging from my "to do list" of responsibilities and from all things cyberspace – almost seems impossible. Silly me! I have to remember:

> **"With man this is impossible, but with God all things are possible."**
> Matthew 19:26

My God deserves my undistracted, undivided worship. My God deserves a full day set aside as holy to Him. And it will be with my God, and through His love, that this will be made possible. To keep a day set aside to rest from my work, to let God restore my soul and my body. To keep a day to honestly and humbly live out the truth that neither I nor my work is of utmost importance! A day for me to take Jesus up on His loving "Come with me" invitation – because all things are possible with God!

> **"Come with me by yourselves to a quiet place and get some rest."**
> Mark 6:31

Do I believe it?
And if I do, what am I going to do about it?

Lord, please let me hear your voice, your love, your wisdom, your grace and truth.

NOTHING GREATER

Many of us want to do great and important things. We have dreams and aspirations we want to see become tangible realities in our lives. We have goals we want to reach. We have plans we want to accomplish. We have things – great and important things – for which we want to be known by others for having done them.

Jesus wants us to do great things, and He wants us to be known for doing these great things. He wants us to do the most important thing we could ever do with our lives. And Jesus makes that most important and greatest thing clearly known to us in His answer to a teacher of the law who asked,

"Of all the commandments, which is the most important?"

"The most important one," answered Jesus, "is this:
'Hear, O Israel, the Lord our God, the Lord is one.
Love the Lord your God with all your heart and with all your soul
and with all your mind and with all your strength.'
The second is this: 'Love your neighbor as yourself.'
There is no commandment greater than these."
Mark 12:28-31

There is no commandment greater than these. There is nothing greater than love. And there is nothing greater by which we could be made known as followers of Jesus. Nothing.

"A new command I give you: Love one another.
As I have loved you, so you must love one another.
By this everyone will know that you are my disciples,
if you love one another."
John 13:34-35

Today, by the love and power, by the grace and truth of our Lord Jesus Christ, may each of us choose to truly love God and love others and love ourselves. May each of us choose to love – really love – as Jesus loves us, with all our heart and with all our soul and with all our mind and with all our strength.

Today, may we choose to love in spirit and in truth, with our every thought, word and action. May we choose to love in small ways and big ways, in obvious ways and unobtrusive ways. May we choose to love more tangibly. More sincerely. More sacrificially. More humbly. More wisely. More freely. More fully. More quickly. More gently. More generously. More faithfully. More kindly. More patiently. More fervently. More purely. More protectively. More playfully. More joyfully. More thoughtfully. More thankfully.

May each of us choose to love God and others and ourselves more and more in these same ways tomorrow and the next day and the next day and the next...

We know that every day that we love, in every way that we love, will be of greatest importance to our God. And as we love as Jesus loves, we will be known for doing the greatest thing we could ever do with our lives.

Because nothing is greater than love.

Do I believe it?
And if I do, what am I going to do about it?

Lord, please let me hear your voice, your love, your wisdom, your grace and truth.

October 23

TANGIBLY EVIDENT GENTLENESS

Let your gentleness be evident to all. The Lord is near.
Philippians 4:5

Your gentleness is to be evident to all. Better make this personal: *My gentleness* is to be evident to all. To all people with all kinds of different personalities, with all kinds of different perspectives, with all kinds of different priorities, with all kinds of different lifestyles, with all kinds of different beauty and body types, with all kinds of different gifts and abilities, with all kinds of different backgrounds – ethnically, culturally, economically, socially, educationally, spiritually. With all kinds of different habits and quirks.

Lord, my gentleness is to be evident to all of these people? Darn good thing You are near!

It is God's nearness – God's encouraging and convicting nearness – that will fill me and move me so that my gentleness will be evident to anybody in any way at all. I need the gentleness of the Lord – the fruit of His Holy Spirit placed within me – to expand in my heart, my mind, my mouth, my eyes and my body language whenever I interact with anyone. I need the Lord's gentleness to gentle everything within me that would too quickly or too self-righteously respond to others with annoyance or judgment, with sarcasm or dismissal, with impatience or petulance, with pride or pig-headedness.

Our God wants me, and all of us as His children, to reflect His character in all we are and in all we do. Our God wants us to think, speak and act more and more like Jesus. The gentleness of Jesus has been poured into us by God's Spirit. And this beautiful, powerful and very good fruit of the Spirit is to be poured out from us to others and made tangibly evident to all with whom we interact. No matter what our own inner, self-focused, initial reaction to them may be. Offering and responding in gentleness towards those who are hard for us to deal with, is our way to obey God's freedom-bringing call on our lives to *get over ourselves*!

Yet! We never have to do this in our own strength. Our God is near. Always. Our God is intimately and constantly present with us and within us through the gift of His Holy Spirit. And because of the power of this transforming, grace-filled truth from our God, we can choose to let our gentleness be tangibly evident to all, in all we do, in all circumstances, at all times. Not just in our quiet time. Not just in our prayer time. Not just with our favorite friends or family members or with an adorable, happy child or with a playful little puppy or with a sweet-tempered elderly lady or gentleman. Oh, no! Our God wants us to make His sacrificially-given, Christ-like gentleness tangibly evident in all our relationships, responses and encounters with all others – regardless of who all those others may be! We need to give this gentleness from Jesus to all others so that they, too, will know that the Lord is near!

And we all need this gentleness from our Lord for ourselves, for our own lives, for our own self-criticism, self-doubt and self-disappointment. The Lord is near to love us and strengthen us, to comfort us and forgive us, to renew us and refresh us. The Lord is near with His powerful gentleness to transform us.

May we each trust our Lord's loving presence in all we are experiencing, at all times, in all circumstances, with all kinds of people. Our Lord is near. May this life-changing, grace-filled truth move us to be gentle to all, including to ourselves, in tangibly evident ways.

594

Reflections – Responses – Challenges – Encouragements – God-breathing Thoughts

Do I believe it?
And if I do, what am I going to do about it?

Lord, please let me hear your voice, your love, your wisdom, your grace and truth.

A 360-DEGREE PERSPECTIVE

***...in humility value others above yourselves,
not looking to your own interests but each of you to the interests of the others.***
Philippians 2:3-4

In the business world there are performance appraisals that are called "360-Degree Reviews." Here, not only does the immediate supervisor evaluate the performance of the employee, but the people, the peers and subordinates, all around the one being evaluated, also have input for this professional review. Thus, a "360-Degree Review."

How good it would be if I took more time to sincerely look around me at the people in my life – whether they are my nearest and dearest or acquaintances and strangers. But not to evaluate their performance. Rather to sincerely look around me to evaluate their needs and interests.

I need to be more aware of and more interested in the other people around me. Because, if I am honest, I still have a tendency to be most aware of my own needs and most interested in my own interests. Yet, everyone around me has needs and interests – in the practical, tangible, physical, emotional, relational and spiritual realms – that need to be met in order for them to survive, and to thrive, on this side of heaven.

I need to actively and intentionally, with compassion and concern, look around me to see what the needs and interests of others may be. Some may be in desperate need of food and shelter. Some may be in need because of illness or pain. Some may be in need because of the deep grief caused by the death of a loved one or the destruction of a marriage. Some may be in need because of loss – loss of a job, loss of reputation, loss of hope, loss of peace. Some may be in desperate need because of addiction and the desperate mix of selfish, self-loving, self-loathing behavior. Some may be in desperate need of a kind smile, a gentle touch, a bit of joy, a bit of playfulness, a listening ear or a caring friend. Some may be in desperate need of a courageous intervention done with the grace and truth of God.

All of us are in desperate need for Jesus. We all need God's love, forgiveness, salvation and transformation in our lives. Some of those around me, and around you, are still lost in the brokenness of this world and their own sins. Their deepest soul needs – to know they are loved unconditionally, to know they belong to Someone forever, to know their lives matter, to know the peace of forgiveness and the hope of eternal life with God – are still unfulfilled.

We each need to *look not only to our own interests, but also to the interests of others.* We need to take a 360-degree perspective to see how we could meet some of those needs and interests of others in some way. This is really all about love. This is about choosing to actively and intentionally look around us with God's love towards others and, then, love others in active and intentional ways – in practical, tangible, physical, emotional, relational and spiritual ways. As we share God's love in the lives of others, they will not only survive, but they will thrive in the love of Jesus who is able to make us all "more than conquerors" (Romans 8:37).

May the compassionate, eternal, life-transforming love of Jesus move each of us to take a 360-degree perspective of those around us. May God's love fill us and move us to be more sensitive and more responsive to the needs and interests, to the hearts and souls of others. And may we do it all for the glory of our God!

Reflections – Responses – Challenges – Encouragements – God-breathing Thoughts

Do I believe it?
And if I do, what am I going to do about it?

Lord, please let me hear your voice, your love, your wisdom, your grace and truth.

DECISIONS! DECISIONS!

Decisions! Decisions! We make hundreds of them each and every day. Some of which we are not even necessarily all that conscious of when making them. Other decisions are about the minutia of life, and some of those we can often make too big in our own minds.

Some of our decisions will be highly significant for our lives and for the course our lives will take here on earth. Decisions about:
What we want to be when we grow up…what steps to take to reach that goal…what school to attend…what training, certification, trade-apprenticeship or course of study to take…what job to take…which relationships we build…who to trust…who to date…who to marry…or not to marry at all…to have children or not…and if "yes" to children, then, when and how many…how to best care for and how to best raise our children…to have pets or not…and if "yes" to pets, then, when and how many…how to earn money…how to save…how to spend…how to use our money to help others…where to live…where to worship…when to leave…when to stay…how to best use our time, energy, efforts and resources at work and in our personal time…when to retire…to downsize or not…to have surgery or not…to have chemo or radiation or both…home-health care or assisted living or a nursing home for our loved ones and for ourselves…and on and on. And there will be oh-so-many other highly significant decisions we will need to make for our lives over the course of our lives.

However, there is no decision – there is no choice – that any one of us will make that will more significantly impact our lives and the course of our lives for all eternity than to make the decision to choose, trust, serve and love God as the Lord of our lives.

> *I have set before you life and death, blessings and curses. Now choose life,*
> *so that you and your children may live*
> *and that you may love the LORD your God,*
> *listen to his voice, and hold fast to him.*
> *For the LORD is your life.*
> Deuteronomy 30:19-20

> *Choose for yourselves this day whom you wil serve*
> *…But as for me and my household, we will serve the LORD.*
> Joshua 24:15

> *For God so loved the world that he gave his one and only Son,*
> *that whoever believes in him shall not perish but have eternal life.*
> *For God did not send his Son into the world to condemn the world,*
> *but to save the world through him.*
> John 3:16-17

> *"I am the way the truth and the life. No one comes to the Father except through me."*
> John 14:6

If the ultimate decision of our lives – made in our minds and in our hearts – is the decision to choose, trust, serve and love the Lord, then the course for our eternal life is set in Christ's sure hope and transcending peace. With this ultimate decision made, our Lord will guide us by His Word and by His Spirit, giving us an eternal balancing point and strong foundation from which to make all of the other decisions we will have to make in the course our lifetimes here on earth. *Decisions! Decisions!* Make God your first choice!

Do I believe it?
And if I do, what am I going to do about it?

Lord, please let me hear your voice, your love, your wisdom, your grace and truth.

LIGHTEN UP!

A happy heart makes the face cheerful,
but heartache crushes the spirit.
Proverbs 15:13

We need to lighten up a bit! God wants to shine His light in us and through us spiritually and physically!

I know there is heartache in our world, in our own personal lives and in each one of us personally – in some way, to some extent. Some of the heartache we experience is absolutely overwhelming and life-crushing. Some of the heartache is unavoidable and inescapable – as it comes at us by the cruelty of others, or by the death of our loved ones, or by the havoc wreaked by natural disasters. Some of the heartache comes directly as a consequence of our own personal decisions, words and actions. All of this heartache is unwanted. Yet, this is what comes from the truth that we are living in a broken and imperfect world. This is what comes from living as a broken and imperfect person.

But heartache does not have to rule us! Jesus offers us His peace and declares that He has overcome the world! Jesus has overcome – by His love, by His sacrifice, by His resurrection – all the power of everything that would crush our peace and break our hearts.

"I have told you these things so that in me you may have peace.
In this world you will have trouble. But take heart! I have overcome the world."
John 16:33

Our God is with us. Always.
Our God loves us. Unfailingly.
Our God pours the fruit of His Spirit into our lives with its power to heal every heartache that comes against us. And as we feed on the fruit the Spirit provides, we will have more power to walk away from every temptation that would cause heartache to ourselves and to the other people in our lives.

The fruit of the Spirit is love, joy, peace, patience, kindness, goodness,
faithfulness, gentleness and self-control. Against such things there is no law.
...Since we live by the Spirit, let us keep in step with the Spirit.
Galatians 5:22-23,25

We need to lighten up a bit! We need to let all of the Spirit's fruit fill our hearts to overflowing. Filling our hearts so much that our faces cannot help but be happy. We need to let all of the Spirit's fruit flow so freely through us to others, that they cannot keep themselves from smiling. And, if only for just a few moments, the heartache that would crush our spirits has been crushed by the light in our eyes and the smiles on our faces! And in those few moments, God's love and joy and peace have, once again, declared the truth that Jesus has overcome the world! Because of all that Jesus has done on our behalf, let's be who He declares us to be – in our lives, in our attitudes, and even on our faces!

"You are the light of the world."
Matthew 5:14

So, let's lighten up!

Reflections – Responses – Challenges – Encouragements – God-breathing Thoughts

Do I believe it?
And if I do, what am I going to do about it?

Lord, please let me hear your voice, your love, your wisdom, your grace and truth.

October 27

SO, WHATCHA TALKIN' 'BOUT?

Have you ever entered into a conversation late and asked or, at least, wondered inside your curious head, "So, whatcha talkin' 'bout?" Have you ever had anyone else enter late into a conversation you were having with others, and you were asked, "So, whatcha talkin' 'bout?"

Did those you asked hesitate to let you in on their conversation? Did you hesitate to let others in on what you were saying? There can be many good and right reasons for those hesitations. Maybe it truly was a private conversation between the speakers. Maybe the one who asked was either too young or ill-equipped to handle the depth or serious nature of the conversation. Maybe the conversation was a sweet and intimate exchange between a husband and wife, meant only to be shared with each other.

But maybe the hesitations were because of what or who was being talked about, and the way they were being talked about was inappropriate and immoral. Maybe the hesitations were because the direction the conversation was taking was just plain wrong, filled with self-righteous judgment, cruel criticism or destructive, ego-fed gossip.

As followers of Christ, our God has much to say about how and what we should talk about, and what our tongue, our mouth – our words – should be like.

> *My tongue will proclaim your righteousness,*
> *your praises all day long.*
> Psalm 35:28

> *Do not let any unwholesome talk come out of your mouths,*
> *but only what is helpful for building others up according to their needs...*
> Ephesians 4:29

> *The mouth of the righteous is a fountain of life...*
> Proverbs 10:11

God is righteous. God is good. God is loving and present, sovereign and intimate. God is holy and faithful. There is so much to say about the One who has given us life. There is so much to say about the One who has saved our lives through the death and resurrection of Jesus. There is so much to say about the One who transforms our lives by His love. There is so much to say about our God – and to say it with so much thankfulness in our hearts, minds and words!

May God quiet all of our tongues (Or shut them down completely!) whenever anger or self-pity, judgment or selfishness come from our mouths or typing fingers. May God, instead, direct and use our mouths and our typing fingers (in emails, devotionals, texts, social media and books) to speak more and more of God's love and God's righteousness. May our God direct and transform all of our mouths to be fountains of life in the lives of others. May our words more greatly nurture and nourish, strengthen and heal, encourage and bring peace, offer refreshment and hope, kindness and forgiveness, grace and truth, wisdom and life to all with whom we speak.

If we will let God help us do all this, the next time we're asked, "So, whatcha talkin' 'bout?" we'll happily and thankfully bring others into our conversations!

Do I believe it?
And if I do, what am I going to do about it?

Lord, please let me hear your voice, your love, your wisdom, your grace and truth.

SITTING AT GOD'S FEET AND RESTING IN GOD'S ARMS

Truly my soul finds rest in God...
Psalm 62:1

My soul, my mind, my whole body truly find their fullest, refreshing rest only in my God.

There in the quiet, that I so desperately need, alone with God in a quiet space – setting everything down and sitting down at God's feet and resting in His arms, I am able to let God's Spirit, God's Word, love and peace be my only focus. Everything else that would pull me and push me, distract me and disillusion me is put in God's care as I let Him care for me.

There in the quiet, everything is put into focus through God's greater, eternal perspective. My soul, my mind and my whole body all acknowledge that I am frail, flawed and finite – and still a precious child of my God and my King. There in the quiet, I am safe to come honestly and humbly, stumbly and bumbly, with all my limitations before my God who knows me and loves me with no limits at all.

There in the quiet, that I so desperately need, sitting at God's feet and resting in His arms, all the limitations of my perspective, strength, energy, abilities, knowledge and understanding, righteousness and love are gently and powerfully soothed, renewed and refreshed by God's breath and God's love, by God's grace and God's truth. Forgiveness is given. The shame of my sins is removed.

There in the quiet, as my soul, my mind and my whole body rest alone with God, I am given a glimpse of eternity – a glimpse of the hope of heaven. There as I rest with my Abba, God's unfailing love is poured out to me in ways and measure beyond my comprehension. God's transcending peace lifts me out of all my earthly limitations and brokenness.

...in quietness and trust is your strength...
Isaiah 30:15

Renewed and refreshed, my soul, my mind and my whole body – all that I am – are ready and able to enter back into the realm and realities, responsibilities and relationships of my temporal life here on earth. As I do, all of my circumstances and challenges, duties and deadlines are viewed from God's greater, eternal perspective. I breathe much more deeply, I respond with truer wisdom and calm, I offer love and peace more fully and freely. I rejoice in God's good truth that I am His little girl; He is Big and I am small. I don't have to do anything on my own. I am held in God's good truth (that I know and must always remember) that my Abba is with me always and my soul, mind and body are kept safe, for all eternity, and continually renewed in His love, care and holy rest.

God's rest is so good, and so desperately needed, for my soul, my mind and my whole body. I'll return very soon to sitting at God's feet and resting in His arms...and maybe I'll stay there in the quiet a little longer.

Return to your rest, my soul, for the LORD has been good to you.
Psalm 116:7

Do I believe it?
And if I do, what am I going to do about it?

Lord, please let me hear your voice, your love, your wisdom, your grace and truth.

October 29

ALWAYS STRIVE TO DO GOOD!

You've probably heard someone say, or you've said yourself, "Okay. I'll try." Not an uncommon answer to being told (maybe asked) to do something. To that response, I have often heard the *Teller's* reply (which is sometimes my own voice), "I didn't say to *try*. I said to do it." Ouch!

> *Make sure that nobody pays back wrong for wrong,*
> *but always strive to do what is good for each other and for everyone else.*
> 1 Thessalonians 5:15

As followers of Jesus we are to be sure that we don't pay back wrong for wrong to anyone. At any time. That is mercy. That is grace. That is the way Jesus did it and does it still! We are even called to help and encourage our brothers and sisters in Christ to choose this way of mercy and grace. This way of Jesus. Returning wrong for wrong in God's eyes is just wrong.

But we are not only told to be sure that we do not act in any vengeful, self-seeking-justification kind of ways, we are also told to go well beyond that. *We are to always strive to do good.* That demands that we develop a mindset that chooses to think and listen, a mindset that chooses to not respond too quickly from our own initial (ticked-off) gut reaction whenever we are in the midst of a tense or frustrating circumstance with another person. *To always strive to do good* will require a mindset that is completely set on allowing God to lead and direct our thoughts, our words and our actions. We will need a mindset that is conformed to the mind of Christ.

> *Do not conform [any longer] to the pattern of this world,*
> *but be transformed by the renewing of your mind.*
> *Then you will be able to test and approve what God's will is*
> *– his good, pleasing and perfect will.*
> Romans 12:2

And God's will is this: that we are *to always strive to do good*. Always. This is not just the absence of doing something wrong as payback to those who have wronged us. This is not a denial of the wrong that has been done. Rather, in choosing *to always strive to do good*, we fully yield ourselves to the truth that Jesus has already taken on the full punishment – the full payback – for every wrong ever done by every one of us. As we follow Jesus closely, we will be empowered to make proactive, intentional, unselfish choices to be good. Always. God calls us *to always strive to do good* for those within our closest, most intimate circles, for those we know well, for those we know as acquaintances, for those we know only superficially and fleetingly, for those we may never see again…and for everyone else.

We are called to let the mindset of Christ – His goodness, kindness and love, His mercy and grace – move us to live in and walk like Him. Our God knows we are not yet perfect. Still, He calls us *to always strive to do good* for each other and for everyone else. And whenever our God calls us to do something, He will also give us the strength to do it!

> *I can do all things through him who gives me strength.*
> Philippians 4:13

Our God is the God of no loopholes. In our Lord Jesus and through His loving, merciful, compassionate power, we are given the strength *to always strive to do good for everyone*. So, let's do it!

Reflections – Responses – Challenges – Encouragements – God-breathing Thoughts

Do I believe it?
And if I do, what am I going to do about it?

Lord, please let me hear your voice, your love, your wisdom, your grace and truth.

KEEP PRAYING! KEEP GROWING! KEEP KNOWING!

...since the day we heard about you, we have not stopped praying for you.
We continually ask God to fill you with the knowledge of his will
through all the wisdom and understanding that the Spirit gives.
Colossians 1:9

Holy Lord, we all need You! We all need prayer. We all need to have You continually fill us – each and every one of us – with the knowledge of Your will. We need You to open us up fully – open our minds, our hearts, our ears, our thinking, our perceiving, our speaking, our acting – to receive and obediently live out all the spiritual wisdom and understanding that You desire to pour into us. All the spiritual wisdom and understanding by which You empower us to grow into the likeness of our Lord Jesus Christ with ever-increasing glory.

Holy Lord, let each of us be tender and merciful towards our brothers and sisters in Jesus whenever we see an area in which growth is needed. Let us be persistent in prayer, faithful in love, giving of encouragement and filled with grace when we need to correct (If that's Your call on us!). Holy Lord, let each of us be the Body of Christ to each other as we love, support, encourage, teach and correct our brothers and sisters, Your children, so that all of us may grow in the knowledge of Your will and in all spiritual wisdom and understanding.

Holy Lord, continually correct me, teach me, keep me growing more and more fully in the knowledge of Your will. Help me to always seek Your heart, Your mind and Your ways so that I may grow in all spiritual wisdom and understanding. Holy Lord, continually grow me and offer through me to others the love, grace and truth of Jesus. Transform me and use me to be Your light and Your voice, Your mercy and compassion to those who believe and follow You now – so that they may know You better. And, Holy Lord, let me be Your light and Your voice, Your mercy and compassion to those who are not yet believers so that they may know You too. And, then, together with all of Your children, we may grow in the knowledge of Your will and in all spiritual wisdom and understanding as we get to know You better.

I keep asking that the God of our Lord Jesus, the glorious Father,
may give you the Spirit of wisdom and revelation, so that you may know him better.
I pray that the eyes of your heart may be enlightened
in order that you may know the hope to which he has called you,
the riches of his glorious inheritance in his holy people,
and his incomparably great power for us who believe.
Ephesians 1:17-19

Oh! Our God loves us so very much! Our God has so much to give us and fill us with through His Spirit and His Word, His eternal hope and His incomparably great power!

Let us each never stop praying for others and for ourselves, asking our Holy Lord to fill us with the full knowledge of His good and perfect will and with all spiritual wisdom, understanding and revelation. Let us never stop praying that the eyes of our hearts will be enlightened so we may know the beauty and power of our Lord Jesus in intense and incredible ways. Let us never stop praying that each one of us will be continually, increasingly transformed into the likeness of Jesus! Amen and amen!

Reflections – Responses – Challenges – Encouragements – God-breathing Thoughts

Do I believe it?
And if I do, what am I going to do about it?

Lord, please let me hear your voice, your love, your wisdom, your grace and truth.

TASTE AND SEE! COME GET DRESSED!

Today many little ones, and some not so little ones, will be walking in their neighborhoods, going door-to-door seeking treats from both friends and strangers and eating lots and lots of candy. All the while they'll be dressed up in some pretty funny, scary and crazy costumes. Clothed in some rather unusual wardrobes.

Our God has something far better for us to taste than even the sweetest, most yummy candy. (Yes! Even better than dark chocolate!)

Our God has given us His living and active Word, His unfailing love and His omnipresent Spirit. And these are absolutely delicious and eternally lasting!

> *Taste and see that the LORD is good!*
> Psalm 34:8

If we would only ask our God for what He wants to give us, seek our God and His kingdom and knock on His door, we would receive more than we could have ever hoped or imagined.

> *"Ask and it will be given to you;*
> *seek and you will find;*
> *knock and the door will be opened to you."*
> Matthew 7:7

> *See what great love the Father has lavished on us,*
> *that we should be called children of God! And that is what we are!*
> 1 John 3:1

> *Grace and peace be yours in abundance*
> *through the knowledge of God and of Jesus our Lord.*
> 2 Peter 1:2

And as for dressing up, why don't we, as God's deeply loved children, choose to dress ourselves in the clothing – in the eternally beautiful and transforming wardrobe – that God has provided for each of us by the power of His Spirit and the victory of Jesus over sin and death?

> *Therefore, as God's chosen people, holy and dearly loved,*
> *clothe yourselves with compassion, kindness,*
> *humility, gentleness and patience.*
> *Bear with each other and forgive one another*
> *if any of you has a grievance against someone.*
> *Forgive as the Lord forgave you.*
> *And over all these virtues put on love,*
> *which binds them all together in perfect unity.*
> Colossians 3:12-14

Let's each taste and see that our Lord is good! Let's each get dressed in the eternally beautiful and transforming wardrobe designed for us by our Heavenly Father! In Christ, we'll never eat better or look better! Or live better!

Reflections – Responses – Challenges – Encouragements – God-breathing Thoughts

Do I believe it?
And if I do, what am I going to do about it?

Lord, please let me hear your voice, your love, your wisdom, your grace and truth.

OUR GOD IS FAITHFUL! I AM CONVINCED!

...I know whom I have believed, and am convinced that he is able to guard what I have entrusted to him for that day.
2 Timothy 1:12

What a statement of faith! It's not about trusting in who we are or in what we do or in what we have. This is all about unabashedly, unreservedly believing in the faithfulness of the One who we know! This is all about intimately knowing the One we can absolutely and eternally trust with our very lives!

This is all about a powerful love relationship with the One who is faithful forever.

The sovereign God of all creation has given the life of His One and Only Son Jesus Christ for our salvation. And God did this all out of His love for each and every one of us.

And for us who have believed in Him, our Mighty Lord has...

Rescued us from the dominion of darkness and brought us into the kingdom of the Son he loves, in whom we have redemption, the forgiveness of sins.
Colossians 1:13-14

Once our Lord Jesus has delivered us from condemnation to forgiveness, from darkness to light, there is nothing and no one, no circumstance, no challenge, no power on earth, no power from heaven, no power from hell that could ever take us out of God's love grip He has on our lives! We are God's beloved children forever. God's love is trustworthy, faithful and unfailing!

For I am convinced that neither death nor life, neither angels nor demons, neither the present nor the future, nor any powers, neither height nor depth, nor anything else in all creation, will be able to separate us from the love of God that is in Christ Jesus our Lord!
Romans 8:38-39

Our God holds us eternally and *is able to guard what we have entrusted to him.* And what is it that we as God's children should trust over to Him?
All of our lives.
All that we are in body, mind and soul.
All that we do in thought, word and action.
All that we have in every possession, every priority, every opportunity.
Every relationship we have.
Every circumstance we face.
Everything.

Our God, the One who we know and believe as our Savior and Lord, is able to guard all that we entrust to Him! "God is love" (1 John 4:16).
And love can be trusted because "love never fails" (1 Corinthians 13:8).

Our God is faithful! I am convinced!

Reflections – Responses – Challenges – Encouragements – God-breathing Thoughts

Do I believe it?
And if I do, what am I going to do about it?

Lord, please let me hear your voice, your love, your wisdom, your grace and truth.

A BOLD SUGGESTION – FULLY DEPENDENT ON JESUS

What you heard from me, keep as the pattern for sound teaching,
with faith and love in Christ Jesus.
2 Timothy 1:13

The Apostle Paul wrote this very bold suggestion to Timothy (and to others): "What you have heard from me, keep as the pattern for sound teaching..." Wow. That really is bold. Bold about the certainty of his teaching. Bold about what he had taught was worthy to be held to "as the pattern for sound teaching." This bold suggestion could sound extremely arrogant and self-righteous. But in his very next words, in his very next breath, Paul makes it clear that his teachings are completely dependent on being in unity with Christ through faith and love.

It is not because of who Paul was or what Paul did (or who we are or what we do) that gives this bold suggestion. No. It is because of who we have come to know Jesus Christ to be – the Lord's Messiah, the Son of God who revealed the fullness of the Father's eternal love for us through His life, His sacrificial death for the forgiveness of our sins and His victorious resurrection – that we have put our faith in Jesus as our Savior and Lord. It is in believing God's outrageous, unfailing love for us that we have been made children of God by faith. It is in faith that we respond to our Heavenly Father's love for us with love for Him.

It is in yielding ourselves to knowing, trusting and loving our Lord, more and more throughout our lives, that we are given the faith and love in Christ to live according to God's good ways. It is in humble and true dependence on Christ that we are given the powerful responsibility to teach others about the salvation and transformation offered in Jesus alone. How thankful I am that it is God's divine power through the knowledge of our Lord Jesus that equips us with everything we need for life and godliness! How thankful I am that it is God Himself who gives us the boldness to encourage others to follow our pattern of teaching, our pattern of living, so that Christ will be made known!

God's divine power has given us everything we need for a godly life
through our knowledge of him who called us by his own glory and goodness.
2 Peter 1:3

I need to constantly keep myself aware of how utterly and fully dependent I am on Jesus, on His Word and on His Spirit for anything and everything I teach in His Name – for anything and everything I would suggest "as the pattern for sound teaching" that anyone should keep.

This is true for all of us who are believers. With Jesus as our Savior, each one of us has been called to be an ambassador of Christ. We are all, therefore, in one way or another, teaching others what it looks like to live as a Christian through the patterns of our lives. We are teaching others, in one way or another, through our words and our actions, through our choices and our attitudes, the patterns that a follower of Jesus is meant to keep. Are they *sound teachings*?

May we each ask our God to hold us tightly in unity, in faith and in love with our Lord Jesus so that the patterns of our lives will reflect our own absolute dependence on Christ. Only then, will we be able to boldly suggest that others "keep as the pattern for sound teaching" anything they have heard or seen or learned from us. Only then, will it all be for the glory of our good God!

Reflections – Responses – Challenges – Encouragements – God-breathing Thoughts

Do I believe it?
And if I do, what am I going to do about it?

Lord, please let me hear your voice, your love, your wisdom, your grace and truth.

GOD'S PATHWAY TO STRENGTH AND MIGHTY POWER

Be strong in the Lord and in his mighty power.
Ephesians 6:10

Only in God's strength and mighty power can we truly be strong. Only in God's strength and mighty power can we conquer the situations in our lives that would twist our minds, destroy our peace and wreak havoc in our relationships with God and with others.

Only in God's strength and mighty power, made known to us by His love, Word and Spirit, are we able to live the lives God intends for us to live. Only in God's strength and mighty power are we able to face the most difficult, challenging and painful experiences of our lives with hope, peace and courage. Only in God's strength and mighty power are we able to face the most mundane and monotonous days of our lives with purpose, joy and thanksgiving.

The truth is: We are just as desperate for and dependent on God's strength and mighty power to hold us, empower us and encourage us every day of our lives. No matter what our days may bring. We are no more desperate for or dependent on God's strength and mighty power when our lives seem to be in the midst of absolute madness and chaos than we are when our lives seem to be going sweetly with some semblance of order and ease.

Our God never changes. Neither does our need for God's strength and mighty power. And the pathway for receiving these never changes either. It is never about us "bucking up" in our own strength or in our own power. No. It is always about becoming "a bucket" to receive what we so desperately need from our God. The pathway through which God's strength and mighty power are released into our lives is always through humility before our God, trust in our God, and obedience in doing things God's way.

This is the same pathway Jesus walked. A pathway marked by extravagant humility, absolute trust and sacrificial obedience before His Heavenly Father. It is this pathway that brought Jesus to walk among us here on earth, to walk to His death on the cross and to walk out of that grave as the strong and mighty King of glory!

Who is this King of glory?
The LORD strong and mighty, the LORD mighty in battle.
Psalm 24:8

It was in humility, trust and obedience to His Father that Jesus looked beyond His suffering and the fierce and brutal battle He had to fight against sin and death on our behalf. And in the humility, trust and obedience of Jesus, we are called to keep...

...fixing our eyes on Jesus, [the author] the pioneer and perfecter of faith.
For the joy set before him he endured the cross, scorning its shame,
and sat down at the right hand of the throne of God.
Hebrews 12:2

The victorious strength and mighty power of our God are fully available to each of us every day of our lives. We need only to walk on the pathway Jesus forged for us by His humility, trust and obedience!

Reflections – Responses – Challenges – Encouragements – God-breathing Thoughts

Do I believe it?
And if I do, what am I going to do about it?

Lord, please let me hear your voice, your love, your wisdom, your grace and truth.

GOVERNING GOD'S WAY

This is the time of year when many of us in the United States will be making decisions and casting our ballots to vote for our elected officials. The men and women who are the victors of the vote will then be entrusted with the responsibility of governing over us – in some way, to some extent. Some will govern at the local level. Others will govern at the state level. And still others will govern at the national level. A wise and right response for us as believers, whether the people we voted for won or lost the elections, is to pray for all those who hold positions of influence and power as they govern us.

Not many of us as everyday people, non-government employees, are necessarily governing anyone. Or are we? At least in some way? To some extent? At some level?

Think about who is affected by the decisions you make.
Who is guided by the actions you take?
Who takes your words to heart?
Who takes your opinions seriously?
Who is it that you influence – in big ways or small ways, intentionally or unintentionally?

Whether you are an official government representative or not, we all govern in one way or another. We govern whenever we influence others by our decisions, actions, words and opinions. In one way or another, whenever we hold some measure of power to sway the way other people decide, act, speak and perceive, we govern. Those people who we *govern* – who we influence in any way – are our spouses, our children, our grandchildren, other family members (near or far, young or old), our friends, our co-workers, our superiors, our subordinates, our clients, our customers, our students, our teachers, our fellow believers and not-yet-believers, and on and on and on. And a wise and right response for us as believers is to pray for ourselves – praying, as did King Solomon, that our Sovereign God would give us what we most need in order to use our influence and power over others.

> *"Give your servant a discerning heart to govern your people*
> *and distinguish between right and wrong."*
> 1 Kings 3:9

Are we *governing* – are we using our influence and power in the lives of others – with a discerning heart? Do we seek God's wisdom? Do we ask God to lead us with His depth of understanding and clarity of perception, for the people and the circumstances involved, as we use our influence and power in the life of another? Do we seek God's discerning heart – His heart flowing with love, mercy, compassion, wisdom, righteousness, grace and truth – to lead our hearts, our mouths, our actions and our interactions as we influence other people in any way?

If we don't do this, or at least not often enough, a wise and right response for us as believers is to pray that we will! And, just as God did for Solomon, I'm pretty certain our God will answer these particular prayers. Our God loves to answer every prayer that will transform us and make us more like Him in any and every loving, wise and right way!

Reflections – Responses – Challenges – Encouragements – God-breathing Thoughts

Do I believe it?
And if I do, what am I going to do about it?

Lord, please let me hear your voice, your love, your wisdom, your grace and truth.

UNSWERVING HOPE! FAITHFUL GOD!

Have you ever been in a car where suddenly you are swerving out of control? Maybe you drove onto an unavoidable oil patch or a sheet of ice. Maybe your car started hydroplaning during a heavy downpour. Maybe you were hit by someone else who was driving out of control. Maybe you swerved out of control because you just weren't looking where you were going; your attention was elsewhere.

Our faith walk can be a lot like driving a car. It requires our constant, intentional attention because there will always be some kind of unexpected or unwanted circumstance that suddenly shows up on our path. Circumstances, events, people and consequences that we didn't want. Maybe our faith walk gets pushed off its path by an illness or accident that takes a cruel toll on us or someone we love. Maybe a precious family member or a close friend died - and it's hard to see the way through our tears. Maybe our faith walk gets turned upside down by someone who hurts us or angers us, disappoints us or shocks us, betrays us or lies to us. Their attitudes, words and behaviors are out of control - from uncaring to cruel, from dismissive to dangerous. They have no love for us. No respect for us. No time for us.

Maybe our faith walk took an out of control swerve, or a way-out-of-God's-way detour, because we allowed ourselves to become too distracted, or too complacent, about purposefully and passionately following Jesus as our Lord. We got too busy, too big. We allowed other things, other people, other desires, other activities and other priorities mark out the paths of our lives.

Maybe we're not even sure how to return to living out our faith – how to return to living out our love for Jesus.

We each need to remember that it is our Holy God who came to us first to give us the fullness of His love through our Lord Jesus Christ. And our God has never left us. He never will. Seek God's heart. Seek God's path. Our God is faithful and will show us where and how to go.

"I am the way and the truth and the life."
John 14:6

Whether you turn to the right or to the left,
your ears will hear a voice behind you,
saying, "This is the way; walk in it."
Isaiah 30:21

Let us hold unswervingly to the hope we profess,
for he who promised is faithful.
Hebrews 10:23

You may have taken a detour or swerved out of control. But! You have never gone so far that our loving God cannot reach you. Let God speak to your soul – with His love for you, with His truth that sets you free, with His life given for you, with His eternal, holy and hope-filled way.

May we each choose, moment by moment, to hold unswervingly to the hope we profess and to trust in our God who is always faithful to His promises! May we each hold onto our God who holds onto us unswervingly and constantly in His loving and everlasting arms!

Reflections – Responses – Challenges – Encouragements – God-breathing Thoughts

Do I believe it?
And if I do, what am I going to do about it?

Lord, please let me hear your voice, your love, your wisdom, your grace and truth.

THE GATE, THE WATCHMAN AND THE SHEPHERD
Part 1 – reflections on John 10:1-18

Our Lord Jesus is Immanuel – God with us. And this passage from John 10:1-18 speaks so strongly of Christ's presence with us and passion and love for us. Twice He emphatically states, "Very truly I tell you..." Throughout this passage, Jesus speaks with righteous authority and passionate words of warning and protection for us. Jesus wants all of us who would follow Him, all of us who are His sheep, to know the truth about the lies and dangers that come at us, attempting to keep us away, or pull us away, from Him. Jesus knows far better than we how very high the stakes are. They are for our very lives. And Jesus knew He would be giving up His own life to save us – now and for all eternity. More than anything, Jesus wants us to know the truth about who He is and how much He loves us.

> *"Very truly I tell you Pharisees, anyone who does not enter the sheep pen by the gate, but climbs in by some other way, is a thief and a robber. The one who enters by the gate is the shepherd of his sheep."*
> John 10:1-2

By this point in His ministry, Jesus had deeply shaken some of the religious leaders' confidence in their own self-righteous ways and measured lives of piously following the letter of the law, though not embracing the heart of God's law. Many of these religious leaders were jealous as people turned to Jesus as Rabbi – as teacher of God's word and ways – rather than following their instructions, religious practices and authority for teaching *all things godly*.

Many of Jesus' listeners had witnessed His humble yet authoritative presence and teachings, His miracles of healing, casting out of demons and feeding thousands of people. Those listening to Jesus were probably aware of His claims to be Messiah, to be the Son of Man, to be the Son of God, even calling the Almighty and Sovereign Lord His Father. Many had heard Jesus boldly and gently forgive sins. An audacious act of mercy and authority reserved for the Almighty and Sovereign God alone.

Jesus makes it clear that He is telling us the truth! The truth that there is a world of difference – a life of difference – between Him and all others who want us to follow them. Jesus warns us passionately and persistently that any person or doctrine, any teaching or religious practice that does not line up with God's holy truth that salvation comes through *the one who enters through the gate* – through Jesus alone – is nothing more than a thief and a robber. It would be a dangerous and deadly move for us to entrust our lives to such a person or doctrine.

We are to be on guard against any and all who come to teach us – to gather us as his or her sheep – and yet profess anything other than Jesus Christ as the only way to eternal life. It is not by good works that we receive the gift of eternal life. It is not by strict adherence to even the most pious, holy, righteous and good religious practices that we receive the gift of eternal life. It is not by working out some good karma so that we will be aptly rewarded in a future life.

Only through Jesus are salvation, eternal life, eternal peace and being in the eternal, loving presence of the Lord Most High possible! If we are putting our faith in any other teachers, doctrines or practices, or our own goodness, we are trusting in thieves, robbers, liars and killers. Jesus Christ is God with us – *the one who enters through the gate*. And Jesus alone is the One who enters into our lives with the fullness of God's grace and truth and life!

Do I believe it?
And if I do, what am I going to do about it?

Lord, please let me hear your voice, your love, your wisdom, your grace and truth.

THE GATE, THE GATEKEEPER AND THE SHEPHERD
Part 2 – reflections on John 10:1-18

"The gatekeeper opens the gate for him [the true shepherd],
and the sheep listen to his voice. He calls his own sheep by name and leads them out.
When he has brought out all his own, he goes on ahead of them, and his sheep follow him
because they know his voice. But they will never follow a stranger; in fact, they will run
away from him because they do not recognize a stranger's voice."
John 10:3-5

We who have accepted Jesus Christ as our Savior, we who have put our faith in Jesus as Lord, are called and known as His sheep. We have been brought into a loving and intimate relationship with our God. He knows each of us by name. We are His and He is ours. Our Shepherd leads us and we follow – knowing Him and knowing His voice. Knowing His words and His ways. We follow in trust.

We are also called, and are to be known as, the Shepherd's gatekeeper. Each one of us.

As God's gatekeepers, we are to be able to readily recognize our Shepherd Jesus Christ. Recognize His presence, His Spirit and His truths so that we will fully open the gates of our hearts and lives to Him, to His love, to His leading and to His authority.

As God's gatekeepers, we are to know His eternal truths so that we may discern what is truly from Jesus and what is not. As God's gatekeepers, we are to be able to discern the loving, life-giving, transforming truths that come from Jesus alone so that we will recognize and separate out all things – thoughts, words, practices and doctrines – that are ugly lies or the twisted truths. No matter how subtle or blatant these may be. We are to be on watch against everything that comes at us from the thief, robber, liar and killer of our souls.

And as God's gatekeepers, we are not just on watch for ourselves. We are also to be on guard to open the gate only to Jesus and His truths so that those who are already His sheep – our brothers and sisters in the Body of Christ – will know His voice even better and follow Him more closely. As God's gatekeepers, watching out for each other, we will be on guard and more fully protected from being led away by any false teachers and their fruitless, lifeless, twisted teachings. As God's gatekeepers, watching out for each other, we will more tenaciously guard against all of our inclinations towards selfish, sinning ways that would lead any of us out and away from our Shepherd's intimate protection and peace. In love we are to be on watch. With grace we are to protect our brothers and sisters in Christ.

Our Shepherd comes into our lives. He comes right into the midst of our muddled-up mess to bring us into His loving care and into His true Shepherd's pen. Our Shepherd Jesus intimately calls each of us to follow Him, calling us each by name. Calling us to listen to His voice, to follow Him and to be on guard – watching out for all our brother and sister sheep – as our Lord lovingly leads us by His words and ways.

May we open the gate only to the Lord Jesus, following only Him, recognizing His voice as the voice of our true Shepherd! May God grow each of us up to be discerning, protective gatekeepers over our own hearts and lives, also watching, in love and grace, over our Shepherd's other sheep.

Reflections – Responses – Challenges – Encouragements – God-breathing Thoughts

Do I believe it?
And if I do, what am I going to do about it?

Lord, please let me hear your voice, your love, your wisdom, your grace and truth.

THE GATE, THE GATEKEEPER AND THE SHEPHERD
Part 3 – reflections on John 10:1-18

*Jesus used this figure of speech, but the Pharisees did not understand
what he was telling them. Therefore Jesus said again, "Very truly I tell you,
I am the gate for the sheep.
All who have come before me were thieves and robbers,
but the sheep have not listened to them.
I am the gate; whoever enters through me will be saved.
They will come in and go out, and find pasture."*
John 10:6-9

Although this passage addresses the fact that the Pharisees didn't understand what Jesus was saying about the gate and His sheep, I'm sure there were others listening to Him who also were not comprehending the full meaning of Jesus' words. And I'm pretty certain I would have been one of these dense ones. Jesus says, once again, "Very truly I tell you" to emphasize the truth and authority with which He is speaking. We each need to listen to Him, and with the help of His "Spirit of truth" (John 16:13) we will understand!

In this passage, Jesus wants to lay down the fundamental truth of salvation. He wants to set before all of us the sole and irrefutable way of entrance into eternal life with our Holy God. Jesus Himself is the entrance. Jesus Himself is the gate. Period. Salvation and eternal life with our Holy God is completely, uniquely dependent on Jesus Christ. It is only through His sacrificial death on the cross for our sins and His glorious resurrection to life eternal that we are able to enter into the presence of the Lord Most High.

Jesus repeats His lesson, knowing how desperately we need to understand and believe all that He is *very truly* telling us. Jesus addresses the Pharisees specifically, the teachers and leaders of the religious laws, because He loves them, as He loves all people, and needs to shake them up and out of their self-righteous thinking and hypocritical practices that almost entirely exclude and dismiss the mercy of God as the only true way to forgiveness and salvation. Jesus knows this is a deadly and damning practice for any who would follow those teachings. Jesus alone is Savior. Jesus alone is the gate, the only entrance point, to eternal life with our God.

*Salvation is found in no one else,
for there is no other name under heaven given to mankind by which we must be saved.*
Acts 4:12

Jesus holds Himself open to all who would enter humbly by faith into the full mercy of our God. His sheep will do this. They will not listen to the teachings of lies. The sheep who truly belong to Jesus – those who have not followed the spiritual thieves and robbers of this world – "will come in and go out, and find pasture." His sheep "will come in" to be loved, cared for, fed and protected. His sheep "will go out" always following Him. Even into unknown and uncomfortable areas. His sheep know His voice, know His teachings and they trust His love and provision to be their "pasture." No matter what their circumstances may be.

Jesus – the gate, the shepherd, the Savior of the world – can be trusted *with* His sheep and *by* His sheep now and forever! Amen!

Do I believe it?
And if I do, what am I going to do about it?

Lord, please let me hear your voice, your love, your wisdom, your grace and truth.

THE GATE, THE GATEKEEPER AND THE SHEPHERD
Part 4 – reflections on John 10:1-18

"The thief comes only to steal and kill and destroy;
I have come that they may have life, and have it to the full."
John 10:10

The thief comes. No doubt about it. No choice about it.

The thief comes against our souls, coming against the truth of the Living God with the sole, and very definite, purpose: Only to steal and kill and destroy us. The thief has no other plan or passion except to steal our hope, kill our faith and destroy our lives. The thief comes only to steal and kill and destroy every shred of peace we have. To steal and kill and destroy every relationship we have – beginning with our relationship with the One True God, our Lord Jesus Christ – the one relationship upon which our very lives depend, now and for all eternity.

Our Lord Jesus, the Lord who has conquered sin and death, proclaims that He not only comes, but that He has already come for us. Jesus has come for us to offer us true life, full life. The thief gives us no choice about what he will do in, and to, our lives. Yet, the Lord Jesus will not force Himself on us. Instead, Jesus offers Himself and His life to us.

Jesus tells us that in Him we *may* have life. It is up to us to make the choice as to whether or not we will put our lives in His hands. Into His good and holy hands that were nailed to the cross for the forgiveness of sins. Into His good and holy hands that were raised in eternal, magnificent triumph through His resurrection from the dead! Jesus Christ offers us life – life without the certain condemnation and punishment for our sins that we deserve, which He took upon Himself. Jesus has already come to set us free and to offer us fullness of life.

We have a choice to make. We *may* have life in Jesus – a life that holds the absolute promise of eternal life. A life that holds the absolute richness and abundance of the fullness of life that we *may* have only when we choose to live our lives in the grasp of Christ's intimate love as our Savior and Lord. Jesus has already come to give us a full life beyond what we could ever imagine, both for an eternity with Him and for right now as we walk with Him daily, listening to His heart of love for us, obeying His word and letting Him lead us in everything we do.

Having life to the full in Jesus does not, and will not, protect us from hardships and hurts on this side of heaven. To believe that would be a lie from the thief who comes only to steal and kill and destroy our lives – our minds, our bodies, our souls and our trust in God. Life to the full in Jesus means that we are fully loved by our Heavenly Abba, fully held in the presence of God at all times, fully filled with His promised Holy Spirit, fully made new in God's sight, fully given access to God's throne of grace, fully offered transcending peace in all circumstances, fully assured that there is nothing and no one in all creation that will ever be able to separate us from the love of God that is in Christ Jesus our Lord.

This full life that Jesus offers is a life filled with God's unfailing love, grace, truth, forgiveness, resurrection power, freedom, peace, wisdom, courage, joy, hope and great eternal purpose! And there is nothing and no one who could ever steal or kill or destroy what Jesus gives to us. May we each enter into the full life we *may* have – the full life Jesus offers to each of us and for which He has already come!

Reflections – Responses – Challenges – Encouragements – God-breathing Thoughts

Do I believe it?
And if I do, what am I going to do about it?

Lord, please let me hear your voice, your love, your wisdom, your grace and truth.

THE GATE, THE GATEKEEPER AND THE SHEPHERD
Part 5 – reflections on John 10:1-18

"I am the good shepherd. The good shepherd lays down his life for the sheep.
The hired hand is not the shepherd and does not own the sheep.
So when he sees the wolf coming, he abandons the sheep and runs away.
Then the wolf attacks the flock and scatters it.
The man runs away because he is a hired hand and cares nothing for the sheep.
I am the good shepherd; I know my sheep and my sheep know me – just as the Father
knows me and I know the Father – and I lay down my life for the sheep."
John 10:11-15

It's not that the hired hand is essentially bad that causes him to run away. He's just not the Good Shepherd. The sheep don't belong to the hired hand. The sheep belong to the Good Shepherd. And the hired hand may be doing a fine job of protecting and directing the sheep, at least until real danger – or real pressure or real temptations – come at him. In the end, the hired hand is just that, a hired hand with no real ownership and no real commitment to the sheep. The hired hand is human, caring more about himself than the sheep. And he will choose to run away from the danger, run away from the pressure or run head on into fulfilling the desires of his temptations. And the flock is attacked. And the flock is scattered.

Our Lord Jesus, the Good Shepherd, is the one who owns the sheep. He is the one who owns our lives, yet gave His own life for ours. It is Jesus alone who willingly laid down His life for us. To protect us. To save us. To rescue us from certain destruction. To give us eternal life. It is only our God who loves us in such an outrageous, unchanging, unselfish, unexpected, sacrificial and victorious way. No human – no hired hand – loves us, cares for us and protects us as does our God. No matter how good those humans may be. Not our moms or dads, not our husbands or wives, not our children, not our friends, not our pastors or our faith-teachers.

Everyone, except our Good Shepherd Jesus, will fail us in some way at some time. Everyone else will hurt us, disappoint us and abandon us in some way at some level – in order to save themselves or to fulfill their own self-centered, sinful desires. Both of these motivations will in some way, at some time, at some level take priority for all those humans, those hired hands, who we trust to love us, care for us and protect us – physically or emotionally or relationally or spiritually. Because we don't belong to them. We belong only to our God.

I have failed all those I truly do love, in different ways at different times at different levels. They, like I, must put the ultimate trust for our lives – for love, for care and for protection – now and eternally, only into the good and holy hands of Jesus Christ, our Good Shepherd.

Anything else that we would put our trust in to take care of us and protect us – our wealth, our health, our jobs, our intellect, our education, our reputation, our charm, our fame, our wisdom, our will power – can never give the security that only Jesus is able to give. Jesus offers what we truly need – a life-giving relationship with Him, our Good Shepherd who gave His life for us.

As His sheep, we know Jesus, just as He and the Father know each other. Within these eternally intimate, loving and *knowing* relationships, we can trust with all certainty that Jesus, our Good Shepherd, passionately and fiercely loves us, cares for us and protects us – from the wolves (the thieves) that would attack and the hired hands that would abandon us.

Reflections – Responses – Challenges – Encouragements – God-breathing Thoughts

Do I believe it?
And if I do, what am I going to do about it?

Lord, please let me hear your voice, your love, your wisdom, your grace and truth.

THE GATE, THE GATEKEEPER AND THE SHEPHERD
Part 6 – reflections on John 10:1-18

"I have other sheep that are not of this sheep pen. I must bring them also.
They too will listen to my voice, and there shall be one flock and one shepherd."
John 10:16

The God and Father of our Lord Jesus Christ sent Him – as the promised Messiah and Savior declared throughout Scripture – first to His sheep, the Jews. But! God's salvation was never intended for the Jews alone, but for all non-Jews, for all Gentiles. These are God's sheep *that are not of this Jewish pen.*

It is the power of God that brings salvation to everyone who believes:
first to the Jew, then to the Gentile.
Romans 1:16

All of creation belongs to the Lord. All of the peoples of this earth – from every tribe, from every language, from every nation – belong to the Lord. And God reaches out in His love, reaches out to all, with the truth of His eternal gospel.

Then I saw another angel flying in midair, and he had the eternal gospel to proclaim
to those who live on the earth—to every nation, tribe, language and people.
Revelation 14:6

The eternal gospel declares that the full price for the redemption and salvation of every person has been fully paid through the sacrificial death of Jesus Christ, the one and only Son of God. And the full assurance of eternal life with our Holy God has been fully promised through the conquering resurrection of Jesus Christ. There is only one shepherd over all creation, over all peoples – whether Jew or Gentile. There is only one Messiah, one Lamb of God – our Lord Jesus Christ who gave His life for all.

And [in heaven] they sang a new song, saying:
"You are worthy...because you were slain,
and with your blood you purchased for God persons
from every tribe and language and people and nation."
Revelation 5:9

And Jesus Christ will bring in all of His sheep. Jesus *must* bring them in because He is the only one who can – He alone is the faithful, eternal God of all! And His sheep, "in Jerusalem, and in all Judea and Samaria, and to the ends of the earth" (Acts 1:8) will hear His voice and be told the truth that Jesus Christ is Lord!

His sheep will listen to His voice. His sheep will believe. His sheep will be saved. And the sheep – wherever they live, whoever they are, whatever their tribe or language or nation or people – will join as one flock in unity, love and victory with the Lord Jesus Christ as the one true shepherd of all for all eternity!

Do I believe it?
And if I do, what am I going to do about it?

Lord, please let me hear your voice, your love, your wisdom, your grace and truth.

THE GATE, THE GATEKEEPER AND THE SHEPHERD
Part 7 – reflections on John 10:1-18

"The reason my Father loves me is that I lay down my life – only to take it up again.
No one takes it from me, but I lay it down of my own accord.
I have authority to lay it down and authority to take it up again.
This command I received from my Father."
John 10:17-18

Jesus Christ, in His intimate oneness and love relationship with the Father, knows that the love between them is based, is *reasoned*, on an absolute trust in each other and an absolute willingness of the Son to follow and obey whatever is the Father's will. No matter what the cost. Because this love they share is inexplicably more perfect, more transcendent and more eternal than my imagination can even begin to grasp. Jesus fully and humbly obeys His Father, laying down His life. And Jesus fully and victoriously obeys His Father, taking His life up again!

It is the passionate love of the Father that commands Jesus, His beloved Son, to do this. It is the passionate love of the Father for His lost and dying sheep that commands the death and the resurrection of His one and only Son, so that unity will be restored and reconciled between mankind and the holy, righteous God, the Lord of all creation.

Here we get a glimpse of the holy, inseparable unity of Father and Son as the One True God. Even as Jesus obeys *the command He received from His Father*, He also declares that he *has the authority to lay down His life and the authority to take it up again*. In these words Jesus declares Himself as one with the Father – in both sovereign authority and amazing, sacrificial love for His lost and dying sheep. A mind-altering, perception-changing, paradigm shift for all who would grasp the words Jesus speaks. Jesus, the Son, is God in human form. Separate, yet in complete unity with the Father's eternal authority and love.

The Son is the image of the invisible God, the firstborn over all creation. For in him all
things were created: things in heaven and on earth, visible and invisible, whether thrones
or powers or rulers or authorities; all things have been created through him and for him.
He is before all things, and in him all things hold together. And he is the head of the body,
the church; he is the beginning and the firstborn from among the dead,
so that in everything he might have the supremacy.
For God was pleased to have all his fullness dwell in Jesus,
and through him to reconcile all things, whether things on earth or things in heaven,
by making peace through his blood, shed on the cross.
Colossians 1:15-20

The Father's full love for His Son always was, is and will be unconditional and intimate beyond comprehension. The Father and the Son are one. Yet, it is through the interweaving of the Son's obedience to the Father's command – through the outrageous sacrifice Jesus made and the ultimate victory Jesus accomplished – that the love relationship between the Father and the Son, and their love for us, is magnificently revealed. And we, the sheep of the Lord Most High, are the benefactors of this benevolent, unconditional, intimate and eternal love.

May we, like our Lord Jesus Christ, choose full obedience to our Father's commands and know His love ever more intimately, passionately and powerfully in our own lives! Amen!

Do I believe it?
And if I do, what am I going to do about it?

Lord, please let me hear your voice, your love, your wisdom, your grace and truth.

SPIRIT SPURRED!

Let us consider how we may spur one another on toward love and good deeds.
Hebrews 10:24

There may just be far too many times that we realize, and need to admit, that we *spur* – poke, prod and push – others around us, in big ways and small ways, in intentional and unintentional ways, *on toward* annoyance, frustration, anger, sadness or silence by our own self-focused and self-centered, thoughtless and inconsiderate words and ways. And sadly, we'll too often consider ourselves justified, because of the words and ways of others, when we do this.

Well! Our God calls us to *consider*, actively and intentionally, doing something very differently within the Body of Christ.

As followers of Christ we are to help build up, not tear down, the Body. We are to help increase the light of Christ that shines among us as believers and through us to the world. Our God calls us to consider how we are to use our own lives, our own examples, our words and our actions to help spur – poke, prod, push – and encourage our brothers and sisters in Christ on toward attitudes and actions of love and good deeds.

Since this is the call for each member of the Body of Christ, then you and I also must consider that God is very likely using some of His other children to keep spurring us on toward attitudes and actions of love and good deeds – even today. The Body is to help build up the Body. Even if we're the ones that need the building up or a major reconstruction job!

This can only happen when each of us allows the Spirit of the Living Christ to spur us on to be more like Jesus in very real ways. Ways that are both visible and invisible to the people in our lives.

As we let God do this within us, actively and intentionally, our God will put us in circumstances and relationships where we can help spur, help encourage, our brothers and sisters to be more like Jesus. And as we each are spurred by the Spirit to be transformed into His likeness, we will be living, more actively and intentionally, in love and doing good deeds within the Body of Christ and within the world.

So, let us consider…

What do you need to let God transform within you so that the way you spur others on will only reflect the spurring of God's Spirit of love and goodness within you and through you?
In what ways has God been spurring you on toward love and good deeds through the words, actions and examples of others?

Who are the ones that need assurance of God's love and your love today?
Who needs to be the recipient of good deeds – deeds that are within your power to do?
Who needs to sense God's presence, mercy, grace, forgiveness, kindness, justice, generosity, gentleness, peace, joy or encouragement from you and through you today?

May we each invite the Spirit of our Lord Jesus to spur us on toward love and good deeds in all we are and in all we do – today and every day. And in Christ's love, with His grace and truth, may we do the good deed of spurring others on toward doing the same!

Reflections – Responses – Challenges – Encouragements – God-breathing Thoughts

Do I believe it?
And if I do, what am I going to do about it?

Lord, please let me hear your voice, your love, your wisdom, your grace and truth.

BEAUTIFUL IN GOD'S SIGHT – A GLIMPSE OF GOD'S GREATNESS

Your beauty should not come from outward adornment,
such as elaborate hairstyles and the wearing of gold jewelry or fine clothes.
Rather, it should be that of your inner self,
the unfading beauty of a gentle and quiet spirit,
which is of great worth in God's sight.
1 Peter 3:3-4

Our God is not telling women, or men for that matter, not to take care of our outward beauty. Our God made us with a heart that seeks and enjoys beauty and loves to be beautiful or handsome or good-looking (Whatever that word is for you!). This inner wiring in us is reflective of our God's heart and mind – reflective of the truth that each of us is made in the image and likeness of our God. God takes great pleasure in creating and displaying beauty. Just look around you at the wonders of nature – from the tiniest of flowers to the majesty of the greatest mountains to the unfathomable depth of the seas to the incomprehensible expanse of the stars and galaxies that make up our universe.

Our God is the designer and revealer of amazing, stunning and breathtaking beauty that moves us to get a glimpse of His majesty and greatness. That is exactly what our own beauty should be all about. Our beauty should give all others with whom we interact in any way at any time, a glimpse of the greatness of our beautiful God. Even if they never actually see us.

Wanting to look good on the outside and taking care of our appearance – whether with exercise or accessories – are not bad in and of themselves in any way at any time. But, they just don't, nor can they ever, add any value in any way, now or in the grand scheme of eternity, to our true beauty – to how beautiful we truly are as men and men of God.

When it comes to our own beauty, God wants to encourage each of us to keep as our deepest concern and first priority: that people will see – in us, from us and through us – the true and transforming beauty that comes only from an intimate relationship with our Lord Jesus Christ. Our beauty, and confidence in our beauty, should flow from – and touch others with – the beautiful, eternal knowledge that we are loved unconditionally by the Lord Most High.

And as our true beauty – our inner self – is transformed more and more into the beautiful image and likeness of Jesus, there will be a grounding and a deepening of our souls, expressed and revealed in a gentle and quiet spirit that trusts our God in and for all things. As men and women, as followers of Jesus, we will increasingly exude a beauty that comes from the confidence of who we are in Him – without any need to be perfectly coiffed, amazingly buff or fashionably clothed. By the Spirit of Christ shaping our beauty, we will have no need to be aggressive or showy or loud or point attention to ourselves. Our beauty will point instead to the eternal and majestic beauty of the Lord. And all those around us will get a glimpse of our God's great beauty.

In quietness and gentleness of spirit Jesus came to us. In confidence of who He was and the value of His life, Jesus fully trusted His God and Father to fully reveal His eternal beauty as the Son of the Lord Most High. And our God did this through His unfailing love and sovereign power. God's greatness and God's beauty are inseparable.

May each of us – men and women alike – fully trust our God for who we are, for the value of our lives and for the beauty that fills us as children of the Living God. May our Lord use each of one us, with the beautiful Spirit of Jesus within us, to give all others around us a glimpse of God's greatness and beauty!

Do I believe it?
And if I do, what am I going to do about it?

Lord, please let me hear your voice, your love, your wisdom, your grace and truth.

O LORD, LET US BE WISE!

Let the one who is wise heed these things
and ponder the loving deeds of the LORD.
Psalm 107:43

The author of this psalm asks us the readers – the people of God, the worshipers, the hearers, the singers – to *heed* the Lord's words and ways and to *ponder* the loving deeds of the Lord.

Heeding these things would prove us wise. The entire psalm is encouraging us to praise the Lord our God for His incredible, unfailing love to us who call out to Him and trust Him. To acknowledge, and thank our Lord for the truth, that it is out of His great love for us that He hears and He answers our prayers. It is out of our Lord's great love for us, and by His loving deeds worked on our behalf, that we are saved from our foes, rescued out of disaster and set free from oppression. And these things we should ponder.

It is wise to heed God's words. It is wise for us as God's people to heed the Lord's call for righteousness in the way we live our lives. It is wise to place our full trust in our Lord alone.

It is wise to ponder the loving deeds of our Lord. It is wise for us as God's people to give thanks and acknowledge and ponder who our Lord is and what our Lord has done for us. It is wise to remember, celebrate and ponder all of God's saving, rescuing, *loving-deed-doing* ways in each of our lives.

Heeding the Lord's words, following and obeying His ways, brings us into a more intimate walk with our Lord, giving us assurance of His sovereign and loving presence to our souls.

Yet, there have been far too many times in my life when I have foolishly chosen not to heed and follow the Lord. And I know there will be far too many more times (Darn it!) when I will choose to heed my own thoughts and ways rather than following and trusting my Lord. And in those times, I am left feeling foolish. And alone. Knowing I know better. Knowing God only wants the best for me. Knowing that heeding the Lord's ways is always His very best for me. How foolish I can be.

Pondering the loving deeds of our Lord, meditating on and calling to mind the loving ways He has worked in our lives, comforts and strengthens us, bringing peace and joy to our souls.

Yet, there have been too many times in my life when I have chosen to ponder over my problems and my predicaments rather than thinking of the truth of God's unfailing love for me and His loving deeds already done in my life. Too many times I have focused on my frustrations and my fears rather than on trusting my Lord to work out His loving deeds and good plans for my life. And I am left feeling foolish. And helpless. Knowing I know better. Knowing the Lord's love for me is more true and eternal than any of my temporal tempests. Knowing that the Lord's loving deeds will triumph in the end. And it's never the end until His love triumphs. How foolish I can be.

O Lord, let us be wise! May we each heed more fully and more quickly all of Your words and ways! May we each ponder more fully and more often all of Your loving deeds!

Reflections – Responses – Challenges – Encouragements – God-breathing Thoughts

Do I believe it?
And if I do, what am I going to do about it?

Lord, please let me hear your voice, your love, your wisdom, your grace and truth.

HELP! WHO DO YOU CALL?

Our help is in the name of the LORD,
the Maker of heaven and earth.
Psalm 124:8

Who do you call out to when you acutely feel, and honestly admit to, your need for help? Do you call your husband? Your wife? Your closest friends? Your mom? Your dad? Your siblings? Your children? Your pastor? Your church family? Your co-workers? Your neighbors?

All these people can be such good people to call. And if we have any of these precious people in our lives who we can trust to share our very real need for help and support on this side of heaven, then we are amazingly and abundantly blessed! I do not want to take my precious ones for granted. Ever. So, let's take even a moment right now to thank our God for each and every one of these people we have in our lives! Thank You, Jesus!

Yet, we also need to give thanks as we realize that there is no One who loves us like the Lord! There is no One who knows us more intimately than our Maker! There is no One who is able to be with us at every single moment of every single day in each and every one of our circumstances and situations. Our God is with us! He is able!

And our Lord wants us to call out to Him, as His children who trust Him, His love and His power to help us at all times in all the ways we need Him. Our Lord wants us to call out to Him for the help that He alone can give. Our Lord's help always comes to us out of His perfect love, out of His perfect will and His perfect and eternal perspective of all things. Our Lord's help always comes to us with our absolute best on His mind.

The Lord's help offered to us is generous beyond our imagination. The Lord's help is sure. God's love and presence, His grace and truth, His peace and hope, His strength and courage, His wisdom and power, God's Spirit and Word are always and limitlessly available to us, His beloved and eternal children.

Let's choose to call out to our Lord before (during, after and continually) we call out to anyone else - even the most precious ones with whom we share our lives and our very real need for help and support. Let's each call out to our Lord, the Maker of heaven and earth to help us...
In every circumstance.
In every bit of pressure we feel.
In every bit of fear or worry we experience.
In every pain we endure - inflicted on us by others or by ourselves.
In every loss of a loved one.
In every loss of our hopes or dreams or plans or security.
In every bit of confusion and chaos that crushes our minds, bodies, relationships and spirits.

Our help is in the name of the Lord, the Maker of heaven and earth. And it is, always and only, in the name of the Lord - our Lord Jesus Christ whose name is above all names - that all of our true and eternal, peace-giving and hope-restoring, life-saving, life-transforming and God-glorifying help comes! Thank You, Jesus, our Help and our Savior!

Do I believe it?
And if I do, what am I going to do about it?

Lord, please let me hear your voice, your love, your wisdom, your grace and truth.

UNLESS THE LORD…

Unless the LORD builds the house, its builders labor in vain.
Unless the LORD watches over the city, the guards stand watch in vain.
Psalm 127:1

Unless the Lord…
This is quite a phrase – a challenging, in-my-face phrase. And it makes me stop and think.

Unless the Lord is the builder and protector, anything and everything that I do – everything that each of us does – is actually in vain. It is all just temporal and, eventually, will prove to be completely unimportant and irrelevant, if not downright false and foolish, in the grand scheme of eternity.

Unless the Lord is the builder and protector of our lives, we live our lives in vain.

I don't want that! I want my life to count for something. Something that counts in God's eternity, even in the smallest way. Something that counts in the lives of others, even in the smallest way. Yet, there it is, challenging and in-my-face: *Unless the Lord…*it is all in vain.

And this is true for everything we do and every relationship we have. This is true for any place, any position, any perspective and any person we put our hearts, minds, energy, gifts, time, talents and finances into without the Lord being the builder and protector. Unless the Lord is the builder and protector of all that we do and every relationship that we have, they will always be desperately lacking in the eternal love, grace, truth and value that only the Lord can give.

Without the Lord being the builder and protector of our lives, of all we do and the relationships we have, we will either be experiencing a disconnect with our God at some level in our spirits or we may, even now, be well on our way towards a major demolition project. And our lives, our efforts and our relationships will need to be overhauled in small and big ways, in tangible and deep ways by our Lord – the builder and protector of all that is of eternal value.

With the Lord as the builder and protector of our lives, of all we do and the relationships we have, we will be filled with God's good assurance that nothing is in vain!

My dear brothers and sisters, stand firm. Let nothing move you.
Always give yourselves fully to the work of the Lord, because you know that your labor
[your life, your efforts, your relationships] ***in the Lord is not in vain.***
1 Corinthians 15:58

In the Lord, our lives, our efforts and our relationships will be infused with an indestructible joy, peace, purpose, hope and strength. They will be held in the love, grace, truth and eternal value with which our Lord has built them, and by which our Lord protects them.

Is the Lord the builder and protector of your life? Of all areas of your life?
Of all that you do?
Of all of your relationships?

May we each invite the Lord to be so, so that we may live in the joy of knowing that who we are and what we do is held in God's good, loving and eternal hands with great eternal value!

Reflections – Responses – Challenges – Encouragements – God-breathing Thoughts

Do I believe it?
And if I do, what am I going to do about it?

Lord, please let me hear your voice, your love, your wisdom, your grace and truth.

PLANS, PERSPECTIVE AND POWER

Sometimes, okay, really far too often, we make plans and decide to do things because we want to do what we want to do...when we want to do them...with whom we want to do them...how we want to do them...and where we want to do them! Our focus settles all on us. And we feel we have every right to make those plans and decisions for all the stuff, all the experiences, we want in our lives.

The truth is we do have a right to make decisions and plans for ourselves. God, in His perfect and passionate love for us, created each of us with the ability to make choices. God made us in His image, and although we're definitely not as bright as God, as good as God, nor as wise as God by any stretch of the imagination, we still were given the gift of thinking and perceiving and choosing to do things in our own power. We were created in the likeness of the Living God, not a puppet.

The thing we don't realize is that during those choosing times (which, of course, are numerous times each day), our focus is often self-absorbed, if not blatantly selfish. And in that mindset, the plans and decisions we make have a very limited perspective, and will never be for our very best. So, although we absolutely have a right to make those choices, they're just not usually the right choices we should make.

During those times, we become way too big and powerful. Our self-absorbed desires become way too big and powerful. We think only about what we want – not about what is truly best for us, or even truly good for us. We don't take time to consider how these choices might adversely affect our health, our peace, our character or our security. We seem to let go of, dismiss and deny, all sincere thought of what the future consequences to our choices will be. And we're certainly not thinking about anyone else in our lives (not even our nearest and dearest) who will be affected by the plans and decisions we make when we're thinking only of ourselves. It is all about us and our limited-immediate-moment.

We need to remember that our God focuses on us, too! Every moment of our lives. Yet, God's focus on us is far more loving, far more gracious and far more truthful than our own focus is. Our God has an absolute and perfect knowledge of the good plans He has for us, a right and eternal perspective of all things, and unfailing power to carry out His plans, now and forever.

> *"For I know the plans I have for you," declares the LORD,*
> *"plans to prosper you and not to harm you, plans to give you hope and a future."*
> Jeremiah 29:11

God knows the plans He has for us. We each need to take time to know, and trust, God. We need to step out of ourselves – get over ourselves – and take time to focus on what God wants for our lives. I am absolutely convinced that the plans God has for each of our lives are very good. And I believe God is always thinking about the very best for all of those around us. Our God's plans are always and only for our good. Our God's perspective is never limited. It is eternal. Our God's plans always give us hope and renew our hope in a future that is held, now and forever, by our God's eternal power.

Take time, even now, to ask God to help you to want what God wants for your life. Then, choose, consciously and deliberately, to trust God's plans, perspective and power more than your own. Starting right now.

Do I believe it?
And if I do, what am I going to do about it?

Lord, please let me hear your voice, your love, your wisdom, your grace and truth.

WHAT BRINGS US TO TEARS?

For, as I have often told you before and now tell you again even with tears,
many live as the enemies of the cross of Christ.
Philippians 3:18

Thinking of others who live as enemies of the cross of Christ brought the courageous and passionate Apostle Paul to tears.

Thinking, and writing to the believers, about the many people who live as enemies of the cross of Christ filled him with sorrow and tears. Not with rage or frustration? Not with self-righteous indignation or judgment? Not with hate or condemnation? But with tears? Yes, tears. Tears for all the lost and broken lives of people, the enemies of the cross of Christ, who would not choose to receive the love, mercy, forgiveness and salvation of Jesus Christ. Tears for all the people who allow their pride to keep them shut off from the power of humbling themselves before God. Tears for all the people who stay locked in, and blinded by, their own private hell, and wreak havoc in the lives of others here on earth. Tears for all the people who refuse to acknowledge their need for forgiveness and the sacrifice of Jesus – the sacrifice that made it possible for all of us to receive God's perfect and full forgiveness through His death on the cross. Tears for all the people who choose death instead of life. Tears for all the people who choose destruction rather than the full, free and abundant life, now and eternally, in the presence of our loving Abba, our Holy God.

Jesus wept over Jerusalem (Luke 19:41). He cried for the many lives in God's holy city who had rejected their true and holy King. He cried over their rejection of what would bring them true and eternal peace. God had come to them in human form – teaching them, healing them, feeding them, revealing Himself as their Deliverer. Jesus had come to them as the ultimate fulfillment of all prophecy for their long-awaited Messiah. Jesus had come as the fullness of God's grace and truth. Jesus had come to offer the fullness of God's love, salvation, mercy, forgiveness, redemption and eternal life. Yet, in their stubbornness and pride, they remained enemies of God. And Jesus wept for them, as I believe He weeps for all who still reject Him and the sacrifice of His life on the cross for our reconciliation with our holy God.

For God was pleased to have all his fullness dwell in Jesus, and through him
to reconcile to himself all things, whether things on earth or things in heaven,
by making peace through his blood shed on the cross.
Colossians 1:19, 20

What brings us to tears? Not to fear. Not to hatred. Not to judgment. Not to religious pride. But to sorrow?

May our God fill us with the love, concern and compassion that He has for all people. May God move us to tears for the enemies of the cross of Christ – whether we know them as our family members, our friends, our co-workers, our neighbors. May God move us beyond tears to acts of sincere, tangible and compassionate love for all who are lost and still live as enemies of the cross of Christ. May we pray for them. May we lovingly, honestly share our faith with them. May we share our own very real need for the forgiveness, salvation and eternal life that the cross of Christ has brought to us!

And may we all be brought to tears of joy as many who were once, as were we, enemies of God, come to the fullness of faith in Jesus Christ – receiving His salvation and gift of eternal life that came through the cross!

Reflections – Responses – Challenges – Encouragements – God-breathing Thoughts

Do I believe it?
And if I do, what am I going to do about it?

Lord, please let me hear your voice, your love, your wisdom, your grace and truth.

_____

_____

_____

_____

_____

_____

_____

_____

_____

_____

_____

_____

_____

_____

_____

_____

_____

_____

_____

_____

_____

_____

_____

November 20

A MUSICAL INTERLUDE – SOMETIMES, YOU JUST GOTTA SING!

Sometimes, you just gotta sing! Lately, in the midst of some very sad times and hard circumstances for some of my dearest ones, God keeps speaking and singing to me of His love, grace and truth. And I hear and sense God's words and music filling and freeing my heart, mind, body and soul with greater power than any earthly sadness could ever hold. God's music declares who He is. And God is the One who loves us more than we can possibly comprehend. God is the One who holds all creation and all eternity in His all-powerful hands. God is the One who holds us tenderly and tightly in His unfailing love and transcending peace forever – no matter what our times or circumstances are like here on earth. God is the Almighty One and He is our Heavenly Abba.

And, *sometimes, you just gotta sing* in response to God's love, grace and truth! There is great blessing for each of us – there is healing of our hearts, transforming of our minds, refreshing of our bodies and lifting of our souls – whenever we speak and sing in thanksgiving to our eternal, faithful, righteous, loving Lord. So, today, I invite and encourage each of you to join me in this musical interlude – for our hearts, minds, bodies and souls – as you read, think about, meditate on, pray through, and *sing* **Psalm 98**:

Sing to the LORD a new song,
for he has done marvelous things;
his right hand and his holy arm
have worked salvation for him.
The LORD has made his salvation known
and revealed his righteousness to the nations.
He has remembered his love
and faithfulness to Israel;
all the ends of the earth have seen
the salvation of our God.

Shout for joy to the LORD, all the earth,
burst into jubilant song with music;
make music to the LORD with the harp,
with the harp and the sound of singing,
with trumpets and the blast of the ram's horn –
shout for joy before the LORD, the King.

Let the sea resound, and everything in it,
the world, and all who live in it.
Let the rivers clap their hands,
let the mountains sing together for joy;
let them sing before the LORD,
for he comes to judge the earth.
He will judge the world in righteousness
and the people with equity.

May our God, who "sings over" us (Zephaniah 3:17), bless you with renewed hope, joy, peace and love because of who our Lord is and who you are to Him!

Sometimes, you just gotta sing!

Reflections – Responses – Challenges – Encouragements – God-breathing Thoughts

Do I believe it?
And if I do, what am I going to do about it?

Lord, please let me hear your voice, your love, your wisdom, your grace and truth.

PLEADING FOR THE BODY TO LIVE AS THE BODY!

Therefore, my brothers and sisters, you whom I love and long for,
my joy and crown, stand firm in the Lord, dear friends!
I plead with Euodia and I plead with Syntyche to be of the same mind in the Lord.
Yes, and I ask you, my true companion, help these women
since they have contended at my side in the cause of the gospel.
Philippians 4:1-3

At the writing of this letter, the Apostle Paul is in prison. Yet, his love and passionate concern, for those to whom he ministered and for those who ministered alongside him, are so very clear. With all of the deep, spiritual truths of God that Paul wants to pour into these brothers and sisters, Paul takes time to address two women by name, and asks another believer, his *true companion*, to be a mediator to help them reconcile their relationship and re-establish their unity, their like-mindedness, in the Lord Jesus Christ.

Maybe you know Euodia and Syntyche. Maybe you know two sisters in Christ, or two brothers in Christ, or two groups in Christ, who have taken a hard line of disagreement with, and separation from, one another. Feelings are hurt. Frustration is real. Judgments are made. Anger is clearly present or just barely kept under a tight mask of calm or self-righteousness.

What are we to do? Well, if we're Euodia and Syntyche – or Ed and Sidney – we need to get over ourselves really quickly. We need to humble ourselves before our Lord Jesus. We need to give up all of our pride, our stubbornness, our self-righteousness, our self-indignation and that horrible death-bringing attitude of needing to be right – and believing we always are!

What are we to do if we're the sisters and brothers in Christ who are aware of this brokenness and disagreement within the Body? We also need to get over ourselves really quickly. We, too, need to humble ourselves before our Lord Jesus. And we need to stand firm in Jesus. Stand firm in His Word, in His Spirit, in His love, in His grace, in His truth, in His wisdom. And as we stand firm in our Lord Jesus, we will be given His ways and words to listen, to speak and to encourage the healing and unity of God's beloved children within the Body of Christ.

These truths are for all of us – whether we are in the midst of the disagreement or we are the observers. We all must fully focus on Jesus. Fully focus on what is truly of eternal value and importance. And get over ourselves about anything that isn't!

Like Paul, who pleads for unity, humility and focusing on Jesus, so do I. First, I plead for myself and for how I relate to others, asking God to remove all of my pride and stubbornness, constantly and continually, so that my energy and my efforts will not be spent in self-focused attitudes, self-justification, critical judgment or just plain stupid and petty thoughts, words and actions that contend against another of God's beloved children in the Body of Christ. I plead with God to, instead, keep transforming me so that I may, by His love and power, passionately contend for the souls and lives of others on behalf of the gospel of Christ!

And I plead with God on behalf of all of us in the Body. May we each allow God to keep us humble and living in peace with all our brothers and sisters in Christ for the sake of His glory. May we each reflect Jesus beautifully and truly to those who do not yet know Him as Savior and Lord. May we, as members of the Body of Christ, live like the Body of Christ!

Do I believe it?
And if I do, what am I going to do about it?

Lord, please let me hear your voice, your love, your wisdom, your grace and truth.

November 22

THE LORD'S WORD TO THE WEARY – THAT WOULD BE ME

Not long ago, my heart was breaking, with an almost inescapable sadness and a sense of complete helplessness, for someone I love beyond expression. This precious one was lost in pain and trauma – physically, mentally, emotionally, relationally and spiritually. In my heartbroken, worn out and helpless state, I sat with my Abba and His living and active Word. I listened to Him and I shared my heart in uncovered and raw ways.

Here is a piece of our conversation as I read, prayed and wrote about God's eternal words from **Isaiah 40:28-29.**

Do you not know? Have you not heard?

My Lord, I do know. And, yes, my Lord, I have heard.
And I believe You, my Lord, even now when my heart is breaking for this precious one.

The LORD is the everlasting God, the Creator of the ends of the earth.

Thank You, my Lord, that You are the eternal, everlasting God.
Thank You that You are the Creator of the ends of the earth.
Thank You that You are the Sovereign God who rules for all eternity.
Even when circumstances and people are so unruly. Even when I am so heavy-hearted.
Lord, You are still God. And You are good.

He will not grow tired or weary, and his understanding no one can fathom.

Thank You, my Lord, that You do not grow tired or weary. Because I am so tired.
I am so weary. My eyes are heavy from crying and my heart is so very sad.
Thank You that Your understanding, Your wisdom and Your knowledge are unfathomable.
Your mind and Your understanding are so far beyond mine. Thank You for that.
You are omniscient, Lord. There is nothing You do not know.
There is nothing You do not understand. You alone have the perfect knowledge and eternal perspective that I do not have. That I will never have on this side of heaven.
Thank You, Lord. I trust You in my tiredness. In my weariness.
I trust You in my seriously limited understanding.

He gives strength to the weary and increases the power of the weak.

I don't feel strong or powerful right now, Lord. Not at all, Lord.
But I do know...and I have heard...and I have experienced...Your strength and Your power.
And I know You are faithful and true to Your Word. I know that Your strength and Your power are here with me and within me through Your Spirit.
For now, my Lord, I will just rest. Rest my breaking heart, rest my weary soul and trust You.
I will curl up in Your love and press into Your faithfulness.
I will trust that You have all that I need.
And I will trust that You have all that the one for whom my heart is breaking needs too.
Thank You, my Lord, my God and my King. Thank You, my Abba.

Sometimes the only thing any of us can do is trust God. Trust, in itself, is God's Spirit with us, comforting our breaking hearts and holding our weary minds, bodies and souls. May our Lord increase our trust in Him – with our own lives and with all those precious ones we love so deeply and dearly.

Do I believe it?
And if I do, what am I going to do about it?

Lord, please let me hear your voice, your love, your wisdom, your grace and truth.

THE CALL OF SALT AND LIGHT

"You are the salt of the earth...you are the light of the world."
Matthew 5:13, 14

Jesus tells us that we as His followers are called to be the salt of the earth. We are called to be the light of the world. That is quite a formidable job description!

The value of salt cannot be overstated. Salt is used widely, and in almost every culture around the world, as a flavoring for so very much of what would nourish us and satisfy our taste buds. Salt is used as a preservative, as a cleanser, and in various medicinal, healing and rejuvenating ways for our bodies.

The value of light is beyond our full comprehension! We have no power on our own to see anything at all unless there is light. Even the tiniest of flame or ray of light is necessary to reveal the size, shape, substance and shades of color of everything that exists. Only in the light is there any vision in our lives.

And Jesus calls us, you and me, the salt of the earth and the light of the world. I am so deeply humbled (And just a little bit terrified!) by this call when I think about what that really means as a follower of Jesus. Do you and I live and act as His salt and light to those around us?

As the salt of the earth –
Do our words and actions help to preserve and protect God's image as reflected through us?
Do our words and actions help to preserve and protect the dignity of those around us who are also made in the image of God?
Do our words and actions leave people with a good and flavorful "taste in their mouths" about who Jesus is? Do our words and actions leave people with a sour, bitter or bland taste?
Do our words and actions encourage others to "taste and see that the Lord is good?"
Do our words and actions leave people hungering and thirsting for more and more of Jesus?
Do our words and actions bring gentle cleansing, deep healing and rejuvenation to others?

As the light of the world –
Do our words and actions reveal and shed light on the love – the unfailing, faithful, passionate, grace-filled, forgiving, transforming love – of God for all people?
Do our words and actions reveal and shed light on the darkness and evil that work to destroy our lives here on earth and for all eternity?
Do our words and actions reveal and shed light on Jesus as the Way out of this darkness?
Do our words and actions reveal and shed light on an attitude of thanksgiving, humility and joy for all that Jesus is and what He has done as the Savior of the world – as our Savior?
Do our words and actions point the spotlight on Jesus as King of kings and Lord of lords? Or do we attempt to grab the spotlight and get the close-up shots?

May God transform each of us to be His pure salt and true light to everyone with whom we interact – in every relationship, in every circumstance, and even in the briefest encounters we have with others. May God teach us and shape us to be His preserving, protecting, healing, rejuvenating, revealing, brilliant vessels – all for His glory and the salvation and transformation of many, many lives through the love and power of our Lord Jesus Christ! Amen!

Reflections – Responses – Challenges – Encouragements – God-breathing Thoughts

Do I believe it?
And if I do, what am I going to do about it?

Lord, please let me hear your voice, your love, your wisdom, your grace and truth.

A HUMBLED, THANKFUL, LITTLE CLAY JAR

For what we preach is not ourselves, but Jesus Christ as Lord,
and ourselves as your servants for Jesus' sake.
For God, who said, "Let light shine out of the darkness,"
made his light shine in our hearts
to give us the light of the knowledge of God's glory
displayed in the face of Christ.
But we have this treasure in jars of clay
to show that this all-surpassing power
is from God and not from us.
2 Corinthians 4:5-7

It is the gospel of Jesus Christ – the all-surpassing power of God's love to conquer the power of sin and death, shame and brokenness of every sort – that we as Christ's followers preach.

It is this all-surpassing power of God's eternal, unlimited love and His outrageous, unthinkable sacrifice of Jesus in order to bring us to Himself, that puts me on my knees, literally and figuratively, in awe of my God. In awe of my God's intimate and sovereign love. God's love that changes everything. God's love that has changed me and my entire life. It is this all-surpassing power of God's love that brought my life out of the darkness of crippling abuse and self-hate and into the glorious light that shines in the face of my Jesus.

And God has chosen to place His all-surpassing power – the knowledge of His grace and truth and love given through Jesus Christ – in me, a frail, flawed and finite human being. God's eternal treasure has been placed in me, in all of God's children, by His eternal Spirit.

Amazing. Incredible. And I am one very humbled and thankful little clay jar.

Do I get this, do I really get this? Do I grasp at any real level of truth that our Almighty God has not only bled and died on a cross for the forgiveness of our sins and destroyed the power of death through His resurrection, but that our Almighty God also pours out His all-surpassing knowledge of these truths into us? And we – by God's all-surpassing power and with the light of knowledge we have been given about Jesus – are to be the vessels, albeit clay jars, that our God uses to preach the gospel of Jesus to all the world!

Amazing. Incredible. And I am one very humbled and thankful little clay jar.

And Paul, in passionate and humble clarity, makes sure it is understood that we, the clay jars, are not preaching ourselves or about our ability to be righteous or holy or even to be loved by God because of something we have done. No. We are just servants of our fellow brothers and sisters of the earth, offering the light and the knowledge and the all-surpassing power of the glory of God that is made known through our Savior and Lord Jesus Christ.

The clay jar is only a vessel. It is the Master Potter, the Creator, the Lord of heaven and earth who has formed us for such a task, fills us with the message we are to share, and pours out of us what He has placed within us – the light of the knowledge of God's glory displayed in the face of Christ! And all of this has come to all of us through the all-surpassing power of our God! Amazing. Incredible. And I am one very humbled and thankful little clay jar.

Reflections – Responses – Challenges – Encouragements – God-breathing Thoughts

Do I believe it?
And if I do, what am I going to do about it?

Lord, please let me hear your voice, your love, your wisdom, your grace and truth.

THIS IS, AFTER ALL, GOD'S WILL!

There have been so many times I've been asked by all kinds of people in all kinds of circumstances, "What is God's will for me? What does God want me to do?"

And many times the deep and detailed answers of what God's will is for a particular person in a specific set of circumstances will be far different from what God's will would be for another person in a different set of circumstances. Prayer to seek God's heart – to seek God's leading, to have God's peace for the pace and path our lives are to take – is absolutely essential. And it may take much time to discern and clearly sense God's will.

Yet, there are other times when God makes His will absolutely and irrefutably clear through His living and active Word. The revelation of His will at those times is not only for a particular person in a specific set of circumstances, rather, these revelations are God's will for all of His children all of the time.

> *Rejoice always;*
> *pray continually;*
> *give thanks in all circumstances;*
> *for this is God's will for you in Christ Jesus.*
> 1 Thessalonians 5:16-18

This passage even closes with "for this is God's will for you in Christ Jesus." It certainly can't get much more absolute or irrefutable about what God's will is for us here!

But, still...
Rejoice always? Pray continually? Give thanks in all circumstances? This is God's will for us? Really?

The absolute and irrefutable answer is: Yes! Easy? No. But absolutely possible.

Our God never asks us to do anything for which He will not also equip us. And God never asks us to do anything that is not for our very best and to accomplish His very highest will and purpose for each of us: "to be conformed to the image of his Son" (Romans 8:29).

Are circumstances in your life frustrating? Overwhelming? Sad? Frightening? Of course they are. We're living in a broken – frustrating, overwhelming, sad, frightening – world. And this truth about our broken world, and our need for God's love and help, should give us more than enough reason to *pray continually*! But! The brokenness of this world is not the end of the story. Nor should it be the foundation of our focus.

Instead, we are to let God's love and good news be our focus and give us all the reason we need to *rejoice always and give thanks in all circumstances*! Jesus Christ has died and is risen! His Word is living and active! His Spirit is with us and within us, at every moment! Jesus is the King of all eternity! And our Lord Jesus Christ will return to rule with power and majesty for ever and ever!

So! Let's rejoice always. Pray continually. Give thanks in all circumstances! This is, after all, God's will for us – "his good, pleasing and perfect will" (Romans 12:2)!

Do I believe it?
And if I do, what am I going to do about it?

Lord, please let me hear your voice, your love, your wisdom, your grace and truth.

A BEAUTIFUL DAWN, A SUNSHINY DAY – GOD'S WAY

Many of us, in one way or another at one time or another, in big ways and small ways, have had to deal with being misunderstood, mistreated, misinterpreted and misjudged. Whether this happens within our personal relationships, within our public and social connections or in the legal domain, being wrongfully treated, accused or perceived can be painful and frustrating.

Sometimes there is absolutely nothing we can do to ensure that the truth about us – about who we are, what we do or what we have done – will be made known, received and believed by those who have come against us. And this can be absolutely maddening.

Or not.

If we know, receive and believe the eternal truth that our holy and righteous God knows us full well, knows every detail about our lives, knows every nuance of our thoughts, words, actions, circumstances and interactions with every person, we can be held in God's peace instead of our anger. Even in knowing we have been wrongfully treated, accused or perceived by others, we can commit our ways – all that we are and all that we do – to our God who knows the absolute truth, and absolutely loves us.

> *Commit your way to the LORD;*
> *trust in him and he will do this:*
> *He will make your righteousness shine like the dawn,*
> *your vindication like the noonday sun.*
> Psalm 37:5-6

I love to watch the sun rising at dawn. I love bright, sun-bathed days. And our God likens these beautiful, natural experiences to what can happen for us on the emotional, mental, spiritual, relational, social, practical and even legal levels when we commit our way to Him. When we fully trust in our God as a righteous and just God who fully knows us, and will fully vindicate us – justify us, exonerate us and free us – from all wrongs!

Whatever righteousness there is in us, whatever is true about us and about our interpretation of our circumstances, may seem for a time to be completely hidden by the darkness of mistreatment, false accusations and misjudgments. But, wait. Trust God. Commit your way to the Lord and your righteousness will shine like the dawn. Your vindication – your being set free from all the lies from the pit of hell – will be like the noonday sun.

Our God will never let falsehood, wrong judgment or cruelty of any kind have the final victory. Our God is the righteous, true and just God. Our God will remove everything that would foolishly or cruelly attempt to overshadow anyone or anything that is committed to His ways – His eternal righteous, true and just ways.

So, wait.
Trust God.
Commit your way to the Lord.
And the beautiful dawn, the bright sun of who we are in God, as His children sealed by His righteousness, will one day be fully revealed!

Reflections – Responses – Challenges – Encouragements – God-breathing Thoughts

Do I believe it?
And if I do, what am I going to do about it?

Lord, please let me hear your voice, your love, your wisdom, your grace and truth.

IT'S THANKSGIVING SOMEWHERE!

When we get up in the morning, we often have a variety of habitual things we do as we begin our day. And the same is true of the way we often close down at the end of our day, as we begin our evening, doing a variety of habitual things.

Two beautiful and powerful habitual things that would be good for us to do would be to take time to give thanks to our God at the beginning of each day and, again, as evening falls at the close of our day.

Our Lord gave us a great example of this in the habitual things that His priests were instructed to do. As priests who served the Lord in the temple, the Levites had many duties – including to be the regular and habitual voices of thanksgiving to our God.

> *They were also to stand every morning to thank and praise the LORD.*
> *They were to do the same in the evening.*
> 1 Chronicles 23:30

God's priests were instructed to stand and to offer thanksgiving and praise to the Lord every single morning and every single evening. This habitual thing called them to lift their voices – and their hearts, their minds, their souls and even their bodies (since they were to stand) – and pour out thanksgiving to the Lord. And I have to believe that all of those around them who sincerely listened to these voices of thanksgiving and praise to the Lord, were themselves lifted in heart, mind, soul and body.

There is power and freedom when we offer thanksgiving to our God! We are filled with the powerful truth of our God's holiness and sovereignty, His love and goodness, His eternal hope and transcending peace. We are set free by God's eternal perspective that who we are and all we go through will one day be fully redeemed and renewed. We are filled with freedom as we give thanks for God's eternal truth that…

> *Our light and momentary troubles are achieving for us*
> *an eternal glory that far outweighs them all.*
> 2 Corinthians 4:17

Our mornings and evenings will bring many things to us over the course of our lifetimes. No matter what they are, may we choose the habitual thing of bringing our thanksgiving to our Almighty God every morning and evening!

May we each let each day be thanksgiving because this is the day our Lord has given us!

> *This is the day the LORD has made;*
> *let us rejoice and be glad in it.*
> Psalm 118:24

It's Thanksgiving somewhere! Happy Thanksgiving, everybody!

Reflections – Responses – Challenges – Encouragements – God-breathing Thoughts

Do I believe it?
And if I do, what am I going to do about it?

Lord, please let me hear your voice, your love, your wisdom, your grace and truth.

OUR GOD – OUR SUN AND SHIELD FOREVER

For the LORD God is a sun and shield;
the LORD bestows favor and honor;
no good thing does he withhold
from those whose walk is blameless.

LORD Almighty, blessed is the one who trusts you.
Psalm 84:11-12

Our God is the very light of life. God's sun light – God's Son Jesus – shines His holy light into this dark world. Our God is the eternal and perfect light that gives sight to our eternal eyes so that our spirits may see and know our God. In His light we are saved. In His light we are set free from all the shadows of sin and the darkness of death.

When Jesus spoke again to the people, he said, "I am the light of the world.
Whoever follows me will never walk in darkness, but will have the light of life."
John 8:12

God has delivered me from going down to the pit,
and I shall live to enjoy the light of life.
Job 33:28

There will be no more night.
They will not need the light of a lamp or the light of the sun,
for the Lord God will give them light.
And they will reign for ever and ever.
Revelation 22:5

Our God is the shield that is set before us to protect us from being overtaken by the hurts and hardships that come at us in this life. Our God is our guardian and protector who shields us from eternal destruction by the power of His love and the fullness of His mercy. No matter what we go through in this life, our God is with us. And we are His beloved and may rest our hearts and minds, our bodies and souls fully in the knowledge that in our sovereign Lord we are eternally secure, safe and protected.

Let the beloved of the LORD rest secure in him,
for he shields the beloved all day long,
and the one the LORD loves rests between his shoulders.
Deuteronomy 33:12

As for God, his way is perfect: The LORD's word is flawless;
he shields all who take refuge in him.
2 Samuel 22:31

As we follow Jesus, walking in His brilliant and eternal light, allowing our Lord to be our shield, lifting us up onto His strong and eternal shoulders, we are bestowed with great favor and honor as the children of God. And to us, our Heavenly Abba withholds no good – and eternal – thing from us. He lavishes us with His unfailing love, mercy and salvation, His Word, His Spirit, His peace and wisdom, His hope and joy. How blessed we are as we trust the Lord Almighty!

Do I believe it?
And if I do, what am I going to do about it?

Lord, please let me hear your voice, your love, your wisdom, your grace and truth.

QUESTIONS FROM OUR LORD

Through the prophet Isaiah, our Lord asks us some pointed and piercing questions about how we respond to Him and what our perceptions are of Him.

> *"When I came, why was there no one?*
> *When I called, why was there no one to answer?*
> *Was my arm too short to deliver you?*
> *Do I lack strength to rescue you?"*
> Isaiah 50:2

Too often our understanding of the Lord can become completely skewed by our own limited thinking and self-focused perspectives. We can become discouraged, self-serving, resentful, angry – and even turn our backs completely on the Lord – because God does not seem to be there when we want Him. God does not seem to answer us when we call to Him. At least not in the way that we think God should answer us. Our inability and our unwillingness to trust that our God is loving and true, good and faithful, present and strong keep us locked into a place filled either with doubt or prideful self-reliance – or some unhealthy mix of the two.

The truth is our Lord comes to us constantly and continually. He comes to us to answer our deepest soul, and eternal, needs. Our Lord comes to us with His unfailing love, eternal salvation, mercy and grace, forgiveness and freedom, deliverance and renewal. Our Lord comes to us with His passionate, life-healing, life-transforming presence. Our Lord comes to us with His peace and purpose, with His joy and hope. Will we be there when our Lord comes to us? Will we recognize that He is here with us now?

And just as our Lord comes to us, so, too, our Lord calls out to us in all the same ways. Will we let ourselves hear our Lord's voice? Will we answer Him? Will we listen to His passionate heart for us? Will we let His unfailing love, grace and truth speak into our lives?

Our Lord delivers us by the reach of His loving and powerful arm. Our deliverance for the forgiveness of our sins and the gift of eternal life cost Jesus Christ His life – as His loving and powerful arms were nailed to the cross in utter and complete humility. Will we take hold of the Lord's arm, letting Him deliver us from everything that put Jesus on the cross?

Our Lord has the almighty strength to rescue us in each of our present moments and for all eternity. Our Lord is able to rescue us, heal us, help us, renew us, rebuild us and transform us in all circumstances – in all ways. All things are possible with the almighty strength of our Lord. Will we trust our Lord's strength? Will we humbly let God be the Almighty Lord of our lives?

Our Lord comes to us. May we welcome Him in humility and love!
Our Lord calls to us. May we answer Him with joy and thanksgiving!
Our Lord's arm reaches to deliver us. May we let God deliver us from all our darkness, and the darkness of this world, into His light!
Our Lord's strength is able to rescue us. May we let God rescue us from everything that would weaken and destroy us – including ourselves!

These are the answers our Lord wants to His questions. These answer all that we need for all of our lives!

Reflections – Responses – Challenges – Encouragements – God-breathing Thoughts

Do I believe it?
And if I do, what am I going to do about it?

Lord, please let me hear your voice, your love, your wisdom, your grace and truth.

IT CAN WAIT. BE STILL. BE QUIET.

Shhhhh…It can wait. I know there is so much for all of us to do. So much time pressure at home, at work, at school, at church. And, oh my! We're right in the midst of the big holiday season. Thanksgiving just came and Christmas is fast approaching. There are so many things we need to finish, deadlines to meet and commitments to fulfill.

Shhhhh…It can wait.

Breathe deeply and take some moments, some grace-filled moments, to let God lift you out of the worry and the warring, the pressure and the panic. Take some moments, some grace-filled moments, to listen attentively to our Lord's holy love and holy messages about being still and being quiet.

"Be still and know that I am God…"
Isaiah 46:10

This is what the Sovereign LORD, the Holy One of Israel, says:
"In repentance and rest is your salvation,
in quietness and trust is your strength…"
Isaiah 30:15

The fruit of that righteousness will be peace;
its effect will be quietness and confidence forever.
Isaiah 32:17

He makes me lie down in green pastures,
he leads me beside quiet waters…
Psalm 23:2

From heaven you pronounced judgment,
and the land feared and was quiet…
Psalm 76:8

Better a dry crust with peace and quiet
than a house full of feasting, with strife.
Proverbs 17:1

Be still before the LORD and wait patiently for him…
Psalm 37:7

The LORD your God…[will quiet you with his love]
in his love he will no longer rebuke you.
Zephaniah 3:17

Breathe deeply and slowly, taking in our Lord's holy love and holy messages to us. Shhhhh…It can wait. Be still. Be quiet. Let the truth of our Lord's absolute sovereignty over every moment and our Lord's eternal perspective over every circumstance, strengthen us in the understanding that: Whatever it is, it can wait – at least for these few grace-filled moments of being still and being quiet with our Lord.

Reflections – Responses – Challenges – Encouragements – God-breathing Thoughts

Do I believe it?
And if I do, what am I going to do about it?

Lord, please let me hear your voice, your love, your wisdom, your grace and truth.

EVERY PRESENT MOMENT WE HAVE

Happy December 1st!

It may seem silly, but I always like to acknowledge the first day of a new month. And the first day of a new week. And, yes, I especially like to welcome and celebrate each new day – it's always a first! I like being cognizant of the marking of time. It keeps me keenly aware and very thankful for my life and that God has a purpose in each of my present moments.

Marking time by intentionally acknowledging each new day helps me to live more fully in the present moment. It helps me to recognize that this new day is a gift from God. It is God alone who is my life-giver and my life-sustainer. And, quite honestly, this practice of being present in the moment keeps me humbled and very mindful that this present moment is all that I truly have. Yesterday is gone. Tomorrow may or may not be here for me – at least on this side of heaven. I have been given the gift of this day. The gift of this present moment. Today.

> *So, as the Holy Spirit says: "Today, if you hear his voice,*
> *do not harden your hearts as you did in the rebellion..."*
> Hebrews 3:7-8

> *Teach us to number our days,*
> *that we may gain a heart of wisdom.*
> Psalm 90:12

> *Satisfy us in the morning with your unfailing love,*
> *that we may sing for joy and be glad all of our days.*
> Psalm 90:14

> *Your eyes saw my unformed body;*
> *all the days ordained for me were written in your book*
> *before one of them came to be.*
> Psalm 139:16

> *My times are in your hands...*
> Psalm 31:15

All of our times, all of our days, all of our present moments are in God's hands. He lovingly, perfectly, wisely, with His eternal purpose in mind pours them out to us as a gift.

How good it would be for all of us to be keenly aware and thankful for this truth, celebrating each day and each of our present moments. I don't want my life to pass by without truly living it. I don't want to miss the present moments I've been given.

How good it would be for all of us if, today, we would listen to God's voice and keep our hearts soft and pliable to His words and ways. If, today, we would let God lead us, transform us and use us in His loving, healing and holy ways – in all we are, in all we do, in all our interactions. As we do, I absolutely believe that all of our present moments will have deep and eternal value and beauty – just as God intended them to have!

Do I believe it?
And if I do, what am I going to do about it?

Lord, please let me hear your voice, your love, your wisdom, your grace and truth.

AS LONG AS THE EARTH ENDURES – AND FAR BEYOND IN CHRIST

After the devastating flood in the days of Noah, the Lord gave a new beginning to human beings, and to all living creatures. The Lord promised that the cycle of life would continue once again in all of its expected rhythms.

> *"As long as the earth endures,*
> *seedtime and harvest,*
> *cold and heat,*
> *summer and winter.*
> *day and night will never cease."*
> Genesis 8:22

Many things can completely wipe out the expected rhythms of our lives – from the small and temporary frustrations with our computers and phones to the gravely destructive forces within this physical world that can shatter innumerable lives through earthquakes, fires, floods, tsunamis, tornadoes, mud slides, hurricanes, super-storms, snow and ice storms.

Our own personal, expected rhythms of life can be altered significantly by the hard things in life we mourn and by the things in life we celebrate. By the loss of loved one. By the birth of a new child. By a wedding. By a divorce. By a loss of a job. By a promotion.

In all of our ups and downs, in all of the changes in our lives – in all of the times when our expected rhythms of life have taken unexpected turns – we can be assured that God is still in control. God is still allowing this life and this world to go on in all of its seasons. For all of its appointed days. As long as the earth endures.

And we can be assured that God is still present with us, loving us always, calling out to us continually so that we would know Him and receive the gift of His merciful salvation and eternal life that He offers to us – that will last far beyond the time that this earth endures.

Our God is eternal. Our God never changes. Nor does His love for us ever change. Yet, our earthly lives, and this world as we know it, will not and cannot go on as they are now. Not one of us knows what will actually happen from one day to the next. We don't know if our own personal, expected rhythms of life will go on for us as we expect them to do. Our assurance of eternity is completely rooted and established, offered and received, only in the love of our God and the hope we have in Jesus.

> *Praise be to the God and Father of our Lord Jesus Christ!*
> *In his great mercy he has given us new birth into a living hope*
> *through the resurrection of Jesus Christ from the dead...*
> 1 Peter 1:3

We each need to take a moment. And be thankful for our lives. Thankful for each day. Thankful for each moment of life. And be even far more thankful that our God – who is not limited by time or seasons as are we – reaches out to us with His unlimited, unfailing love and salvation. May any of you who do not yet believe, trust in Jesus as your Savior today and receive this *new birth into a living hope* so that each of your days will be filled with the assurance that you will live eternally with our God and in His love – far beyond the time that this earth endures!

Reflections – Responses – Challenges – Encouragements – God-breathing Thoughts

Do I believe it?
And if I do, what am I going to do about it?

Lord, please let me hear your voice, your love, your wisdom, your grace and truth.

December 3

THE VERDICT IS IN – AND IT IS HARSH

This is the verdict:
Light has come into the world,
but people loved the darkness instead of light because their deeds were evil.
Everyone who does evil hates the light, and will not come into the light
for fear that their deeds will be exposed.
But whoever lives by the truth comes into the light, so that it may be seen plainly
that what they have done has been done through God.
John 3:19-21

Pretty harsh verdict, but God's truth: People love their darkness more than God's light.

I have to admit that I don't really like it when people shout out – whether from the pulpit or from a public corner – the verdict against evil in this world. But it's only their style that makes me a bit uncomfortable. God's judgment against sin doesn't make me uncomfortable. It's the truth.

But what does happen within me, when faced with God's verdict against sin, is this: I am ripped apart by God's truth, and then put back together again by the blood of God's grace. His light exposes my every ugly and sinful, hateful and shameful thought, word, action and attitude. Coming into God's light can be scary. But look at the Hands that are beckoning us to come into God's light. They are nail-scarred and loving. They offer forgiveness and salvation, freedom and transformation, hope and eternal life in the light of our Savior Jesus.

Yes, God's verdict against sin, against our human nature that would prefer to keep on sinning and prefer to stay in the darkness, is exceedingly harsh. And rightfully so. The consequences of staying in our sins only bring death to us. Maybe not immediately, but eternal darkness and separation from our God, who loves us so much, is the certain destiny of all who will not come into the light of Christ. God's verdict against sin, against our human love of the darkness, compelled God to give His Holy Son Jesus over to death to pay for the forgiveness of our sins. Because God so loved the world. Because God so loved us, we lovers of darkness.

Did you know God's harsh verdict against sin? Did you know the harsh punishment Jesus suffered, out of His perfect and passionate love for you? Come into God's light now! God wants to shed His light into your mind and into your spirit. Admit that you have sin in your life and you need God's forgiveness. Jesus Christ has already died for your sins. Ask Him to be your Savior. He will be. Jesus Christ has already conquered death through His resurrection. Ask Him to give you His promised gift of eternal life. He will give it.

If Jesus is your Savior already, celebrate the eternal life in God's light you have been given! Then, check yourself and your light level. Are you living in the light of God's truth? Or are you living in the shadow lands, believing that what you think, say and do aren't really all that bad? Please, think again. If we have to justify and rationalize anything we think, say and do – then I'm pretty sure we're still living in the shadow lands. Jesus is not a God to be taken for granted. He cannot be mocked. He cannot be fooled. He is the truth. Jesus, out of His love, wants all of us as His precious, passionately loved children, to stop living a lie. To stop living in the dark since He has already given each of us the full light of life through His death and resurrection! God's verdict against sin is harsh. But His gifts of light and life are here! Live in His light!

Do I believe it?
And if I do, what am I going to do about it?

Lord, please let me hear your voice, your love, your wisdom, your grace and truth.

GOD'S MAJESTY IN THE MIDST OF THE MESSY

Life can be very messy at times. Life can move at a pressured pace. Life can be filled with things that we never want mentioned. Life can be filled with crazy circumstances and even crazier people. Life can be mundane. Life can be maddening.

But! Always our Lord is majestic! And it is so good and so right for our souls to remember that! It is so good and so right to lift our eyes up to our majestic Lord and off all of the messy and maddening, the mundane and the unmentionable things in our lives. It is so good and so right to lift our eyes to see and acknowledge the clear evidence of our Lord's majesty all around us. No matter how messy our lives may be!

Take time to let the words of Psalm 8 enter deeply into your heart, mind and soul – right in the midst of the messy. And lift up the truths of this hymn of praise to our majestic Lord!

LORD, our Lord,
how majestic is your name in all the earth!

You have set your glory in the heavens.
Through the praise of children and infants
you have established a stronghold against your enemies,
to silence the foe and the avenger.
When I consider your heavens,
the work of your fingers,
the moon and the stars,
which you have set in place,
what is mankind that you are mindful of them,
human beings that you care for them?

You have made them a little lower than the angels
and crowned them with glory and honor.
You made them rulers over the works of your hands;
you put everything under their feet;
all flocks and herds,
and the animals of the wild,
the birds in the sky,
and the fish of the sea,
all that swim the paths of the seas.

LORD, our Lord,
how majestic is your name in all the earth!
Psalm 8:1-9

Taking the time to really meditate on (And sing about!) the majesty of our Lord helps my heart, mind and soul to breathe more deeply and my smile to come more easily. Taking time to push back from the messiness and the *messed-up-ness* of this life – every moment we will take – to focus on the eternal majesty of the Lord is always so good and so right!

Take those majestic moments regularly – especially right in the midst of the messy!

Do I believe it?
And if I do, what am I going to do about it?

Lord, please let me hear your voice, your love, your wisdom, your grace and truth.

December 5

THE GOOD NEWS OF GOD'S GRACE

I consider my life worth nothing to me;
my only aim is to finish the race
and complete the task the Lord Jesus has given me –
the task of testifying to the good news of God's grace.
Acts 20:24

I am so deeply aware that my life is of great worth and value, as is the life of each person.

Our lives are of such great worth and value that Jesus, our Holy God in human form, chose to die in our place. Jesus, in outrageous love for us and with extravagant humility, received God's holy and harsh judgment against all sin. Jesus, in outrageous love for us and with extravagant humility, took on the agonizing and brutal punishment for the forgiveness of our sins through His death on the cross and the horror of being spiritually separated from His Father so that sin and death would no longer have any power to separate us eternally from our God! And Jesus is the Risen King over all eternity – just as He had proclaimed, and the messengers sent from God declared to the women at His empty tomb.

"Why do you look for the living among the dead? He is not here; he has risen!
Remember how he told you, while he was still with you in Galilee:
'The Son of Man must be delivered over to the hands of sinners,
be crucified and on the third day be raised again.' "
And the women remembered his words.
Luke 24:5-8

This is the good news of God's grace!

This is what makes me absolutely convinced of the great worth and value that each of our lives has to our Holy God! This is why – apart from Jesus, apart from this great love of God and apart from the purpose of testifying to the good news of God's grace – I consider my life worth nothing to me, but everything to my God!

...for us there is but one God, the Father,
from whom all things came and for whom we live;
and there is but one Lord, Jesus Christ,
through whom all things came and through whom we live.
1 Corinthians 8:6

I am alive because of Jesus. I planned suicide. He gave me life. In His love and by the power of God's forgiveness, I am set free from the shame of my own sins and now live as *more than a conqueror* over the cruelty that came at me from others. Apart from Jesus, apart from this great love of God and apart from the purpose of testifying to the good news of God's grace – I consider my life worth nothing to me, but everything to my God! And God is everything to me.

May each of you know and believe in Jesus as your Savior who died, who is risen and who will come again as the eternal King of kings and Lord of lords to welcome all of His children Home!

This is the good news of God's grace!

Reflections – Responses – Challenges – Encouragements – God-breathing Thoughts

Do I believe it?
And if I do, what am I going to do about it?

Lord, please let me hear your voice, your love, your wisdom, your grace and truth.

WHATEVER!

Our God wants to be the Lord of every *whatever* in our lives!
Whatever we think.
Whatever we say.
Whatever we do.
Whatever we want.
Whatever we care about.
Whatever relationships we're in.
Whatever circumstances we're in.
Whatever we need to forgive.
Whatever we need forgiveness for.
Whatever condition of mind, body and soul we're in.
Whatever gifts we've been given to serve God.
Whatever we need to carry out God's plans for our lives.

> *Whatever you do, whether in word or deed, do it all in the name of the Lord Jesus,*
> *giving thanks to God the Father through him.*
> Colossians 3:15

> *Each of you should use whatever gift you have received to serve others,*
> *as faithful stewards of God's grace in its various forms.*
> 1 Peter 4:10

> *Whatever happens, conduct yourselves in a manner worthy of the gospel of Christ.*
> Philippians 1:27

> *But the LORD said to me, "Do not say, 'I am too young.' [Or 'I am too old!']*
> *You must go to everyone I send you to and say whatever I command you."*
> Jeremiah 1:7

> *"You did not choose me, but I chose you and appointed you*
> *so that you might go and bear fruit – fruit that will last –*
> *and so that whatever you ask in my name the Father will give you."*
> John 15:16

> *Commit to the LORD whatever you do, and he will establish your plans.*
> Proverbs 16:3

> *Finally, brothers and sisters, whatever is true, whatever is noble, whatever is right,*
> *whatever is pure, whatever is lovely, whatever is admirable –*
> *if anything is excellent or praiseworthy – think about such things.*
> Philippians 4:8

Whatever. Wherever. Whenever. However. With whomever. Let's each choose, as children of God, to do everything in the full awareness of who we are in Jesus Christ. Choosing to live in the love and freedom, grace and truth, power and purpose to which our God has called us.

May we each let God be the Lord of every *whatever* we have in our lives!

Do I believe it?
And if I do, what am I going to do about it?

Lord, please let me hear your voice, your love, your wisdom, your grace and truth.

LET "THAT DAY" BE TODAY!

"In that day," declares the LORD, "I will gather the lame;
I will assemble the exiles and those I have brought to grief.
I will make the lame my remnant, those driven away a strong nation.
The LORD will rule over them in Mount Zion from that day and forever."
Micah 4:6-8

The Lord sees and knows the full outcome for all of eternity. And it is in God's almighty power to accomplish and achieve all that He has planned and promised for *that day*!

"...so is my word that goes out from my mouth:
It will not return to me empty,
but will accomplish what I desire
and achieve the purpose for which I sent it."
Isaiah 55:11

In *that day*, through God's conquering, unfailing love and His faithful acts towards His people, our Lord will gather all of us who are weak, hurt, discouraged and dismissed – the lame of body, mind and spirit – and bring us fully to Himself. In Jesus every brokenness, every wound and every weakness we have experienced in this life will be healed. We will be made new.

...by his wounds we are healed.
Isaiah 53:5

In *that day*, our Lord will draw back to Himself all of His people who have either been captured and carried away as exiles by the evil, prideful and selfish acts of others or by their own evil, prideful and selfish acts. Our God will assemble and redeem all of His people!

In *that day*, for each of us who has turned away from the Lord and suffered the grief of our sinful choices, the Lord's compassionate love will not fail us. In *that day*, for each of us who has repented and turned back to our Holy Lord, we will receive the gift of His mercy and salvation. Through the blood of Jesus, we are reconciled to our God!

...by making peace through Jesus' blood, shed on the cross.
...he has reconciled you by Christ's physical body through death
to present you holy in his sight, without blemish and free from accusation...
Colossians 1:20, 22

In *that day*, we will be gathered to our Lord as His people. We will be made strong, for all eternity, as the Lord's remnant, as His nation, as the Body of Christ. In *that day*, the Lord will rule over us in His holy, perfect love and authority for ever and ever. No more weakness, no more exile, no more grief.

May each of us recognize that our Lord's full love and power are available to save us, gather us, heal us, strengthen us, renew us and embrace us in His eternal care and rule right now!

Let *that day* be today for each of us who live as the children of the Lord!

Reflections – Responses – Challenges – Encouragements – God-breathing Thoughts

Do I believe it?
And if I do, what am I going to do about it?

Lord, please let me hear your voice, your love, your wisdom, your grace and truth.

ONE. JUST LIKE GOD.

After the Israelites returned from exile in Babylon, Nehemiah was instrumental in directing the rebuilding of the wall around Jerusalem. He cared deeply for his people and for the holy city of Jerusalem. He wanted both his people and Jerusalem to be rightly and righteously protected – both physically and spiritually.

Nehemiah used his God-given authority to place others in positions of leadership throughout the city of Jerusalem. Hananiah was one such man.

> *After the wall had been rebuilt and I had set the doors in place,*
> *the gatekeepers and the singers and the Levites were appointed.*
> *I put in charge of Jerusalem my brother Hanani,*
> *along with Hananiah the commander of the citadel,*
> *because he was a man of integrity and feared God more than most men do.*
> Nehemiah 7:1-2

Nehemiah's description of Hananiah, *a man of integrity, who feared God more than most*, is so powerful, so filled with meaning for all of us who seek to be God's people – whether we are appointed to obvious leadership positions or not.

This description of Hananiah makes me wonder:
Does my integrity – as an individual, as a follower of Christ, in the ways I interact with others, in the ways I fulfill my responsibilities – show as clearly as Hananiah's?
Is my faith – my fear of God as the Sovereign Lord over all that exists – as obvious to others as was Hananiah's?

Are my integrity and my faith in God consistent? Always? In all circumstances?
Or do my integrity and my faith show more obviously when I'm in my Christian circles? When I'm in church? Or in a Bible study? Or in a small group? Or on a mission trip?
How do my integrity and my faith in God show when I'm at work? Or at school? Or when I'm driving? Or when I'm alone? Or when I'm in a hurry and hassled?

Are my integrity and my faith in God consistent? Always? With all people?
Or do my integrity and my faith in God show more fully when I'm with my favorite people? Or with those easy-to-get-along-with and really fun people? Or with people I want to impress?
How do my integrity and my faith in God show when I'm with those people who disrespect me, dismiss me or dishonor me? Or with those people whose habits annoy me and whose quirks drive me crazy? Or with those people whose life choices are so different from mine?

Our God is one. Always the same. Always love. Always grace and truth. Always faithful.

And our one God wants each of us *to be conformed to the image of Jesus* (Romans 8:29). We are to be transformed to be more and more one person. Just as our God is one. We are each to become one consistent person, full of integrity and faith in God – in all of our relationships, in all of our responsibilities, in all places, in all of our interactions with all people, in all that we are, in all that we think, in all that we say and in all that we do. One. Just like God.

Do I believe it?
And if I do, what am I going to do about it?

Lord, please let me hear your voice, your love, your wisdom, your grace and truth.

PROCLAIMING AND PLEADING – BEING REAL

Unabashed in his proclamation and praise of his Lord, David lets all who will hear know about God's righteousness, saving help, faithfulness and love. And David is just as unabashed and uncovered as he pleads for God's mercy and help because of his circumstances and his sins.

David knows he can be real with his God whose love and faithfulness to him are absolutely perfect and far greater than his own are, or ever could be, to his God. David does not hide his praise for God or his sins from God. He rejoices in God's love and faithfulness. He is rescued by God's mercy.

> *I proclaim your saving acts in the great assembly;*
> *I do not seal my lips, LORD, as you know.*
> *I do not hide your righteousness in my heart;*
> *I speak of your faithfulness and your saving help.*
> *I do not conceal your love and your faithfulness*
> *from the great assembly.*
>
> *Do not withhold your mercy from me, LORD;*
> *may your love and faithfulness always protect me.*
> *For troubles without number surround me;*
> *my sins have overtaken me, and I cannot see.*
> *They are more than the hairs of my head,*
> *and my heart fails within me.*
> *Be pleased to save me, LORD;*
> *come quickly, LORD, to help me.*
> Psalm 40:9-12

David puts forth his absolute assurance of who God is, lifting His name high – proclaiming and praising the Lord *in the great assembly* (with a whole bunch of people) as the One who is righteous and saves us, as the One whose love and faithfulness are eternal and good.

Is this how we know our God? Is this how we make our God known to others – with joy and thanksgiving, with proclamation and praise for our God's righteousness and saving acts, for His boundless love and faithfulness?

David reveals his vulnerability and his desperate need for God – pleading with Him to pour out His mercy, to save him, to help him, to lift the blinding shame of sin from his eyes and to heal his sin-broken heart.

Is this how we come to our God? Do we come in all *real*-ness and repentance, in trust and vulnerability to receive what we desperately need from our God – His mercy and forgiveness, His love and faithfulness, His help and salvation?

Our God knows us full well. Our God loves us full well. And whether we are proclaiming His love and faithfulness or pleading for His mercy and help, our God wants us to be fully real with Him at all times!

Do I believe it?
And if I do, what am I going to do about it?

Lord, please let me hear your voice, your love, your wisdom, your grace and truth.

IN OUR COMFORTER'S EMBRACE

You are my Comforter in sorrow, my heart is faint within me.
Jeremiah 8:18

There are days in each of our lives when we just need our God to show up as our faithful and tender, kind and compassionate Comforter. We need our Comforter to hold us in His loving embrace. To comfort us with the truth that He is with us and loves us. And that He, as our Comforter and the Sovereign Lord of all time and space and circumstances, will one day make even our sorrow "beautiful in its time" (Ecclesiastes 3:11).

This is one of those times for me. There is nothing yet beautiful about the sorrow I feel for another. I have no power to change the sad things that have happened to someone I love very much. I can only pray. I can only love. And even as I try to be a vessel of God's comfort to this precious one, I, too, desperately cry out for my Comforter to hold me in His loving embrace.

I have no strength of my own. And my heart is faint. It actually hurts.

Yet, I know that God is my Comforter. And God is the Comforter of my precious one. I can't fake feeling better – I won't even try. But, I can say in all truth that God is comforting me. God is strengthening me on the inside. Massaging my soul. Quieting me with His love. Holding my mind with His peace. God's promise of unfailing love and comfort are mine. And yours.

May your unfailing love be my comfort, according to your promise to your servant.
Psalm 119:76

I am not alone. None of us are. Not ever. Our Comforter is with us always. "To comfort all who mourn" (Isaiah 61:2). We just need to let ourselves snuggle into – with all of our sadness and sorrow – our Comforter's loving and powerful, peace-bringing, soul-quieting, heart-healing embrace.

In the embrace of our Comforter, may each of us come to know Him more powerfully and intimately as "the Father of compassion and the God of all comfort, who comforts us in all our troubles" (2 Corinthians 1:3).

In the embrace of our Comforter, may we let God tenderly and mightily strengthen and restore us in our sorrow, so that one day we can "comfort those in any trouble with the comfort we ourselves receive from God" (2 Corinthians 1:4).

In the embrace of our Comforter, may we trust God's loving and faithful promise that there will come a day when "He will wipe every tear from [our] eyes" (Revelation 21:4).

In the embrace of our Comforter, may we put our full hope, even when our hearts are broken, in the astounding transformation – from sorrow to comfort and joy – that our God will bring into our lives in the fullness of time. And it will be beautiful in its time.

Then young women will dance and be glad, young men and old as well.
I will turn their mourning into gladness;
I will give them comfort and joy instead of sorrow.
Jeremiah 31:13

Reflections – Responses – Challenges – Encouragements – God-breathing Thoughts

Do I believe it?
And if I do, what am I going to do about it?

Lord, please let me hear your voice, your love, your wisdom, your grace and truth.

December 11

THE TWO-SIDED TREASURE KEY

The LORD will be the sure foundation for your times,
a rich store of salvation and wisdom and knowledge;
the fear of the LORD is the key to this treasure.
Isaiah 33:6

Things can seem so shaky and insecure in all of our lives at different times. Maybe your job or your finances are unstable or suddenly diminishing or gone. Maybe your relationship with your husband or your wife or your child or your friend is tense, confusing, painful or ending. Maybe your health is weakening, your prognosis is uncertain, complicated, devastating or terminal. At those times, do you have and know the Lord as your sure foundation? For all of your times? No matter what?

Things can seem so empty in all of our lives at different times. Maybe you feel that every personal resource you have of energy, hope, peace, strength, sustenance and survival are completely depleted. At those times do you have and know the unfailing, exceeding and abundant riches that come from the Lord? That come from our God's eternal storehouse? That come from the Lord's loving and merciful offer of salvation and wisdom and knowledge?

Our Lord makes known the key to His eternal treasures. Whether we're feeling shaky and insecure or empty and depleted. The key to God's treasures – for every circumstance, situation and relationship here on earth and which opens up eternity with our God – is to have *the fear of the Lord.*

Fear of the Lord. What does that truly mean for how we are to relate and respond to the Lord? I have come to understand it this way: An honest and deep sense of humility before the Lord. An acknowledgment that the Lord, and the Lord alone, is the Sovereign God, the Almighty Creator and the Eternal One. A profound, even trembling, reverence and respect for the Lord's power and majesty as the omniscient, omnipotent, omnipresent Lord over all of life, over all that exists in every realm we know and understand and in every realm that is far beyond our comprehension. An authentic embracing of the truth that each of our own lives on this earth and our eternal lives and destination are completely in the hands of the Lord. Fear the Lord!

I believe there are two sides to this treasure key: Fear of the Lord and Trust in the Lord. Knowing who the Lord is should cause us to deeply *fear* Him. Our lives depend on Him.

For the LORD is your life
Deuteronomy 30:20

Knowing who the Lord is should cause us to fully *trust* Him with every breath of our lives, now and eternally, because the Lord alone loves us unfailingly.

I trust in your unfailing love; my heart rejoices in your salvation.
Psalm 13:5

This two-sided key, *fear of and trust in the Lord*, opens our lives to the eternal treasures our Lord offers to each of us. The Lord will be our sure foundation. The Lord will generously pour out the riches of His salvation, wisdom and knowledge to all who fear and trust Him.

Do you know where you put your two-sided treasure key?

692

Reflections – Responses – Challenges – Encouragements – God-breathing Thoughts

Do I believe it?
And if I do, what am I going to do about it?

Lord, please let me hear your voice, your love, your wisdom, your grace and truth.

DO NOT FRET. DO NOT BE ENVIOUS. TRUST GOD.

Do not fret because of those who are evil
or be envious of those who do wrong;
for like the grass they will soon wither,
like green plants they will soon die away.
Psalm 37:1-2

Sometimes it seems that the evil within us and around us overtakes what is good and true and right. Evil, whether subtle or viciously blatant – that comes from our own words, attitudes and actions or from the words, attitudes and actions of others towards us – destroys relationships, destroys trust, destroys peace. Fret and worry can overtake us.

Sometimes it seems that those who do wrong – those who lie, manipulate, bully, cheat and push their ways on others – are the ones who are getting all the good stuff in life. It seems that these wrongdoers receive a greater share of the wealth, the better job, the special recognition. When wrongdoers prosper more than those who are people of integrity and honor, people who are hard-working and humble, our hope in justice and fair play is greatly diminished. We want what others have. Jealousy rises. We start to wonder if it makes any real difference at all whether we do things according to God's righteous ways or not. Envy can overtake us.

Yet, our God tells us: *Do not fret. Do not be envious.* But this is not the "Hakuna Matata – No Worries" kind of directive heard in *The Lion King*. This directive comes from our Sovereign Lord, the *Lion of Judah who has triumphed* (Revelation 5:5). Our Lord tells us not to fret because of evil men or be envious of those who do wrong because He is in control – even when, according to our experiences and feelings, everything seems out of control and the bad guys are winning. Be still. Our Lord is always in control. Our Lord can always be trusted.

It is in trusting God as our "Prince of Peace" (Isaiah 9:6), instead of letting our fret and fear rule us, *that our hearts and minds will be guarded by God's transcending peace* (Philippians 4:7) whenever we are confronted with the evil words, attitudes and actions of other people. It is in trusting God's unfailing love for us that all of our fret and fear will be removed as God's "perfect love drives out fear" (1 John 4:18). It is in trusting that God has our backs – and our fronts and our sides, and our present and our future – in His eternal, protective care, that we will have the full eternal assurance that "no weapon forged against [us] will prevail" (Isaiah 54:17).

It is in trusting God as the Provider of everything we truly need, for now and all eternity, that we will be fully released from all our envy towards anyone and anything. It is in trusting that our *God has lavished us as His children with His great love* (1 John 3:1), that all our envy of other relationships will be crushed. It is in trusting that in Jesus we have received full forgiveness and are now viewed by God as "holy in His sight, without blemish and free of accusation" (Colossians 1:22), that all our envy of anyone else's life or looks, position or power will be obliterated. It is in trusting that our God "has blessed us in the heavenly realms with every spiritual blessing in Christ" (Ephesians 1:3), that we will be set completely free from the deceptive envy of all earthly, temporal and material wealth.

Do not fret. Do not be envious. The Lord is our Prince of Peace and our Eternal Provider. Our Lord is always in control. Our Lord can always be trusted.

Do I believe it?
And if I do, what am I going to do about it?

Lord, please let me hear your voice, your love, your wisdom, your grace and truth.

ALWAYS, IN ALL WAYS

The law of the LORD is perfect, refreshing the soul.
The statutes of the LORD are trustworthy, making wise the simple.
Psalm 19:7

All the time, compared to the Lord of all wisdom, I am *the simple*! Sometimes, I'm just a plain fool! That's every time I go my own way, even if it's in my own head. That's every time I ignore God's perfect law that would refresh my soul and fill me with His wisdom. Always, in all ways.

The precepts of the LORD are right, giving joy to the heart.
The commands of the LORD are radiant, giving light to the eyes.
Psalm 19:8

It's true! The precepts of the Lord are right! And I just don't feel right, in any way at all, when I ignore and dismiss, deny and reject my God's rule over my life – over all of me. My thoughts. My attitudes. My reactions. My words. My behaviors. God has a right to rule me and lead me. My life belongs to Him and He loves me unfailingly. Following my own ways, responding in any hateful, prideful ways to anyone or anything at any time – even if no one else ever knows – is heart breaking to my God who loves me like crazy. And by His love He breaks my heart too, in order to draw me back to His ways, His precepts of love, grace and truth. Always, in all ways.

And there is joy. Real joy. Deep joy. Sweet joy. Surprising joy – every time my first thoughts, attitudes, reactions, words and behaviors flow from the uniting of God's Spirit with my spirit – with my mind, mouth and behaviors! God's commands are radiant! It is so good whenever all that I am – seen and unseen – can come fully into the radiance of God's light with joy! My eyes shine with the light of thankfulness in those moments. And I believe God's eyes also shine with His love for me, knowing that doing things His ways is for my very best. Always, in all ways.

The fear of the LORD is pure, enduring forever.
The decrees of the LORD are firm, and all of them are righteous.
They are more precious than gold, than much pure gold;
they are sweeter than honey, than honey from the honeycomb.
By them your servant is warned; in keeping them there is great reward.
But who can discern their own errors? Forgive my hidden faults.
Keep your servant also from willful sins; may they not rule over me.
Then I will be blameless, innocent of great transgression.
Psalm 19:9-13

To purify and strengthen gold all of the dross, all that is impure within it must be burned away. And so it is with me. My sins, hidden and willful, must all be burned away. For my strength and for my purity as a child of the King. God's Word warns me. In listening to Him, in obeying Him there is great reward. And it is sweet. And it is strong. And it is pure. Always, in all ways.

May these words of my mouth and this meditation of my heart
be pleasing in your sight, LORD, my rock and my Redeemer.
Psalm 19:14

Yes, Lord! This is my prayer. Purify me in all I am – in all that I speak, write, think and do. Purify me. Always, in all ways. Amen!

Reflections – Responses – Challenges – Encouragements – God-breathing Thoughts

Do I believe it?
And if I do, what am I going to do about it?

Lord, please let me hear your voice, your love, your wisdom, your grace and truth.

LET'S COUNT DOWN, CALM DOWN AND CONSIDER JESUS

In ten days from today it will be Christmas Eve! If that just sent a little, or a big, shiver of panic through you because of all the things you still need to get done – sending out cards, buying gifts, wrapping gifts, mailing gifts, planning for and preparing for special meals, special events and extra guests – then, please join me in seeking God's heart for this season. Let's remember to truly focus on the great celebration of the birth of our Savior and Lord Jesus Christ!

Let's count down, calm down and consider Jesus. He is the Holy One who came to interrupt and intervene in our lives so we would know His love. So we would know His salvation. So we would know His peace. So shhhhh...

Consider Jesus. Let the panic and the pressure of our rushing around to meet the cultural (Crazy!) expectations for what Christmas should be like, just stop. Let Jesus, the Prince of Peace, the Eternal One rule our hearts, heads, spirits, time, energy, efforts and wallets. Amen!

Let's count down to Christmas. Let's stop all of our rushing, panic and pressure that we allow to overwhelm us and take over too much of our lives far too easily. Instead, let's count the eternal blessings we've been given by the Almighty Sovereign Lord who let nothing stop Him from showing us His passionate, interrupting, intervening, transforming love for us.

Jesus wasn't stopped by the humility of being born as a helpless human baby.
Jesus wasn't stopped by the darkness and disease, disbelief and dismissal He encountered and confronted, touched and transformed as He came to us as a man and as Immanuel.
Jesus wasn't stopped by the shame of being killed on the cross for the forgiveness of our sins and the renewal and redemption of our souls.
Jesus wasn't stopped by death!

Let us stop and be thankful that nothing stopped Jesus from coming to us!

> *For to us a child is born, to us a son is given,*
> *and the government will be on his shoulders.*
> *And he will be called Wonderful Counselor, Mighty God,*
> *Everlasting Father, Prince of Peace.*
> *Of the greatness of his government and peace there will be no end.*
> *He will reign on David's throne and over his kingdom,*
> *establishing and upholding it with justice and righteousness*
> *from that time on and forever.*
> *The zeal of the LORD Almighty will accomplish this.*
> Isaiah 9:6-7

> *...fixing our eyes on Jesus, [the author] the pioneer and perfecter of faith.*
> *For the joy set before him he endured the cross,*
> *scorning its shame, and sat down at the right hand of the throne of God.*
> *Consider him who endured such opposition from sinners,*
> *so that you will not grow weary and lose heart.*
> Hebrews 12:2-3

Let's count down, calm down and consider Jesus in this season and in every season of each of our lives!

Reflections – Responses – Challenges – Encouragements – God-breathing Thoughts

Do I believe it?
And if I do, what am I going to do about it?

Lord, please let me hear your voice, your love, your wisdom, your grace and truth.

_____

_____

_____

_____

_____

_____

_____

_____

_____

_____

_____

_____

_____

_____

_____

_____

_____

_____

_____

_____

_____

_____

_____

_____

LET'S COUNT DOWN, CALM DOWN AND CONSIDER JESUS

In nine days from today it will be Christmas Eve.

Take a breath right in the midst of all the time pressures you're feeling at work, at home, at church and with all the extra things you need to get done during this holy (?) season – all the running around and buying gifts and wrapping gifts, ordering gifts and getting them delivered, writing out cards, decorating the inside and the outside of your home, planning, hosting and attending all kinds of special gatherings. Calm down and take a breath.

Take a deep breath. Take a moment to recognize that the deep breath you just took is a gift from the Living Sovereign God of all Creation. The One who loves all of us beyond measure.

Today, all that our lives are right now, is a precious gift that we have been given. Today, Jesus wants each of us to know Him and trust Him and consider His great love for us.

Consider Jesus. Consider His love and let that perfect love of Jesus calm you from stressing about having to make everything perfect or, at least, appear perfect for the perfect Christmas.

The perfect Christmas has already happened! And it happened in a stable in Bethlehem in the land of Judah. The midwives didn't make it. The animals smelled. So did the awestruck shepherds. The star shone brightly. The angels sang brilliantly. Mary and Joseph trusted their God. And Jesus our Savior was born! No Christmas could ever be more perfect than that.

Consider Jesus. Consider His love and let that perfect love of Jesus lift you from all the imperfections of this life, from your sadness and disappointment, your agitation and frustration, your sin and your shame, your loneliness and loss. Let the perfect love of Jesus hold, calm and comfort your heart, especially now when you're not feeling any of that stuff the Christmas songs are singing about.

Consider Jesus. Consider His love, the love from the One who is our…

Immanuel – God with us
Matthew 1:23

Consider His presence with us as the greatest present any of us could ever receive.

Consider Jesus. Consider His love, the love from the One who is absolutely sovereign, eternally present and almighty in power. Consider the One who delights in us, loves us deeply in such tender ways and sings over us, and to us, with joy!

"The LORD your God is with you, the Mighty Warrior who saves.
He will take great delight in you, in his love he will no longer rebuke you
[he will quiet you with his love], he will rejoice over you with singing."
Zephaniah 3:17

Let's count down, calm down and consider Jesus in this season and in every season of each of our lives!

Reflections – Responses – Challenges – Encouragements – God-breathing Thoughts

Do I believe it?
And if I do, what am I going to do about it?

Lord, please let me hear your voice, your love, your wisdom, your grace and truth.

LET'S COUNT DOWN, CALM DOWN AND CONSIDER JESUS

In eight days from today it will be Christmas Eve.

I pray that each of us are choosing to breathe deeply, quiet our minds and allow ourselves the time and perspective to honestly count down, calm down and consider Jesus more and more as we move toward Christmas.

Yes, we can acknowledge that we have much yet to do – much that we want to do, much that we should do and, just maybe, some things we only think we need to do. Let's intentionally choose to consider Jesus. Actively choose to acknowledge Jesus as the King of kings and Lord of lords, making Him our focus and the ruler of our heads, hearts, hurried schedules, hopes and plans, actions and attitudes. Allow the mindset of Jesus to shape all that we do and every way we interact with all others.

In your relationships with one another, have the same mindset as Christ Jesus:

Who, being in very nature God, did not consider equality with God
something to be used to his own advantage;
rather, he made himself nothing
by taking the very nature of a servant,
being made in human likeness.
And being found in appearance as a man,
he humbled himself
by becoming obedient even to death –
even death on a cross!

Therefore, God exalted him to the highest place
and gave him the name that is above every name,
that at the name of Jesus every knee should bow,
in heaven and on earth and under the earth,
and every tongue acknowledge that Jesus Christ is Lord,
to the glory of God the Father.
Philippians 2:5-11

Consider Jesus. Choose His mindset.

Give thanks to our God who interrupts and intervenes in our lives through the giving of His life for ours; giving Himself humbly and sacrificially – first in a manger and then on a cross! Give thanks to our God who knows exactly what each one of us most desperately needs and knows Who alone is able to triumphantly and eternally give it all to us: our Lord Jesus Christ! Jesus alone is our Savior, Redeemer, Rescuer and Lover of our souls. Jesus, the King of kings and Lord of lords, is the only One able to fill our lives with unfailing, incomprehensible love, joy, peace and freedom – now and for all eternity! That is something to seriously consider.

So, as we continue with all of our gift-giving and celebration preparations and plans, let's slow down enough to reflect on God's truest and most perfect love gift of all, our Lord Jesus.

Let's count down, calm down and consider Jesus in this season and in every season of each of our lives!

Do I believe it?
And if I do, what am I going to do about it?

Lord, please let me hear your voice, your love, your wisdom, your grace and truth.

LET'S COUNT DOWN, CALM DOWN AND CONSIDER JESUS

In seven days from today it will be Christmas Eve.

We are just one week away from Christmas Eve – a season that seemed to begin as early as July with certain stores offering "Christmas in July" sales. Even before Halloween arrived, many merchandisers in the brick-and-mortar stores and throughout cyberspace were ramping up for the Christmas hoop-la and its marketing mayhem. Commercials were filled with all kinds of commercialization of this holy (?) season. An abundance of catalogs and fliers came to our mailboxes, and an overload of emails and pop-ups came to our screens. Arrrgghh!

Don't get me wrong. I love Christmas decorations and Christmas music. Christmas plays in the theaters and Christmas shows on TV. I love the sparkle of Christmas lights and the sound of Christmas bells and the smell and taste of Christmas cookies. I love the sense of anticipation and celebration in the air as we approach Christmas. But! There is so much more to consider!

Consider Jesus. Consider and consciously choose to not allow the pretty lights and presents, the glitz and glamor, the great food, music and magic of this season to diminish in any way our focus on the truth about the birth of Jesus and the purpose of His life.

Consider Jesus. Consider and consciously choose to not allow the pretty lights and presents, the glitz and glamor, the great food, music and magic of this season to overshadow in any way the true light of Jesus Christ. Jesus, God in human flesh, came to dwell among us – to light up our darkness and remove our blindness and to show us the only way to our Heavenly Father so that we may dwell in the light of His eternal presence and perfect love for all eternity.

Consider Jesus. Consider and consciously choose to not allow the truth of Christmas – the truth that Jesus came to us so that we might come to the Father – to be lessened or put aside, hidden or made hollow by all the holiday hoop-la. Consider Jesus. Consider Jesus first and well before we consider Santa and sleigh bells, plans, preparations, parties and presents.

Consider Jesus above all else. Recognize Him. Receive Him. Believe in His name. Let Him bring you to the Father to be born as His child. Consider Jesus and let the light of His life, His grace and truth fill and flow through you with wonder and joy, amazement and hope!

The true light that gives light to everyone was coming into the world.
He was in the world, and though the world was made through him,
the world did not recognize him. He came to his own, but his own did not receive him.
Yet to all who did receive him, to those who believed in his name,
he gave the right to become the children of God...
The Word became flesh and made his dwelling among us. We have seen his glory,
the glory of the one and only Son, who came from the Father, full of grace and truth.
John 1:9-14

"I am the way and the truth and the life.
No one comes to the Father except through me."
John 14:6

Let's count down, calm down and consider Jesus in this season and in every season of each of our lives!

Do I believe it?
And if I do, what am I going to do about it?

Lord, please let me hear your voice, your love, your wisdom, your grace and truth.

LET'S COUNT DOWN, CALM DOWN AND CONSIDER JESUS

In six days from today it will be Christmas Eve.

There are so many Christmas lights shining in windows, on houses, on trees, in luminaries, in storefronts and on lamp posts. Christmas lights are showing up in some pretty creative and unusual places. In earrings and belt buckles, in necklaces and sweaters, in dresses and down pant legs, on baby strollers and car seats, on dog-leashes and bird-houses.

Beyond some of the other Christmas displays and decorations, and even beyond much of the commercialization of this season, it seems that the lights, more than almost every other adornment, are what fill our world – our homes and surroundings – during this season. And they are beautiful and bright. They bring an unnatural sparkle and glow to the shorter and darker days of winter.

These Christmas lights will be eventually taken down and put away. They'll be put out of sight until next season. These lights add some temporary sparkle to our lives. But that's all they can do. That's the fullness of their power and purpose. Not so with our Messiah, our Lord and Savior Jesus Christ!

Consider Jesus. Jesus has come to bring His true light to all people. Jesus is the eternal light of God's love, grace and truth. Jesus, our Messiah, has come to illuminate God's gift of salvation and forgiveness that is offered to all of us whose lives are shortened and darkened by the reality of our sin and our eventual death.

Consider Jesus. Consider the inextinguishable, true light that He brings to our lives.
Consider Jesus. Consider the truth of our darkness and our need for His eternal light – for the light of His Word and the light of His ways as we walk through this life.
Consider Jesus. Consider the Father's kingdom of light to which Jesus alone can bring us.

The people walking in darkness have seen a great light;
on those living in the land of the deep darkness a light has dawned.
Isaiah 9:2

"I am the light of the world.
Whoever follows me will never walk in darkness,
but will have the light of life."
John 8:12

...giving joyful thanks to the Father, who has qualified you to share in the inheritance
of his holy people in the kingdom of light. For he has rescued us
from the dominion of darkness and brought us into the kingdom of the Son he loves,
in whom we have redemption, the forgiveness of sins.
Colossians 1:12-14

Our Holy God, our Messiah Jesus, is our light, our hope, our very life! When we receive the light of Christ's salvation, darkness flees and death loses its grip on us. And we will walk as His rescued, redeemed and holy people in the Father's kingdom of light for all eternity!

Let's count down, calm down and consider Jesus in this season and in every season of each of our lives!

Reflections – Responses – Challenges – Encouragements – God-breathing Thoughts

Do I believe it?
And if I do, what am I going to do about it?

Lord, please let me hear your voice, your love, your wisdom, your grace and truth.

LET'S COUNT DOWN, CALM DOWN AND CONSIDER JESUS

In five days from today it will be Christmas Eve.

Five short, fast days. Many of us may still have far too many things to do in order to feel and be fully prepared for Christmas. Fully prepared at work. Fully prepared at church. At home.

How about your heart? Is your heart fully prepared for Christmas?

This would probably be a good time for each of us to take care of our hearts. To take just a few extra minutes, right now, to take a deep breath, or two or three or ninety-seven, as we count down to Christmas.

This would be a good time to calm down and put down our gotta-do-that-and-that list.
This would be a good time to calm down in the midst of our sadness, loss, frustration or hurt.
This would be a good time to calm down in the midst of the madness of the struggles and stresses we're having with some of the people we'll be spending Christmas with this year.
To calm down period. Even if some of the plans that have been planned just aren't our plans.

This would be a very good time to consider Jesus. To intentionally and actively consider Jesus. Consider His love. Consider His joy. Consider His peace. Consider His hope. Consider His sacrifice. Consider His utter humility. Consider His victory over sin and death. Consider the gift of eternal life that is given by the Father to all who believe in Jesus!

God gave His Son Jesus to us out of His incomparable, incomprehensible love for us. Jesus came as a baby born to us. Born to die for us. Born to obliterate the power of sin and death over us. Jesus was born to die and rise again so that we, who believe, would be birthed into eternal life with our Holy God. Consider Jesus.

> *For God so loved the world that he gave his one and only Son,*
> *that whoever believes in him shall not perish but have eternal life.*
> John 3:16

> *Whoever believes in the Son has eternal life,*
> *but whoever rejects the Son will not see life,*
> *for God's wrath remains on them.*
> John 3:36

> *"Very truly I tell you, whoever hears my word*
> *and believes him who sent me*
> *has eternal life and will not be judged*
> *but has crossed over from death to life."*
> John 5:24

> *And this is the testimony: God has given us eternal life,*
> *and this life is in his Son.*
> 1 John 5:11

Let's count down, calm down and consider Jesus in this season and in every season of each of our lives!

Reflections – Responses – Challenges – Encouragements – God-breathing Thoughts

Do I believe it?
And if I do, what am I going to do about it?

Lord, please let me hear your voice, your love, your wisdom, your grace and truth.

LET'S COUNT DOWN, CALM DOWN AND CONSIDER JESUS

In four days from today it will be Christmas Eve.

So many things may be consuming our time, our thoughts and our energy during these last few days before Christmas. Many of these things consuming us are probably very connected with whatever we still have to do, or think we have to do, to get ready for Christmas. And there are undoubtedly many other, and possibly overwhelming, things that are consuming our time, our thoughts and our energy that have absolutely nothing to do with Christmas.

Calm down. Breathe deeply. Let's seek our God's perspective and peace, inviting God's love and strength to hold us. To calm our hearts and our minds as we consider Jesus.

Consider Jesus whose offer of peace is never dependent on our circumstances, but on us choosing to be held in His peace. Choosing to be held in the victorious peace of Jesus that overcomes everything that ever would attempt to consume us.

> *"...in me you may have peace. In this world you will have trouble.*
> *But take heart! I have overcome the world!"*
> John 16:33

Consider Jesus whose peace will fill us and surround us as we bring Him all of our consuming situations – all of our anxious and frustrating, hurtful and confusing, stressful and demanding situations. Bringing them all to Jesus with prayer and with thanksgiving. Trusting in His peace.

> *Do not be anxious about anything, but in every situation,*
> *with prayer and petition, with thanksgiving, present your requests to God.*
> *And the peace of God, which transcends all understanding,*
> *will guard your hearts and minds in Christ Jesus.*
> Philippians 4:6-7

> *Let the peace of Christ rule in your hearts...And be thankful.*
> Colossians 3:15

Consider Jesus. Consider our Lord's great love and great faithfulness. Consider all that God has given to us through the humble birth, holy life, sacrificial death and victorious resurrection of Jesus Christ. Consider Jesus and be assured that in Him we can never be consumed by anything that comes at us in this life. Nor will we ever be consumed by the finality of sin and death as we place our trust in Jesus as God's Son and our Savior. Consider Jesus. God's fullest and most magnificent evidence of His great love for us and His great faithfulness to us.

> *Because of the LORD's great love we are not consumed,*
> *for his compassions never fail.*
> *They are new every morning;*
> *great is your faithfulness.*
> Lamentations 3:22-23

Let's count down, calm down and consider Jesus in this season and in every season of each of our lives!

Do I believe it?
And if I do, what am I going to do about it?

Lord, please let me hear your voice, your love, your wisdom, your grace and truth.

LET'S COUNT DOWN, CALM DOWN AND CONSIDER JESUS

In three days from today it will be Christmas Eve.

Calm down. Let the true, eternal, transcending peace of Jesus calm our hearts, our minds and our pace. Let's take a few deep, slow breaths to calm down and slow down in spite of whatever pressures we may have on us and in spite of whatever presents we may still need to find. Let the eternal love of God hold us as we consider Jesus.

Consider Jesus. Consider Jesus who came to interrupt and intervene in our lives with His love. Consider Jesus and know that the full, true, eternal meaning of Christmas goes far beyond that precious little baby boy born in a barn and laid in a manger. Far beyond that star shining brightly and the angel choir giving a magnificent sound and light show to some bewildered shepherds in a field.

Consider Jesus. Consider the full, true, eternal meaning of Christmas and the fullness of who Jesus is. Consider Jesus who is our amazing, sovereign, almighty God, our Messiah, our Savior, our Shepherd, our Lord and our Life. Consider Jesus who loves us beyond all sense and reason. Consider Jesus so we will know how very deep and intimate, and truly beyond measure, is the fullness of God's love for us. Consider Jesus so we will know and trust how very constant and powerful His presence is with us and how very unfailing and unending is the fullness of His love poured into us.

> *I pray that you, being rooted and established in love,*
> *may have power, together with all the Lord's holy people,*
> *to grasp how wide and long and high and deep is the love of Christ,*
> *and to know this love that surpasses knowledge –*
> *that you may be filled with all the fullness of God.*
> Ephesians 3:17-19

Consider Jesus and let our God speak to each of our hearts so that we will know the truth of how very precious we are to our Lord, and how eternally protected we are by our Lord. Consider Jesus so that we will each be completely convinced that there is nothing – no circumstance, no situation, no person, no power, no danger, no dilemma, no fear, no failure, no suffering, no shame – that could ever separate us from the unfailing love of our God. Consider Jesus and believe that it was out of God's unlimited, unfailing, outrageous love for us that Jesus was born to us, to die for us and to rise again to give us eternal life!

> *For I am convinced that neither death nor life,*
> *neither angels nor demons,*
> *neither the present nor the future,*
> *nor any powers, neither height nor depth,*
> *nor anything else in all creation will be able to separate us*
> *from the love of God that is in Christ Jesus our Lord.*
> Romans 8:38-39

Let's count down, calm down and consider Jesus in this season and in every season of each of our lives!

Do I believe it?
And if I do, what am I going to do about it?

Lord, please let me hear your voice, your love, your wisdom, your grace and truth.

December 22

LET'S COUNT DOWN, CALM DOWN AND CONSIDER JESUS

In two days from today it will be Christmas Eve.

It's a really good time to calm down our hearts, minds, souls and bodies and consider Jesus. It's a really good time to take some deep, life-giving, mind-clearing breaths, and ask ourselves gently: How's my heart? How's my pace? How's my perspective?

Consider Jesus. And let our hearts belong fully to our God who loves us fully – at all times, in all ways. Let our hearts reflect the heart of Jesus whose love for us holds us for all eternity. Consider Jesus and let our hearts be calmed and comforted. Consider Jesus and let our hearts be joy-filled and hopeful. Consider Jesus. Let His love and kindness, mercy and compassion fill and flow through us to others in real and tangible, generous and true ways.

May the Lord direct your hearts into God's love and Christ's perseverance.
2 Thessalonians 3:5

In your hearts revere Christ as Lord. Always be prepared to give an answer to everyone
who asks you to give the reason for the hope that you have.
But do this with gentleness and respect...
1 Peter 3:15

Consider Jesus. And let our pace be kept fully and beautifully in step with the Spirit of our God. Consider Jesus and let our pace be strong and gentle, courageous and purposeful, wise and peaceful, humble and honest, loving and kind – in every thought we think, in every word we say and write, in every task we take on and in every interaction we have.

The fruit of the Spirit is love, joy, peace, patience,
kindness, goodness, faithfulness, gentleness and self-control.
Since we live by the Spirit, let us keep in step with the Spirit.
Galatians 5:22-23

Consider Jesus. And let our perspective be held in eternity's lens. Let our focus be on Jesus, on His presence with us in the midst of all of our circumstances and all of our relationships. Consider Jesus and let our perspective be lifted far beyond whatever chaos or craziness, problems or pressures we may be experiencing in our lives as a part of the reality that we live in a broken world. Consider Jesus and let nothing and no one diminish our view of God's unfathomable, unfailing love and care for us and God's amazing, eternal plans and life for us.

For our light and momentary troubles
are achieving for us an eternal glory that far outweighs them all.
So we fix our eyes not on what is seen, but on what is unseen,
since what is seen is temporary, but what is unseen is eternal.
2 Corinthians 4:17-18

Consider Jesus in the midst of all the demands and plans of this Christmas season, in all the other things going on in our lives, and let Him be Lord of our hearts, our pace and perspective!

Let's count down, calm down and consider Jesus in this season and in every season of each of our lives!

Reflections – Responses – Challenges – Encouragements – God-breathing Thoughts

Do I believe it?
And if I do, what am I going to do about it?

Lord, please let me hear your voice, your love, your wisdom, your grace and truth.

LET'S COUNT DOWN, CALM DOWN AND CONSIDER JESUS

In one day from today it will be Christmas Eve.

It's the day before the day before Christmas. And every day that we have been given is a good day for us to take a few moments to calm down, breathe deeply and deeply consider Jesus. Consider Jesus. Consider the refreshing and cleansing He brings into our lives. Consider the renewal and purity He pours into us.

In the little corner of the world where I spent my childhood and most of my adult years before I turned forty (many years ago now), our winters along Lake Ontario were long and deeply covered in snow. Throughout the winter, there would never be too many days that would pass from one snowfall to the next. Although the length of our winters was sometimes a little hard to be thrilled about, I did love the fresh falling snow.

The snow would float down from the sky and cover the entire ground, every field, every hill, every house, every church, every building, every sign, every tree, every plant, every single thing that lay between heaven and earth. And it was beautiful. When the sun shone on this freshly fallen snow, it was lovely, absolutely sparkling with the sun's reflected light. Everything looked fresh and clean, new and pure. And brilliantly white.

Consider Jesus. The beauty and the purity of the snow covering everything in its path is such a beautiful picture of our how our God makes everything new with His love and His forgiveness. Consider Jesus. Consider the holiness and purity of Jesus and all He poured out in the giving of His life to us – first as that humble, helpless baby in a manger and then as that humble, atoning sacrifice for the forgiveness of our sins on the cross. Consider Jesus. And not just at Christmas. We need Him always. We need His blood, His love and His mercy to make us clean. We all need Jesus to make us whiter than snow. To make us pure and new.

...wash me and I will be whiter than snow...
Create in me a pure heart, O God,
and renew a steadfast spirit within me.
Psalm 51:7, 10

In him we have redemption through his blood,
the forgiveness of sins,
in accordance with the riches of God's grace...
Ephesians 1:7

To Jesus Christ who loves us and has freed us from our sins by his blood,
and has made us to be a kingdom and priests to serve his God and Father –
to him be glory and power for ever and ever! Amen.
Revelation 1:5-6

This is the time to celebrate the birth of Jesus! And it is always the time to celebrate the truth that Jesus was born to die so that we would be forgiven and made clean, pure and new! In Jesus we are made whiter than snow to reflect the Son's light in all we are and in all we do.

Let's count down, calm down and consider Jesus in this season and in every season of each of our lives!

Reflections – Responses – Challenges – Encouragements – God-breathing Thoughts

Do I believe it?
And if I do, what am I going to do about it?

Lord, please let me hear your voice, your love, your wisdom, your grace and truth.

LET'S COUNT DOWN, CALM DOWN AND CONSIDER JESUS

Today is Christmas Eve. I hope and pray that all of us are done with all of our preparing, planning, shopping and rushing around now. It's time now to let Christmas be Christmas – deeply, completely and truly.

Consider Jesus. Consciously and gratefully choosing to let Jesus be the full focus of our minds and hearts now. Consciously and purposefully inviting Jesus, the Holy Child of God, to be born fully into each of our lives.

Just as newborn babies are surrounded with adoring love and attention by those who are intimately connected to them, so it is time for each of us to fully turn our love and attention to Jesus, the King of kings and Lord of lords, our Deliver, our Messiah and Savior whose birth we celebrate.

Consider Jesus. Consider the interrupting, intervening birth announcement about Jesus the angel gave to the shepherds in the field – *the Messiah, the Lord, has been born! Good news of great joy!* Consider the interrupting, intervening, sky-filling group of heavenly host who joined the angel to give glory and praise to God, declaring peace to those on whom God's favor rests!

And there were shepherds living out in the fields nearby, keeping watch over their flocks at night. An angel of the Lord appeared to them, and the glory of the Lord shone around them, and they were terrified. But the angel said to them, "Do not be afraid. I bring you good news that will cause great joy for all the people. Today in the town of David a Savior has been born to you; he is the Messiah, the Lord. This will be a sign to you: You will find a baby wrapped in cloths and lying in a manger." Suddenly a great company of the heavenly host appeared with the angel, praising God and saying, "Glory to God in the highest heaven, and on earth peace to those on whom his favor rests."

Consider Jesus. Consider the terrified, humbled, immediate response of the shepherds to the interrupting, intervening, human history-changing, message they received from the angels!

When the angels had left them and gone into heaven, the shepherds said to one another, "Let's go to Bethlehem and see this thing that has happened, which the Lord has told us about." So they hurried off and found Mary and Joseph, and the baby, who was lying in the manger. When they had seen him, they spread the word concerning what had been told them about this child, and all who heard it were amazed at what the shepherds said to them. But Mary treasured up all these things and pondered them in her heart. The shepherds returned, glorifying and praising God for all the things they had heard and seen, and which were just as they had been told.
Luke 2:8-20

The shepherds responded immediately by turning their full focus and attention on being in the presence of the Holy One! But they didn't stop there! They interrupted and intervened in the lives of all who would listen to them, telling others all they had heard and seen. *The Messiah, the Lord, has been born! Good news of great joy!*

The count down to Christmas is done. It's time to fully celebrate the birth of Jesus, our Messiah and Lord! Celebrating all that this means in every season of our lives – and for all eternity!

Do I believe it?
And if I do, what am I going to do about it?

Lord, please let me hear your voice, your love, your wisdom, your grace and truth.

A GOD-INTERRUPTING, GOD-INTERVENING CHRISTMAS!
Scripture references are from Matthew 1 and Luke 1

God loves us so much that He will interrupt our lives and every single one of our plans so that He may intervene with the fullness of His grace and truth, love and power.

God has always done this to call His people to Himself. Jesus Christ interrupts our own broken and sinful ways of doing things as He comes to intervene in our lives with His grace and truth, love and power for all eternity.

Jesus did just this through His birth in a manger on His way to the cross.

Mary, a young virgin pledged to marry Joseph, was suddenly and shockingly visited by the angel Gabriel who told her that she will be with child; that the Holy Spirit will come upon her and the power of the Most High will overshadow her and the holy one to be born will be called the Son of God.
Mary's response: *"I am the Lord's servant...May your word to me be fulfilled."*

These weren't Mary's plans, but God totally interrupted her life, to intervene in her life – and in the lives of everyone who would believe – with His grace and truth, love and power.

Joseph's plans for his life were also suddenly and shockingly interrupted when he found out that Mary was with child. Yet, even in the hurt and betrayal he must have felt, Joseph planned to quietly divorce Mary so she would not be publicly disgraced. However, before Joseph could carry out his plan, an angel of the Lord appeared to him in a dream, telling him to not be afraid to take Mary home as his wife; assuring him that "what is conceived in Mary is from the Holy Spirit. She will give birth to a son, and you are to give him the name Jesus, because he will save his people from their sins."
Joseph's response: *He did all that the angel of the Lord had commanded him.*

These weren't Joseph's plans, but God totally interrupted his life, to intervene in his life – and in the lives of everyone who would believe – with His grace and truth, love and power.

May we each choose to let God interrupt our plans, interrupt our lives, interrupt our worries and our self-focused thinking – and even interrupt our usual ways of doing Christmas – so that we may allow the full grace and truth, love and power of our Savior Jesus Christ to interrupt and intervene in our lives. May we each respond in awe and thankfulness, and put our full faith in Jesus, our Immanuel, God with us – who interrupted and intervened against all the powers of hell – to be born to us so vulnerably as a baby in a manger with the purpose to die humbly and sacrificially on a cross for the forgiveness of our sins.

Christmas and the cross of Jesus are fully intertwined as God's greatest gifts to all who would believe. Jesus put aside all His heavenly glory to come to us here on earth – interrupting and intervening in the time-space continuum. Jesus came to save us from our sins. Jesus came so that we would each know the fullness of God's interrupting and intervening grace and truth, love and power in each of our lives! Every day of our lives! Today, at Christmas, and forever.

Have a beautiful, wonder-filled, God-interrupting, God-intervening Christmas!

Do I believe it?
And if I do, what am I going to do about it?

Lord, please let me hear your voice, your love, your wisdom, your grace and truth.

IT'S NEVER OVER FOR OUR GOD

Christmas gift giving and gatherings may be nearly over for most of us. But the offer of His gifts to us is never over for our God.

Our God offers all that is good and true and eternal to each of us, each and every day. Our God – through our Lord Jesus Christ, through His Word and through His Spirit – offers Himself continually. Our God desires to save us. Our God desires to be with us. Our God desires to pour His Holy Spirit into us. The offer of His gifts to us is never over for our God.

For the grace of God has appeared that offers salvation to all people.
Titus 2:11

"I am with you always, to the very end of the age."
Matthew 28:20

This is how we know that we live in him and he in us:
He has given us of his Spirit.
1 John 4:13

Our God's love, grace, truth, kindness, compassion, mercy, forgiveness, righteousness, justice, faithfulness, protection, provision, strength, wisdom and light of life are continually offered to all of us who will accept and receive what our God has to give us. Our God's loving and lavish gifts are not offered to us for just a day, or even for just a season of celebration.

So, let's celebrate the outrageous love and unending presence and presents our God has for each of us, each and every day of our lives.

Your love, LORD, reaches to the heavens,
your faithfulness to the skies.
Your righteousness is like the highest mountains,
your justice like the great deep.
You, LORD, preserve both people and animals.
How priceless is your unfailing love, O God!
People take refuge in the shadow of your wings.
They feast on the abundance of your house;
you give them drink from your river of delights.
For with you is the fountain of life;
in your light we see light.
Continue your love to those who know you,
your righteousness to the upright in heart.
Psalm 36:5-10

We have a choice to make. May we each choose to continually accept and receive all that our God offers to us, according to His love, wisdom, timing, grace and truth. Our choice, just as it was with the Christmas presents we were offered from family and friends, is to accept and receive God's gifts fully and with full thankfulness and, then, fully make them our own! Just as the offering of His gifts to us is never over for our God, neither are the blessings for all of us who will accept and receive them!

Do I believe it?
And if I do, what am I going to do about it?

Lord, please let me hear your voice, your love, your wisdom, your grace and truth.

WHAT TO DO NOW?

What to do now that Christmas is over? The birth of Jesus has been celebrated. Presents have been given. Presents have been received. Guests have come and gone. Or maybe you've gone and returned from your own Christmas travels. What to do now?

Let's take our cue from Mary and Joseph. Their journey with Jesus had just begun. So what did they do after the humble birth of the Son of God? Mary and Joseph put their full trust in God for their baby Jesus and for their own lives. And they obeyed God's Word as it was revealed in the Law of Moses and as it was spoken to them by angels.

On the eighth day, when it was time to circumcise him, he was named Jesus,
the name the angel had given him before he had been conceived.

When the time came for the purification rites required by the Law of Moses,
Joseph and Mary took him to Jerusalem to present him to the Lord
(as it is written in the Law of the Lord, "Every firstborn male is to be consecrated to the
Lord"), and to offer a sacrifice in keeping with what is said in the Law of the Lord:
"a pair of doves or two young pigeons."
Luke 2:21-24

Mary and Joseph were far from their Nazareth home when Mary gave birth to our Messiah Jesus in Bethlehem. They had obeyed the decree issued by Caesar Augustus that required them, along with all the occupied people of the region, to register for the census in their families' hometowns. God used even the orders of a pagan emperor to ensure the fulfillment of His Word given through the prophet Micah:

"But you, Bethlehem Ephrathah,
though you are small among the clans of Judah,
out of you will come for me one who will be ruler over Israel,
whose origins are from of old, from ancient times."
Micah 5:2

God's Word matters. Mary and Joseph knew that.

As faithful followers of the Lord and as people who trusted in God's Word given to them, both through the Law of Moses and through angel visitations, Mary and Joseph obeyed God. In trust and obedience, they had their baby boy circumcised on the eighth day and gave Him the name Jesus – just as the angel had already proclaimed His name should be. Then, also according to the Law of the Lord, Mary and Joseph, after the completion of the forty day purification period, took Jesus from Bethlehem to Jerusalem to consecrate him to the Lord.

So, what to do after the celebrations have stopped? What to do after the crowds are gone? What to do when our lives start going back to our daily-day routines? The question really is: *What to do with Jesus?* The answer is, as it has always been with regards to our Lord: Trust and obey God's loving, good, holy and faithful Word. And His Word is Jesus! As we follow Jesus our lives will have more joy, purpose and peace – right in the midst of our daily-days, in times of celebration and in times of crisis and sorrow – than we could ever experience on our own, and far more than we could ever imagine!

What to do now? Let the Lord lead our lives!

Do I believe it?
And if I do, what am I going to do about it?

Lord, please let me hear your voice, your love, your wisdom, your grace and truth.

OUTSIDERS R US!

Not long ago I was on an airplane which was approximately the length of a school bus, and maybe even a little narrower. Personal space had no more meaning than what I imagine the inside of a sardine can would feel like. And, yep! I was surrounded by a family of four – two of them being under the age of four. Their need to hop up and down, move constantly and change seats continually, parents included, was phenomenal. (And I was the one who had the triple shot of espresso in my cappuccino before boarding!)

Within the first thirty minutes, at cruising altitude, my cup got knocked over, my laptop was firmly gripped by the little boy's very sticky fingers (pressing several keys at once while I was trying to write) in an effort to keep himself from falling onto my lap as he got trapped in his iPod cord. And the background noise of pages being ripped from the airline magazine during the last half of the trip was far better than the screaming, crying, slapping demands of the youngest child during the first half of the trip.

Did I mention that I was hoping to have a peaceful, reflective time of prayer and writing while on the plane in order to prepare for a ministry event? I hope you're laughing. I had to!

I was actually grinning. And shaking my head a little. But not at the hyperactive family. I was shaking my head at me and laughing at me because of God's truth that continually reminds me that: *Life and life's circumstances and life's interactions with others are just not all about me. And certainly not about my plans.* I have come to know this so very well, so very often!

> **Be wise in the way that you act towards outsiders;**
> **make the most of every opportunity.**
> **Let your conversation be always full of grace,**
> **seasoned with salt, so you may know how to answer everyone.**
> Colossians 4:5-6

God is good. And God wants His goodness, His love, His wisdom and His grace to flow freely and continually through each of us who are His children by faith in our Lord Jesus. Even when our plans are changed. Even when our peace is disturbed. The members of this precious, albeit hyperactive, family were still sadly "outsiders" to knowing Jesus Christ as Messiah and Savior – as evidenced by the yarmulkes and hair locks worn by the father and his young son.

God called me, first, to laugh at myself, laugh at my plans and get over myself really quickly so that I could get with His plans that He had presented to me on this very small plane! God calls each of us to be His representative with all people, in all circumstances, at all times. Some small but potentially eternally valuable interaction can happen whenever we do things God's way. So, for this very energetic family of four, and because of the saving and transforming grace that God has poured out to me, I could put down my laptop and set aside my plans to be present in the moment with them. I could offer smiles and kindness, patience and grace as I chatted with all of them and played with the children during our flight – during this very short time we had been given to share a portion of our lives, and share a portion of our stories.

May God use everything for His glory and to bring all people to His love and salvation. Because all of us, who now know Jesus as our Savior and Lord, were once outsiders too.

Reflections – Responses – Challenges – Encouragements – God-breathing Thoughts

Do I believe it?
And if I do, what am I going to do about it?

Lord, please let me hear your voice, your love, your wisdom, your grace and truth.

December 29

TEMPORARILY OUT OF ORDER!

Two times over this past week I read what I consider to be very optimistic signs which stated: *Temporarily Out of Order.*

I like that. The things upon which this sign was displayed were not to be discarded, nor were they to be considered as permanently out of order. There was hope for them yet! They were only *Temporarily Out of Order.*

So, there's hope for me, too. There's hope for all of us, always, who trust our eternal lives over to the King of kings and Lord of lords, our Savior Jesus Christ! We will walk through this life where things and our bodies and our relationships break down and suffer. But in Jesus Christ, we are only temporarily out of order!

We won't always be broken. We won't always have to struggle with temptation and sin. We won't always have to suffer from disease and death. We won't always have to face crises and deal with the evil within our world, within our country, within our neighborhoods, within our churches, within our families and within ourselves. Jesus Christ has rescued us and redeemed us from the dominion of darkness and the power of sin! We are only temporarily out of order!

...[that you] may have great endurance and patience,
and giving joyful thanks to the Father, who has qualified you to share in the inheritance
of his holy people in the kingdom of light. For he has rescued us from
the dominion of darkness and brought us into the kingdom of the Son he loves,
in whom we have redemption, the forgiveness of sins.
Colossians 1:11-14

What a great and amazing hope we have in Jesus! We can hold onto the glorious promise that all things will yet be made new – for all eternity! We can hold onto the glorious promise that the old order of things, that are temporarily out of order, will pass away!

Then I saw "a new heaven and a new earth,"
for the first heaven and the first earth had passed away,
and there was no longer any sea.
I saw the Holy City, the new Jerusalem, coming down out of heaven from God,
prepared as a bride beautifully dressed for her husband.
And I heard a loud voice saying,
"Look! God's dwelling place is now among the people, and he will dwell with them.
They will be his people, and God himself will be with them and be their God.
He will wipe every tear from their eyes.
There will be no more death or mourning or crying or pain,
for the old order of things has passed away."
Revelation 21:1-4

Thanks be to our almighty God who makes all things new! Our Lord redeems and transforms all of us who trust in Jesus as Savior! Our God has promised that the old order of things – all that we experience here on this earth as temporarily out of order – will pass away and leave no trace. All things will be made new for all eternity!

He who testifies to these things says, "Yes, I am coming soon."
Amen. Come, Lord Jesus.
Revelation 22:20

Reflections – Responses – Challenges – Encouragements – God-breathing Thoughts

Do I believe it?
And if I do, what am I going to do about it?

Lord, please let me hear your voice, your love, your wisdom, your grace and truth.

FOLLOWERS OF CHRIST – BODY OF CHRIST

As we get close to this year's end, many of us may find ourselves being a bit reflective about our lives and our faith journeys as followers of Christ and as members of the Body of Christ. When it comes to our faith and how we live it out, it's always a good idea to honestly ask some introspective questions and to ask some broader perspective questions as well. It's always a good idea to invite our God into our question-asking sessions, courageously inviting our God to be the One who answers us – because our God always has each of us intimately in His focus and our God always keeps His eternal perspective and purposes in His sight.

With honesty, and with courage to hear God's loving, grace and truth filled answers, let's each ask ourselves some of those introspective questions about our faith journeys:
How does my life – my mind, my heart, my words, my actions, my reactions, my interactions, my relationships, my stewardship of my body and of all my resources of time, energy, talent, money and material goods – reflect the passionate love that Christ has for me? Reflect that I belong to Jesus? That I am His follower? How does my life reflect the sacrificial, unfailing love that cost Jesus His holy life to save me, forgive me, set me free and to transform me to be more and more like Him?

With honesty, and with courage to hear God's loving, grace and truth filled answers, let's each ask ourselves some broader perspective questions about our faith journeys:
What am I doing, not just for my own spiritual growth, but to help grow the Body of believers right where I am in my own home church, in my own community, in my own region? What am I doing to help grow the Kingdom of God? What am I doing to help strengthen the Body of Christ? Since we are to be ambassadors of Christ, what am I doing to care for, protect, support and encourage the whole Body of Christ – locally, nationally, internationally – so that we, as the Body, may represent our Lord more truly and beautifully and lovingly to those who do not yet know the truth, beauty and love of Jesus?

As we honestly ask ourselves these questions and courageously open ourselves to seeking God's perspective, passion and purpose for both our personal and universal Body of Christ growth, I have no doubt that our God will answer!

> *The end of all things is near.*
> *Therefore be alert and of sober mind so that you may pray.*
> *Above all, love each other deeply, because love covers over a multitude of sins.*
> *Offer hospitality to one another without grumbling.*
> *Each of you should use whatever gift you have received to serve others,*
> *as faithful stewards of God's grace in its various forms.*
> *If anyone speaks, they should do so as one who speaks the very words of God.*
> *If anyone serves, they should do so with the strength God provides,*
> *so that in all things God may be praised through Jesus Christ.*
> *To him be the glory and the power for ever and ever. Amen.*
> 1 Peter 4:7-11

Let's each allow God's Spirit and God's Word to minister to us and challenge us – whatever life season and circumstances we may be in, whatever gifts we may have been given – to live and grow personally as a follower of Jesus and, as an ambassador of Christ and a member of His Body, to live with purpose and passion to help grow the Body of Christ and to make known Jesus as Lord to all those around us – all for the glory of God the Father!

Do I believe it?
And if I do, what am I going to do about it?

Lord, please let me hear your voice, your love, your wisdom, your grace and truth.

IT'S FINISHED – AND IT'S JUST BEGINNING!

It's finished. This year is done. We can't change anything that has happened to us over this past year. Not the things that were wonderful and beautiful. Not the things that were frustrating and ugly. We can't change anything that we have experienced – from thrilling adventures and calming vacations to deep and hard loss, suffering and grief. We can't change anything that others did to us out of kindness and love or out of cruelty and spite. We can't change anything that we thought or said or did to ourselves or to others either.

How does that leave you feeling? Are you regretting or celebrating this past year? Are you ready to say a quick and final "Good riddance!" to this past year? Or are you sad to see such a sweet and meaningful year go? No matter what we may be feeling about this past year, are we willing and able to see and embrace – even in the midst of our struggles and our successes, our heartbreaks and our joys, our shameful acts and our shining moments – God's eternal truths that are able to make a difference for each of us, each and every day of each and every year? God's eternal truths that declare:

God is still God.
God loves us unfailingly.
God is with us constantly.
God is our eternal Abba.
God is our eternal Savior.
God is our eternal peace.
God is our eternal hope.
God is our eternal joy.
God conquered sin.
God conquered death.
God is the Resurrection and the Life.
God makes all things new.
God makes all things beautiful in its time.
God is in control.
God doesn't change.

Yet, our God is able to change everything for us! He did it through the death of His Son Jesus who finished the work on the cross for the forgiveness of our sins. Through His death and resurrection, all of us and all things may be made new! In Christ there is a new beginning!

> *Later, knowing that everything had now been finished,*
> *and so that the Scripture would be fulfilled, Jesus said, "I am thirsty."*
> *...When he had received the drink, Jesus said, "It is finished."*
> *With that, he bowed his head and gave up his spirit.*
> John 19:28, 30

> *He who was seated on the throne said, "I am making everything new!"*
> *...He said to me: "It is done. I am the Alpha and the Omega, the Beginning and the End.*
> *To the thirsty I will give water without cost from the spring of the water of life."*
> Revelation 21:5-6

Our God is eternal and is able to make all things new! May we each choose to embrace the finished work of Jesus Christ who loves us passionately and offers us grace and renewal, life and hope today and every day of our lives! Let's celebrate each new moment by living our lives with Jesus as our Lord, our Alpha and Omega, beginning now and for all eternity! Amen!

Reflections – Responses – Challenges – Encouragements – God-breathing Thoughts

Do I believe it?
And if I do, what am I going to do about it?

Lord, please let me hear your voice, your love, your wisdom, your grace and truth.

Coming from a background of horrendous emotional, physical and sexual abuse, Sylane is unflinchingly convinced that God is greater than our greatest pains, shames and fears. With passionate strength, vulnerability, wisdom and humor, Sylane shares God's Word and her own faith journey in all she writes and in all she speaks at conferences and retreats. Sylane encourages her audience, whether readers or listeners, to more fully trust our Lord Jesus and His unfailing love that is able to radically and eternally transform each of us in beautiful and powerful ways.

Here in *Grace Moments*, God's love for us is passionately and purposefully made clear as we take time to daily journey with our God and His Word. Sylane encourages and challenges us – and herself – to reflect on what we believe and, then, choose to do something about it. God's grace and truth are meant to be trusted and lived out daily – moment by moment by moment!

Sylane and her husband Tim (Who she's just crazy in love with!) live in Princeton, NJ – an easy train ride into NYC, where their two beautiful, all-grown-up daughters and their "sons-in-love" live. Travel, hiking, biking, leisurely meal times and being at the ocean are favorites for Sylane – all made that much more special when enjoyed with close family and friends!

Interested in scheduling a speaking event with Sylane Mack – nationally or internationally? Please contact us at Transformed by Grace:
Website: **www.transformedbygrace.org**
Email: **Info@transformedbygrace.org**
Phone: 215.497.0882
Address: PO Box 976 - Newtown, PA 18940

Made in the USA
Middletown, DE
26 November 2014